HISTORY OF MEDICINE
IN THE
UNIVERSITY OF ST ANDREWS

HISTORY OF MEDICINE
IN THE
UNIVERSITY OF ST ANDREWS

JOHN S G BLAIR

1987

SCOTTISH ACADEMIC PRESS
EDINBURGH

Published by
Scottish Academic Press Ltd,
33 Montgomery Street
Edinburgh EH7 5JX

ISBN 7073 0525 X

© 1987 John S.G. Blair

Phototypeset by
Waverley Graphics Ltd., 6 Canongate Venture, New Street, Edinburgh.
Printed and bound in Great Britain at
The Camelot Press Ltd, Southampton

Contents

Illustrations

Foreword

by SIR JOHN REID KCMG. CB. TD. MD. DSc. LLD FRCP. FFCM. DPH

Scotland's senior University has always, as John Blair puts it, had 'the wish for Medicine'. This fascination has made itself manifest in many ways, from the time of the mediaeval origins of the University, through the 18th century Chandos chair (a ducal munificence originally proposed to establish a Chair of Eloquence) until at last a true faculty of medicine came into being towards the close of the 19th century. Establishing the likely quality of any particular medical degree, as in the case of a bottle of wine, raises questions of where and when. There were times when the University's degrees, which were in competition with licences awarded by the various non-university colleges of physicians and surgeons, were granted lightly; but, on the other side of the coin, and in the present century, there were periods of excellence in medical education at the University of St Andrews. The triumphs and tribulations of medicine in that university over a period of some five and half centuries, are chronicled by Mr Blair.

As scientific and clinical medicine developed, St Andrews inevitably had to look towards Dundee for its hospital resources of patients and specialist skills; and this immersed the faculty of medicine in the complex, and all too often unhappy, relationship between the moieties of the University which were geographically sited in St Andrews and in Dundee respectively. Indeed, medicine became one of the pawns in an unseemly game of academic chess. The situation, as is so often the case in human affairs, was complicated at various stages by personalities on both sides of the river Tay; and problems were all too often aggravated by the unfair and one-sided distortions perpetrated by what Mr Blair describes as 'the third party'.

This book traces St Andrews' involvement in medicine from the earliest times to the most recent stage following the 'disruption'[1], when the new and fruitful linkage between St Andrews and Manchester was successfully forged. As had historically been the case with Dundee, Manchester has since supplied not merely the clinical facilities required by medical undergraduates, but also the social and environmental contrast which has made the association of each of these two industrial cities with the delightful, if ethereal, university atmosphere of St Andrews itself so well-balanced an arrangement. Mr Blair appositely quotes from Lord Reay's 1885 Rectorial address at St Andrews, 'On this side of the Tay you have the old associations; on the other side you have the vitality of modern progress. Remain separated and you are weak on both sides; unite, and you double your strength. The distance will be smaller than that between a west end and an east end hospital belonging to the new London University, . . . The idea of a University is the blending of ancient and modern'.

The disruption which gave birth to the separate University of Dundee was a facile and politically attractive means of being able to declare that a further University had been founded at a time when the government of the day was committed to the expansion of tertiary education. Yet it was a tragedy which, by a stroke of the pen, undid the work of generations of students who had striven to keep the geographically separate components of the University together recognising, if certain of their teachers did not, that there was a true complementarity between St Andrews and Dundee. The separation was the more tragic in view of the advent of the Tay road bridge, which made the maintenance of unity so much easier than the former state of affairs which, for many decades, had necessitated the irksome journey by train, or by ferry-boat and road vehicle, directly from St Andrews to Dundee or, after sociable evenings, round the long circuit through Perth.

The history of medicine in the University is the history both of students and of their academic mentors. Analytical descriptions are given of the roles played by many of the latter through the centuries—the first Professor Simson, whose efforts were nullified by his inward-looking Senate colleagues; Reid, who restored prestige to the Chandos Chair; Day, whose ununited arm fracture came at perhaps the most critical date in five hundred years; Pettigrew, who fought and finally won the battle for medical teaching in the United College; Principal J. Yule Mackay, who saw the worth of the enlarged university. There were the clinical teachers, Price, Patrick and all their successors; Tulloch, that memorable teacher; Hill and Hunter in the post-1950 era of expansion; and Douglas, who joined them in importance when Ninewells Hospital was being built. The intellectual giant and polyhistor, Sir D'Arcy Wentworth Thompson, has his high place. The contribution and personality of Dr James Lawson is assessed. And in the post-1967 period, by contrast, no professor, but three doctors, Tristram, Bayne and Smith, merit St Andrews' remembrance and gratitude. Accounts are given of the careers of many more of the staff; and there are also references to the diverse fields of medical endeavour which medical graduates of the University of St Andrews have entered.

From time to time in the history of medicine in that University, a sad lack of vision was displayed, and this at various stages affected the appointment of staff and access of students to the hospital facilities in Dundee. No lack of vision was, however, manifest in the long saga which ultimately led to the opening of Ninewells Hospital, with its combination of medical school and general hospital, perpetuating the Scottish traditions of teaching hospitals serving the generality of the local population. The establishment of the new hospital was a bold move by St Andrews although, as fate would have it, Ninewells had become part of the new University of Dundee by the time it opened its doors to patients and to medical students.

Scotland has always welcomed students from less fortunate parts of the United Kingdom and from overseas and, in turn, has produced graduates who have practised their art and craft in their native countries and elsewhere. During the present century the University has gained a justifiable reputation for producing doctors well versed not only in medical theory but also in practical

clinical and laboratory skills. Many of those graduates will read this book and, in so doing, will discover new facets of the history of the faculty of medicine in their University; and they will also recognise situations and individuals whose interplay contributed to their preparation for entry into what will always be a profession full of the most diverse fascination. The medical degrees of the University of St Andrews have passed into history, but its diminishing number of extant medical graduates will never doubt that their alma mater served them well.

JOHN REID

Introduction

> Every Scottish graduate, if he thinks about it . . . will realise in his heart that he has two universities . . . his own . . . and St Andrews. For St Andrews is not only older . . . it is unique.
> *Professor Sir Ian Hill, last Professor of Medicine in the University of St Andrews at his retiral presentation.*

This is an account of Medicine within the oldest of our Scottish Universities, from its earliest beginnings until by the Universities (Scotland) Act 1966 it was no longer permitted to grant degrees in medicine to new matriculating students. The last medical graduation at St Andrews took place on 30th June 1972 and in the ten years since, medical preclinical training has continued within the Faculty of Science. 'St Andrews Medicals' then go on to complete their clinical training at other medical schools where they obtain a place, but particularly at the University of Manchester in England. There has come to an end, then, a half millenium of medical graduation. How that medical teaching appeared, expanded, prospered and faltered, and then firmly and steadily developed after clinical training became available from Dundee, is the substance of most of this book. Like so much of history, the documentation of the earlier centuries is scanty and often very irregular, and the real mass of records do not become comprehensive until the eighteenth and nineteenth centuries are reached. This story progresses almost like a novel—the account of a great family which had traditions, breeding and great worth—but had fallen upon hard times. By a marriage of convenience with a new stock having these attributes in reverse the older line seemed to have been so strengthened that its posterity was assured, especially after a serious disagreement, engineered largely by neighbours, was successfully overcome. And then, almost unexpectedly, and from within the family, the bond was broken. But St Andrews has suffered so many disasters in the past that there can be no certainty that the present arrangement will be permanent—and it may be that a future historian will be able to take up the story again.

1

The Mediaeval Background

The Reformation and After: Early Medical Men

Medicine was the third subject to be taught at St Andrews. Its foundation charter listed these as 'divine and human law, medicine and the liberal arts and faculties'. By 28th February 1412, when Bishop Wardlaw issued this 'charter of incorporation and privileges ... to the venerable men, the doctors, masters, bachelors and all scholars dwelling in our city', St Andrews already had a long and distinguished history. A centre of Christian activity from the sixth century, its earliest known name *Kinrimund* ('headland of the King's mount') suggests a political importance confirmed from other sources and perhaps reaching its climax under King Angus MacFergus (c. 729-761). It may also have been in his time that the relics of St Andrew were brought there, and his adoption as the patron saint first of the Picts and then of the Scots not only gave the place a new name but ensured a continuing religious and cultural eminence. By the early 900's it seems to have become the seat of the principal Scottish bishopric, under whose auspices a striking new pilgrimage church ('St Rule's') was built about the year 1070. It was to this church that Augustinian canons came in the 1120's from the royal abbey of Scone near Perth, and, once they were firmly established, work began in 1160 on a great new cathedral.

It was Bishop Fraser of St Andrews who, by his appeal to King Edward I to decide the royal succession, could be said to have given the pretext for political and subsequent warlike invasions by the English, and it was Bishop Lamberton, Fraser's successor, who played a considerable part in the eventual success of the Scottish resistance. His political activity in France and Rome as well as at home, and his early choice of Bruce rather than Comyn, showed him a shrewd patriot who, though not ranking with Bernard de Leynton, perhaps deserves a larger memorial than he has at present. And in July 1318, four years after Bannock-burn, Bishop Lamberton saw the fulfilment of the other great part of his life's activity, when the consecration of the great Cathedral of St Andrews, by far the largest and most glorious church ever built in Scotland, took place in the presence of Robert Bruce, King of Scots, and all the clergy and great men of his Kingdom. 'It was something of a national thank-offering'[1]. Its associated Priory was an acknowledged centre of learning while the *burgh* created by the Bishops was now a sizeable and prosperous town well equipped to be the meeting-place of Parliaments and other assemblies. It was this ecclesiastical and national background which led to its becoming the earliest University in Scot-

land, and which ensured its predominance over the years until the Reformation and beyond.

St Andrews University's first teachers were Paris graduates. But unlike the University of Paris, its corporation embraced both masters and students and as its Common Seal states, it was a 'University of Doctors, Masters and Scholars'.[2] The place of study was a *studium* in mediaeval times, and a *studium generale* was an institution into which students in all 'faculties' and from all parts could be received. In the fourteenth century, schools of higher learning began to secure their status of *studium generale* by means of a Papal or Imperial Bull, and this normally carried with it the *ius ubique docendi*, the right of a master to teach in any *studium* in Christendom. The power to grant this licence, the power to confer the degree of Master of Arts, was, as it remains today, the distinguishing mark of a University. Oxford's earliest College received confirmation of its rights and privileges by Pope Innocent IV in 1254, Cambridge was similarly confirmed by Pope John XXII in 1318, and St Andrews by the Avignon Pope Benedict XIII, Pedro de Luna, in 1413. The first professors were Laurence of Lindores, who was Rector (corresponding to today's Principal) and also Dean of the Faculty of Arts, Richard Cornel, Archdeacon of Lothian, and John Litster, Canon of St Andrews; John Shevez, official of St Andrews and William Stevens, later Bishop of Dunblane 'expounded the doctrines of the canon law, from its simplest elements to its most profound speculations'. And John Gill, William Fowles, and William Crozier taught philosophy and logic.

These were the 'academic staff'. The mediaeval student entered the university about the age of fourteen or even earlier. His main qualification for entry was an ability to converse in latin. The *trivium,* or three-fold course, consisted of latin grammar, logic, and rhetoric, the last being in effect the study of a latin version of Aristotle's treatise. After passing the test of disputation both in logic and rhetoric the student, now an 'incepting' or 'commencing' bachelor, passed to the *quadrivium* or four-fold course of arithmetic, geometry, music and astronomy. He was now, in old and recent St Andrews parlance, a 'magistrand'. On completion of the *quadrivium* at the end of his fourth year, he was qualified to proceed to the degree of Master of Arts and then himself engage in teaching; he had the *ius ubique docendi* on graduation. Such was the mediaeval arts course. For a doctorate in theology, canon law, civil law, or medicine, a further period of at least eight years' study was required. During these years the graduate could travel and study elsewhere, and was free to return to his original university for his doctoral disputation either at the end of his required minimum period of study, or later.

All undergraduates were therefore 'Arts' students; there was no under-graduate faculty of medicine or indeed of specialist law or even theology. Those who had passed through the first university years of learning almost always entered the Church. Having entered and taken Holy Orders, they gained the Church's privileges. Those with special skills or abilities were encouraged—as directed by Scripture—to use these (1st Corinthinas, 7) and especially for the benefit of the needy and the poor. But they were clergy first; in Scotland just as the ecclesiastic taught as one of his duties, so he treated the sick and attempted

to heal as another part of his duties. It was through the Church that all social services were delivered to the public. Nor had the priest-physician any lack of supporting background knowledge. He had the mediaeval world-model, the mediaeval physiology and pathology, and the mediaeval pharmacology, and he used these just as reasonably and scientifically as the present-day physician uses his equivalents in physiology and pathology[3]. By contrast there were the full-time professionals of the day who came from the unlettered walks of life— the barber-surgeons, the apothecaries, the handywomen. Theirs was strictly practical, word-of-mouth knowledge. What could be called the full-time professional physicians from the university walk of life were uncommon in England and rare in Scotland, though the more developed lands of Italy and France possessed them, as did those parts of Europe still under Mohammedan rule. For in continental Europe mediaeval universities had sometimes arisen because of the need to teach and learn matters not entirely ecclesiastical. Thus the first European medical school was not Edinburgh but Salerno, whose fame was well established by the middle of the eleventh century. Greek dialectic and Roman law were also studied keenly; such knowledge was as necessary for the mediaeval statesman as scholastic training was essential for the churchman.

It seems important, at the outset, to record that these mediaeval students did not invariably matriculate, follow a course of study, and then graduate at the end of this period provided they passed their examinations, in the fashion of today. It was commonplace for a scholar to study at a university but go elsewhere for further study and graduate at a third centre later. It was therefore entirely in order for a mediaeval university to graduate by examination a person whose studies had been carried out in another place. This was not regarded as in any way unusual. Being peculiarly concerned with clerical studies, as befitted the ecclesiastical capital, and being accustomed to the free movement of students and scholars which was one of the great strengths of pre-reformation Europe, St Andrews easily and quickly fell into such a pattern. It was never, from its foundation, an entirely 'local' university. This acceptance for graduation of students who had studies elsewhere became established in St Andrews from the earliest days, and remained in the minds of the masters into the eighteenth century. It may, indeed, have helped to formulate the attitude of some of them to the doctor of medicine degree.

The university developed and expanded. Bishop Wardlaw's successor Bishop Kennedy—one of Scotland's greatest figures—founded the College of St Salvator in 1450 on the site it has occupied ever since. Its foundation was confirmed by a Papal Bull of 1458. It quickly provided a student community of the sort that universities have continued to provide up to the present. Its closest parallels, in Dr Cant's view, are found in the foundations of New College Oxford and King's College Cambridge. The founder's concept was of a college on a scale of considerable grandeur, and the Collegiate Church was no more than one element in this. Various chaplainaries became attached as the years went by, and subjects other than theology were taught[4].

In 1472 St Andrews was raised to an archbishopric, during the episcopate of Bishop Kennedy's nephew Patrick Graham. Graham's successor Alexander

Stewart, who became Chancellor in 1509, was persuaded by John Hepburn, the Prior, that the hospital and church of St Leonard might provide another suitable base for expansion, and in 1512 St Leonard's College was founded. As a city, St Andrews reached its highest point of glory at this same time, in the late fifteenth and early sixteenth centuries. It shared the good years of King James IV's reign, when for a brief spell there was unbroken success in home government. About 1516 John Hepburn surrounded the monastery on its north, east and south sides with the wall which is still impressive today. In the priory was held the great annual fair, the Senzie market. It began after Easter, and, during the fortnight it continued, it is said that 200 to 300 vessels would be in the harbour. It was Scotland's International Festival of the Middle Ages. A little later, in 1537, Archbishop James Beaton began his foundation of St Mary's College. It was to be a college of 'theology, canon and civil law, physic, medicine and other liberal disciplines' but became, like St Leonard's College, predominately a centre for teaching clergy.

In the fifteenth century, two other universities began in Scotland. William Turnbull, Bishop of Glasgow, obtained a Bull in 1451 from Pope Nicholas V for the establishment of a *studium generale*. The first principal, Andrew Melville, was a St Andrews graduate. At Aberdeen Bishop William Elphinstone obtained the necessary Bull from Pope Alexander VI in 1494, and King's College was granted its charter in 1505. Aberdeen's first principal, Hector Boece, was educated at the Grammar School in Dundee (now Dundee High School) and was probably also a St Andrews graduate.

Outside Britain, scientific stimulus in medicine made a large leap forward as dissection of the human body began to be practised, and anatomy, 'that very vast and beautiful subject' as Professor Sir D'Arcy Thompson used to call it, was studied in Italy more by artists of the Renaissance than by doctors. Vesalius' *De humani corporis fabrica*, published in 1543, was significant not only as the foundation of modern anatomy, but because Vesalius had begun as an enthusiastic follower of Galen; from 1538 his doubt led him to carry out more and more detailed dissections by himself, inventing on the way new techniques and new instruments, and he made the description of what he actually found the basis for his writing. His was the first step towards the work of William Harvey, when physiology was added to anatomy, and basic medical sciences could develop further. From the wealth of Renaissance Italy came also the anatomical studies of Bartolemeus Eustachius the Professor in Rome, and of Colombo and Fabricius, Vesalius' successors in Padua. Several Scots moved to the continent and became distinguished professors there—Duncan Liddle at Helmstadt, Gilbert Jack at Leyden, Thomas Forbes at Pisa, and James Leith at Paris—but all these were from Aberdeen. David Kinloch, a St Andrews M.A., later became a Doctor of Medicine in Paris and was taken by the Inquisition in Spain but later released. Many unknown others, doubtless, went to the continent and practised there, to become the first of many generations of Scots doctors who had to move to lands where they could obtain a more profitable living than they could at home. For the Scotland of St Andrews University—and of her sisters in Glasgow and Aberdeen—was a poor country in every way and

remained so for almost two hundred years after 1500. As well as the long record of tragedies which make up Scottish history in the fifteenth and sixteenth centuries—the successions of failure of policies by the Stewart Kings, the selfishness and lack of principle of the nobles, the privileges of the middle classes quickly lost by their own failure, the continuing weakness of the Scottish Parliament—poverty affected everything from architecture to writing. Poverty then as now made for disease, and Scotland was not spared that greatest of mediaeval disasters, bubonic plague. War and destruction, whether in the wake of invading English or revengeful nobles, repeatedly produced famine and misery.

So it is hardly surprising that education had little chance to flourish. Details of teaching are absent probably because there was no exciting teaching to record. The very date of foundation of St Andrews was too late for the first revival of letters, too early for the second. Renaissance had begun in Italy in the fourteenth century but in 1411 Scotland was effectively cut off from Italy by its prolonged allegiance to Benedict XIII. Of the ecclesiastics who manned the new university 'these were the last people in the world to be touched by the spirit of Humanism. They had no idea beyond 'reading' the *libri consueti*, that is, the latin version of certain works of Aristotle. This was done *more parisiensi*, that is to say, by dictating sections of the text along with the paraphrases of whoever were the approved doctors of the time'[5]. The door to progression in medicine which Vesalius had opened through dissection was far distant from Scotland. Also, Professor Butterfield makes the point strongly that the Middle Ages had received from earlier times writing of such authority, especially from Aristotle, that the notion of research did not arise, and as 'Galen had performed the experiment in the past, and if we could not make the answer come out correctly we were well aware that we ourselves were in the wrong'[6].

One medical ecclesiastic who was a graduate was William Schevez— Schevez was probably born in 1438, of St Andrews parents, matriculated at 14 years of age, and was a resident master from 1456 to 1470. To graduate in Arts, he had to take Holy Orders. He studied medicine in Louvain and on his return to Scotland was in active practice as a physician; in 1465 he was appointed Master of the Maison Dieu at Brechin in Angus. Later he was physician to King James III and at the age of 40 became Archbishop of St Andrews and Chancellor of the University. Though criticised by certain authorities, a scholarly study by Cowan[7] supports him and describes two of his medical books in some detail, as well as mentioning his copy of the works of the great Arab physician Almansor, in Flemish, which deals particularly with neurological disease. Disease of the nervous system was his special interest, and his reputation as a physician spread to the continent.

In 1469, Andrew Goreth was named as a Master and Doctor of Medicine when appointed to the academic staff at St Andrews. As a teacher he was also associated with Glasgow University, and may have had an interest in Astrology[8]. Sixty years later, in 1529, when John Mair came from Glasgow to be Principal of St Salvator's College, he brought with him William Manderstone, who had been a student of Montaigu College in Paris, and had graduated Doctor of

Medicine. In Paris, where he was Rector of the University in 1525, he had joined the School of Terminists under Mair's leadership, and with Mair in 1539 he was associated in the foundation of a chaplaincy or bursary in St Salvator's College. His published writings are scholastic, but in the dedication of his *Tripartitum Epithoma* to Archbishop Forman of St Andrews he is 'Medices professor', (sic) and in the copy of his *Bipartitum in Morali Philosophia* in Edinburgh University is a dedication 'Robertus Gra. medicinae amator preceptori suo vilelmo Mandersto apollonie artis professori peritissimo'; in St Andrews documents Manderstone is consistently described in a manner which probably confirms that he lectured in medicine there. For example, in 1535, in 'King James the 5 his grant to the Ministers of the Universitie to be fre Taxationes' there is:

> We heirfor, and for certain utheris guid caussies and reasonable
> consideratiounes moving ws, be the tenour of their presentis, exonoris
> and dischairges our lovite masters James Brady, archdeacon of
> Cathnes, now rector of our said universitie; John Mair, Provost of St
> Salvatoris College, within our said citie, and dean of facultie of
> theologie of the said Universitie; Peter Clepham and Martin Balfoui,
> channones of the said College; and William Mandirstoun, doctour in
> medicine, persoun of Gogare, maisters and actuall lectoures of our
> said Universitie, of all manner of payment to ws.

At this time in history there was no requirement for a source of clinical material for teaching purposes as there is today. Yet there is no doubt that the apprentice system of learning applied and it is certain that St Andrews as the Archbishopric and Metropolitan See had hostel accommodation for pilgrims and travellers in these centuries. Records of them exist in scattered entries in old deeds and charters. St Leonard's hospital had been in the care of the Culdees in the twelfth century, continued as a hospice for pilgrims with a hospital attached, but by the early sixteenth century had become a home for elderly women— what would now be called a geriatric hospital. Archbishop Alexander Stewart made use of its buildings at the time of his founding of St Leonard's College. But it was by no means the only hospital—from 1529 records exist of 'the Hospital and leperhouse beside the city of St Andrews', and of a further hospital in 1611. The fact there appeared to be a range of institutions is not surprising, since in mediaeval Scotland there were four basic types—the hospital for an abbey or convent, the hospital for travellers, the hospital in towns for the elderly infirm, and lastly the isolation hospital for leprosy, syphilis, plague, mental disease and rarely erysipelas. St Andrews was important and large enough to merit all these types[9].

Though the Stewart dynasty did not pass from the throne of Scotland till long after the death of James V, within twenty years of his death the old alliance with France was broken and the Catholic Church crashed down into ruin. The events of 1560 changed the character of the nation far more than did the Union of the Crowns. Several of the best-known of the earlier reformers were students or staff, from Patrick Hamilton, who was martyred below St Salvator's Tower in 1528, through to Andrew Melville. John Knox may have been a student at one time; his later associations with the city are common knowledge. On the

other side were the Beatons and Hamiltons—Cardinal Beaton's diplomatic skills were considerable but his execution of George Wishart in 1546 by burning and his own subsequent murder are remembered by more than those who watch the Kate Kennedy procession each year. Archbishop Hamilton ratified the city's rights as far as the golf links were concerned in 1552, and pleased the citizens. The Hamilton family were also connected in varying degrees with the religious assassinations of the next ten years; in April 1571 Archbishop Hamilton, the last Catholic Bishop of St Andrews, was hanged at Stirling for his complicity in them. At a very different level, the justifiable anger of the citizens and the excesses of the mobs must be seen against the long-standing grievances they had against payment forced upon them by the lower clergy whom they so often despised. And at yet a third level, the politics of the rulers of England, France and Spain, and the series of changes through the two-year period around the death of Frances II in December 1560 and the return of Queen Mary can only be called bewildering.

How bewildering the year 1560 was for scholars in the three colleges—for St Andrews was very much a collegiate institution in these years—is not known. The damage to the cathedral following Knox's sermon of 1559 must have seemed like the end of the world for many—for the citizens and clergy, its ruin must have been a daily reminder of the loss of their greatest possession. Nor was there any prospect whatever of its restoration. Even if the state of the nation in political terms had made it possible, there was as ever no money available from any source. Perhaps the university, too, would be destroyed.

But the *First Book of Discipline,* which manifesto included the reformers' views on how education in Scotland was to develop, made St Andrews the 'first and principal' of the three universities of the land. Further, while Glasgow and Aberdeen were each to have two colleges, one for Arts and one for Law and Divinity, St Andrews was to have three—the first for Arts and Medicine, the second for Law, and the third for Divinity. At St Andrews, the duties of the office of Chancellor—formerly the Archbishop—were to be carried out by his replacement, the 'Superintendent of Fife'.

The *Book of Discipline* is popularly dismissed, as its creators often are, as bigoted and illiberal. In fact its tone is realistic, and its proposals extremely far seeing both in respect of education and in the provision of social services[10]. As far as university teaching is concerned, they look forward to Medicine, Law, and Divinity becoming what would now be called second or higher degrees, the 'first degree' being the Mastership of Arts. Further, they were proposed by what would now be described as a 'select committee' and were to be imposed on the universities from without. The committee consisted of John Winram, Dean of the Faculty of Theology and Superintendent of Fife, John Douglas, Provost of St Mary's College and Rector,[11] John Row, a St Andrews graduate, John Knox, John Spottiswood and John Willock.

And in the first Universitie and principall, which is Sanctandrois, thair be thre Colledges. And in the first Colledge, quhilk is the entre of the Universitie, thair be four classes or saigeis (chairs): the first to the new Suppostis, shall be onlie Dialectique; the nixt, onlie

Mathematique; the third of Phisick onlie; the fourt of Medicine . . .

In the fourt classe, shall be ane Readar in Medicine, who shall compleit his course in five years after the study of the whiche tyme being by examination fund sufficient, thei shall be graduat in Medicine.

That nane be admittit to the classe of the Medicine bot he that shall have his testimoniall of his tyme weall spent in Dialectigue, Mathematique, and Phiscque and of his docilitie in the last.

For the stipend of everie Readar in Medicine and Lawis, ane hundredth threttie thre punds vi s viii d.

The first three classes were to take one year each. Medicine, like the other special disciplines, was to extend over five years after the completion of the Arts course.

It is of interest that Aberdeen University, which had had a teacher of medicine provided since 1497, was now directed to have this readership abolished. This directive was never carried out. But the proposals for the development of St Andrews were never fully carried out either. This may have been due to the usual lack of money, but was also probably due to inertia on the part of the masters. In 1563 what would today be called the 'George Buchanan Report' followed the visit of a commission from the Scots Parliament. The College system was to be retained but the tasks of the three colleges were to be re-arranged; the first college was to become a college of Humanity—in effect a Grammar School, the second was to teach Arts but have a reader in medicine, and the third was to be for Divinity and have a reader in Law. And in 1579 when a further visitation, this time acting under instructions from King James VI, produced the report which led to the so-called New Foundation, the Provost of St Salvator's College was 'Mr James Martine Principall Professor of Medicine thairin'. One of the proposals of this commission was, in fact, that the Principal of St Salvator's was to be the Professor of Medicine; details of his contract required him to teach four times a week, on Monday, Tuesday, Wednesday and Friday 'at the hours to be appointed by the electors and maisters of the universitie'.

In 1580 another of the great figures of Scottish history, Andrew Melville, became first Principal of St Mary's College in its new guise as a seminary of reformed Theology, and with a figure of Melville's stature occupying the stage, it is not surprising that other elements in the life of the university tended to pass unnoticed. Most of the report of the next visitation, in 1588, concerned inadequate college finances and the refusal of the masters to adopt the professorial system. The regents, instead of confining themselves to the subject of one year, as the Book of Discipline and the New Foundation had visualised, insisted on taking their students through the entire four years' course in turn. The report did however record that the Provost said he taught medicine 'according to the Act' since 1590 twice a week, (though this was denied by certain of the masters) and that teaching in law was also proceeding. By the time of the 1597 visitation it was again recorded that the Provost had 'teichit medicine according to the Act' but by now the unfortunate William Walwood, lecturer in Law, had been compul-

sorily retired 'it being fund that the Professioun of the Lawes is na ways necessar at this time in the Universitie'.

The next fifty years saw continuing strife in Scotland, both political and religious. Once again the Archbishop of St Andrews was to become the controlling force in St Andrews University. The visiting commission of 1608 included prominent Anglicans, and an attempt was made to model St Andrews very closely upon Oxford and Cambridge in its constitution. The Doctorates in Divinity and Laws were restored. Attempts to establish a library were, as ever, hampered by lack of money. After various private benefactors had been encouraged to pass their private collections to St Andrews and the King himself donated 200 volumes, a collection did exist by 1612, but did not achieve a proper building to house it until thirty years later. A few medical books were included—Actius, Almansor, Celsus, Dioscorides, Galen and Mesue in St Mary's, Albertus Magnus, and the *Alchemy* of Geber in Arabic.

In 1600 the duty of teaching medicine fell to the second master of St Salvator's. At the visitation of 1642-49 the *third* master of St Salvator's was to function as a Professor of Medicine, providing a compend of anatomy for final year students in Arts. And after the Restoration Dr. Robert Burnet, until his death in 1663, and Sir Andrew Balfour, between 1667 and 1670, are recorded as medical teachers[12]. One other teacher's name is of interest in the seventeenth century, and one student's. John Wedderburn was the teacher. He had been on the staff of St Mary's College in Divinity, but had transferred to St Leonard's in 1620. (He was later physician to King Charles I and was knighted). But it was the student who is of the greater interest.

John Makluire was probably born in 1602 or 1601. He first matriculated at St Leonard's College as a ternar in 1618 and graduated M.A. in 1622. In 1630, by which time he was a physician in Edinburgh, he published two medical books—*Sanitatis Semita—cum tractatu de febre pestilente praefixe* and *The Buckler of Bodilie Health*. In 1634, he published the third book in his set, *The Generall Practise of Medicine*. But in his dedication of *The Buckler of Bodilie Health* to James Montgomery, a fellow student and son of the first Viscount Hugh Montgomery of the Ards, in Ulster, he 'acknowledges to his generous friend that the book was hatched in the University of St Andrews eleven years since'—that is, in 1619. He began to make notes for the book, he indicated, while studying medicine at St Andrews and it seems that he was encouraged by Wedderburn. This first book is quite short and 'mediaeval' in content; it contains a full range of diet for various disorders. His *Generall Practise of Medicine* is, however, a more mature work, and is largely concerned with prognosis and therapy. As well as being a student of medicine known to us through his three pamphlet-like medical books, Makluire is of special interest as being the author of the 1630 petition for instituting a College of Physicians in Edinburgh. The story is told by Dr. J.F. McHarg[13] and the association of the seven-year-old Hugh Montgomery, son of Makluire's student friend, with Charles I and William Harvey is recorded by him also. Makluire's records are clear; if this was one St Andrews graduate who certainly pursued medical studies while a student—and whose medical studies led him to write, publish

and act on behalf of the Edinburgh physicians—and who is therefore known to posterity—there must surely have been others who belong to the anonymous mass of mankind only because they did not leave any written records which have survived.

In the first quarter of the seventeenth century, St Andrews again enjoyed a bright period—again the ecclesiastical capital, again being sought for the education of sons of great and burgh families. While changes and counter-changes occurred in theology in the second half of the century, there was still some medical teaching quietly continuing in the background. In 1668 there was discussion about whether a new chair be founded in either medicine or the re-emerging discipline of mathematics. Mathematics was selected, and the university had the enormous fortune to have the great James Gregory as its first professor, but the decision which new chair be founded could have gone the other way.

Over the whole of the Reformation and Post-Reformation periods, then, there was medical teaching in St Andrews. The fact that the first Book of Discipline said as much as it did about medicine has been taken by Dr. Buist[14] as evidence that active teaching had been taking place before 1560. Evidence continues after 1560 also, as the system of the regents by which a student was taken through his entire *quadrennium* by a single tutor was gradually overcome. Records in the Arts faculty describing attempts to improve special subject teaching through the sixteenth and seventeenth centuries show what resistance the regents made. The evidence for special teaching in philosophy, literature, science, and even Greek is no more than it is for medicine. Historians of these other disciplines have bewailed the lack of evidence for regular special teaching[15]. The reason why medicine has traditionally been held up as the subject which 'was never taught at St Andrews' was the undoubted failure of the teachers of the later eighteenth and earlier nineteenth centuries to do so, and it is generally assumed that this had always applied. The very fact that St Andrews was so occupied with church and national affairs and had for its Chancellors men who were national figures, ensured that Church matters and doctrine predominated in its records, diminished by contrast the accounts and records of other subjects of university study and activity. But while Arts and Theology continued to develop in the later centuries Medicine did not, and in fact reached its lowest and most unhappy level.

2.

St Andrews Falls Behind

The Chandos Chair of Medicine: The First Missed Chance

The ecclesiastical dominance, the political status, and the geographical position of St Andrews—near to the continent of Europe yet isolated within the Kingdom of Fife, were facts which gave her an importance which Glasgow and Aberdeen could not match. Glasgow and especially Aberdeen were favourably placed to develop in relative security. They had active men of the highest ability in charge of their affairs. But they lacked involvement in the highest level of Church and State. By 1690 St Andrews had been firmly placed at this level for close on three hundred years; even today, St Andrews retains this sense of seniority, which links her with Oxford and Cambridge more than any other British University. It would be both her strength and her weakness as the centuries pass. As soon as the support of the Church and Crown was lost, the city and the university declined. Since the south of Scotland was now spared repeated invasions of the English, use could be made of the resources there as never before. Before the Reformation Edinburgh, Perth, St Andrews and Aberdeen were the most populous cities[1]. But by now, at the end of the seventeenth century and the beginning of the eighteenth, trade and industry were beginning to develop and the south west, having access to the American colonial trade, began to preponderate in population as it has done since.

On the East coast, trade and other contracts with France and the low Countries declined during the eighteenth century wars, and the activity and importance of its ports declined correspondingly. Throughout the seventeenth century, the Reformation lessened the popularity of Italy and France as places of study for Northern Europeans. The Papal decree excluding all non-Catholics from Italian universities reinforced this change. And then a succession of outstanding men, including one or two of the greatest figures in world medicine, appeared in a small new university at the edge of European civilisation and far from the favoured circle of Italian States and the Kingdom of France. For a hundred years Leyden became the centre of European medical teaching, from the middle of the seventeenth to the middle of the eighteenth century. Leeuwenhoek, inventor of the light microscope, his colleague the microscopist Swammerdam, Peter Paaw, who had studied in Padua under Fabricius in the late sixteenth century and was one of the earliest of the Leyden school, were followed by the anatomists Sylvius, Rusch, and Nicholas Tulp—remembered as the prosector in Rembrandt's 'The Anatomy Lesson'. Regnier de Graaf was

11

their physiologist (describer of the Graafian Follicle), van Deventer their obstetrician, and the great Hermann Boerhaave (1668-1739), the greatest name of them all, their professor of Botany and Medicine. Almost as if by Providential arrangement, the abilities were great and the range of abilities remarkable: Lipse in History, Jan Vossius in Literature, Ruhnken in Philology, and Gomarus and Arminius in Theology, were the best known professors. With men of such high talent as teachers, it was not surprising that young Scots students left home to join the Leyden school—along with their young English counterparts—and they returned home full of new ideas to develop in their own lands. The Dutch Renaissance being not confined to medicine, they returned with exciting ideas in other sciences.

It is usually said that St Andrews declined to an alarming degree in the eighteenth century, but it is perhaps more true to say that Edinburgh passed St Andrews and Aberdeen by because it was in Edinburgh that the Scottish Renaissance reached its highest flowering. Just as in Leyden, a new medical school in an out-of-the-way land was founded, was peopled by a range of men of the highest ability who 'all somehow appeared, one after another', and outstripped not only its sister universities in its own country but all other medical schools in the Western World. Edinburgh succeeded Leyden after Boerhaave's death as Leyden had succeeded Padua; the first Edinburgh medical men were Leyden trained, as the contemporaries of Peter Paaw had been Padua trained.

St Andrews, as far as medicine was concerned, was no worse off than the other Scottish universities[2]. Medicine in Aberdeen had been taught between 1632 and 1649, when Dr. William Gordon was mediciner, with more enthusiasm than at any time since the foundation of the university, but this activity had declined while Dr. Andrew Moore, and later Dr. Patrick Urquhart—who held the Mediciner's chair for fifty-three years from 1672—were in post. Dr. Urquhart did not give any public lectures until the early eighteenth century, in 1719. In Glasgow a Chair of Medicine had been established in 1637 when Mr Robert Mayne, an M.A. who apparently obtained the M.D. abroad, was appointed professor. The University visitation of 1642 decided that the Chair was not required, but allowed Dr. Mayne to hold his post during his lifetime. It was re-instituted in 1714 and continued from that date onwards, but regular teaching did not take place till the second half of the century[3].

So the next period in the history of medical teaching in St Andrews is concerned with reactions to developments in Edinburgh, and the setting up of St Andrews' own first medical Chair. But to understand the subsequent events, and the way they progressed as they did, it is first necessary to examine earlier developments in the two major centres of population.

The Surgeon's Hall to be described shortly by Defoe on his visit to Edinburgh was built by successors of the Barbers and Surgeons of Edinburgh, whose first charter had been granted in 1505. The Faculty of Physicians and Surgeons in Glasgow was founded by Maister Peter Lowe in 1599, with the support of King James VI. The faculty had the power to examine the 'literature, knowledge and practize' of those professing to be surgeons, and to admit them 'if found worthy'

(i.e. to be an *examining* body), to investigate sudden or suspicious deaths, to make statutes of medical practice, to prevent persons from practising medicine 'without ane testimonial of ane famous universitie quhair medicine be taught', and lastly, to inspect those who sold drugs, in the City of Glasgow and in the West of Scotland. Its sphere of influence included Lanark, Renfrew, Ayr, and Dumbarton, as well as Glasgow, and licence from the faculty was a legal requirement for medical practice in all those parts. But this did not deter the many who practised without licence. Similarly, the licence of the Edinburgh surgeon-apothecaries was required for legal practice of surgery or pharmacy in the Lothians, and in the counties of Fife, Roxburgh, Berwick, Selkirk, and Peebles, as well as in the City of Edinburgh. These licences thus did not apply to physicians—till now surgeons and apothecaries had continued in their separate and lower status, as in Mediaeval times. They remained the non-university element in the profession.

Edinburgh physicians attempted in the seventeenth century on three occasions to obtain a charter to found a college—in 1617, in King James VI and Ist's reign, in 1630, in King Charles Ist's reign, and in 1656 during the time of Oliver Cromwell. This last attempt in particular was fiercely resisted, not only by the Glasgow Faculty of Physicians and Surgeons but by the Edinburgh surgeons, and, most strongly of all, by the University of Aberdeen. The arguments from Aberdeen are worth quoting in more detail—(in Aberdeen) 'there had been an active Profession of Medicine many years erected, established, and stipended, with a learned Doctor of Medicine in the place for some years ago, exercing and orderly teaching and professing medicine in all its parts'. Because by its charter Aberdeen (like St Andrews) could 'licence every one of their graduates to teach and exerce their respective professions, into which they are graduated, as wide as any who take their degrees at Paris or Bolonga *id est hic et ubique terrarum*', that University argued that the powers being sought by the proposed Colledge of Physicians in respect of granting licences and imposing examinations would 'exceedingly injure ... their just rights and powers'[4]. These views were stated verbally at a meeting held in July, 1657, not in St Andrews, but in Dundee, between physicians from Aberdeen and Edinburgh alone. Finally in 1681, the Edinburgh physicians were successful. The King accepted their petition. The local Apothecaries and Surgeons agreed to the terms of the charter and the 'Colledge of Physicians of Edinburgh' was formed. The Charter of the College of Physicians of Edinburgh laid great stress on the examination of those seeking to practise medicine, and their own importance as an authorising body. Specifically mentioned was Edinburgh's 'pre-eminence as Metropolis and seat of the Highest Courts of Law'. One regulation in the first Charter obliged the new College to confer without examination or fee a licence to practise on any applicant possessing a degree of any Scottish University.

During this time, as the end of the seventeenth century was approaching, Leyden was the pre-eminent seat of medicine in not only Northern Europe, but in the whole of Europe—yet Boerhaave had not yet been appointed as Professor of Botany and Medicine—he would not be appointed till 1709, and would only have *twelve* beds allotted to him in this Dutch town of 40,000 inhabitants. At

home, the massacre of Glencoe happened in 1692, the Bank of Scotland was opened in 1696, and in 1696 the ill-fated Darien Scheme began, with Fort St Andrews as its capital. Within two years it had failed, and only a few broken survivors made the journey home. In 1707 the union of the Scots and English Parliaments would take place, and nominally at least, there would be equal access of Scots to the English colonies and to professional and business enterprise in England.

Defoe's accounts of his travels in Scotland within the first quarter of the eighteenth century set the scene as the Edinburgh Renaissance was beginning to develop.

> (In St Andrews) the old church has a noble structure; it was longer than St Paul's in London by a considerable deal, I think ... The city is not large, nor is it contemptibly small; there are some very good buildings in it and the remains of many more. The colleges and handsome buildings are well supplied with men of learning in all sciences, and who govern the youths they instruct with reputation; the students wear gowns here of a scarlet-like colour, but not in grain, and are very numerous ... Were [St Salvator's] supported by additional bounties and donations, as has been the case in England; and were there sufficient funds appointed to repair and keep up the buildings, there would be few colleges in England go beyond it for magnificence ...

Aberdeen, too, is commended for its past as well as its present. In Glasgow he notes that while 'the merchants of Edinburgh have attempted to trade with the American Colonies ... The Glasgow men are always sure to outdo them'—but makes no mention of the University whatsoever.

Defoe noticed the 'stench and nastiness' of central Edinburgh, and the 'thronged buildings from seven to twelve storeys hight'. The college of Physicians he saw: 'a hall and adjoining to it a very good garden ... they have a fine museum, or chamber of rarities, which are worth seeing, and which, in some things, is not to be matched in Europe'.

> But I must not omit the seminaries of learning, and the attendants upon them, nor the surgeons and apothecaries, with the great hospital, all which stands on the south side of the city; the first of them is the surgeons' hall—or surgeon-apothecaries, for here they make but one profession. They have set up a large building all at their own charge. They have also a Chamber of Rarities, a theatre for dissections, and the first bagnio in Britain; 'Tis perfectly well contrived, and exactly well finished, no expense being spared to make it both convenient and effectively useful ...

This was the contrast between old and new, and between poverty of financial support and its abundance.

The details of the foundation of the Medical Faculty within the University of Edinburgh do not concern this history of St Andrews. Edinburgh's 'Town College' was opened in October 1583 and it was not for another century that a Medical School was started. But much of the impetus for the promotion of a

school of Medicine certainly came from the Fellows of the newly formed College of Physicians.

Four years after the establishment of the College, three of its Fellows, Sir Robert Sibbald, James Halket, and Archibald Fitcairns were appointed Professors of Medicine by the Town Council without salary and without duties. It is recorded that they gave no lectures[5]. Professor Sibbald began private classes in 1706, and in 1726, four Fellows were appointed Professors of Theory and Practice in Medicine, and of Medicine and Chemistry—four Chairs in all. These, together with Mr Alexander Munro, the Professor of Anatomy, made up the five original Professors of Medicine in Edinburgh University. All had matriculated at Leyden, but only one, Andrew Plummer, Professor of Chemistry, had actually graduated there.

What is of significance in all these events is the fact that the Town's College had been up till now limited to Arts and Divinity—much as St Andrews had, although in St Andrews Divinity had attracted more important figures[6]. In Edinburgh, as in St Andrews and Aberdeen, the system of tutorials by regents on the mediaeval pattern had been broken down with difficulty. There was the same reluctance for change by the College Patrons. Had there been no 'College of Physicians' and no pressure from outside the Town College by determined men with ideas from outside Scotland, the Edinburgh Town College and University might have drifted on. It was surely then the College of Physicians who deserve the credit for establishing 'a new faculty' into the University, which when planted grew so quickly that it became the most famous faculty of all within fifty years.

It may have been realisation that the Edinburgh physicians were in process of setting up something of great import that stirred the other Scottish universities. St Andrews University records include no evidence of dealings with the Edinburgh Surgeons or the Faculty of Glasgow. The masters were, however, considerably exercised over the pretensions—as they saw them—of the College of Physicians in Edinburgh. For while the original charter of the College had not required Scots medical graduates to come to them for licence to practise, or to be tested (tryall) by them, the Fellows during the last decade of the seventeenth century began to press various noblemen, in particular the Earl of Perth, to support a petition to King William that all candidates for medical practice 'in any tym coming, whether they be Graduate either at home or abroad, shall be tryed and examined by the said Colledge, to the effect that they may be admitted if they shall be found sufficiently qualified, or otherwise they may reject them . . .'

The account of the discussions, from the point of view of the College of Physicians of Edinburgh, is detailed in Professor Craig's History[7]. That account shows the fairness of many of the proposals coming from the College, but also the clear intention to exercise control over medical education in Scotland. This account, from St Andrews records, completes the picture from the other side.

Following the 'encroaches by the College of Physicians' in 1702, several years of correspondence continued.

Dr. Alexander Dundas, the College President, wrote not only to St Andrews but also to Edinburgh, Glasgow, and Aberdeen Universities in July 1704. He proposed, on behalf of the College, that until medicine was taught in their own universities to a satisfactory standard, students should be 'committed to the colledge of physicians for examination, always provided that they apply to the university first', before they could be granted a medical degree. Robert Ramsay, the Rector, replied on behalf of St Andrews on July 25th, informing Dr. Dundas that his masters 'heartilly agreed' to the proposals . . . until a publick profession of medicine be established in our university'. And a few days later, William Carstares, the Principal, replied on behalf of Edinburgh that his professors also agreed to the proposals 'about conferring the degree of doctors of medicine'; 'I doubt not', his letter ended, 'but it will show how willing this university is to keep in a friendly correspondence with the colledge of physicians'.

The College of Physicians must have taken the matter further. Having obtained this degree of consent from St Andrews, Glasgow and Edinburgh, they next sought an Act of Parliament to confirm and consolidate their proposals and with them their aim to become the only legally constituted body with authority to examine and licence medical graduates. The alternative view is that their aim was solely to protect standards, but from the correspondence it appears that the former, to establish themselves as the most important and superior medical body in Scotland, was the real aim. The initial enthusiasm of the other universities cooled. At St Andrews it was suggested that a conference be held in Edinburgh and the Senatus minute of April 20th 1705, instructed Provost Ramsay their delegate as follows:

(1) That this university resolves upon any occasion of conferring the Degree of Medicine, they will call three or four of the licentiates or fellows of the said College of Physicians be examiners of the candidates and if it be necessary for satisfying the College of Physicians they are willing to advertise the president of the College of Physicians that he may send any one whom he thinks proper to join the said examinors.

(2) That this shal not take effect till the Act of Parliament mentioned in the proposals made by the College of Physicians, be obtained.

(3) That although the Act of Parliament be obtained not yet the above concession is only to continue until there be a professor of medicine in this university—actually working—in which case the university can allow no encroachment upon their privileges such as is demanded in the second part of the said proposals anent examining those Graduates by the universities who come to reside within the said college libraries.

(4) That if agreement is made, there be regulations as to the emoluments and that this university have their equal proportions thereof.

(5) The delegate from this university before any agreement be entered upon with the other universities or college of physicians, shal wait upon the Duke of Athol (formerly the Earl of Tullibardine, a

confidant of King William III, who as Chancellor was also 'Conservator of the Privileges') and acquaint his Grace with the proposals of the College of Physicians and the universities instructions anent extracted forth of the records of the University.

The delegate from St Andrews chosen to attend this meeting in Edinburgh was Mr Thomas Forrester, Professor of Philosophy in the Old College. But on June 1st 1705 a letter was produced at the Senate meeting from the 'Principal of the College of Glasgow to the Principal of St Leonard's College concerning the faculty of physicians' proposals about the not graduating any Doctor of Medicine degree in any university unless recommended by the society and desiring there might be a meeting of correspondents from the several universties in this Kingdome at Edinburgh in time of this running session of Parliament to consider what may be most fit to be done' . . . and on this occasion the Provost of the Old College (Provost Ramsay) was chosen to attend in Edinburgh on June 15th. It seems from this that the earlier meeting did not take place.

The College of Physicians of Edinburgh now shifted their ground. On July 3rd, the Rector, James Hadow, produced a further letter from them. This asked that the universities would not graduate in medicine anyone other than candidates approved by the college, until the universties had a Professor of Medicine in post. The College for its part would only admit as licentiates or fellows 'those that have taken their degree at one of the Universities at home'[8].

Their proposals were in effect for reciprocity—the universities were asked not to allow a candidate to graduate until he have been examined and recommended by the College of Physicians; once they had a professor of medicine of their own who could examine them on the university's behalf, however, this obligation to send candidates to Edinburgh would cease, and the several universities would conduct their own examinations. The College of Physicians, on the other hand, were now undertaking not to grant a licentiate or fellowship to any candidate who did not have a medical degree from one of the four Scottish Universities. And further, they were combining forces with the universities to obtain parliamentary backing for legal restraint against practice of medicine by anyone who had not so graduated. The proposals were a step upon the road which finally led to the Registration of Medical Practitioners Acts, which conferred the legal right to practise.

In the late seventeenth and early eighteenth century at St Andrews some of the distinctions and style of earlier times remained. In May 1698 Magistrands were told to stop 'powdering of wigs and hair' on Sundays, but on other days, 'wigs can be powdered as you like'. Archery had not disappeared from the extra-curricular activities and while golf was regularly played, it would not be till 1754 that the last Silver Arrow competition was held, and the Society of St Andrews Golfers, which became the Royal and Ancient Golf Club, would be formed. In St Andrews more students 'lived in' than in Glasgow or Edinburgh, and the proportion was only rivalled by King's College in Aberdeen. 'To suit the finances of different walks of life there were first and second tables—at the former the wealthier lads paid £2.15 or £2 per quarter for their food—of which oatmeal, broth, and ale formed a large proportion—and at this common table

the principal and regents sat'[9]. The term 'Hebdomadar' was given to the regent on duty each week to superintend the students—there is still a 'Hebdomadar's room' at St Salvator's College today. The poorest students, who could not afford fees, lived at a very low level of subsistence in lodgings.

In St Andrews the first years of the eighteenth century found the Senatus concerned with the state of the library and the loss of books and papers from it, and not with a Chair of Medicine. Failure of students to pay their 'library money' filled its discussions through the summer of 1701. The library, its finances, and the duties of the librarian filled almost every record in 1702 also. But the 'encroaches of the College of Physicians' and subsequent events brought the question of medical teaching on to the agenda.

Equipment came before staff. An opportunity arose for the university to acquire a skeleton. The source of this may have been the body of a suicide, possibly one of the university watchmen or porters. On January 30th 1707, 'the university appointed Mr Scrimgour to give four dollars of the library money to the Rector to be given by him to Mr Arnot, chirurgeon, for his assisting at the dissection'. On February 17th 'six fourteins shilling pieces' was advanced, again out of the library money, to pay the cost of transporting the bones to Dundee. The skeleton was prepared and articulated there by Mr Patrick Blair, who was the first man in the British Isles to dissect an elephant and whose account of his 'Osteographia Elephantia' is a classic and is preserved in the *Philosophical Transactions of the Royal Society* for 1710[10].

'May 22nd, the University being met, and it being proposed that Mr Blair having now brought over the sceleton, should be pay'd for ane hundred merks Scots, out of the library money, for the said Mr Blair his pains and expenses for making the said sceleton, and bringing it over, and three pounds Scots to his servant, of drink money, and to give out two pounds sixteen shillings Scots upon incidental expenses'. A glass case was then to be made, and this was done. (In 1714, on January 23rd, is the entry: 'The University being met, there was presented to them an inscription relating to the skeleton, set in a frame and covered with glass, which glass was broken. Whereupon the University appointed the library keeper to hang up the said inscription on the case of the skeleton').

The first formal suggestion that there be a Chair of Medicine appears in the Senatus minute of 20th March 1715, when Dr. Robert Wood 'desired a favour of the Rector to call an university meeting this day and there to ask the mind of the members whether or not they would at this present juncture recommend a man to be professor of medicine in this university'. Dr. Wood reminded the Senate that since he understood there was a professor in Glasgow, Aberdeen, and Edinburgh already, 'it might be reasonable that there should be one at St Andrews'. The Senate were however entirely concerned with the provision of finance at this meeting, and the suggestion was dismissed unanimously.

So another tactic was tried. Dr. Hay, a friend of Dr. Wood's, left for London ostensibly to 'procure a patent' for there being a professor of medicine at St Andrews. This stimulated the Senate to appoint a sub-committee of Principal Dean and Messrs. Young, Rymer and Duncan, who were to write to the Dukes of Montrose and Argyll and seek their advice. Help however came from an

entirely unexpected source. In 1720 the son of the Duke of Chandos was on a tour of Scotland. While visiting St Andrews, he got into certain difficulties and was helped out of them by university staff. In recognition of this kindness shown to his son, the Duke offered one thousand pounds to the University with the suggestion that it be used to endow a 'Chair of Eloquence'. The offer was made through his son's tutor, Dr. Charles Stuart. It was then suggested verbally that a Chair of Medicine was a higher priority. Back and forward went the correspondence; Dr. Stuart worked hard to convince the Duke that literature was a more deserving subject for a new chair. One of his letters, of November 28th 1720, included argument against medicine being established which was frighteningly prophetic:

Oxford

Reverend Sir,

I take this first opportunity of thanking the University for the honour of the letter I lately receiv'd from you by their appointment, I was present with the Duke of Chandos when your letter came to his hands, and upon reading it he desired me to let you know that he was very willing to consent to the alteration you inclin'd to make in the disposition of his donation in favours of Medicine ... I hope you will not suspect me of any partiality to Eloquence or any other faculty in preference to Medicine to which I have the honour to belong, when I tell you that while it was under deliberation here how his Grace's bounty might be usefully imploy'd Medicine was not forgotten, but it was carried against it for reasons which I mentioned in a letter to Mr Pringle, and to which I must confess I can not find an answer: the Theory and Practise of Medicine are not only considered as distinct professions in some of the Universties abroad, but there are likewise other Sciences such as Anatomy, Chemistry and Botany, which are unseparable retainers to that Science and absolutely necessary to the study of it: now there are no foundations in your University for any of these Sciences, nor perhaps will be for these hundred years to come, and as one man can hardly be sufficient for more than one or at most two of them, I can not see of what use a Professor of Medicine wou'd be at St Andrews where an Anatomist may be ten years in looking for a body to dissect: I think I plainly forsee that this Profession wou'd quickly fall into the hands of some young Physitian who, wanting imployment, should have interest enough to get himself chosen to it for a livelyhood to him, without having so much as one scholar to teach, and if this should be the case in my Lord Duke's own lifetime I leave it to you to judge if his Grace would have great reason to think that he had imploy'd his money well ...

However by December, the Duke agreed to alter his disposition in favour of a Chair of Medicine. He then seems to have hesitated, and the Senatus sub-committee tried to hurry things along by drawing up a draft of regulations for the Chair, in anticipation of his final agreement. The Senatus next became hesitant; the sub-committee's letter to the Duke was produced on Christmas

Eve, but they were then directed to write to the Chancellor to keep him, as would be said today, in the picture. A week later the Senate decided to send drafts of regulations for both a Chair of Rhetoric and Eloquence, and a Chair of Medicine, to the Duke of Chandos, but when this suggestion was put to the vote, it was decided that the Medicine Chair regulations be sent. In early January, several drafts were produced, and Messrs. Gregorie, Young and Petrie were asked to combine these; their combined effort had its second paragraph altered. The altered letter was produced the next week, finally agreed, and was to be despatched signed on behalf of the University by the Rector and along with a covering letter from the Duke of Atholl, the Chancellor, on January 10th. By the 6th May, it had apparently not yet been sent away. The interval had been used in drawing up a further draft!

Finally, however, all was well. The details of the appointment were agreed. The appointing sub-committee was selected and the short list drawn. The person elected was to defend two theses on subjects laid down by the university in public after his election and before his admission. Immediately after his admission, he was to give his inaugural oration. It was agreed in early November, 1721, that a university apothecary be appointed, in whose shop the new professor 'would teach materia medica to his scholars'. After some discussion about whether the appointment be made at once or after the professor's election 'Mr Andrew Watson apothecary in St Andrews' was named to be elected, 'who shall be subject to such regulations as the University shall see meet, and continue in that office *durante bene placito*'.

Next, after commendatory letters on behalf of the various candidates had been circulated, on December 4th, almost a year after the earlier deliberations had begun, 'This day there were produced to the University by Thomas Simson, James Stuart and John Rutherford their several diplomata of their being Masters of Arts, and Doctors in Medicine, which being read and considered by the University, they approved of them as agreeable to the terms of the Regulation of the Chandos Professor in those points'.

'The University agreed that the following order be observed in the masters' voting in the election of the Chandos Professor ... and in case of an equality that the Rector (Robert Ramsay) have the casting vote'. Fourteen men were to vote, uncluding the two principals and the Dean of the Faculty of Arts.

On the next day, the 5th, Doctor Thomas Simson was elected. He was to defend theses on two subjects. On January 10th, Dr. Simson defended his theses. He was appointed by the Rector at 2 p.m. and gave his inaugural lecture immediately after. The appointment was confirmed by the Duke of Chandos on January 15th and he took his seat in Senate on March 26th 1722.

The two subjects which professor Simson had to 'defend' had been agreed at the Senate meeting of December 6th 1721. They were, in present-day terms, a physiological one and a gastro-enterological one: *De Motu Muscularis*, and *De Ventriculi Concoctione Laesa*. On December 29th, the University had agreed to invite the following physicians 'to impugn the said theses against the time appointed, viz. Doctors Wood, Bruce, Lindsay, Bothurn, Hay, Balfour, Arnot, Scot, Blair, Wedderburn, Fotheringham, Rait, and in order therto that the

Rector write a letter to each of them with a copy of the theses therein inclosed; which letters to be delivered to Mr John Rymer to be sent by express to the several persons mentioned'. There was obviously no lack of physicians available to constitute this large examining committee, and no lack of clerical help to copy and distribute the theses.

Thomas Simson was one of the most able and efficient of the medical professors in the Scottish Universities at this time. He was a brother of Robert Simson, Professor of Mathematics in Glasgow, whose *Euclid* was a standard work in Scotland for over a century. Born in Kirktonhall, in the parish of West Kilbride in Ayrshire in 1696, he was the third son of John Simson. He took his M.D. at Glasgow in 1720, with a thesis 'De Fluxo Menstruo'. About 1724 he married a daughter of Sir John Preston, of Preston Hall, Fife, who was deprived of his estates after the 1715 Jacobite rising, and it is possible that this Fife connection had attracted him to St Andrews. After defending his theses in St Andrews, his inaugural oration was entitled 'De Erroribus tam veterum quam recentiorum circa materiam Medicam'. This covered physiology, the natural history of disease, and testing the worth of medicaments by experiment.

Now elected and his inaugural lecture safely over, what was Professor Simson to do? He had a skeleton, access to the apothecary's shop to teach students *materia medica*, the use of what books there were in the library, but nothing more. He had medical colleagues, but no hospital beds—any clinical teaching he could develop would depend on a supply of patients. Further, his contract required him not only to dissect any available body in public and have prelections in the university hall 'four time in the first year, to be published, and six every year thereafter'; but he was obliged to teach any scholars that shall apply to him, and that once a day, at least every Monday, Wednesday and Friday . . . any system of Anatomy and Medicine that likes him best, and be allowed to take such premium from his students as the University shall agree to'. And not only did Professor Simson teach, but he taught in Scots and with success. His inaugural lecture along with three others were reprinted in 1771 and re-issued by Dr. Andrew Duncan, a St Andrews student who did a great deal for the development of the Edinburgh Medical School, as the first of the *Miscellanies* which he later transformed into the *Edinburgh Medical Journal*. Professor Simson also published, in Edinburgh, 'De re Medica' in 1726, and the same year, 'De Erroribus circa Materiam Medicam. His 'System of the Womb' was published in 1729, and his fourth major publication, 'An Inquiry how far the Vital and Animal Actions of the more perfect Animals can be accounted for independent of the Brain: in five Essays: being the substance of the Chandos lectures for the year 1739, and some subsequent years', also in Edinburgh in 1752. In 1744 he was made an Honorary Fellow of the College of Physicians of Edinburgh, evidence of the considerable esteem he was held in there. St Andrews had a chance with Professor Simson *primus* to begin a Medical School. His date of appointment coincided with the beginning of medical teaching in Edinburgh and was before Edinburgh 'took off'. But Simson had no colleagues, apart from Mr Andrew Watson and local doctors; he had no clinical beds; worst of all, he had no money. St Andrews could never have

become even a second to Edinburgh in this early eighteenth century, but could have at least begun an *annus medicus*, had Professor Simson had some support. He tried to progress along similar lines to those of the Gregorys in Aberdeen— John, following his brother James as mediciner in 1755 also taught in Scots and went beyond Simson in trying to set up both a chemical laboratory and a dissecting room. John Gregory moved to Edinburgh in 1766, where he became a major figure amongst the physicians[11]. By then Edinburgh Medical School was at the height of its fame and everyone who was anyone was drawn to it. Unfortunately once the first Chandos Professor was appointed, the university interests returned to what they had been before—the library, Arts and Theology. Yet Professor Thomas Simson remained seriously concerned about medical education in the university he never deserted, as his action over the granting of degrees would show.

3

The St Andrews M.D.

The Empty Century of Chandos Professors

From the later seventeenth and early eighteenth century began the granting of Doctor of Medicine degrees. The practice of the granting of these degrees is perhaps the best known story about medicine in St Andrews University, and is regularly told with scorn— the name of Jean Paul Marat, one of the prominent leaders of the French Revolution, being always quoted to show how ridiculous the system became. In fact Marat had practised as a doctor in London, especially with female patients, and had impressed a number of people there before he was given his St Andrews degree on June 30th, 1775. His practice and graduation were not discreditable, given the easy-going standards of the day.

The period of the 'St Andrews M.D.' (in its popularly remembered form) corresponds to the next century of medical activity from about 1750 to 1850. Although St Andrews gained an especial notoriety over granting of degrees in medicine, it should not be forgotten that the other Scottish Universities, even Edinburgh, granted similar degrees over this period and were, like St Andrews, sharply called to account in 1830.

Scots doctors had been granted the degree of Doctor of Medicine from universities outside the country at earlier times. The degree was granted to an already experienced practitioner, who had to be supported by prominent members of the profession, undergo an examination, and usually but not invariably submit a thesis. Aberdeen University had granted the M.D. degree in 1637 and 1654. In Glasgow the first recorded M.D. is in 1703 and in Edinburgh in 1705. The first M.D. at St Andrews was granted on 11th September, 1696, to John Arbuthnot—famous in another context as originating the nickname John Bull to the true-born Englishman. Whether this was in fact the first St Andrews degree of this sort is by no means certain, as before 1696 the Senatus records of higher degrees are not generally preserved. But the fact that the granting of this medical degree began to occur at this same period in Glasgow, Aberdeen and Edinburgh suggests that the idea was not confined to St Andrews.

On August 3rd, 1696, the Senatus heard that 'Mr John Arbuthnot student of medicine hath desired of this Universitie that he graduate Doctor of Medicine by a letter upon his own hand to the Rector'. It was decided that he should first satisfy the university that he was a graduate, second satisfy them at a trial, third prescribe to the Protestant religion and fourth, in the usual careful academic

23

parlance, 'perform what else in use to be required of candidate to be graduate'. Mr Arbuthnot was written to and asked what date he could attend. The examiners chosen were Dr. John Watson of Dundee, Dr. Douglas of Kinglassie and Dr. Robert Wood in St Andrews 'educate in this Universitie to be assessors to assist at his tryal'. The Rector also wrote to Mr Arbuthnot asking him the subject for his thesis, 'to prepare a discourse upon the same'. Finally, the minute ends 'Mr Robert Ramsay is appointed to write to Provost Munro to be careful in making tryal at Dr. Wood and Dr. Steel where the ornaments that are used at doctoral graduation are to be found'. This does suggest that a previous such graduation had taken place, but not in the very recent past, or may of course have referred to the doctorate in divinity. Mr Arbuthnot appears to have satisfied the examiners, and duly graduated.

What could be called the process of post-graduate examination, where the candidate for a 'lower' post-graduate diploma—in effect the membership of a specialist college—has to pass a *viva voce* and written examination, and the candidate for the 'higher' degree (M.D. or Ch.M. or equivalent) has to submit a thesis on a subject of his own choosing, and be prepared to defend it, was laid down in Britain in the eighteenth century. In some universities the thesis alone is nowadays required, while others retain a clinical 'tryal' where the questions asked are different in character from those of the college examinations. The candidate is expected to comment on a clinical case or cases to show mature judgement and prognostic skill, rather than mere knowledge of facts and their application.

At this time, too, the granting of a degree *honoris causa* to men of great distinction, and the admission *in eundem gradum* of the graduate of another university, began to occur—these too have found themselves a permanent place in our university degree system. But what could be called the 'ordinary' candidates for the higher degree had always to face an examination of some sort; it was the practice of granting degrees *in absentia* on the nomination of others which produced the disrepute. Over the eighteenth century the system of higher degrees allowed men who had begun their professional lives at a lower level to pass into the higher grades if they had the ability and the necessary degree of support from senior colleagues—just as happens today. Thus medical men who had served overseas in the colonies or the armed forces could take advantage of the system and a significant number did. Their fees were always welcome to the poorly-endowed university professors, and their theses were useful additions to the university libraries. In England too, because of the close monopoly of the Royal College of Physicians of London and the Royal College of Surgeons of England, it was extremely difficult for anyone who was not an Anglican and a graduate of Oxford or Cambridge to get a medical degree or in fact any other form of professional qualification. England had not had the benefit of the liberal education policy of the First Book of Discipline. The same applied in Ireland. The availability of an M.D. degree from a Scottish university was therefore an enormous benefit to those who were otherwise denied advancement in their profession because of non-conformity or failure to belong to the correct social class. It should be remembered also that in the provinces of

England the majority of 'doctors' (surgeons, apothecaries, physicians) were self-taught or taught by the apprentice system, and of this majority, most did not seek a qualification from a university at any time in their careers.

St Andrews was traditionally Scottish in its respect for ability in all walks of life. Lists of Bursary holders began to be published; in December 1698 the six recommended included the sons of a burgess, a major in the Army, a deceased skipper from Ely and miner from Biggar. Class lists had included 'paupers' from well before the Reformation; indeed from the fifteenth century. Such candidates as appeared for the degree of *Doctoratus in Medicina* in the first quarter of the eighteenth century were all carefully assessed before even being requested to attend 'for tryal' and were few in number. Academical ability and experience, not ability to pay, was demanded of these very first medical graduates. John Munro, already a graduate of St Andrews with medical training, was admitted without comment in March 1698. William Hamilton, a former student of St Leonard's College and also a graduate, had his diploma approved on May 18th 1700. One or two local physicians were granted a diploma *ad eundem gradus doctoratus*, but not more.

In Novermber, 1705—seventeen years before Professor Simson's appointment, the earliest written regulations for the M.D. appeared. As well as requiring that the candidate show evidence of training and good character, they allow the degree to be conferred *in absentia*. This was new, and this was a change as far as St Andrews degrees were concered. The fee was £5 sterling, plus 40 merks to the promoter (in effect one of the professors) and 20 merks to the Arch-beadle. This substantial fee was a significant change also. Unimportant changes were added in 1728. But considerably modified, and more stringent written 'Regulations for the Degree in Medicine' were produced by Professor Simson in 1756, and were debated by the Senatus on May 4th of that year. They were as follows:

1) That no degree in Medicine be given in absence.
2) That no one be admitted as a *candidate* until he produce certificates of having studied at some University, and "gone through the several arts and sciences commonly requisite of his being Master of Arts".
3) That if the candidate has not got the degree of Master of Arts that he undergo the usual trials for that degree.
4) That he produce proper certificates of having the several parts of Medicine at a public University.
5) That upon the Professor of Medicine being satisfied concerning the above certificates, he examine the candidate in presence of two or more of the members of the University, upon the several branches of Medicine.
6) That in presence of the whole University the candidate deliver a comment on an Aphorism of Hippocrates, and a solution of a Practical Case to be prescribed to him by the Professor of Medicine some time before and shall answer such questions relating to both as shall be proposed by any Member of the University.

7) That notwithstanding the above, the University reserve a freedom to confer Honorary Degrees as they shall see occasion.

These regulations are unexceptionable. They equate closely to those of today, having the same sort of requirements for evidence of previous approved training to exclude unsuitable and untrained candidates, and of requirements for a *viva voce* and a clinical examination, which a prospective applicant for the clinical part of the St Andrews M.D. degree would have found in the University Calendar of ten or twenty years ago. They show Professor Simson's preference for using English and not Latin. They also involve other members of the staff in the examination, though who these might be are unknown. They also possibly suggest that the professor had a source of clinical material which he was prepared to use for the purposes of the examination.

The proposals were well discussed. 1) was agreed. For 2) and 3) was substituted 'that none be admitted a candidate until he produce a diploma of Master of Arts from this or some other University'. To 4) was added 'That the certificates be under the hands of the Professors with whom they had studied the several branches of Medicine'. 5) was altered to 'The Universities being satisfied concerning the Certificates' instead of 'The Professor of Medicine being satisfied concerning the Certificates'. 6) was agreed unchanged and 7) was thought unnecessary. And then the Senatus spoiled its good day's work: 'Upon the whole vote being put, whether the above articles, with the alterations and amendments thereof should be passed into an Act just now, and it carried not'. Professor Simson made no attempt to raise the subject again, at least not formally, in his lifetime. A real chance of progress in medical graduation at St Andrews had been lost.

Of Professor Simson's conditions the first was the most important. The fact that a degree was granted *in absentia* was the real reason for the disrepute in which Scottish medical degrees were held in the southern part of England, and especially in London. The frequently quoted letter of William Hunter to Dr. William Cullen, referring to the resentment at 'the brokers of Scotch degrees' by the College of Physicians of London described the situation entirely[1]. But while such 'graduation by post' was indefensible, it must be remembered that the Southern English resented any intrusions into their monopoly of power, and hostility to 'Scotch Practitioners' extended into the nineteenth and twentieth centuries; the derisory 'get yourself a proper Fellowship—or Membership' to a young Scottish doctor aspiring to a post in London or the Southern peninsula is still heard today.

Professor Simson attended the Senatus Meeting on 5th January, 1764 for the last time and died on 30th March.

On 6th April, 1764, it was agreed that Wednesday 9th May be fixed for the appointment of a successor, and that each member of the Senatus was 'to satisfy himself concerning the character of the candidates' before the vote was taken. It was also agreed that the new professor was not to keep an apothecary's shop 'either *per se* or *per alium* '. There was some dissent about the question of whether or not 'a public comparative tryal' of the candidates was required, led by Professor Brown and Mr Gregory, and the point was made that it was

important for each candidate 'to solve a practical case to be presented to him by the Professor of Medicine'. But since there was no other method of election than by perusal of the *curricula vitae* of the candidates, and no Professor to assess them—since the idea of external assessors had not yet been conceived—the dissenters were outvoted. During all this discussion, a further clause was agreed for insertion into the new Professor's contract, that 'fees arising from Degrees in Medicine were to be under the Direction of the University'.

The candidates were Dr. James Simson physician to the county hospital at Northampton, Dr. James Walker physician in London, Dr. Robert Menzies physician in Cupar in Fife, and Dr. Alexander Douglas physician in Dundee. 'And the Roll being called and the Votes marked it carry'd for Dr. James Simson by the votes of all the members, excepting Principal Tullidelph who declined, and Professor Brown and Mr Gregory the Mathematics Professor who refused to vote.' And so two months later on July 17th Dr. James Simson, Professor Thomas Simson's son, duly arrived from Northampton, agreed not to keep an apothecary's shop, nor to take the Doctor of Medicine fees, but otherwise to have the fees 'enjoyed by his predecessor'. He was admitted the next day in the Common Hall of St Salvator's College. Had the well-favoured Dr. Alexander Douglas been appointed, might the whole subsequent history of medical teaching in the University of St Andrews been different?

Professor James Simson was himself a Doctor of Medicine of St Andrews University. His thesis, 'De Asthmate Infantium Spasmodico', was presented in 1760. It is an essay of twenty-four quarto pages, and is divided into twenty sections. After some general observations on the specific qualities of tissues and the liability of muscles to contraction he shows why the laryngeal muscles should be easily excited in the infant, then assesses the influence of cold, as followed the custom of taking infants to Church for baptism within a day or two of birth, and next describes disturbances of teething and infection by thrush. He discusses differential diagnosis from whooping cough and putrid angina (diphtheria), and finally discusses forms of treatment. These include bleeding from the jugular vein, blistering, the use of specific antispasmodics, especially valerian, the use of purgatives, avoidance of raw milk except that of the mother or wet nurse, and the use of 'inunction' and of bland diet and white wine whey. This essay may appear crude and ignorant to present-day students, but represents a clear and careful study based on ideas of etiology then held, and of therapeutics as practised routinely. As such it would have been perfectly acceptable in its own day and age by practising physicians, and showed its author certainly a man who in the present day and age would be considered worthy 'of consultant status'. Within the University at this time, Professor David Gregory in Mathematics, Professor Watson in Logic, and Professor William Wilkie in Natural Philosophy were the best of the staff. The period after the union of St Salvator's College with St Leonard's had been marked by one of the many upsurges of activity among both staff and students which have been a feature of St Andrews over the centuries. The loss of St Leonard's building had meant restoration of St Salvator's—to be described by Dr. Samuel Johnson in 1773 as 'The neatest place of worship he had seen'.[2] The library had improved very greatly since the

early years of the century, and was enlarged considerably in 1765 to accommodate its increasing number of books. The Earl of Kinnoull became Chancellor
at this time, and during the period of his Chancellorship he gifted books to the
library, founded undergraduate prizes, and encouraged sons of the gentry to
choose St Andrews as their University. From Fife and Angus local boys came,
including James Wilson, later one of the Fathers of the American Constitution,
and Robert Fergusson the poet from Edinburgh. Student Societies also were set
up in the middle period of the century. Benjamin Franklin was made an
honorary LL.D. in 1759, indicating perhaps that the Senatus were not entirely
limited in vision as far as the wider world was concerned.

As far as medicine was concerned, Professor James Simson's appointment
coincided with the first increase in the number of applicants for M.D. degrees. It
is not clear whether this was a true coincidence or whether it began to be known
that a St Andrews medical degree was an easy option. What does seem clear
from the Senatus records is that there was disquiet about the method of
appointment of the new Professor, and that this disquiet did not disappear after
he was in post. During a long debate after which suggestions for making the
appointment of a medical Professor much more strict in future were finally
dismissed, it was noted that the person elected was *obliged* to read and defend
two theses in Medicine and two in Anatomy, and to read an inaugural oration.
It was also noted amusingly by Dr. Haddow that 'as no member of this
university is obliged to have any knowledge of Medicine or Anatomy, no one
has or pretends to have any—so they are not of a capacity to take any tryall of
a candidate'! It was also suggested that the choice in future might be committed
to the physicians of Edinburgh, but this too was stupidly turned down; 'it does
not at all appear that we would be better enabled to make a right election by this
method, than by that proposed in the resolution of the University which was so
happily successful in the Election of our late worthy Professor of Medicine'.

This debate has some of the features of limited view and a parochial, almost
smug attitude which has saddly afflicted the Senior Members of the University
of St Andrews on certain occasions. There seems no doubt that Senatus wished
for a medical teaching department. Edinburgh was by now at the height of its
fame as a medical school. An Edinburgh appointee with energy, vision, and
medical skill might have attained the apparently impossible, to found a teaching
hospital in the town of St Andrews. Its small size was not the absolute bar to
progress that has often been alleged; Leyden was not a large town when its fame
was beginning to spread. The house in Robertson's Close Edinburgh had at
first only six patients. Whereas the Senatus members of the early years of this
century had involved themselves with both the College of Physicians and the
other universities about medical teaching, those of sixty years later did not seem
able or willing to look farther than the walls of their Senate room. The long
justifications which were recorded to support their views are almost the best
evidence of this; they protested too much about unimportant detail. A rush of
M.D.s followed, and the numbers of doctorates of divinity also increased for a
short while.

Professor James Simson last attended the Senate on 4th August, 1770; he

died on 30th August. He does not appear to have carried out any medical teaching beyond 'displaying the skeleton'. Before the appointment of the next Professor, a further attempt was made to make conditions of appointment more stringent but this was turned down by the Rector, Dr. James Murison. On December 4th a leet was made of the candidates— Dr. Robert Menzies, Dr. James Flint, Dr. Andrew Duncan, and Dr. Patrick Wright. The vote was for Dr. Flint a physician in Dumbarton. It was agreed to inform Dr. Flint 'as he was at present in Town. He was elected that day at 3 o'clock p.m.' He 'listened to the Regulations in the Duke of Chandos' original Bond and promised to pay all due attention to the same'. The whole election sounds extraordinary—there is no record of Dr. Flint's background, or medical training. Notwithstanding his promise on the day of his election not to open an apothecary's shop, he was allowed to do this in 1777 because 'the present circumstances of the University as well as others in this place rendered it expedient'.

Although the numbers of M.D. degrees granted by St Andrews in the period of office of James Simson had increased, study of the records shows that there was still reasonable assessment of each candidate's merits. Most of the supporters appeared to be men of standing—Professors and readers at Universities, Fellow of the Royal College of Physicians on the staff of London hospitals, the Professor of Chemistry at Cambridge, Fellows of the Royal Colleges of Edinburgh, and some of lower status. As well as on Marat, the M.D. was conferred *in absentia* on Edward Jenner. In December, 1778, it was recorded that one candidate, James Clephan, had gone through a regular course (apparently in medicine) at St Andrews in Dr. James Simson's time. He had previously been an M.A. of St Andrews. Dr. Clephan had been a surgeon in the Royal Navy for sixteen years. On the same day as he was accepted for graduation, it is recorded that 'Bell's Surgery' was bought for the library.

Unfortunately there began to appear many obscure candidates, and too many obscure supporters of them. The granting *in absentia* continued, and the memorandum of the Duke of Buccleugh, Chancellor of the University of Edinburgh to Dr. William Cullen in 1774, criticising Aberdeen and Glasgow as well as St Andrews for their practices, followed one of the very rare instances of even Edinburgh University granting an M.D. to an ill-qualified candidate.[3]

And in these latter years of the century, the rate of M.D. graduation at St Andrews in particular accelerated further. Physicians, Surgeons and Apothecaries from English provincial towns—far distant from London—supported by their fellows, began to appear and all graduated, without question. Not all were obscure; on 15th April, 1795, the M.D. was conferred on Francisco Solano Constancio of Lisbon, a physician of international distinction, on the recommendation of two London doctors. About ten per cent of candidates still came for examination locally; Mr Archibald Paton 'was examined by Dr. Flint in presence of a committee of eleven, produced certificates of a liberal and medical education at Glasgow and Edinburgh, and delivered the usual exercises in presence of the University'. The very few Doctorates in Divinity granted at St Andrews over these years were clearly on men of distinction in their fields, and were often noted as 'given gratis'. The University thought of its Doctorate in

Divinity as an honour worth having. But fees were invariably charged to Medicals. Fees for medical degrees had sometimes included contributions of medical books to the library, as for example, occurred following the *in eundem* degree to Dr Cunningham, later President of the Edinburgh College of Physicians, who, already an M.D. of Leyden, was admitted in 1725. In 1747 the fee was raised to £10 for all higher degrees. For medicine this was divided as follows: '£3 to the Professor of Medicine for degrees in medicine; eleven shillings, one penny and four twelfths of a penny to the library keeper and the same to the Archbeadle; the remainder to the library'. Thus a fairly steady though small number of medical books continued to be acquired for the library, and a few were presented by their authors, suggesting a degree of medical interest. More than one edition was sometimes bought. Because of this supply, the library— and the library keeper—benefited financially.

28 M.D.s were granted in 1796, the years of Burns' death, after 10 in 1795. A surgeon in Botany Bay graduated *in absentia*, on two letters of recommendation, in March 1797. On 5th June, 1797, Mr Patrick Mitchel, surgeon to the 63rd Regiment (the King's Regiment) graduated, on supporting testimonials from two Dundee physicians—Sir Alexander Douglas, M.D. and John Wilson, M.D.—the first ever support from that city, though Dundee doctors regularly helped to examine. Sometimes the subjects of the dissertations were mentioned. A good example is Alexander Milroy of Edinburgh who delivered a commentary upon an aphorism of Hippocrates *de apoplexia* in Latin and dissertation *de incibu* (nightmare) in English—'both approved'. Dr. Milroy received his M.D. on 24th July, 1797, and on 5th March 1798 he himself sent a testimonial to support Mr Julian Michael Huet, also of Edinburgh, who then graduated 'the degree of Doctor of Medicine in common form'.

The numbers did vary from year to year. Their notifications became by far the commonest item of business to report in university records. On 13th April, 1798 Mr Hugh Moises of Pimlico graduated, supported by two fellows of the London College of Physicians. On 18th April 1798, it was moved in the Senate that 'the fee for the Degree of M.D. be £14 sterling without any deduction excepting only when the graduated has previously taken and paid for the degree of M.A. of St Andrews University'. On 21st March, 1799 came the first warning to St Andrews that something might be wrong with their Doctors of Medicine. They received on that day a letter from Dr. Hugh Moises of London 'who is engaged in a lawsuit before the Court of King's Bench—where it was necessary to verify the Diploma which he had received from this universitie on 13th April, 1798 . . . he requested . . . the universitie to subscribe a Certificate authenticating the Diploma which he now laid on the table . . . this request being considered as just and reasonable, an extract of the minute was made that the said extract was true and faithful, and that the Diploma had been signed by the Rector, Principals, and all the Professors, and the seal of the Universitie' . . .

On June 15th, a newspaper report noted 'that Dr. Hugh Moises had lost his slander suit against Dr. Thornton who had called him a quack'; 'notwithstanding the mode mentioned in the minute of March 21st, 1799, by which the members of the University had authenticated their subscription the Lord Chief Justice

Kenyon had given it as his opinion upon the trial of the said action that 'there was not sufficient evidence that the Parchment produced by Dr. Moises' Counsel was a Diploma of the University of St Andrews'; that while his Lordship testified his respect for the character of the University, he 'exprest his disapprobation of their practice of conferring Degrees of Medicine upon persons not their own students', and that upon the 8th of this month the Court of King's Bench refused to grant a new trial. After consideration, the Senate directed that the Chancellor, the Right Honourable Henry Dundas, and Lord Kenyon be informed:

The University of St Andrews derive from ancient charters the same rights of conferring Degrees in all the faculties which belong to any other University, and these rights they have uninterruptedly exercised from the time of their foundation to the present day.

The Senate Academicus is a body consisting of the Rector, a Magistrate annually elected who is Preses of the University, the Principals and Professors of the Two Colleges.

The Chancellor of the University in former times appointed a Vice-Chancellor, by whom degrees were conferred, upon those persons whom the Senatus Academicus judged worthy of that honour. During the greatest part of this century, there had been no University Chancellor and the Rector, or the person chosen Preses in absence of the Rector is styled promoter, because he, in name of the University confers degrees, *promovet ad honores.*

The instrument authenticating a Degree is a roll of Parchment subscribed by the Rector, Principals, and Professors; to which is appended the seal of the University.

As there is not a regular and compleat course of medical lectures in the University of St Andrews, Degrees in Medicine can not be conferred by this University upon any who have not prosecuted the study of Medicine elsewhere. But the University have never considered themselves as debarred by this circumstance from conferring such degrees upon those who appeared to them worthy of that honour, in whatever place they had acquired their medical education.

When the Candidates present themselves to be tried by the University they are not admitted to trial unless they bring certificates of their moral character, and their previous regular education. They are strictly examined by the Professor of Medicine in presence of some of his Brethren: and they are required to deliver in presence of the Senatus Academicus discourses of difficult kinds upon topics prescribed to them by the Professor of Medicine from which all the Members of that body may form a judgement of their proficiency in medical knowledge.

When the Candidates do not appear they transmit a Certificate under the hands of not less than two physicians of eminence bearing that their character is inexceptionable, that they have had a regular

education and that the subscribing physicians, from personal knowledge, judge them worthy of obtaining a Degree of Medicine. Upon looking over these Certificates which are carefully kept in retentis, that Certificate which included the Senatus Academicus on the 13th of April 1798 to confer the degree of M.D. upon Mr Moises is found to be subscribed by George Pearson, M.D. of the College of Physicians, London, Lecturer on Physic, and Andrew Thynn., M.D. of the College of Physicians, London, Lecturer in Midwifery, who concur in recommending Mr Hugh Moises to the University of St Andrews for the honour of a Degree as Doctor of Physic.

On 19th April, 1800, a Mr Maughan turned up unannounced and asked for an M.D. degree. He had come from Sunderland, and produced two letters of support, from Messrs. T. Withers and A. Hunter of York, dated 24th December, 1799. He was questioned by Professor Flint on Anatomy and Physiology and answered well. He then asked the local medical men present 'what they would do for a sore case he had under treatment in Sunderland' but they refused to answer. He had no certificates of character, but said he could easily obtain these. He then left, to return home. On the 25th April a letter arrived from him containing a further recommendation, but he asked that the university authorities would please 'not insert it in the papers there'. Even Professor Flint became suspicious. So he wrote to Dr. Withers, who replied that he did not know the man and that his and Dr. Hunter's writing was forged. He asked that the name of the man be sent to him, and after consideration, the professors did this. Nothing further was heard of Mr Maughan—but granting of M.D. degrees continued as if nothing had happened, after this revealing incident.

In 1800 and 1801 there were many more surgeons from the Services, particularly the Royal Navy, awarded the degree. In May, 1802, for no obvious reason, a sub-committee of the Senate examined the existing conditions for granting the M.D. The only change they made was that in future certificates from an 'external' candidate were to lie on the table for two weeks at least; certificates of character and education were required as before, as were testimonials—theses were still to be in Latin. St Andrews was by now hopelessly behind the other Scottish Undergraduate Schools, unable to catch up with all that had happened over the last fifty years. Aberdeen, struggling with medical teaching in both its universities, had nevertheless had a written paper for the King's College M.D. set by Dr. Chalmers in 1782, and had the impetus of the Aberdeen Medical Society in Marischal from 1789 onwards. Yet, as if in ignorance, one or two students of medicine from Edinburgh were reported as coming to St Andrews, apparently for instruction of some sort.

All the new regulations had done was to delay the granting of the M.D. for three weeks or so. If 'there was urgency' (and the reasons for this were sometimes given) the requirement was waived. In March of 1803 an Edinburgh paper reported that a St Andrews M.D. had been given to one Robert Gellathie of Rothesay—this was denied by St Andrews, and the report was refuted in all possible newspapers. The Moises' lawsuit continued to nag local memory, and written reports of the case were eventually received; no comment was made,

UNIVERSITY LIBRARY, ST ANDREWS, *May 14th, 1802.*

RESOLVED that, when a Candidate for the Degree of Doctor in Medicine does not present himself for Trial, he shall transmit a Certificate under the hands of not less than two Physicians of eminence, known to the Senatus Academicus, in the following terms :

We, A. B. *residing at* ___ *and* C. D. *residing at* *do hereby certify that* E. F. *a Candidate for the Degree of* M. D. *is a Gentleman of respectable character ; that he has received a liberal and classical Education ; that he has attended a complete Course of Lectures in the several Branches of Medicine ; and that from personal knowledge we judge him worthy of the Honour of a Doctor's Degree in Medicine.*

N. B. The date must always be annexed.

The MD *in absentia.* Professor Briggs' writing

Robert Briggs

Arthur Connell's chemistry class — quadrangle 1851. One of the oldest university class photographs in existence

John Reid

George Edward Day FRS

Oswald Home Bell

Principal John Tulloch

and the papers were 'ordered to be put in the catalogue'.

1804 showed just how bad things had become. On 21st April, after an application from William Welch, a surgeon in Moffat, had been laid on the table, Dr. Flint read a letter he had written to the University authorities:

> Gentlemen, I beg leave to represent to the University that having for more than half a century practised Medicine, and for nearly 34 years of which discharged the duties of Chandos Professor, and now feeling the infirmities of age advance upon me I am extremely desirous to have my son Dr. John C. Flint, Physician of Gainsborough joined with me in the office.
>
> A physician has no right to take any merit for his solicitude about the recovery of his patients because it is the first duty of his profession; but after a long and kindly intercourse with most of the families of the University, it is impossible for me not to feel much confidence in the goodwill of my brethern when I now submit to their judgement the wish of my heart.

James Flint had done no more than process applications for the M.D. degree. He had not taught students (though he may have had the apprentices) and he had taken no steps to try to develop teaching. Like some St Andrews Professors before and also after him, he had enjoyed a comfortable sinecure. Further, he had been in post for a long time. The University as a whole was the poorest in Scotland and seemed to be moving to extinction. Their pride in their antiquity was unaltered, as the Senate letter to the Chancellor and Lord Kenyon showed, but with this was a refusal to concede any fault in their activities. This request of Professor Flint to have his son succeed him (though there was a precedent, for Professor Simson's son had succeeded him) showed how completely inward-looking and indeed actively damaging in attitude he was. Against this it can be said that no Royal Commissions had disturbed the peace of St Andrews or indeed any of the Scottish Universities throughout the eighteenth century, and none would do so until 1826. Because of the Renaissance of letters of every sort in Edinburgh, the best in all fields of endeavour had gone there, and this protected Edinburgh by ensuring a high standard of ability. Nevertheless nepotism had existed in Edinburgh and would continue to do so, though it would be the nepotism of Edinburgh itself rather than of individual families. In Aberdeen also University nepotism reached a high degree with the Gordons, Gregorys, Gerards, Bannermans, Blackwells, Donaldsons, Beatties, and Skenes. In St Andrews, the last ten years of the eighteenth century and the final twenty of the nineteenth were those of the 'Hill regime', during the time of Professor George Hill, first Professor of Greek in United College and later Principal of St Mary's. He was the outstanding Scottish Theologian of the day, and he too was a staunch encourager of nepotism. This almost certainly explained the subsequent events.

When the next meeting of the Professors took place, there was an attempt to do something. A number of Professors, headed by Dr. Playfair, moved that the foundation of the Chandos Professorship be examined, its regulations and former election be investigated, and a report made. But it was a second motion,

led by Dr. Hill, which was carried. Its length suggests a considerable degree of preparation and lobbying. The minute sets the scene.

'That if the Professor of Medicine shall resign his office, it is competent and expedient for the University after accepting the resignation to elect Dr. James Flint, and Dr. John Flint his son, joint Chandos Professors of Medicine in the University, upon the following terms.

1)	That Dr. James Flint shall have during his incumbency, the sole right of the Salary, Emoluments, perquisites of the Office of Chandos Professor of Medicine.

2)	That Dr. John Flint shall not have a right, during the incumbency of his father, to sit, deliberate, or vote in any meeting of College, University or Faculty.

3)	That the University shall have the right at any time during the Incumbency of Dr. James Flint when they see cause, to summon Dr. John Flint to reside in this place and to discharge the duties of Professor of Medicine in attending the Members of University as physician and examining Candidates for Degrees in Medicine.

4)	That if Dr. James Flint, Dr. John Flint are elected joint Chandos Professors of Medicine, they shall be admitted at the same time, and that previously to their admission they shall subscribe in presence of the University a minute to be kept *in retentis* expressing their acquiescence to the three preceding articles.

5)	That upon Dr. James Flint ceasing by death, by resignation, or in any manner of way, to have right to the Office, Dr. John Flint shall immediately succeed without any new admission to the full enjoyment of the rights, privileges and emoluments of the Chandos Professor of Medicine; and that his standing in the University shall be reckoned from the date of his admission with his father.

From which resolution Dr. Adamson for himself and those who shall adhere to him dissented and protested for remede as accords, for reasons to be given in due course, whereupon he took instruments in the Clerks' hands; for which dissent and protest Dr. Playfair and Dr. Hunter adhered, and the Doctor having obtained permission to leave the Chair also signified his adherence. The said protesters further protested that their continuing to sit in the Meeting and to reason on any further question relative to this business shall not be considered as departing from the above protest, Thereafter Dr. Flint gave in a letter dated April 28th, 1804, subscribed by him and addressed to the Rector, Principals and Professors of St Andrews, and having done so immediately withdrew'. Dr. Flint's letter was of resignation of the Office of Chandos Professor of Medicine and Anatomy.

It had all the features of a pre-arranged deal. The motion that the resignation be accepted was quickly passed, as was the motion that the vacant post be filled immediately. The rest of the account records like that of a stormy board meeting; those against protested and demanded that the election be postponed; the Rector left his Chair and 'craved that it might be recorded that the motion

did not meet with his concurrence'. The protestors next took legal advice, and Robert Meldrum, a notary public, intimated that they would seek a bill of suspension and interdict. The majority agreed that 'admission of the professors elect be delayed till the bill of suspension be advised', and authorised payment from university funds to Mr Walter Cook, their own choice of solicitor, to defend their decision. All this happened on May 1st. On May 6th 'The University agree to confer the degree of M.D. on Mr William Welch, Surgeon in Moffat' whose application had lain on the table since April 21st.

However, the majority voice prevailed. On July 3rd Lord Cullen at the High Court in Edinburgh quashed the interdict. They moved on July 7th that the admission of the joint professors go ahead on the 16th 'upon the terms expressed in the minute of 28th April'. Once again Dr. Adamson, the Rector Dr. Arnot, and the Principal of St Salvator's College, Dr. Playfair, protested. Dr. Playfair quoted some points in the judgement (which had not been unanimous) apparently not made public. He refused to support an election 'so irregular and incompetent, and an admission which eventually may prove highly injurious'. But the majority had its way. These are the first records clearly showing angry discord over the Faculty of Medicine in St Andrews, and would not be the last.

The Senate meeting on July 21st, following the election of 16th July, had all the features of smug satisfaction on the part of the victors, and increased bitterness on the part of the losers. By August 13th, Dr. James Flint was back in his place, laying before the University a further certificate on behalf of an M.D. candidate Patrick Macnamara Brody.

Why did the St Andrews M.D. continue as it did? It was in part economic necessity, since the fees were a regular source of income in the plight of the university in the last thirty years of the eighteenth century. Yet these Professors— Murison, Shaw, Cook, Hill, Haddow, Watson, Brown—and Dr. Flint—were the men who entertained Dr. Johnson to dinner. Dr. Watson exchanged repartee with him and James Boswell, Dr. Shaw breakfasted with him, Professor Haddow walked around St Salvator's with him the day after the dinner, and Professor Hill—at that time Professor of Greek—took the key to the library with him when he went out of the town and so prevented his seeing the newly extended and furnished library. These men were warmly spoken of by Dr. Johnson, and evidently respected by him. There comes through the records of the half century we are at present in—from 1750-1800—a certain continuing determination to maintain a medical presence within the University of St Andrews, in spite of the lack of a 'compleat course of instruction'. This is the old University marking time but not halting, as if in anticipation that if it does so, it will have a base to build upon when the time comes. This view was also held by Dr. Buist (Votiva Tabella),[4] who speaks of 'the wish for a Medical Faculty'. For St Andrews was a continuing University, in spite of adversity—just as other Universities were. The very fact that so much interest, so many records through the years, were devoted to medicine, when it would have seemed much easier to give the subject up altogether and expand other subjects in the Arts and Divinity faculties and soon now the very beginnings of the Science faculty, cannot

but be significant. These professors may have been comfortably parochial, happy to continue as they had been for so long now without external interference, that it could be argued that they simply did not think of dropping an easy source of assured income. But this explanation does not seem enough, in view of what is to be found, either explicitly or by inference, in the records as they are written. In spite of its name as a perpetrator of 'Scotch degrees' in Medicine, St Andrews must have had the drawing power it has always had: James Sims, President of the Medical Society of London, was happy on the 5th of September 1804 to receive the honorary degree of LL.D. So he at least considered a St Andrews honour worth while.

As far as the Flints were concerned, the protesters won in the end. Their joint election was declared illegal by the House of Lords on May 26th, 1809, in one of St Andrews' periodic recourses to litigation. James Flint was re-elected on July 29th, 1809, and died, an old man, on December 16th, 1810. Once again there was argument about the new appointment and the contract of the new Professor. This time, as well as inspecting the previous regulations for the Chair, the sub-committee of the two Principals, Dr. Hunter and Mr Cook, was 'to find out what happened at other Universities'. Various recommendations were produced to press Dr. John Flint's canditature and testimonials. As well as Dr. Flint, Dr. James Davidson, a physician from Dunfermline, and Robert Briggs, an M.D. of the University of Edinburgh, had applied.

On January 19th, 1811, the Sub-Committee reported: 'The Chandos Professor should be a teaching Professor who shall instruct such scholars as may apply to him in such branches of Medicine or the sciences connected therewith as the University may be pleased to direct'. They also suggested that the scale of fees for the M.D. degree should be increased. This report lay on the table. On February 2nd the proposal to increase the M.D. fee to £20 Scots was turned down. On February 9th when the proposals were debated and finalised, three important changes were made. The Professor was to teach, he was to teach Chemistry as well as Medicine and Anatomy, and he was 'to *assist the University* in the trial and examination of M.D. candidates'—those who did not appear in person to be more strictly vetted—rather than to examine them himself. On this occasion, the inclusion of Chemistry (with which was soon included Chemical Pharmacy) in the new Professor's duties was a confession that the Medical Chair required alteration in scope. When Dr. Briggs was appointed on February 16th, on the Rector's casting vote, 'the University, considering that without some addition to our Medical Establishment, and without a Public Hospital, any attempt to teach in his own department must evidently prove abortive, took him bound to give annually a course of Chemistry as an interesting branch of general science, the most nearly connected with Medicine, and provided an Apparatus for the purpose'. The real reason for this change was that a recent endowment for a Chair of Chemistry was not thought enough, and the money was being left to accumulate interest. But as Chemistry was now a regular Arts subject, and required to be taught, the Chair of Medicine and Anatomy was used as a means of introducing it without incurring extra expense.

M.D. degrees continued. There were two dozen in 1824, when a letter was received in November of that year from Dr. Mearns, of King's College, Aberdeen, reporting that Parliament was about to legislate against the granting of medical degrees *in absentia*, and King's College had in mind to stop the practice. The letter sought the views of St Andrews. The letter was sent to Lord Melville, the Chancellor, who replied that the proposed alteration (by Aberdeen) in the mode of granting degrees should not be rashly conceded—and that he himself had never heard of any proposal of legislative interference. In 1825 there were 40 medical degrees conferred, but a number were refused. But in 1825 also the first intimations were received of the wind of change which would blow in 1826. Specific queries were raised by the Lord Advocate in November 1825, and it was clear that the regulations would have to be altered. News came that Aberdeen University was also taking steps to change its medical regulations. And so, in December, a sub-committee of the Senate, consisting of Dr. Mitchell, Professor Briggs, and Mr Alexander was appointed. The certainty of threatening enquiries from outside resulted in the long-delayed improvements actually taking place.

In many aspects, the tightening of the regulations was to what Professor Thomas Simson had proposed a century before. 'No degree was to be conferred on an absent candidate' was the first new regulation. Candidates must be over 21 years of age. Certificates of general education, of 4 years' attendance at a medical school, and of 2 years' hospital practice, were required before a candidate could be considered. The form of the examination was to remain similar, but now the examination was to include 'all branches of Medical Science' (these were detailed, and included Public Health), and the whole proceedings were to be submitted to the Senatus for their consideration. 'In the case of a candidate possessed of a surgical diploma from Edinburgh, London, Dublin, or Glasgow, who had been in practice for some years or who had acted as Surgeon in His Majesty's Navy or Army, or in the forces or ships of the East India Company, one year was subtracted from the attendance on lectures and on hospital practice'. Also, the university could confer Honorary Degrees of Medicine on highly distiguished individuals—who did not have to comply with the ordinary regulations. But every 'such Honorary Degree shall be conferred unsolicited and free of expense'. Lastly, and most important of all, these regulations were to become 'the law of the University on the subject' and were not to be relaxed.

This stopped the flow of candidates. On 8th March, 1828, Richard Scholes Hutchinson was fully examined according to the letter of the law—and in Latin and Greek, and was awarded an M.D. On 5th January 1830, Mr John Geddes' examination was even more closely reported—his two-hour long osteology ('the skeleton put before him was gone thro') myology, neurology, hepatic system, principles of respiration and digestion *viva* was followed by another in Chemistry and Pharmacy. He was allowed to write his answers to his thesis and clinical case in English, as his knowledge of Latin was restricted. (He had been examined in some Latin and on verses of St John's Gospel in Greek). He, too, passed, and graduated *doctorus in medicina*.

This first part of the story of 'The St Andrews M.D.' comes to an end with the Universities Commission Report of 1826-30, which ordered that no medical degrees be conferred by the University of St Andrews till there were Professors teaching classes for at least one whole year of medical teaching—one complete *annus medicus*. The full report of evidence submitted, and Dr. Briggs' replies to questioning by members of the commission in particular, confirm that no formal medical instruction had taken place by Dr. Briggs or by Doctor Flint. Dr. Briggs had, he said, tried to start some teaching, including classes in Pharmacy, but these had collapsed through lack of support. The word 'sinecure' was used to describe the post of Chandos Professor. The commissioners must have realised that the large amount of University administration—on the quaester's side—which Dr. Briggs did, amply confirmed this. Amongst the evidence prepared by the University for the Commission was the information that four fifths of the money from the M.D. graduations had gone to the library and to providing apparatus for the Natural Philosophy and Mathematics classes. The memorandum ended with the suggestion that a special plea would have to be made to retain 'the supply of M.D.s . . . 'because of the great revenue loss that would ensure if it were to cease'.

Yet it has to be said once again that St Andrews was not alone in having difficulties over this period of time. Glasgow and especially Aberdeen were also censured for their practice in conferring medical degrees, and both these Universities had had and were continuing to have serious troubles, Glasgow over the antagonism between the Faculty of Physicians and Surgeons and the University, and between the University and the Anderson's College Medical School, and Aberdeen between King's and Marischal. In Edinburgh, the antagonism between the Town Council and University had led to major litigation. Up to and after 1830 medical degrees awarded by all the Scottish Universities continued to provide a means of professional progress for those English and Irish whose path was blocked by unfair restriction, and some of the anger at Scottish degrees came from the English academic and medical establishment. In the next part of the story, this background antagonism is a factor explaining measures taken or proposed against the Scottish degrees.[5,6]

4

The 1826-30 Universities Commission

Dr. Reid Professor 1841-48

Medicine was not in fact written out of St Andrews after the excitement and anxiety of the 1826-30 Commission. This was the first thorough, external investigation of everything going on in the University for over a hundred years. Every aspect was examined—constitution, curriculum, even the fabric of the buildings. It was, as Dr. Cant says, The Age of Reform affecting the four Scottish Universities.

It must be remembered that the Scottish Universities were not as backward as might be supposed. Nor were they any more inward-looking, any more resistant to change than those in England. Oxford and Cambridge in particular had colleges jealous of outside interference, governing bodies who did not wish for change, and a clerical vote in the majority in almost all the general assemblies of Masters of Arts. The college tutors had little say in the direction of University affairs. Many of the colleges, as rich as the Universities were poor, made little contribution to higher studies. The restrictions of most fellowships or scholarships to founder's kin or to those born in particular places or educated at particular schools led to abuse and filled the colleges with idle and useless members. Written examinations, and a real *viva voce* examination instead of the mediaeval disputations, were only begun for the B.A. degree at Oxford in 1800, and an honours list added to the ordinary pass at the same time. Cambridge was in this respect ahead of Oxford, having had college examinations in St John's in 1772.

In England too, critics of the Universities were as much concered with their denominational exclusiveness as with their educational shortcomings. At Oxford no-one could matriculate without subscribing to the thirty-nine articles. At Cambridge nonconformists might become members of the University, but they were denied access to scholarships, fellowships, or University degrees. These two senior Universities were the training grounds of the Anglican clergy; to those seeking to reform the educational worth of Oxford and Cambridge were joined both the enemies of the establishment and the enemies of religion. So there were several reasons why attempts at reform were resisted, and why there was such a bitter controversy both within the University and in Parliament. It was not till 1871 that religious tests before admission were finally abolished.

The development of studies other than the traditional Classics and Theology was not achieved until later in the nineteenth century. It was not till 1848 that Cambridge began triposes in 'the natural and moral sciences'. It was not until

1850 that honour schools of natural science, law, and history were begun in Oxford. Laboratories for chemistry were not built in Oxford till 1855-60; the Cambridge laboratories were a little later, but with the gift of the Cavendish laboratory by the Duke of Devonshire in 1871, during his Chancellorship, Cambridge had a better centre for research than Oxford—as always, the later laboratory had better facilities than the earlier.

In Scotland, on the other hand, the four Universities were untroubled by such denominational difficulties and accumulation of vested interests. They were cheap; fees and lodging charges were low. Thus Scottish students were drawn from a wider field and included very many more boys of poorer families. The aims of the First Book of Discipline had been achieved at least in part. The age of matriculation was lower than at Cambridge or Oxford, and the standard of examination tests was not very high. More than a third of the students were under seventeen, and more than half under eighteen. Yet the reputation of the Scottish professoriate was high, even amongst the English, and because university education was spread more widely, more secondary school teachers in Scotland were graduates.

At this time non-secretarian university institutions began to be formed in England. The first was University College London, opened in 1828. Because of clerical and medical opposition and opposition too from Oxford and Cambridge, the United University formed from University College and King's College in 1836 did not really begin to function effectively till the 1850s. The University of Durham's foundation followed a gift from the Dean and chapter of 1832, and in 1852 the College of Medicine at Newcastle was connected with the University. A nondenominational college was founded at Manchester in 1851, with a benefaction left by the radical nonconformist John Owens. Colleges of medicine were instituted in 1831 at Leeds, in Birmingham in 1828 and in Sheffield in 1828—these three in towns developed by the booming industry of the times. In 1822 a college at Lampeter was formed, mainly for the education of the Welsh clergy.

As far as Medicine was concerned, the main centres of progress were now continental. By 1800 Edinburgh had lost its first place, and had become, as it has remained, only one of many good medical schools. The twenty years 1770-1790 were the last years of her intellectual renaissance, during which activity covered a commendably wide range. And just as men went from Leyden in the early eighteenth century to Edinburgh, so Gerard van Swieten went from Leyden in 1740 to Vienna where as a Roman Catholic he was acceptable, to found the medical school there at Queen Maria Theresa's behest. It was not for another hundred years, in the mid 1800s, that the New Vienna School became the 'Cathedral of European Medicine'. From then till the First World War a whole succession of great men, Bilroth, Julius Hochenhogg (who performed the first laryngectomy; Vienna became the world capital of the new speciality of otorhinolaryngology), Semmelweiss (of puerperal fever fame), Rokitansky, von Pirquet, and later Adam Politzer, Robert Barany, and Sigmund Freud, appeared and followed one another as if by special arrangement. The applied sciences of pathology, bacteriology and immunology, and biochemistry, were now led by Germans and French. And in Scotland, precedence was passing to Glasgow.

Back in St Andrews, the period of thirty years from 1830 constituted the first phase of the search for a viable medical faculty, and the second phase of the St Andrews M.D. when serious attempts were made to make that degree more respectable. In 1833, the year after the great Reform Bill, it was apparent that St Andrews was entering one of its periodic financial crises, and shortage of money forced reductions in the salary of the librarian to £30 *per annum*, and of his London agent from £50 to £30 *per annum*. And in December 1833, a sub-committee of the Senate (Dr. Briggs, Mr Alexander, Dr. Cook, and Dr. Scott) revised the M.D. regulations yet again. There was the usual insistence upon irreproachable character. Candidates must have attended at least four complete sessions of teaching by Professors in some university—the eleven subjects of anatomy, physiology, materia medica and pharmacy, pathology, physic, and surgery were listed, followed by practical chemistry, obstetrics and gynaecology, and paediatrics. They had to have been apprenticed to an apothecary or hospital laboratory or dispensary, and to have attended a public hospital of not less than 80 beds for at least twelve months. Alternatively, they could have been in regular practice or surgeons to the Armed Forces or to the East India Company.

What was new on this occasion was the appointment of external examiners. These were:

> Robert Liston, Esq. F.R.C.S. Ed., Surgeon to Edinburgh Royal
>   Infirmary and lecturer in surgery at Edinburgh University
> I.A. Robertson, M.D. F.R.C.S. Ed., Lecturer in surgery and
>   materia medica
> I. Mackintosh, M.D. F.R.C.S. Ed., Lecturer in midwifery and
>   practice of medicine
> Alex. Lizars, F.R.C.S. Ed., Lecturer in anatomy
> William Gregory, M.D. F.R.C.P. Ed., Lecturer in chemistry

Any three of these, together with Professor Briggs, would form a quorum.

The examinations were to be held at three dates in the year—the last Tuesday in April, the first Tuesday in August, and the last Tuesday in December. 'The candidates must ... be fully prepared, have attended classes regularly, and must be examined by the Professor of Medicine *alone* ... along with the external examiners'.

Finally, the fee for graduation as M.D. was to be £25.3.0; a deposit might be required. A fee of 10 guineas was also mentioned 'for surgeon's diploma'—what this referred to is not clear from the Senatus records.

This particular attempt to strengthen the rules by St Andrews, as seen from Edinburgh, was the subject of a critical memorandum by the Royal College of Physicians in a College minute dated 28th December 1833. A copy of the proposed St Andrews regulations was sent to the other universities of Scotland as soon as they were agreed. The Edinburgh University authorities passed them to both the Edinburgh professional colleges, and also obtained legal opinion from the Lord Advocate and the Solicitor General. The Physicians' College history notes 'that unmasking of the iniquities of St Andrews University had involved an element of collusion between the College and the University of

Edinburgh ... Mutual expressions of gratitude passed between Edinburgh University and the College, and the latter directed that their Memorial should be published in the Press ... In arriving at this decision the College no doubt derived determination from the opinions of the two governmental experts who were "decidedly against the propriety—and very strongly against the legality of the University of St Andrews' resolutions" '.[1]

The St Andrews Senatus, with some justification, considered the note from the Edinburgh Physicians and Surgeons (a copy of *their* resolutions concerning the new regulations was passed round the Senate meeting of 14th January 1834) somewhat high-handed. They were justified in this annoyance, because it is clear from the record that the regulations were a genuine attempt to rectify the wrongs of the past, and were more precise than anything proposed from St Andrews since the time of Professor Simson *primus*. On February 3rd, a sub-committee of Dr. Cook, Dr. Briggs, and Mr Alexander was given the task of examining the letter from Sir William Hamilton, Secretary of the University of Edinburgh, including the legal opinions of the Lord Advocate and the Solicitor General. The Senatus did not apparently see any need to reply to the Edinburgh Colleges directly, stating it was because they considered it below their dignity to do so, but more probably because they did not want to compromise the distinguished external examiners whose help they had secured.

Five days later, the full text of the reply to Sir William was agreed by the Senate. Summarized, it was:
1) The University expressed surprise at the letter 'having made out that St Andrews is answerable to Edinburgh'.
2) also expressed surprise that Edinburgh had passed their regulations to the Lord Advocate for opinion
3) St Andrews would not have replied had they not been shown such discourtesy
4) while acknowledging that the King by virtue of his prerogative could oblige St Andrews 'to abstain from acting on these resolutions, they do not believe the Sovereign would do so, as St Andrews is only following its powers to grant degrees upon examination in all faculties ratified by Act of Parliament'.
5) In the unlikely event of his doing so, St Andrews would make the 'strongest representations ...'
6) The reply referred to the stringent conditions imposed on St Andrews by the Royal Commission. These had been met.
7) 'the idea of terminating the matter by a Bill of Suspension Interdict and Declaration appears too preposterous to require any notice' (as had been threatened by the Lord Advocate)
8) as far as the resolutions of the Colleges of Physicians and Surgeons were concerned—to which the letter from Sir William referred, St Andrews stated that it 'has no more to do with them than with the regulations of men on the other side of the globe'.

Three Senate members added that while they agreed to the terms of the letter in reply, 'they shall not be precluded from moving that, when they shall see it

expedient, the regulations respecting medical degrees recently adopted shall be rescinded'.

St Andrews University did not however stop at sending their letter to Edinburgh. They published a reply which put the admitted previous and present defects of St Andrews in the best possible light, and also went on to the offensive, for the first time since the early eighteenth century, and attacked the University of Edinburgh—not the Colleges, it must be noted—in a public pamphlet. 'St Andrews', as far as medical degrees are concerned 'does the same as Edinburgh formerly did' when that University lacked clinical teaching. This pamphlet does not find a place in the official Edinburgh Physicians' History, and its main contention deserves to be quoted here.

'For above a century after the erection of that University, there were no medical Professors, and even after such Professorships were founded, candidates for degrees in Medicine in this University have always been regulated by the Senatus Academicus exclusively. The first regulation, under the title *Statuta Solemnia*, prescribing *inter alia*, a course of study, was in 1767, prior to which time the fitness of the candidate for the degree was by examination only'. (In the ten years prior to 1767, about 16 M.D.s were granted annually.) Edinburgh University evidence to the Royal Commission was further quoted: 'Candidates for medical degrees are always examined by the Professors of the Medical Faculty exclusively, to whom all such candidates are directed to be referred by the resolution of the Senatus Academicus in 1726'. Resorting next to quibble, the pamphlet claimed that Edinburgh University still did not *itself* have power of granting medical degrees—they only have power by an act of the Town Council of Edinburgh dated 1724. Further, when University candidates were examined in the eighteenth century, examiners had to be borrowed from the College of Physicians.[2] Finally, the pamphlet ended, 'Oxford University has exactly the same system as St Andrews—there being no curriculum at Oxford, but only a specified time of study and course of examination . . . (candidates) may study where they please'. The new regulations for medical degrees at Oxford were in fact published in the London Medical Gazette on the same date as those of St Andrews, on 23rd December 1833.

What this public argument was saying was that St Andrews University did not merit criticism for its medical degree regulations—these were no different from those in other Universities where there had been, or still were, no clinical facilities. The regulations had been strengthened, and the next step was going to be the establishment of a more complete course of study, whenever means could be found to establish this.

No sooner had this counter-argument been prepared, published, and sent off, than another critical communication appeared before the St Andrews Senate. This was on 15th April, 1834, in the form of a very long letter signed by Henry Warburton, M.P., Chairman of the House of Commons Committee investigating medical education. Some of the questions—and their answers—showed that Dr. Briggs—and the Senatus—had become well practised in putting their case. They replied more skilfully than in the years of the 1826 Royal Commission—

Question 2: What additons have been made to the Medical Professorships since 1724?

Answer: When Dr. Briggs obtained his appointment as Professor of Anatomy and Medicine, he was bound to teach Chemistry, as there was no prospect of forming either an anatomical or medical class in St Andrews where there is no hospital and few medical students. With the exception of Chemistry, which has been regularly taught every winter since 1811, there have been no additions.

Question 8: Are any students at present enrolled at the University of St Andrews as students of Medicine or in what period of its history have medical students been enrolled?

Answer: All students enrolled in the Chemistry Class are or may be considered medical students, insofar as Chemistry and Chemical Pharmacy are important branches of medical practice. No student attending the University of St Andrews could be considered as a medical student before the induction of the present Professor and attendance at his class is considered by the other Universities as sufficient so far as Chemistry is concerned.

This answer is all that could be wished for by anyone whose aim was to criticise or indeed ridicule the University. Dr. Briggs would also have been on surer ground had he referred to the time of Professor Thomas Simson—he was possibly unaware of what evidence there is from earlier times—when medical teaching did take place. He was so obviously making the best of a bad job, as his inclusion of Chemical Pharmacy makes clear.

Question 10: In the session 1832-33 what course or courses of lectures did each Medical Professor give and how many?

Answer: During the session 1832-33 no medical lectures were given in the University of St Andrews excepting those given by the Professor of Chemistry and Chemical Pharmacy, for 6 months, 5 days per week, i.e. at least 100 lectures. In this session ended yesterday, there were exactly 107.

No.34 was another key question: Does St Andrews afford any facilities for the study of Medicine exclusive of the lectures given by the Professors of the University, such as a Dissecting School, a Museum of Anatomical Preparations, hospital or infirmary, libraries of medical books, Botanic Garden, or Societies for discussing Medical Questions? If so state the nature and extent of these and the terms on which they are accessible to students. This was given a straightforward answer: St Andrews affords no facilities for the study of Medicine exclusive of the lectures given by the physician in the University. There is no Dissecting School, Anatomical Museum, hospital or infirmary. There is an excellent library of Medical Books. There is a Chemical Laboratory in the classroom of the College. There is no Botanic Garden and no medical societies for discussing medical questions . . .

wrote Dr. Briggs in his bad handwriting.

Anyone reading these letters would certainly wonder why no-one in St Andrews had had the wit to introduce at least some medical content into the chemistry lectures, so that it could at least have been said in all honesty that medical lecturing was included in the curriculum. But Dr. Briggs had not. It may also seem strange that no attempt had been made to produce an anatomical museum, even on a small scale. The answer to this could hardly be that the Chandos Professor regarded himself as a physician, and so *not* a surgeon, and therefore hardly to be expected to produce a surgical exhibition, since he was by his title Professor of Anatomy also. The reason for lack of initiative seems to be in the general low state of the University as a whole. While the Royal Commission had found much to criticise in the teaching in 1826, they had also found even more to criticise in the University buildings themselves. Their state was such that the King's Architect for Scotland, Robert Reid, had had to make urgent plans for their reconstruction, and these were only just being put into effect. The reconstruction affected all parts of the University—Parliament Hall, the Library, St Mary's College, and especially the United College. This was the period when the quadrangle began to assume its present form.

Later in 1834, reasons for continuing decline in University income were given by Professor Briggs when he was interviewed by a Committee of the House of Commons about the financial grant recently made to St Andrews to make good the loss suffered from reduction in fees from M.D. examinations since 1826. Professor Briggs was probably chosen as the University's representative spokesman because of his connection with the quaestor's side of University administration. The government grant was made to the Colleges, Professor Briggs pointed out, and not to the University. The original endowment of both the Colleges consisted of tithes or teinds from parishes of which they were Patrons. While the tithes had continued with little diminution for many years, there had been a reduction in the previous forty years of income of from £1600-£1700 *per annum*—this was because the stipends of the ministers had been raised, and there was less money available as a result. In response to pleas from the Colleges, a grant in compensation had 'at last been obtained', but this was of £800 only—£500 *per annum* to United College and £300 to St Mary's. The University library got no help from this grant.

Dr. Briggs argued further for increased help. Before the regulations of 1826, he quoted, the very large number of medical degrees produced an income to the library of over £400 *per annum*. In 1825 there were 43 degrees conferred and the average for the four preceding years was 26. (In Edinburgh University, there were 114 medical degrees conferred in 1822, and 122 in 1836). The fee made available to the library for each St Andrews degree was £15.19.3—and these facts had been made fully known to the Government. But since the income from the M.D. examinations went to the *University*, and not the Colleges (cf. above), the Government grant had not helped the University—especially since there were only 3 M.D. degrees in 1826 (excluding an Honorary one) and so small a number since. Not only had the library lost this source of income, but the remainder, derived from tithes, had also now been reduced by £100 *per annum*. With money being as scare as this, it is hardly surprising that scientific museums

and dissecting rooms were a low priority. And once again, in spite of direct pressure by the 1830 report, the Medical Chair was still not abandoned.

The University had made a sincere effort—there seems no doubt of this—to make the M.D. examination a more acceptable and respectable one, and were trying to improve chemistry teaching further in the search for the as-yet elusive *annus medicus*. The form of the examination which was devised and which continued for the rest of the century, did equate very much with what was being done in Edinburgh. Sir Robert Christison's 'Life'[3] details the hour-long examination by Dr. Gregory on the anatomy, physiology, and diseases of the stomach, their treatment, and the chemistry of some of the remedies mentioned. His own examination in 1819 included questions from Professor Alexander Munro *tertius* on concretions in the stomach, and from Dr. Rutherford on 'the symptoms of the descent of a calculus from the kidney'. Sir Robert recalled 'but fortune had favoured me by presenting a characteristic case of the kind about a fortnight before, so that I had the needful answer at my finger-ends'. He also recalled, of the written commentary on an aphorism of Hippocrates, a consultation on a case drawn up by a professor, and the defence of a thesis, that 'as these exercises were all written at home, they were actually often the composition of the candidate's grinder'. His own, he said 'were all done by myself, and I even composed the Latin of my Thesis (on the epidemic fever of Edinburgh), which indeed was never put into English, and was merely purged of a few errors by my father'. Even in Edinburgh there were evidently loop-holes in the examination system. While there was good cause for Edinburgh University to be suspicious of 'the iniquities of St Andrews University' from its past record, it was certainly unfortunate that this attempt to threaten legal action was made. It did nothing to encourage the more forward-looking members of the St Andrews Senate to develop anything better, and it provoked the one or two others—as evidenced by the other threat, to have the new regulations rescinded—to demand a reversion to the old.

So with the background knowledge of a succession of proposals being made to alter the continuing confusion and irregularity of medical practice—practice by surgeons, apothecaries, physicians, and acchoucheurs still being separate, and subject to different legal and university and college restraint—the University ignored the criticism from Edinburgh. And on the 29th April, 1834, when Mr Warburton's paper was laid on the table at St Andrews, it would also be ignored, after the answers seen already were returned to London.

On the same day, the recently appointed external examiners were introduced—Robert Liston and Alexander Lizars, surgeons, and I.A. Robertson, M.D.; I. McIntosh, M.D. and William Gregory, M.D., physicians. All these were the examiners for the degree of medicine at the University of Edinburgh. Later they examined five candidates whose certificates of training, under the new regulations, had been checked by Dr. Briggs:

William Carroll (Ireland)
Henry Giles Lyford (Winchester)
David Boyter (Dundee)
Mackay Burns Vaughan (Liverpool)
William Brewer (Norwich)

All five were passed. A sixth candidate, from Ireland, was withdrawn as his certificates were not approved.

The succeeding years saw this new, stricter, examination continue. They also saw a constant succession of letters between Parliament, through its committees for medical reform, and the University. On the 5th of August 1834, two months after Dr. Briggs' visit to London to give oral evidence before Henry Warburton, 'after full examination by all the external examiners except Dr. McIntosh, Andrew Ross and Frederick McKellar passed for the degree of M.D.' On the 11th October, it was proposed that an Honorary M.D. be conferred on the surgeon to the late King George IV, Mr James Wardrop, and this was agreed on October 25th. Dr. Grace, of Cupar, was allowed access to medical books in the library for research purposes. On December 30th, three candidates out of five passed the M.D. examination. This year recorded medical examinations and activity in a more positive way than for a hundred years.

In April 1835, six candidates passed out of seven, and Mr Lizars, the examiner, had the degree conferred *gratis*. Those who passed were Robert Brydon, James Edwards, David Murray, Thomas Burnford Harness, Charles K. Vacey, and Charles William Coventon. At the August examination, when five candidates passed out of nine, it was discovered that William Smith of Forfar had appeared at the April examination under the name of James Edwards. He was now re-appearing on his own behalf! 'He expressed his deep regret for what had taken place and his hope that the University would deal as mildly with him as, in the circumstances of the case, they possibly could. The Senatus intimated to him that while it was their determination in as far as it was consistent with the dignity of the University to deal mercifully with him, they can come to no final determination till the degree conferred on Mr Edwards, which had been surreptiously obtained, was laid on the table'.

Four days later, on August 8th, Mr Edwards' Diploma was laid on the table by Dr. Briggs. 'Dr. Briggs stated that Mr Edwards had waited on him yesterday and expressed deep sorrow . . . that he was willing to undergo an examination in person with a view to obtaining the M.D. The Senate passed unanimously that Mr Edwards would never be received here as an M.D. candidate and that a press release in the Edinburgh Evening Courant, the Perth Constitutional, and the Dundee Courant, that Edwards had obtained a degree surreptiously by William Smith taking the examination for him, had rendered Edwards' degree null and void; Smith was rejected as a candidate (because of the part he had played) and severely censured'.

Two further external examiners were appointed in 1835—Drs. Hannah and Buchanan from Glasgow. The examinations continued; the numbers remained very small. Queen Victoria succeeded to the throne in July of 1837. In October of that year, a letter was received from the Royal Belfast Institution, giving details of the medical course available there—140 lectures in Anatomy and Physiology, with 100 demonstrations, Practical Chemistry and Midwifery, 100 lectures and so on. The clinical lectures were held in the two Belfast hospitals of 150 and 100 beds. The letter asked that their students be allowed to present themselves for examination by St Andrews; this was agreed. Sir James

McGrigor's report on sickness amongst British troops in the West Indies was received in September 1838. At the end of 1838, and in the spring of 1839, there was further correspondence between the University and the Edinburgh Professors and College Fellows, when yet another attack was strongly resisted.

On July 10th, 1840, Dr. Briggs died. Much of his time at St Andrews had been taken up with general administration and academic politics, and he comes out of the records as a man without a great personality, and as a man who tried for a very short time to set up teaching in Medicine but quickly gave up the attempt. Against this, the considerable changes in introducing external examiners occurred while he was in post, and with it a considerable improvement in the form of the M.D. examination. 1840 brings to an end the empty century of Chandos Professors. From now till the end of the century there would be continuing efforts to place medical teaching on a new footing, and success finally achieved.

The first challenge was to the Chandos Chair itself. A letter from the Royal Commission dated 30th July was read on August 1st to the Senate, the post being quicker in those days. This proposed that the Chandos Chair should be converted into one of Natural History, but that there was no hurry to bring about the change. The Senate replied that they would agree to delay filling the chair, at first by only 'half a year'—this part of the minute was voted to be left out of the record. A motion that the Chandos Chair be for Natural History, and that Comparative Anatomy and Animal and Vegetable Physiology should be principal subjects taught by the new Professor was talked out, and it was finally agreed, following a further motion, that the University decline at present to enter any consideration of whether other subjects be attached to the Chandos Chair. Sir David Brewster, who was to be a vehement opponent of continuing the chair as a medical one, noted that there was now no university appointee who could examine Medicine; this did not deter the University from holding an M.D. examination four days later. There were fourteen candidates this time, and they were examined by five external examiners; ten passed.

By October the University, after hearing that the Royal Commission were not to visit before the start of the session (in the next spring) asked that the Rector pass on their deliberations about the vacant chair to it as required. Lord Melville, the Chancellor, next wrote to the University that the Commissioners could only *advise* change, and not force it.

The arguments over retention or conversion of the Chandos Chair are interesting. One body of opinion, led by Sir David Brewster, maintained that to widen the range of subjects in the Faculty of Arts was essential—and it has to be remembered that pressures for reorganising the Faculty of Arts were just as strong as any—and that a majority of United College regarded Natural History as essential for their curriculum. On March 13th, 1841, a final resolution to fill Dr Briggs' Chair was passed by 7 votes to 3. Strong attempts were made to reverse this at the end of the month. By now a candidate was available—Dr. John Reid, Pathologist and Superintendent at the Royal Infirmary of Edinburgh, and he was a candidate of quality. Dr. Haldane, who had been Principal of St Mary's since 1820 and Moderator in 1827, proposed him, speaking warmly on

his behalf, and Dr. James Hunter seconded. Sir David Brewster countered by arguing that since several individual members of the Royal Commission had indicated that St Andrews should *not* proceed, they should delay. On a vote, he was defeated, and Dr. Reid was then formally proposed as Chandos Professor. This was duly carried by 8 voted to 3.

But Sir David Brewster was not satisfied. The Royal Commission, he insisted, had aimed at converting the Chairs of Medicine and Civil History (the latter considerably more of a sinecure than the medical chair; the incumbent, William Ferrie, also minister of Kilconquhar, had told the Commissioners when he was interviewed by them in 1830 that he had lectured in only two sessions since his appointment in 1808) to Natural History and Modern Languages—as agreeable to Sir Robert Peel's Commission. This was an essential reform, he argued. The Royal Commission had already said there was to be a delay, and the University had pledged to the Royal visitors that they *would* delay. Not to go along with the Royal Commission, he went on, could not fail to disappoint— and annoy—them, and could result in their not carrying out other necessary beneficial measures. The University two years previously had agreed to change the Gray Professorship into Natural Philosophy—this Chair of Chemistry had first been available in 1808, when a Dr. John Gray of Paddington had bequeathed £1500 to its foundation. For various reasons the money was left to accumulate interest till now, Sir David reminded the Professors, and Chemistry had been introduced as a side subject for Dr. Briggs when he was appointed to the Chandos Chair. It has already been seen that Dr. Briggs had maintained stoutly, under examination and cross-examination by the Commissioners of 1830, just how much teaching in Chemistry he had carried out, and had given precise details at the same time as complaining about his lack of apparatus. But Sir David maintained that there was still insufficient money available to provide more than £60 *per annum* for the Chemistry Chair, and that the money which would become available from the Candos Chair, were it abolished, would then provide enough to attract a candidate of the required calibre in these difficult days when there was so much competition from richer centres. As the arguments continued, Sir David, with his supporters Dr. Anderson, the Professor of Natural Philosophy, and Mr Duncan, Professor of Mathematics, went over the same ground more angrily, attacking the Chair of Medicine as a sinecure for ninety or a hundred and twenty years; it was 'altogether inexpedient to make another appointment to this Chair, and thus perpetuate a sinecure in United College'. Finally, they all warned against upsetting the members of the Royal Commission!

But it was all to no avail. On the 21st April 1841, Dr. Reid's appointment was confirmed. Either with or without his prompting, the articles of the contract were altered very significantly:

> The Chandos Professor shall be a teaching Professor, who shall open classes to be regularly taught during the session of the United College for the instruction of those students who may apply to him, in the principles of Medicine and Anatomy, with a view to make an *annus medicus*, and likewise in the principles of Physiology, Zoology, or

such kindred branches as may be found useful in an academic course.

The remainder, that the Professor would be bound as part of his duty 'to attend gratuitously such students of both Colleges as may stand in need of medical advice', that he should assist in the trial and examination of M.D. candidates, and that he would receive a proportion of the fee from such degrees—two guineas instead of £1.13.4—were as before. As well as the Professor's share being increased, the external examiners were to be paid an equivalent account. Mr Connel, who lectured in Chemistry, was to be paid £1.11.6. from each candidate's fee, Drs. Hunter and Cook to receive half-a-crown each (2/6), Professor Gillespie (who examined in Latin) 5/-, the librarian 3/-, and the Archbeadle 5/6. 1/6 was to go to the chemical apparatus fund, and the largest share of all, £7, to the library. If Government money was not forthcoming, the University would earn its own.

Professor Reid took his seat on 4th May, 1841. He was the best qualified doctor since Simson *primus*. A son of Henry Reid, a farmer in West Lothian, he was born in 1809 and graduated M.D in Edinburgh in 1830. He was appointed Assistant Physician at the Royal Infirmary of Edinburgh the same year—at the age of 21!—and moved to Paris until 1832. He was later sent to Dumfries along with three other Edinburgh physicians to deal with the outbreak of cholera there, but the diversity of his ability was shown by the reputation he gained for himself as a demonstrator in Anatomy at Old Surgeon's Hall, by his election as a Fellow of the Royal College of Physicians in 1836, and by his appointment as lecturer in Physiology at the Edinburgh Extra-Academical Medical School the same year. In 1838 he had been appointed Pathologist at the Royal Infirmary. Here at last was a man of ability and even more importantly, of personality and drive.

As invariably happens with a new Professor, Dr. Reid very soon sought changes in the examination curriculum. These were minor and the only two of note were that the Medical Board should consist of two members of University staff, and that a list of medical graduates be published regularly. Further small details were altered in October (when Dr. Lizars resigned as an external examiner, as he had been appointed Professor of Anatomy in Aberdeen); the regulations were now to be printed and circulated widely.

In 1842 Dr. Reid was granted leave to go to the continent to study. His expenses were paid out of the M.D. fund. He was the first St Andrews Professor of Medicine to undertake post-graduate study, and his visit to the continent was to the centres of new progress there. During this year there was a good deal of notice taken at St Andrews of the various medico-political bills which were successively being put forward, and the usual sub-committees were formed to watch over their progress. The University added its voice, too, to the protests of the British Medical Association against attempts by London graduates to establish a monopoly in certain branches of practice. 1843 saw the major row over the election of Rector and the undergraduate unrest which followed it. The number of M.D. candidates had risen again, to approximately twenty at each of the biannual diets of the examination. External examiners came from both Glasgow and Edinburgh. In the later summer Mr Connel applied for the vacant

Chair of Chemistry in Edinburgh, but was unsuccessful.

The next ten years saw a large increase in candidates for the M.D. degree—forty one in 1843, with five failures, fifty-three in 1844, with eight failures. In October of 1844, the newly appointed Professor of Latin, Dr. Pyper, found himself debarred from the fee for examining M.D. candidates in Latin which his predecessors had enjoyed. In 1845, there were fifty-nine candidates at the May examination, with six failures; and nineteen at the August examination—with nine failures. Most of these were from English provinces or Ireland, and very many were members of Royal Colleges. Services candidates, so common in the early years of the century, had now disappeared.

Over this same period, criticisms of the degree continued. That made by Lord Farrell, a judge, in 1844, was a typical example—'There is a College in Scotland, St Andrews, where a Diploma might be got for 30 shillings'—but these were now confidently refuted and public apologies obtained. What did bother the University a good deal more, however, was the continuing threat of legislation by the United Kingdom Parliament which could stop its medical graduation completely. The Senatus records show that its members were aware of this as the real threat—annoyance at articles in the 'Edinburgh Review' was minor in comparison.

Sir James Graham's Medical Bill came before Parliament in June of 1843, and was watched anxiously throughout the summer. In June a 'memorial' was sent to Sir James—the Home Secretary of the day. As before the main arguments were first, that St Andrews University had the legal right to grant degrees in Medicine from its ancient Charters, and second, that loss of this right 'would throw it into a state of pecuniary embarassment and difficulty which would seriously interfere with the efficiency of this seminary of education, and ultimately terminate in the total destruction of its valuable library'. That this is not an exaggerated description must be obvious from the following Statement of Income and Expenditure of the Univerity for the last year.

Income £414.19.0   Expenditure £300.17.5

The strictest of the regulations governing the new M.D. examinations since 1826 were emphasised, and the effect of the reduction in medical income on the salaries of the medical and chemistry Professors.

The 1843 bill had two parts—one dealing with regulations for granting of licences for general practitioners, as this branch of the profession was now called, and the second dealing with regulations for granting degrees in Medicine. The second part of this bill did not expressly propose to remove the privileges of St Andrews for granting degrees, and the University hoped that by offering its M.D. degree as what amounted to a post-qualification degree, suitable for more mature candidates, and with a considerably extended and more strict examination, it was safe to continue. There was also by now what was nearly, but not quite, an *annus medicus*.

But in 1844, in September, a new Bill was brought forward. This was considerably more hostile to St Andrews, in the view of the University. Whereas the 1843 Bill had allowed Universities to confer any degree in Medicine on a person who had attended a prescribed course of study in some medical school

either in connection with that University or, what was important to St Andrews, *recognised* by the University, the amended 1844 Bill enacted that a candidate must have duly attended the course of public lectures prescribed by the *same* University to students in Medicine, 'at the seat of the same University' as the Bill stated, and referred to *two anni medici*. Since St Andrews could not provide more than one year, it necessarily follows that its old-established privilege of granting degrees in Medicine would be abolished.

This 1844 Bill was fiercely resisted. On 8th March, 1845, Dr. Reid went over the provisions of the Bill, and commented: 'It appears that the provisions of this Bill will utterly destroy the ancient privilege of this University of granting Medical Degrees'. Along with Mr Connel, Dr. Pyper and Mr Alexander, he prepared a strong memorandum which was printed, and five hundred copies sent to London for circulation to members of both Houses of Parliament. This memorandum went over the same ground, but in addition quoted from the original Latin Bulls, and from the Act of 4th August, 1621, which specifically confirmed the right to grant medical degrees *to those who had studied in other schools*. It showed the University income for 1844-45 to have been £454.1.0. and its expenditure £461.0.8. But its most telling point was that the only Collegiate Universities in the United Kingdom legally entitled to grant medical degrees were Oxford, Cambridge, London and St Andrews, and the first three of these had been excluded from the provisions of the Bill. And in its breakdown of the apportioning of the £25.3.0 candidate's fee, it noted that the largest proporiton, £10.4.0. now went to pay Government Stamp Duty. Professors Reid and Connel, along with Dr. Skea a newly appointed external examiner who went to represent Edinburgh, travelled to London in May and returned, well satisfied at the result of their visit, on June 4th. Professor Reid was congratulated by the other Professors for the zeal and skill he had shown, and £12 was paid to him to pay the expenses of his mission. Poor Professor Connel had no payment, and at the same meeting, the Reverend Mr McBean was appointed University Secretary at a salary of £10 per annum! Further, there were 50 M.D. candidates examined that July, and 19 in August, as if to demonstrate that a Senior University could continue as it had always done!

This respite coincided with an air of general cheerfulness and renewed optimism. 1844 had seen a grant received of £6000 to allow the new building of United College to be completed. In 1846, Dr. Andrew Anderson, Professor of Physic in the Andersonian University of Glasgow, was appointed an external examiner instead of Dr. Hannay who had died, and in March of 1849 Dr. William Seller, who had been appointed President of the Royal College of Physicians of Edinburgh on November 30th, 1848, instead of Dr. Bennet, who had been appointed Professor of the Institutes of Medicine.

This was a short bright period in St Andrews' medical history. The old University had fought off its Southern foes and Scottish critics, and could attract physicians from those very sources of former criticism as examiners. Its degree was acceptable in a way never previously, and the background of virtually all the candidates was unexceptionable. This was due to the personality, ability, and connections of its Chandos Professor, and to the standards he set.

It was all the more tragic then that Professor Reid developed a carcinoma of the tongue, and suffered for a very long time with this disease. In June 1848 he was unable to go again to London to give evidence before another Select Committee on Medical Registration, and Sir David Brewster and Dr. Alexander had to go in his place. He informed the Senate on June 23rd 1849 that he was no longer fit to examine, and on July 30th, after protracted suffering, he died. His painting hangs in the Bute Medical Buildings at St Andrews, the only Chandos Professor's to do so. His early death was a tragedy for St Andrews University; his time there had marked the beginning of real progress and the likelihood of even more had he lived.

5

Slow Progress

Medical Acts 1850-1875: The Second Missed Chance

On the 9th of October, 1849, Sir David Brewster proposed George Day, M.A.Cantab F.R.C.P. London, as the next Professor of Medicine in the University. This was seconded by Principal Haldane and carried unanimously. The other candidates were George Paterson, M.D. F.R.C.P. Ed., Senior Physician to the Royal Infirmary of Edinburgh, and Peter Redfern, M.D. London, Lecturer in Anatomy and Histology, and University Examiner, King's College Aberdeen. It was agreed that the regulations for the Chair made by Professor Reid in 1841 remain in force, and were not to change 'until the University shall see fit to alter them'. There was no hint whatever of opposition to the Chandos Chair now, and Sir David's opposition in particular was stilled.

While something different had been expected from Dr. Briggs' appointment as a chemistry teacher, and new life had been hoped for when Dr. John Reid came from Edinburgh, there was no very obvious reason why Dr. Day, already a distinguished London Physician and Professor of Materia Medica and Therapeutics at the Middlesex Hospital Medical School,[1] should come to St Andrews. But it could very well have been that the University wanted someone with English connections—particularly London ones—in view of the continuing English inspired legislation. He was born in 1815, the son of a minor landowner at Manarabon, near Swansea. His mother, Mary Hale, was a descendant of Chief Justice Sir Matthew Hale. In 1825 his father invested his money in the Swansea Bank, but this failed six months later, and the family were financially ruined; George was brought up by his grandmother in Worcestershire. The family however retained enough income and connections to allow him to go up to Trinity College Cambridge, where he first studied mathematics. He moved to Pembroke College, graduated as a Wrangler in 1833, and became B.A. in 1837 and M.A. in 1840. He went to Edinburgh to study medicine in 1838, and was awarded five of the top medals and prizes, including the gold medal for anatomy in 1839, Professor James Simson's silver medal for midwifery in 1840-41, and the Edinburgh Harveian medal in 1843. Incredibly by today's practice, he did not graduate in medicine in Edinburgh or in Cambridge, but merely became 'licenced to practise' in Cambridge in 1842. He became Physician to the Western General Dispensary and lecturer in Materia Medica at the Middlesex Hospital. It was from London, then, that he came to St Andrews, but as an M.D. degree was considered essential before he could be appointed to the Chair,

he went to the University of Giessen to obtain one. His whole background, then, was as different as could be from that of his fellow-professors, predominantly Scottish as they were.

At the end of Professor Reid's time, the number of candidates for the St Andrews medical degree had begun to rise. In May of 1847, for the first time, qualifications of each candidate were included after their names, and many were M.R.C.S. of England or of Edinburgh. This increase continued, and Professor Day's years as Chandos Professor saw the numbers rise to their highest of any period. Minor changes continued to be made—new subjects were introduced, and periods of clinical attachment altered. In 1850 the graduation fee was raised to 25 guineas, and the fees to the various members of staff and to the apparatus fund and the library increased. Printed examination papers were introduced in the same year, and each candidate's examination extended over two days. For those wishing to take the exam at times other than the set dates of May and October, the fees were increased to the high figure of 50 guineas (£52.10.0d) At Dr. Day's first examination, in May 1850, 16 candidates passed out of 19, after an examiners' meeting had been held.

From the same year began a series of attempts by Dr. Macdonald, the Professor of Natural History (and a medical graduate) to get himself elected as an examiner for the M.D. degree. Sharp exchanges took place, and his pleas were repeatedly ignored. The 'Edinburgh Medical Journal' was discontinued in 1850 and the Catalogue of the Museum of the Royal College of Surgeons of England was presented in 1851, with the Transactions of the Pathological Society of London the same year. These changes may have been initiated by Dr. Day. In 1852, the year the Duke of Argyll was installed as Chancellor, the Smithsonian Institute in Washington presented volumes with medical content to the St Andrews library, and Continental and Armed Forces journals appeared.

The next four years followed a similar pattern. In January, 1853, the University had £1,429.6.1d. in the Bank on account. Changes were made in the Regulations for Degrees in the same year, when Honours Degrees in Arts were formalised. The three groups reflected the range of subjects taught in the University as a whole:

Group A comprised ancient and modern languages, ancient history, and general philosophy.
Group B comprised logic, metaphysics, moral philosophy, political economy and modern history and
Group C was the 'Science' element in the M.A. Honours syllabus, including mathematics, natural philosophy, chemistry, comparative anatomy and physiology, and natural history.

During this year Dr. Day was delegated to go to London with a deputation from the Faculty of Physicians and Surgeons of Glasgow to oppose clauses in the London College of Physicians' Charter objectionable to Scottish Medicals— the Glasgow Faculty was just as indignant—more so, in fact, than the University. The delegation was formed in April, but did not travel to London till December. By this time, clauses in the proposed Medical Act of that year were also a

subject for objection and protest. Complaints from Scotland were always similar: regulations limiting Scottish medical graduates were so often conveniently relaxed for Cambridge, Oxford or London. Ever since the Apothecaries Act of 1815, the 1830 University Reforms, and the Anatomy Act of 1832, legislation had been threatened or real, and all the Scottish Universities and Medical and Surgical Corporations were affected.[2] Since there is no doubt of the antagonism and jealousy of many members of the London Medical Colleges to Scottish medical graduates, the presence of Dr. Day, himself a fellow of the London College of Physicians, was most useful in these delegations. His election to the Chair in St Andrews proved a shrewd choice.

December of 1853 was an eventful month in St Andrews University. Dr. Macdonald, whose campaign to have himself made an official member of the examining board in Medicine continued sporadically, gave an introductory lecture in which criticism of colleagues was the main text. 'An Academic Chair', said Dr. Macdonald, 'has always been regarded as affording the *"otium cum dignitate"* which frees the occupant from professional cares, and enables him to devote his leisure to the advancement of literature and science. But if the Chair is to become a couch of indolence, in which its possessor is to slumber, and from which he is to pass at the close of the session into a state of *semi-annual hibernation,* then has its dignity been degraded, and its light extinguished'. Not only did he read these words to his students—he had them published in the Fifeshire Journal. He then ignored the inevitable censure from the Senatus, and re-published and re-circulated his attack.

His remarks were directed against the Medical Chair, and were not entirely without foundation. They were made while Dr. Day was absent in London, and became quite amusing when, on his return, he announced that he proposed to teach Anatomy only every second session! In the alternative sessions, he said, he would give a course of about 36 lectures on the classification, structure, and function of animals. He was quickly put in his place by Dr. Alexander the Greek Professor and Mr Mitchell the Professor of Hebrew who reminded him that his original contract was 'that he should open classes on the Principles of Medicine and Anatomy, with a view to make an *Annus Medicus* and likewise in the Principles of Physiology, Zoology, or such kindred branches as may be found useful in an Academical Course'. They proposed formally that the prescribed present course of medical study should *not* be altered. This motion was quickly followed up when Sir David Brewster, who in his different way from Dr. Macdonald was a regular critic of the way medical teaching was carried out, proposed as an amendment 'that as Dr. Day was willing to deliver annually such a course of lectures as would form an *Annus Medicus* along with Chemistry provided the minimum number of students be fixed, the University appoint a Committee to fix this minimum'. This was passed by 5 votes to 3.

The Senate meeting following, on December 13th, was an angry one. Dr. Day was furious at Dr. Alexander's motion—the first of the two—where he had said how notorious Dr. Day's class had been since his appointment—'most inefficiently and badly taught'. Dr. Alexander must either substantiate his

words or withdraw. Dr. Alexander would not, however, but confirmed his remarks in reply to saying he had been misunderstood. Dr. Macdonald protested against the censures on *his* remarks earlier—the previous week, in fact—but his protestations were not impressive. He tried to counter by alleging there was a secret endeavour to substitute another lecturer for him in the Natural History class. Dr. Alexander was undoubtedly offensive in manner towards Dr. Day, and his words were described as intemperate, offensive, and contemptuous— indeed, 'violent', in his own severe censure which was delivered two days before Christmas. Finally, as late as January 14th, it was agreed that Dr. Day had discharged his duties satisfactorily, and no further action was to be taken.

1854 saw an increase in cash at the bank for St Andrews. Further medical legislation saw further protest meetings, and the same pattern of protest from the English provincial centres and from Scotland against London. While reform in medical education and uniformity of graduation standards was progressing, the balance between the need for this and equity was not always obvious to those in what the southernmost establishment lumped together as 'the provinces'. In the Spring the Reform Committee of the Provincial Medical and Surgical Association held a meeting at the Royal College of Physicians in London to consider the Medical Reform Bill which was proposed by the Committee of the Association, and Dr. Day travelled once more south to London to represent St Andrews. And in the late part of the year, on November 9th, a very important figure came to St Andrews in the person of Rev. Dr. John Tulloch, when his introduction as Principal of St Mary's College took place in Parliament Hall.

In each year until 1858 medical bills appeared. In 1855 two Bills were reported by Dr. Day as putting at risk the chartered privileges of St Andrews. There was suspicion in St Andrews that certain of the proposals for a national council to oversee examinations might have come from Edinburgh, but Mr Headlam's Bill of 1856 was opposed by all Scottish Universities. Even when amended, the Bill still excluded St Andrews from membership of the Board of Examiners for a suggested licentiateship in Medicine and Surgery by its clause XI, and this clause was attacked with vigour. The claim to Seniority was made in the St Andrews argument, referring to its legal power by the Royal Charter of 1621 to grant degrees in medicine as well as in other subjects, and earlier under the terms of the original Papal Bull, at a time when the College of Surgeons and Societies of Apothecaries did not even exist. It was conceded that while the Apothecaries Act of 1815 might legally debar St Andrews medical graduates from what was then known as 'general practice' in England, that Act had no force in Scotland, where they were 'universally received as legally qualified practitioners'. But while criticisms of the St Andrews M.D. were something the University was well used to and well able to defend, though with increasing realisation as the nineteenth century progressed that it would have to form a proper Faculty of Medicine if its degrees were to survive, exclusion as a University was something St Andrews would not accept, especially when junior bodies had been given a place. 'To give to every such body in Scotland except St Andrews a voice in the nomination of examiners for the proposed licentiateship

of Medicine and Surgery is, with deference, an act of injustice and a further interference with their vested rights, in defence or palliation of which no plea of public advantage can be urged . . . By the Bill in question the power referred to is conferred on King's College Aberdeen, which possesses only *one* Medical Professor, and on the University of London which possesses *no* Medical Professor and *no* Medical School; while it is denied to the University of St Andrews which has stronger claims than either of those Universities, in so much as it possesses within itself the means of a year's Medical Study, which is recognised as an *Annus Medicus* by all the Corporate Boards . . . the University of St Andrews claims a similar share in the nomination of Medical Examiners as the other Academical Bodies mentioned in Clause XI'.

Copies of the complete paper were distributed widely. By early October Principal Tulloch, who had brought new vigour not only to St Mary's College but to the University since his appointment in 1854, reported that replies had been prompt and satisfactory. The University had wisely chosen to fight this particular battle on the grounds of eligibility to nominate an examiner, and on the unfairness of this particular exclusion. The choice of Aberdeen to criticise was a good one, since 1850 had seen the climax of jealousy between the medical men of King's and Marischal, and King's College was at this period weak in medical teaching. And the choice of London was of course obvious. While there could be no defence against absence of a medical school, there was a good defence against exclusion of an examiner. What St Andrews gained was the right to continue examining for and granting degrees in Medicine; it was not excluded as had been threatened and feared.

1857 was another good year for Medicine in St Andrews. M.D. regulations were made even more stringent, in expectation of forthcoming major legislation. It was certainly not true 'St Andrews still gave the degree of M.D. by post'.[3] While members, fellows or licentiates of the Royal College of Surgeons of Edinburgh, Dublin or England, or the Glasgow Faculty, or of the London College of Physicians, or of the London Apothecaries Society, were eligible as candidates for the St Andrews M.D. on producing their Diploma or licence, those without had a considerable increase in required basic and advanced training before they could apply. And although Dr. Pyper, the Professor of Latin, was still on the Board of Examiners, Professor Andrew Anderson of the Andersonian University in Glasgow, and Dr. William Gairdner from Edinburgh, were external examiners of standing. Various critical members of Parliament and English periodicals were forced to admit publicly that the practice of selling diplomas at St Andrews did not occur, and their apologies received wide publicity.

The Medical Act which mattered was passed in 1858. 'An Act to regulate the Qualifications of Practitioners of Medicine and Surgery' became law that October. Its aim, to allow 'persons requiring Medical Aid to distinguish qualified from unqualified Practitioners' was not at all strange—there was still a medley of practitioners whose training was variable and often irregular, and whose qualifications were variable and confusing. The creation of the General Medical Council ensured the existence from now onwards of consistent standards

in training and especially in examinations before an individual became a Registered Medical Practitioner. What was enacted then continues to this day, and guarantees protection not only for the public against fraud and crime by medical practitioners, but also for the practitioners themselves. The United Kingdom Council had twenty-three members—one each from the three Scottish Corporations, one from 'The University of Edinburgh and the two Universities of Aberdeen collectively', and one from 'The University of Glasgow and the University of St Andrews collectively'. The English bodies had also their representatives from their own Corporations, and from the Universities of Oxford, Cambridge, Durham, and London. There were three Branch Councils, one each for Scotland, England and Ireland. Appointment of any member of the General Council was not to exceed five years, but reappointment was not precluded.

The main duty of the new Council was to keep the Register. Specified qualifications included those of all the Corporations, and also Doctors, Bachelors, or Licentiates in Medicine, or Masters of Surgery, of any University of the United Kingdom. Doctors of Medicine granted before the passing of the Act by the Archbishop of Canterbury—something far more strange than anything practised in Scotland, and oddly immune from the spiteful attacks on 'Scotch Degrees' made in the south—were also eligible for registration.

The other important duty was the supervision of standards of training and examination. Members of the Council, or their representatives, could be present at examinations. And just as an individual's name could be struck off the Register for unethical or criminal acts, so could a University have its right to confer degrees removed. But the Universities retained their rights and have since established themselves as the main source of the first registrable qualification an individual can have; the Corporations lost their previous privilege of conferring the right to practise medicine—from now on it was the General Medical Council alone which conferred legal rights to practice. Further, the Corporations now no longer found themselves the senior Professional bodies, since they were lumped together with Universities several of which—including St Andrews— were older than they.

The particular revision of regulations at this time was carefully designed to put the examination proper on a par with that in the other Scottish Universities and particularly in Edinburgh. If St Andrews had no Clinical School, at least its examination would be strictly conducted and entry to it demand precise, formal conditions. The Medical Circular[4] gave details of the evidence of character and medical training, and of previous licences obtained, required for the candidates. It also detailed very precisely the amount of time which candidates not holding licences memberships or fellowships of the various Royal Colleges had to have spent in approved training in the whole range of medical curriculum subjects— 14 in all—before they were eligible to take the St Andrews M.D. The list of examiners, particulars of the examination itself, and of recommended textbooks, was also included. The Circular ended: 'In connection with the clause stating that Candidates for Honours should be examined at the bedside, Dr. Day stated that the Governors of the Dundee Infirmary had expressed their willingness to offer their wards for that purpose'.

The last paragraph of these regulations was of cardinal importance; what became of this proposed Dundee connection will be seen later.

So medicine was not written out of St Andrews in 1858, after all. But it was enacted that after 1862, the number of M.D.s to be granted annually would be reduced severely, and this limitation would thereafter be strictly enforced. Though the number was to be ten only each year, and the form changed, Ordinance No. 19 Sec. XX of the Universities (Scotland) Act, also of 1858, did in fact concede a continuing special privilege on St Andrews, to confer a small number of medical degrees on a restricted type of candidate. The four intervening years, as a result, were quite hectic in St Andrews, before the new regulations came into force.

There was first of all a rather disreputable attempt by other members of the Senatus to gain a share in the M.D. examination fees. This began with the suggestion that four additional members of staff be appointed annually as *assessors* to the examiners, to assist at all diets of the examination. The argument for this was that the M.D. was a *University* concern, and not a *College* concern. As the four assessors were to get 4 guineas and the external examiner only half a guinea for each candidate, the assessors stood to gain considerably. Later it was proposed that the whole Senatus would become the Examining Board—'as there is no Medical Faculty as such, the other members acting as assessors to those who are at present examiners, and, as well as the examiners, receiving a suitable remuneration'! For some reason the opinion of John Inglis, Dean of the Faculty of Advocates, was asked. He replied simply 'of the expediency of the changes proposed it is not our province to judge'. Re-allocation of fees on a daily basis was then suggested—10 guineas to Dr. Day, 4 to the other local medical examiners, 3 to the external medical examiners, and 1 to the classical examiner. The whole of the funds remaining after these had been paid were to go equally amongst the members of the Senate. There is no good evidence, however, that this share-out was ever adopted.

The next change was the proposal, in November, 1858, that as well as Doctor of Medicine, the degree of Bachelor of Medicine (M.B.) would be conferred at St Andrews. The regulations for this would require a preliminary examination in Arts subjects, all of which could be taken in the University, followed by at least four years of medical professional training. External examiners were to be appointed annually, and approved by the General Medical Council. The Regulations were simplified in 1859, when in October 67 candidates presented themselves and 50 passed M.D. The new M.B. regulations did make it possible for a student to matriculate as a medical in St Andrews, complete his preliminary studies there, and return after a spell of more advanced training elsewhere to graduate. It was a further step towards the still elusive *annus medicus*. The M.D. examination's improved status had however been accepted, and the external examiners were not men who would have made the journey for the fee only—Dr. Alexander Wood, one of the most famous Presidents of the College of Physicians in Edinburgh, and its first representative on the G.M.C., John Struthers of Edinburgh and George Buchanan of Glasgow as surgical examiners, and in Midwifery and Diseases of Women and Children,

Dr. A. Anderson and Dr. J. Matthews Duncan from Glasgow and Edinburgh respectively. These were experienced and distinguished men. Perhaps because of this, the failure rate was now between ten and twenty per cent for the M.D. In 1859, too, the Royal Infirmary in Dundee was used for the first time, and this was an even bigger step; in January 1861 the sum of 10 guineas was sent as a subsription to it, 'out of a connection established between this Institution and the University with a view of rendering the medical examinations more efficiently', and the detail is recorded in St Andrews minutes.

At the beginning of 1861 the Scottish Universities' Commission in Edinburgh was concerning itself with the next round of changes in the ordinances for graduation in the Scottish Universities. The Secretary wrote to St Andrews on February 9th asking for suggestions before changes there were discussed by the Commission. The Draft in reply appeared later in February. It went over the now familiar ground, as far as medical degrees were concerned, as previous ones had done—noting the antiquity of St Andrews, its long-standing legal right to confer degrees, and so on. It noted the C.M. (Master of Surgery) degree was not conferred, and it admitted that a full year of residence for medical instruction proper was not available. But the reply made the good point that London University followed the same pattern as existed at St Andrews, and had been accepted in the South as a fit institution to confer medical degrees. Later in the year, on June 10th, the Ordinance (No. 3) was published. Clause 23 stated clearly that no degrees in medicine would be granted at St Andrews after the first day of January, 1863, except upon candidates who had complied with the terms of the Ordinance. Mildly worded protests were made by the Senate; it looked as if medical graduation would now cease after all.

Prince Albert died later in 1861. For most of 1862, medicine was a subject not formally discussed in St Andrews. And then, in September, with the greatest confidence, discussions began on the proposed academic dress for doctors and bachelors of Medicine: ... 'The Cap and Gown ... are to be similar to those worn by Masters of Arts at Cambridge ... The Gown may be made of silk or stuff, at the option of the wearer ... The hoods are also to be made of the same stuff as the Cambridge hoods, but of distinctive colours and materials. The M.B. hood may be either black silk or stuff, with an edge of purple silk two inches wide inside and outside. The M.D. hood, which is very handsome and elegant, is made of purple cloth and lined with rose-coloured silk'. There was no suggestion of the University not having medical graduates—perhaps a critic might say that this splash of colour was to close the medical chapter in the grandest manner possible, especially as 151 candidates appeared in October! 130 passed; various had honours conferred at their graduation.

December saw not only the largest number of all—213 in the first batch when 190 passed, and 166 after Christmas when 146 passed, and it also saw the request of a single woman to matriculate in medicine. Miss Garrett's application was actually accepted, but later queried by the Senate. She had asked 'to be enrolled in the Anatomy and Chemistry classes.' The request was received very sympathetically, especially by Principal Tulloch, but after much discussion, Counsel's opinion was sought, and, sadly, it was then quashed.

It was not surprising that Dr. Day needed additional helpers with these rushed examinations. It is remarkable that he was still able to contribute as much as he did. For in 1857 he had been on holiday in Hellvelyn, and had fallen down a mine shaft while climbing. His fall had fractured his right humerus, and the fracture had never united. As a result he had a flail arm, and could only write after his arm had been lifted on to a cushion. Arthritis of his right knee also progressed so far that he was almost confined to a wheelchair. He was by now a virtual invalid. In March of 1863 he was allowed £105 from the medical fees (profits in these past five years had been £450 p.a.) as he was known to be about to resign. After some correspondence passed between the University and the Privy Council, a retiring allowance was granted, and he retired officially on 16th May, 1863. He wrote the nicest of letters to his former colleagues before he left.

Dr. Day was the first St Andrews Medical Professor to be made an F.R.S. He was a considerable scholar, especially as a writer and translator. His most important works were *A Practical Treatise on the Diseases of Advanced Life,* and *Chemistry in its Relation to Physiology and Medicine.* He translated Simon's *Animal Chemistry* and the fourth volume of Rokitansky's *Pathological Anatomy* for the Sydenham Society, and Lehmann's *Pathological Chemistry* for the Cavendish Society. He also translated Vogel's *Pathological Anatomy.* His translations of the new science of Pathological Anatomy, from the European schools then leading the world, established him as one of the foremost medical scholars in Great Britain. He was a very important figure indeed, in making this knowledge available in the English language to the English-speaking world. But in addition to his scholarship, Professor Day did all the necessary things a professor needed to do. He retained his connection with colleagues in London, and just as importantly, with John Goodsir the great Edinburgh anatomist; he had known him as a student as he had known his St Andrews predecessor John Reid. He carried out research in Zoology and comparative anatomy and physiology, and it was he whose work on marine fauna encouraged Professor McIntosh to start the Gatty Marine laboratory in due course. And he gave lectures of a very high order. A tall man, with a pale face, prominent nose and dark hair, he used to take his class of six or eight students as often as not to his house where he lectured and showed specimens. He read his lectures clearly, and was said to be able to explain their matter to the whole range of student ability so that they understood easily.[5]

The Institute of Medicine course ran from November to April, and a complete set of Professor Day's notes are preserved.[6] The first lectures included an outline of basic physics, mensuration, algebra, and basic logic. General principles of anatomy and physiology in plants and mammals then followed, with a lecture on 'Dormant Vitality' and the diagnosis of death—including clinical applications. Organisation of the cell, and of basic body tissues—with clinical applications—are described much as they would be today. The systematic description of the gastro-intestinal tract, the anatomy of the cardio-vascular system, with clinical applications, is also entirely modern. The foetal circulation, blood clotting, intracranial haemorrhage and lesions of the venous sinuses, are

in modern detail—as is description of peripheral nerves and the clinical effects of injury to these in the limbs and brachial plexus.

There is good interest in anatomical description of systems whose function was not yet known. An excellent example is the sympathetic nervous system. Lecture 21, given on Friday 22nd February 1885, was taken down as follows:

> The Sympathetic Nerves. This is a set of nerves that is involved in considerable security. This sort of nerves was first observed in dissecting the spinal column. It was found that there were nerves running down forming ganglia; this system passed down till it reached the region of the coccyx, when they unite, forming the bottom of the system. In the region of the neck there are 3—the superior cerebral ganglion, middle c.g. and inferior c.g. They give off brs. to various organs, most of the ns. of the heart come from this system; the lungs and all the blood vessels. As we pass down to the middle of the dorsal region, we observe brs. going off forming one stem, or mass. One of these masses lying at the coeliac axis—is called the Solar Plexus. A man receiving a severe blow on the abdomen falls down and often expires. This is owing to the shocks his N.S. must have received at the S.P. All the small intestines, kidneys, bladder, male and female organs of generation etc. etc. are supplied with these nns. Experiments have added information in regard to these. A frog was taken and its head cut off, its breast was opened, and its heart was still. A galvanic battery was applied to the ganglionic cervical nns, the heart commenced beating at the rate of 150 per minute: when applied to the heart it had no effect.

Lecture 36 was given on Friday 18th April, and after it the student wrote FINIS. The notes also included a list of questions, e.g. 'Describe the digestive process in man and describe the stomach of ruminating animals'. 'Describe the structure of the eye and the mechanism of vision'. 'How does Milne Edwards group the principal instructive actions—give illustrations of each group'.

Dr. Day was a clear lecturer, but had as well a way of expressing himself which recalls Sir D'Arcy Thompson's lectures of a century later—he had the same striking choice of words which his students must surely have remembered to the end of their lives. His lectures were undeniably 'medical' in their content and regular clinical applications, and would have provided anatomical and physiological knowledge sufficient for any pre-clinical student of medicine. Much of their content, in fact, would have served for a second professional examination in Anatomy or Physiology of about fifty years ago. They form a lecture course of the very highest level.

After leaving St Andrews he retired to the south coast to Torquay, where he continued to contribute to medical publications with the help of Miss Otte, a family friend and colleague in translation. She remained with him and his family and helped his efforts to earn enough to provide for his widow and three children, for his pension would lapse on his death. It was kindly said of him that in spite of his physical sufferings he never complained and never lost his kindly disposition. He died on January 31st 1872.

Professor Day's early retiral on account of illness was a most critical event in the history of medical teaching at St Andrews. His appointment and that of his predecessor Dr. Reid were excellent ones, and it has been seen how the University anticipated the type of person who would further its medical interest best in this century of continual reform. The pressure from within the University, notably by Sir David Brewster, to do away with the Medical Chair, and with all medical teaching, had been overcome by the person and prestige of Dr. Reid. And Professor Reid's contribution, to stiffen the examination system, and to enlist the aid of former colleagues in Edinburgh and Glasgow, had come at just the right time. Because of his efforts, and because of the good relations he maintained with Edinburgh, former critics both from there and from south of the Border became fewer and were increasingly easily refuted. Professor Day was able to talk easily to the London physicians, and the journeys he made there were not only to argue the case for St Andrews, but with other Scottish colleagues, for all the other Scottish Universities. But his importance in this political respect of being an ambassador from St Andrews to London was no more important, and in fact, in the longer run significantly less, than his policy decision to seek clinical facilities in Dundee Royal Infirmary.

The Dundee Infirmary had been opened in 1798 after some years of discussion about regulations and constitution, and after the necessary money had been raised and a site for the building acquired. The first Infirmary had accommodation for 56 patients, and in the first full year, 45 patients had been admitted. In the 1840s these numbers had risen to over 900, of which about 500 were 'medical'—including 194 'fever' patients—and 400 were 'surgical'. By the late 40s the numbers rose to over 3,000 in a year when the town, now having a population of 70,000, suffered epidemics of infectious diseases. A mental hospital was opened in 1820, but there would be no separate infectious diseases hospital until the opening of King's Cross in 1890. Ether and later chloroform was used for the still limited range of surgical operations from 1847, and in 1855 a new Infirmary was opened, large enough to take 280 patients. The money was provided by a bequest of £14,500—higher than St Andrews' total revenue income—by Mr James and Miss Elizabeth Soutar of Thornbank. The original Infirmary had received its first Royal Charter as early as 1819, in the reign of King George III.[7]

So here was the obvious place to use as a source of clinical material for the examinations—and Professor Day did so. But his departure, and the failure of his successor to follow his lead, resulted in the tragic failure which represents the second lost chance in the story of medical teaching at St Andrews University.

In November of 1862 Professor Day had requested that Dr. Oswald Home Bell assist him in taking classes—and Dr. Bell was supported by no less persons than Dr. John Struthers and Professor Goodsir. His appointment as the next Chandos Professor was unhappy and ill-fated for the University. Dr. Bell was the son of a Colonel Bell of the Madras Artillery. He was educated at St Andrews and then took his M.D. in Edinburgh in 1857 at the age of twenty-one. He soon returned to St Andrews and entered general practice there with a local doctor called Adamson. While Adamson was a most interesting and able man,

James Bell Pettigrew FRS

W. C. McIntosh FRS

Sir D'Arcy Thompson FRS

Principal William Peterson

The Old Infirmary

Watson's Lectures on the Principles and Practice of Physic, and Williams's Principles of Medicine.

Miller's Principles and Practice of Surgery, or Fergusson's System of Practical Surgery.

Churchill on the Theory and Practice of Midwifery.

It has been resolved that, after the present year 1857, those Candidates who have acquitted themselves creditably in the first two day's examination will be allowed to compete for Honours.

Candidates for Honours will be additionally examined in Comparative Anatomy and Physiology, in the higher departments of Human Physiology and Pathology, and in Medical Jurisprudence, and their practical Knowledge of Medicine will be tested at the bed side.

St Andrews, June 1857.

In connection with the clause stating that Candidates for Honours should be examined at the bed side, Dr Day stated that the Governors of the Dundee Infirmary had expressed their willingness to offer their Wards for that purpose.

It was further agreed that in the event of a Candidate for a special examination being found unqualified, he shall forfeit the sum of Twelve Guineas.

1857 book list for MD. Professor Day's arrangement with D.R.I. (See page 59)

especially in the practice of public health, Bell was lacking in academic distinction and breadth of experience, and his outlook remained that of a small local practitioner—he continued in general practice during his time as Chandos Professor. He did teach some physiology, and conducted the examinations, but showed no initiative in the Councils of the University to develop his subject. His failure had possibly a greater effect than has been realised before, as far as the development of medical teaching in St Andrews is concerned.

As usually happens, the effect of his mediocrity was not at once apparent, and the work and worth of Dr. Day overlapped his first years. The fact remains that while St Andrews was alone amongst the other Scottish Universities in lacking a hospital of any size for clinical training, it had nevertheless managed to argue its way to retaining its power to examine and graduate in medicine. It had indeed extended this power after 1860 to examine not only for its M.D. degree, but also for the recently constituted first degrees of M.B., C.M. Its arguments were strengthened by the fact that its two English counterparts, Oxford and Cambridge—and later, the new London University—continued to graduate candidates who had taken most and often all of their medical training elsewhere. And had the initiative in using medical clinical facilities in the growing City of Dundee been followed up with vigour, the whole subsequent development, not just of medical training, but of the whole University, might have been entirely different. It could be said that St Andrews' problem over the centuries, that of lack of money, was the reason. But the M.D. candidates were going to be men who could afford the cost of a rail journey to Dundee—the majority had made a considerable journey already from their places of work elsewhere in Scotland, England, or elsewhere so a little farther would have made little difference. And if Dr. Bell had had the wit to have a member of the Dundee Royal Infirmary staff appointed an examiner, *his* fees would also have been borne by the candidates. And once an examiner, it would have been a short step to his becoming a clinical teacher for undergraduate students; one or two students were already appearing in the Infirmary records of the 1860s and 1870s as dressers, and these could have become the nucleus of a University class. But the connection weakened, and indeed, as will be seen later, wards in Edinburgh began to be used for M.B. examinations.

The students can perhaps have the last word. In Issue No. 4 of 'The Comet' of November 1865, p.8 appeared the leader:

THE DUNDEE INFIRMARY

The public have recently heard a good deal about the proposed affiliation of the Dundee Infirmary to the University of St Andrews. That this Scheme is practical may reasonably be inferred from the opposition of our Medical Professors. We do not wish to impute unworthy motives to these gentlemen; but we are surely entitled to expect from them a slightly more zealous support to the efforts that are being made to utilise their Chairs. We trust that the subject will not be lost sight of by any who are interested in the prosperity of either institution.

The important change in the examination system after 1862, then, was that the General Medical Council would allow M.D.s to continue at St Andrews, but the candidates must be true *post-graduates*—must be forty years of age at least, and have been established in practice. So the examination was to revert more nearly to what it had been in the earliest years of the eighteenth century, except of course that the form of the examination was to comply with the modern form—written and *viva voce* subjects in the five main clinical subjects, and also a *viva voce* in the basic subjects of anatomy, physiology, and chemistry. Latin had disappeared as a degree subject, and there was no thesis. Degrees of M.B. C.M. could be taken; after a candidate had completed the preliminary first division of Arts subjects, he could proceed to basic medical subjects, and return later after doing a clinical course elsewhere. In this respect, lobbying from St Andrews supporters had put the University in an equivalent position to Oxford, Cambridge and London. And perhaps time would show whether local clinical training could still be developed. New external examiners for 1864 were appointed: Dr. Andrew Anderson, in Medicine, from Glasgow, and Dr. Patrick Heron Watson, in Surgery, Dr. Scoresby Jackson, in Materia Medica and Jurisprudence, and Dr. Alexander Keiller, in Midwifery—all from Edinburgh. New, too, was the formation of a Medical Faculty—consisting of Dr. Bell (Physiology), Dr. Heddle (Chemistry) and Dr. Macdonald (Natural History)— and it must be said that at long last there were enough subjects for a true *annus medicus*.

The next sixteen years consolidated these changes. Never more than ten M.D. candidates were examined; they almost always passed. Because of the seniority of these men, the basic subjects were dropped after 1865—with the agreement of the G.M.C. Correspondence continued with the G.M.C. over details of the M.B. C.M. course. Local examinations for schools became a new requirement of University staff, as did the development of subjects in science. Professor Allen Thomson continued to represent Glasgow and St Andrews on the G.M.C. From 1866, medical examinations were to take place only once a year, in late April—at the end of the University session. Further decisions were taken on acadmic costumes in 1867. Teaching in medical subjects certainly continued: Dr. Bell bought two microscopes for his class for £15 in 1867, and others later. In 1868 Dr. Henry Littlejohn joined the External Examiners. In 1869 Dr. Bell said he would begin an Anatomy class, if enough students enrolled. And in that year, Mr John McVail passed the necessary preliminary examination and matriculated as a student of medicine proper. (He passed in Anatomy and Botany in 1871, but failed Chemistry and Materia Medica. The next year he completed the first professional part of the examination.) In 1871, discussions took place on the setting up of a Scottish Conjoint Board for clinical professional examining: luckily for St Andrews, once again, examinations in the pre-clinical subjects remained in the hands of the individual medical authorities. In 1872 the Secretary of the Commission of Scientific Instruction wrote to all Universities asking what their views were on development of science as a degree subject. Principal Tulloch replied that St Andrews was very anxious to set up scientific instruction, and to make it 'a centre for the diffusion of such

instruction throughout the surrounding country and especially to the large neighbouring population of Dundee'. Soon after, a deputation went to London (Scientific education, like Conjoint Board examinations, was being encouraged from the South) to meet the Commission. In 1872 also, in mid April, Professors Macdonald and Heddle, of the Medical Faculty, reported that a number of lady medical students had applied to have two courses of lectures during the summer, so that they could take the preliminary University examination and later continue medical studies. This was considered very sympathetically, but eventually, after the opinion of the Solicitor-General had been obtained, their request was turned down. While certain members of staff were agreeable, no final resolution could be made. But the ladies were consoled by being told the University was willing to await the National Regulations on Matriculation of women students being discussed at National level, and that the refusal was not final.

The St Andrews University Medical Graduates' Association had been former a little earlier in the century, but it is worth detailing its history now. It began at a meeting called by Dr. B.W. Richardson, M.A., M.D., F.R.S., F.R.C.P. Lond. at his house on May 29th 1867. Following this meeting of a small number of his friends, a circular was sent out to all Doctors of Medicine of St Andrews in the United Kingdom, and a larger meeting to constitute the Association was held at the Freemason's Tavern in London on June 19th. Here the laws were agreed, and the office-bearers elected. While the objects of the Association were declared in general terms to be 'the advancement of the Science and Art of Medicine, and of General Science and Literature, the maintenance of the interest of the medical graduates of the University, and the cultivation of social intercourse and good fellowship', the early and main cause of its foundation was to press the claims of the medical graduates to a vote for the Parlimentary representative of the Universities of St Andrews and Edinburgh.

In his Inaugural Oration as President, Dr. Benjamin Richardson honestly expressed the disadvantages suffered by Medicine at St Andrews. 'Those who take the medical honours from our University', he said, 'must gain their knowledge elsewhere, and merely register it in the College Calendar. Hence it has been common for the most favoured seats of medical lore to look upon us with some distrust; distrust which it is our duty to remove . . . not by boasting, not by contention, not by complaint, and certainly not by despair; but by a manly and truthful exposition of our power . . . our industry . . . and by an earnest determination to prove that, after all, we are worthy of our vocation'.

Four hundred members joined the Association in its first year, and 532 members, 15 associates, and 28 honorary members made up the total by 1868. The Association met annually on St Andrew's Day, and papers covering the main topics of contention amongst medical men of the day were read and printed in book form. The political aim of the Association was quietly realised when in 1868-69 they convinced Parliament of the rightness of their claims to be granted a vote (as were St Andrews Arts, Divinity, and Edinburgh graduates including Medical) in the election of the joint Member. Their arguments were fair and reasonable, and the fact they had to be made at all is yet more evidence

of the considerable antagonism and distrust of 'St Andrews Doctors of Medicine'. They were accepted by the Ministers of the Crown of the day, perhaps more quickly and easily than the office bearers ever expected.

Membership declined over the next three years to four hundred and sixty-three members by 1873. During this time Dr. Richardson had been knighted, papers on Tuberculosis, Syphilis, and Aneurism (sic) had continued to be read, and attempts were made to have the numbers of M.D.s increased beyond ten per annum. Their attempts were lost, as was one to institute a Master of Surgery (CM) Degree at St Andrews. In 1873, on the motion of Dr Sedgwick on December 30th, the Association was dissolved, because 'its aims had been realised'. Its books and papers were to be retained by Sir Benjamin Richardson, who was 'empowered to re-organise the Association should the need arise'. It was thus a short-lived 'pressure group' and although the London Committee of the General Council was largely composed of medical graduates, it was not, by the 1880s, the 'astutely organised' body it has been called.[8]

In its arguments for the inclusion of medical graduates in the General Council of the University, and for them to have a vote for the University seat, some interesting general facts about the character of these graduates emerge. It is clear, for example, that the story of degrees being 'bought' at St Andrews was still widely repeated. Statistics were given to show that there was not the complete preponderance of 'Englishmen' amongst St Andrews Medical Graduates—when compared to those of the other Scottish Universities—as was generally held. The 39 graduates on the staff of the 'top London Hospitals' were proudly quoted, and the recurring complaint of London University medical graduates, who though never *residing* in the University, were yet allowed a vote, made and re-made. More interestingly, the figures showed that while the St Andrews General Council numbered only 368 M.A.s in 1868, it had above 1300 M.D.s and so 'St Andrews may thus fairly be called a Medical University chiefly, for its graduates outnumber the other graduates by three to one and have contributed to a still larger proportion of its revenues'!

But most interesting of all were the figures in support of the standard of the examination. The Army and Navy Boards of the day required every candidate for employment in the Services to pass a professional examination. While 32% of Members of the Royal College of Surgeons of England failed these examinations in the recent past, and 18% of Edinburgh M.D.s, only 8% of St Andrews' failed, and the failure rate in the examination held at St Andrews in the years up to 1862 was one in eight. It was insisted that clinical cases had been used in St Andrews examinations, as yet further evidence of their strictness of standards.

And finally, the records of the Graduates' Association bring together in one table just how important the medical degrees were to the financial support of their *Alma Mater* over the years until 1862, when M.D.s were reduced to the mere ten *per annum*.

Medical Graduates, St Andrews University

1836	11	b/f		592
1837	14	1852		65
1838	23	1853		68
1839	28	1854		65
1840	25	1855		53
1841	21	1856		84
1842	35	1857		68
1843	38	1858		73
1844	45	1859		93
1845	106	1860		83
1846	51	1861		107
1847	39	1862		606
1848	22	1863		10
1849	30	1864		10
1850	56	1865		6
1851	48		1866	10
	592			1993

Fees by M.D.s for Diplomas 1836-66 ....£53,261.5.0d.
of which retained by University .... 33,331.5.0d.
Paid in Stamp Duty .... 19,930.0.0d.
Fees paid by M.A.s during 1836-66 .... 762.6.0d.
No Stamp Duty (by contrast)

Other things were happening in St Andrews over the 1860s and 1870s. The development of the train service was one of these—by 1865 two trains left daily for the North and South, and this new easy mode of travel brought a substantial number of visitors to the town. Visitors were men and women of importance in the ecclesiastical and literary world. Their visits were recorded both by individual writers like Dr. A.H.K. Boyd[9] and in the pages of the local Gazette. Study of these accounts does not give the impression that St Andrews was the complete backwater it was alleged to be, and the range of news in the local press showed a world-wide coverage which surely implies wide interests by its readers. Popular lectures began to be given in Fife by University staff, and academic lectures too; doctrines of philosophy and religion were expounded 'from its simplest elements to its most profound speculations'.

In 1865 work commenced on the building of the Mental Asylum for Fife at Springfield and was completed in 1866. From 1865 the University Golf Club was formed; from March 4th of that year its matches began to be reported. Of as yet unknown significance for the future, St Andrews golf was increasingly reported—the supper in honour of Tom Morris in April 1865, the regular results of competitions, the May and Autumn medals of the Royal and Ancient Club. New golf professionals, trained at St Andrews, went out to Westward Ho! in the South and Aberdeen in the North, and in the 1870s and 80s, professionals' matches at the huge stake of £100 a side, over 72 holes and three

different courses, took place between the top men. All these were recorded with the detail and interest, and with the expert comment, no differently from today's. In these years, too, student activities were initiated along modern lines—athletic and gymnastic clubs, various societies, and student magazines. The newspapers printed details of the 'Gaudeamuses' of Classical and other societies in a way that indicated their lighter side being happily catered for. Student and modern opinions were not lacking: 'The downfall of the Scotch Church' said a student leader in March 1866, 'may be counted upon as certain. It can scarcely hope to survive the next twenty or thirty years of religious action . . .'

The change of the Chandos Chair from an Anatomical one to a Physiological one had been a deliberate choice on the part of the University. Professor R. Walmsley is of the opinion that, long before his fatal illness, Professor Reid had been a saddened and dispirited man by his failure to establish anatomical studies, in spite of his best efforts.[10] Although the substitution of Physiology for Anatomy had had the result of making available a subject which could be studied by students in the Arts faculty as well as by intending medical students, and certainly saved the Chair from extinction or conversion into Chemistry or another Science, it took away the one subject from St Andrews which nineteenth century public and professionals alike identified as the *sine qua non* of a medical faculty. Anatomy was *the* subject unique to a medical faculty in its pre-clinical years at this time, before students went into the wards; students were enthusiastic about comparative anatomy in the new Darwinian era, but human anatomy kept its earlier high status. The whole history of procurement of material for dissection in the nineteenth century, and the sensational crimes and punishment associated with it, preserved Human Anatomy's *mystique*. This mystique remains to this day, in the warning notices still to be seen 'No admittance unless to members of the Anatomy Class'. There was, after all, nothing in Britain as yet of the systematic study of Disease—Pathology—such as existed on the Continent, and Surgery remained limited and primitive until the development of anaesthesia and antisepsis. Medicine too was much more unhelpful in curing disease, and even in reaching a diagnosis, than is often realised. While diagnosis was a little more accurate than it had been a century before, therapeutics was not. And while Pharmacopoeia was purged of many of the more superstitious elements of mixtures, those that were employed were as liable to produce discomfort and harm as relief and cure.

So, although an *annus medicus* did eventually appear, in the years before 1875, out of the three subjects of Physiology, Chemistry, and Natural History, the absence of Anatomy was important. It was the pre-clinical status symbol which St Andrews lacked. Professor Bell-Pettigrew, Dr. Bell's successor, certainly requested funds not only for physiological apparatus, but for anatomical models also, and histology preparations were made and renewed from time to time, so there is good evidence that some anatomy was taught. The use of models instead of dissection material was not time-honoured in Edinburgh or Glasgow, but was widely employed in France, Germany, and Austria. It was not by any means the third-best substitute some allege. And though the number

of students taking first year subjects and returning to take the M.B. C.M. later was a handful, they do appear in the records of these years while they did not appear before.

And then, just as some progress seemed to be being made, and the subjects, if not many students, existed for the start of a Medical Faculty in fact as well as in name, the Government began to talk of the need for *two anni medici*. The developing Northern English Universities all had clinical facilities in their respective large towns. They had locally based industrialists willing to provide money to help their development, and had socially conscious reformers, some of more radical political persuasions than others, to encourage higher education of the academically able members of the working class. They were a contrast to the older English universities in most respects, and were their superiors, as far as medicine was concerned, in having ample clinical material for their Medical faculties. It was clear how things were going. No longer were provincial English doctors going to have to come to Scotland for a University degree which would allow them to practise. They were soon going to have all the facilities they required in Newcastle, Manchester, Leeds, Sheffield, Birmingham, and Liverpool. The only other Scottish University which had lacked clinical facilities now had them. The Act of Union of the two Aberdeen Universities took place in 1860, on September 15th, and there, too, the first degree of M.B., C.M. took the place of the old Aberdeen M.D. Some of the developments earlier may have been helped by the friendship of the Earl of Aberdeen with Sir Robert Peel, at an earlier date, so that treasury money became available, but by the 1860s additional impetus came from the strengthened and improved morale of the united University itself, and from the determination and shrewdness of the Aberdeen race itself. In 1860 there were 145 medical students in Aberdeen.

None of this happened in St Andrews. There was no local industrialist, no rich benefactor, ready to provide finance. The failure of the University staff to take advantage of clinical facilities in Dundee has already been seen, explicable only in terms of the Old University's belief in the security of its own long-established privileges. There was no lack of awareness on the part of Principal Tulloch at least of the need to develop scientific subjects, but the Medical faculty seemed to imagine that students would continue to present themselves in St Andrews because of its past, rather as golfers were by now beginning to present themselves to the town which housed the Royal and Ancient Club, because of its obvious future.[11]

6

University Education begins in Dundee

The General Medical Council visits St Andrews
The Foundation and Early Years of University College
D'Arcy Wentworth Thompson

Dundee had been a manufacturing town and seaport since before the Reformation. It became known on the larger scene at that time on account of its reforming activities, though the claim by its local historians to be 'the first place where the reformed religion was openly confessed' is not substantiated by more major Reformation accounts.[1,2] A century later the soldiers of Cromwell attacked the town; on September 3rd, 1651, while Cromwell was defeating the Scots at Worcester, his General Monk was storming the last Scottish stronghold of resistance to him, the Old Steeple of the Parish Church of Dundee. He did his work so thoroughly that it was said the townsfolk danced with joy at the news, on Cromwell's Day, 1658, that the Protector, who had destroyed more Scottish churches than ever the reformers had done, was dead. The Grammar School had associations with Sir William Wallace, and one of its houses today bears his name. That school had also educated Hector Boece, before he went to St Andrews and thence to Aberdeen. As Dr. Johnson passed by he found nothing of note there, however, since the town had shared the decline of the mid-eighteenth century and had no mediaeval or national associations; he regarded Kirkcaldy and Cupar as better towns. But over the nineteenth century Dundee was prospering as never before. It steadily grew in population from about 25,000 in the early part of the century to nearly 80,000 by 1850, and was moving towards its highest fifty years of importance as a shipping and manufacturing centre. By the 1870s Dundee was on a tide of wealth and prestige it would not experience again, and with it went the confidence and pride which new wealth always brings. And as far as medicine was concerned, its size demanded and had obtained a large and modern hospital.

From the early 1870s interest began to be shown in the provision of higher educational teaching in Dundee, and various ideas were put forward to bring this about. On March 14th, 1874, a 'proposal for erecting a College in Dundee' was sent to the St Andrews University Senate; this was an initiative from Dundee to St Andrews. On March 25th the paper was discussed, but was not proceeded with as it was regarded as an informal one, coming from an individual citizen. A formal letter from Mr Thornton, the Town Clerk, came to the Senate the next winter, about the possibility of starting University education

72

in Dundee. It is of the greatest significance in view of subsequent events and assertions, that this letter's arrival coincided with the year when St Andrews University's poverty in student numbers and poverty in worldly goods reached as low a point as at any time in her sad eighteenth century history. To the request for help, Principal Tulloch, as he now was, replied most civilly on behalf of the University.

University of St Andrews, January 25th, 1875

My dear Sir,

I duly received your letter of the 16th inst. and laid it before a meeting of the Senatus Academicus held on 22nd January. It received very full consideration, and I am instructed to send you the following reply on behalf of the Senatus.

The promotion of Academic culture in Dundee is a subject in which the members of Senatus have long felt a warm interest. It may be in the recollection of some of the inhabitants of Dundee that a statement of special proposals on this subject was prepared and circulated by a member of Senatus in the end of 1871, and another member about the same time availed himself of the opportunity of being examined by the Royal Commissioners on Scientific Instruction to state that it was the desire of the St Andrews University "to meet the Dundee people in any way most likely to advance the Higher Instruction in Dundee".

With such views the Senatus rejoice to hear that "the inhabitants of Dundee have under consideration a proposal to establish a College within the town of Dundee", and they gladly express their willingness to render their "friendly aid" in carrying out the proposal in any manner that seems to the University practicable and expedient.

In the meantime it is hardly possible for the Senatus to say more in the absence of definite information (1) as to the character of the proposed College when established in Dundee, and (2) as to the funds available for founding such a College. When the promoters of the Dundee movement are in a position to communicate more fully with the University, the Senatus will be glad to offer them their best advice as to the details of the College Scheme.

It appears to the Senatus, however, to be necessary to state in the outset that the constitution of the Scottish Universities requires the instruction for the Degree in Arts to be given at certain definite classes at the seat of the University—special provision being made for the passage of students from one University to another during their Arts Curriculum.

It is for the inhabitants of Dundee themselves to consider what is best for their own educational interests. The Senatus have no wish to dictate to them in such a matter. They desire only to point out that they are precluded both by their constitution and by immemorial University usage in Scotland from favouring any proposal to give a complete training for the Degree in Arts anywhere save at St Andrews.

It does not follow from this that the College to be established in Dundee should be "a purely scientific one". The Senatus see no reason why the proposed College should not embrace certain Chairs in Literature as well as in Science—leaving the relation of these Chairs to the general graduation system of the University to be afterwards considered and determined.

While expressing these views the Senatus desire once more to assure the Committee representing the inhabitants that they regard the movement with much interest and hopefulness, and will be ready to forward it to the utmost of their ability, consistently with their position, and with the principles which as one body in the community of Scottish Universities, they are bound, in behalf of the higher education to maintain.

I am, my dear Sir, Yours very truly,

(Signed) J. Tulloch

T. Thornton, Esq. Dundee.

It is unreasonable to see in this letter deceit and evasion or writing with an eye to any outside national body. Principal Tulloch, from the many accounts of him both in press and private, was too honest and liberal a man to mean other, in this personal reply to Mr Thornton, than exactly what he said.[3]

The next step came in October 1875, when there were suggestions that scientific subjects should be taught in Dundee by St Andrews professors. The scheme of Dr. John Boyd Baxter for the foundation of a University College in Dundee paid for by £150,000 of his money and with the need for a further £75,000 if six professorial Chairs were to be endowed had fallen. Professor Bell had died that June, and his successor had not been appointed, but Physiology was one of the three scientific subjects offered for the coming winter, the others being Chemistry and Geology. The University representatives, Dr. Heddle the Geologist and Chemist and Dr. Nicholson the Geologist and Zoologist met Sheriff Cheyne, Rev. William Knight, Mr Thornton, as representatives of the Town Council, Mr Thoms, Chairman of Directors of the Dundee High School and Mr Morrison, the Science Master at the Science and Art School in Dundee. In the Dundee party was also Mr Leng of the *Dundee Advertiser*, the publication which was to be the third party in all subsequent dealings between Dundee and St Andrews. Being aware of the various major proposals which had been made and which were being made about higher education in Dundee, the St Andrews professors made it as clear as they could to the Dundee representatives that they did not wish to discuss the merits or advance the interests of any of these. All they wanted to do, they said, 'by directly offering, as Professors of the University of St Andrews, to deliver certain courses of lectures during the forthcoming winter, to test whether there existed in Dundee enough interest in higher education for them to think of putting University lectures on a more permanent basis at any later date. They had previously ascertained, (as they said later in their report of the meeting to the University) that the Dundee representatives had a special interest in the establishment of an educational connection between Dundee and the University of St Andrews. It seemed that

before the formal meeting took place, informal discussions had been held, and informal letters exchanged, and that both the St Andrews and the Dundee members were in agreement about what was actually being sought.

It is clear that this meeting was an important one, and that it went into very considerable detail. Even the proposed location of the winter lectures, the mathematics class-room of Dundee High School, had been inspected already by Drs. Heddle and Nicholson from St Andrews. The lectures were to take place in the evenings, and so be available to a mature adult as well as a youthful audience. Drs. Heddle and Nicholson had urged that as well as scientific lectures, some classical or literary subjects should be included, but this suggestion was 'met by the strongly expressed opinion of all the gentlemen concerned that in the present circumstances, and for the first year at least, a systematic course in such subjects would not be advisable'. (In the winter, however, classical lectures of general interest were in fact given, but these were given in the Albert Institute, opposite the High School, were individual, and did not constitute any sort of systematic course).

Two points are worth noting here. It has been suggested that there was some hidden reason why the Dundee Committee 'declined to grasp the nettle proferred by the Professors in rejecting any systematic course connected with classical literature'.[4] It is very much more likely that they chose scientific subjects rather than Arts for the very good reason that the former would be much more acceptable to a Dundee audience. The second follows: these were not *University* lectures leading to any sort of degree. They were very much the sort of lecture offered today to a class of adult, or further education—of the non-vocational type. The large size of audience showed general interest as well as the interest of novelty, and the St Andrews Professors, as their reports later showed, were well aware of this. The insinuation that the result of their single winter session at once convinced them that large *University* classes would immediately become available comes from the *Dundee Advertiser* and not from their considered opinions when expressed later.

Details of the guinea fees for participants were worked out, and the sum of £150 was subscribed by the Dundee gentlemen themselves towards expenses. It was also stressed that the lectures were not to be 'given by any sort of private arrangement, but were to be officially sanctioned by the University and be seen as an extension of University facilities'. The University also agreed to provide some funds to cover costs.

After the courses of the three scientific subjects had been agreed, Drs. Heddle and Nicholson called in person on Mr Morrison, one of the teachers of the Science and Art School of Dundee, which was connected with the Science and Art Department of South Kensington Institute in London, to see, as they put it, 'whether the proposed courses might be regarded with jealousy, as trespassing on the ground already occupied by the Certified science teachers'. But they were pleased to find that not only were the science teachers not at all jealous of the new enterprises, but were most enthusiastic about it; and several of them had arranged to attend themselves.

The choice of Dundee High School as the site of the courses was not sur-

prising. This School, the continuing Academy of Dundee for six hundred years, had in the last ten years and more an arrangement that St Andrews University staff inspect its examinations and facilities, and this was now done on an annual basis. The request for this had come from the School and not the University, and relations between them were obviously very good. Dundee High School, as the nearest centre of higher secondary education, was a natural relation, and St Andrews University received its share of its best pupils.

There was certainly no suggestion in these records that the St Andrews Professors were desperately anxious to hurry to Dundee or to join with a proposed College there. Principal Tulloch had expressed in his quiet way the policy of wishing to help. The Arts and Divinity Professors were not involved. Professor Heddle was unhappy over the recent protracted battle he had been waging with the Senate over the exclusion of his subject, Chemistry, from the stipulated course in the faculty of Arts, but he was the only staff member anxious for change. The other science staff were involved because it was acknowledged that science subjects were applicable and of interest to citizens of an actively expanding industrial town, and the object of the lectures was, as was said, to estimate the amount of interest they might arouse as well as to give information.

There was no teacher of Physiology represented in the October meetings, but the new Chandos Professor of Physiology and Medicine appeared on the 6th of November for the first time in the St Andrews Senate. The Minute did not even say who he was! As he was to become such an important figure in the early years of the new Medical School, both before and after its foundation, he requires a better introduction here.

James Bell Pettigrew was born on the 26th of May, 1834, at Roxhill in Lanarkshire. He was related on his mother's side to the Henry Bell who built 'The Comet'. Educated at school in Airdie, he was an M.A. of Glasgow and then studied Medicine at Edinburgh. His under-graduate career there was so remarkable as to defy belief, and he almost deserved the word 'genius' applied. In 1859 he was awarded Professor Goodsir's Senior Anatomy Gold Medal for a paper 'On the arrangement of the Muscular Fibres in the Ventricles of the Vertebrate Heart'. As a result of his dissections, still preserved in the Anatomical Museum in Edinburgh, he was invited *while still a student* to give the Croonian lecture at the Royal Society in 1860 on the musculature of the heart. In the same year he was awarded a gold medal for his M.D. thesis on 'The Ganglia and Nerves of the Heart'. Like his predecessors Reid and Day, he was invited to be the President of the Royal Medical Society in Edinburgh, a singular honour for a non-Edinburgh man.

Pettigrew moved next to London, where he was appointed the Assistant Curator of the Hunterian Museum of the Royal College of Surgeons of England. He worked there until 1867, when he resigned on account of the ill-health his overwork had brought on. It was while in London that he began his work on the flight of birds. When his health recovered, he became Curator of the Museum of the Royal College of Surgeons in Edinburgh and also pathologist to Edinburgh Royal Infirmary. In 1869 he was elected F.R.S. and in 1873

appointed a lecturer in Physiology in Edinburgh. This was the outstanding man who now appeared at St Andrews in 1875, a man who had met and matched the highest scientific minds in the Kingdom.

As soon as Professor Pettigrew had arrived, a suggestion was made by Drs. Humphrey and Barclay, the external assessors for St Andrews from the G.M.C. They suggested that *all* the candidates whose credentials were suitable under the St Andrews regulations should be examined, and only the best ten passed. This was extremely advantageous to St Andrews, as it would undoubtedly strengthen the M.D. degree further—as well as providing an increased revenue from fees. At the discussion on this on the 11th December, Professor Pettigrew considered that it should be accepted, as he felt it would help the University retain its privilege of granting medical degrees.

The winter passed, and the first Dundee lecture courses were given. The two Principals, Tulloch and Shairp, had had an almost full room in the Albert Institute for their open lectures. Professor Pettigrew had given a course of twenty lectures on Human and Comparative Physiology at Dundee High School. 'The audience was usually about three hundred'. The lectures, Professor Pettigrew reported, were 'strictly scientific' . . . as he 'is in the habit of delivering to medical students and others who intend to graduate'. They were illustrated by six or eight microscopes, brought from his department, and by experiments specially designed for the course.

While Professor Heddle, who was still fighting his battle over the inclusion of his Chemistry lectures into the Arts course, was moderately complimentary, Professor Bell-Pettigrew was positively flattering to his Dundee audience. 'In Dundee', he said, 'there is a numerous class of well-educated individuals of both sexes who not only desire University lectures and higher instruction, but are prepared to purchase this at very considerable sacrifice . . . The examination papers were exceptionally well answered . . . for questions quite as difficult as those usually set to medical students'. For the first time in his life he had awarded full marks to one candidate at each of the two class examinations. The good results overall he thought, however, might have been due to those attending the class doing no other course. He was full of enthusiasm, and said that, for himself, he would have much pleasure in delivering a second course in 1876-77.

In the M.D. examinations of 1875, when Professor Bell was ill and the University was experiencing the latest of its periodic crises of numbers, two assessors from the General Medical Council visited St Andrews. Their report's suggestion, that a larger number of M.D. candidates than then should be examined was supported, as has just been noted, by Professor Pettigrew that December. But in addition the assessors had criticised the examination. They had noted the Regulations for the M.B. M.C., which allowed candidates from elsewhere to be examined in the First, Second, and Third Professional examinations, and had given their opinion that the small number of candidates (only one or two a year) was at least partly due to the nature and stringency of the regulations. 'There can be no doubt that a Regulation, which requires the candidate to have passed two years, at least, of his four years of Medical and

Surgical study at one of the British or Irish Universities or Colleges, would, of itself, in most instances, prevent the student from resorting to St Andrews for a Degree; inasmuch as only one Annus Medicus can be kept there, and that very imperfectly; and he would naturally prefer to pass the Examinations, and take his Degree at the University . . . where he had studied'.

One such candidate had appeared, trained in Edinburgh. He offered himself for all three parts of the Final Examination, but failed. 'His answers, which we read, showed a certain amount of knowledge on all the subjects, but not sufficient to justify the University in granting him a Degree. Copies of the questions are appended. His clinical examination had taken place in the Infirmary at Edinburgh on the preceding Saturday'. Details of this man's M.B. M.C. examination were given, with the report: 'This examination, therefore, although conducted with a good deal of care, can scarcely be said to come up to the modern requirements of a Pass Examination. Nor does it appear that there are, at present, at St Andrews, the means of conducting such an examination with efficiency'. In each preceding year to 1871 there had been one candidate for one or other or more of the various Professional examinations. Only half of these had passed.

As far as the M.D. examination was concerned, the vistors described the selection. Applications accompanied by testimonials (of which they saw several signed by men of eminence in the profession) were received from aspiring candidates. Ten of these were selected by the University Court and directed to appear for the examination. If any failed to attend, those next on the list of acceptances were told to come—this year, two had been summoned by telegraph a day or two before. The two-day examination was described. There were four tables, one each for Medicine, Surgery and Midwifery, and the fourth for Materia Medica and Jurisprudence. Though various specimens were used, no microscope slides were shown, or practical tests required. The main and serious criticism was that only a moderate amount of practical knowledge was required by the candidates, and that the answers were of no high order. Two of the ten failed.

What the visitors were really saying was that the practical standard was just not adequate. Their conclusion was not that the degree should be abolished, but that its standard should be raised to make it a really worth-while attainment. 'On the whole we must confess that the manner in which the privilege of granting ten M.D. degrees annually as exercised by this University, does not appear to us satisfactory. We cannot think that the conferring of the highest Degree in Medicine in consequence of a Candidate having presented testimonials and passed an Examination as we witnessed can be fraught with any real benefit to the profession or the public, or even to those who seek and obtain the Degree. It fails to afford any sufficient stimulus to induce the Candidates to take pains in making preparation, or in the maintaining that higher culture which such a Degree should indicate. This is the more to be regretted because we cannot but feel that a very beneficial influence might be exerted by a judicious mode of exercising this privilege and giving to practitioners, who really merited the distinction, an opportunity of obtaining the doctorate of medicine which they

could in no other way reach, and of connecting themselves with an institution of much antiquity and interest. This end would probably be, to some extent at any rate, effected, if, instead of sending for ten practitioners only to come up, and so limiting the Candidates at the Examination to the number of Degrees to be conferred, a larger number were admitted, and a selection made upon well defined grounds of professional distinction, and the possession of such superior knowledge as may be indicated by an Examination of a higher order'. This report was eminently fair and reasonable.

The questions set for this year were not very inspired, and it is interesting to speculate how different things might have been had a fit Professor Day been in post, and had patients at Dundee Royal Infirmary been used for a practical clinical examination as he had wished to do. But Professor Day was not in post, his successor was ill, and there was no local medical man of worth even to make excuses. This task had to be undertaken by the external examiners, all from Edinburgh, who sounded indignant that their own standards were being called in question. There is no evidence whatever in the University Senate records of fear and alarm at this critical report[5] and the reply of the external examiners was firm.[6]

In March 1876 Professor J. Bell Pettigrew M.D. F.R.S., now styled 'Dean of the Medical Faculty', wrote a formal comment on behalf of the University to the General Medical Council. In this he quoted in full the Regulations for the M.D. degree and examinations, as laid down by the Ordinances of the University Commissioners of 1858, noted that the University itself had no power to alter them, and made the point that the St Andrews M.D. was not the usual 'first degree'; it was a true post-graduate qualification for those already on the Medical Registers, and therefore should be judged differently from degrees given to young men in the ordinary circumstances of the day. Professor Pettigrew once again made the point that the very regulation which restricted candidates to men over the age of forty meant that while their knowledge of Medicine, Surgery, and Midwifery should be wide, they could 'not be expected to possess the same knowledge of the minutiae of subjects, such as Anatomy, Chemistry, and Physiology, which may reasonably be asked from candidates just fresh from the Schools. It would not be fair, nor expedient, that candidates over forty years of age, who have been for many years engaged in active practice, should be tested by an Examination precisely similar to one which would be suitable and proper for a candidate who had just completed his Curriculum of Study. This undeniable fact was recognised by the Commissioners in framing the Regulations for the Examination'.

Professor Pettigrew went on to say that the character of the Examination could not be materially altered while the present Regulations remained in force. He freely conceded the demerits of the present Examination, and said he would be willing to modify it at the General Medical Council's instruction, provided the Regulations could also be modified. The St Andrews Senate did not agree with the recommendation of the Visitors that the Examination be made a competitive one, as the present small number of candidates allowed did this already. But he did agree that the degree could be made competitive if the age

of admission were reduced from forty to twenty-six years 'this being the age fixed for the admission of Candidates to the Fellowship of the College of Physicians of London', and if more than ten candidates were allowed in a year. He was clearly, as the just-appointed Professor from Edinburgh to St Andrews, very eager to make the standard higher if he possibly could. The point about making the examination a much stricter one was not lost on him. And so while the G.M.C. criticism of the St Andrews Medical Examination can undoubtedly be used to denigrate the University by anyone who wishes to do so, it can also be seen as constructive and useful. Nevertheless the criticism of the lack of clinical material for practical examination was entirely justified, and Professor Bell's failure in this respect remains. The character and personality of the first of the two assessors, George Humphrey, is however another factor in the sort of criticism offered.

George Humphrey had been born at Sudbury, Suffolk, in 1820, the son of an advocate. Educated locally, he had been apprenticed to J.G. Crosse, surgeon to the Norfolk and Norwich Hospital at the age of sixteen. When he was nineteen he went to St Bartholomew's Hospital in London, where he won the Gold Medal in Anatomy and Physiology, but did not graduate. Instead he became a licentiate of the Society of Apothecaries in 1842, after being admitted M.R.C.S. (England) in 1841. He applied for the unexpectedly available post as surgeon at Addenbrooke's Hospital Cambridge in October 1842, and after appointment became the youngest hospital surgeon in England. A succession of Honours of the highest levels followed over the years, including an F.R.S. in 1859. But he did for Cambridge what he must surely have realised another could have done for St Andrews—he converted the hospital there—having in 1842 only 70 in-patients and 120 out-patients per annum—into a School of Medicine. The criticisms of the Anatomy part of the Examination certainly came from him; he had been elected Professor of Human and Comparative Anatomy at Cambridge in 1866 on the retiral of the Reverend Dr. William Clark. He had been instrumental in obtaining anatomical specimens from several sources—including Dublin—and arranging their transport to Cambridge. He had, in fact, shown just what could be done by a man with vision and drive, and the fact that he was a man 'without an introduction, poor, and with no influence in the England of the day', testifies to his ability being of the very highest.

The very last word must be given to Professor Bell Pettigrew. His reply on behalf of the University brings out a fact of the greatest significance about medical graduations at this time, and this was that the Regulations themselves had succeeded in limiting the examination very much indeed. The Regulations were, in fact, very particular to St Andrews, and the University were not hiding behind them when they asserted what they did about their M.D. degree. They were confined by them. The examination had to be seen within the context of the 1858 Regulations; because this was not realised at the time, and has not been appreciated since, the degree continued to be ridiculed.[7]

After the initial enthusiasm of the first winter's lectures at Dundee, further serious discussions continued. In May of 1876 Principal Shairp moved that

matriculated students of St Andrews be taught in Dundee. The Professor of Divinity, Dr. Crombie, forced and carried an amendment that such an important decision required a special committee to report. Dr. Crombie had shown himself a stickler for correct procedure in other matters, and not just over this particular one. Later in 1876 the University approved the giving of the Higher Certificate of Education to women, angry student complaints about Professor Heddle's Chemistry class continued, and interest was beginning to be shown in measures to make the students more physically fit. But Dr. Crombie's delay ended in February of 1877, when it was agreed to hold matriculated student classes in Dundee in Science subjects, and also in Mathematics, Education and Humanity. This decision was approved by the University Court on April 7th.

Because the agreements of February 10th, 1877, were important, they deserve recording in detail.

1) Principal Tulloch moved that it was desirable that matriculated classes in Science be begun in Dundee with a view to graduation in Science. This was agreed.

2) Professor Knight (moral philosophy) moved that the classes should be in Natural History or Geology, Physiology, Chemistry, Experimental Physics and Mathematics. This was agreed, with Dr. Crombie dissenting.

3) A class in Education should be started; this was agreed.

4) Principal Shairp stated it was desirable that a Latin class be established, to be conducted by the Professor plus assistants as necessary. Dr. Crombie dissented from this also.

5) Finally, it was agreed that the Senatus enter into negotiations with Dundee to establish University education there on a more permanent and academic basis. This was agreed, with no dissent.

It is clear from the records that Dr. Crombie's dissent was personal and unimportant.

Discussions, proposals, and counter-proposals continued throughout 1877—and into 1878—copies of the minutes being sent to Mr Thornton for information. In 1877 a request for students' tickets at competitive rates was made by the University for the rail journey between Dundee and St Andrews on the opening of the Tay Bridge. In December of 1877 Professor Pettigrew became the G.M.C. representative for Glasgow and St Andrews Universities. In January 1878 it was agreed that Professor Meiklejohn start classes in English Literature in Dundee, and that Professor Pettigrew give a lecture course on the physiology of 'The Senses'. While Professor Pettigrew's course was to be paid for by funds from Dundee, those of Professor Meiklejohn (and Professor Nicholson, lecturing in Geology) were to be paid for by funds from the Gilchrist Trust, from St Andrews. Good results were reported that June on the success of the ladies in the Arts and local examinations. The M.D. candidates passed, and two passed M.B. C.M.; 20 guineas from forfeited fees were used to purchase medical specimens.

The year 1878 also saw another chapter in the age-long difficulty St Andrews had in attracting finance because of its small numbers. 'This is no new fact' the

University complained, 'the public now regards prestige solely by the test of numbers'. The want of valuable bursaries and fellowships at St Andrews was stressed, as was the fact that professors in other Universities whose classes were even smaller than those in St Andrews were to get a salary increase. However, student numbers were starting to rise again, and the University still lived.

In 1879 a proposal was laid before Parliament to amend the 1858 Medical Act, and a petition was sent from the University to Lord Selborne, the Rector, and the Rt. Hon. Lyon Playfair, M.P. for Edinburgh and St Andrews Universities, to present to their respective Houses. One Dr. James George Beaney donated £1000 for the better endowment of the Chair of Medicine and Anatomy—this was invested in New Zealand Government loan at 4½%. And in December, shortly before the Tay Bridge disaster, the Railway Company threatened to discontinue the students' train from Dundee unless St Andrews bought a further four tickets, bring the total to eighteen.

1880 saw quite considerable development of the Natural History Museum, in which Professor Pettigrew had an interest. 1881 saw further satisfaction expressed at the efforts to establish a College of Higher Education in Dundee, but the progress hoped for on the St Andrews side had slowed. The year also saw a Government Committee active with proposals to change the Medical Acts, and a series of questions was sent to St Andrews as well as to all other Universities with medical faculties. The question of licensing of graduates was raised, but no change in this was advised. If any change was recommended, the University recommended a Conjoint Examining Board of the four Scottish Universities, which should hold examinations in rotation in Aberdeen, Glasgow, and Edinburgh. 'It is to be understood that in making this recommendation the Senatus does not intend that it should apply to the special privilege granted to the University of St Andrews by Ordinance No. 19 Sec. XX, of the Commissioners under the Universities (Scotland) Act of 1858. These replies included financial returns which emphasised the poverty which had haunted St Andrews since the Revolution of 1689. As well as the 10 annual M.D. graduates, 7 men had graduated M.B. C.M. since 1867. The average net income from all of these to the University (after Stamp Duty and examiners' expenses) was £357.4.11d. The '50 guinea men' as a source of income was not only a sneer, it was an inaccurate sneer. Other sources of income to the University in this recent period from lands, interest, matriculation and Arts and Divinity fees was less than £1300 *per annum*.

In 1882, University College was founded in Dundee following the offered gift of £140,000 mainly from Miss Mary Ann Baxter of Balgavies and from Dr. John Boyd Baxter of Dundee. For the Royal Commissioners' Report of 1878 had not taken the line which those most anxious for the establishment of higher academic education in Dundee wished.

> It appears from the evidence that has been laid before us, that the inhabitants of Dundee—a large and increasing town and the seat of many important industries—very naturally desire to bring within the reach of their children an education as good as that which is obtainable by the citizens of Aberdeen, Glasgow and Edinburgh, and

that they would not be unwilling to provide the funds for that purpose. Now that a bridge over the Firth of Tay has been completed, St Andrews will be within about half-an-hour's journey of Dundee; and as the University of that place possesses complete Faculties of Arts and Divinity, and the rudiments of the Faculty of Medicine, various projects have been formed for combining the educational resources of Dundee with those of St Andrews in such a manner as to minimize the loss of teaching power and of endowment which would attend the co-existence of wholly independent teaching institutions at the two places.

It might be suggested that the seat of the University of St Andrews should be transferred to Dundee; but to this there are so many objections, both sentimental and practical, that it is probably not worth detailed consideration. The proposal to transplant the oldest University of Scotland from its ancient site is hardly likely to be received with much favour. Any such transfer would involve the sacrifice of the large capital represented by the present University buildings; and it may be justly urged that the quiet and retired situation of St Andrews renders it much better fitted than the thickly-populated and busy town of Dundee for the residence of students who do not belong to the locality. Another conceivable plan is to strengthen the University of St Andrews by the addition of new Chairs in Science and in Medicine, and to enlarge its buildings in accordance with their wants. But it cannot be denied that the distance between Dundee and St Andrews, small as it is, would interpose serious obstacles in the way of the attendance of students from Dundee, who might not desire to go through a complete curriculum in Arts and Science, and that this difficulty would be especially felt in the case of Medical Classes, on account of the necessary separation between the hospital and the school. Moreover, it is doubtful whether those wealthy citizens of Dundee who might be willing to contribute largely to the establishment and support of an educational institution in Dundee itself would be equally ready to supply funds for the enlargement of St Andrews.

A third alternative is the institution at Dundee of a College, which should be affiliated to the University of St Andrews, and stand in the same relation to it as the College of St Mary and the United College do at present. Such a College would contain a complete set of Chairs of Arts, of Medicine, and possibly of Law; and the Professors would be members of their respective Faculties in the University of St Andrews. This plan has the advantages of getting over the difficulty of distance; of completing the organization of the University of St Andrews, and rendering needless its present anomalous power of granting degrees in a department in which it is not in a position to afford full instruction; and of giving the people of Dundee everything they can want in return for their contributions. The chief disadvantage

would be the reduplication of the Arts Chairs and, unless it were
found possible to devise some plan by which the work of the Arts
Classes could be carried on both in Dundee and in St Andrews under
the superintendence of the same Professor, this objection appears to
us so serious as to be fatal to the scheme.

Finally, it has been proposed to establish at Dundee a College
affiliated to the University of St Andrews, and the Professors of which
should be members of the Faculties of Arts and Medicine of that
University, but which should be devoted entirely to the Mathematical
and Physical and Natural Sciences, and to Medicine, leaving the
literary moiety of the Arts Faculty in St Andrews. Considering the
importance of applied science to the great industrial interests of
Dundee, we cannot doubt that advantage would be largely taken of
the opportunities for instruction in Chemistry, in Engineering, and the
like, which would be afforded by such an institution to persons who,
for want of time or other reasons, might be unable to go through the
whole course required for a Degree in Arts or Science. On the other
hand, those who have the means and leisure to pass through the
curriculum, either for the Arts degree or for the Science degree, would
probably find the short distance between Dundee and St Andrews no
serious obstacle to obtaining their instruction in Arts at the latter
place. On the whole, we are inclined to think that the best solution of
the difficulty would be found in the adoption of some plan as that last
indicated.

The new University College had been founded without reference to St
Andrews; Miss Baxter had insisted that it be established before any question of
affiliation be raised. In the events which led up to Miss Baxter's final decision to
endow a University College, the third party—the *Dundee Advertiser*, had been
prominent and could even be argued to have precipitated her action.[8] By its
ready suggestion of what it hoped for or wanted rather than what was actually
happening or possible, it caused over-alarm in St Andrews and over-expectation
in Dundee which would not otherwise have existed, and provoked by the force
of its leaders ill-advised and in later times hysterical letters of reply or of
justification. It is therefore very easy to quote matter from its columns to
support widely differing interpretations of what actually happened, before,
during and forever after the foundation of University College, Dundee. During
this period, for example, letters are referred to in a way which gives the
impression that St Andrews Professors were almost all highly critical of the
University and seeking salvation in their transfer to Dundee.[9] Of four letters
published together, three were entirely in support of the University and one
only, from Professor Heddle the Mineralogist who was still desperately unhappy
in his Chair of Chemistry, seriously critical of it.[10]

The apparently satisfactorily smooth progress after 1878 towards setting
up matriculated classes in Dundee, so that students could take them and then
graduate at St Andrews University, had come to a halt. There were various
reasons for this, among them lack of necessary money on the St Andrews side

and uncertainty on the part of certain possible benefactors on the Dundee side about what they really wanted. In retrospect, this delay was the first tragedy in relations between Dundee and St Andrews, and with it went the sad failure on the part of the Dundee sponsors to acknowledge and co-operate with the liberality and fairness, as well as the long-sightedness, of Principal Tulloch. No blame can be attached to him, even by the most biassed observer. On the 25th of November, 1882, he gave a talk on 'University Reform' at St Mary's. Mentioning 'the somewhat anomalous state of the Medical Faculty, which needs to be set right without touching upon ancient privileges' he said of Dundee 'The relation of the University to the new College in Dundee may also form a subject of legislation in the near future. That the two institutions will in any legitimate sense be rivals is too ridiculous to be thought of; but it appears to many that their affiliation in some way would add much to the efficiency and future success of both'. Principal Tulloch was coming to the end of his years of service as a major university figure in the country. Unlike certain of his counterparts and successors, he maintained his fairness and clearness of outlook, and saw farther ahead than perhaps any of them.[11]

In the same November the *St Andrews Citizen*, on the 4th, recorded the introduction of a new Professor. He was William Carmichael McIntosh, Professor of Natural History. As he, with Professor Pettigrew, is to occupy a long period in the history of the Faculty of Medicine, and become an important figure in its ultimate growth and form, his is the next formal introduction to be made. McIntosh was born in St Andrews on 10th October 1838. His father had known Sir Hugh Lyon Playfair, whose initiative had helped the town to regain a status it had not had for a hundred years, and had begun the transformation of the Royal and Ancient Golf Club which came to make St Andrews 'The Mecca of Golf'.[12] As a local builder, he had built the new Town Hall in 1859 and many fine houses of this renaissance. William attended Madras College and was later a student at the University. Here he followed the *annus medicus*, and went on to Edinburgh for his clinical training and graduation. He thus did his early medicine at St Andrews, but both as a schoolboy and student he had played in the pools in the harbour and around the coast, and learned the fascination for marine biology which continued throughout his long life.

After a good undergraduate career—well above average but not as outstanding as Bell Pettigrew's—McIntosh graduated M.D. in June, 1860, at the usual age of twenty-two years. But what he did achieve was a Gold Medal for his Graduation Thesis—not in Anatomy, or Surgery, but in Zoology. His desire now was to follow an academic career, but not having the financial means to do so, he applied for a post as assistant physician at the Murray Royal Hospital at Perth. Appointed in August 1860, he remained there for three years. He then moved to another mental hospital, the newly opened Perthshire District Asylum at Murthly, as medical superintendent. Here he remained for the next nineteen years. During this time he published papers on mental disease, but his main work was Annelids. He wrote two volumes, and next turned to the marine fauna of St Andrews Bay, presented as a paper in 1867 at the meeting of the British Association in Dundee. By the time of his appointment as Professor in St

Andrews (he had applied unsuccessfully in 1875) he was a good deal older than many Professors on first appointment; forty-four years in fact. But he would become one of the great zoologists of his day, hold his chair till 1917, and live a longer natural life than even his successor at St Andrews, Sir D'Arcy Thomson.

Perhaps the only recent member of St Andrews University to maintain such detailed notes and letters, both of professional and social life, as Professor McIntosh was Principal Wimberley. Professor McIntosh, or his sisters, must have retained every academic invitation, every social event attended, and every letter received or written. His papers cover such a range of activities and opinions that it is very easy to assess him as a more important source of information than perhaps he is; there is just so much which can be quoted, while most of his colleagues' contributions appear in Court or Senate records and nowhere else.

On his appointment, Principal Tulloch asked his views on two subjects of immediate interest—first his attitude to the teaching of women undergraduates, and second his attitude to teaching in Dundee. Professor Pettigrew was at this time still enthusiastic, though less so than he had been four years earlier. He was not particularly interested in the entrance of women students. But Professor McIntosh was the opposite: he told the Principal that he would be happy to teach women and would encourage their entry into University classes. On the other hand, he expressed from the very start of his St Andrews career no interest in lecturing in Dundee. This seems to have been largely because he had such a strong ambition to set up a marine biology research establishment in St Andrews, and was determined to give this ambition all his time and energy. While in Murthly he had already created a large and important enough collection of marine specimens that students came from other centres to study it, and the transfer of this to St Andrews, and its further improvement and modernisation, was his immediate aim.

In January, 1883, Miss Baxter gave a further £10,000 to the University College of Dundee; this for the building of a new chemical laboratory. It was her money which had founded the institution and was now furnishing it, and it was her trust deed which provided its constitution, embracing the following authorities: 1) The Governors, 2) The Council, and 3) The Education Board.

The Governors were the ruling body. Anyone who donated £50 or more, and representatives of bodies donating £250 or more, or indeed anyone who undertook to subscribe £5 *per annum* or any organisation which undertook to subscribe £10 or more *per annum*, could become a Governor. This was the nineteenth century way of subscribing. Each Governor would then have one to six votes, depending upon the size of his contribution—a similar system to that for the Dundee Infirmary. As well as these, there were six *ex officio* members— the Lord Lieutenant of Angus, County convener of Forfarshire, M.P.s for the County of Forfar, and the Montrose District of Burghs, the Sheriff Principal of Forfar and the Dean of Guild of Dundee, and a representative each of the Dundee Chamber of Commerce, the Dundee School Board, the Directors of the High School of Dundee, and the Management Committee of the Dundee Free

Library. The number of Governors was completed by 'all Members of the Council'.

The detailed management of the College was assigned to the Council, its powers including the appointments to professorial Chairs. Half the Council members were to be chosen by the Governors, and the others were, once again, five *ex officio*: the Provost of Dundee, the two Dundee M.P.s and the two Forfarshire Sheriffs Substitute, and three others—one elected by Owens College, Manchester, one by the Privy Council, and one member elected by the Principal and Professors of the College who was not 'a Professor, permanent teacher, or other salaried officer'. The original Council included James Donaldson, Professor of Latin at Aberdeen University, the Professor of Chemistry from Owens College, Manchester, and the Earls of Dalhousie and Camperdown, as well as local business men and ministers and the *ex officio* members. No St Andrews University representative was included, even though power 'to affiliate or unite the College with any University, College or Society' could be entrusted to the Council. Representation of St Andrews was actively excluded by these foundation terms and arrangements, while Miss Baxter's recorded sentiments excluded its University in any form. The first Education Board comprised Professor Peterson (Classics and Ancient History) who became Principal, Professor Steggall (Mathematics and Physics), Professor Carnelly (Chemistry), Professor Ewing (Engineering) and Professor Gilroy (English). From the beginning, there was to be a summer session.

This instant University College was set up very smoothly. There was no doubt of the value of ample financial support. At first, students were advised to go to London University for their graduation, since London had the privilege of granting degrees to students without any necessity for residence. Further, candidates did not require to go to London to take their examinations, but could sit them at a number of centres around Britain. Recognition was quickly obtained for the Chemistry class by the Royal College of Physicians of London, who also had St Andrews' privilege of examining without residence requirement, and for Science and Medicine in Edinburgh. The only mention of St Andrews in the first College report was the fact that courses were suitable for her L.L.A. examination.

The next year a library was started, and immediately concern was beginning to be felt by the new young Principal about the lack of further endowments. He believed this was because of the commercial depression existing in the City. The confident list of hoped-for Chairs in his first public report was replaced in the second by a much more factual account of work done. But the ability and the dedication of the staff augured well for the future. As well as lacking financial support from major contributors they were lacking the small revenue support which individual students' fees should bring.

On January 30th 1885, a new Rector was installed at St Andrews. The occasion set the pattern for Rectorial installations to the present day—the singing students, the chorus 'coming to an end amid hilarious laughter' at the arrival of the Academic Procession—the honorary graduation ('The Doctors of Divinity covered a range from the Waldensian College in Florence to the

Union Chapel, Islington')—and the Rectorial Address. Lord Reay, born
Donald James Mackay in the Hague, had become a citizen of Britain in 1877.
He would soon depart to India for a career of the highest distinction there. In his
address he expressed the outsider's view of the relation of the University and the
Dundee College:

> The Science and the Medical Faculties of this University have a
> splendid opening, if they make the most of Miss Baxter's great
> foundation in the neighbouring town. Science itself is paving the way,
> bridging over the difficulty. On this side of the Tay you have the old
> associations; on the other side you have the vitality of modern
> progress. Remain separated and you are weak on both sides; unite,
> and you double your strength. The distance will be smaller than that
> between a west end and an east end hospital belonging to the new
> London University. You are the oldest family among the Universities;
> take heed that by haughty isolation you may not meet with the tragic
> fate of extinction. And to my Dundee friends I would say—you have
> the means of building your future glory on the sure foundations of the
> experience of centuries. Let your College be the fourth constellation in
> the St Andrews planetary system. The idea of a University is the
> blending of ancient and modern.

It was a warning to both that co-operation and sharing was the way to achieve a
prosperous future.

From the very earliest years of the University College, indeed, a basic fact of
which the business men and women involved were ignorant, quickly became
evident. This was that large sums of money did not, by itself, create a university.
The foundation of University College, Dundee, by Miss Baxter was done
without reference to St Andrews—and it could not guarantee that the students
who studied its various courses would get university degrees. For this they had
to seek accreditation from a university proper, with the established right to
confer the Master of Arts degree. If no proper university would accredit them,
no amount of financial endowment would help. Endowment money could not
buy a university degree. So while the Secretary of St Andrews University may
have forgotten that the Dundee business element had plenty of money, this was
less serious than the Dundee business element's forgetting that only a university
could confer degrees. In 1886 Principal Peterson acknowledged that 'Dundee
Science students have at once preferred St Andrews to London for graduation'
and also that the best of his Arts students had left Dundee for St Andrews and
Edinburgh, where they had done well and gained class medals. And by the next
year, the St Andrews Graduation Regulations in Science exempted *only
Dundee* students from residence—these were 'entitled to complete their entire
course at the University College'. In spite of the 1882 rebuff to St Andrews—
whose members and income were now above the crisis level of eleven years
previously—both by the actual foundation of University College and also by
the ignoring of the fair and far-seeing offers of Principal Tulloch to the Dundee
side—the old University continued its earlier offers of help and support to the
new College. This fact has been ignored so often that it must be noted and

stressed before the foundation of the Medical School, and events subsequent, are examined.

In 1886, an appointment was made to the Dundee Chair of Biology, and the man chosen would become one of the greatest scientists St Andrews University has yet had. D'Arcy Wentworth Thompson was born on 2nd May, 1860, in Edinburgh. He was an only child. His father's family had come from Maryport, in Cumbria; their forebears were Scandinavian. The D'Arcy Wentworth of his father's name had come from a Captain of that name in the 63rd Regiment of Foot (The King's Regiment). He had been present at the child's christening in Australia—D'Arcy Thompson the elder having been born to Mary Thompson, the wife of John Skelton Thompson, just before his ship landed in Australia. For John Skelton Thompson, shipowner at Maryport, had been obliged to take a number of convicts to Australia to keep in business in hard times. His wife, together with the officer commanding the detachment of soldiers guarding the prisoners and his wife and daughter, had accompanied him.

D'Arcy Thompson the elder was a classics master at Edinburgh Academy, and had as pupils Robert Louis Stevenson and Andrew Lang. His first wife died tragically of puerperal sepsis a week after D'Arcy the younger's birth. Later he moved to Ireland and became Professor of Greek at Queen's College, Galway, when D'Arcy the younger was only three years old. This represented a serious loss of income—compared with his previous post as a master at Edinburgh Academy, from which he had resigned on the issue of corporal punishment. After schooling at Edinburgh Academy, D'Arcy junior went up, in 1878, to Edinburgh University to study medicine. He remembered his time there vividly—especially Professor Turner's anatomy lectures—and still told stories about them seventy years later. But he did not take to Medicine, and sought and obtained a Scholarship to Trinity College, Cambridge. On May 1st 1881 he wrote home 'The Prize-lists of our last exams were published last night, and you will be delighted to hear that I stand at the top, and become a Scholar of Trinity. I am no richer, but on the contrary somewhat poorer in money, but very much richer in honour and position ... My four keenest competitors came to supper last night at ten, and we had great fun. I gave 'em champagne, and two or three other fellows came in also'. At Cambridge he met, learned from, and talked with, the greatest biologists of the day. But as well as Biology, he had a keen interest in Greek, German, and Mathematics.

By 1884, D'Arcy's ambition above all else was to gain a Natural Science Fellowship at Trinity. He failed in 1884, and again in 1885, when 'another man was ahead of him'.[13] He tried yet again, in 1886, after he had come to Dundee. His appointment there as Professor of Biology was made in December 1884, and Principal Peterson said at his Inaugural Lecture on 25th January 1886 that the new Chair combined Zoology and Botany, and it was precisely because of Professor Thompson's width of interest that he had been appointed.

In the new College he quietly made his presence and personality felt. He quickly took up a variety of causes in Dundee—his department, which soon became as popular as any—perhaps the most popular of all—showed concern for the poor of the City. But as far as the Faculty of Medicine was concerned, he

was the first Professor on the Dundee side to do anything practical towards medical academic teaching. His work in background and foreground had not only the object of establishing a Medical School from small beginnings rather as Sir George Humphrey had done in D'Arcy's Cambridge less than twenty years before, but it had also the aim of providing greatly improved facilities for the care of the sick and ailing poor in the tenements of the town.

This led him to begin practical projects, and encouraged others to give their support. The knowledge that bacteria were the cause of infectious diseases was becoming accepted and applied to sanitation, and Professor Carnelly shared experiment and investigation with him in this field. He invited Dr John Scott Haldane, whom he had known at school, to come to Dundee and work both in academic research and as a pathologist associated with the Infirmary. Like McIntosh in St Andrews and so many other investigators of the day, he was an eager collector of specimens and enthusiast in museum display. He helped Dr. Haldane to start and develop a pathological museum for teaching purposes, and he had also thoughts about making use, again for teaching purposes, of the museum at the Royal Asylum set up by Dr. Rorie the medical superintendent. He also saw from an early stage the value of co-operation with St Andrews University, though as will be seen shortly, his discord with Professor McIntosh was another factor in denying both College and University the happy start their friendship would have provided.

Thus it was D'Arcy who wrote to the *Dundee Courier and Argus* at the end of 1885 publicly expressing the thanks of the University College to St Andrews. Of the University he said:

> Her real gain is the honour of lending a helping hand to a young
> school, and of endowing it with a great privilege. The vague and
> impossible notions of rivalry with St Andrews that were rife in
> Dundee when University College was endowed are already forgotten
> and St Andrews has taken the first step in linking the fortunes of the
> two schools. The new connections with St Andrews should be the
> greatest possible encouragement for the extension of the work of
> University College, Dundee.

7

The Beginning of Medical Education in Dundee

The Formation of the Conjoint Medical School

In the initial formulation of ideas about higher academic studies in Dundee, in 1874-75, the subjects proposed were 'Higher branches of Literature and Science', but not Medicine. The very first notion seems to have been that a few classes in Dundee would be conducted by Professors from 'a neighbouring University' during two or more evenings in the week. From this start the movement developed, and the foundation of the College has been shortly described. But while during the preliminaries 'Medicine was thought of', it 'was decided expedient to defer this question to a future period . . . Medicine could come later if the first College prospered'. The *Dundee Advertiser* of this time was quite certain of the prospects for Medicine—'It is more than doubtful if a School of Medicine would flourish in Dundee. The medical science of our time tends to go to the great centres long established. Even the medical degree of the University of London, famous though the University of London is, is held in less esteem throughout the country than the degree of Edinburgh and Dublin. Of what value would be a degree newly founded in Dundee? Is it likely that it would be sought even by young Dundonians studying for the profession of Medicine'?[1] At this date, too, the local newspaper supported the scheme of lecture courses run by St Andrews University. It quoted the success of these in the midlands of England, arranged and run by Cambridge University, and saw the good sense of a connection with an existing University.

Two years after the foundation of University College, however, in 1884, the Principal and Professors mentioned in their Annual Report the possible establishment of a medical school. And although the academic interest shown by Professor D'Arcy Thompson has already been noted—being given particular mention in 1886, when it was also suggested that he teach some elementary Physiology—it seems certain that the political interest was that of Principal Peterson.

For nearly twenty years before the foundation of University College, Dundee Royal Infirmary had made available facilities for medical students to act as dressers. Any medical student, on payment of a guinea to the Treasurer, could get a ticket entitling him to attend the Infirmary daily 'along with the visiting physician or surgeon, to be present at all operations, to be allowed to peruse and take extracts from the case books'. Any approved student could be

91

appointed a dresser, and every dresser was entitled to a certificate 'of diligence and skill from the Medical Superintendent' when he left.[2] Although there were no outstanding figures amongst the medical staff there was ample clinical material. This established background of material had in fact been used in the quite recent past, when M.D. candidates of St Andrews University were examined at the Infirmary. What Dundee did not of course have were any established pre-clinical Chairs. These were at St Andrews. It would have been interesting to find if any of the very few students who *did* make individual use of the clinical material in Dundee subsequently attempted the M.B. C.M. examination at St Andrews, but there is no evidence for this, one way or the other.

While the new College was being founded and was feeling its way in Science subjects and Mathematics, the medical side at St Andrews was continuing the efforts of so many years to improve its medical teaching. As a University approved for medical examination and graduation, St Andrews was approached by the Medical Acts Commission in 1881 about the licensing of medical graduates, and about the possibility of setting up a Conjoint Examining Board of the four Scottish Universities. And though the numbers of those graduating M.B. C.M. were tiny—seven by 1881—some had done their pre-clinical study at St Andrews, and some who had similarly been pre-clinical students there completed their M.B. course in Edinburgh. In 1879 too, there had been an unexpected and very welcome support to the Chandos Chair of Medicine and Anatomy, as it was still called, in the form of a donation of £1000 from Dr. James George Beaney. And in 1885, at the same time as the Senatus sub-committee approved the admitting to graduation of Dundee Science students who had received the whole of their education in Dundee, it gave an additional report about Medicine, proposing the provision of *two Anni Medici* in the University of St Andrews. To effect this, it was recommended that two new lecturers be appointed—one on Anatomy and one on Materia Medica. For these a sum of at least £400 *per annum* would be required—viz. £150 for each lecturer, and £100 for class and other expenses.

The correspondence between Principal Peterson and the University throughout 1885, beginning with his request in the February for revision of the rules of residence and also for reduction of the class fee from three guineas to two, made no mention of Medicine. But 1885 was a key year in the development of Medicine, and in Dundee, Principal Peterson was thinking and planning.

The lecture given in Dundee on 27th June of that year by Professor William Gairdner, of the Chair of Medicine at Glasgow University, and previously a lecturer in Edinburgh, has received great prominence in Dr. Southgate's account.[3] A close study of the events before and after put it in the context of a probable larger background strategy; it was not a speech made by accident.

Professor Gairdner had been specifically asked by Principal Peterson to come to Dundee, and had to leave his own University during the course of his clinical examinations to do so. Professor Thompson had been sent through to Glasgow to see to the arrangements. For any Professor actually to leave his department during examinations is unusual, and his opening remarks made this clear. In introducing him, the Principal spoke plainly. He saw 'the undertaking of medical

teaching is (as) one of the means by which a College such as ours may take a short step in advance towards the development of a complete University'. It was not Engineering, or Technical Sciences, or Law which Principal Peterson appeared determined to set up first nor, most interestingly, was it Arts subjects. It was Medicine. Professor Gairdner referred to recent conversations he had had with Principal Peterson. Pressure of work from the clinical examinations had not allowed him to prepare 'a formal and elaborate address'. It rather sounded in fact as if he had been pressed to come to Dundee at short notice. He went on to say that the question of higher education for Dundee was already settled. 'At present the question is whether medical education is to be a part of the future ambition of Dundee in this respect. Now, I not only think Dundee justified in entertaining this ambition, but I think she is bound to entertain it'. He went on to instance the large working population, the very high incidence of disease, and the excellent range of hospital services—'as stated by Principal Peterson'—in other words, the established necessary background for clinical teaching. But he warned that in the wish to set up a medical school in Dundee, his audience must be realistic about the necessity of co-operation with St Andrews. 'In considering this subject, it is not possible to overlook the fact that Dundee has not at present, and is not likely, as matters go, to acquire the power in itself of giving degrees. It is equally impossible to overlook the fact that only a few miles away there is the most ancient University in Scotland . . .' He criticised the power of St Andrews to give medical degrees without being connected with and supported by an equally valid power of teaching—and noted that there was at that time increasing criticism of London University, which in spite of its large income was in exactly the same position as St Andrews as far as its power to graduate in Medicine was concerned. But he welcomed an involvement in clinical teaching by St Andrews, seeing it as a natural co-operation. 'I clearly thought of this . . . many years ago . . . while I was for a time an examiner in Medicine at the University of St Andrews and in those days (when as yet, too, and for many years thereafter in Scotland, clinical examinations were things unknown, and not even spoken much about) I always made it a point to bring the honours students with me to Dundee to undergo a strictly clinical examination in the Royal Infirmary, and many of the men so examined remain in my memory to this hour as some of the best men I have ever had to deal with. The physicians of the hospital in those days lent themselves most kindly to my efforts, and owing to that circumstance the association, in my mind, has always existed between Dundee and St Andrews'. This part of his talk may not have been quite what his listeners wanted, and certainly all later local press comment avoided it most pointedly. But of the rest of his address, with his ideas about how a medical curriculum be organised, was accepted with pleasure.

Professor Gairdner was one of the many Scots before and since who had been impressed by the snobbery and exclusiveness of the educational system in England. He gave as example the need of the bulk of general practitioners in England to be apprenticed at an age which precluded their receiving a university education, and the attitude of the small number of wealthier born men who could afford such education towards this large majority. 'In England the

average practitioner had to be an apprentice like any other workman, and who had hardly been taught in those days to admit into his mind even the merest notion of scientific training'. The 'Senior Universities and Colleges' ' almost supercilious attitude towards the general practitioner of the day annoyed him, and it may have been this antagonism which had led him to see no good in 'the view of Oxford and Cambridge that they taught a man science for two or three years and then turned him over to a London Hospital to teach him the practice'. Professor Gairdner believed that although this system might suit England, what was needed in Scotland was 'the presence of a field of disease' from the very start. He believed too, that exposure to an Arts and Theology Faculty was of great importance in broadening the background of the medical student, and showing him Christianity as well. He ended by expressing the view that a wholly new system could begin in Dundee, with men going from the Chemistry or Biology class to be tutored by Physicians at Dundee Royal Infirmary on the application of their basic science—he foresaw the 'integrated medical course' of the twentieth century. He did not advocate immediate foundations of Chairs in the major clinical specialities, and his lecture, in fact, was not the clarion call for Dundee to found a comprehensive medical school it was later selectively quoted to be. His main theme was the need to apply basic science to clinical practice from the first year of a medical course.

Of great interest was what the various speakers following took from Professor Gairdner's address, and their comments then were consistent with their actions later. Principal Peterson considered 'that the time had come when they should aim at founding a Medical School in Dundee'. 'With the Dundee Royal Infirmary and the other Public Hospitals on the one hand and *the facilities for graduation which existed at St Andrews on the other*' (author's italics) he thought that 'the materials for such a school lay ready in their hands'. Professor Thompson saw a role for St Andrews other than as a legalising Service Agency; he supported the idea of Medicine, and said he thought their guests from St Andrews would thank Professor Gairdner for 'taking the initiative in a scheme which may bring new work and usefulness to their old and famous University'. Professor Knight, formerly of St Enoch's Church in Dundee and now Professor of Moral Philosophy at St Andrews, said he spoke as a Dundee man, aware of the needs and aspirations of the City. He spoke of 'the relationship which may yet be established between St Andrews and University College, Dundee' (not yet, it must be emphasised, having any University status nor even the sure prospect of any) 'fills our minds—we hope for a union which will make the work of both University College and University durable and useful'.

The Third Party comment in the Dundee Advertiser began carefully, quoting Professor Gairdner as 'advocating the establishment of a Medical School in Dundee incorporated with St Andrews University', but quickly became boastful. This was 'a big boost for how good Dundee would be' . . . 'we have a splendid Infirmary, equipped and maintained in a way that makes it a model throughout the country' . . . 'In Dr. Gairdner's words, it is not only in our power, but it is our bounden duty, to make use of these conditions, and when we

do it will be as plainly the duty of St Andrews to help us by giving us facilities for graduation to the medical students who are taught here'. Professor Gairdner had not, of course, made any such demand.

While this was happening in Dundee, an assessment was being made in St Andrews of the scientific equipment available in teaching Physiology, Anatomy, and Biology, with reference to pre-clinical teaching of medical students. The efforts made were considerable and have not been recorded before. Physiology models were described as excellent, but microscopic specimens 'few'. The same comments applied to teaching diagrams. Anatomical models, which Professor Pettigrew collected from Glasgow as and when he could, 'were fairly well presented and in good condition'. The excellence of Professor McIntosh's catalogue of Natural History specimens was praised.

The later part of 1885 recorded the opinions of Counsel on the graduation of Dundee students who had studied there and not in St Andrews, and confirmed the legality of graduating such students. In 1885, too, Dr. Rawdon Macnamara and Dr. Joseph Magee Finny, both of Dublin, and Dr. Robert Barnes of London, were visitors to the M.D. examination from the General Medical Council. For the first time actual marks of candidates were recorded in the visitors' report, which was also more detailed than the previous one of 1875. The visitors noted that the M.D. at St Andrews could be conferred upon those who had recently graduated M.B. C.M. after completing 'a four years' curriculum under regulations similar to those in force in the other Scotch Universities'. During the past six years only eight such young men had presented themselves. Six had graduated M.B. C.M., one had failed and the last had passed on part of the final examination, but not as yet the other two parts. These undergraduates *did* have a clinical examination, it must be stressed, which was held in Edinburgh at Chalmers Hospital. Unfortunately there was no M.B. C.M. candidate in 1885, and the visitors recorded this fact with regret.

The 'traditional St Andrews M.D.', on mature men already on the *Medical Register*, was assessed by Drs. Finny, Macnamara, and Barnes as requiring 'to be considered simply in the light of an examination for a supplementary, if not a higher title. Looked at in this light, the University of St Andrews may fairly claim credit for endeavouring to fulfil a useful function'. The full report was a mixture of criticism with some praise. Of the candidates, it was said that they were all English, and that only two had Scotch qualifications—one an F.R.C.S. Ed. and one an M.R.C.P. Ed. One was a fellow of the English College of Surgeons. All the applications—and not the ten selected (still mainly by priority of application date, it seems)—were examined. The examiners criticised an absence of desire on the part of the candidates to reach 'a higher position in the profession' and considered that many were men in General Practice who had little time or opportunity for advancing their knowledge. 'The majority of candidates sought the degree for the purpose of being thought more of by the public by obtaining a legal right to add to their names the highly esteemed letters of M.D.—a title which usually testifies to a special knowledge of medicine'. Some discrepancy was noticed, too, between tributes in the testimonials and the performance in the examination. There were six hours of written papers. Four

papers were set, one by each of the four examiners. Medicine and Surgery were in the forenoon and Midwifery and Materia Medica with Jurisprudence in the afternoon. The Medicine paper had five questions, the Surgery six, the Midwifery four, and the Materia Medica and Jurisprudence, seven.

The Medicine paper (Paper 3) had three essay-type questions, which could have been set at any date up to the present, and two case descriptions for diagnosis. While discussions of the *differential* diagnosis of these would seem to have been required as a test of the candidate's knowledge, a single diagnosis with its treatment was all that was asked. The Surgery paper too began with questions applicable to surgical practice, and the two cases for diagnosis were described in much greater detail and so were a good deal more satisfactory than those in the Medicine paper. The Materia Medica paper was applicable to its date. The Jurisprudence and Midwifery papers could be set today, with only a little change in terminology.[4]

Details of the oral examination, on the next day, were also given. It began at 9.30 a.m. and ended at 11.30. The external examiners sat at four tables at different corners of the hall, Professors McIntosh and Purdie (the Chemistry Professor) sat at two of the tables as extra assessors, and asked questions also. Each candidate had fifteen minutes at each table, an hour of examination altogether. Each table had specimens of medical or surgical pathology, surgical and obstetric instruments, tests and glasses for examination of urine, and 'various articles of Materia Medica'. There was a microscope at each table as well.

There were two main criticisms of this part of the examination. The first was that while a period of fifteen minutes was enough to assess a quick candidate who answered well, it was not enough for a 'slow man whose information is of a fairly moderate standard'. The questions were adequate, the visitors thought, but 'from the answers accepted it appeared to us that a very moderate acquaintance on the part of the candidate with any subject was all that was expected or required'.

The second criticism in the general part of the report was that more use could have been made of the practical material available. But this was inconsistent with the detailed reports which the visitors made on their own subjects. For example, Dr. Finny praised Dr. Balfour's skill as an examiner; he went on to detail with approval the form of the oral examination. Each candidate was first asked to look at and recognize two pathological slides already placed under a microscope. While some candidates were poor at this part of the examination—as much because they were unskilled at using the microscope itself, 'others made more or less accurate answers'. The description given would fit that of the Primary or Second Part of today's Fellowship or Membership examinations. Slides included sections of catarrhal pneumonia, pulmonary tubercle, amyloid liver, cancer of the kidney. Some of the wet pathology specimens in pots were old and barely recognizable, but others were 'well-mounted and well-prepared'. 'These exhibits included Bright's fatty kidney, amyloid disease of the kidney, Phthisical lung in the third stage, larynx and bronchi in croup, transverse sections of hypertrophied heart, Taenia Solium, Ascaris lumbricoides, etc.'.

James Walker

J. L. Henderson

J. Crooks

J. P. Duguid

R. E. Coupland

I. S. Smillie

The Duke of Hamilton and Principal Sir Malcolm Knox discuss Medical
School development

Ninewells Hospital under construction

'The questions which followed were in many instances suggested by the specimen shown, and after a brief inquiry as to pathology, the diagnosis and treatment of various diseases formed the main topics of examination'.

The description of the surgical *viva voce* examination suggests that this followed the same lines. There was a plentiful supply of pathological specimens, both dry and moist, with splints, bandages and instruments. Candidates were asked the use of these last, asked to name certain other surgical instruments, and describe their use. They were asked to outline in ink incisions on their own persons for various operations. Operative surgery was not otherwise discussed, and no anatomical dissections were shown. As far as the obstetric part of the examination was concered, Dr. Barnes reported 'The written questions were, in my judgment, well drawn, and the answers given were, in most cases, very fair. At the Oral Examination, a pelvis and foetal skull, some preparations, and the common instruments used in obstetric and gynaecological practice, were on the table. These suggested in many cases, the question put, testing to some extent the practical knowledge of the candidate . . .'

The one general criticism of the oral part of the examination, that considerably more time should have been allowed, and that the fifteen minutes at St Andrews rendered the examination unsatisfactory, was answered firmly by Professor Pettigrew (who had taken no part in the examination itself) in his comments on the report. He attacked the 'insinuations' about the source and background motivation of the candidates with figures to show that 1885 was an unusual year as far as the first was concered, and with rather unconvincing arguments about the second—their motivation for seeking a St Andrews M.D.

As far as time allocated to the oral examinations was concerned, the St Andrews examiners from Edinburgh brought up once again the criticism of St Andrews because of the background of its bad reputation in times past. Not only were oral examinations allowed to continue for longer than fifteen minutes in other years, but 'what is regarded as an offence at St Andrews is not commented on elsewhere. The Visitors complain of the brevity of the oral examinations at St Andrews, while they pass no strictures upon the Universities of Glasgow and Aberdeen, where, according to their own showing, the time allocated for Oral Examination is precisely the same as at St Andrews'. They went on to quote directly from the examiners' reports of these Universities' oral examinations.

This account of medical examination in St Andrews, while containing plenty of criticism, shows that the examination compared well with those held in other centres. There was certainly nothing to suggest that the examination was a sham, as was declared by so many critics with preconceived ideas or who, like the Third Party, were looking for any way of discrediting the University they could find. But where St Andrews failed was in the absence of a clinical examination. Even though Dr. Finny, the medical visitor, was clearly mixed up in his comments about whether the examination he had just seen was to admit an undergraduate to the *Medical Register* or to confer an additional qualification upon an experienced practitioner, he put his finger on exactly the right place

when he said: . . . (the clinical examination) 'is perhaps of all the parts of the Examination the one to which Candidates for the Degree of M.D., St Andrews, who have been in the practice of their profession for some years, should be subjected, and upon which—in contra-distinction to book learning—a judgment could be justly based as to their practical bedside knowledge. The absence of any hospital or Infirmary at St Andrews, wherein a Clinical Examination could be conducted, was assigned as a reason for its omission. This, however, can hardly be a valid objection to instituting such an Examination, for if it be practicable and be the rule, as I was informed it is, to include a Clinical Examination for the Degree of M.B. St Andrews, I can see no difficulty in the Medical Faculty of the University conducting a similar Clinical Examination in the Royal Infirmary of Edinburgh for the degree of M.D.'

The latter part of 1885 saw protests from Professor Pettigrew against the privileges granted to students from the Dundee College. He was on very unsure ground in his arguments against this 'new departure' and was almost curtly refuted in the November by the University and the Court. It was made clear that the privileges granted to Dundee students were justified, and that in any event they were no more than similar accreditations given by Edinburgh University to externally trained students. Dr. Pettigrew was told, quite pointedly, that he should hardly criticise the recognition of Dundee Science students and ignore the recognition of training elsewhere implicit in the University's medical degree regulations!

In January, 1886, Principal Tulloch was granted six months' leave, on account of his ill-health. He died suddenly on the 13th of February, while in Torquay. He was Professor of Divinity for thirty-two years, and had been Principal for twenty years. Tributes to him were warm and long—his scholarship, forward thinking, and sincerity were universally acknowledged. He remains one of the great figures in the University of St Andrews, and Dundee.

On the 10th April, Dr. James Donaldson, Professor of Humanity at Aberdeen, was nominated and inducted as the new Principal. James Donaldson was a man of middle age—of fifty-five years. He was born in Aberdeen in 1831, a son of an engineer of the same name in that city. He graduated A.M. of Marischal College in 1850, and four years later had become Rector of Stirling High School. In 1856 he had moved to the Royal High School in Edinburgh, and in 1882 had become Professor of Humanity at his own University. Most of his career had been as a teacher, but he had been appointed a member of the original Council of Miss Baxter's University College in 1882, and so had a full knowledge of its constitution, its working in practice, and its early difficulties. Perhaps more important, he had come to know the business men who were its prime movers, and in this respect he was at a great advantage. He knew the sense of civic pride and loyalty they had for their flourishing city, and there is evidence that he was concerned about the problems of its poor which several of these men shared. He had begun by regarding the local University very much from the side of this new College, and now he found himself its major administrative head. It therefore seemed that this background was an excellent one, and that he was a sound choice as Tulloch's successor.

During 1886, St Andrews was again showing an improvement in its student intake, in its numbers graduating, and even in its financial income. The Ladies' Arts Examination was increasingly popular, and becoming more highly regarded. 391 candidates entered from 16 centres throughout Britain—till 1886, a grand total of 1168 had entered for the examination. In 1886, 386 had actually sat, and 328 passed in one or more subjects; only 75 that year, however, passed the full number of subjects and so could be entitled L.L.A. The fees were of the welcome order of £600.

Throughout the summer, thoughts and preparations, and as much improvement in equipment as could be afforded, continued to be made. The second *Annus Medicus* was a prize of great worth, and the hope of a clinical component in Dundee made its realisation seem possible after so many years of trying to make the best of the impossible task St Andrews had had in keeping its medical teaching. A new Universities' Bill was promised. Although the earlier offers of help to Dundee to share education facilities—as distinct from merely providing the legal means whereby Dundee based students could *graduate* at St Andrews, which the Dundee Principal had accepted so gratefully—had been rebuffed, this seemed an excellent chance of sharing in the setting up of a true Medical Faculty.

On October 2nd it was moved by Professor Crombie and seconded by Professor McIntosh that a Memorial (Memorandum) be sent from St Andrews to the Secretary for Scotland, asking that two new Medical Chairs be set up, out of monies to be voted by Parliament under the promised Universities Bill, to allow medical students to take *two* years of their total course in United College. On November 6th, a verbal report was given to the Senate on the details of the 'Memorial', and, very importantly, it was agreed to approach University College first, and agree on a common approach, before the Memorandum was publicly circulated.

At the prize-giving ceremony at University College, now in the third year of its existence, in June, 1886, Mr W.E. Baxter noted that one B.Sc. degree for a Dundee student had been conferred by St Andrews University without requiring residence there, and said what a good thing this was. Progress in constructing the Pathology Museum at the Infirmary was mentioned but 'they were no farther forward as regards the Medical School'. At the Annual General Meeting of the College Governors in October, the forthcoming University Bill was mentioned and the minute read 'Dundee will be very blind to its interests if it allows a big lump of public money to go to St Andrews without striving to get some equitable working arrangement for the local institution'. There was no suggestion of co-operation, and the tone was hostile. The meeting also commented on Professor Thompson's contribution 'by making the Biology Department acceptable to the University of St Andrews'. At this time Professor McIntosh's Marine Biology Studies were beginning to achieve national and international acclaim: he was far from being the limited figure he has been painted.[5]

On 19th November, the sub-committee of the College Council charged with safeguarding the interests of the College with regard to expected proposals by

Government met under the chairmanship of the Principal. The other members were Professor Thompson, Dr. Sinclair, and two local gentlemen from the business world, Mr J. Martin White and Mr James Cunningham. A letter from St Andrews, signed by Professor Pettigrew, was read. Addressed to the Council, it asked for a conference 'with regard to the desirability of forming a complete Medical School between the University of St Andrews and University College, Dundee, on the lines indicated in Clause VI, page 3, of the enclosed memorial'. This was that by developing the Medical School to enable the University to give two *anni medici*, it would be in a position 'to utilise for the remaining two years of University study required for Medical Degrees the larger hospital at Dundee and the practical classes which may be instituted in connection therewith at University College, as well as the extra academical classes in other parts of the United Kingdom. While few better centres than St Andrews could be found for the first two years of medical study, it would be difficult to find a more suitable centre than Dundee for the last two years—the last two years embracing the more strictly practical subjects. By this arrangement the burden of forming a fully-equipped Medical School, consisting of eleven Professors, would fall more or less equally between St Andrews and Dundee: St Andrews providing the Professors of Anatomy, Pathology, Chemistry, Natural History and Botany—these Professorships being important to St Andrews for her Science Degree and for the general training of her students; Dundee providing the Professors of Medicine, Surgery, Pathology, Midwifery, Materia Medica (including Pharmacy) and Medical Jurisprudence (including Hygiene)—these Professorships requiring for their operations an extensive population and a large well-equipped hospital such as Dundee possesses'. The letter ended by requesting a meeting at St Andrews, but at a date to suit the Dundee Council.

This was in effect a plea for co-operation. The St Andrews Chairs were in being—except Anatomy and Botany. None of the Dundee Chairs mentioned was even immediately proposed, but it was implicit in the Memorandum that agreement between the University and the College, and a joint approach to Government, would present a strong case. The suggestion of sharing was eminently fair, and something of the spirit of Principal Tulloch was in the offer.

But the Dundee College Minute only read:
>   It was resolved to draw up a report on the subject to be submitted to the Council showing:
> 1) The claims of Dundee to the establishment of a Medical School in the Town.
> 2) The requisites for such a School.
> 3) How far and in what way the proposals of St Andrews University would affect the establishment of such a School.
> Signed W. Peterson

A fortnight later, on December 1st, the sub-committee met again. Four members were present. The draft report was studied, and unanimously approved of'. No details were given, but 'the report was to be printed, for the information

of Council members'. On 6th December a further letter from Professor Pettigrew was discussed by the whole committee under Principal Peterson's Chairmanship. This was 'a letter covering a packet of eighteen open, unaddressed envelopes, each containing a printed memorial and also a letter addressed to the Council of University College, Dundee'. The 'letter' was the same as that sent to the sub-committee on November 19th. Professor Pettigrew asked particularly if the memorial and a copy of the letter could be sent to each member of the Council, but the memorial only to Principal Peterson and his five sub-committee colleagues. This was all minuted, and it was also reported that the University College report—from the Principal's sub-committee—had been now circulated to Council members but had not been made public.[6]

On the motion of Mr John Sharp, seconded by Ex-Provost Brownlee, the report of the sub-committee was generally approved: there were eleven members present, including Principal Donaldson. The Sub-committee was then ordered 'to confer with St Andrews and report'.

The St Andrews report on the meeting of December 9th, 1886, was brief. It was summarised as 'a very amicable meeting, though no formal decision was taken. It was agreed to have the memorial circulated to Members of Parliament and others'. At this same time, further privileges were granted to Dundee matriculated students—they were now allowed to vote in the election of the Rector, and have the use of the University library. But the College minute was much more interesting. Principal Peterson reported to the seven Council members on 13th December:

> Principal Peterson protested against the notion that in advocating the Cause of Medical Education in Dundee his Council was actuated by any spirit of rivalry, much less of hostility, towards the University. Their highest expectations he said would be fulfilled if they could get the University to recognize that the conditions of medical teaching in the present day and in the circumstances of the district, made it desirable that the whole medical curriculum should be provided at Dundee in connection with the University, University College, and Dundee Royal Infirmary. Principal Peterson also showed how such a scheme would not necessarily involve the transferrence of existing Chairs from St Andrews to Dundee.
>
> Professor Bell Pettigrew then proceeded to criticise the Report of the Council, dwelling especially on the statement that St Andrews was already a centre of medical education, capable of immediate and appropriate development. Dr. Bell Pettigrew's arguments were replied to on behalf of the deputation by Dr. Sinclair who called special attention to the inexpediency of divorcing the more theoretical from the practical part of a Medical Curriculum and by Professor D'Arcy Thompson who proved that according to the Regulations of Edinburgh University the College at Dundee is able to give at present an *annus medicus* 'though not under the most advantageous circumstances'. After some further conversation general regret was expressed that, as the Medical Faculty of the University adhered to

the position that the first two years of classes should be taught at St
Andrews leaving only the last two years for Dundee, no common
basis of action was in the meantime discernible.

The view was adopted on both sides that the foundation of a
Chair of Anatomy on either side of the Tay would at once settle the
question with regard to which the present difference of opinion has
emerged.

This report was signed, on behalf of the deputation, by Principal Peterson.
'The meeting approved the Report'.

Principal Peterson *immediately* announced that he had received
the following letter from Mr Thomas H. Cox of Maulesden intimating
a donation of £12000 for the foundation and equipment of a Chair of
Anatomy in the College.

On the motion of Mr Brownlee the Meeting resolved to return its
hearty thanks to Mr Cox for his munificent donation for the
foundation and equipment of a Chair of Anatomy

The Council is fully sensitive of the advantages which the town
and district will derive from the Institution of Medical teaching and it
hails with great satisfaction the foundation of a Chair which is
universally regarded as the central pillar of a Medical School.

And then, in quick succession, the Committee agreed

1) to send copies of the Report with extracts from the present minute
   to the Secretary of State and the Lord Advocate
2) to send a deputation to both these officials—if they agreed to see
   them, to express their views about the establishment of a Medical
   School
3) to see the Lord Provost of Dundee, and ask that donations for
   the Queen's Jubilee be made towards the founding, etc.—by
   starting a subscription to raise the necessary funds
4) to take any steps the Committee think necessary by way of
   Conferences with the Senatus of the University of St Andrews for
   promoting this object and from time to time to report
5) to ask the Secretaries of the Forfar Medical Association and the
   Royal Infirmary for any suggestions they might have in
   connection with a Medical School.

This swift and comprehensive action of Principal Peterson's sub-committee
continued. It met again on the 17th with Mr Thornton and Mr J. Martin White
present, when arrangements were made to inform the public of the nature and
objects of the proposed Medical School and to show the peculiar advantages to
be derived from its establishment in Dundee. Arrangements were also made to
get as many members of the main Council as possible to join the deputation to
the Lord Provost to seek his support. On the 21st December, Principal Peterson,
Professor Thompson, Dr. Sinclair, Rev. W.J. Cox and Messrs. R.B. Don and
James Cunningham heard that copies of the College Report had now been sent
to the Secretary for Scotland and the Lord Advocate, with the request that these
officers of state would receive their deputation.

Mr Cox's intimation of his donation of £12000 towards the endowment and equipment of a Chair of Anatomy was made public in a letter published in the *Advertiser* of December 14th. The leader in the *Advertiser* commended Mr Cox, and observed that 'The Exchequer will not now have to provide for a *second* Anatomy Chair'. It went on to extol 'the vested interests of Dundee'. But from now on the 'Third Party' became fiercely involved.

For from now began the series of angry attacks which continued in the local press, at varying intervals and with varying degrees of intensity, for seventy years. On December 17th Professor Bell Pettigrew wrote to the *Advertiser* making public the proposals put to the Dundee College Committee by the St Andrews Medical Faculty. He quoted in full the proposals about the sharing of Chairs, which, he said 'will show that St Andrews while not prepared to give Dundee the whole loaf, is, nevertheless, quite willing to give her the half'. The letter was in no way aggressive, but the reply from the Editor deliberately avoided the offer of sharing, and attacked the University. 'St Andrews students will still have to go to Dundee for clinical training, even if new Chairs are available in St Andrews', it began. This was exactly what the St Andrews proposals themselves had said, and they had also praised the hospital facilities which those same students would find in Dundee. The *Advertiser* went on: 'All that St Andrews wants it may have if it will cease to think so much of vested interests and heartily co-operate with University College, Dundee . . . If the University under its new Principal would make the slightest sign that it is willing to identify itself with the large population and vigorous College established at its doors' . . . and so on.

On 6th January, 1887, it was reported to Principal Peterson's sub-committee that favourable replies had been received from the Chairman of the Royal Infirmary Board and from the Forfarshire Medical Association, and that deputations had met the Lord Provost. The pamphlet being prepared for publication was scrutinised and gone over at the sub-committee meeting on the 7th, corrected again on the 10th, and finally approved on the 13th. On the 17th the whole Council met, with Rev. W.J. Cox in the chair. A letter from the Forfarshire was read. The Association 'had learned with pleasure that a Chair of Anatomy had been founded', and asked that measures to set up the first two years of a medical course be begun as soon as possible. The letter went on 'It is the opinion of the Association that the time has now arrived when a close alliance in medical teaching between the University of St Andrews and the Dundee College has become more than ever desirable in the interest of both institutions'. The letter was signed by 'A.M. Stalker, M.B., Secretary'. Professor Peterson's pamphlet was further altered by the main Committee and a thousand copies were ordered to be printed *gratis* under the sanction of the College.

On the same day, a letter to be well-quoted in future times was published by the *Advertiser*. It was 'The Proposed Joint Medical School for St Andrews and Dundee' and was signed 'By an old Medical Student of St Andrews University'. (The 'old student' was Professor W.C. McIntosh.) This very very long article quoted the student's own experience in the *annus medicus* at St Andrews before going on to clinical studies (in Edinburgh). He continued by declaring that St

Andrews has entered vigorously in the movement towards higher education in Dundee, and had helped as well as it could when Dundee had no available Professors of its own. He was very restrained in what he said about the foundation of University College, making no mention of the ignoring of the University and the complete ignoring of Principal Tulloch's more than generous offers, both about University sharing in general and indeed about provision of medical teaching in Dundee in particular, but contented himself with 'Yet when University College was opened in the presence of members of the Senatus of St Andrews, co-operation was not favourably entertained'.

'St Andrews had given Dundee students privileges willingly, without requiring residence. St Andrews gave Dundee all it asked'. This was true. As far as a Medical School was concerned, the wish for the establishment of a complete one was not new. But it had been said on behalf of Dundee, Professor McIntosh continued, that the obstacle was want of money, and that until there was a union between the two bodies, the suggestion was held in abeyance.

He next referred to the meeting of December 9th. The Dundee College Council (in fact, Principal Peterson's sub-committee) had insisted that as a *sine qua non* all the medical classes should be located in Dundee. These were the inflexible views of the Dundee side at the conference of December 9th. The Medical School was to be for Dundee, not St Andrews, and not even one class in the curriculum was to be left at St Andrews. The Medical Chairs at St Andrews were to be suppressed. Dr. Sinclair's argument about the need to have medical students studying from the beginning of their course within a hospital context he answered by showing that the *exclusion* of medical students from hospitals in their early years was exactly what happened everywhere at present. He agreed, and instanced points in support of the pre-clinical student working beside his hospital, and said also that 'on the other hand, the student would have to carry out his work in an atmosphere uncongenial both to health and study, and he would lose the culture which to a large extent attached itself to all the old Scottish Universities. Nor can it be said that opportunities for studying pre-clinical subjects are better in Dundee than St Andrews'. The development of research was important in a pre-clinical school, and the Professors were as important as money in this respect, and in general. 'Dundee has nothing to gain by competing narrowly with St Andrews. On the contrary, it would be for the best interests of Dundee if future donors aided St Andrews, with a view to founding a Joint Medical School as between St Andrews and Dundee'.

The *Advertiser's* leading article, it goes without saying, ignored the positive points of 'Clause VI', the proposals which Professor Pettigrew had made public and Professor McIntosh had repeated. Attacking the old medical student's 'hints and conjectures' and 'demands', the leader, containing its own share of hints and conjectures, exemplifies precisely the attitude of mind which was so upsetting and exasperating to members of the University. Its tone is contemptuous, its arguments superficially fair but in fact extremely unfair. St Andrews will give; Dundee will take. Professor McIntosh's letter may have been spoiled by being long, but it was reasonable and in no way offensive or belligerent. Professor Pettigrew's previous signed letter had been conciliatory; he had said,

almost diffidently, that the Dundee Press had perhaps not been altogether fair to St Andrews. It was entirely reasonable for the St Andrews Professors to wish to retain their teaching and their Chairs. It was very reasonable to ask for an extension of pre-clinical medical teaching at St Andrews, especially since there was now the developing association with Dundee, and so a source of clinical material and clinical teaching was in prospect after so many centuries. There was no wish to suppress a Dundee department (although Dundee had sought to suppress the St Andrews Chair of Chemistry)—but only to preserve St Andrews ones. And further, the newspaper's arrogance implied a corresponding attitude on the part of the new College academic staff which was not by any means always present; indeed, one of the difficulties of trying to give an objective account of these and subsequent proceedings in the setting up of the Conjoint Medical School is the frequent discrepancy of College records in their private form and the expanded form to be found in the *Advertiser's* accounts. So many of the University College records exist as newspaper cuttings that the information available tends to be weighted towards the latter and not towards the probably more accurate former.

Nor were fears lessened by a letter from Mr Alexander Robertson, of Broughty Ferry, who wrote to the *Advertiser* on the very next day:

'In your article of yesterday as to the Dundee Medical School you state that: "nothing to our knowledge has been said of late years about the suppression or transference of any of the teaching Chairs at St Andrews". Allow me, however, to inform you that your knowledge as to what has taken place within the last three years is not entirely accurate as to the facts. About three years ago I was—and still am—of opinion that a Medical School should be gradually built up and established in Dundee in connection with the University College of Dundee. I accordingly had conversations with the Earl of Dalhousie and also with Mr Frank Henderson, M.P. as to the transference of the St Andrews Chairs of Natural History and Pathology (he presumably mixed up *Physiology* with Pathology), but not of Chemistry, to the University College of Dundee; and thereafter with their sanction, and for their approval, I forwarded each of them a copy of a clause which I had drawn up for the purpose of transferring the above two Medical Chairs to the University College of Dundee, and as an amendment on the Scotch University Bill of 1883 or 1884. I have further to state that the noble Earl and the junior member of Parliament for Dundee consented to move the adoption of the clause I had prepared ... the Committee stage of the last Scotch University Bill was never reached and, as far as I know, nothing was done in regard to the clause I sent ... I have not the slightest particle of hostile feeling against the University of St Andrews ...

But perhaps it was the calm assumption that Dundee would make use of St Andrews which was hardest of all to bear—especially after the help which had continued to be given after 1882. And here the paper spoke openly on behalf of the College Council. On January 18th it published a long statement 'on behalf

of the Medical School which it is proposed to found in Dundee under the sanction of the Council of University College'.

St Andrews has already freely given us in respect of our science students all that we need or ask for our medical students—the right to a University degree upon the results of our College teaching . . . this straight path to a recognised University degree in medicine is not an ordinary or common thing. It is a condition that comparatively few Medical Schools possess. Those which lack it can and do prepare their students for the qualifications of the Colleges of Physicians and Surgeons, or send them up for the higher examinations of the University of London . . . The Owens College, (Manchester) for instance, worked successfully for years in this position without the right to confer a degree; and the great school of University College, London, is only now acquiring the same privilege. But we, with the St Andrews degrees before us, would start possessed of a great natural advantage, which no new Medical School of recent years has been born into immediate possession of; and the prospect of this privilege, though it does not create, yet immeasurably strengthens our claim to undertake this new teaching work.

The *Advertiser* went on to press the view that 'while the success and the honour of the new school are intimately bound up with St Andrews University', there is no place for splitting the medical course, as has been suggested by the St Andrews side, into two 'pre-clinical' years there, and two 'clinical' years at Dundee. 'Such a scheme', the College Council paper goes on 'has never been accepted as workable; and, very briefly given, the following are the chief reasons for this opinion:

1) That it is unnatural, inexpedient, and wholly unusual to exclude medical students, even in their first two years, from the practice of a hospital. Even if students are not actually attending lectures in connection with their hospital work, they should have daily opportunity of acquiring experience in the wards.

2) That such a line of demarcation between the "scientific" and the "professional" periods would be a very artificial one. For where students are passing through their course in the minimum of time, as the great bulk of Scottish students do, the class for surgery, for instance, finds its natural place (as in Edinburgh) in the second winter session.

3) A still more crucial objection is that since students generally go up for examination in anatomy and physiology at the end of their third session they would, on such a scheme, be debarred from all fair opportunity of revising their work for a whole year before presenting themselves for examination.

4) That were the laboratories and dissecting rooms located in St Andrews it would be exceedingly difficult, and probably impossible, for us to organise the third and fourth years' work in Dundee. For on any possible scheme for the organisation of these

two latter years' work in Dundee we should be dependent on the medical profession for very great effort and sacrifice—at least in the earlier years of the undertaking.
5) That under any circumstances a forced break in the middle of the course would be undesirable and hazardous. For students turned adrift at the end of their two years from one school would reconsider their position, and would have before them the strong attraction of London, of Edinburgh, and of other great hospital centres.
But above and apart from these mere arguments, there is the simple fact that we already possess the endowment for our Chair of Anatomy and where the Chair of Anatomy goes the rest of those two years' work must of necessity be done'.

Requirements of the proposed school were then listed. Of the six (or seven, if surgery were included) Chairs required for the first two years' curriculum, only two were functioning—Chemistry and Biology. Physiology, Pathology and Botany Chairs were essential; Anatomy had just been endowed but no more. 'We may assume', the paper goes on, 'in the outset that our business for the present lies with the work of the first two of the four years constituting a full course of medical study. The remainder is not wanted for a while; it will cost little to endow, and very little to equip, and we have every reason to believe that when the first half is gained the rest is to all intents and purposes secure'.

Surgery, Medicine, Midwifery and Diseases of Women, Materia Medica and Pharmacy, and Medical Jurisprudence and Public Health were the curriculum subjects of the third and fourth years, and it was noted that:
provision will have to be made for the teaching of clinical medicine and surgery. All of these subjects can be, and habitually are, taught in conjunction with medical and surgical practice; and an endowment for each of about £100 a year, with the prospect of students' fees, is a not unfair allotment for work, in itself attractive which involves a partial sacrifice of professional income. In not one of these departments need we look beyond the limits of our towns for our future teachers.

This Medical School will give our College completeness along a new line of educational work. It will quicken into new usefulness departments that already exist . . . As to the practical result of the success of such a movement, Dundee would, in fact, become a University town . . . it ought not to be forgotten that the influx of a class of students which we do not at present reach would involve a considerable addition to the material prosperity of the town.

The diary of 'Dr. Munro, Professor of Medicine in Edinburgh University in the beginning of this century' was quoted: "During the last 48 years 13,404 students, or nearly two fifths of the number, came from England, Ireland and other countries; and, they brought into Scotland £466,480 sterling". 'A like calculation made now, on the basis of the present number of students, would yield far more astonishing results' . . .

The obvious inconsistencies and several errors of fact in this really very poor leader as published were immediately replied to by Professor Pettigrew. His letter was published on January 24th. Again not surprisingly the *Advertiser* had nothing to say to his corrections to the Dundee Council's list of arguments in support of its determination to have the Medical School. In this letter his comments on the *Advertiser's* wilder statements were sharper, but still restrained. He did not conceal his anxiety that the Dundee Council were in fact opposing the formation of a *joint* Medical School, and intended to ask the Government for new medical buildings when the University was also doing so. Recalling the demand in the *Advertiser* that when the Chair of Chemistry became vacant at St Andrews in the recent past it be suppressed in favour of the Chair of Chemistry in Dundee, he complained that it was now being suggested that St Andrews abandon her bid for a Chair of Anatomy because one was being endowed in Dundee. He was restrained enough not to point out that the new Dundee Chemistry Chair's position had been strengthened by the University's agreement to recognise its classes for graduation. As well as printing his long letter in full, the *Advertiser* attacked him and medical teaching in St Andrews, ridiculing St Andrews as a 'medical authority' and its medical faculty an 'examining board'. Of St Andrews and London medical graduates, the editorial commented that 'there is as much difference between the two sets of graduates as between Falstaff's Army and the German Guard'. The best point which the newspaper made was to quote the opinion of the University Commissioners of 1876, who had been against new Medical Chairs in St Andrews and in favour of the formation of a *College* which would be affiliated to St Andrews University 'and stand in the same relation to it as the College of St Mary and the United College do at present. Such a College would contain a complete set of Chairs of Medicine, and the Professors would be members of their Faculty in the University of St Andrews'. This suggestion of a Medical College is important to record, since a not too dissimilar idea would be suggested eighty years later.[7] But in the interval between 1876 and the present, the *Advertiser* failed to point out, the University College now founded in Dundee was in no way a College standing in the same relation to the University as the College of St Mary, nor ever would be. Its founder and its founder's requirements had made certain of that. So the newspaper's insistence that 'the promoters of a Medical School in Dundee stand by the report of the Commissioners' was calculated to mislead.

This unfortunate behaviour continued. St Andrews was subjected to ridicule and contempt, and proposals were vigorously made on behalf of Dundee, and in stronger, and often violent terms, at every opportunity. Whether a different attitude by the local press, and by members of the local community in Dundee encouraged to contribute, would have altered the subsequent history of the relations between the Colleges, and made for smoothness of co-operation is not difficult to answer; it undoubtedly would. Indeed it can be said that the unfortunate and unnecessary exchanges of these years established a tension and distrust which persist to the present day. Successive letters made points and counter-assertions which often did not answer previous ones, but merely

increased annoyance and hardened attitudes. When the *Advertiser* quoted at length from selected General Medical Council criticisms that (for St Andrews M.D. degrees)... if the 'St Andrews M.D. examination were like those of London it would be different... the graduates of London are tested by a series of examinations the most searching known in this country... the Degree fails to afford any sufficient stimulus to induce the candidates to take pains in making preparation or in maintaining that higher culture which such a degree should indicate', Professor Pettigrew replied at equal length, quoting figures and reports by visiting bodies, and quoting in detail, though apologetically, criticisms recently made of the University of London examinations—'There was no clinical examination; no operations were required on the dead subject; no testing as to bandaging was employed... a candidate may present himself for the M.B. examination without ever having attended a course of lectures on Systematic Medicine or Systematic Surgery' and so on. He quoted in support of St Andrews Medicine the written testimony of the leading medical men in every division of the Kingdom, such as Sir Dominic Corrigan, Sir George Burrows, Sir William Muir, Sir James Paget, Sir William Jenner, Sir Andrew Clark, Sir William Ferguson, Sir T. Spencer Wells, Sir Joseph Lister, Sir William Gall, Sir Henry Thompson, Sir Joseph Fayner, Sir John Rose Cormack, Doctors Humphreys, Jackson, Matthews, Duncan... etc.

The background to all this acrimony does not need re-stating. There was the long-standing lack of money and the recent horror of threatened extinction of the University. But had St Andrews had commercial undertakings and consequent wealth to endow Chairs—which she had not—it would have made no difference. St Andrews had no hospital of any size and so no source of clinical material. The St Andrews professors were just as aware of this as any others. Professor Pettigrew had like several predecessors tried desperately hard to make Anatomy viable—there are reports of his journeys back and forwards to Glasgow, collecting and replacing specimens and dissections—and by now he was getting older and tired, and he was disappointed that his enthusiasm over Dundee had come to nothing. And so he, and Professor McIntosh, made the best they could of their case. And now a new College over the River Tay had appeared and was advancing quickly, and was about to take over the medical teaching which the University had always wished to provide. It was hardly surprising that the St Andrews side viewed these developments with alarm and even with jealousy, and that the enthusiastic and self-confident Dundonians were equally alarmed at what they saw as their own Medical School's subordination to an elderly and to them effete institution in a tiny little Fife town. It was rather like the old story of the poor but proud heiress of a noble family being courted for her title by a brash newly-rich young man who sought her only for her name and social connections and whose own commercial wealth was in her eyes a doubtful attraction.

But there was more to this sudden incursion into the pages of the local Dundee press by two St Andrews Professors than a background of general concern. Both letters, first Professor Pettigrew's and then Professor McIntosh's, had followed closely upon the meeting of the 9th of December, but more

importantly, on the most significant meeting of Principal Peterson's small sub-committee four brief days later.

This meeting, just reported, was full of significance in the whole future relations between Dundee and St Andrews over the Medical School. When the St Andrews minute is read, it is no different from the usual Senatus records of those days. But Principal Peterson's minute is very different. In particular, its last sentence is not found in the St Andrews minute, and is incongruous with what has gone before.

'The view was adopted on both sides that the foundation of a Chair of Anatomy on either side of the Tay would at once settle the question with regard to which the present difference of opinion has emerged'. But the foundation of a Chair of Anatomy had not been stated to be the crux of the matter. When Professors Pettigrew and McIntosh wrote later, they made no reference to this particular 'question with regard to which the present difference of opinion had emerged'. Professor McIntosh's long article, in particular, almost certainly puts into print words and arguments actually used at the meeting. The person who wrote the other minute, laid it before the sub-committee, and had them approve it, was Principal Peterson. Why Anatomy—when a whole *range* of Chairs was in the discussion? Principal Peterson immediately announced—in the next sentence to his report being approved—that he had received a letter from Mr Cox with his £12000 offer for a *Chair of Anatomy*. It is a little hard to believe that this letter had just happened to come into his hands, absolutely unexpectedly, in the very brief period between his visit to St Andrews and the Dundee Council Meeting.

The statement that Principal Peterson had had his intention to have a Medical School formed in and for Dundee alone settled finally by remarks Professor McIntosh had made at a house party[8] is as ridiculous as the story that Principal Irvine's hatred of Dundee was the result of overhearing some remarks critical of St Andrews University at lunch one day in the Eastern Club. From his very first College reports he had talked of the Dundee Medical School, and the evidence of the records before and especially after the meeting of December 9th make it very likely indeed that he had known all along about Mr Cox's offer, and had indeed made the Dundee location of a Medical School the *sine qua non* when he met the St Andrews Professors. It is probable that he went to St Andrews having already decided to make the meeting fail. The speed with which the list of subsequent decisions, all designed to put one over on St Andrews, was gone through, is highly suggestive of a prearrangement. Armed with the background knowledge that money was forthcoming to support his aim, and probably with the knowledge of forthcoming support from the Leng press, he could not see himself lose.

If the institution of the University College, and especially the constitution of its Council was the first tragedy in the unhelpful attitude Dundee showed to St Andrews, the behaviour of Principal Peterson over these first negotiations was the first tragedy in the foundation of the Conjoint Medical School. He showed himself entirely unsympathetic to St Andrews and completely determined to get what he could out of her to suit his Dundee policy. From this early hardness of

attitude arose an increasing suspicion of Dundee and its real intentions which was certainly not present before. Principal Peterson's behaviour and attitude in the nineteenth century towards St Andrews mirrored Principal James Irvine's attitude in the twentieth towards Dundee, and was no less reprehensible.

While the crude boasting of the *Advertiser* and its attacks on the unfortunate St Andrews Medical Professors continued, discussions about the incorporation of University College within the University of St Andrews were proceeding. Extensions to the present Scottish Universities, with incorporation of the recently formed technical colleges within them, were discussed at a large public meeting held on February 1st, 1887, in Perth. Formation of a new technical or other college tended to follow the same sequence of events—the first rush of novelty interest was not invariably followed by steady increase in numbers or achievements, but by a disappointing reduction. This was happening in University College also, where the Technical Institute was actually competing for students with the College and with some success. Professor Carnelly, in his annual report for 1887-88, regretted the lowered standard of work, and noted that Chemistry classes had opened at the Technical Institute. Inadequacy of space was complained of by Professor D'Arcy Thompson. And while the Principal reported that 25 science students—including Chemistry ones—had matriculated at St Andrews, he was not as confident as he had been six months earlier. 'In my own Department' he wrote 'I have never felt so much as in this session the disadvantages of working without a definite University connection. The London University examinations are not popular with our students, though they afford the only opportunity within our reach of graduation in Arts'. He again looked forward to the Dundee College gaining improved status through the forthcoming Universities (Scotland) Bill, and towards the foundation of a School of Medicine. An Anatomy Chair 'will be a useful advantage, and a Physiology one would follow'. For although the Universities (Scotland) Bill had proposed 'that the University and Colleges at St Andrews, be incorporated into one body named the University of St Andrews', and 'that the University College of Dundee be affiliated to, or incorporated with, the said University, with the special object of establishing a fully equipped University School of Medicine there', it had not been proceeded with during the Parliamentary session. In the 1887-88 session there were 127 students at University College and 170 evening students. The decrease from 144 and 199 of the previous session, was said to be because of 'stricter regulations' for entry. Women students' numbers had also fallen from 60 to 36. On the credit side, a Chair of Botany was founded that July, by a gift of £6000 from the family of the late J.F. White of Balruddrey. This was to be 'for the School of Medicine'. But as far as this school of Medicine was concerned, all the unseemly correspondence published by the *Advertiser*, and the planning and pronouncements of Principal Peterson, had ignored the most telling sentences of all. These were written on January 24th, 1887, by Professor Pettigrew, in reply to the Third Party demands:

Anyone reading these passages would naturally infer that University College, Dundee, had applied to the University of St

Andrews to recognise *its medical teaching* and that such recognition had been accorded. Such, however, is not the case. The subject has never been before the University. Moreover, if the University College had a complete Medical School tomorrow, only two of its four medical years could, according to existing regulations, be recognised by the University of St Andrews. This follows because two out of the four years required for medical graduation *must be spent at a University*. This is a most important consideration for the citizens of Dundee.

University College might lose after all. Even the financial advantages of uniting St Andrews with Dundee—rather than uniting Dundee with St Andrews—were now less relevant. And within two years, they would become possibly irrelevant. The sensible solution which sensible men were hoping for was that University College would become a College of St Andrews and as such an integral part of a University. Everything else would follow this.

The importance of the Medical faculty in the move towards such a unity was considerable. Principal Peterson had spoken of 'Medicine' in his very first public report to the Committee of the Coucil of University College on 4th February, 1884, as his second priority—the first being to try to complete a Science Curriculum. The larger Universities, he said, could only handle the work being crowded upon them by developing their extra-mural teaching; he saw 'no reason why part of this work should not come to Dundee, which can boast of an Infirmary for clinical instruction'. As soon as he had won recognition for Science undergraduates from St Andrews, his next move had been to demand a complete course of Medicine for Dundee. The St Andrews medical Professors had resisted this, and in spite of the best efforts of the press, had held their ground. They were continuing to challenge for two new Medical Chairs out of money hoped for under the coming University legislation, in spite of having no men of wealth like Mr Cox and Mr White to endow them. In fact, they were proving extremely tiresome adversaries. Principal Peterson's tactics in the meetings of November and December, 1886, and the subsequent public press war, had hardened their attitude considerably.

At this stage, there was fortunately action on more than one level. Provost Thornton was a good friend of St Andrews as well as a loyal supporter of Dundee. He saw the need for co-operation and not confrontation.[9, 10] The letter from Provost Ballingall of February 12th, 1887, requesting Principal Donaldson to allow his name, and those of other Senate colleagues, to be put forward as members of a committee to promote the foundation of a Medical School in Dundee, was exactly what was required, and produced a measured and friendly reply. This level of co-operation went on in parallel to, but much more quietly than, the public pamphlet of the Principal's Sub-Committee and its College Council. There would be a number of later occasions over the years when constructive action was brought forward, sometimes behind the shrill destructiveness of the Third Party.

In 1887, a draft Universities Bill was brought forward which included a clause allowing the amalgamation to be made:

Clause 14 Without prejudice to any of the powers herein before
conferred, the Commissioners shall, with regard to the
University and Colleges of St Andrews, and the University
College of Dundee, have power to make ordinances.
  (i) as regards the University and Colleges of St Andrews,
  for incorporating them into one body under the name
  of the University of St Andrews under such conditions
  as may seem just, having due regard to vested
  interests.
  (ii) as regards the University College of Dundee, for
  affiliating it to, or incorporating it with, the said
  University, with the special object of establishing a
  fully equipped University School of Medicine.

The Sub-Committee of the College Council discussed the proposed Bill at
their meeting of 12th December, 1887. The legislation Sub-Committee, as it was
called, was very much Principal Peterson's Committee—he was its convener,
and frequently the only members present were himself and Professor Thompson
or a lay person or two on other occasions. Principal Peterson minuted that on
this occasion he made two alterations to the draft—first, that separate representation of the College Council on the University Court of St Andrews University
be provided, and second, that para. (ii) above continued . . . 'of Medicine,
having due regard to the Constitution of the said College as set forth in its Deed
of Endowment and Trust'. These amendments went to the full Council, where
just as St Andrews had its Professor Crombie, so Dundee had its Rev. W.J.
Cox—he dissented from the otherwise unanimous approval of the Bill and the
recommendation. And just as St Andrews had its Dundee opponents in
Professors Pettigrew and McIntosh, so the Dundee Council had its Mr W.C.
Leng, who that October attacked the proposal in the Bill to divide £47,000
amongst the four Scottish Universities, attacked St Andrews for its 'very few
students', (some 200) and demanded a share for Dundee. And just as these two
St Andrews Professors were talked down by other members of the Senate, so
was Mr Leng, on this and other occasions, by other members of the Council.
Rev. Colin Campbell, Dr. Sinclair, and Mr R.B. Don answered him. 'If Dundee
affiliated to St Andrews', Dr. Sinclair pointed out, 'it will gain access to money
also. The grant to Scottish Universities is not a thing which an Institution like
ours can lay claim to, because it is given in commutation of the ancient
endowments which belong to the Universities'. And Mr Don added: 'It would be
unfortunate if an impression went out that it was the wish of the Governors of
the College to claim upon what I think we have no claim'. These quieter
arguments ensured that good sense prevailed.

The legislation Sub-Committee then asked the Council to take the recommendations, if they approved of them, to the Secretary for Scotland. This was
agreed—with Rev. W.J. Cox again dissenting. On the 14th, when the death of
Lord Dalhousie was reported, amalgamation was again voted as most desirable,
but further reference to the whole Council was insisted upon. The whole College
Council met on the 21st, when Principal Donaldson was present and took the

Chair. Yet further discussion took place; Mr James Cunningham moved, and Mr G.W. Baxter seconded, that the second paragraph of Clause 14 be changed to ... College of Dundee, of effecting *some form of union* with the University of St Andrews ... and this was carried unanimously. Other amendments were approved, but the draft itself was not recorded. By the 28th, Principal Peterson was in London pressing the points in Dundee's case he wanted agreed by Government. He saw Sir Francis Sandford, the Secretary of State for Education, who assured him that there was 'every disposition' on the part of the authorities to meet his views, and reassured him that the omission of the phrase covering the Dundee 'vested interests' was unintentional. Peterson wrote in haste to make sure the Council did not forget to communicate these points to the Lord Advocate.

It was interesting that no copy of the earlier report was included in the College Council meeting—or, for that matter, appears to exist now in Dundee University records—so important was it for the future of the College. The printed Report of what was actually transmitted by the deputation of the Council to the Secretary for Scotland and the Lord Advocate is dated 12th January, 1888. It had had final approval by the whole Council on the 8th, except for Principal Donaldson, who 'reserved himself as to the third alternative' and for Rev. W.J. Cox, who reserved himself as to the whole Report.

Principal Peterson's first point was that the Constitution of University College, Dundee, was only seven years old. It had several features from which they were bound never to depart—he instanced the declaration that the College was founded for the education of *both sexes*, and for the *study of science, literature, and the fine arts.* He also instanced the prohibition of any religious tests for students or professors. Following Mr Cunningham's amendment, his wish for union was in vague terms in the preamble: 'It is natural' he wrote, 'that we should desire to be united with St Andrew's(sic) University, which has always interested itself in the work of higher education in Dundee, and which has recognised the Science teaching of University College, as qualified for its degrees. We recognise the value of a systematic connection with a Degree-giving institution, and we are sensible also of the benefits which will be derived by the University from the extension of its work in this great centre of population. The Council of the College is therefore ready, under Article 43 of the Deed of Endowment and Trust, to take the present opportunity of effecting "some sort of union" with St Andrew's "upon such terms and conditions as may be desirable" '.

Principal Peterson had already shown himself, however, as far as the Medical Faculty at St Andrews was concerned, to be entirely unsympathetic. His attitude was entirely logical, seen from his own tactical point of view. St Andrews was lacking large benefactors, and Dundee had a continuing supply of these, or so it seemed. Obviously he was determined that these expected endowments remain firmly in the control of the College Council, of which he was not yet a member but which he was working towards becoming. And of course he did not need to voice any suggestion that a St Andrews Senate or Court representative be appointed to the Council, since the Dundee College's foundation deed did not allow this.

It was the third alternative which had set the alarm ringing in the University Senatus and about which Principal Donaldson had made reservations. For this, Principal Peterson had suggested a position be given to his College equating it, on a one-third share basis, with the United College and St Mary's. Again, his starting point was the assured authority of his governors and Council. 'It is doubtful', he wrote, 'if the University Court even if mixed with representatives from Dundee, would be better qualified than our present administrators to take in hand the special features of our work in this large industrial centre. We have a large and growing technical side; the department of evening classes is an essential feature in our scheme of education; and we have women students'.

He then went on to describe the Victoria University of Manchester with its Colleges. All of these were centred within a large local population, and each was under the independent control of its own governing body. The only control the University Court exercised was over the educational curriculum of each college. He therefore suggested that United College, St Mary's, and University College would each send members to the Court so that the special features of each of the component colleges might be preserved, and their development encouraged . . . 'Unity in Educational Matters would be secured by the jurisdiction of the University Court; so unnecessary duplication of Chairs would be avoided. To the University Court would also belong the right of determining whether a Chair which it might be proposed to found should be considered a University Chair, i.e. one inside the degree curriculum of the University'. This seemed a little unclear, as from what he had just proposed, *all* Chairs would be inside the degree curriculum of the University. It is possible that he was thinking of the University as it existed at that moment. If the objection were made that such a step would dissociate St Andrews from the pattern of constitution of the other Scottish Universities, Principal Peterson answered that a radical change of this sort 'seemed to be demanded by the interests of the University itself and of the district'. It might, he thought, be *advantageous* to St Andrews, by 'giving it greater freedom of action in dealing with such subjects of action as the higher technical education, and the education of women'. He could certainly have been correct in his suggestion that a three-college University was worth while, and it is interesting to speculate what might have followed if this third alternative had been accepted by the University. The stumbling block in their eyes remained the autonomy of the College Council and the fear that the New Dundee College would quickly grow to become the predominant College within the University, nourished by sources of income which the older foundations could never match.

His paper ended with a reference to Medical teaching, and the hard line he took confirmed the suspicions of Pettigrew and McIntosh:

> We highly appreciate the reference in Clause 14, 2, to the scheme for establishing a fully equipped University School of Medicine in *Dundee*: but the wording of the clause ("with the special object of establishing") has been thought to limit the Commission too narrowly to one department of our operations. A verbal change would meet this difficulty'.

W. Peterson, 23rd January 1888.

On February 20th Peterson's legislation Committee received the reply of the Senate. As he must surely have expected, they objected entirely to the radical change in his third alternative, and declined 'to entertain or assent to any proposal that would destroy the integrity, alter the constitution, or impair the rights and privileges of the University founded on its ancient Charters'. They approved paragraph (ii) of Clause 14 as it stood, and felt that this agreement be made known to the Secretary for Scotland and the Lord Advocate at once, as should their resolution against Principal Peterson's third section. While Peterson minuted that he would call a meeting of the full Council, he did not do so, but called a further meeting of his legislation Committee for the 27th. On that date he admitted no compromise: his Committee did not see their way to recommend to the Council to withdraw from the third alternative of their report, 'as they considered that it was desirable that the whole question should, for the present, be kept as open as possible as difficulties might arise in carrying out either of the Proposals'. However, the very same Monday, the 27th, Rev. W.J. Cox, James Cunningham, and Robert B. Don met and *called* for a meeting of the whole Council. This was duly held, apparently later in the day, when the Council agreed that a meeting should be held with the Senate to exchange views. The joint meeting took place on the 9th of March, three professors and three business men attending, and it was a very friendly one. The Senatus had said they would re-formulate their own proposals and send them back to the University College Council. It may have been that some council members were a little concerned at their young Principal's handling of the negotiations, since the full meeting moved and passed a motion that the legislation Sub-Committee was to be enlarged, and that more members were to attend its meetings.

Throughout 1888, as well as the diplomatic, tactical, background and public campaigns over the Bill to affiliate or incorporate the new College with the old University, so that the college would obtain the statutory right to confer degrees on all its students who completed their examinations and so obtain the *ius ubique docendi*, progress also continued in Dundee and St Andrews towards the establishment of a Conjoint School of Medicine. In April, concern was expressed by the finance Committee at the urgent need to reduce expenditure in Dundee, so that its debts could be reduced. The Principal's assistant and the College fireman were dispensed with, and grants to the Physics, Engineering, and Chemistry departments were reduced. Expenditure on prizes was to be limited to £35. In May, Professor Carnelly, who had taken the post of Professor of Chemistry in Aberdeen in January, wrote anxiously about the delay in providing equipment for Dyeing and Bleaching in his former department. These, plus anxieties over falling numbers of local students in degree-type courses, all produced a picture very different from that in the Principal's memorandum arguing for his third alternative.

In St Andrews, two petitions were presented to the University in the spring—one, from Arts alumni that higher degrees in Classics and English be instituted, and the other, from medical graduates, that the medical regulations be altered to allow those graduated for ten years to be eligible to take the M.D.

On 14th April, lectures in Botany were approved to begin, and Mr R.A. Robertson was named as the lecturer. These were to be specifically for medical students, and details were to be given in the forthcoming calendar. University funds were declared 'in a satisfactory state', and 'cordial approval' given to the points in the Universities (Scotland) Bill relating to the constitution of the Court. The incorporation of the Colleges and the University into one body—while retaining the colleges nominally—confirming the rank of the University, and the provision of the Consolidated Fund at at least £50,000—as well as to Clause 14 (ii) 'connecting University College, Dundee with the University of St Andrews, understanding this clause likewise to be permissive', was also welcomed.

In April there was a great deal of activity over medical teaching and medical examining. The Medical Faculty petitioned the University yet again to seek provision in the forthcoming Bill for St Andrews to have its former rights in conferring medical degrees restored. Durham and London Universities had the same privilege—to give a medical degree to 'all comers', and the three Royal Colleges were petitioning likewise. The discussions over the early part of 1888 were probably the frankest and most realistic statement of the University's shortcomings over provision of medical teaching that had ever been made. It includes the complaint that St Andrews was in fact not remiss in its mode of graduation—as the external examiners and Professor Pettigrew had already pointed out to the G.M.C. assessors; they were shackled by legislation which thwarted their attempts at improvement. They could not, for example, *require* a thesis. Any continuing examination would have to be very strict indeed—and to ensure this, *annual* direct supervision of the G.M.C. would be welcome. At present the M.B. C.M. *clinical* examinations were held at Chalmers Hospital, Edinburgh, but there were no clinical examinations for the M.D. The medical Professors drew special attention to the absence of a dissecting room and fresh specimens for Anatomy, Surgery, and Physiology. 'Neat dissections of the several regions of the body', said Pettigrew, 'are a *sine qua non*'—the Senatus Academicus, with the sanction of the Court must provide money for a dissecting room. The Dean, Professor Pettigrew went on, had endeavoured to the utmost of his ability to strengthen this weak link in the St Andrews system by importing a large number of specimens from Glasgow—but these were detached portions, used from year to year, not useful for teaching, and indeed unfair to students. 'We would be lacking in foresight ... especially as far as the M.B. C.M. is concerned . . . if we did not take *steps forthwith* to erect a dissecting room with fresh bodies'. Something also had to be done about Medicine and Surgery ...

> the backbone of the final examination ... as Anatomy is of the
> Second Professional ... we must have Anatomy and Botany Chairs,
> or at least lectureships within the three Chairs presently available, to
> give us the *two anni medici* which the Scottish Universities all
> require ... the imperfect nature of the medical school at St Andrews
> has, no doubt, retarded the development of the University as a whole;
> and this, to us, is a source of great regret, as the increase in the

number of students attending the other Scottish Universities has of late years been largely, and indeed principally, due to an influx of medical students'.

Professor Pettigrew was also realistic in his attitude to the developments in Dundee. He was by now a man of fifty-four, who had worked hard and had suffered illness. His words and his behaviour at this time belie the reputation he has been very unfairly given as being no more than a narrow-minded, selfish blocker at Senate meetings and of every attempt at medical development in Dundee, and the just cause of the new College, although later as he grew older and his abilities diminished, he did become progressively more difficult and unco-operative, and he faded sadly from the medical scene which he had formerly dominated. He knew by this spring of 1888 that the St Andrews M.D. was an anachronism, and its mode of examination unsatisfactory. He knew, too, that its seniority—as indeed that of the University—cut little ice with the eager generation of young men in the new College and even less with the business men and newspaper owners who supported them. He had appealed with Professor McIntosh for a degree of co-operation with them, but Principal Peterson ignored his efforts and the *Advertiser* ridiculed him. It would have been odd if he was not frustrated and disappointed. But he kept up his insistence that St Andrews be not denied a share in medical teaching as had been her hope for so long, and in 1888 he argued strenuously for the urgent development of what medical school already existed 'to the extent of giving *at least two anni medici*'.

On March 5th in Dundee, Patrick Geddes was appointed to the new J.F. White Chair of Botany. Professor Geddes was from Perth, where his father had been a quartermaster in the 42nd Highlanders. He had studied in London at the Science Institute in South Kensington, and in 1874 spent a session as a junior assistant in the great Huxley's laboratory. He was appointed Sharpey Physiological Scholar in University College, London in 1877 under Professor Burdon Sanderson, then moved in succession to Paris and to Edinburgh. In Edinburgh he was first extra-mural lecturer in Natural History at the Medical School in 1880, and then lecturer in charge at the Botany Department. He now came to Dundee to start an entirely new department. No other candidate was mentioned.

The other new Chair was Anatomy. The Sub-Committee of Principal Peterson, Dr. Sinclair, Messrs. R.B. Don and J. Martin White, met throughout June. The list of applicants for the Chair was:

Henry St John Brooks, B.A. M.B. B.Ch., Chief Demonstrator in the University of Dublin.
David Hepburn, M.B. C.M. Edinburgh, M.R.C.S. Eng., Senior Demonstrator in the University of Edinburgh.
Joshua Low Kerr, C.M. M.B., Manchester, a practitioner holding two Union Medical appointments.
John Yule Mackay, M.D., Senior Demonstrator, University of Glasgow.
A. Melville Paterson, M.D. Master of Surgery, University of Edinburgh, M.R.C.S. Ed. Demonstrator, Owens College.

G.H. Heston, B.A. Camb., Honours National Science Tripos,
M.R.C.S. Eng. of Polesworth near Tamworth.
In St Andrews, 10 candidates out of 12 graduated M.D.—some were from
Scotland, and 2 graduated M.B. C.M. On July 25th voting took place on the
proposals Professor Pettigrew had made earlier to improve the Medical Faculty
teaching: restoration of the 'ancient M.D. privileges' was passed by 5 votes to 4,
and it was agreed to provide fresh specimens for a new examination in Materia
Medica. But Pettigrew's plea for a dissecting room, on which he placed such
urgent importance, received only two votes. Instead an amendment was passed,
that the University Commissioners be asked only to 'consider the propriety of
setting aside money for a dissecting room and fresh subjects', by 7 votes to 2.
The St Andrews Professors too were unhelpful to Pettigrew and McIntosh, and
this was just as damaging to them, and as frustrating, as the policy of Principal
Peterson. The M.D. and Materia Medica votes were of nominal worth only, and
gave no practical help to the struggling pair of Professors. It was not, by now,
that there was no money available; £3000 was voted for the better endowment
of the new Chair of Education.

It was not all plain sailing in Dundee either. In spite of the publicity
surrounding the building of the new Chemistry Department with Miss Baxter's
gift, which had led to the Third Party calling for the abolition of the St Andrews
Chair when vacant, Professor Stegall's assistant Mr Capstick reported to the
Council in August that he had gone to Cambridge, and after spending only
three weeks in the Cavendish Laboratory there, had found the advantages of
that laboratory over Dundee so great that he wished to leave, and work in
Cambridge from now on. He resigned from the end of September. Professor-
designate Geddes also queried his terms of appointment that August. He had
discovered, he said, that the salary proposed with two-thirds of the fees would, if
he estimated his maximum class numbers at 20-25 students, give him an income
less than his present one as an assistant at Edinburgh. Even if he got fees from
an evening class of the same number as his College students, he would still be
out of pocket. He had been told informally by Mr White that his salary would be
£200 annually, but the College were now only offering £180. So it was agreed
after discussion to raise the salary to £200.

The short list for the Anatomy post was Brooks, Mackay, and Paterson.
After interview by Principal Peterson's Sub-Committee on September 12th, Dr.
Andrew Melville Paterson was offered the post. He had begun his undergraduate
career in Manchester, then moved to Edinburgh where he graduated M.B. C.M.
in 1883 with first-class Honours. The next year he had been awarded a Gold
Medal for his M.D. thesis on 'The Spinal Nervous System of the Mammalia'. He
had spent all his graduate career in Manchester, as lecturer first in Owens
College and then in the Victoria University. (In a curious way, the Council only
then *minuted* that they were prepared to receive applications for the Cox Chair
in Anatomy.) It was stipulated that the appointee was to start work by October
1st and was to *give his services to the Council (sic)*. But although the Third Party
applauded the appointment and stated that this meant the Medical School was
now almost complete, the reality in logistic terms was very different. Professor

Paterson, on his arrival at the beginning of October, met first with the Anatomy Department Sub-Committee—i.e. with the Principal and Professor Thompson, where his suggested class syllabus was 'scrutinised', but second with a local architect. There was no available accommodation whatsoever, and 'a workshop was to be taken over, and adapted as an Anatomy Department'. The architect required £250 for the structural work and £150 for fittings. £100 was also agreed to be made available for 'instruments, Osteology, books, etc.' It would be pleasant to record that an invitiation had been sent to Professor Pettigrew to meet Professor Paterson, but this did not happen.

The necessary framework for a new Medical School was further weakened by the absence of a Professor of Chemistry in Dundee. Professor Carnelly had left with some reluctance, he said, but the inducements offered in Aberdeen were very considerable. The College Council decided not to intimate his vacancy publicly, and not to advertise for a successor. Instead, they began to select a list of likely candidates themselves.

So although 1888 was a year when superficially there was progress towards a Medical School, and when according to the *Dundee Advertiser* everything continued well, there was in fact continuing set-back. Professor Paterson found he had to ask for more money than his original allocation for his basic needs, and asked for a laboratory assistant also. At the end of October the College finances were worse, not better. The Council agreed to draw up a statement of their financial difficulties and 'to consider if it be not possible to raise enough money by private subscriptions to clear off the existing debt to the bank'. The Education Board was asked for further ideas for saving. Although details were carefully witheld, shortages must have been serious—there was even discussion on whether money could be afforded to pay for drains in the Anatomy room.

The Universities Bill was still not passed, and there was evidence of increasing anxiety on Principal Peterson's part that his plans for the way the Bill should go would not succeed. He expressed concern in the early summer, and also in November—in the early part of the year he tried, apparently unsuccessfully, to change his ground on the options of the second alternative, and in the later part of the year, found that some disturbing detail had been re-introduced in the Commons which he thought had been removed in the Lords. But November did see Professor Paterson's first Anatomy Course proposed— a course of twelve lectures in *Artistic Anatomy* at a fee of one guinea—and approved by the Council. Predictably the *Advertiser* made no critical comment. In November also, Dr. Percy F. Frankland was appointed Professor of Chemistry. He was from the South Kensington Institute, and his syllabus was to include dyeing. It was in November 1888 that the first use of the term 'Medical Faculty' appeared in print in College minutes. At this stage it was anticipation rather than certainty, but this tactic, to anticipate and win the public relations battle in the educational world, was employed very successfully. As earlier, and in later years, the policy of presentation of what was hoped would come about before it happened was not however merely a public relations tactic; the evidence that a Medical Faculty was certainly in prospect was strong enough for the College

Council to be correct in acting as it did. A true Medical Faculty was in prospect, and not the sadly restricted number of departments so described in St Andrews University. Yet it has to be remembered that in St Andrews, too, the tactic of anticipation was used, and the persisting desire for worthwhile medical teaching associated with the University was the reason for it. In this respect, the two sides of what would in due course become the enlarged University were at one in what they wanted to happen.

Development of Medicine in Dundee in 1889 was slow and followed the same pattern as 1883—appointments were made, but there were few or no students to be taught by those appointed. The financial difficulties were helped by a further bequest, from the Trustees of the late J.B. Baxter, of £500 to help to reduce the College's debt, and £1200 to properly endow a Chair of Biology. Professor Thompson's Chair had not been on a permanent footing up till now. In January Professor Paterson had reported from the Dundee Education Board that he had secured the agreement of Dr. McEwan, of the Royal Infirmary, to begin teaching of Surgery. It was at once agreed to 'organise a Department of Surgery' before the Summer term. When this news was passed on to the Council, Principal Peterson explained that 'what was really meant was not to create a Department of Surgery on the scale which this subject will ultimately fall to be treated, but merely to institute a course of instruction in operative surgery to supplement the medical teaching already available in the College'. Peterson was very clever at public relations, for this proposal when agreed to by his Council and immediately given leader coverage and confident forecast of still more to come by the Third Party, gave the impression to the local community of more content in Dundee Medical training than existed in fact. The course was to consist of an hour's lecture two days a week during April, May, and June—twenty-four lessons in all. Dr. McEwan was to receive an honorarium of 25 guineas, and the course was to be advertised at once in the *Lancet, British Medical Journal, Scotsman, Glasgow Herald, Dundee Advertiser,* and *Courier and Angus News.* It was not recorded if any students took this course, but it may be that none did—Professor Paterson in May told the Council that his Tutorial Class in Anatomy were taking no other course in the College. This Anatomy course was being given free, though the Professor asked that a guinea be charged to each participant. The Anatomy course was in difficulties after a gas stove had over-heated in March and had caused a fire in the Anatomy room. The fireman was sacked in May. No further course in Artistic Anatomy was planned, but a Miss Patti Jack of St Andrews was engaged in March to come over to the Technical Institute and give a course in drawing and painting. She had no difficulty in travelling from St Andrews to take this course, and in June the Principal reported that her class had earned eighteen guineas in fees.

The Universities Bill moved onwards to its completion in this year of British expansion in South Africa. Principal Peterson continued his close supervison of its progress, and continued to make journeys to Edinburgh or London to lobby a member of one of the Houses of Parliament, or a Minister, to press a point he wanted made, or a clause altered, just as he had done in the previous years. He

called an urgent meeting of his legislation Committee in May when a newspaper reported that representatives of the St Andrews Senate had met the Secretary for Scotland, Lord Lothian, to put points of *theirs*. He remained the hard negotiator, ready to lobby his view, angry if the other side did the very same thing, and especially indignant when Principal Donaldson and his colleagues now complained about changes made in the Bill against their wishes and without their knowledge.

Since the Conjoint Medical School's formation was dependent upon the final form the Bill and the connection University College would obtain from St Andrews would take, some consideration must be taken of the general events of 1889. It remains very difficult to select from the mass of public, private, open, background, records, what were the most significant statements and what were the most significant facts. Perhaps for the purposes of this account four only may be selected. The first was the continuing voice of the Third Party. On December 16th 1874, the local newspaper had declared: 'For good or evil we are concerned, not about the wants of St Andrews or of Scotland, but of Dundee'. The local press remained local in its attitude. Quick to attack, it was quick to commend, but only if its policy was being fulfilled or its wish granted. The prolonged campaign against St Andrews over its medical faculty had turned Professor Pettigrew from a friend into a suspicious enemy, had alarmed the whole Senate, and had encouraged quite unnecessary antagonism in the Court. And while those who did read other major Scottish newspapers—the *Scotsman* and especially the *Glasgow Herald*—could see leaders questioning the actions and even the motives of the young staff in the Dundee College, the local business men in Dundee and other citizens who did not, were soon heavily indoctrinated. While the Third Party would be calm and complimentary in 1889, when its tactics demanded, the damage had already been done.

The second was the personality of Principal Peterson. He had been kindly received by the fair-minded Principal Tulloch. He had the very highest ability, but was impatient—'a young man in a hurry'. He was too ready to demand concessions for his new College without the good manners to defer to the older and in certain respects less clever—though equally academic—St Andrews staff. Even his formal requests by letter to the Senate in the earlier years about privileges for science students were almost too obsequious, when compared to his statements when in Dundee. And unfortunately his strong support by the Dundee press reduced his acceptance by St Andrews, and much of his entirely fair and justified concern for the Dundee College was viewed with needless suspicion as a result.

Principal Donaldson was the third element. He was a mature individual very agreeable to giving help to the new University College of whose Council he had been a founder member, but was more far-seeing than Principal Peterson. This was because he was not in a hurry; his University was now secure. He signed the agreement to associate University College with the University, but he was able to look beyond the local Dundee interests and ambitions and see that the agreement was unsound. He saw the contradictions in the independence which the Dundee College Council and Governors retained, which could not be

questioned by the University, with their claim to be yet part of it and have immediate access to all the academic privileges which affiliation would bring. He wished to have University College become a College of St Andrews University in the same way as the United College of St Salvator and St Leonard, and St Mary's College, already were. His ideas on this form of incorporation were near to Principal Peterson's 'Third Option', and earned him suspicion by those Court and Senate members in St Andrews who, like their Dundee equivalents, lacked his length of vision. In many ways he was the nineteenth century counterpart of Principal Knox.

The fourth was the student body. These were, after all, the persons who stood to benefit most from a wider range of academic instruction which a union would bring. Of all the individuals quoted in both the St Andrews Senate and the Dundee Council, Professor Pettigrew was the only one to refer to their needs, and point out that certain staff members seemed more concerned with their own ambitions than with the requirements of their students. Throughout 1889, events in Dundee were closely followed by the students of the University. There had been some mixing, both informally and through the University Volunteers, of students of both sides.[10] The financial reports from University College, and the attempt to secure affiliation with the University, were reported in 'College Echoes'. Nor was the Third Party un-noticed. In 1889 it became known publicly that a large bequest of £100,000 was to become available to the University from the estate of the late Mr David Berry of Coolangatta, Shoalhaven, New South Wales. On 21st November, 1889, the Editorial from 'College Echoes' commented: 'It is amusing and a little disgusting to note the change of tone adopted towards St Andrews by the Dundee papers since the announcement of the Berry Bequest . . . their tone of habitual insolence was as absurd as it was impolite . . . St Andrews, poor as it then was, could have continued to exist with honour and usefulness, independently of Dundee. Dundee, rich as it was supposed to be, could never, without affiliation to some degree-giving institution, have risen above the position of a superior Mechanics' Institute'. Now that St Andrews had obtained the one thing needful to her, the student voice went on, a more realistic appreciation was essential. And it is noteworthy what the students *at this time* saw as Dundee's contribution to their University. 'The St Andrews students believe, as they have always believed, that Dundee, as an affiliated Medical School, may be of service and an added honour to this University. But they hold, as they have always held, that the advantages to be derived from any form of union will be very largely on the side of Dundee; and that it is not for an inferior and suppliant institution to dictate to its superior the terms of its own affiliation'.

An Act for the Better Administration and Endowment of the Universities of Scotland, 52 and 53 Vict., 30th August, 1889 laid down the terms. As far as Medicine was concerned the Government of the day, and later the Commissioners acting for it, were more receptive of the arguments of the Senate than those of Principal Peterson. For the Commissioners were empowered (Sec. 16 (i)) 'To affiliate the said University College to and make it form part of the said University, with the consent of the University Court of St Andrews, and also of

the said College, with the object, *inter alia*, of establishing a fully equipped Conjoint University School of Medicine, having due regard to existing interests, and to the aims and constitution of the said College, as set forth in its deed of endowment and trust'.

8

The Conjoint Medical School
Starts to Develop

The Marquess of Bute, Lord Rector
William Peterson, Principal

Although the Articles of University College 'had to be preserved and maintained', the College Council did have power to alter them, and in the summer of 1889 they were amended to allow Principal Peterson to become a Council member. Both at his legislation Committee and now, with the full Council, the Principal described his policy of trying to have the term 'Conjoint' deleted from the Universities Bill (5th July, 1889, and 10th July). On the latter date, the Principal had raised the question of a Chair of Physiology, and it had been agreed to proceed with this. He also reported that he had applied for the same Treasury Grant, for Dundee—£1,800 or £1,200—as the other Scottish Universities were being given, but had only been offered £500. As far as the endowment of the Physiology Chair was concered, the happier news was that several sums were assured, bringing the total to £7,000. On September 10th, when the Council had agreed to ask the University Court to consider their request for affiliation under the terms of the newly published Act, a further £2,000 was promised towards the Chair's endowment. Principal Donaldson was asked to chair several Council Meetings over this year, and there was evidence of the quiet progress which had been seen in previous years beginning once more. Later again, when the total amount available rose to £12,000, it was agreed that the Physiology Chair in University College should be advertised. £5,000 had first been given by Mr John Bett, and the benefactors of unspecified amounts, Mr Valentine, Mr Robert Fleming, and an anonymous donor of £2,000, made up the rest.

The usual Sub-Committee was formed, of Principal Peterson as Convener, Professor Paterson, Mr J. Martin White, Mr Robert B. Don, and Dr. Sinclair. Professor D'Arcy Thompson's name had disappeared from the Principal's and other committees in 1888 and 1889, but he agreed to serve on this one. On the 21st and the 25th October the Committee considered Dr. G.N. Stewart, of Owens College, and Dr. A. Waymouth Reid, of St Mary's College, London, and unanimously elected Dr. Reid. Like Professor Day, Professor Reid was a Cambridge man—and was a Southerner as far as all his training was concerned. Born on the 11th October, 1862, in Canterbury, he was the fourth son of James Reid, a surgeon there. He was at Sutton Vallance Grammar School, and won a scholarship to Cambridge, where he matriculated in 1878, took his Tripos first

part in Natural Science in 1882, and his second part in 1883—both with First Class Honours. He then decided to qualify in medicine, and moved to St Bartholomew's Hospital, graduating in 1885. From there he went to St Mary's at once, as Demonstrator and then Lecturer in Physiology. He was formally appointed on October 30th. The rules of his appointment specified that he was to give all his time to the Chair, to lectures, demonstrations, and practical work. He was 'subject to the rules of the College' except that he was *not* to have to undertake evening classes for the general public. He was to begin work at once, on November 1st.

On November 13th at the meeting of the full Council, after arguments that the now vacant Chair of English should not be filled till May of 1890 on account of the present financial position of the College, it was reported that the Town Council had given Professor Reid £100 of their total authorised sum to equip the Department of Physiology and also to engage an attendant at ten shillings per week. As with the Professor of Anatomy, Professor Reid had at his appointment no class room or laboratory. Two days before, he had given his opening lecture in the Mathematics class-room in the presence of 'a considerable number of students as well as of the general public'. Principal Peterson began by saying that the lecture they were about to hear marked another stage in the forward movement of their medical school, and he did not think they had any reason to complain of the rate at which things had been progressing lately in that direction. He answered criticisms he had heard that the Chair had been founded on an endowment of £9,000 when £15,000 had been asked for; the additional sum was however to be used to equip the department and to carry out certain alterations in the College buildings, which the audience could see on a plan available for inspection. ('The plans', the *Advertiser* report added, 'showed how, at comparatively little expense, the building could be converted into an imposing structure'). The Principal went on to say that he had to take the opportunity of congratulating (what he described as) the sister University of St Andrews on the munificent legacy which he understood had been left to it by an Australian gentleman. If it was the fact that St Andrews University was the recipient of £100,000, it became their duty and pleasure to offer their sincerest and heartiest congratulations upon this stroke of good fortune. In introducing the new Professor, Principal Peterson said he trusted his lectures would be attended by the general public as well as by the students.

The new Physiology Chair was the other especially 'Medical' Chair to be endowed as a College Chair, for all subsequent ones followed the formation of the 'Conjoint' Medical School and so were 'University' ones. Thus would arise an anomaly in the Faculty of Medicine which would persist for sixty years. It would have been pleasant to record that Professor Pettigrew had come over to hear Professor Reid's Inaugural Lecture, or Professor McIntosh, but there is no record that either did so.

One of the decisions the legislation Sub-Committee of the College Council had taken a little earlier, at the end of October, looked towards the new University Bill becoming law. This was that members of the Education Board should be added to the legislation Committee, and that Sub-Committees be

formed for each of the faculties of Arts, Science, and Medicine, to consider the curriculum and any other necessary developments of their own Faculty. The medical Sub-Committee was to consist of the Principal, Professors Thompson, Paterson, and Frankland, and Messrs. James Cunningham junior, and R.B. Don. The Convener was to be Dr. Sinclair. It was also agreed, most importantly, that the Medical Committee should have power to confer with the Directors of the Dundee Royal Infirmary.

The full draft of the proposals for union of the College with the University were debated at the end of December, and the published accounts of the discussions and debates from then through March of 1890 and later, show the moderating views of quiet progress. Mr Thomas Thornton continued to appear as perhaps the best exponent of this reasoned discussion with the aim of reaching fair agreement.[1] He thought in terms of the whole University and his belief that the inclusion of the new College would benefit what he termed 'the enlarged Univerity' was expressed in such a way that even the most suspicious St Andreans could not have found fault. He stressed the need for compromise. He hoped, he said, the fairness and reasonableness of the proposals would commend them to the Council. The governors followed the Council in their agreement on January 10th, and the *Advertiser* added its approval the next day. 'This agreement is creditable to both parties. The banns have been duly proclaimed, it now rests with the University Commissioners to declare the union complete. The union is intended to be permanent, dissoluble only by Act of Parliament'. Mr Cox, deeply aware of Miss Baxter's wishes, was agreeable to the terms ... 'This should reassure any that may have had misgivings that the terms of union contain nothing inconsistent with the broad and comprehensive basis upon which University College was constituted'.

The St Andrews students were not so compromising. *College Echoes* of January 8th had said of the proposed scheme 'While its accomplishment will mean nothing less than salvation to Dundee, the future alone can show whether its results to St Andrews are to be good or evil'. And later, after listing the advantages for Dundee in being raised to the level of a University, with all the degrees and privileges enjoyed by the national seats of learning, having its Professors obtain seats in the Senatus Academicus, and being entitled to share in the Annual Parliamentary Grant, the students again expressed their anger at Press attacks on their University—'more or less deliberate attempts to mis-represent our position in the eyes of the public: and none know that better than those who raised it'. Later still, at the end of March, when the affiliation was confirmed, the students were even more sharp in their magazine ...'The world-renowned University College is now a part of ourselves ... she hopes to become the sudden attraction to all aspiring youthful medicals and eager nondescripts ... (The *Advertiser* was in fact to comment that it appeared a thousand students could be accommodated in the Medical School) ... it is too painful a subject'.

Just before confirmation of the union, there were discussions about how medical teaching was to develop. In St Andrews on January 13th, a long Senate discussion was taken up with distribution or possible re-distribution of Chairs.

The opinion that 'St Andrews should continue with Theology, Arts, and Pure Science, while Dundee should seek its development in the direction of Medicine and Applied Science' was once again set down. But since it had been 'especially provided in the Universities Act that the new Medical School was to be a Conjoint one', the St Andrews Professors suggested that the first summer's session at least in the Medical Curriculum, including Botany, Natural History, and optionally Chemistry, should be at St Andrews. They suggested also that the University Chairs in these subjects should be located there, and that the First Professional Examination in the Medical Curriculum should be held at St Andrews. And to make money available to create further Medical Chairs in Dundee, the Senate also considered that some of the Chairs in Dundee which were duplicates of Chairs that had long existed at St Andrews might, as opportunity allowed, be dispensed with, and their endowments then be used for this purpose. Professors Pettigrew and McIntosh did not, as might have been expected, press for the *two anni medici* they had previously sought. They asked for no more than one *annus medicus*—not a term only—and that Physiology be added. As would be expected, they wanted First Professional Examinations to continue. All they said about Anatomy and Materia Medica now was to express the hope that 'some provision' for these subjects might some time be made.

At University College, the Medical Committee, as it was called, met for a similar discussion on February 27th. Dr. Sinclair was in the chair as Convener, and Professors Reid, Paterson, Frankland, and Thompson were joined by Mr Don and by Dr. McEwan, the surgeon. Principal Peterson was also present. Dr. Sinclair was an excellent chairman and guided the discussion well. It was stated that the Medical School could be 'completed for an annual sum of from £1,800 to £2,000, and it was agreed to set out a Preliminary Report of what was necessary to accomplish this.

The Report was drawn up within a week. It was discussed on Monday, March 3rd, by the same Committee, except Mr James Cunningham was present instead of Mr Don. The present equipment was detailed first. Five chairs were already endowed and equipped. The best of these was Chemistry, whose endowment was worth £420 *per annum*, and whose laboratory was in an excellent separate building—this was the £15,000 of Miss Baxter's put to use as she had ordered after her initial gifts. It had a lecture theatre, and laboratories as well as a museum of chemical specimens. As well as the Professor, there were two demonstrators and a lecture assistant. Biology came next, with a lecture room, library, workshop and stores. Laboratories were well equipped and there was 'a considerable nucleus of a museum but no accommodation for its protection or display'. Botany was confined to the summer months as Professor Geddes was absent for much of the rest of the year. The Anatomy buildings were temporary, consisting of a small dissecting room, private laboratory, lecture room, offices, etc. Some students from Edinburgh had made use of the facilities in the vacations, and a course of 100 lectures, practical and tutorial classes, and demonstrations, was offered. The 'nucleus of a museum' had been formed, by the purchase of anatomical models and by donation of normal and

G. R. Tristram

J. D. E. Knox

K. G. Lowe

J. W. Smith

J. Lamb

O. M. Wrong

D. Brynmor Thomas

W. Russell

A. Seraffini-Fracassini

pathological specimens from the Infirmary. Physiology, lastly, had a laboratory, and a course of 100 lectures was being offered. Courses in all these subjects were already recognised by the Universities of Edinburgh and Glasgow as qualifying for the first two years of medical study. It was an impressive basis for a pre-clinical school.

Clinical works and instruction had begun formally by an offer of operative surgery lectures and demonstrations, and would be available, when required in due course, in the wards of the Royal Infirmary. The clinical Chairs in Medicine, Surgery, Materia Medica and Therapeutics, and Midwifery and Gynaecology would be occupied by those in active practice, and so an honorarium of £100 *per annum* would be all that was required, for each occupant, from University Funds. It was thought, however, that the Professor of Pathology should be a full-time Professor, and so this Chair would require a sufficient endowment to put it on the same footing as those of Anatomy and Physiology. Lectureships were needed in Medical Jurisprudence and Hygiene, Mental Disease, and Ophthalmology; an endowment of £50 would be needed for Medical Jurisprudence and Hygiene, and £25 *per annum* for each of the others. Later, lectureships might be needed in Diseases of Children, Laryngology, Dermatology, and others, but not immediately. Two demonstrators would be required, in Anatomy and Physiology, each at an annual salary of £120. An annual grant of at least £450 would be needed to set up and maintain the teaching museums—including the wages of an attendant. Lastly, it was thought that £200 *per annum* would be needed to set up and maintain a medical library.

Arrangements for graduation in Medicine should observe the same regulations as in the other Scottish Universities. But it was proposed that students be allowed to take their Professional Examinations, except the Final, at the end of the various courses of study, provided that at least two subjects were taken together. It should be compulsory for students to take the classes for the first Professional Examination before starting their medical studies proper (experience in the other Scottish Medical Schools had shown the inadvisability of students doing clinical work—as Professor Gairdner had suggested—from the very start of their course. In Glasgow some years earlier, some clinical disasters had occurred when two junior students had interfered with patient management.[2]) Physics should form part of the First Professional. Operative Surgery and Opthalmogy should form part of the Final Examination, as this 'would enhance the value of the Surgical Degree (C.M.)'.

The full Medical Curriculum of St Andrews University would therefore be as set out overleaf.

This was good a curriculum as could be asked for. All that was required was students to fill the classes and provide the revenue to keep the Faculty going. University College had suffered student lack already and the lack of student numbers would continue to be a problem for many years to come. The difference was now that University College was a part of a University. Things augered well. The arguments over the number of Dundee representatives on the University Court were got over, but were a source of discord. However, when the University College Professors attended the Senate as full members on

166
MEDICAL CURRICULUM AND EXAMINATIONS
FIRST YEAR

WINTER—
Chemistry
Practical Chemistry
Physics
SUMMER—
Zoology) With Practical
Botany) Instruction

Examination on
Chemistry and Physics
at end of Winter

Examination on Zoology
and Botany at end of
Summer

FIRST
PROFESSIONAL
EXAMINATION

SECOND YEAR

WINTER—
Anatomy
Practical Anatomy
Physiology
Hospital
SUMMER—
Practical Anatomy
Practical Physiology
Hospital

THIRD YEAR

WINTER—
Anatomy (Demonstrations)
Practical Anatomy
Surgery
Pathology
Hospital
SUMMER—
Practical Pathology
Practical Materia Medica
Practical Surgery
Hospital

Examination on Anatomy
and Physiology at end of
Winter

SECOND
PROFESSIONAL
EXAMINATION

FOURTH YEAR

WINTER—
Materia Medica and
   Therapeutics
Medicine
Clinical Surgery
Hospital
SUMMER—
Mental Diseases
Medical Jurisprudence and Hygiene
Operative Surgery
Opthalmology
Hospital

Examination on Pathology
and Materia Medica at
end of Winter.

FIFTH YEAR

WINTER—

Medicine	Final examination at end
Midwifery and	of Winter.
Gynaecology	
Practical Midwifery	
and Vaccination	

Clinical Medicine
7th March, 1890.

April 2nd, it was Professor Pettigrew who seconded the nomination of Professor Ewing of Dundee by Principal Peterson to the Court in place of Principal Cunningham.

On April 12th, the Declaration of the Scottish University Commissioners affiliating the University College of Dundee to, and making it part of, the University of St Andrews in terms of Section 16, sub section 1, of the Universities (Scotland) Act, 1889, was received at the Senate. From now, any new Medical Chairs would be University and not College ones, and arrangements had to be made to provide them. But before this, something had to be done about medical teaching in the United College of the University. Also, the General Medical Council in the early summer of 1890 had made alterations in the length and arrangement of the Medical Curriculum which applied to the whole country. These were a) the extension of the curriculum to five years b) the first year to be devoted exclusively to science c) Physics was introduced as a Degree subject for the first M.B. Professional Examination. Again the Medical Committee considered what to advise the Senate and the Court, and their second report was made on July 2nd.

Physics was duly introduced into the first year of study. It was agreed that graduates in Arts and Science be exempted from the First Professional, if they had passed Science subjects of that examination as part of their first degree. A forward-looking suggestion, that the fifth year of study consist mainly of clinical work, with an alternative of six months 'pupilage with a Medical Practitioner', was made. The fourth year of the curriculum's winter term would be as before, but Mental Diseases would be omitted in the Spring, or Candlemas, term. In the fifth year, Medicine was omitted during the winter, Mental Diseases, Infectious Fevers, and diseases of Children added during the Candlemas term—with an attachment to a practitioner if authorised; the Final, Fourth Professional would then be at the end of the summer.

The first medical degrees should be M.B. Ch.B. instead of M.B. C.M. but operative surgery and ophthalmology should be retained 'to make the examination for the latter degree a serious one'. 'The Doctorate in Medicine should be granted either by thesis or examination. In the latter case the examination should be mainly clinical and conducted in two or more of the practical subjects of the Medical Curriculum. The Mastership in Surgery (C.M.) should be of equal rank with the Doctorate of Medicine and should be granted in the same way either by thesis or by examination'.

The views of this Committee on the abolition of St Andrews' power of

granting medical degrees without reference were sound, fair, and unexceptionable. There was no intrusion by the Third Party, no attempt to score points or belittle a supposed opposition. Thought was now being given by Dr. Sinclair's Committee to the enlarged University as a whole in the way Mr Thornton would have approved. The first point made was that the St Andrews M.D. was given under conditions which, compared with those elsewhere, appeared insufficient—neither thesis, residence, or clinical examination being required. The second was that, as the Universities' Act recommended the establishment of a complete Medical School in connection with the University of St Andrews with a full teaching curriculum, and facilities for regular students obtaining their qualification in Medicine and Surgery, the present degree-conferring power would not only detract from the value of the ordinary degrees, but would also tend to lower the character of the Conjoint Medical School, and put it at a disadvantage when compared to the other Scottish Universities. Its present form detracted from the value of the other degrees of St Andrews, and could give an erroneous impression of the inferiority of all Scottish degrees. The number and distribution of M.D. graduates of St Andrews was next analysed. While this analysis could be taken by a biased observer to ridicule and attack the University if selectively reported, there is absolutely no suggestion in the original paper that this was the Committee's intention. The fact that the bulk of graduates were from England, Ireland, or abroad, and so relatively far from Scotland, was reckoned to show that no important service was given to the profession in Scotland by its availability. Medical practitioners in England of the type seeking a higher qualification were now provided for by the University of Durham, or in a different way by the University of Manchester.

A further consideration supporting its abolition was the greatly increased number of students taking their first medical degrees at *Universities*—in Scotland, Cambridge and the Northern English Medical Schools, and most recently in the Teaching University Schemes for London. Fewer and fewer men were taking the licences of the Colleges alone, and as the bulk of candidates for the St Andrews M.D. were now such College licentiates, as time went by these numbers would reduce very considerably. Compensation in financial terms should certainly be given to the University were the degree abolished.

As far as the other details of teaching and examining arrangements were concered, the Medical Committee's proposals were once again sensible and non-compromising. No change was asked for the Chandos Chair—when the present incumbent's tenure of office came to an end, the Court could decide what was best. If it were to be abolished, the revenue should be used to benefit the Medical School. There should be no reduction in Science Chairs in United College—*duplication of the first year of medical study should be recognized*. Medical Faculty meetings should be held in Dundee, as should examinations. But the First Professional Examinations—of basic Sciences—should be held in both St Andrews and Dundee, as being more convenient for the students of the respective colleges.

In St Andrews, the affiliation of University College was received by the University Court at its meeting on April 18th. Those present on that date were

Principal Donaldson, Principal Peterson, and John Paterson, the Provost of St Andrews; Hugh Cleghorn M.D. LL.D., of Stravithie, John Campbell-Smith LL.D. Sheriff-Substitute at Dundee, and George Balfour from Edinburgh were General Council Assessors. The Senate Assessors were Rev. Lewis Campbell, LL.D., Professor of Greek, Professor J.A. Ewing, Professor of Engineering, and Professor James Bell Pettigrew. There were apologies from Principal Cunningham of St Mary's, Lord Elgin, the Chancellor's Assessor, Mr Munro Ferguson, M.P., the Rector's Assessor, and Viscount Cross, appointed by the General Council. At the same time meeting, a sealed Declaration by the Commissioners constituting the new University Court was delivered, and 'a new University Court' duly constituted.

The next month, on May 15th, Mr Thomas Thornton and Dr. Sinclair joined the Court, to serve as Dundee representatives. Agreement was quickly reached on the length of the session—to be three terms of from nine to eleven weeks, on the plans for the new Chemical Laboratory at United College, and on the formal letter about the proposed Teachers' Training College in Dundee. There was full agreement that the Chair of English at University College should be advertised—although there had been doubts about this at Council meetings, the Court encouraged University College to proceed. But on the 26th of July, there was some disagreement about the Medical Ordinances, although most of these were agreed. Principal Peterson asked for the course in Botany to be extended from 50 to 75 lectures, but this was lost. Professor Pettigrew forced a vote on retention of authority to maintain the M.D. and was apparently supported by Dr. Sinclair, as his motion had five votes from the seven members present. Principal Peterson had only Professor Ewing in his support. It was also decided, by two votes, to retain the authority of St Andrews to graduate anyone, not necessarily a local student, who had completed a five year medical curriculum. Arguments against these two motions made the same points the Dundee Medical Committee's Second Report had made, but both motions were carried after a vote.

Anyone whose interests and enquiries were limited to Dundee or St Andrews would have dismissed these motions as yet more evidence of the antagonism of Professor Pettigrew to any progress, or to his yet again trying to cling to outmoded things. There was however a background of wider extent at this particular time. The three Scottish Corporations—the Royal Colleges of Physicians and of Surgeons of Edinburgh, and the Royal Faculty of Physicians and Surgeons of Glasgow, were still licensing between them some two hundred practitioners each year, and these individuals did not require local residence to sit the qualifying examination—they could have studied anywhere. The English Corporations and the Irish Colleges had been in competition for such students, with the English Universities having authority to grant medical degrees without a residence requirement—Durham and London. While the London University degrees were till now post-graduate degrees and in effect 'Honours' degrees (the *Advertiser* had either been unaware of this distinctive feature or had ignored it), there were moves afoot by the English Colleges and the London Medical Schools to establish a University in London which should grant qualifying

degrees after examination less severe than those presently made at London University. Gresham College was thought to be about to be used for this purpose. Because the Scottish Corporations were afraid this new foundation would put the English Corporations at an advantage over them, they were currently asking not only that their Triple Qualification continue, but that the University of St Andrews should be available to grant medical degrees to the licentiates of theirs, and to them only. They asked therefore that the University of St Andrews be given power to grant qualifying degrees for young men *without residence*. This request re-opened the whole question of the usefulness of St Andrews for this sort of degree-giving purpose, just when it seemed to have come to a natural end with the proposed foundation of a Conjoint Medical School. A Paper on the whole subject was in fact presented at the Univerity Court in April of 1892, when these arguments were set out in print, and the assertion made that this special arrangement need not interfere with any new Medical Ordinance allowing the University to graduate its *resident* medical students.

But apart from this small disagreement, progress towards a Conjoint Medical School moved smoothly on. The University College accounts showed that the measures to keep running costs down were being successful, when they were reported to the Finance Committee in July. The Chair of Biology was renamed Natural History. Although Professor Meiklejohn had thought of applying for the vacant Chair of English he withdrew, and William McCormick, later to become an especially distinguished Professor, was appointed from Glasgow. In September Professor Paterson asked for and got a Demonstrator, because of the likelihood of his work increasing in the coming session. He also wanted someone to help prepare a museum. Dr. David M. Greig, a local surgeon, had volunteered for the Demonstrator post, and was appointed at an Honorarium of 25 guineas a year. And Mr David C. Thomson of the *Dundee Courier and Argus* sent a letter to the Council offering £50 to one or other of the Departments of Chemistry, Engineering, or Anatomy. It was decided to accept the offer, and give the money to the Anatomy Department.

Further proposals for the Medical School came from University College in October. Arguments against the old degrees were repeated, but the main part of the paper concerned the times students sit their Professional Examinations. The first year was equally suitable for students at University or United College— Chemistry and Physics at the end of the Martinmas (Winter) Term, and Zoology and Botany at the end of the Whitsun (Summer) Term—or all together then—at the end of the First Session. The Second Professional also suited United College—since it was already known informally that there was the hope of a Materia Medica lecturer being appointed there if the funds could become available: Physiology and Materia Medica at the end of the Second Session, and Anatomy and Pathology not till the end of the third Academic year.

At the end of 1890, in mid-December, the Senatus decreed that Deans were to be appointed in all Faculties. Although Professor Pettigrew 'reserved his legal rights, conferred by the terms of his appointment to the Chandos Chair of Medicine and Anatomy' it was resolved that each Dean would from now on be

appointed by his Faculty, subject to approval by the Senate. The term of Office was to be three years, and the details of the elections were fixed. Professor Pettigrew moved that the Senatus appoint Deans, but had not support either from the United College Professors, or from the University College Professors, now members of Senate.

In 1890 there were other events taking place besides the affiliation of University College. In St Andrews the local press, in complete contrast to Dundee, hardly mentioned the events leading to the union—they were more concerned with Mr Parnell and Mr Gladstone, and with issues elsewhere in the world. But golf was more and more of a news item, and this year, on Friday, September 19th, was published the first issue of 'Golf—a Weekly Record of "The Royal and Ancient" Game'. This weekly magazine was to become in due course 'Golf Illustrated'. The first issue gave details of the Autumn Meeting of the Royal and Ancient, when the Silver Club, the Royal or King William IV Medal, the Royal Adelaide Medal, and the Gold Medal of the Club were to be competed for as they are today. The Annual Ball was to take place two days later, showing that twentieth century beliefs that women had never taken part in Club activities were wrong. The interest in the sixteen page magazine was the evident ascendancy of St Andrews in the Golf World, even at this date—the spread of the game from Scotland, the advice on how to play the Old Course, the accounts of the one-hundred-pounds-a-side matches between the professionals, even the advertisement for Rusack's Marine Hotel on the links, were all described from the viewpoint of the centre of the whole game. Reports of students' activities—sporting, political, and of the volunteers—have a modern ring. The red gown was seen in increasing numbers in St Andrews, and the *Advertiser* had suggested it would soon be seen in Dundee. The coldness and wetness of Leuchars junction was already well known. In University College, student corporate life was beginning to develop also. Professor Paterson was an ardent supporter of the gymnastic club in University College as Professor McIntosh was of the gymnastic club in United and St Mary's. And the first steps were being taken to admit women undergraduates, in old St Andrews as well as in modern Dundee.

1891 saw the beginning of the sequence of events which were to worsen relations between the old University and the new College. At the start of the Candlemas term, there was dissent from the University College Professors in the Senate about the provision of teaching in Modern European languages. In October, Professor Scott Lang began his campaign against double chairs in Dundee as well as St Andrews, a campaign he was to continue for many years and with increasing bitterness. This was the month when Principal Peterson protested against the late appearance of a resolution from the University Court at a Senate Meeting, which had been brought to the notice three days previously of a small minority only. His protest was entirely justified, for this was an attempt to push through business without the knowledge of other University colleagues. But Principal Peterson himself was guilty of acting behind the backs of colleagues also. He had arranged for University College to apply to the University of London for recognition of graduation in Medicine and Surgery

for his few medical students, none of whom had matriculated at the University of St Andrews as they were supposed to do. This action was reported to the Court, of which he was now a member, on the 14th of November—it had only become known through a newspaper report—and although his 'explanation of the informality' was minuted as being 'satisfactory', the Court resolved that all students of University College attending classes qualifying for graduation were henceforth to matriculate at St Andrews University.

Although Principal Peterson had not acted as straightforwardly as might have been wished, there was a real difficulty about the placing of medical students. The United College had been ridiculed for having to send its few students elsewhere for clinical teaching. But University College did not possess a clinical school either at this time—although there was an active Infirmary with a large source of clinical material, there were no clinical departments in the Dundee side of the Conjoint School. Nor would there be for several years to come. So University College had the same problem as the United College now—its pre-clinical students were, once they were matriculated, students of a University, but they had no outlet after they had passed their First and Second Professional Examinations. In fact, lacking a Pathology teaching department they were perhaps barely able to complete the Second M.B. Their only advantage over their few counterparts in the United College, in fact, was their Professor of Anatomy, with access to material for fresh dissection. As had happened a year or two before, the Third Party had created the belief that there was a near-complete Medical School available, when there was certainly not. And Principal Peterson had certainly not corrected this public belief either.

It was not until May 1892 that a formal request was received by the Court for University College to be given the means of setting up a third year in Medicine in order to retain these same medical students locally. The requests were similar to those made by Professor Pettigrew when he still retained some hope that co-operation would come along—£100 for a lecturer in Materia Medica and the same for a lecturer in Surgery. Perhaps there was the suggestion of co-operation, too, in the request for extra help in teaching Physiology from the University College. For their request continued 'It is for the (University) Commissioners to determine whether there is to be one Chair of Physiology with one assistant, and where the Chair is to be or whether the two Chairs are still to continue, each with an assistant'. Just before this, prospects of quiet movement forward seemed possible after a good compromise motion on double Chairs by Professors Lang and Steggall together at Senate that February.

The quarrel about provision of new chairs arose partly also because of lack of finance. St Andrews had known poverty for so long that a certain anxiety was not unexpected. In Dundee, the continuing realisation that a large initial endowment did not ensure large revenue was also producing fears for the financial future. Principal Donaldson had written to Mr Hay, one of the executors of the Berry Bequest in July saying openly how crippled St Andrews had always been for lack of funds, and asking that salaries could be increased as a first priority. St Andrews had received £10,000 from the Bequest already, but was now asking for more.

On 21st July, a letter was received by the University Court from the Scottish Universities Commission. As this letter set in motion the unfortunate events of the next three years it requires to be looked at with some care. At this time, both United College and University College wanted cash to endow new Chairs. The United College argued that money should go to new Medical Chairs, and Applied Science teaching in University College. Some of the University College staff were pressing for extra Arts teaching there. And Professors Pettigrew and McIntosh were continuing to press for additional Medical Chairs located in United College, as they were desperately anxious not to lose Medical teaching in what they still saw as the University proper. All of these three outlooks had enough to commend them. There was the additional factor of the imbalance between the salaries at the United College and those at University College; hence Principal Donaldson's request to Australia. As usual, he seemed to see the priorities more clearly than most. For the St Andrews salaries to be raised would take away some of the resentment which Professors Pettigrew and McIntosh certainly, and Professor Lang probably felt. Finally, the St Mary's College professors were in a separate category—their chairs were funded in such a way as to remove them from the immediate argument.

The letter from the Commissioners noted the disputes about double chairs. They pointed out, immediately, that they had not enough information about the revenues of University College (because its Council was independent) and the fees drawn by its professors, to know whether it was practical to set up a fee system for University College similar to the fee fund they were proposing to set up for the United College. They were unsure whether to have a separate fee fund for University College or to have a common fund with the United College.

Their academic proposals were quite decided. Besides Arts, the United College was to provide one *annus medicus* located at St Andrews. There must be a Chair of Botany, or the present short-service lecturer continue. There was no money available at present to provide other Medical Chairs. In Dundee, the main object was the completion of the Conjoint Medical School. Therefore they proposed to provide Chairs of Medicine, Surgery, Pathology, Materia Medica and Therapeutics, and Midwifery and Gynaecology. They did not propose to abolish any Chair in either College, except with its consent, but suggested that United College give up Physiology to have a Chair of English, and University College surrender English, to complete the Clinical Medical School.

> They are further of the opinion that it is indispensable for the efficient and harmonious conduct of the University affairs that the union of the various Colleges should, if possible, be more perfect than under present arrangements. They therefore recommend that the Agreement for affiliation should be modified (1) by giving the University Court a more direct control of the finances of University College, Dundee (2) by giving the University Court the patronage of the existing Chairs at University College, Dundee and also all future Chairs for which the founders have not stipulated that it shall be in other hands.[3]
>
> Sgd. Robert Fitzroy Bell
> Secretary, Commissioners

Mr Thornton, one of the Dundee representatives, moved acceptance of the proposals. He was seconded by Professor Knight. This letter put into official words what Principal Donaldson—and others also—had already said: the original agreement needed improvement if it was really going to succeed, and that a few sensible changes were all that was immediately required.

Throughout 1891 and 1892, Principal Peterson was reporting monthly to his Council his efforts to have the Government Grant increased from £500. In May 1891 he had interviews with the Secretary for Scotland and the Secretary of the Scottish Education Department. In June he produced a letter for the Lord President of the Council he had written. It was approved by the Dundee Council and then went out on Mr G.W. Baxter the Chairman's signature. He wrote again in September, and so on—all to no avail. He had more success with a circular he prepared in June, and had published locally—this resulted in a succession of subscriptions, from £5 to £100 being sent in, but by local men only.

Quiet progress continued. In July the College Council agreed to ask the Visiting Physicians and Visiting Surgeons of Dundee Royal Infirmary to give clinical lectures there. They had first to obtain the agreement of the Infirmary Directors. The Medical Committee on Teaching—consisting of Principal Peterson and Dr. Sinclair alone—met on July 27th and recommended that Dr. McEwan—already engaged to teach operative surgery—when students became available—should give a course of Systematic Surgery, and that Dr. Rorie of the Royal Asylum give lectures on Mental Disease. At the full Council Meeting in August these were confirmed; Dr. McEwan was to give the lectures and receive an Honorarium of £50, but only 'in the event of a class being formed'. Besides Dr. McEwan, Dr. Steele Moon was appointed a clinical teacher in Surgery, and Drs. J.B. Macleod and A.M. Stalker appointed clinical teachers in Medicine. The Directors of the Infirmary and of Westgreen Asylum duly confirmed the appointments in September, when the Chairman of the D.R.I. Directors was suggested as an *ex-officio* member of the College Council. In the December, Professor Paterson sought and obtained a Demonstrator in Anatomy. Dr. E. Tenison Collins, from Cambridge, was appointed for a year at a salary of £120.

In 1892 a move was instituted in Dundee to set up a complete course in Agriculture—two of the necessary four years were already available, and it was said that the further two would follow without difficulty when a lecturer was appointed and suitable farmland bought. Expectations were raised in other spheres than Medicine. There were useful costings of the essential outlays for the Medical School—at times in the various minutes having the word 'Conjoint' added, clearly as an addition—and a round sum of £2,500 was reached initially. Professor Paterson asked repeatedly for money to extend his rooms, and this came along from March onwards. The University Court asked the Council on February 10th to communicate their estimates directly to the University Commissioners. But later estimates raised the expected sum very considerably indeed—to £8,160.

A point of interest in this year was the resignation of Dr. Steele Moon as

clinical lecturer in Surgery, not because he was moving elsewhere, but because his contract as Visiting Surgeon at the Infirmary had expired, and the Directors would not renew it. Thus was established a precedent which would have repercussions forty-eight years later. Records showed, too, that the College and the Directors had sufficiently serious differences of view that special meetings were held to resolve them.[4]

Towards the end of 1892, two events of note occurred. In mid-October, Charles Henry Gatty gave £2,000 to set up a Marine Laboratory in connection with, and to be the property of, St Andrews University. Professor McIntosh's St Andrews work on fisheries had now been going on for ten years, and he had achieved an international reputation in this field. Although this new laboratory would not realise the hopes he had for his fishery research, at this time its endowment was a high point in his own life, and in the development of Science in the whole University. The other event was the unanimous election by the student body, on November 24th, of the Most Honourable the Marquess of Bute, K.T. as Rector. His assessor, nominated to Court on December 3rd was Rev. Dr. William Metcalf.

Lord Bute's predecessor, Lord Dufferin, had shown no interest in his duties towards the University in general or to the Court in particular. But Lord Bute had been a member of the Scottish University Commission of 1889 and so was fully aware of the problems besetting St Andrews. From his first appointment he took an active part in University affairs—his opponents said too active a part—and worked hard for what he saw as the best way forward for his espoused University.

The problem remained one of allocation of funds, and of the conflict between what Principal Peterson saw as his legitimate aims, and a minority of his colleagues on Senate and later Court saw as a progressive take-over of their University by this new College. Professors Pettigrew and McIntosh had the additional quarrel with not only the University College Professors, but also with the Arts and Divinity Professors in the United College and St Mary's, over their determination to maintain a medical presence. From their point of view, failure to press their objective would mean certain disappearance of medical teaching in St Andrews. They knew of the struggles of the past century to retain this presence, and they represented both the strength and the weakness of the old University. Their strength lay in their often undeclared faith in their University's past record in keeping medicine against all odds: their weakness lay in their progressive narrowing of attitude and refusal to look for compromise. It has already been seen that Professor Pettigrew at least had not always been like this, but had become soured by events. Professor McIntosh had always a tendency to quarrel and take offence—his earlier exchanges with Professor D'Arcy Thompson over Professor Thompson's article in *The Scotsman* of 1st January 1886 permanently spoiled what should have been a successful and rewarding relationship. Their personal animosity was just one of several which would do serious harm to quiet progress in the Faculty of Medicine over the ensuing years.

As far as the development of the Faculty of Medicine was concerned, the

events of the next few years were less concerned with the Common Fund than with who should support the new Medical Chairs financially and whether the United College would gain a viable pre-clinical school. And as far as the University of St Andrews was concerned, the contribution of Lord Bute towards the setting up of a viable pre-clinical school was probably of more long-term significance than the unhappy way he went about trying to sever the attachment of University College, Dundee.

On 21st January, 1893, the Court met for the first time with Lord Bute in the Chair. A further draft from the University Commissioners was read concerning the principle of payment of professional salaries. Principals Donaldson and Peterson successfully overcame an attempt to reject the new draft. This draft or Schedule 'B' was however modified in February, and the Schedule could then have provided a reasonable basis for agreement. The Schedule proposed that the Funds and Estates of the Dundee College should henceforth be under the control of the University Court, which was now to control them in the way the College Council was presently authorised to do under the terms of the existing Agreement. But the Titles to the Dundee Funds and Estates were always to remain in the names of the Trustees of University College. There were to be Financial Committees for both St Andrews and Dundee—the Dundee Council managing and administrating their funds as the Dundee Finance Committee of the University Court. The representatives of the Dundee Council on the Court were now to be entitled to sit and vote in all matters, and the provision limiting their right to vote, as it existed under Article 4 of the original agreement, was to be cancelled. On a Dundee Chair becoming vacant, the Court would appoint his successor, and the Court would appoint to all *new* Chairs to be founded. But the Dundee Council would continue to elect its Principal. The present floating debt of £4,800 of the Dundee College was to be paid off by gifts and bequests in five years.

There was a real fear that the amended Act would transfer the liabilities of University College to the 'Funds and Estates' of the University, and since the Dundee side looked as if it was set on endowing further Chairs without any corresponding certainty of students appearing in sufficient numbers to produce a revenue return, Principal Peterson's motion, in Senate, that finance should be available 'for the adequate equipment of the Chairs of the Conjoint University School of Medicine in Dundee—viz. Chairs of Anatomy, Physiology, Pathology, Materia Medica, Medicine, Surgery, and Midwifery, so far as not already provided for by the endowments attached to these Chairs, including the remuneration of assistants, etc.' was altered, on Professor Scott Lang's amendment by inserting the words 'and by the funds of the Dundee College' after the word 'Chairs'. But the St Andrews Professors, including Professor Lang, agreed that the Chandos Chair should, if not retained after the present incumbent was no longer in post, go to provide a new Chair in Medicine or Science, or its money be used to increase the endowment of such another Chair: at this time they were anticipating its disappearance.

In February, a special meeting of the General Council was held. The General Council, the Senate, and the Council of University College, had all previously

agreed with the amended Schedule, and had asked for the Secretary for Scotland to introduce a Bill into Parliament at the earliest opportunity. But there was by now a hardening of attitude by St Andrews elements against Dundee. This was perhaps the second tragedy in the early relations between the two sides. There was reasonable cause to find the present arrangement of affiliation unsatisfactory. This had been Principal Donaldson's view all along. But if the proposed modified arrangements had been allowed quietly to move along, and become law, the upset of the next few years would have been avoided. The Bute Medical Buildings would certainly still have been built, the pre-clinical school in the United College still developed, and Lord Bute would not have been cast in the role of monster in the way he was—even his photograph and personal letters might have been chosen differently.[5] The Third Party would have had less excuse for a further series of outbursts, to indoctrinate a new generation of Dundonians who did not read other newspapers, against St Andrews. And many unhappy consequences might never have occurred.

Over 1893, a series of events raised the level of discord. The summons by the Church of Scotland Ministers' Widows' Fund against University College, Dundee *and* the University Court, asking the Court of Session to declare that the Principal and Professors of University College were not entitled to become contributors was probably not so important, had it not been that it was used by Professor Scott Lang, Professor of Mathematics at United College, to question the status of University College Professors to attend the Senate and to vote. He continued this tiresome and spiteful tactic over a period of years, and so did the United College Medical Professors. Although Professor Lang was voted down heavily by 10-4 in the Senate that March when he moved the University College Professors incompetent to vote, he continued undeterred.

From March 1893 onwards developed the split between the Senate and the Court over policy. In Senate, it was agreed that first B.Sc. Degree Examinations, and Preliminary Examinations in Arts, could be taken in Dundee as well as St Andrews; in April the usual ten M.D. candidates passed, and in April it was also carried by a clear majority that St Andrews recognise the lectures on Medicine given by staff of the Edinburgh Medical School for Women, with a view to having their students admitted to examination for graduation at St Andrews University. It was a little inconsistent of University College professors to support a move such as this and yet protest against the Ordinance retaining the right of St Andrews University to examine and graduate those who had studied their Medical Curriculum elsewhere. But at the Court that March it was agreed not to adopt the Commissioners' Report (on the Schedule) by a single vote. And when Mr Thomas Thornton, and Dr. Sinclair, both the most reasonable of men, moved that the Bill be approved *simpliciter*, the Marquess of Bute declared their motion incompetent. At the General Council Meeting in late February, an *incorporating* union of University College was asked for, and that the Professors of University College be made subject to *all* the provisions of the 1889 Act. But the way the meeting was organised raised real anger in the Dundee representatives, and in some St Andrews ones, just as the packed Dundee Governors' meeting would do to Principal Wimberley fifty years in the future.

The action was continued at the Court on April 8th, when the split was widened further. The University Commissioners had reminded the Court that a common fee fund would have to be agreed by the College Council (which it was refusing to do), as would proposals for the future founding of chairs. It is worth recording, however, that at this particular meeting, when Provost Paterson of St Andrews moved that since the Council and University College Dundee were insisting on remaining independent from the University, and since the original agreement had led to discord and hostility, steps should be taken to dissolve it, Dr. Cleghorn, a St Andrews M.D., supported strongly the amendment against. The amendment was carried by 6 votes to 5, and so the motion was lost. At this meeting a letter from the St Andrews professors was read—the first of several—urging that the Bill and Schedule go forward, as a 'sense of unsettlement' was affecting the University badly.

As in every dispute of this sort, exchanges became more and more angry. The Dundee Council was alarmed as well as angry. Its small student numbers were looking likely to become even smaller. The Duke of Argyll, the Chancellor, almost certainly directed by the Rector, wrote directly in October to say that in his view the University had been led to an agreement which was unworkable, and should be re-negotiated. Various letters suggesting that the original agreement's validity be now called in question were sent to the Court. The Rector in October refused to accept Professor Purdie's vote as assessor, because the Dundee professors had voted for him.

Alarm grew stronger in Dundee. It was now the turn of the young College to feel insecure—its very existence threatened. But the United College were also concerned, though now for different reasons. Its members knew that they had enough financial backing to survive, but, having no medical axe to grind, they saw the value of University College. So they and the St Mary's Professors wrote again to the Court in November asking it to approve Schedule 'B', and on December 1st a similar letter was sent by the University College Professors— not from the Principal. Professor Thompson had contracted out of political argument earlier—his original support for Peterson had waned somewhat. The letter came from the quieter stream of the background movement which had not ceased in Dundee or St Andrews. 'We believe that Schedule 'B' places the Dundee College under all the Sub-Sections of Sec. XIV, of the Universities' Act, and thereby puts it upon the same basis as the other Colleges of the University, the union between University College, Dundee and the University would work smoothly if a definite financial arrangement were made'. The settlement should take place speedily—this was important for the welfare of the University. The letter was signed by Professor Paterson and Professor Waymouth Reid, supported by the recently appointed Professor Fiddler.

1893 at least saw further quiet background progress as far as Medicine was concerned. Professors Pettigrew and McIntosh, by now a source of irritation to their colleagues for their progressively more antagonistic attitude, received a boost for their medical policy by a letter from Australia, at the end of the year, from the executors of the Berry Bequest. This letter said that the University of St Andrews was indebted for the Berry legacy to the fact that the Chandos Chair

of Medicine existed within the University. Because he had begun his medical study at St Andrews, Mr Alexander Berry had gone on to 'acquire his profession', as the letter put it.

> It was this fact that caused his love for the Institution and his determination to do what was possible towards cancelling the obligation under which it has placed him. And it was solely with the view of carrying out his late brother's wishes that Mr David Berry made the bequest ... in evidence of the leaning of Mr David Berry towards the furtherance of the interests of Medicine we may point out that by his will he devoted towards the founding and endowment of an Hospital on his own estate of Coolangatta a sum equal to the amount left to the University. We cannot help feeling that so far from the Chandos Chair being abolished it would, under the circumstances of the case, be much more appropriate to establish additional Chairs in furtherance of the Science of Medicine ... the rank and emoluments, instead of being reduced, shall be quite raised to the standard of those determined upon in the case of any other of the professors. The gift to the University was made by Mr David Berry at a time when he had no knowledge of the contemplated affiliation with any other University, and we are satisfied that if either he or Mr Alexander Berry had had such knowledge, such gift would not have been made, or, at all events, conditions would have been imposed with the view of preventing the proposed removal of the Chandos Chair.

The executors of this huge award, Sir John Hay and Mr James Norton, had just as much right as Miss Baxter to impose conditions—and this letter was a powerful support to Professors Pettigrew and McIntosh—especially since only a tenth of the bequest had been paid, and the rest was not by any means guaranteed! Another event which helped in a different way towards the establishment of the pre-clinical school in United College was the Sir William Taylor Thomson bequest for medical bursaries at St Andrews. This had been made public earlier, in the summer of 1892, but further details were now known. The bursaries were to be for both sexes in equal numbers, and were especially provided to allow women to follow 'a proper *medical* curriculum in St Andrews with a view to becoming medical practitioners'. The existence of these bursaries, and the warning from Australia, encouraged Sheriff Campbell Smith to propose that the Chandos Chair be preserved after all; he won his motion on the casting vote of the Rector after Principal Donaldson had tried to block him.

At the end of 1893 the Special Committee on Finance reported. It consisted of a majority of St Andrews members of the Court, and its recommendations do not support the belief that St Andrews was trying to do down Dundee over allocation of Government Grants. Of a total grant of something over seven thousand pounds, the Finance Committee allocated three thousand to Dundee to pay the salaries of the new Medical Chairs which were necessary to complete the clinical, senior, Medical School. The money was specifically allocated. Any over was to be used for equipment for the Clinical Chairs (being Clinical, the salary was in effect nominal to whoever would be appointed to the part-time

Chair—his principal income coming from his professional fees), and to sustain Medical Teaching in Dundee. Had the St Andrews side wished to stifle medical teaching in Dundee, their majority on this committee would have allowed them to do so. And the Court adopted the Report as policy—although against the vote of Rev. Dr. Anderson and Dr. Metcalf. The same day, the 9th of December, Principal Peterson reported this hopeful result, and the Council agreed to give their representatives power to vote for Schedule 'B' on the basis of the acceptance of the fixed sum of three thousand pounds for Medical Education in Dundee. This time, the St Andrews side had specified *in Dundee* also.

The Dundee Council were having good cause to be genuinely upset at the way things were going. It was the University Court which had caused the troubles. There could be no doubt of that. The previous year, the Council had almost pleaded at their April 1892 meeting that they had a claim 'to form part of St Andrews rather than be "merely affiliated" '. Their minute of 21st April 1892 had stressed the useful discussions, the proposal by the Dundee authorities that the whole annual revenue of the College should be handed over to the Court, but that this had been objected to by the St Andrews representatives, who had proposed that the Dundee College should manage its own finances, and should undertake at the same time to transmit to the Court a copy of its annual accounts. The Council had agreed that the appointments to Chairs remain from now on in the hands of the College but become subject to Court approval. They had accepted the express stipulation that they would have no jurisidiction or power over University teaching given in University College, or over courses for graduation or class fees. On much less sure ground was the anomaly of representation on the Court by Council representatives but not *vice versa*; again they pleaded that if sufficient importance was attached to membership of the Dundee Council, its Constitution was so elastic that the necessary changes could be made without any appeals to parliament or University Commissioners. (All in all, their line was much softer than their Principal's). They had had what they thought was a final meeting with six members of the Court—when a dozen of their own members were present—on January 27th of this year when they had added their future agreement to alteration and re-designation of Chairs in both Arts and Science subjects—had had provision for lectures in University College in Logic, English, French, and German—all at Dundee in their own Council room, and all apparently sincerely agreed. They had even minuted that suggestions for Medical School Accommodation, with estimates, had been sent to the *Medical Faculty* of the University of St Andrews—though they did not say so, their recognition of this was an enormous good-will concession. And when all the above, constituting what they thought was the agreed Schedule 'B' had been modified by the Court, they had even agreed, though resolving to stick to the original 'to defer to the pleasure of the Commissioners' should they agree to those modifications.

But their loyalty was stretched too far by the demand for full incorporation made by the General Council. The ensuing months had caused them to retract several agreed points in Schedue 'B' and reading both accounts makes it clear how it could all have been avoided, had the Rector and chairman of the

University Court not been so obviously partisan. On the other hand, Lord Bute's support in Court was not in fact as great as might be supposed, and he had no support from the majority of the Senate. He has been built into a giant monster which perhaps he never really was. For it did seem to come as something of a surprise when in April of 1895, the House of Lords upheld the action Rev. Dr. Metcalf had previously lost in the Court of Session. This judgement said in effect that the Commissioners had had no power to affiliate the new College with the old University. While this meant that students now matriculated at University College were not in fact truly matriculated after all, since their college had no University status, it also meant that St Andrews University at once lost the large Parliamentary Grant it was anticipating with the object of setting up the Conjoint School of Medicine it had hoped for for so many centuries. So both sides were harmed. But the final judgement by the House of Lords, came, in terms of lawyers' time-scales, very quickly indeed. In July of the next year, the action by Rev. Dr. Metcalf against the University Court, the Senatus, and the University College Professors and Dundee Council members—all with their names included, was finally quashed. So the danger of disaster to Dundee was over.

As far as the teaching of Medicine in the University of St Andrews was concerned, the mass of who-said-what-and-when in this dispute is not of as much interest as the question of involvement of St Andrews medical graduates in background antagonism to developments in Dundee, the inclusion of medical ambitions in the legal arguments made, and the subsequent medical developments in the United College. The first two of these seem important in assessing whether there was any real strategy of stifling medical development in Dundee.

While holders of the St Andrews M.D. may have written letters of support for its continuance in its old form, and certainly did write letters asking that the University be given authority to graduate licentiates of the Colleges who had not studied locally, there was no good evidence that the 1893 General Council Meetings were packed by such medical graduates. Newspaper reports from elsewhere than Dundee list the supporters in the sort of detail added to give interest to what was a good issue for the press to report, and do not refer to graduates from the south, where most of them were, gathering in large numbers. No St Andrews M.D. was a main speaker—the majority were in fact Parish Ministers.

As far as the arguments about medical ambitions are concerned, these continued to follow the lines laid down by the Dundee press, the Third Party, since the later 1880's. In the campaign it ran against medical teaching being continued at all in St Andrews, it repeatedly attacked the University for abstaining 'from acknowledging Dundee as its only possible Medical School' from the time of Principal Donaldson's appointment as Principal onwards. St Andrews was attacked for being poor, and when it began to ask for money, was attacked that it was not asking the money for Dundee. Courteous replies by other than Professors Pettigrew and McIntosh pointed out that the University's aim *was* to identify St Andrews with Dundee for the realisation of a complete Medical School. So the earlier attempts to gain a sharing of facilities continued

to be overshadowed by demands that all teaching in Medicine must be in Dundee. This 'medical' campaign can be followed in the Dundee press from 1886 onwards. Leaders were scathing in their condemnation.

> In Scotland no medical student dreams of going to St Andrews for his professional education. He would as soon think of going to Iceland to study snakes ... some of its (St Andrews') pleas for a grant of public money will cause a hard-headed Chancellor of the Exchequer to smile. All that St Andrews wants it may have if it will cease to think so much of vested interests and heartily co-operate with University College Dundee.

This was in December, 1886.

Attacks continued sporadically over the next seven years. Not only was the St Andrews University Medical degree attacked, but the Arts degree came in for severe criticism also. The main themes were the inadequacy and unworthiness of St Andrews, contrasted with the large size and evident superiority of Dundee.

On January 7th, 1889, a long article developed the theme:
'It is a fact that St Andrews is desperately short of money—what is the cause of this state of Affairs?' This letter was in reply to an anonymous one, almost certainly by Professor McIntosh, which had appeared earlier, asking for support for the development of Science and Medicine in St Andrews.

> Professor Carnelly is quite an ideal worker but he did not gain his knowledge at a sea-side village, but in busy centres of industry like Manchester, Sheffield and Dundee. Anyone acquainted with the facts knows that the University of St Andrews deserves the castigation it received the other year in Reports to the General Medical Council ... The marine station for Zoology at St Andrews, the Botanic Garden, the practical teaching of physiology, chemistry, and practical physics—sound magnificently but are little more than sound ...
>
> In view of the languid, sluggish intellectual life at St Andrews, the lack of energy on the part of the professors, and the want of love on the part of the youthful Scots for this out-of-the-world University, what ought Parliament to do? Far better would it be to move the whole establishment to Dundee where the larger civic life, the larger population, the more ardent students ... I hope to see a Radical University Commission appointed which will make short work of the pretentions of University institutions more remarkable for lofty aims than for work

wrote COMMON SENSE, expressing exactly the newspaper's own sentiments.

The Third Party regularly gave the impression that there was a nearly complete Medical School in existence when there was not. As early as 1891, eight years before the Medical School really took off, the *Advertiser* made use of the announcement that Professors Stalker and McEwan were to begin clinical teaching to declare, on August 28th:

> The hospital and the mortuary are the foundations on which the

whole superstructure of Medical Education rears itself. Whenever these are found on an extensive scale, there should also be found a flourishing Medical School. In Edinburgh a hospital with 600 beds provides a training ground for 2000 medical students. In the Dundee Infirmary there are 250 beds. At the same rate as Edinburgh this should accommodate nearly 1000 medical students. But clinical teaching in Edinburgh is too scanty and thin-spread to be copied as a model. All the more reason why Dundee, within two hours of the overcrowded University, should relieve it of its overflow. Aberdeen Infirmary has fewer beds than the Dundee Infirmary. The wards of the Aberdeen University with some 350 medical students are not in a congested state. The total day students attending all classes (Arts, Sciences, and Medicine) in University College Dundee number only 163. And of these only a small proportion are medical students, though their quality would seem to be unimpeachable ... no lack of raw materials for the training of doctors in Dundee ... the machinery necessary to utilise it consists of professors, laboratories, class-rooms, and scientific apparatus. The acquisition of this is the simplest matter of supply and demand. The possessor of sixpence is master of mankind to that extent. The accumulated wealth of Dundee could command the best teachers and teaching appliances as readily as two coppers will purchase a pound of sugar. The excellence of the raw material is such that if there were machinery to match, there would be no fear of a dearth of students. Great sums have been given to Glasgow and Aberdeen. It is now the turn of Dundee.

The Leader writer now turned on St Andrews. 'The coveted degree (M.D.) is virtually vended yearly to a limited number of candidates in much the same way as the American Universities were once in the habit of scattering broadcast Doctorates of Divinity' ... he taunted the examiners and the Senatus for their use of this device to obtain money.

On August 31st, Principal Donaldson's angry reply was printed in full: 'I think you can scarcely have been conscious of the horrible accusation which you bring against honourable men' he said. He went on to defend the examination, and especially the external examiners. He listed them, and then said the *Advertiser* was implying that they gave this degree to obtain a sum of money, which he denied strongly. He also denied that implication that the Senatus looked only for financial gain. The clever editorial Leader as usual did not answer directly, but attacked him in general terms: 'Principal Donaldson plays an excellent hand at the game of bluff. His logic is as rational as that of the man who, when accused of ruining his constitution by too much brandy, urged in extenuation that it was prime Bordeaux'. It also drew a red herring, of the number of English students at *all* the Scottish Universities, over the arguments.

The other constant feature which recurred periodically over these years was the accusation that St Andrews was demanding to teach Medicine and *exclude* Dundee from its rightful position as a centre deserving a Medical School. But

the evidence of where the medical ambition lay points rather to a strategy in the reverse direction. It has already been seen how reasonable and co-operative proposals and arguments were upset by the policy of the Principal, whose efforts to have the word 'Conjoint' removed both by statement in the Council and in what he wrote in his own Sub-Committee minutes, continued in his written arguments against Lord Bute's Bill of 1895. While he was correct in criticising the 'certain dissentient parties who object to the interference threatened by the Commissioners with the anomalous system of graduation' at St Andrews, he was not correct in stating that there was a wish to continue teaching at Dundee exclusively for Science and Technical subjects—even Professors Pettigrew and McIntosh had never denied that Dundee was the place for clinical medical teaching. All they were fighting their own St Andrews colleagues and the Dundee Principal and his staff for was the retention of a pre-clinical element. His statement that the St Andrews side was trying to found a rival Medical School in the town of St Andrews 'to make St Andrews still more independent of Dundee and in spite of the fact that there is no proper Hospital or Infirmary or other appliances for clinical and practical teaching' was untrue and certainly misleading. The Law Lords ignored these statements completely in their published comments.

While Lord Bute has been firmly elevated to the status of a major figure of Evil in Dundee mythology, the contributions of Principal Peterson to the troubles of this period should not be forgotten. While his place as a brilliant scholar and determined pursuer of his College's early general development is assured, his strategy over the development of the Faculty of Medicine in the University is suspect both in design and execution. His concern for medicine to help the poor of Dundee is never recorded—unlike that of so many of his colleagues. Had he allowed progress to take place, shown the capacity to see another side as did Sir Thomas Thornton, and been more accommodating to Professor Pettigrew initially, the Bute interlude might never have occurred in the way it did. He left the University, almost abruptly, in 1895—his scrap book, left by him to his University College, did not even have its later cuttings trimmed and gummed in place but left in a single pile inside—and his successor would contribute infinitely more to the success of the development of medical teaching than he ever did. By contrast, the individual who did show generosity and a patient capacity for seeing things in the context of an enlarged University—while maintaining loyalty to his own Council, Sir Thomas Thornton, deserves a more honourable mention than he has so far had. Criticism of Principal Peterson did not occur in the writings of the Third Party, but was certainly made in other major Scottish newspapers, especially the *Glasgow Herald*. From the early 1890s its occasional observations on the Dundee-St Andrews controversy had pointed out with unpleasant sharpness facts which were carefully avoided more locally.

> There is no disguising the fact that a very considerable degree of friction has been occasioned by the steady bid for supremacy in University matters on the part of the very young and ambitious College at Dundee. In the United College, the Senate, the Faculties

and Committees, the Dundee College aspires to leadership. This is all the more remarkable as it is a College almost without students, its *bona fide* students last session numbering only 21 as against 226 attending the St Andrews Colleges. The Dundee College, rightly or wrongly, pursues a policy of keen competition with the Colleges at St Andrews. This is especially the case as regards Science and Medicine, and signs are not wanting of a similar competition in Arts. The competition in Medicine amounts to hostility, and the Dundee College has done everything in its power to appropriate the St Andrews Medical School. These tactics pertinaceously pursued are beginning to bear bitter fruit ...

This was in October 1891, well before the years of litigation. The *Herald* was equally sure whom to criticise. In 1895 it said of the University College Principal:

He it was who got the archaic authorities of the Fifeshire University to sign an agreement all in favour of Dundee, and it is he who year after year compiles the wonderful statistical tables showing the Dundee institution to be the most powerful, prosperous, and best-attended seat of learning in Europe ... A languid, eye-glassed savant of some forty years of age ... he is understood to hold the barbarians of Dundee in supreme contempt.

Sarcastic and over-drawn as this leader was, it nevertheless provides a view of Principal Peterson from elsewhere than St Andrews which agrees remarkably with his policies as they can be read in his many minutes and memoranda about the Medical School.

9

Real Progress Now 1895-1911

With the departure of Principal Peterson to McGill University, the atmosphere seemed to change. The Marquess of Bute remained as Rector, but after the House of Lords' decision, made no further serious effort to deny the association of University College with the University. Instead he made certain provisions which were of more permanent importance for the Faculty of Medicine than the law-suits he had inspired, and although it is easy to instance his dreams for St Andrews University as fanciful, his very real contributions to restorations of the ecclesiastical buildings in St Andrews, as well as to University buildings and staff endowments, were of permanent value. Indeed, the very fact that progress in academic development was so relatively little delayed during the few years of his legal dissent leads to the view that even this was not nearly as huge an upset as has been alleged.

The evidence for this is largely in the records of the Council of University College. From early in 1893, suggestions came from the Court that salaries of the already endowed Medical Chairs, and for those proposed, should be increased. The amounts were specified on February 13th but the salary of the Principal was not. At the Council meeting that day it was also agreed that it should 'however be in the power of the College to appoint a person as Principal who is not and has not been a Professor in the College'. In March, Dr. J. Mackie Whyte was invited to become a lecturer in Clinical Medicine on the death of Dr. J.M. Macleod. In the autumn, Mr Thornton protested at the overspending in the pre-clinical medical departments; Professors Reid and Frankland obtained vivisection licences to allow them to undertake animal experimentation. In December, the Council thanked Lord Bute for his recently endowed Scholarship at University College, which had just been awarded to a Lochee student, Mr Thomas Pettigrew Wylie. Difficulties between the Directors of the Royal Infirmary continued into the next year, and when Rev. Mr Hamilton complained to the Council that his daughter had been refused admission to instruction in Clinical Surgery by them, it admitted that the Council was powerless to help. Professor Frankland was re-appointed a Dundee assessor on the Court in March, supported by both Professor Pettigrew and Professor McIntosh, but resigned and left Dundee in June. He was replaced by Professor Walker. Professor Paterson resigned next, in June, to move to the Chair of Anatomy in Liverpool. Although of Scottish background—his father was a Presbyterian minister in Manchester—and having married while at Dundee—he had been looking for a move back to England. There were six applicants for his post: the

150

only one named was Dr. Mackay of Glasgow who was selected on 30th July, 1894.

John Yule Mackay was born in 1859. He too was a son of the manse, and his father ministered in Inverkeithing before moving to a parish in Glasgow. John Mackay was educated at Glasgow Academy and graduated M.B. C.M. in Glasgow in 1881. He became an assistant in Embryology under Professor John Cleland, took his M.D. in 1885, and had been a candidate at the time of Professor Paterson's appointment. He co-operated with Professor Cleland in their Textbook of Anatomy, published later in 1896, and also wrote a manual of dissection. His research work was concerned with the branchial arches of birds, but a notable part of his contribution while in Glasgow University had been in organising the Students' Representative Council there.

The total financial requirements to complete the Conjoint Medical School in Dundee have been seen already. They were a major item in the arguments of 1894-95. Their details were worked out by the Medical Committee and are of interest when compared to today's monetary value:

A— Estimate for Building for a Medical School   £12,000

B— Initial Expenditure for Equipment of Medical School Chairs

1— *Apart from Buildings:*   2— *Including Buildings:*

Materia Medica	£1,000	New Chairs, etc	£2,570
Pathology	1,000	Anatomy	500
Medicine	30	Physiology	500
Surgery	60	Library	150
Midwifery	30	Museum	150
Medical Jurisprudence	400		
Mental Diseases	25		
Ophthalmology	25		
	£2,570		£3,870

C— Annual Expenses of Medical School

1— *Apart from Buildings:*

	£ Salary	£ Annual Upkeep	£ Service	£ Demon-stration	£ TOTAL
Anatomy	400	125	78	120	723
Physiology	400	125	78	120	723
Materia Medica	350	50	13	—	413
Pathology	350	100	13	?	463
Medicine	100	30)		—	130
Surgery	100	50)	?	—	150
Midwifery	100	30)		—	130
Medical Jurisprudence	50	50	13	—	113
Mental Diseases	25	10	—	—	35
Ophthalmology	25	10	—	—	35
Museum	—	120	100	—	220

Continued overleaf

	£	£	£	£	£
		Annual		*Demon-*	
	Salary	*Upkeep*	*Service*	*stration*	*TOTAL*
Library	—?	100	150	—	250
Advertising, Printing, etc.	—?	100	—	—	100
Miscellaneous	—?	75	—	—	75
					3,560
Revenue Anatomy	Endow-			433	
Physiology	ments			418	851
					2,709

2— *Including Upkeep of Buildings:*

Annual Expenditure on Chairs, etc. as before		£3,560
General Account	£250	
Gas, Coal and Water	25	
Repairs	25	
Insurance	50	
Rates and Taxes	50	
Cleaning	50	
Fireman	62	
Watchman	50	
Purser	78	590
		£4,150
Revenue as before		851
Deficit		£3,211

Summary

A— Medical School Buildings   £12,000
B— Initial Expenditure:
    1— Apart from Buildings   £2,570
    2— Including Buildings   £3,870
C— Annual Expenditure:
    1— Apart from Buildings   £3,560
    2— Including Buildings   £4,150
D— Estimate of Amount necessary to conduct a fully equipped
    Medical School on the line suggested in the agreement
    with St Andrews without *loss*:
    Expenditure:
    1— Apart from Buildings   £3,560−£851   £2,709
    2— Including Buildings   £4,150−£851   £3,299
    Revenue: Endowments of Anatomy and Physiology   £851
    Deficit:
    1— Apart from Buildings   £2,709
    2— Including Buildings   £3,299

On November 3rd 1894, the Medical Faculty met in Dundee and discussed the Senate's directive that a Dean was to be elected. Professors Pettigrew, McIntosh, Purdie, D'Arcy Thompson, Reid, Mackay, and Walker were present. Professor Pettigrew attended only to explain that the minute of the University Court of 1875 had not been rescinded, and he reserved his rights. After he left, Professor Mackay moved that since the Ordinance dealing with the appointment of a Dean of the Faculty of Medicine had not yet become law, no action be taken. This wise suggestion was accepted by everyone present: even Professor McIntosh did not dissent! 1894 also saw first proposals made for a Hall of Residence for women students in St Andrews. There was some initial hope that this might lead to the formation of a Women's College like Girton, but as ever there was no money available, and these hopes faded.

The use of the Berry fund to endow new Chairs, as well as to raise salaries in the United College, continued to be debated over the next two years. The University Court proposed funding two new Medical Chairs out of the money in late 1894 but this was defeated in Senate, in spite of a counter-motion by the two medical professors, on 9th February 1895. 1895 was the year when Court and Senate were in disagreement about St Andrews developments as well as St Andrews litigation. On the same day Professor Pettigrew gave a report from the Faculty of Medicine about the additional Medical Chairs in Dundee—the clinical ones—agreed in January by Professors McIntosh, D'Arcy Thompson, Reid, Mackay, and Walker. It was as if they were all in a different world from that of the Court, in this year when the litigation was at its most angry. The earlier suggested lectureships in Medical Jurisprudence and Public Health, Mental Diseases, and Ophthalmology had also been agreed—even by Professors Pettigrew and McIntosh—and the full report had been signed by the Dean. In Senate, however, the two were obstructive once again, but received no support. Back and forward went the arguments about the use of the Berry Fund. The usual sequence of events was that a Berry Chair of English Literature would be approved—with Professors Pettigrew and McIntosh dissenting, and that Berry Chairs of Materia Medica and Anatomy would be proposed by Professors Pettigrew and McIntosh—with all the other Professors, and sometimes the Principal—dissenting. In late March of 1895 the Secretary of the Students' Representative Council wrote to Senate stating that the students, at a mass meeting, had voted by 93-3 against two more Medical Chairs being created as there were 'more pressing wants'. The appointments of Charles Templeman, M.D. D.Sc., James Rorie, M.D., and Angus McGillivray, M.B. Ch.B. to the Jurisprudence, Mental Diseases, and Ophthalmology lectureships respectively were confirmed by Court and Senate. There was no slowing of this steady progress, and Rev. Dr. Metcalf's case might not even have existed.

On 14th December, 1895, it was formally reported to the Senate that the Marquess of Bute had been re-elected Rector, by 120 votes against 80 for Viscount Peel. This second term of office by Lord Bute coincided with the development of medical teaching in the United College, and to some extent also with the consolidation of science teaching there, which would have the permanent effects already mentioned.

The disruptive litigation was almost over—it could be said that for practical purposes, it *was* over. Though Lord Bute remained, his major policy now took a more positive direction, as far as Medicine was concerned, and perhaps as far as the whole enlarged University was concerned too.

In 1896 the Berry Chair was now designated for History, not English. The Senate became less antagonistic to Medicine, and no objection was raised to the suggestion—as had been made now several years before—that an Anatomy lectureship be tried in St Andrews for a trial period. Appointments were quickly made—Dr James Musgrove from Edinburgh, as lecturer in Anatomy, Miss Alice Martin Umpherston, L.R.C.P. and S. from Glasgow, in Physiology (to teach women students) and Dr. W.H. de Wytt, Glasgow, in Materia Medica. Dr. James KcKinnon was appointed lecturer in History—all these early in 1897.

But the main event of 1897, as far as Medicine in the United College of St Salvator's and St Leonard was concerned, was the new Medical Building 'The Bute'. It had been known the previous year that Lord Bute had in mind to provide money to build a pre-clinical Medical School—as was going to be built also in University College. On 27th January, 1897, a special meeting of the Senatus Academicus was called—at five p.m.—to consider the proposed new Medical Building. Lord Bute had earlier provided money to improve the Students' Union and dining hall facilities, but his major provision now was for Medicine. The Court had already appointed a sub-committee of its own to carry out his plans, and this particular Senate meeting was in protest. The Court's sub-committee had proposed that a large and self-contained medical development be built to the south of the St Mary's College quadrangle—in just the site it now occupies. At this meeting of Senate, Professors McIntosh and Pettigrew tried to block proceedings because, they said, 'it was not the business of the Senatus Academicus to interfere with the new medical buildings' and that the Court had already a specially appointed committee to deal with the project.

The Senate majority, however, after thanking the Marquess of Bute for his financial donation, and acknowledging his warm interest, asked that the site be in the United College and *not* in St Mary's. Their arguments were three: Medicine had always been associated with St Salvator's College, all class rooms for Medicine would remain together—if the new site were used, Anatomy, Botany, Materia Medica and Practical Physiology would be separated from the rest, and lastly that the new building would complete the quadrangle. It could then be called the 'Bute Wing'.

The above arguments to the Court from Senate noted that there had recently been considerable differences between the two bodies, but ended with a hope that a new chapter was beginning. Although they were wrong about the location of the Bute building, they were right about the new chapter. All the Dundee Professors were present at the Senate meeting of February 13th, when the Principal said he had asked them to be present as Ordinance 46 (St Andrews No.5) had now received the approval of Her Majesty in Council. The needless protest by Professor Lang was quickly dismissed, and from then on the full Senate continued to meet and function. But one dissentient was absent. Professor

Pettigrew sent a letter intimating his ill-health—constant worry, the accompanying medical letter certified, had largely brought about the unsatisfactory state of his health: he could not attend 'any meeting liable to lead to excitement'.

This really marked the end of Professor Bell Pettigrew's career in the Senate and indeed in the University. By now sixty three years old, old enough indeed to be the elderly father of any of the young University College Professors, he was a tired and unhappy man. Though he would recover and attend Senate again, he would fail progressively, and soon even his class teaching would fail—in the coming November he would ask for assistance. His letter on this occasion was a pathetic one, ending with the dissent from Ordinances St Andrews Nos. 4, 5, 6, 7, and 8 . . . 'I further beg to state that I feel it my duty to uphold the University of St Andrews as it existed prior to the issuing of the above specified Ordinances, I am, dear Principal Donaldson, Yours sincerely, J. Bell Pettigrew M.D., F.R.S., Chandos Professor of Medicine and Anatomy, Dean of the Medical Faculty, and representative of the University at the General Medical Council'.

The second most important medical event in St Andrews University of 1897 was the last examination for the M.D. under the old regulations. On 26th March, 1897, the last list read:

Charles GRINLING BUNN, London
Ed. BUXTON, Liverpool
Thos. Arthur DIXON, Surgeon Major Army Medical Department
Ed. Morton GARSTANG, Bolton
Walter Robt. HADWEN, Gloucester
Arthur Herbert HOFFMAN, London
Thos. Wm. JACKSON, Chorley
Alex. MALLAGH, Barrow-in-Furness
Howell WILLIAMS, Richmond, Yorks.
Roland Philip WILLIAMS, Holyhead

Examiners: Drs. Balfour, Littlejohn, Watson, and Halliday Croom.

Below this list was the first name on the New Order: David Munro passed the First Professional M.B. Ch.B. in Physics. The new Ordinance had required the Old Order to cease, and cease it now did.

Earlier in March, Mr G.W. Baxter informed the University College Council of his decision not to accept the position of Principal. It had been moved and passed that he take this post at the February meeting, for a period of three years, and that Professor J. Yule Mackay be his deputy. But he declined, and Professor Mackay agreed to take the post—for three years initially. Professor Mackay's appointment was not agreed unanimously and there was an opinion led by Mr W.R. Valentine, that University College should engage someone unconnected with it as Principal.

And so 1897 passed, with the final end of litigations and major protests, the revival of the Kate Kennedy procession, the raising of £21 by the Senate towards the cost of the new Cottage Hospital, and the award of the C.B. to Professor D'Arcy Thompson for his work in connection with fur seal fisheries on behalf of Her Majesty's Government. In the wider British scene, Chamberlain

was at the Colonial Office and engaged in the events leading to the Boer War; Campbell-Bannerman, Asquith, Sir Edward Gray—and David Lloyd George—were emerging on the Liberal side. The Workmen's Compensation Act was passed. And 1897 was the year of Queen Victoria's second or Diamond Jubilee. Although doubts about the supremacy of Great Britain's position and even about imperialism were growing, the people's enthusiasm for their now elderly sovereign was as unanimous as ever.

James Musgrove, whose lecture course of 80 lectures in Anatomy began in United (St Salvator's) College, plus 20 lectures in Anthropology and 50 hours of laboratory work, had been born in Kendal in 1862. As ever he was an Edinburgh M.B. of 1886 and M.D. of 1888. He had been demonstrator in Anatomy under Sir William Turner, and lecturer to the Royal Colleges. Though arriving in St Andrews in 1896, he had not managed to get his course started till the next year.

1898 saw an acceleration of activity. From January, the Board of Studies in Medicine began to function. From the start, it met in Dundee. At the first meeting on January 29th, those present were Professor Bell Pettigrew the Convener and Dean, Principal Mackay, Professors McIntosh and Purdie (Chemistry), Drs. Musgrove and de Wytt, Miss Umpherston, and Mr Robertson (Botany at St Salvator's College). Class hours for the two Colleges were agreed and the times of these classes continued for fifty years largely unaltered—in United College Botany was followed by Natural History with Anatomy after lunch in the Martinmas Term. Chemistry was included in the Candlemas Term, and Physics 12-1p.m. after its practical class 11-12 midday in the Summer Term. Materia Medica lectures were to be arranged in the lecturer's home—as there was no space available for him in the college buildings. In University College, Principal Mackay reported: Botany—for the Summer Term—would have its lecture at 12.30p.m. and its practical 2.30-4.30, and Natural History its daily lecture for 'medical and other students' in the elementary course also in the Summer Term, but at 9.00a.m. The practical class was 10-12. His own Anatomy class lectures were at 10.00a.m. for the bejant year, in the Winter and Summer terms, and for the second year, at 12.00 midday. Practical work could be carried out daily except on Saturdays from 9.00a.m. till 5.00p.m.—on Saturdays the dissecting room was open till noon. 25 Embryology lectures were added for the first year Summer Term at 12.00 midday and, as at St Salvator's College, Anthropology would be offered 'if sufficient students present themselves'. Physiology was on Mondays, Tuesdays, and Wednesdays from 2-3p.m., with an extra tutorial at 4.00p.m. on Mondays, 80 lectures in all, for the bejant year. The advanced course, of 40 lectures in continuity with the above, followed in the second year on Thursdays and Fridays at 2 o'clock. The practical course was on Tuesdays, Wednesdays, Thursdays, and Fridays at 2p.m. for Medical and junior B.Sc. students. Microscopes and reagents were to be supplied, but students had to buy their own microscope slides and cover glasses. Physiological Chemistry was included in the second year. Chemistry was on three days a week during the winter for two hours from 2.00p.m. and laboratory work would be done throughout. Finally, Physics was from 9-10a.m.

daily except Saturdays, in the Martinmas (Winter) Term.

Physics was taken by Professor Kuenen, who left almost at once for London, Botany by Professor Geddes, Chemistry by Professor Walker, Anatomy by the Principal, Physiology by Weymouth Reid and Natural History by D'Arcy Thompson. All courses in both colleges fully satisfied the new Medical Ordinances for the University. The report was agreed unanimously by the Board of Studies, as also by the Senate. Both the very recent litigation and Peterson's campaign to erase the word 'Conjoint' were forgotten. The report was signed by Professor Pettigrew as Dean of the Medical Faculty.

On March 25th, 'the following candidates for the Degrees of M.B. Ch.B. of St Andrews University had passed the first division of the First Professional Examination:

Cyril W. Burrows	in Physics
James Monie	in Chemistry
Harry Overie	in Physics and Chemistry with distinction
Hugh S.W. Roberts	in Botany and Zoology, Physics and Chemistry
Mary L. Walker	in Botany and Chemistry

Signed J.B.P.

Dean of Medical Faculty'

There was no question of these students being other than undergraduates of the University of St Andrews—no taking of sides. This was quiet progress, without Principals' letters or press comment—and how refreshingly it all reads in the records. Nor did the University College Council press for money, as would have happened only three years earlier. They now knew that time and good will were on their side. On 13th April, the University Court—with Lord Bute still there—agreed on the apportionment of the Grant. £3,000 *per annum* was for the Medical School. It also agreed to make University money available for building the Medical School premises in University College, when the full State Grant came to St Andrews. It was agreed further to seek the co-operation of the Directors of Dundee Royal Infirmary with regard to the provision of facilities there for clinical teaching. And on June 8th, 1898, Principal Mackay would report to the Dundee Council that as the direct result of this harmonious approach by representatives from both Colleges of the University, the Secretary for Scotland had made available 'all the necessary money' for the completion of the Conjoint Medical School. The D.R.I. Directors were less forthcoming, but offered weekly meetings with the University.

The slight unease which marked relations with the Directors increased in early July, when they announced that they would be prepared 'to approve of the nominations in each case of either of their present attending physicians or surgeons', but that they would also fix an age limit and a time limit to the services of their medical officers. Thus while appointments in Medicine and Surgery could go ahead, the Directors required delay over the Midwifery appointment because they had not yet made an appointment themselves. This insistence virtually demanded that only a person given a contract to be on the Infirmary Staff could become a University teacher, and would have repercussions many years later.

In May, a Draft Scheme for the Diploma in Public Health of St Andrews University was agreed by the Board of Studies, by Professors Bell Pettigrew, McIntosh, Reid and Walker, and Principal Mackay. The Diploma should not be conferred on those with the 'Triple Qualification' (i.e. licentiate of the Royal Colleges) but only on University medical graduates.

Candidates 1) Must have held a medical degree for at least twelve months.

2) Must have attended, in a laboratory of the University of St Andrews, six months of practical training in Chemistry, Bacteriology, and Pathology of the diseases of animals transmissible to man.

3) Must also have done six months sanitary work with a Medical Officer of Health of a County, Burgh or District of a population of at least thirty thousand people.

4) Must have had three months of clinical instruction in an Infectious Diseases Hospital.

There were to be 2 Examinations:

1) Chemistry, Physics, Meteorology—written and practical.

2) Sanitation, Sanitary Law, Vital Statistics, Medicine in relation to Public Health (including Epidemiology, Endemiology and the Pathology of Infectious Diseases).

The fee was 5 guineas for each examination.

The only discordant note at this time came from the University College Council in July. While it agreed that 'University status was of the greatest importance to Dundee', and seemed pleased that 'all University subjects taught at Dundee were now recognized for graduation at St Andrews'—which it might well have been—it was a little complaining about its Grant. It commented 'Council of University College Dundee remains financially independent and will receive no relief of any kind from the University, and will continue to be charged as previously with the whole maintenance of the College work'. It is rather hard to see the need for this complaint. It was after all the unsatisfactory constitution of this College which made it financially independent and made it insist on retaining its degree of independence from the rest of the University. At this time, the Court had voted all the necessary *university* money for the part of the medical school situated in Dundee, and in due course would provide almost all the required amount.

The College Council now, on 15th July, requested the Court to consult it over the new Medical Chairs, and asked for a report on the appointments. It then nominated the Senior Acting Surgical Officer at D.R.I., David McEwan M.D., as Professor of Surgery. He had been surgeon there for more than twenty-two years, and had since 1891 given some surgical lectures. It nominated Alexander Mitchell Stalker, M.D., who held the equivalent position on the medical side and had been over ten years at D.R.I., as Professor of Medicine.

There was therefore no question of the Chairs being advertised, and appointments then made, allowing open competition. Again, this was because of the policy of the D.R.I. Directors, but these included Mr R.B. Don and Mr Robertson of the Council, and had always included one of the University College staff—Professor Paterson in 1889, Claxton Fidler in 1892, and now Principal Mackay himself.

At their meeting three days later, these names came before the University Court. Drs. McEwan and Stalker were duly elected; though Lord Bute tried to delay their appointment, with Dr. Metcalf, on the grounds that no public advertisement had been made, he was defeated by nine votes to five. But at the next Court meeting, on the 20th, when a proposal appeared once again that a Berry Chair of Anatomy and Anthropology be founded, it was Principals Mackay and Donaldson who tried to block the proposals, the first attempting to have the Chair designated 'Anthropology' only, and the second by attempting also to stop extra money being voted from the Berry Fund to boost the salary of the Chandos Chair. This was the first Court meeting at which 'new' External Examiners were appointed—the 'old' ones having disappeared with the old M.D. They were Dr. Richard J.A. Berry, F.R.C.S. of Edinburgh in Anatomy—preferred to Principal Mackay's nomination of a friend from Glasgow, and R. Barclay Ness, Professor of Materia Medica and Therapeutics of Anderson's College, Glasgow also Principal Mackay's nomination. They were both appointed for three years. D.R.I. lecturers in Medicine were appointed examiners in Medicine for the University—just thirty-eight years late.

The later part of 1898 saw three more appointments—one which lasted, and two which ended quickly for different reasons. It also saw the election of a new rector, James Stuart. The lasting appointment was that of Professor Kynoch in Midwifery. He was preferred to Dr. R.C. Buist. Dr. Kynoch was born in Forres in 1863, educated at Dollar Academy, and graduated M.B. C.M. at Edinburgh in 1887 with honours in Midwifery and Surgery. He spent several years in post-graduate training, working first in centres of highest excellence in Vienna, Berlin and Munich; he then came to Dundee Infirmary as a house physician in 1889. Following this he trained at the Samaritan Women's Hospital in London and next at the great Rotunda Hospital in Dublin. He was now back in Dundee once more, an assistant physician and Member of the Royal College of Physicians of Edinburgh, but his interest was in obstetrics and gynaecology, housed in the new block at the right side of the main Infirmary building.

Robert Muir was born in 1864 at Balfour in Stirlingshire. His father and one of his grandfathers were parish ministers, and his mother was the daughter of a Dundee merchant William Duncan. From Hawick, where his father ministered, he went as a scholarship boy at the age of sixteen to Edinburgh, graduated M.A. at twenty, and M.B. C.M. with first class honours in 1888. He worked under Professor Greenfield in Edinburgh, and quickly became interested in research. He was a demonstrator in Pathology and later Bacteriology. Very early in his career he began to write, and the *Manual of Bacteriology* which he wrote with Dr. James Ritchie, lecturer of Pathology at Oxford, and published in 1897, went

through many editions. But within a year of being appointed to this new Pathology Chair in the University of St Andrews, he left to be Professor of Pathology in Glasgow where he remained for thiry-six years, becoming a Kingmaker in the world of Pathology (placing eight of his assistants in Chairs throughout the United Kingdom), and the author of the celebrated Muir's *Pathology*. Both Professors Muir and Kynoch were appointed in September of 1898.

The third Professor, and the other who would have a very short stay in St Andrews, was Dr. de Wytt. On October 19th, in Court, the voting arrangements were extraordinary. On the first count, Dr. C.R. Marshall received most votes, but de Wytt's votes were then counted against those of other candidates and by a series of further proportional voting, was finally elected.[1] Dr. de Wytt was of uncertain origin, but was certainly a medical graduate of ability from the University of Glasgow. He had already treated Lord Bute, and it was Lord Bute who now pressed his appointment in the teeth of opposition from Court and Senate. The two Principals, Professors Steggall, Herkless and Burnet, and Lord Provost McGrady asked that their dissent be recorded. De Wytt had already been teaching from his home as a lecturer, but now he was Professor. And so, William Henry de Wytt was induced as Professor of Materia Medica and Therapeutics by Principal Donaldson with the four others on November 12th. Very soon afterwards, he was called to the Senate to answer questions over a certificate he had given, but did not attend, and in fact left St Andrews. There is no real evidence of any legal proceedings ever being undertaken,[2] however. He very soon afterwards bought and developed a private nursing home in London, which he ran successfully to the end of his life. On December 29th, Dr. C.R. Marshall was appointed, four days after de Wytt resigned. At this Court meeting, it is interesting that Professor Steggall moved, and had passed, that Dr. Marshall, when appointed, would teach in St Andrews as well as in Dundee. On 21st January 1899, Charles Robertson Marshall, M.A., M.B.Ch.B. became Professor, and was inducted on February 11th. He had come from Owens College—being born in Bradford in 1869—but had moved in 1894 to Downing College Cambridge as assistant to Professor Bradbury. So successful had he been in organising the School of Pharmacology that he was elected Bradshaw lecturer in 1895 and Croonian in 1897, and made an M.A. (*honoris causa*) of Cambridge in the latter year.

As well as people, buildings were being provided apace for the Conjoint Medical School. Here Lord Bute fortunately had his way: on these developments his was the farther-seeing eye. At the meeting when de Wytt was appointed, Principal Donaldson once again blocked the proposal, supported by the Rector, to provide grants for the Physiology and Anatomy Departments in the United College. At the meeting in December, the Senatus Academicus by a majority of 18 votes to 4 passed a resolution *against* new Chairs of Anatomy and Physiology (in St Salvator's College) because (1) their previous decision of 1896 had agreed only to a 'tentative and experimental scheme of providing two *anni medici* in the United College' and (2) the University Commissioners had recently refused to institute a new Chair of Anatomy when their full grant was awarded and (3) the

Privy Council had proposed abolishing the Chandos Chair and applying its endowments elsewhere. At this meeting Professor de Wytt, in post, had added his protest to those of Professors Pettigrew and McIntosh. Even the General Council, which voted *for* the new medical Chairs, did so by only 52 to 31 votes. Following the Senate resolution, however, Principal Donaldson and Mr James Stuart, the new Rector, had proposed in Court that while the various departments produced their priorities for finance, the Court 'continue medical teaching in United College for two sessions longer than at present arranged for'.

They really had no option but to do this. The new Bute Medical Building was progressing—some increased expenses had appeared but Lord Bute had said he would not pay more than he had promised already—but this increased cost did not result in delay. In December, Principal Mackay asked that another sub-committee of the Court be formed, to take further the resolution of the Business and Finance Committee about the building of medical premises in University College. There was not the slightest suggestion of antagonism or rivalry by Principal Mackay over this period; in fact, he went over the estimates for the new Anatomy department in the 'Bute' in March 1899, and approved of them, subject to a few suggestions for savings. The Court at once adopted his helpful recommendations.

On April 15th Professor Muir, less than seven months after his taking office, resigned as Professor of Pathology. Dr. James Gray, who was assistant to Professor McEwan, was asked to teach Pathology, to any students who appeared, until the end of the session. A little earlier, Dr. Arthur T. Masterman, B.A. D.Sc. was appointed lecturer in Embryology in the United College, and Mr Henry Llewellyn Heath was appointed assistant to Professor Marshall. And a little later in 1899, in July, Professor Bell Pettigrew was finally relieved of his teaching duties. Dr. Harris was to teach now. Bell Pettigrew had already been succeeded in January as Dean by Professor Weymouth Reid, and he now passed quietly and sadly from the scene.

At the end of July, applications for the new Professor of Pathology's post were received. Drs. Bolam, Dean, and Lazarus applied again. They were joined by Dr. D.A. Welsh B.Sc. M.B. C.M. M.D. M.R.C.P. from Edinburgh University, and Dr. Lewis R. Sutherland, M.B. C.M. from Glasgow. Dr. Sutherland was appointed 'as specified in Ordinance No. 46 (St Andrews No. 5), Professorships in the Faculty of Medicine in the University of St Andrews.' Lewis Robertson Sutherland was born in Gibraltar, yet another son of the Manse. He had been at Glasgow Academy before graduating with commendation in the University in 1890, and after house posts in the Western Infirmary became assistant to Professor Coats at the Royal in 1892. He studied on the continent in Paris, Frankfurt and Berlin, where he worked in Virchow's laboratory. He returned in 1895 to Glasgow as senior assistant in the Department of Pathology. He too would spend his professional life at St Andrews University and would not retire until 1932. But perhaps as interesting a fact about him as all of these is that he was married to a daughter of the Professor of Medicine in Glasgow, Sir William Gairdner. This connection may have had something to do with his application and his appointment.

It was now the turn of University College. The sub-committee of the Court Principal Mackay had asked for had met through this year, and on 16th September it held an important meeting in Dundee. The Principals, Lord Provost McGrady, Professors Steggall and Herkless, and Mr J. Gordon Stuart were present. 'Section 16 (1) of the Universities' (Scotland) Act of 1889 dealing with the affiliation of University College and for establishing an adequate and suitably equipped Conjoint University School of Medicine, and the Ordinances of the Commissioners' bearing thereupon' were read. Principal Mackay reported that careful consideration had been made of three separate plans, drawn by Mr Murray Robertson, a Dundee Architect, for possible sites. These were: 1) on the West of the College, 2) northwards from the Centre of the College, 3) on the site of the old St John's Free Church at the back of the College. The sub-committee inspected the plans and the sites, and agreed that the church site was the most suitable.

Back to the United College. On October 31st, the equivalent medical buildings committee—Principal Donaldson, Provost McGregor, Rev. Dr. Anderson, Rev. Dr. Scott, and Dr. Dow the Convener—met in St Andrews. The Bute Medical Building was complete. The Convener submitted a draft inscription to be inscribed on the stone over the main entrance (though never in fact placed there):

The Bute Medical School
Erected A.D. 1899
By the most Honourable
JOHN PATRICK CRICHTON STUART
Third Marquess of Bute
Lord Rector of the University of St Andrews from 1892 to 1898
For the advancement of Medical teaching in the University and
City of St Andrews

The completion of the 'Bute', as it has been known ever since to medical students of the United College, was an event of great significance in the history of the Faculty of Medicine. Not only did it provide a secure and impressive base for medical teaching, but Botany and Natural History would very soon be included there, followed shortly by Physiological Chemistry. And it provided classrooms, laboratories, and most of all dissecting rooms for Anatomy, and equivalent facilities for Physiology—all the life sciences, in fact. It was completed before its University College counterpart in terms of time, and time would confirm its worth for what Mr Thomas Thornton so often liked to call 'the enlarged University'.

Just a month later, the Medical Building Committee met in Dundee. This time the Principals were joined by the Very Reverend Principal Stewart of St Mary's; Mr Joseph Gordon Stewart, Provost McGregor, Dr. Dow, Professors Herkless and Burnet were the other committee members. More important decisions were taken, following preliminary meetings and discussions over much of the year. The College Council had in May agreed to recommend that that site for the new medical buildings be at the west end of the ground extending

from the Technical Institute to the Nethergate. But now, on November 25th, the Building Committee agreed with the revised suggestion that what had become known as 'the Church site' be used—that is, behind the building presently in use. At this meeting also, site valuation figures were given by Mr Murray Robertson the architect, and the estimates gone over yet again. Principal Mackay in particular was happy with the Court's vote of £12,500 from its accumulated medical funds—'since the estimate is £15,000', he said, 'building can proceed in the confidence that friends of the University in Dundee will raise the difference and any further sum which may be necessary to make the buildings and their equipment worthy of the City and of the University'. Though Rev. Dr. Dow dissented, the detailed estimates were agreed.

For reasons which are not exactly clear, the greatest part of 1900 saw no good progress on the new buildings in University College. But in United College, a further large forward progress took place. On January 8th Lord Bute insured the new Medical Building for £8,000, and the apparatus now removed from the former medical classrooms in North Street for £600. It was agreed that the Botany department should also move, and its equipment was insured for £325 in its new home. Correspondence was begun with Lord Bute's agents that the new Medical Building be used for purposes other than those associated with medical teaching. While nothing came of this move, the new Lord Rector proposed that the Physiology department attic be used for teaching Materia Medica in the United College—as the students had petitioned—and that Natural History be moved also to Bute. So over this short period, these sciences were placed within the Bute Medical Building complex, where they remain. July 1900 saw another major event. A letter was received on the 28th by the Court.

Dear Sir,

I have been authorised by Lord Bute, whose health does not at present admit of his writing personally to you, to inform you that his Lordship proposes to offer to the University of St Andrews a sum of twenty thousand pounds, to be held as a fund for endowing a Chair of Anatomy. Should this proposal be acceptable, Lord Bute will grant an undertaking binding himself and his executors to provide the money under the following conditions:

1) That the said sum of twenty thousand pounds shall be paid to the University not later than ten years hence. The exact date cannot be specified, as it will depend upon certain works at Cardiff. Interest at 3% will be paid to the University from the time of the appointment of the first Professor until they receive the principal sum;

2) That the first presentation to the Chair shall be in favour of Mr Musgrove, the present holder of the lectureship in Anatomy at St Andrews;

3) That the lectures shall be given exclusively at St Andrews;

4) That the course shall meet the requirements of the two first *anni medici*;

5)   That before the beginning of the University session 1901-02 the
     approval of the Universities' Commission of the Privy Council to
     the establishment of the Chair under the foregoing conditions be
     maintained; and that the approval of Lord Bute or his
     representatives be obtained to any further conditions embodied in
     the ordinances instituting the Chair. I shall be much obliged if you
     will submit this proposal to the University Court at their meeting
     on 28th inst.

I am, yrs. very faithfully,

A.R.S. Pitman (Law Agent)

P.S.   This letter is written on the understanding that the University is
       prepared to make adequate teaching arrangements for
       completing the permanent provision in St Andrews of teaching
       necessary for the two first *anni medici*.

James Stuart Esq., M.P.

Lord Rector,

St Andrews University.

Principal Mackay and Professor Steggell were delighted at this offer. The
Principal reported it to the University College Council at its meeting on August
8th. It was discussed, and minuted 'No action to be taken'; there was no dissent.
The press had no comment; indeed, the last two years had seen a change for the
better in the attitude of the Third Party. This change is worthy of comment;
while the *St Andrews Citizen* had certainly published letters giving rival
opinions about the policies and supposed hidden intentions of Lord Bute, it had
never attacked University College or Dundee in the same consistently unfair
way that the Dundee press had attacked St Andrews. The *Citizen,* indeed, had
published a speech of Principal Donaldson criticising Lord Bute on October
9th, 1897, which the *Advertiser* did not, in as harsh terms as anything the
Dundee paper ever wrote. But for the most part, its reports were published
without comment. But in the last three years of the decade the *Advertiser* ceased
its campaign of attacking St Andrews, and made no comment whatever on
events it would previously have seized upon. This perhaps started in the summer
of 1896, when on July 24th, 28th and 29th, the reports of the final House of
Lords' judgment for Dundee in the last of the major litigation hearings were all
reported without any comment whatsoever, and thereafter St Andrews University began to be praised. By the time the new Rector had arrived, there was
an understandable stepping up of this praise: 'The new Lord Rector has sent a
breath of modern spirit over St Andrews University. Not that we would have it
supposed that the University ever belonged to the cloistered order of institutions;
on the contrary, St Andrews has been among the first of the Universities to
adapt itself to the developing needs of the age' . . . The leader added 'Academic
culture is not necessarily to be sacrificed to the claimant desires for professional
training'. The *Advertiser* spoke of St Andrews as 'our University'. It was as
complete a change as could be imagined.

On September 1st it was agreed 'cordially to accept' . . . and to request the
Lord Rector to inform the Marquess of Bute of the University's decision to do

so. The United College, St Mary's and University College representatives were all in agreement. Arrangements were to be begun 'with the view of making permanent provision for the teaching in the United College necessary for the first two *anni medici*,' and the Court was to proceed at once 'to the creation of a Professorship of Anatomy in St Andrews to be endowed ... subject to the conditions stipulated by his Lordship—the first presentation to the Chair being in favour of Dr. Musgrove—as soon as the Ordinance is approved by Her Majesty in Council'. Next, the present temporary lectureship in Botany was to become a permanent lectureship, and lastly, it was resolved 'to proceed at once with the creation of a Professorship of Physiology to come into effect on the death or resignation of the present Chandos Professor of Medicine, to be endowed with the revenues presently payable to that Professor; for the interim, the present lecturer, Dr. Harris, would continue to teach'.

A special sub-committee drafted the required Ordinances; on the 29th of September Mr Pitman wrote to say that they were acceptable to Lord Bute. But before these could be passed to Senate—now twenty-one members strong including the three Principals—Lord Bute died, at the early age of fifty-three. On October 20th, they recorded his death with sorrow:

'For six years (he) was Rector and strongly attached as he was to St Andrews from his youth he discharged all the duties of the office with much earnestness and devotion. He showed great generosity in the contribution he gave for the Students' Dining Hall and Union. He was munificent towards the Medical School in St Andrews, supplying it with handsome and commodious buildings and endowing a Chair of Anatomy'. Deep sympathy was expressed to the Marchioness and her family.

And on the same day, as if to emphasise that rejuvenated medicine was at long last beginning for St Andrews University, it was reported in Senate that eight students had passed the first M.B. Ch.B. Professional Examination, three second Professional, and one the second part of the Diploma in Public Health Examination. On December 1st the Senate agreed to Draft Ordinance No. 1 (The foundation of the Bute Chair of Anatomy) and to Draft Ordinance No. 2 (The foundation of the Chandos Chair of Physiology); slight changes of detail were necessary as a consequence of Lord Bute's death and on December 10th the Seal of the University was affixed.

And so, in the short space of two years, changes took place which revolutionised the way the Medical Faculty would develop within the enlarged University. United College had its Medical Building, and its vital pre-clinical Chairs were secured. University College would soon have its Medical Building and its life sciences concentrated within it, and the two would now start to feed their students into the clinical part of the Conjoint Medical School. All were part of the University of St Andrews, and pleased to be so.

This was surely just. For centuries the University had 'wished for Medicine'. The strategy of Principal Peterson and the heavily biased writings by the Third Party had sought to deny a share in medical science teaching—and, perhaps in other science subjects also—to the old University, and much of the bitterness which had grown until it had raged into fury was the result of this strategy and

sedulous newspaper support, which the Principal was all too eager to use. The litigation and the interruption it had caused were a sad and unnecessary interruption of the quiet progress of sensible men in both new and old colleges, but it now seemed as if they could be forgotten by this new spirit of co-operation. Sadly, however, they would pass into mythology and be recalled in later years for purposes as partisan as their initiators' strategy had been.

In this sudden transformation Professors Pettigrew, McIntosh, Reid, Thompson, Dr. Metcalf—even Principal Donaldson—were somehow the smaller figures. The prime mover was Lord Bute, and, as has been seen, his plans were supported, in greater measure than has perhaps been realised, by Principal Mackay and Professor Steggall of University College. As a benefactor, more-over, Lord Bute does not deserve the sneer[3] that his wealth came from toiling workers unless the same observation is made of the jute owners whose wealth endowed so much of University College. At this time, Dundee had some of the worst slums in Europe, and the jute lords were neither then nor indeed many years later the most considerate of employers.

The next ten years saw quiet co-operation continue. In 1901, in January, Queen Victoria died, and the great Victorian era ended. The Chancellor of the University, the Duke of Argyll, died in April. Professor McIntosh received the Gold Medal of the Royal Society. And on July 18th, Alexander Cunningham, from Campbeltown, was the first M.B. Ch.B. to be capped under the new regulations. In the Fourth Professional Examination earlier that month his marks were high—74% for Medicine, 70% for Surgery, 70% for Midwifery and Gynaecology.

The Faculty of Medicine worked well over this period. On 7th March, 1899, it recommended to the Senatus that Professional Examinations in Medicine be conducted simultaneously in the United College and University College, and it supervised the development of both pre-clinical and clinical parts of the course diligently. But the numbers of Professors who actually attended Faculty Meetings remained very small; in the first five years Professors Thompson, Walker, and Weymouth Reid the Dean were often the only three. Professors Musgrove and Purdie attended periodically; the clinical Professors no more frequently. What remains striking about their minutes is their obvious interest in the University of St Andrews they belonged to, and their desire to further its good name by working towards the good of their own Faculty.

The other major development was the completion of the new Medical Building in University College. Of the three suggested sites—the 'West', the 'North' and the 'Church', the last, which was within the College precinct, had been chosen. The cost of the new building was to be borne by the Court of the University, and so the site had to be bought from the College. The anomaly of the Council's position required this. But progress was straightforward. Mr Murray Robertson had completed his detailed estimates by late 1900, but unfortunately died the next year. Mr James Findlay took over the work. Unfortunately, too, the earlier estimates were too low (it is of interest, and almost amusing, that the addition of one sum already shown on page 152 is incorrect. The correct addition should be £3359 for the deficit (the Council

members apparently did not notice the mistake). By the end of May 1901 the lowest tender for the building and its fittings, including painting, ventilation and lighting, was £18,332. The architect's fee of £917 brought this total to £19,240. But as there was enough money available to make a start on the building, work was commissioned to begin.

On 1st July the Council discussed where the extra could come from, and decided it would try the Carnegie Trust first, and failing that, attempt to raise the money by local appeal. It is certainly untrue that the Council asked the Carnegie Trust only to provide extra money *after* the local appeal had raised a large sum; the opposite was in fact the case. Nor did the University Court delay; on 25th July, a Draft Agreement between it and the Dundee Council was produced, and completed in October and December. Further help came the next year, in 1902, from Sir William Ogilvy Dalgleish, Bt. One of the problems which had arisen for the new University College was its considerable debt. As has been seen, its original businessmen benefactors were able to give large sums to *endow* Chairs or departments, but because Universities were not factories, they could not ensure the revenue income to maintain them in profit. Their debt by now was of the order of £7,500, and this continual burden had been a strong reason why some older University figures feared earlier St Andrews would be over-whelmed by Dundee—not by its profit, but by its debts. Sir William now offered to donate £5,000 towards the completion of the new Medical Buildings in the University, and said he would give a *further* £5,000 to clear off University College's debt *provided the remaining* £2,500 were raised by other means. The Court happily accepted his offer, and the College Council began the task of encouraging a further round of public subscriptions in Dundee and district. Final agreement on the site between the Council and the Court was not concluded until late January of 1902,[4]—there could be no blame laid on the late Lord Bute for this continuing delay—and the foundation stone was eventually laid on 24th October 1902 by the Lord Rector, Mr Andrew Carnegie. Of the final cost estimates, £12,500 was to be met by the University out of the Parliamentary Grant, £11,139.12.11d. out of its accummulated funds put by for the Conjoint Medical School, and the remainder, 'an amount not exceeding £6,000' by the College Council. These details are in the Council minutes for 1902, as is the considerable correspondence over loans of money it was endeavouring to raise for its own University College costs. Sir Ogilvie Dalgleish delivered his £10,000 to the Council on July 2nd 1902—half for the Medical Building Fund, and half 'towards the extinction of the debt'—for by now the shortfall had been raised by local donors. The College Council minuted that as it had no immediate use for the money, it should 'be lent or placed on deposit'. 1904 saw the completion of University College's equivalent to the Bute. 1904 had also seen the unsuccessful application of Professor Steggall to leave St Andrews for Aberdeen. The new Medical Building was opened, with considerably more ceremony than the Bute, by the Chancellor, Lord Balfour of Burleigh, on 17th October 1904. Above the door is inscribed 'University of St Andrews' with the Seal of the University below, and below again, 'School of Medicine'. The date is 1902, when the first stone was laid and the legal agreement concluded.

Cost of upkeep was now the responsibility of the Court of St Andrew University, but 'in the event of the said School of Medicine being at any time discontinued the Council of University College are bound to purchase the building and equipment.'[5] The Council decided to provide a silver key for the Chancellor to use when he opened the building, and the Court declared the day a holiday in the whole University.

The Faculty of Medicine of the University of St Andrews now had all the necessary buildings, clinical material, and staff for a full five *anni medici*. Principal Mackay had looked forward to their use when he wrote his report earlier in the summer.

> New buildings are now almost completed, and the Departments of Anatomy, Pathology, and Surgery have already been transferred to them; they will be in full occupation at the commencement of the session in October. There will be accommodation for about one hundred students. The old Anatomy work-rooms—inconvenient, inadequate, and unsightly—are in course of demolition, their presence interfering with the lighting of some of the new laboratories; but over-pressure on original college buildings will be eased when Physiology and Materia are transferred to the School of Medicine.

The Dundee press reported the opening ceremony in full detail, and the *Advertiser's* excellent account stressed throughout that the occasion was a *University* one. This was the consummation of a long-cherished scheme, and good-will was everywhere. In honour of the occasion a large number of professors and students had come from 'the grey city' to lend their assistance. The student 'drag' carried the Chancellor and the three College Principals along the Nethergate; the *Advertiser* approved heartily. 'The unusual spectacle attracted great attention', and the whole event 'evoked great interest in the city'. The Gaudeamus was sung. It was a happy and exciting occasion. The speeches, though all warm with praise and congratulation, were of interest as showing the different—but largely united—viewpoints of the main characters. The Chancellor, Lord Balfour of Burleigh recalled how the events of the day were a great step which had been the aim of the earliest reason for union between the new College and the University. 'Before 1897', he said, 'Dundee had two Chairs which at any rate provided for students in the first two years of their medical course'. It was only since the union that the University had added the other necessary Chairs. Principal Donaldson mentioned the benificence of the Rector, Andrew Carnegie. His main praise was for what the Dundee townspeople themselves had done in providing facilities for the treatment of disease; he instanced the new Maternity Hospital, and the Cancer Hospital. The Earl of Camperdown spoke warmly in praise of Principal Donaldson who was, he said, 'the working head of the Dundee College just as he was of the St Andrews, and when he was in Dundee they claimed him as the head of the University of which they were so proud to form a part. This was said not only on behalf of the Dundee governors but also on behalf of the doctors who belonged to the Dundee College'. Principal Mackay, like Principal Donaldson, spoke first of the hopes now for the alleviation of sickness and disease, mentioning the good work of D.R.I., but

also said that it was a matter of congratulation to St Andrews University that after a growth of nearly five hundred years it had at length acquired a fully equipped Medical School. And lastly Sir William Ogilvie Dalgleish spoke as a Fife man, both of his feelings for the need of a Medical School in Dundee and also for the ancient University of St Andrews; the union would benefit both. All in all, this was a *University* occasion, and the press happily presented it as such.

1904 also saw another event of interest and significance for the Faculty of Medicine. This was the first inspection of Medicine in St Andrews Universitry by the General Medical Council since 1888. Sir John Moore, M.D. and Mr Thomas Bryant were the visitor and inspector from the G.M.C., and they reported on the final Professional Examinations held in June and July. Their preliminary remarks were especially interesting, as they detailed the development of the medical degrees offered by the University over the last half century. Noting that 'The Qualifying Examinations for the Degrees of M.B. and Ch.B. at the University of St Andrews are of recent origin', they continue:

> The Commissioners under the Universities (Scotland) Act of 1889 made an alteration in the titles of the qualifying degrees in Medicine of the Scottish Universities, as previously framed by the Commission of 1858.
>
> Before the passing of the *Medical Act* of 1858 the degree for practice given was M.D. in spite of the fact that instruction in Surgery was included in the curriculum. This M.D. gave the holder a title to practice both Medicine and Surgery.
>
> The Commissioners of 1858 substituted M.B. for M.D. as the degree qualifying for ordinary practice, and provided that the candidate might, if he pleased, also receive a degree of C.M. (master of Surgery), to which his education and acquirements were supposed to entitle him.
>
> The degree of M.D. *was made a higher degree*, to be taken two years after M.B. C.M.
>
> The last Commission of 1889 amended this work of the 1858 Commission by substituting *Bachelor* of Surgery (Ch.B.) for the *Master* of Surgery (C.M. of the 1858 Commission) as the degree to be taken with M.B., "so that the degree qualifying for ordinary practice should be of the same denomination in both departments". Neither of the degrees M.B. and Ch.B. is conferred on any person who does not at the same time obtain the other. The degree of C.M. thus became a *separate higher degree of the same order as M.D.*, and is conferred only upon those who have obtained the Ch.B. A full account will be found in the "General Report of the Commissioners under the Universities (Scotland) Act 1889." *Eyre & Spottiswoode*, 1900.
>
> The United College, St Andrews, offers full opportunities for the study of all the subjects of the first two years of the medical curriculum, and has excellent classrooms and distinguished Professors.
>
> One candidate from St Andrews University passed in 1901, one in

1902, three in 1903, and upon the present occasion there were six
candidates. No candidate has yet been rejected.

It has, therefore, so happened that this is the first occasion upon
which an Inspector accompanied by a Visitor from the GENERAL
MEDICAL COUNCIL has visited this University.

The subjects of Pathology and Forensic Medicine and Public
Health, having been included in the Third Examination, were excluded
from the Final Examination.

One or both of us attended all these Examinations except the
Written, and followed the six candidates who appeared before the
Examiners in all their work.

Their main criticisms were of the clinical examinations. 'The examination in
Clinical Medicine as leading to a qualifying examination appears to us to be
somewhat limited; more evidence of clinical knowledge should be required of
every Candidate, and better evidence of good knowledge of ward work brought
out, than was exhibited in the Examination as we visited'. Details of criticism
were given—in a case of chronic kidney disease no reference was made by either
the Candidate or the Examiners to the condition of the heart. The candidate
concerned had been awarded a high mark for his clinical—24 out of 30.
Another candidate had 'correctly diagnosed acute pneumonia, but did not
allude to the sputum as an important item'. In Surgery, too, 'the evidence that
the Candidates had acquired a fair knowledge of the diagnosis and treatment of
disease by personal observation was by no means so well marked as could be
wished'. In their oral examinations, too, the students were criticised for lack of
practical knowledge. Midwifery came in for no criticism—this part of the Final
Examination was 'most satisfactory'—thus establishing a reputation for the
Midwifery Finals in St Andrews which would continue over the years. Examinations were also carried out in Ophthalmology—which were praised as 'excellent',
in Mental Disease—'good and highly interesting', and in Ear and Throat by Dr.
Guild—'very full and satisfactory'.

Now it was the turn of Professor Waymouth Reid, following his predecessor
Professor Pettigrew as Dean, to refute what criticisms had been made, and to be
able to report to the Faculty and Senate that the final Professional Examinations
of the University of St Andrews had been reported 'sufficient' by the General
Medical Council Examiners.

A report was also made by an Examination Committee consisting of Sir
Patrick Heron Watson as Chairman and including Sir Charles Ball, and Sir
William Thomson. This covered the same ground as the Visitor and Inspector
had done, and also supported the local clinicians in surgery who had been
indirectly criticised by them over the method of treating fractures in general and
a fracture of the arm in particular. Their comments were supportive and
helpful—Sir Patrick Heron Watson perhaps continuing as the friend of the St
Andrews Medical Faculty which he had been for many years in the past. The
most interesting feature of all, perhaps, in this account is that the criticism of the
'old' St Andrews examination—of the *clinical* knowledge required and the way
it was treated—had occurred again in the 'new' examination.

So the early years continued. The 6 candidates at the 1904 Final Examination all passed. The number would rise only a little—in 1908 there would be 11 candidates, and the Bute would have 8 pre-clinical Second M.B. students, its largest number to date. There would be a slight fall in 1911 following the Lloyd George Insurance Act, as will be seen later. All these students taking their finals were students of St Andrews University. For the Conjoint Medical School was the School of St Andrews University. In University College, the numbers of Arts students would begin to fall in these years, and this trend would continue into the future with future significant results; what should be remembered is that this fall begins as early as it undoubtedly did, before there was any possible imputation of pressure by the United College side or neglect by the Senatus or Court. It was not in fact stricty true that in these pre-First World War years the two larger colleges developed equally. Already students were following the tendency Principal Peterson had noted twenty years earlier. They were preferring St Andrews.

This period, which ended with the quincentenary celebrations of the University in 1911, also saw the first of the 'new' M.D.s; although provisions for an M.D. had existed since 1897, definitive Regulations for the 'new' degree were put out by Faculty on 18th January 1907.[6]

It was not long before the first candidate appeared. She was an M.A. M.B.Ch.B. of St Andrews University. On 6th June, 1907, the Dean, now Professor Marshall, 'presented the reports of Professors Kynoch and Sutherland on the thesis entitled "A classification of the pathological changes affecting the endometrium" offered by Miss Elizabeth H.B. Macdonald for the degree of M.D. Both examiners agreed that the thesis was satisfactory and sufficient'.

On July 5th, 1907, eleven students sat their finals, and one failed. On the same date, the Dean intimated that Miss Elizabeth H.B. Macdonald had completed the clinical examination for the M.D., had complied with the Regulations; Professors Stalker, Kynoch, and Marshall reported that her work was safe and sufficient, and the thesis presented by her having been previously passed, the Dean was empowered 'to ask the Senatus Academicus to confer the degree of Doctor of Medicine on Miss Macdonald'. And so Miss Macdonald having satisfied the examiners 'at a tryal and by a thesis' almost became the twentieth century opposite number of John Arbuthnot of 6th August, 1696.

Others soon followed. On November 5th, 1907, Alexander J.H., Russell, M.B. Ch.B. requested leave to take a special examination for the clinical part of the M.D. at the end of January, or early in February next, before sailing to India to join the Indian Medical Service. On March, 1908, Professors Stalker and Marshall reported that they 'had examined Mr Russell and that they had found his knowledge to entitle him to pass this part of the examination for the degree of M.D.' This set the precedent for many successors, who took the clinical part of the examination soon after qualification, and could then proceed to the thesis at their leisure, possibly many years later.

In July 1908, three more candidates presented themselves. The account reads:

Thesis: W. Arnott Dickson, M.B. Ch.B.
            'Arteriosclerosis in Coal Miners' (examined Professors Stalker
            and Sutherland)
            Robert Malcolm, M.B. Ch.B.
            'Remarks based on a careful study of 120 cases of Influenza'
            (examined Professors Stalker and Marshall)
            Thomas J. Mitchell
            'An investigation into the causes of an epidemic of Typhoid
            Fever in Perthshire during 1906, with clinical notes and treat-
            ment'
Clinicals: Examiners—Professors Stalker, Marshall, Dr. Mackie Whyte
            and McGillivray.
            All candidates passed.

Except for the detail of the theses, the Senate report reads like one from a half
century earlier. The old University had accepted the new examination and had
now recorded it in its traditional examination form. But there was one impoitant
difference. These recent degrees, respectable as they were to public enquiry,
lacked one highly important element the old ones had had: no external examiner
was present for either clinical or thesis. In this respect, they were inferior, and
strict criticism by a destructive external critic would certainly have pointed out
the defect.

In 1910, the Regulations were altered. Candidates who possessed the
degrees of M.B. Ch.B. could now proceed to the special degree of M.D. after
having been engaged for one year in special medical practice or for two years in
general practice. Details of the clinical examination, with at least three medical
cases and written report and commentrary, were given. Election of a special
subject remained. Regulations for the Thesis were specified and would remain
for the next sixty years:

Theses   2 typewritten copies, foolscap size, with 1½ inch internal margin,
         must be lodged with the Dean on or before 30th April.
         Candidates are expected to give precise reference to the literature
         of their subject.
         No thesis will be accepted unless it bears evidence of original
         observation: mere compilations will not be approved.
         The clinical examination and thesis may be taken in different
         years.
         Candidates may submit published papers as additional evidence
         of their ability, but such papers alone will not be accepted in place
         of a thesis.
         The fee will be 10 guineas.

Small changes within the Medical Faculty continued in the years till the First
World War. After some discussion the Governors of Dundee Royal Infirmary
agreed in 1909 that students pay the quite considerable sum of £10 for a
perpetual hospital ticket for their clinical years, or 10 guineas if it were paid in
instalments. In 1909 Professor Kynoch became Dean, the first Clinician to hold
the post. Professor Musgrove joined the Dean and Principal Mackay in a

conference called by Glasgow to frame new Ordinances for medical degrees. Clinicals and practicals in Midwifery and Gynaecology were instituted as part of the final M.B., and a Certificate for each student, that he or she had conducted not less than 20 cases of labour and attended a lying-in hospital for such experience, became required. For graduation, while two of the five years had to be spent at the University of St Andrews, either in the University College or partly there and partly in United College, the remaining years might be spent in any specially recognised University, or under any specially recognised teachers—a little known decision of the Faculty.

Two men who would in due time become greatly revered and important members of staff appeared in these pre-war years. They were Mr Lloyd Turton Price and Professor Percy Theodore Herring. Mr Price was appointed assistant to Professor McEwan at University College in 1906. He was born in Shrewsbury and educated at schools at Oswestry. Inevitably he went to Edinburgh to study Medicine where he won the Lister prize for the best surgical thesis, and the Crichton Research Scholarship. He had graduated in 1901, and taken the Fellowship of the Royal College of Surgeons of Edinburgh in 1905. Between graduating in 1901 and going to Dundee Royal Infirmary he was house surgeon to Sir Harold Stiles in Edinburgh and at the Royal Infirmary, Manchester. He was assistant demonstrator in Anatomy, and later surgical tutor at Edinburgh. So he had done the necessary right things before obtaining this more senior post. He quickly made his mark as an incisive teacher with a barbed wit, and as a skilful practical surgeon.

Professor Herring was very different. Born in Yorkshire in 1872, his family emigrated while he was very young to New Zealand. He went to school in Christchurch and University in Otago, but returned to Edinburgh for his medical degree. He graduated M.B. Ch.B. with First Class Honours in 1896, and his residency was spent in the Royal Infirmary and the Simpson Memorial Hospital. In 1897 he was awarded the Murchison Memorial Scholarship in Clinical Medicine and one year later, the Crichton Research Scholarship in Pathology. During this year he wrote his M.D. thesis on 'A study of the Malpighian Bodies of the Kidneys', and was awarded a Gold Medal. During this year also he formed a friendship, which was to become a life-long one, with Professor Robert Muir of Glasgow. His aptitude for histology continued after he joined Professor Schafer in the Physiology Department in 1899—as Goodsir Memorial Fellow, and he began his important work on the posterior lobe of the pituitary gland. Soon he was a full member of staff, and his outstanding gifts as a teacher became widely known. He was President of the Royal Medical Society of Edinburgh in 1898. Now, in 1908, on the death of Professor Bell Pettigrew, he became Chandos Professor of Physiology in the United College of St Salvator and St Leonard, St Andrews University. He would hold this till his retiral in 1948, and became a dearly remembered teacher to several generations of students. His appointment was a happy one and now 'the Bute' had a Professor who would look forward to a new era there. All the age-long arguments about this Chair were forgotten, as it seemed, overnight.

Very soon the Medical Faculty would share in the quincentenary celebrations

of the University of St Andrews. It is still possible to share the sense of pride and excitement which this produced, in all three Colleges of the University. But the celebrations were not only proud, they were sincere, even poetic.

Alma Mater is indeed difficult to classify. Other Universities may win an easy victory over her in any single contest for superiority ... but what the friends of *Alma Mater* all feel and are all more or less conscious of, is the manifest appeal to all sides of their personality ... the more complex the character of the student the more interest or delight he or she can experience during College days and from their memory. Hence it comes that the best men St Andrews sends out are also her truest lovers.

The essence of romance lies in the wonder of unexpected charm, and this is the secret of *Alma Mater's* spell. You think our University a lonely outpost of learning and you find, on studying its history, that its contact with European thought has been close and intimate in all but a very few years of its life. You think it insignificant in these modern days of great educational developments, and forgotten by the world, and then on its five hundredth birthday you find a pilgrimage from all the habitable globe to its shrines. You think the town a 'grey city' and suddenly a day comes when the shore vibrates with colour waves—blue sky, clear green water, and red-white sand—and the aged stones are warm with light ... and the blue fades from the sea, while the visitors are still ... over the last putting green ... the light fades from the sky, the serious golfer cannot follow his ball after a full drive. The links are deserted, the seabirds and the white mist have it to themselves ... but striding home, through the chilly haar, with scarlet gown pulled closely round him, the student sees, even through the mist that hides material things, the ghosts of a great past, the immanence of a happy present, the shadows of a noble future.[7]

10

The Students

Their beloved University

There were others closely involved in this history—more perhaps than the Professors, more probably than the business men, and certainly more than the Third Party—and these were the students. While the nineteenth century saw the development of easy travel and communications for those going up to St Andrews University, and the emergence of a way of life not so very dissimilar to that of the twentieth, its earlier years were those of students like Duncan Dewar who went up in 1819 and was an undergraduate until 1827.[1] He completed a course of seven years—first in Arts and then Divinity—at a total cost of £101. In King George IV's reign he *walked* from Kenmore, where his parents farmed, to Perth, took the steamer from Perth to Dundee, another ferry to Newport, and then walked the rest of the way to St Andrews. Perhaps the only part of his journey which remains as it was then was the eighteenth hole in the Old Course and the bridge over the Swilcan burn which he crossed on his way into the town. His class fees for Latin and Greek in his first session, to Dr. John Hunter and Dr. Henry Hill respectively, were one-and-a-half guineas each; (157 pence) carriers' charges were three shillings and elevenpence ha'penny for his luggage; his new gown an expensive item at one pound, two shillings, and his Scots English Dictionary one and ninepence. Taking £15 with him, he spent only half this between the beginning of November and the beginning of May. Students then had one Monday off each month, but only three days at Christmas and New Year, and so did not go home for six months. As so often at St Andrews, its small size did not equate with the distinction of its teachers; Professor Hunter was described as the most learned classical scholar in Scotland at the time, and his distinction was to edit a number of Latin authors in a text-book form suitable for higher education.[2] Professor Hill was a brother of Principal Hill and author of a series of essays on ancient Greece. But the Greek student had no separate editions of individual writers—most works of a classical writer were of the whole of his works, and often in quarto or folio.

Dewar apparently bought a new gown when he went up, though then as now a second hand one could be bought much more cheaply. He had to wear his gown only in class, in the College Chapel, and in the Common Schools. These were on the left of the quadrangle, running north from the janitor's house. He also had to wear his gown in University Hall, which was on the ground floor of the library to the east of the entrance door.

Students were classified as Primars, the sons of noblemen, Secondars who were equivalent to Gentleman Commoners at Oxford or Cambridge, and Ternars 'of the Common rank of life'. Primars paid six guineas (£6.30) each for a class, Secondars three, and Ternars a guinea and a half. The Professors exacted no fee but accepted what the student gave. In 1829 a uniform fee of three guineas for all students for each class was instituted, following evidence given to the University Commissioners. Whether by coincidence, the numbers of students fell at once—the average to 1828 was 200, but for the next three years, 138. These small numbers continued for fifty years, and the small numbers were the reason for the so-called 'crisis year' of 1876-77. In fact, however, it was in the 1839-41 period when numbers were lowest, and by 1880 they had increased to 188.[3] From the 1860s, accounts of student affairs began to be published in the Fife press which tell of the day-to-day activities and anticipate the modern era. In St Andrews these tell especially of golf—from 1865, University golf matches against Fife or Perth clubs were regularly reported, and football match reports appeared also. *Gaudeamuses* of student societies next began to be reported. In this decade, when the formal act of graduation became more necessary, there were about 50 ordinary M.A. graduates at St Andrews and 9 Honours in a year; the corresponding figures for Aberdeen were 200 and 16, for Glasgow 97 and 3, and for Edinburgh 141 and 14. Edinburgh and now Glasgow continued to have large numbers of medicals graduating, and these medical faculties were large, active, and flourishing.

In the decade 1885-1895, numbers at St Andrews itself had increased to over 200, and there were now some dozen science students, and a tiny handful of medicals. Divinity students were 30-40. But in University College, Dundee, the number of matriculated students was also very low indeed, the published totals always including evening class and adult students who were not proceeding to graduation. The selected quotation: 'Meiklejohn would tell the Commission that in St Andrews he could lecture to ten: in Dundee, for ten two-hour sessions on Saturdays, to eighty-seven' is mischievous and misleading,[4] as are the innuendoes that St Andrews needed every student it could get. For University College graduates were also tiny in numbers—this point was made strongly by Dr. Metcalf and his compatriots in their arguments against the affiliation of Dundee, and Principal Peterson himself, in his written evidence to the House of Lords in February of 1895, while listing the total numbers of science students taking classes as ranging between 10 and 89 said that in the eleven years to 1895, only 19 graduated. (Principal Peterson said also that in 1893 his own class on the History of First Century Rome was attended by 5 ladies and gentlemen, and even wrote to the *Advertiser* on 28th January that year complaining of how he spent hour after hour with tutorial classes in Greek and Latin 'in which the class numbered only 1 or 2'; popular lectures in Dundee too, he said, were not successful. In a leader, the paper commented: 'there is indeed a danger that we are over-lectured ... very regrettable that so few attend instruction on great subjects'.) The Anatomy class had decreased from 16 in 1891-2 to 7 in 1894-5, and in Physiology the numbers had only once reached double figures. So far as University College was concerned, even medical student numbers were small

until the end of the century and beyond, and this in spite of the huge publicity given locally to the prospects for the Conjoint Medical School. For St Salvator's College, it would not be until the early years of the twentieth century that pre-clinical medical students would appear consistently at all—not, in fact, until the missing Anatomy class became established—and in succeeding years their numbers would equal and overtake those in University College.

The background to any consideration of medical students, then, was one of very small numbers of matriculated undergraduates. So individual personal accounts are few in number. Happily, those available provide the very best antidote to the official records and public reports, and show both individual staff members and their departments in a different light from the formal accounts in annual College reports or in the statutory retiral or laudatory obituary minutes.

St Andrews in the last decade of the nineteenth century was not very different from the University her students in the recent past have known so well. The 200 students 'lived in one family' and most lived in town lodgings. The undergraduate publications were a 'terror to evil-doers' and often produced the cleverest of skits on members of staff. One in the 1880s was so sharp that the Senate tried hard, but without success, to find the writer. According to J.R. Strachan, whose account of student life then appeared in Blairgowrie in July 1924, this was the later editor of the Oxford English Dictionary Dr. Craigie. Craigie was one of a few students who visited Dundee regularly by train. In this decade, too, the wearing of gowns in Chapel was re-instituted, following the initiatives of Professor McIntosh. He said often that Universities were for students and not for the ambitions of Professors, and was a popular figure both in the College and in his University Volunteer and gymnastic club activities. Professor Scott Lang, so often depicted as the narrow antagonist of the just claims of Dundee, and so often appearing bigoted in the Senate and Court, was another 'students' friend'—private accounts from members of the Battery, of his class, and of those who knew him only as the staunch supporter of 'Dines'— agree about his popularity. Professor Purdie was another well-loved Professor, but Professor Crombie, who opposed affiliation with University College Dundee and queried the development of science and medicine in St Andrews, was known as much for his sarcasm as for his Biblical Scholarship. And Professor Pettigrew—was it *really* true that he was 'the real discoverer of the aeroplane' as students said?—whose invention only failed because it could not develop the power to lift off—was regarded as a rather quaint old man. His 'Design in Nature'—though hardly a 'Growth and Form'—had impressed Rev. J.R. Strachan enough that he recalled its interest many years later. And finally, Principal Tulloch was remembered with the respect and affection reserved by the student body for *very* few—'Queen Victoria' it was said 'once declared that Tulloch was the noblest form of a man she had ever beheld'.[5]

This was the part of the University comprising the United and St Mary's Colleges, but the Dundee side could not be better accounted for than by the recollections of Elizabeth Macdonald, who was born in Dundee in 1880 and whose story fills the student years from 1896 to 1905. Elizabeth Macdonald's autobio-

graphy is particularly fascinating for its account of a Dundee schoolgirl's travel to
St Andrews University, there to take first her M.A. and later her M.B., Ch.B., and
of her complete surrender to the University which she regarded as a whole in the
same way that so many, many medical students who followed the same path
subsequently did over the next sixty years. A 'lass o' pairts', she came from a
rather poor family in Dundee, the fourth of nine children, and by no means the
only intelligent member of the family—her younger brother and sister were also
St Andrews graduates. She educated herself by bursaries—first school ones,
then university ones. It was she who spoke of 'The Beloved University'.[6]

Her account turns so much of what the three parties said on its head. For
her, there was no 'them and us'—

> University College Dundee, was opened in 1883, and by the building
> of the new Tay Bridge, the ancient University of St Andrews had been
> brought within an hour's distance by train from Dundee. Everything
> was conspiring to bring the University to our very doors. As a
> schoolgirl and aspiring student, this was how it appeared to me ... as
> early as 1877, the year in which the fighting medical women were
> admitted to the Royal Free Hospital in London, the University of St
> Andrews devised a scheme for granting an Arts Degree to women
> who, though not admitted as students, were allowed to sit the M.A.
> examinations; those who reached the required standards were given a
> new degree of L.L.A., signifying Lady Literate of Arts ... the next
> significant year for women was 1883, when Sir William Taylor-
> Thomson K.C.M.G., C.B., left "the residue of his estate to the
> University of St Andrews as a fund for the purpose of founding
> Bursaries *for students of both sexes in equal numbers,* and *in the case
> of females to assist them in qualifying for the medical profession*"

... she saw St Andrews as coming to Dundee, and not the reverse, and saw St
Andrews as having a liberal and indeed revolutionary attitude to the acceptance
of women undergraduates: in fact, the very reverse of an ancient and morose
institution, suspicious of change and quick to demand subservience. For her, Sir
James Donaldson was 'the wise Principal'.

She described arriving in October 1896 and gazing in wonder at a group of
women pointed out to her as

> M.A.s—the first women graduates of this almost five-hundred-year-
> old University. One of these was Janet Philip, already known to me as
> a member of a remarkably clever Dundee family: she married almost
> immediately after graduating, and by a late second marriage became
> Lady Beveridge ... Twenty-three women "came up" in my year,
> among them being a number of English girls of whom two ... were
> daughters of the then Poet Laureate ... England had indeed been
> quick to recognise the unequalled attractions of St Andrews as a
> residential University centre for women.[7]

While the majority of the women students lived, as did the men, in 'bunks',
(University Hall being too expensive for most) a number of Dundee dwellers
travelled daily by train. For her, there was nothing shameful or politically

undesirable about this, or disloyal to the city of her birth; this was the way she got to her beloved University.

My advent as a "travelling" student had been a joyful experience. I was young, unsophisticated, and poor—ignorant also of the plans for the care and accommodation of women students. My clothes were of the simplest, home-made, but Academic dress was compulsory and would cover all deficiencies and hide any inequalities. At the University we were all students and all equal, and when I put on my Red Gown I was "drunk" with joy—St Andrews "belonged" to me!

The 'equality' was one of her deepest memories. She was aware of the 'rich'—especially the 'rich English girls' who could afford the fees for residence in University Hall—but bore them no ill-will. For she noticed . . . 'residence has never been compulsory in St Andrews. Neither has there been, in this ancient University, any separation of the sexes in classes or lecture halls—not even in medical classes and Hospital clinics when the new Medical School of St Andrews University came into being in Dundee.' It remained Dr. Macdonald's firm belief that this record was unique in Britain, and certainly accounts of the treatment of aspiring women medical students elsewhere at this time would seem to confirm her feeling.[8] Her years in Arts have all the incidents St Andrews students cannot help but recall—the 'hecklings', the 'gaudeamuses', the Rectorial, (for her the election of Lord Bute was 'exciting'), the 'Capping Days'—when 'Professor Scott Lang, the students' friend, was also their butt'—and seems to have taken it all in the best humour—Meal Monday, formal Balls and other less formal flirtations—she describes a special Ball when she and her friends did not get back to Dundee until the early morning train—since it had not finished until 2 a.m. There was the First Class Honours pass in English, followed by the cruel disappointment of not getting the Scholarship which went with it as this was reserved for a man.

Her years in the Medical Faculty in fact began not in University, but at United College. She took the Botany Class Medal there, and in the winter session of 1900-01 took out her very last class—lectures in Anatomy—there also.

St Andrews—"little city, worn and grey"—why was I so loth to leave you? Andrew Lang found the simple words to express your uncanny charm.

> "St Andrews by the Northern Sea
> It is a haunted town to me".

A haunted town indeed! The very stones speak. Approaching the old College Tower you see cut into the cobbles under your feet the initials P.H.: they mark the spot where the student martyr Patrick Hamilton was burnt at the stake in 1527, and you tread gently as you pass under the arch into the Quadrangle . . . the past is with you as you go to "the rugged pier" . . . and sometimes, when you are young, you go down, on a misty night,

> "to where beside the rugged pier
> The sea sings low"

and the mystery and magic of the eternal sea lays its spell upon you and chastens you. All this, and much more, St Andrews had given me. These memories and emotions, intangible things of the spirit, are what remain for ever, woven into the very texture of thought and feeling.

Her move to University College followed the institution of the Carnegie Trust, and her personal thanks to this as a source of help in the four last years of her medical course are described with heartfelt and sincere thankfulness. Now she was only ten minutes walk from her home to classes. Now she had no more early trains to catch. Here too she felt entirely a St Andrews student—Court, Council, Third Party—all might not have existed for her. She too was overwhelmed by D'Arcy in the Zoology class—which she seems to have taken before her Botany and Anatomy at United College—and remembers him 'at the height of his mature manhood, forty and as yet unmarried. Devastatingly handsome, tall, broad, erect, bearded in the tawny colour of a lion—friendly yet unapproachable—awe-inspiring yet kind—so far above ordinary mortals both physically and mentally that he semed to stoop to communicate...' She remembers how the 'Botany and Zoo labs were such friendly "Common Rooms" in the College that they were frequented by many students other than the few medicals'. She remembers 'Anatomy had also been taught in the College. The early accommodation had been a small basement with a stone floor in an outhouse behind the main building: and the dissecting room—a small room up a narrow stair—had to be seen to be believed'. It was a very different account from those of the First Principal, his Council, and the *Dundee Advertiser* in earlier years. But now the new Anatomy and Physiology Departments were in being in the new buildings—though they were the only ones there, the remainder being unfinished—and Principal Mackay was a teacher this brilliant young girl adored. 'We called him The Chief, and Chief he certainly was. A man of unusual charm, humble, brilliant, with a gentle sense of humour . . . his lectures on the Human Brain enthralled me. I can in memory see and hear him now . . . how he elucidated the staggering complexity, the sheer miracle, of the human brain, so that for ever after I would think of it with reverence and awe!' She tells of how she and her two girl student compatriots would dissect on 'after the Chief had gone' till 'closing-time', sometimes making tea to which they added a penny-worth of milk. They were, as girls, happy because 'quite simply we belonged to the generation born in time for the new Medical School of St Andrews University—a Medical School that never knew what it was NOT to have women in lectures and hospitals'. Professor Waymouth Reid was apparently remembered best for his ability to make candy and fudges, as well as for his 'keen brain and caustic wit'. He had tried unsuccessfully to leave Dundee for a Chair elsewhere.

She progressed in her course. 1904 for her was most important as seeing the opening of the Students' Union in University College, because it gave accommodation for both men and women students within its walls; as seeing the total numbers there, now forty percent of the entire University, and as including the opening of the new Medical School, when she remembered 'the feel of Mrs

Carnegie's Russian sable coat and how its deliciousness cured me for ever of any desire to own one'. She took the Pathology class, in the completed new building, and though Professor Sutherland was 'one of the most delightful of men, friendly, quietly kind, and greatly liked', she did not enjoy his subject, and 'hated her first Post-Mortem'. 'Materia Medica did not appeal much either, although the teaching of the new Professor Marshall was enlightening'. The major clinical subjects were more to her liking, and they had practically individual tuition from the clinical Professors.

The difficulties of teaching must have been considerable before the completion of the new building. One account, published at the same time as the official opening took place, presented a grim picture: 'The dissecting room was a weird place in more senses than one, and from the exterior always struck one as being more like a pigeon loft. Dispensing i.e. Materia Medica used to be taught in a queer old corner room next neighbour to the women students' sitting room, while Professors D'Arcy Thompson and Waymouth Reid could unfold harrowing tales of the hardships and privations suffered by themselves and their students'. The clinical Professors were even worse off: 'Professors McEwan and Stalker had to beg borrow or steal a room if they did not wish to camp out with their class in the corridor!'

By now the class had stabilised into three women and six men—nine students in all. Their day started with a formal lecture in Medicine 'the Professor arriving in a hansom, all leisurely and full of wisdom, reading the morning paper until his cab stopped and woke him to the reality of waiting students'. This was Professor Stalker. After the lecture, the students 'dashed off—up on the rising ground behind the College, through various wynds and lanes and bypaths and an enclosed area of park, to the Infirmary—D.R.I.' This was the path St Andrews medicals would tread for the next half century—up Small's Wynd, over Blackness Road, down Blinshall Street and up towards Dudhope Park (first crossing the Lochee Road with its carts, lorries, and tram cars), up the steep path, to emerge eventually by the bus shelter on Infirmary Brae—and over the road to go in past the stern but friendly head porter at the Infirmary doorway. Miss Macdonald came on the outpatients we all knew, surgical first and medical 'farther into' the Infirmary. Skirts were ground level when she began 'walking the hospital'—she remembered

> one of the next year's group of five (girls) appearing in a skirt at least six inches off the ground, and attracted a great deal of attention especially from the men: we gazed in wonder at her boldness: when she spoke she tossed her head. Soon we were all wearing shortened skirts! With our shortened skirts we wore washable shirt blouses with long sleeves fastened at the wrists with cuff-links. For practical work we wore white surgical coats—we were very smart.

Where did the students of these years come from? They were for the most part local—in 1904 Tom Fyfe from Alloa, David Gillespie from St Andrews, L.M. Moncrieff and Cecil Morrison from Stravithie, Harry Pearson and Albert Rusack from St Andrews, and Thomas Schollay from Strathkinness, passed the 1st M.B. Examination in Botany in United College. G.N. Anderson,

Edinburgh, Elizabeth Morgan, St Andrews, Lily McLean, Broughty Ferry, and Elizabeth Pithie, Ceres, passed the 1st M.B. in Physics. In University College Andrew Cunningham from Dundee, Charles Lilley from Arbroath, Arthur Mills from Tayport, William Munro from Kirkden parish, Ernest Murray from Aberdeen, William Nairn from Dundee, Madelaine Newton from Barnhill and Elizabeth Paisley from Newport passed Botany and Zoology. In March of 1905, Messrs. Cunningham, Mills and Nairn passed Chemistry, as did a Dundee student of whom more would be heard, William John Tulloch. All of them were going to their nearest-to-home sources of University training; there were only two—Fyfe and Murray—from farther afield. Being so few, they would enjoy the almost individual attention of their teachers. The senior years, smaller in numbers still, included an Edinburgh and a Dollar girl, and the single Final Year graduate of this session, A.G. Malcolm, was another Dundonian. At this date there was only one final M.B. but following a suggestion from the students that a 'double' examination be allowed, a December re-sit was agreed by the Senatus. From Elizabeth Macdonald's account, the clinical teaching was an extremely personal affair. This was the feature of St Andrews medicine which continued as long as the Faculty existed and which was such a source of enjoyment to the students over the years. 'Individual teaching from a physician as subtle and unpredictable as our Professor Stalker is something to be remembered' she said. Her experience in the learning of physical diagnosis must be that of all honest medical students: 'Well I remember the day when I first really *heard* through a stethoscope! Day after day I had listened after being told what I should hear, and had nodded my head wisely, but all I had heard was a confused babel of sounds. Then one day I actually *did* hear not only with my ears but with my understanding, and I looked up quickly to be met with a quizzical "Ah! a look of intelligence at last!" ' (Nearly fifty years later, some unkind St Andrews students put cotton wool in the tubes of the class medallist's stethoscope, and unkindly noted how she still nodded wisely when questioned by Professor Adam Patrick.)

Elizabeth Macdonald retells the story about Professor Stalker and the man with the obscure symptoms, of whom he said, when pressed for a diagnosis after a long silence 'Well, a man who's lived in Patagonia for fifteen years might have—ANYTHING!' This story was also told of Dr. Foggie, a physician of later years. Another story about Professor Stalker was of how he would sometimes sit at a patient's bedside in silence while the students gathered round, awaiting his wisdom. After what seemed an interminable period, he got up, and sat by the next patient's bedside, still without saying a word.

Professor McEwan 'was one of the old Surgeons who were doing necessary operations before the days when Asepsis displaced Antisepsis and made things safer. There was still to be seen in the dark recesses of the Surgery department a frock-coat with cuffs stiff with clotted blood—the coat kept for operating in the days before anaesthetics or asepsis had come to the aid of the surgeon and the patient'. She recalled, many years later, her memory of Professor McEwan 'in the operating theatre wandering round with a nurse following him almost on her knees trying to wipe the blood from his boots. By now an elderly man, he was

called 'Old Mac' by his students. 'He was a slow but safe surgeon'.

A young member of the surgical staff who was a popular personality and a popular teacher was Dr. James Gray, the Professor's assistant. He was young, boisterous, happy, full of life and jokes. One day at a post-mortem examination he pricked his finger and developed septicaemia. He appeared to recover, to the great joy of Professor McEwan and the students, but a few weeks later was found dead in bed, supposedly from heart failure.

Surgery at this time continued to include amputations, and abdominal surgery was only in its beginnings. Tuberculosis was the Captain of the Men of Death in Surgery as well as in Medicine, as far as the young were concerned, and because of the frequency of bovine tuberculosis, from infected milk, 'excision of glands of neck' was the commonest children's operation and every operating list had at least one of these cases on it.

Anaesthetics was an important part of the students' training. Elizabeth Macdonald recalls this too. 'Chlorofrom was part of the magic of medicine to me: and I never had any fear of taking or administering it. We were taught most carefully how to give it: the lessons were rigid and serious and skilful: and we were strictly supervised in our administration until we proved our expertness. This extreme care was the price of safety and success'.

Professor J.A.C. Kynoch was known as 'Jack' by his students. He had gynaecology wards, but most of the maternity experience the students gained came from 'the district'. He was a vivid lecturer, humorous, though not always consciously, and his department got the best pass rate of all in the Final Examinations.

What were the examinations like, for these students? The Second and Third Professionals were much as they would be over the next half century—a written examination, a practical, and an oral. Those near the border-line for a pass, or 'up for a merit' got special attention in the practicals and orals. The written examination in the Finals were also to continue unchanged for many years— each major subject had a paper of six questions, of which five only were to be answered. In Medicine, any five could be attempted, in Surgery and Midwifery, there was one compulsory question. These were held in the College.

The clinicals were held at D.R.I. In Medicine, each candidate had a major or 'big' case to examine and write a detailed report on, and for this one hour was allowed. He was not examined orally on this case, and was allotted fifty marks to it. He had next a 'small' case, to be examined in thirty minutes, and on this he was examined orally for fifteen minutes. He also had quarter of an hour's urine testing, and another quarter of an hour's examination of eleven microscopic slides of clinical conditions. These could gain 30, 10, and 10 marks respectively. Surgery followed the same pattern, except that there were two small cases. These were the clinical examinations which the G.M.C. externals had thought insufficient in 1904. An examination on operative surgery and surgical anatomy was practical: a male model was used in the bandaging questions as well as the traditional cadaver. Each candidate had to perform two 'operations'—the first group were ligatures of various arteries—the radial, brachial and femoral, and exposure of the median nerve at the wrist and the sciatic nerve in the leg, and the

second were disarticulation at the wrist, amputations in the lower third of the forearm, middle upper arm, Syme's amputation, left inguinal colotomy, and gastrostomy. Medicine included a section on diseases of the skin, and there was a separate examination on mental disease. Surgery included ophthalmology and ear and throat surgery. Written papers were both 'modern' and 'early century' in the questions set.[9]

While the University was indeed forward-looking in its attitude to woman students, the Royal Infirmary was not, and no recently graduated woman doctor could hold a house doctor's post there. Their inability to continue in hospital after graduation was an obvious disappointment to the girls of the years, but nothing could be done, as the Infirmary Governors had the final say in this as well as in the selection of more senior clinical staff.

The progress was the same into and through the first World War. Prospective medical students, like those for other faculties, camp up in September to sit 'The Bursary Comp'. The range and value of student scholarships at all the three Colleges was excellent, and those who were placed high enough up the bursary list were comfortably off financially, if not exactly rich. But no-one who had already a bursary of £20 annually or more, awarded from his or her school or elsewhere, could be awarded a University one. This rule made the bursaries 'go around' better, and prevented any single student from coming up with an excessively high bursary income. Most prospective students bought their *sine qua non*, their red gown, from Ritchie's shop in South Street, and the women their trenchers with the tassel for each year—blue for a bejantine, red for a semi, yellow for a tertian and thereafter black. In United College, no other mark was worn, but in University College, students often though not always wore the fleur-de-lys of the City of Dundee on the left breast.[10]

The next priority was the bunk. Most of the bunk-wives mothered their students, male or female, as they continued to do until the recent past. A room might cost five or seven shillings weekly, including coal for the fire and cans of hot water for washing. Rents were low because the bunk-wives then as now made their principal income from summer visitors, and were glad to have their rooms occupied by students through the winter. Food charges were about six pence per day for a two-course midday dinner, and this brought the total to well under a pound a week. By contrast, University Hall for Women, the only student residency then in St Andrews, had much higher charges, ranging from 30 shillings to £3 per week. Some of the places in 'Hall' were taken by girls, usually wealthy and English, who had been sent to St Andrews instead of to the Continent to finish their education. And indeed a few of these did not even matriculate, but took only a few lectures in English, History, or French. Their presence provoked some resentment, as they were certainly not *bona fide* students.

Most students arrived by train—'Leuchars Junction. Change for St Andrews' was heard then, and no-one who heard forgot. At St Andrews, they were taken by horse wagon to their bunk, either with their luggage, or without if it had been sent already by train 'in advance'. For students, 'Leuchars Junction' was cold, windy, and wet, but it had for them something about it which adult visitors

never had. It was a release point on their journey from elsewhere to their University.

In this pre-war period, the numbers at University College were starting to fall a little and this applied especially to women Arts students. Principal Mackay, in analysing this trend in his 1910-11 report, attributed part but not all of it to new Regulations. In his 1911-12 report he wrote 'in our shrinking number of medical students I cannot but recognise as one factor our conspicuous inferiority of garden resources to St Andrews'; Professor D'Arcy Thompson also noticed a fall in his Zoology Class from a recent average of 30 students to 'about 6, all of them medical'. In fact, however, the numbers in University College were now about the same as those in St Salvator's. The combined clinical classes were about a dozen in size, with University College students still in a slight preponderance. Total numbers graduating were still tiny—4 in 1905—Elizabeth Macdonald M.A. with her two girl friends Jean Balsillie and Alice Jean Donaldson, and Robert Linton; there were 4 in 1912, and 7 in 1913. In 1912 7 passed the Diploma in Public Health. In 1912, too, when 9 passed the final M.B. Ch.B., two of them were women; an Indian, a Sikh, also passed; Bakhshi Kartar Singh. He was medallist in Obstetrics and Gynaecology. A second graduate from India was Panna Lal Gupta, in December, 1914, and others followed.

Names appeared which would be amongst the best-known of St Andrews clinical teachers: George Ranken Tudhope, who passed his first M.B. in 1911, W.J. Tulloch, who left St Andrews on his appointment as Demonstrator in Bacteriology in Durham in 1911, and Margaret Fairlie, one of 11 graduates in 1915—she had begun in Bute, they in University College. Margaret Shirlaw, who later as Margaret W. Menzies Campbell became a distinguished medical historian in her own right, came up in October 1912. She recalls her first day 'On the Monday morning, the redoubtable Coutts, head janitor and master of works at the United College, known to many generations of professors, lecturers, and students, was true to form and repeated his annual quip when directing the bejants to the Upper Hall that it was always better to be sent up than down (indicating Heaven rather than Hell)! Actually, he considered his purpose in life was to keep everybody in order from the Principal downwards, and did not hestiate to do so, if he considered circumstances warranted his interference'. Margaret Shirlaw remembers

> only five students in St Andrews and very few in Dundee [there were in fact seven on the Dundee side of her year in the last three clinical years]. The reason was Lloyd George's Insurance Act of 1911, which was expected to ruin the medical profession for ever. In 1913, however, the numbers were greater—medical practitioners in the poorer districts were discovering that the Act might prove a blessing in disguise to the profession, because doctors were receiving fees, albeit small, for work which they had previously done free of charge, patients being too poor to pay.[11]

Her student life was really no different from that of Elizabeth Macdonald— she had come from England although a Scot, but this was the only contrast. Her

parents had wanted a Scottish medical education for her as 'the cost was considerably less, and doctors with Scottish degrees were popular everywhere'. For her too there was Raisin Monday, extreme formality of speech between men and women students in classes, Sunday mornings at Chapel followed by the pier walk, and the dances and *Gaudeamuses*. She however did her first two years at 'the Bute' and describes how the women students never failed each forenoon to visit Armit's, the baker next to Henderson's in Church Street (now Fisher and Donaldson) to buy two cream cookies costing a penny each. 'The first winter we attended practical chemistry in the United College at 9.00 a.m. and Anatomy lectures at 10 in the Bute (already 'the Bute' was becoming a mini-college for medicals) Medical Buildings, so we fled down Westburn Lane swallowing cookies and cream as we ran'. Miss Shirlaw's account is different from Miss Macdonald's mainly because she was living in St Andrews and not returning by train nightly to Dundee. And so she paints, and paints so well, the picture of the Women's Union, Mrs Andrew Carnegie's gift, at 79 North Street, with its various rooms and membership costing eight shillings (40p) *per annum*, the active societies—Debating, Celtic, Total Abstinence, Missionary, Musical, Conservative, Liberal, Golf, Rugby and Association football, Hockey and Cricket. 'Her' society was the Town Students' Association for Women, which met every Saturday evening in the Union, or in the gymnasium. Miss Hodge, the physical instructress for women, came to almost all meetings and taught Scottish Country Dancing. The members had dancing amongst themselves and sing-songs mostly from R.F. Murray's *The Scarlet Gown* and the *Scottish Students' Songbook*. There were *Gaudeamuses* too, with men students: 'Every function started with one or more verses of *Gaudeamus igitur,* the women, of course, never singing the fifth verse, and always someone recited Andrew Lang's *Almae Matres*. Other favourites were *Beloved Peeler,* After Many Days, Reflections of a Magistrand, John Brown's Body, There is a Tavern in the Town, Clementine, and Riding down from Bangor, to name only a few'. She remembers also the S.R.C.-run dances, two each term, and 'conducted on truly Victorian lines, with professors' wives acting as very strict chaperones'.

Margaret Shirlaw, like Elizabeth Macdonald, gives her own simple view of arrangements between University and United Colleges—and very different it is too from those of the adults of the previous twenty years. She was well aware of the extremely small size of the enlarged University, but aware too of the remarkable talent of the teachers in spite of this: Taylor in Moral Philosophy, Stout in Logic and W.M. Lindsay and John Burnet in Latin and Greek. 'Strangely there were in some subjects Chairs in both Dundee and St Andrews, in others a Professor in the one and a lecturer in the other. This state of affairs was due to the fact that the College in Dundee was founded in 1881, but not affiliated to St Andrews until 1897, and to conform with the terms of the union, holders of Chairs there, automatically became University Professors and members of the Senate whether or not there was already one in St Andrews'. For her, the union was a natural thing: she saw no harm in duplicate Chairs, and she was seeing the Colleges as naturally forming part of the University, some

offering some subjects, others others. She clearly regarded her clinical classes as being 'St Andrews University classes'; and not 'University College Dundee classes'.

She was much more of a critic of her teachers than Elizabeth Macdonald—who tended to idolise all of them. For Professor Irvine's abilities she had the highest possible regard: 'a marvellously clear and lucid lecturer; if you did not know your subject when it came to the degree examination, the fault could certainly never be laid at his door . . . He was a genius at Chemistry, and the country was very grateful to him for his work on sugars both before and during the First World War . . . Actually, I was almost sorry when he was appointed Principal in 1921, because I thought that Chemistry had lost a great scholar'. Professor Butler was often absent on account of illness, and his cockney lecturer Mr Bagot did most of the teaching. Professor (later Sir) Patrick Geddes held the Botany Chair in Dundee; 'generally speaking he was more interested in town planning in India and Sociology, but did appear for our degree examination, although he spent most of his time in the gardens around the Bute Medical Buildings'. From her account, Professor Geddes saw no difficulty about working in both Colleges. R.A. Robertson was praised: 'if you attended him, you could scarcely fail'. 'The professor of Natural History was W.C. McIntosh, but so little impression did he make that I do not even remember him, because we were mostly with the lecturer, Mr Shann, whom I can still picture'. D'Arcy Thompson she remembered clearly, however: 'such a learned man that he could correspond with Professor Lindsay in Latin; he also winced, and corrected (under his breath) Principal Colquhon Irvine, when he made a mistake in the pronunciation of a Latin word'. In the winter of 1912-13 she attended Professor Musgrove's junior Anatomy lectures, and in the summer of 1913 'started practical Anatomy under Dr. (later Professor in Dundee) Rutherford Dow—his first term!' Finally, she loved, as did so many subsequent students, Professor Herring: 'a most understanding man with a great sense of humour and a marvellous understanding of students . . . he was the only lecturer or Professor from whom I ever had a tutorial class . . . every Wednesday morning in the Summer term'.

She had no problems over her arrival in Dundee, although it was 'a strange town, new lodgings (there being no residence then) and new friends'. She had the same experience of so many of her later fellow-students of finding new friends in the other faculties in University College but also 'of having to become cquainted with senior medical students who had left St Andrews before we started there. One of these was Margaret Fairlie, later to become the first medical woman Professor in Scotland'.

Her comments on the Clinical Medical School were also more critical. Of Professor Marshall's class of Pharmacy she said 'this subject was my *bete noire*, because it seemed to have neither rhyme nor reason, requiring merely a hard swot' . . . she remembers dashing up the hill immediately after for clinical surgery at 10.15 after Professor Marshall's class and dashing down by 1 p.m. after a 'two-course dinner en route at Draffen and Jarvie in the Nethergate, then the finest draper in Dundee, which cost 9d.' Segregation in the Union she found

silly, especially since men and women students met equally in class. Professor David McEwan she remembers as 'elderly' and she had no recollection of ever seeing him operate. His lecture was at 1 p.m. and was followed by Pathology: 'Professor Sutherland was reputed to spend his time drinking tea. He was not a stimulating lecturer—in fact, I wrote to my parents that he would have been a very nice kindly grandfather'! The class on fractures was held by Mr Anderson and his class over-ran its time so often that Miss Shirlaw eventually borrowed her landlady's alarm clock and set it outside the door to ring just after 5 p.m. 'to the amusement of Mr Anderson and the horror of the senior students, who always repeated the class in their final year'. These students explained that if the surgeon who would normally have been taking this class had not been absent on war service, she would never have dared to set the alarm as she had done. This was Mr Lloyd Turton Price, whom she did meet sooner than expected as he was invalided home after Christmas 1914 following a mastoid operation. She freely admitted being scared of him and of his sarcasm, and regretted the exit of Mr Anderson, but acknowledged Mr Price's skill as an operator, and that 'those who liked him just worshipped him'. She preferred Mr David Greig who was also a very good operator and the neatest bandager she ever saw in her long life. 'He was a keen researcher but war conditions prevented him from making full use of his investigations'. David Greig was undoubtedly a keen student of research, greatly interested in congenital malformations and surgical Anatomy and Pathology. Professors Stalker and Kynoch too she found good lecturers, especially Professor Stalker 'who could pack more into forty minutes than many of the others in an hour or more'.

The First World War produced an immediate shortage of doctors, and so the women students found themselves doing a good deal more practical work in the wards than they would have done in normal circumstances. Margaret Shirlaw's account of these includes all the sorts of story which have entered the lore of medical student life—the frightening poverty and masses of fleas on the midwifery 'district', the teetotaller physician (here Dr Mackie Whyte) who would not allow any brandy on his wards, but whose lobar pneumonia patients were tided over their crisis by brandy borrowed secretly from the Professor's wards; the popular lecturer who allowed the undergraduates to do smaller operations (here 'Bobby' Mathers), and, for her, the Medical Society. Being more senior and less shy, she took a greater part in student activities in University College than she had in St Salvator's. Even while a student she had an interest in medical history, and she became co-editor of the student magazine in 1916. That Autumn, she became the first President of the St Andrews University Medical Society, and its first lecture was given by Professor Stalker.

In United College, the Bute Medical Society was formed the previous year, in 1915, and had she been founder of this, too, she would have been a unique figure. But the founders of the 'Bute' were bejantines and bejants of 1914—Miss Mildred Clark, Calum McCrimmon, Clive Mackie Whyte, Cecily Thistlewaite, Mary Ellison: another was W.G Robertson. Though its numbers were small it flourished from the start—its aim to provide lectures on clinical subjects to those

otherwise isolated pre-clinical medical students becoming of even greater importance later in the century. Its early records were lost, and the names of the founders were only re-discovered when Mary Whitfield, the president in 1947-48, in her attempts to preserve a history which she knew would otherwise be lost, found a St Andrews graduate who supplied the missing information— Peter Robertson.

Peter Caw Robertson came up in 1916. His clear recollections of the University just before, during, and again after the Great War, and his subsequent friendship with a later Professor of Medicine in the Second Wolrd War, make him the next in the series of students whose accounts must be included in any history of medicine in St Andrews. A native of Cupar, he was a much better than average student academically. In contrast to the ladies he was a first-class athlete—a triple blue—captain of hockey and cricket, and one who when he returned from his brief military service just missed international honours in hockey. His sporting prowess made him close friends outwith medicine—one was J.H. Williams, also a member of the cricket team, who became lecturer and subsequently Professor of History. When in Dundee he had a degree examination on a day when he should have run against Eric Liddle, and although he was rushed over to Fife by car along with a half-miler and fellow member of the team, Cohen, was too late for the sprint.

He recalls being taken by his older brother, W.G. Robertson, to the University sports day in the summer of 1914, before the outbreak of war, and seeing Principal Donaldson, now an elderly man in his eighties, surrounded by enthusiastic students clearly very fond of him. He began his career in United College, where he first took a B.Sc. including medical subjects—Zoology, Physiology and Anatomy. By the time he had come up John Herkless was Principal, but seemed a remote figure to Peter Robertson as indeed he seems to have been to most students. Professor McIntosh was by now so far past his best that his assistant Mr Collinge tried very hard to get him retired—he eventually persuaded the science and medical students to sign a round robin stating that he was ineffectual, and Peter Robertson felt it was this request from the students which finally led him to resign. By contrast he remembers particularly the kindness and decision of Professor J.C. Irvine the Dean in making it possible for him not to have to sit his Physics degree examination—he had gone to ask Professor Irvine's advice, as the Physics Professor Butler was again very elderly and indecisive—as his class marks had been good enough to merit a degree pass. He had been told to report to Perth for call-up on the day of the degree examination.

In his B.Sc. class there were three who intended to proceed with medicine and no pure science students. The others were James Webster, a Dundee High School former pupil who in later years succeeded Sir Bernard Spilsbury as Home Office Pathologist, and Gordon Dacomb (Tubby) Laing, a heavy-weight boxer and rugby player, who went to South Africa as a medical officer of health and whose son returned to St Andrews medicine after the Second World War. Gordon Laing later married Jean, one of the daughters of Dr. R.C. Buist the obstetrician at Dundee Royal.

Peter Robertson, like the lady students, grew to love St Andrews as they did. He told of the happy start and excitement of his first years just as Elizabeth Macdonald and Margaret Shirlaw did. A 'bunk' student like all the men, he recalled how students would whistle the first bars of the *Gaudeamus* at the door or window of another, as a sort of pass-word. This he found he could not do when he moved to University College after the War, at least not at first, and he expressed the feeling many students from the United College undoubtedly had, when they crossed the river, that the University College students living at home had missed a part of university life they had enjoyed. But once friendships were made, and tales were told of the other professors by students from both Colleges, an over-riding companionship prevailed. Dr. Peter Robertson M.D. is the best of student bridges between the First War and the changed world after it, and will be heard from several times in the future.[12]

11

The First World War and Its Aftermath

Principal Sir John Herkless

In the year after the five hundredth anniversary of the founding of the University, the British Association for the Advancement of Science held its annual meeting in Dundee. Much of the pressure to have Dundee as the host city had come from Professor D'Arcy Thompson. There was great and justifiable civic pride expressed; the local handbook believed that an earlier meeting of the British Association, in 1867, had led to an increase of industry and activity, and looked forward to the population following this 1912 meeting increasing to something like two hundred and seventy thousand by 1942 from yet more industrial expansions. With this population would grow a steady expansion of the city boundaries, and of its influence and wealth. Its development as a health resort was also anticipated:

> the bracing air of Broughty Ferry, with its open face to the North sea,
> the superior facilities for recreation—especially in golf—provided on
> the links and sand-dunes of Monifieth, combined as they then will be
> with the high standards of City public services, must increasingly
> attract visitors, and mark out suburban Dundee as likely to prove the
> most attractive summer watering-place on the east coast of Scotland.

Dundee as a higher educational centre was described in two articles, a long one about the University of St Andrews by Professor McIntosh, noting in the most friendly terms the affiliation of University College and the 'formation of the Conjoint Medical School, for which the populous City of Dundee, with its large Infirmary, is well adapted', and a shorter one by Professor Mackay. This noted the Deed of Endowment and Trust, the management function of the Council:

> it directs and controls the expenditure of the finances, and exercises its
> authority over all the Departments of the College save those
> belonging to the later years of the School of Medicine; these are
> supported by funds coming through the University Court from a
> Government Grant, and although they are part of the College, they
> are retained by the Court under its own management.

His article also traced the development of St Andrews over the centuries, described University College as an 'adopted daughter of the University', and praised its progress . . .

> but it is not to be forgotten that success could not have come so
> quickly or in the same measure had it not been for the co-operation of

191

the University of St Andrews. The gift of University status has been all-important. The gratitude of the City is due to those academic statesmen at St Andrews through whose wisdom and foresight the idea of union was approved and under whose labours the scheme was matured and accomplished.

One of the Principal's greatest virtues was his support of the idea of the enlarged University[1]

With this happy background, it is a little surprising that the medical student numbers continued to be so small—as did those in the science faculty—in the newest College. In 1910 there were three students in Anatomy at University and four at United College, and five and three respectively in Physiology, and this equal distribution continued into the war years. There was still some money available for extra staff; in May an assistantship in Regional Anatomy to Professor Musgrove was approved—'to live in St Andrews' and an equivalent to Principal Mackay—'to live in Dundee'. There continued to be some difficulties with the Infirmary governors, who liked to maintain their authority; in 1911 the students asked the Board of Studies of the Faculty that priority be given to St Andrews students applying for clerkships at Dundee Royal Infirmary. The Dean had to write formally with this request, and received the reply that 'The Governors agreed, *provided application was made early*'. Because of Infirmary rules Professor MacEwan had to retire from active clinical practice that year, and it was agreed that Mr Greig, Mr Don, and Mr Price act as teaching surgeons to the hospital. But this arrangement where the Professor continued to lecture at the University, and the staff surgeons at the Infirmary taught to rotation, produced difficulties. In 1912 two senior women students, Miss Adeline Campbell and Miss Annie Mitchell, wrote to the Dean complaining about the teaching of clinical surgery. The Faculty meeting called to discuss this complaint was one of the very few Professor D'Arcy Thompson attended. Various motions were put, but finally it was his which was accepted. This placed groups of senior students in their final year in the wards of one of the senior surgeons, and it is interesting that this probably led to the 'intensive' attachments which persisted until quite recently where final year students spent a whole term doing one of the principal final M.B. subjects on one unit, but junior ones rotated in groups between various clinical units.

In 1914 the Faculty agreed that all theses for the M.D. without the candidate taking a clinical examination should be submitted to an additional examiner under regulations similar to those for the D.Sc. This involved the return of external examiners in the M.D. examination—but only for theses. Also, to bring St Andrews into line with the other Scottish Universities, a thesis could be awarded a gold medal or commendation if thought good enough (In June 1915 Dr. W.J. Tulloch's M.D. thesis 'The Mechanism of Coagulation' was awarded commendation, just when he was appointed lecturer in Bacteriology and assistant to the Professor of Pathology).

The outbreak of war in August 1914 immediately produced staff shortage when younger staff members were mobilised. On the 8th of October, 1914, as Dr. J. Mackie Whyte was on service, his assistant Dr. Kerr had to take his junior

students in medicine, Professor Stalker to take his senior, and Professor Marshall to share teaching with Professor Stalker. Professor Stalker was also to take over the medical children's department while Dr. J.S.Y. Rogers was away, and Professor Marshall the skin department while Dr. Foggie was on service. And although the small numbers of students did not mean that the teaching load was onerous, the increased clinical load certainly was. While the clinicians were able to cover the vacancies from their own resources, the Pathology Department was less fortunate. Professor Sutherland found it impossible to get an assistant from local graduates, and had to advertise the vacancy in his department in the press.

As far as students were immediately concerned, the changes the war brought are described in general in the History of the Officers Training Corps.[2] In particular, every effort was made to bring forward examinations for a student to sit before call-up, and many others besides Peter Robertson benefitted from this arrangement. Failure in undergraduate examination meant, then as later in the Second War, immediate liability for call-up.

The most important event of 1915, as far as St Andrews University was concerned, was however the death of Sir James Donaldson on March 9th. He was by now an old man of eighty-four years, and from his middle age had guided the University through one of the most difficult periods in its long history. He had had the eye to see farther than most of his contemporaries, and had seen the unsatisfactory nature of the relationship of the new college of the enlarged University with the old colleges. He had resisted the threatened disruption, and by his service in the Dundee College Council had kept alive the friendship and contacts he had established there, so that his presence remained a stabilising influence for those on both sides of the River Tay who wished for co-operation. Only the most extreme statements of the Third Party provoked him to reply, and in this he was wiser than some older professional colleagues. Mrs Christian Tudhope recalls being told by her father of Principal Donaldson being happy to speak, even on formal occasions, in the Doric, and this seems to have been one of many endearing qualities about him which contemporaries remembered.[3] But he had become so infirm that his capacity as a Chairman and his effectiveness as a Principal were now seriously lacking, and this was perhaps why tributes to him were somehow rather muted. His death was intimated shortly at the College Council meeting on March 10th in Dundee, and almost as shortly in the Senate Meeting the same day in St Andrews. The St Andrews minute also outlined the funeral arrangements, and reported that his library of books were bequeathed to the University.

His successor was appointed very quickly indeed, and on 14th April, 1915 simultaneous meetings were held in United College and at the University College Council announcing the appointment of the Very Reverend John Herkless, Professor of Church History in St Mary's College, as Principal and Vice-Chancellor of the University. John Herkless had been born on 9th August, 1855 in Glasgow. He had never graduated M.A. as in spite of his academic gifts he had not passed the examination in mathematics. Appointed Professor of Ecclesiastical History at St Mary's in 1894, he was made a D.D. of Glasgow

University in 1898. In Senate and Court he had shown considerable administrative ability, and a political achievement had been to be elected Provost of St Andrews from 1911 till 1913.

Said the College Council, in a combined minute of valediction and welcome: (they) 'resolved to put on record their sense of great loss . . . at . . . the great ability of Sir James Donaldson, his literary gifts and his zeal in the whole fields of educational matters . . . his kindly interest in the students endeared him to them all'. There was no mention of his efforts to maintain the union during the troubles of the 1890's, nor indeed of his very real earlier good service on the first College Council. The next paragraph welcomed the new Principal with considerable warmth:

> The Council of University College Dundee very heartily congratulate
> Principal Herkless on his appointment to the high office of Principal
> of the University of St Andrews . . . The Council know well the great
> love of Principal Herkless for the University . . . confidently look
> forward to an extension under his supervision of the usefulness of the
> University, and an enhancement of its name as an educational force in
> Scotland.

This was on 14th May. It was not until June 5th that a formal resolution came from the Senate. This did speak of the growth of the University during Principal Donaldson's twenty-nine years as Principal, the University Act of 1889, the addition to the University staff of U.C.D., the admission of women students, the foundation of the Carnegie Trust, and, like their business friends in Dundee, stressed his unfailing sympathy with the young.

Just after this, what could be called a 'flash-back' occurred. On June 17th the College Council wrote to Principal Peterson of McGill University congratulating him on his Knighthood, his Knight Commander of St Michael and St George— the diplomat's decoration. In a very formal, almost stiffly formal note, 'many pleasant memories were evoked by this signal honour to one who did so much in past days for University College', and Dr. Sinclair, seconding the congratulatory motion by Sir George Baxter, 'reminded the meeting that (he) had seen the College through much stress and trial, and had acted in no spirit of rivalry or narrowness but maintained a wide, comprehensive, and liberal outlook on the Educational rights and requirements of the district'.

The distinction was briefly noted on the St Andrews side also. The minutes then reverted to their usual succession of incidents and interests. The College Council continued its consideration of College accounts: cleaning, indemnity for loss of income due to the War, appointment of gymnasium instructor, and so on. On October 13th, 1915, Principal Herkless took his seat as Principal in the College Council for the first time. 'All in St Andrews', he said, 'regarded the Dundee College as a valued part of the University of St Andrews which they were desirous should be recognised by the University in every way so that they might all work together for the welfare of our ancient University'.

Although external events were constantly presenting themselves throughout the war period, internal ones which affected teaching within the Medical Faculty came to be not unimportant. Through the war almost the whole range

of teaching departments were established—those added being anaesthetics, bacteriology, clinical pathology and radiology. And in the war some fundamental research of national importance was done by Professor J.C. Irvine, Professor of Chemistry in United College, and Dean of the Faculty of Science, and by Professor P.T. Herring, Chandos Professor of Physiology in the Bute. Professor Irvine's application of the 'silver oxide reaction', discovered before the war by W. Pitkeathly, a St Andrews graduate and member of Professor Purdie's staff, to the isolation and later constitution of disaccharides and other compound carbohydrates, made him one of the greatest organic chemists in the world. He was probably, at this time, as great a chemist as D'Arcy Thompson was a biologist, and at this date the United College School could safely be bracketed with that of Emil Fischer of Berlin. The war application of the work was in the production of bacteriological sugars and related substances required by the Allies for military purposes. Novocaine, a local anaesthetic drug which could be used instead of cocaine, was also produced at St Andrews, and the chemistry laboratories of United College were transformed into what was practically a research factory. Teams of chemists worked in shifts, by day and night. The contribution of St Andrews was out of all proportion to its size and financial resources. Professor Herring's contribution was his work on the properties and effects of war gases, particularly mustard gas. It therefore came later in the war. Though more limited, it too was out of all proportion to the small department it was carried out in. Professor Herring's arms were permanently scarred by the experiments he courageously carried out on himself.[4]

The third staff member who made a noteworthy contribution was Dr. W.J. Tulloch, the Bacteriology lecturer. On joining the RAMC, he had gone first to the Royal Army Medical College at Millbank. At this early part of the War, the two main problems for Army Health were the incidence of tetanus in wounds in the field, and outbreaks of meningococcal meningitis amongst recruits in barracks. Tulloch's work on tetanus and later on meningitis earned him membership of the special wound infection team, mention in despatches, and the award of the military O.B.E. His work on tetanus was applied to handling of the wounded; he himself later thought it his chief contribution to medical science.[5] At the end of the War, he was commended especially by Sir David Bruce himself.

On the St Andrews side of the Faculty, Professor Musgrove was succeeded on his retiral in 1914 by David Waterson. Waterson had Dundee connections, his father having been a Free Church minister in the town for many years. Though born in Glasgow he was at school in Dundee before going to Edinburgh. There he graduated M.A. before doing Medicine, and after graduating M.B. Ch.B. he studied in Europe, Canada, and the U.S.A. He returned to Edinburgh as Anatomy demonstrator in 1897, and since 1909 had been Professor of Anatomy in London University. While there he was Dean of the Faculty of Science (Medical) in King's College. He was therefore the first Professor in the Faculty of Medicine to leave a previous Chair on his appointment to St Andrews University. That he was prepared to leave a London Chair to return to Scotland may have been partly due to his Scottish background and his

enthusiasm for golf, but there was enough prestige attached to a medical post in St Andrews to give it academic attraction also. Here he would remain for twenty-eight years, and here he would become a notable anatomist and anthropologist—he would be one to deny the authenticity of the Piltdown skull against claims of many more famous colleagues including Sir Arthur Keith and subsequently be proved correct in his doubts. As a later traveller he would be excelled by no-one, and his prehistoric studies would take him from the Pacific and Australasia to Africa, the Mediterranean, and the Americas. He was undoubtedly a Professor many Universities would have been happy to appoint.

Criticism by External Bodies, and the changes made in the much more senior Scottish Universities' Medical Faculties, produced certain administrative and examination procedural improvements at St Andrews. The whole of the Final Examination regulations were re-issued in May, 1915. The Internal Examiner had to be present when the papers were given out. The whole examination was to be conducted by the Examiners jointly. Written, clinical, and oral examination, and the Operative Surgery practical, were to be marked out of 100. Any candidate who failed to get 50% in total in the three major final subjects would fail, and any candidate who failed the written and clinical would not proceed further to the oral. The clinical pass mark was raised to 60%, the specialist subjects of 'Eyes, ENT, Skins and Psychiatry' were to be marked each out of 25. Mark sheets when signed were to be sent immediately to the Dean and then by him to the Meeting of Examiners. Finally, to graduate with Honours, a student had to score 75% in his second, third and fourth Professional Examinations.

As the War continued and more doctors were clearly going to be required, the numbers of students, and especially of women students, started to increase. In June 1915, eleven passed, including Miss Fairlie. Her Midwifery marks for paper, clinical, and oral were 60, 75, and 70%. The Second Final examination was held in October; three passed and one failed. The records show differences between numbers at various stages in the curriculum which are confusing until it is remembered that they mirrored the variable Government policies towards medical students—first increasing, then decreasing the numbers allowed to enter, sometimes ordering students to continue their course, sometimes ordering them to leave for service after one or two years.

An event in 1916 was the foundation of the kindred School of Dentistry. This followed the initiative of a Dundee family of dentists, Walter Campbell and his sons William Graham and Henry Gordon Campbell. The Dundee Dental Hospital had been opened in 1914, and the next logical step was to begin teaching there. Regulations for the new School were put before the Faculty of Medicine on 25th January, 1916, and passed on to Senate. On 2nd February, at the next Faculty meeting, Dr. Graham Campbell was invited to attend to speak to the requirements for the new licentiate in Dental Surgery (L.D.S.) Degree. The first Degree Examinations were held in 1917. In that year too, Mr W.R. Tattersall, later to become a distinguished President of the British Dental Association, asked leave from the Faculty of Medicine to qualify as a dental

surgeon, which he did in 1918. This new Dental School, like the Medical School, was the responsibility of the University Court and not the University College Council. There were therefore now two Schools of the University physically situated in Dundee with no constitutional relationship to United College or to University College, but nevertheless parts of the University of St Andrews.

The Principal was knighted in the New Year of 1917, and a warm letter once again went to him from the College Council on January 10th. Professor Purdie died that month also. On February 14th, Sir John spoke at the Standing Joint Committee of the Court and Dundee Council to a proposal from the University to establish a hostel or home for women students attending the Medical School. The University Grants Committee supported the proposal, he said, and women students who had lived in University Hall had said they would like somewhere similar in Dundee. The way he went about this proposal brought out again the unsatisfactory nature of the position of University College Dundee and its Council—part of the University yet holding its separate status. Because the University Court was prevented from applying in Dundee to such a purpose any money or funds within its control, he said he was having to make a strong representation to the College Council in the hope his scheme would be taken up in Dundee. The Science Dean, Professor Irvine, submitted the statistics and expenses of University Hall, and said, applying these to Dundee, that it was likely such a hostel would have a reasonable expectation of success. If opened in Dundee soon, it could begin with about ten first year students, increasing yearly until by the fourth year there would be about fifty. In the first year, the residence could be run by a cook housekeeper with a lady assistant as interim matron giving free service; after two or three years a larger permanent staff would be required. He warned that during the first year the hostel would have to face a financial deficit as the charge to the individual students could not exceed thrity-six pounds *per annum* or thereby.

The full Council agreed to support the project, and the business men arranged that a statement with costs be circulated. As always, delays and further enquiries raised the sums involved,—the furniture estimate for example rising from five to seven hundred pounds, and by May the letter to prospective donors had still not been sent out. On May 17th, Sir George Baxter and Principal Mackay reported that Lord Camperdown, the Council President 'did not approve' of the letter to be signed by him about the women students' hostel, and so other arrangements had to be made. Each member of the Council was asked to select a number of likely donors and speak to them personally. By mid-June No. 1 Airlie Place had appeared as a suitable place for the new residence— it was the house owned by Dr. Moon, a former surgeon at the Infirmary, who had recently died. Promised donations totalled £1515. Dr. Moon's trustees refused to consider a possible lease of the property, but were prepared to accept an offer to purchase. Principal Mackay had the good idea of circulating a letter asking for financial help to open the hostel to those likely to be interested in Perth, Forfar, Montrose, Brechin, and Blairgowrie, as these towns were the source of medical students outwith the city. Negotiations with Mrs Moon and the trustees concluded in August, when No. 1 Airlie Place was bought for

£2528-10-3, and preparations began for opening at the beginning of the session in October. The Council agreed to apply to the Carnegie Trust *via* the University to make up the difference, and this was later done. On August 8th Mrs Watt, the new Warden, attended the Finance Committee meeting which settled details—and a saving of one hundred pounds was possible on the cost of furnishings. This, the first University residence in University College, was another advance in the growing Dundee side of the enlarged University.

So 1917 continued. In October George Ranken Tudhope, the President of the Union in University College, wrote to the Council asking help to clear a financial deficit of twenty six pounds. Eighteen pounds was voted. As Professor McIntosh had resigned, his Chair became vacant, and Professor D'Arcy Thompson applied and was appointed. The Council sent him a laudatory letter in October. His large work *On Growth and Form* had been printed that summer, and made a great impression from the start. As his biographer said 'This, his greatest work, shows him for what he was, a scholar-naturalist; and under scholar one must group together the classicist, the mathematician, the philosopher, and the poet ... for D'Arcy's knowledge of the classics, his wide general reading, and his style, influenced by his love of Bunyan and the Bible, were a revelation to other biologists'[6]. Of his move to St Andrews, 'there were many advantages—St Leonard's School nearby for the children, the University library at hand, and the social life both within and without the University circle was totally different from anything he had known in Dundee'[7]. As his biographer says, he had become frustrated by the lack of opportunity to use his great gifts in the narrow circle in which he had been working; he felt isolated in Dundee. And so he moved naturally to St Andrews where he could meet and talk to the men there of European standing in their several fields.

Medical teaching was described as satisfactory throughout 1917, except for Anaesthetics. Dr. Mills had been called up, and an attempt to get him demobilised was unsuccessful. In March 1918 Dr. Templeman the Forensic Medicne lecturer died, and his work was carried on by other staff members. In the early part of 1918 arrangements were made to allow medical students to fulfil their Officer Training Corps commitments which would be repeated twenty-five years later—the Faculty allowed classes for students aged under eighteen to be arranged so that they could complete their eight hours' commitment in each week. Five of these hours were done after four o'clock each weekday, followed by three hours every Saturday. Because second and subsequent year students were once again being allowed to continue their studies, they were advised to give only a minimum of their time to military training.

Numbers graduating remained very small. In December 1915, the third Final Examination that year, eight passed Medicine and two failed, five Surgery with four failures. Nine passed Midwifery. In June 1916, a total of eight passed the Final Examination, and four passed a special Final that October. The first Licentiate in Dental Surgery Examinations appeared in 1917—one passed the First Professional, four the Second. In June 1918, eight again passed the Final M.B. But in this year, the numbers coming into medicine increased considerably—for example, twenty sat the First Professional in Zoology and fifteen passed,

and in the summer of 1918, there were forty in the Physiology class. The number of women students increased greatly. 'Distinction' passes were introduced for Second and Third Professional Examinations in these years.

On the 13th of November 1918, the full Council of University College met, when an apology for absence from W.L.S. Churchill was recorded. Remarkably, there was no mention of the end of the War! Very quickly arrangements were made to accommodate the men returning from service with the forces. On December 5th, Dr. Norman Walker, the Commissioner of Medical Service for Scotland, came to Dundee to discuss demobilisation of both teaching staff and prospective students still serving. He was given a list of the former, with the request that they be released soon. Later, agreement was reached on what relaxations the Senatus might allow in regard to the duration of courses. Dr. Peter Robertson remembers this, though he did not return till the next year. Arts students, he said, had a good deal more leeway allowed them than medicals did; this was largely because the G.M.C. insisted that regulations for the training of doctors must not be relaxed.

In early 1919, the Senate approved the setting up of memorials to those killed in the War. Professor Scott Lang had made himself responsible for keeping the records of these, and other casualties, and he did this, for the whole University, with much more personal dedication than anyone except Professor E.P. Dickie in the Second War. In the summer of 1919, Professor MacEwan resigned and Mr Lloyd Turton Price, M.B. C.M. FRCS Ed. was appointed Professor of Surgery in the University in his place. Dr. James Fairlie Gemmill M.A. D.Sc. M.D. was appointed Professor of Natural History at University College in Professor Thompson's place. A Divinity Professor of distinction, D.M. Kay, returned from service with the D.S.O. to his Chair of Hebrew, and George Simpson Duncan O.B.E. M.A. B.D. who had been Field-Marshal Haig's Chaplain during part of the War, came as Professor of Divinity and Biblical Criticism.

1919 saw the anticipated large numbers applying to enter the Medical School of St Andrews. In the summer of the year, one hundred and four, of whom thirty-nine were ex-service, applied to enter. Several had started their course elsewhere during the War. It was agreed by Senate to admit them all, with the usual proviso that their qualifications—including the standard of courses they had begun elsewhere—were adequate. For some, return to University meant virtually a new start, for others, a continuation where they had left off. An item of social interest in the autumn of 1919 was that a post-graduate course in Venereal Diseases was asked for, because of the numbers of ex-servicemen who had contracted these diseases while abroad. Another was the introduction by Professor Herkless, at the Standing Joint Committee of the University Court with the UCD Council, of the need for developing aero-engineering and hydro-electrical engineering, and Professor Gibson was intro-duced by the Principal as an expert in these fields. This was an initiative by the Court to the Dundee side of the University, proposing a new development in technical subjects to be taught there. And at the end of 1919, in November and December, a committee of the Senatus considered designs for academic hoods,

including that for the Ch.M. Degree. They proposed that this hood be the same as the M.D. one, but without the white lining. They also proposed designs for the Ph.D., Ed.B., and the new Bachelor of Commerce degree—this Dundee development had also been initiated by Court and Senate.

The excitement of this first post-war year is well recalled by the record of Dr. William Cunningham, who sixty years later would become the President of the Scottish Society of the History of Medicine. He and 'my school friend Ben Rycroft (later Sir Benjamin Rycroft, the ophthalmologist) both aged sixteen and a half' found themselves in St Andrews in the October and signed the Matriculation Roll 'under the keen eyes of Andreas Bennett, Registrar of the University'. 'Now we were *Cives Universitatis Sancti Andreae*, and like many others we fell under the spell of the ancient city'. Here was the picture of Elizabeth Macdonald, Margaret Shirlaw and Peter Robertson all over again:

> The streets were a gay sight in those days when the hours of ten,
> eleven, and twelve noon struck and classes were changing. On Sunday
> too College Chapel was filled with wearers of the Scarlet Gown and
> after service the old pier was bright with their presence[8]. The 'Bejant
> smoker' followed the usual lines. How fortunate we were to sit at the
> feet of D'Arcy Wentworth Thompson ... (in Anatomy) we were more
> fortunate than the students of Edinburgh and Glasgow in those years,
> as they were short of specimens for their large post-war influx of
> students ... Professor Herring gave us a very good grounding ...
> John Pryde, later Professor at Cardiff, was his assistant, and I must
> not forget the kindly Frank Weston (technician) known to many
> generations of students ... a special song at Sir Peter Scott Lang's
> house on the way back from University Hall ...[9]

But there was a difference. The majority of the new students were ex-service, and William Cunningham and Ben Rycroft were as overawed by the maturity of these men and women, and often by the distinction of their war records, as their successor boy and girl students would be in 1946.

In October of 1919, Professor Marshall having left to go to the Regius Chair of Materia Medica and Therapeutics in the University of Aberdeen, Francis James Charteris, M.D. was appointed to succeed him in St Andrews. He was the second son of Matthew Charteris, Professor of Materia Medica in Glasgow, and a nephew of the Very Rev. A.H. Charteris, Professor of Biblical Criticism at Edinburgh and founder of *Life and Work*. Born in 1876, he graduated with commendation in 1897, and took his M.D. with commendation in 1907, both at Glasgow University. Soon after graduation he became first assistant and then lecturer in the Materia Medica Department, and so had had twenty-two years of experience in a large department with very big student numbers. He was also assistant physician at the Western Infirmary, and so was a senior practising clinician. He had been an applicant for the Regius Chair in Aberdeen, and when Professor Marshall was appointed, the University Court decided to appoint him without further advertisement. While his application included an impressive list of thirty-one publications, his subsequent time at St Andrews would be characterised by a marked lack of research and activity, and he would become

one of the least active Professors in the Faculty.

At the beginning of 1920, there was a further initiative from Senate towards improving facilities for medical students—men this time—in Dundee. St Mary Magdalene's Rectory was examined as a possible house, but was found unsuitable. But pressure for a men's hostel continued, and investigations did not stop. In January also the G.M.C. required that rules of medical ethics must be taught to students, and the Faculty and Senate agreed that this could be done by the Forensic Medicine lecturer. No successor had so far been appointed for Dr. Templeman, but in May Dr. David Lennox, a Dundee practitioner and police surgeon, was appointed to fill the lecturer's post. Applications to enter the Conjoint Medical School were lower than the previous year, but still rather more than before the War; twenty-two had been received by February. Because of the large 1919 intake, which in another year would pass into the clinical part of the School, more lecturers were appointed: Professor Charteris, Drs. Foggie and Kerr were to join Professor Stalker and Dr. Mackie Whyte. Dr. Kerr resigned soon after, and was replaced by Drs. Malcolm, James Stalker, Douglas Scott, and Rankine—beginning the tradition of Dundee families of general practitioners acting as clinical tutors at the Infirmary. Professor Kynoch resigned as Dean, and Professor Charteris was appointed to succeed him. Mr D.M. Grieg left to become curator of the Royal College of Surgeons of Edinburgh's museum (where Professor Pettigrew had once worked a half century earlier), and Professor Price took over from him as lecturer on Surgical Diseases of Children.

This was the list of staff appointments. There were three other happenings affecting the Medical School in this year, one minor and two major. In May, 1920, Dr. George A.S. Gordon, the Honorary Secretary of the St Andrews University Club of London, wrote in some anxiety to the Senatus Academicus with the news that the University of London were proposing to adopt a robe and hood for their Ph.D. degree of the same colour as those of M.Ds of St Andrews. This was obviously not a sensible suggestion, but it seemed at first as if nothing could be done. In the June, however, a Dr. David Heron D.Sc., reported to the University that he had attended a meeting of Convocation of London University, had pointed out their error, and recommended they change the colour of their Ph.D. hood. This they had agreed to do.

The first major event affecting the Faculty was a further visitation by inspectors from the General Medical Council. Dr. H.H. Tooth C.B. C.M.G. M.D. inspected the Final Examinations in December, and not, as previously, the main finals in June. The written, clinical, and viva voce examinations in Medicine were for practical purposes the same as they had been at the last visitation. He regarded the examination as 'sufficient' but was critical of it: 'The examination as a whole is a sufficient test of knowledge, but it can scarcely compare in scope with that of the other Scottish Universities'. He was also critical of the clinical examination, complaining that the 1915 Regulation about the local and external examiners acting jointly was not observed. Sir Hector Cameron was the surgical inspector, and was less critical. While there were only three candidates in Medicine, there were eleven in Surgery, five women and six

men. He noted the clinical diagnoses of the patients used for the examination: epithelioma of the tongue, vertebral caries with psoas abscess, rodent ulcer of the face, carcinoma of the stomach, sacro-iliac joint disease, and enlarged mass of glands in the neck of a man from whose lower lip an epithelioma had been removed two years before, simple fracture of the tibia, adenoma mammae, tubercular disease of cervical glands, syphilitic periostitis, tubercular disease of a knee-joint, infantile paralysis, and harelip with complete cleft palate. He praised the fact that 60% was required as the pass mark 'this exceeding by 10% that of any licensing authority', and found the examination 'searching, well organised, and conducted with great regularity'. Mr F.R. Brown FRCS, the Professor's assistant, was praised for his help with the clinical part of the examination.

Sir William J. Smyly M.D. was the Midwifery inspector. Twenty-two candidates had entered for this part of the examination, and eighteen had passed. The discrepancies between numbers sitting the three parts of the Final was greater at this time than at any other; in subsequent years numbers for each would become more equal. This part of the fourth Professional received the highest praise, and was described as admirable in every way. There was one minor criticism only of one of the written papers. In due course Andrew Bennett, the University Secretary, sent its acknowledgement to the Registrar of the General Medical Council.

This report was the best received so far by the Faculty of Medicine on its academic standard. There was by now an increased confidence among the staff which had grown with their increased experience in student teaching and organisation. Yet again, the small numbers of students meant very personal tuition—just as William Cunningham told how valuable this was in the pre-clinical classes, so he told of it in the senior classes also. It was noticeable not only in the major, final year subjects, but also in the smaller classes of Public Health, where Dr. W.L. Burgess taught, and Forensic Medicine. William Cunningham remembers 'facing the great Professor John Glaister of Glasgow University as External Examiner. A man of small stature but what a keen eye he had. He was old then and the weather was cold—and I noted that he kept on his overcoat and his tall hat lay on the table beside him'.

By now staff members known to many graduates were being appointed: G.R. Tudhope in Pathology, Mr Anderson and Mr Robertson, visiting surgeons at D.R.I., as lecturers, Mr F.R. Brown and Miss M. Fairlie as clinical tutors. The stage looked set for further developments and further expansion, now that the immediate post-war difficulties had been overcome.

But on June 11th Principal Herkless died. He had had a urinary obstruction for prostatic disease, and had died in a nursing home in Dundee. Dundee was now the natural place to go for surgical and medical care and the fact he went there and not to Edinburgh is of significance. Although a man of whom very little is known—perhaps because of the fact that he left virtually nothing in the way of letters, papers, or notes, his death was received with real sorrow. This was particularly so in Dundee. He had regularly attended College Council Meetings, and seems to have gained both the respect and the confidence of Sir

George Baxter, Robert Don, Robert Sinclair, and J. Ernest Cox who had welcomed him to their inner Council meetings only five years before. He had made proposals to extend and improve the academic field there—in commerce, law, and new types of engineering, as well as in medicine. The fact that students in the newer departments in University College did not flood in in large numbers was no fault of his—indeed, Professor Gibson, who had been introduced very recently by him to open new fields of engineering, left for Manchester at the end of June, apparently finding there was not the opening in Dundee he had anticipated. So their letter of condolence of July 14th caught the point of real significance about his short contribution: it was known to the Council, whose meetings he frequently attended, from his own words, that the advancement of the University as a whole was his supreme care. 'How well during his too brief tenure of office, he carried out his pledge is known to all members of the Council, who now lament the loss of a good friend and wise guide'.

In 1921 occurred an event which finally closed the nineteenth century chapter. This was the death on January 4th of Sir William Peterson. He had returned to England two years before following a hemiplegic stroke. Although not referred to by Court or Council except when he was knighted, he had in fact written on a number of occasions to his successor Principal Mackay. These letters were always seeking information—he wrote in February 1903 'Kindly send me an abstract and forward any testimonials you can spare' these on behalf of candidates for the Chair of Philosophy in St Andrews—'I have no time to add more at the moment, as I am just off to Boston, but hoping that you are flourishing no more than you deserve'. They were always demanding— 'Mind you send me the testimonials of the candidates for the Logic Chair at the earliest possible moment' ... 'Can you tell me, by return post, what the St Andrews people are doing with their Chair of Chemistry? Is it open? Is it going to be advertised and when will the election be made. I rather fancy that our Dr. Walker here might be interested to know'. (This was in May of 1909, before Professor Irvine was appointed). He asked for a copy of the constitution of the University Club in Dundee in 1909 also, as a guide for the setting up of a similar club in Montreal. In 1916, when he required a new Professor of Physiology, he wrote the longest of all his letters to Principal Mackay, who by now seemed less prepared to act as a messenger for him.

4/5/16

Are you there? I hope you are alive and well, although you have been strangely silent of late. Can you tell me everything you know about P.T. Herring? I don't know that he would be interested, and the place is practically under offer to a man (Carlston) in Chicago, etc. It was only the other night that one of my medical colleagues spoke of H as a man whom he knew personally and who, he thought, would suit us equally well. Personally, I have had H's name on my private list for a year and a half, but till the other night I have never heard anyone here speak so warmly of him, prob. because people here are strongly disposed to consider mainly physiologists on this side of the water.

You might speak to Reid about Herring. Of course, if he is quite happy at St Andrews, and gets enough work to do, he would have no reason for change. But he is just about the right age; and he may be enterprising enough to think of coming over here to make the greatest School of Physiology on the American continent!

We may hear from Carlston within a few days, and if his reply is favourable I should not been to trouble you. But you might write me your impressions as to whether Herring would be interested in what we are doing, and as to whether you would recommend him unreservedly in every way as teacher, investigator and colleague.

6/5/16

The Chicago man has received promotion and intends to stay where he is. Can we possibly borrow a man for a year? Perhaps H would think of it if there is no great rush of work at St Andrews. See what you can do, and please speak to Waymouth Reid about any others you might have available.

Yours v. truly

W. Peterson

The series of letters show that Sir William Peterson had not changed since his promotion to the New World. He remained the manipulator he had been when in Dundee, and his calm assumption that Principal Mackay would arrange things to suit his interests, as well as a certain contempt for his successor, comes out of his correspondence all too clearly. The letters confirm the view that the faults in the negotiators of the late ninetenth century between the New College and the University were not all on one side.[10]

12

Between the Wars

Sir James Irvine, Principal

In January of 1921 the chemistry classroom in United College was
packed from floor to ceiling. Professor James Irvine came into the
class at the usual hour of 11.00 a.m. The students cheered, and kept
cheering. He looked very serious—he always had a sense of drama,
you know. Then there was a silence. A student nicknamed 'Plunker'
Menzies called out: "Just tell us how you wangled it, Sir". This broke
the ice, there was laughter and applause, and the new Principal said
he thanked them all for their support, and that he promised he would
do his best for the students as long as he was in the job.

These are the words of Dr. Harry Graham, who had come up to study
medicine the previous October, after demobilisation from the Royal Flying
Corps. He recalls as clearly the other local candidate.

D'Arcy missed a lecture one day the previous term and the day after
told the class 'I was in Edinburgh yesterday. I told them there was no
need to go outside the University for Principal'. He was obviously
down in the dumps for two or three weeks after Irvine was appointed,
but he wouldn't have made a good Principal. J.C.I. brought a business
mind to the job that no-one could have surpassed.

Peter Robertson's opinion was the same.

We knew J.C. Irvine as highly respected for his ability. Most students
thought he would be more efficient than D'Arcy. But we all knew how
brilliant D'Arcy was—like one of the Ancient Greeks. J.C. Irvine was
very precise as Dean (of Science). He was very decisive. He was very
powerful. But it was never terribly wise to joke with him. Perhaps not
quite a gentle man. We felt then that the University was everything to
him and that he loved the University.

James Colquhoun Irvine was born in Glasgow on 9th May 1877. His father
was a manufacturer of light iron castings, descended from a family of yeomen
Ayrshire farmers. His mother's ancestors were highlanders, and her forebears
had been at sea in either the Merchant Marine or the Royal Navy. He won a
scholarship to Allan Glen's School in Glasgow at the age of thirteen, and took
advantage of the special training that school offered in the experimental
sciences. From school he went to the Royal Technical College in Glasgow, and

then to St Andrews in 1895. After graduating in 1898 he became an assistant in Professor Purdie's department, worked for some time in Leipzig, and in due course succeeded him as Head of the Department. But as well as being a brilliant chemist, he showed an unusual aptitude for organisation and administration—this was his business sense. He became Dean of the Faculty of Science in 1912, and this appointment brought him membership of the Medical Education Board. As well as all this, he was an athletic man, a good swimmer, golfer, and tennis player. Professor Herring now succeeded him as Dean of the Science Faculty.

Because Principal Irvine is such a large figure, and of such importance to the University's recent story, he has to be shown in as fair a light as is possible. For he too, like the Marquess of Bute, unfortunately became depicted as a monster, who did University College untold harm[1] and was responsible for much damage to the whole University as a result. And since there is later good evidence that he did develop a deep antipathy, not to say hatred, of Dundee, it seems important to determine how and when this arose.

Perhaps the fact that he was a scientist and not a classicist or theologian by academic profession tended to bring him into conflict with the scientists who predominated in University College. Professional jealousy could explain some of the feeling by subsequent chemistry staff on this side of the University. There is much evidence that in his early years he and Mrs Irvine went out of their way to welcome new students who had come up to that College—Mrs Tudhope recalls the parties for bejantines the Principal and his wife always gave in these early years, actually within their house in St Andrews, and recalls that life-long friendship followed meetings of girls from the two main colleges on these occasions. He had a human side which Dr. Harry Graham says must be recorded. Harry Graham like others before and after him commuted from St Andrews until only six months before his medical finals, and was Secretary of the Union in United College and captain of the Rugby Football club in the University. He therefore got to know the Principal well:

> You could crack a joke with him. Some of us went every morning at
> seven o'clock to the Step Pool from April onwards for a morning
> swim before catching the train to Dundee. He—and Professor
> Herring—used to join us from the beginning of May onwards. He did
> his best for students—as Secretary of the Union, I passed messages to
> him via Dr. Ettie Steel his secretary about any students who were in
> financial difficulties. And he used to help them.

> There were however some difficulties over the Rugby Club. In
> 1920, a new Rugby Club was formed at UCD and their players
> refused to turn out for the University XV unless at one of the four
> inter-university games. We had a combined meeting in 1923-24 when
> I was captain and the Dundee representatives said I was running a
> college club in St Andrews and calling it St Andrews University. J.C.I.
> chipped in and said Graham was running the only team recognised by
> the University Court. The trouble really was that the majority of
> mature rugby players were senior medicals and we had poor
> communications between the two sides of the University.

On the other hand, Peter Robertson's hockey team had no such difficulties. But there was a desire for a special identity which the University College players were beginning to seek, and this special identity was desired by some members of the staff also. These years saw a certain sharpness shown by the new Principal towards the Dundee side: Mrs Tudhope's 1923 Arts year were assured by Principal Mackay, now somewhat failing and with personal problems of his own, that they could have a Special History class as well as a General one. 'The Principal was very hard on Principal Mackay and Principal Mackay was frightened of him. He told him off severely about the Special class. Professor Williams had to come over and lecture in UCD. He rather despised J.Y. Mackay and was openly contemptuous of him. This didn't help.'

These students' recollections paint more clearly than a third-person account the two elements which were to progress and cause trouble in future years: the determination of some University College elements to demand an identity different from that of the rest of the enlarged University, and the dislike the new Principal was beginning to show for some of the University College staff.

Against this background, the decades between the Great Wars unfolded. In the Faculty of Medicine, the older names were now accompanied by those known to later students of the century. On 8th April, 1921, Mr R.C. Alexander, one of the visiting surgeons at Dundee Royal Infirmary, was appointed a lecturer in clinical surgery. In June of that year, there were two M.D.s—Robert Davidson and Frances Braid, twelve M.B.s—all local except one student from Glasgow, and six of them women; six D.P.H.s and two L.D.S. In July Lord Balfour of Burleigh, the Chancellor, died, as did Professor Sir Peter Scott Lang: 'he had never hesitated to express fearlessly his opinions', his obituary said. Earl Haig was the new Chancellor. And towards the end of the year, the system of teaching anaesthetics was altered by having a course of introductory lectures by the lecturer, followed by practical instruction by the senior hospital staff— Drs. S. Clark, J.M. Stalker, and W.E.A. Buchanan. They were paid twenty-five pounds *per annum* for their teaching services.

At this time the rate of payment for University and hospital staff followed the time-honoured principle that those who had an income from private practice—including the Professors of Medicine, Surgery, and Midwifery and Gynaecology—were paid a very small salary from the University because the bulk of their income came from their private fees. Professors of Pathology, Materia Medica, and pre-clinical subjects were paid three hundred and fifty pounds. For lecturers and clinical tutors, smaller amounts were paid, but these again followed the principle of nominal amounts for those in private practice. The insinuation that these small payments were the result of local deliberate policy on the part of the University Court is nonsense.[2]

Numbers in the two sides were not balanced at this time. The 1920-21 session had begun with more students at University College than in United— 467 against 365. In October 1921 there were 463 matriculating in Dundee against 344 in St Andrews. 1922, the seven hundredth anniversary of the foundation of the University of Padua, saw the first Ch.M. thesis submitted. This was from T.J. Mitchell, D.S.O., M.D. on 'Oriental Sore', and was accepted.

He had not however come to sit the clinical part of the examination. William George Robertson, brother of Dr. Peter, graduated M.D. with commendation. Eighteen passed the finals that June. In 1923, Principal Mackay attended the eight hundredth anniversary of the founding of St Bartholomew's Hospital in London.

In 1920, one of the greatest figures in British medicine of the century retired to St Andrews. He was Sir James Mackenzie, the inventor of the polygraph and a pioneer in cardiology. He went into the Bute at least once a week, talking to the students, teaching them, and encouraging them. One of his aphorisms which several remembered was: 'The more you are told that anything in medicine is an established fact, the more you are to doubt it'. He had come to St Andrews to set up, many years before the days of computers, an institute to keep a full and complete record of all persons in the town of St Andrews, their births, illnesses, and deaths, so that the earliest factors associated with disease could be studied. He was supported enthusiastically by Dr. Orr, one of the local practitioners, but after they both died the enterprise gradually failed and ultimately disappeared. Although this was a scheme the University might well have supported, it never did so to more than a nominal degree.

A feature of this decade was the number of Indian undergraduates who came to study at St Andrews. Immediately after the War, a few had tried to have their Indian qualifying courses approved; some were successful, others not. As there was then as now a certain doubt about the authenticity of some of these qualifications, the G.M.C. continued to press British Universities not to accept them unless they were absolutely certain of their validity. St Andrews had its share of these, and in 1924, J.S. Gurawara was refused leave to graduate with the thirty-one others, because although he had passed the examinations, he had failed to pay the fees! The number of Indian students was high enough for the UCD Council, in November, 1928, to moot the appointment of an Adviser to them selected by the Indian High Commission.

Another temporary difficulty arose in 1925. W.S. Duke Elder, although failed in his Ch.M. clinical by Professor Price, passed his clinical M.D., and was to be awarded a Gold Medal for his Thesis 'Reaction of the Eye to Changes in the Osmotic Pressure of the Blood'. But no Gold Medal existed, and the Senate asked the Medical Faculty to prepare and submit a design for this, along with an estimate of its probable cost. It was first agreed that the specimen medal be struck from a die belonging to Professor McIntosh, but this was later found to be unsuitable, and a new one was prepared. Duke Elder was finally presented with the prototype medal, and capped, on October 9th. This was not however the medal which became used permanently at St Andrews. The next summer, Dr. James Rutherford of Harrogate, who had just seen his son graduate, offered to provide a gold medal and silver medals for the St Andrews M.D. to the two candidates who had the highest marks. He donated an endowment of 100 guineas for the cost of the medals plus the cost of the necessary dies. This was the origin of the Rutherford Gold Medals.

In the wider world, this decade was full of political and industrial tensions. The Irish Free State was set up in 1921. Mussolini established fascism in Italy in

1922. The post-war Lloyd George ministry fell. The first Labour Government, dependent on Liberal support, had lasted for eight months in 1924 and in this year, 1925, there was a temporary relaxation of European tension when the Locarno Treaties were signed. But unemployment in the Western European world and in the United States of America was rising, the General Strike in Britain only a year, and the world financial slump and financial crisis only five years, into the future. The days of Dundee's wealth as the centre of the jute trade were soon to be over, and the recession meant that once more financial depression was upon the city. This widespread uncertainty in the financial and political worlds had its inevitable effect on education, and as always in these times the governments of the day had less and less to spare for the Universities. St Andrews University shared with others in this shortage of confidence, and would have to rely more and more on its own efforts while the industrial depression continued. This was the reason for the failure of the expansion which had been so hoped for in 1912.

In the University world, one of the keys to survival was the ability of the individual institutions to attract students whose fees would maintain income for revenue expenses. The days of the huge fortunes were over, and this source of capital was no longer available in Dundee. It had never been available to St Andrews. But the name of St Andrews, used in a business-like way by her ambassadors, could produce a return from benefactors farther afield. This was precisely where the new Principal's abilities were so valuable, and it should not be forgotten that at this time they benefited the whole University. He was responsible, in 1924, for improving the terms of scholarships already established—Tyndall-Bruce and Berry, making them more appropriate to the new conditions students required, and he was the first Principal to go to the New World to seek, and obtain, a source of replenishment for the University's capital.

In 1925 Edward S. Harkness of New York sent a friend from Yale University, Max Farrand, to London to found the Commonwealth Fellowships. Representatives from Oxford, Cambridge, London, and Principal Irvine as the representative of the Scottish Universities met with him, and Irvine made such an impression on the visitor from Yale that he was invited to become the Chairman of the British Committee. Instead he elected to become permanent vice-chairman, and in due course he met the philanthropist himself. Again he impressed Harkness so much that his suggestions for the composition of The Pilgrim Trust were accepted, and 10 million United States dollars were donated to finance it. In 1925, the year Principal Irvine was knighted, Harkness received the Honorary Degree of L.L.D. from St Andrews. Two years later, in 1927, came his princely donation of £100,000 to be used in great part for the provision of a residence for men students in United College (St Salvator's Hall) and in association with it, the endowment of residential entrance scholarships. Harkness Scholarships, of £100 annually for 3 or 4 years, made the recipients (a maximum of five in a year being obtained by Open Scholarship plus an interview to assess the personality and character in addition) among the wealthiest undergraduates in the kingdom. In later years, St Salvator's Hall

and the Harkness Scholarships, because they were available only to United College students, produced bitterness in Dundee. But this did not occur in the 1920s, when they were regarded as a great status symbol for the whole University.

The 1920s saw major staff changes in Medicine. Professor Stalker retired and was succeeded by Adam Patrick as Professor of Medicine from 1st October 1923. Nineteen passed the 1922 finals, including W.S. Duke Elder, who as President of the Union in University College had arrived to meet the Rector, Sir James Barrie, at Taybridge Station in a coffin on a horse-drawn hearse, and twenty passed in 1923 including W.F. Dorward, later lecturer in Forensic Medicine, Dr. J.D. Saggar, who became a Dundee institution with his brother D.R. Saggar, and Peter Robertson who had had scarlet fever in 1923 and had been unable to sit until autumn.

Peter Robertson was Professor Patrick's second houseman after his arrival. The new Professor had come from Glasgow, where he was a visiting consultant physician at the Glasgow Fever Hospital and Bellahouston Hospital. Born in Greenock on 29th June 1883, he was educated at the Academy there. He took an Honours M.A. in Classics in 1904, and his M.B. Ch.B. with Honours in 1908. His M.D. thesis won the Bellahouston Gold Medal in 1913. After graduation and house physician and surgeon posts, he went to Ruchill Infectious Diseases Hospital, and here he began his interest in the infectious fevers which continued throughout his life. He also did a spell at the Royal Hospital for Sick Children, and was assistant to the Professor of Medicine, before joining the R.A.M.C. at the outbreak of War. He was posted to Malta as bacteriologist in the hospital there, and by the end of the war was officer in charge. After the war he became a Fellow of the Royal Faculty of Physicians and Surgeons of Glasgow in 1919, and had become a member of the Royal College of Physicians of London not long before his appointment to St Andrews. Young Dr. Robertson had had Professor Stalker for his undergraduate training, and thought the new young Professor a complete contrast and 'very much better'. His opinions of his teachers, as opinions of students and younger graduates in general, depended very much on how old they were when he encountered them. Students usually take to a younger man, nearer them in age and outlook, forgetting or not realising that the old men were once young, active, and modern too. Professor Waterson in the Bute had a very high regard for Professor Stalker, and told his students so before they went over to their clinical years.

Orthopaedics entered the Medical Syllabus in 1926, following a recommendation from the G.M.C. In October 1925 Principal Mackay resigned his Anatomy Chair, and Dr. David Rutherford Dow crossed from United College to fill it. In the same month a successor to D'Arcy Thompson was appointed to UCD—Professor A.D. Peacock. And on 30th March, 1927, Professor MacEwan died. He was the first of the original clinical Professors to pass from the scene. Peter Robertson remembers being examined by him in his surgery final in 1923 as the external examiner, Barrington Ward, was ill. The MacEwan prize in surgery, in his memory, was instituted in the next year.

The regular succession of small happenings continued. The Report of the

Education Committee of the G.M.C. was answered in 1928, and its absurd inclusion of mechano-therapy tactfully dismissed. An article in the *Yorkshire Evening Post*, that a medical degree in St Andrews could be bought, was reported to the Senate and a denial sent by the Principal. The viability of St Mary's College was called in question—how often the viability of the Old University has been questioned in this way. Miss Jessie Balsillie, Dr. Macdonald's class-mate, had her M.D. thesis on the use of ultra-violet light in rickets turned down. One of the earlier graduates who had achieved high distinction (W.A. Young, of 1911) as Director of Tropical Research in the Gold Coast died of yellow fever. An eloquent tribute was paid to him by Professor W.J. Tulloch; later Professor Peacock asked to be associated with this tribute also. Professor Kynoch—still unmarried, still a keen golfer, resigned. Sir William Craigie, whose anonymous criticism of the staff in the *College Echoes* of an earlier age had led to such alarm on the part of the Senatus Academicus, was congratulated on his work upon the *Oxford English Dictionary* by that same body. Walter Gordon Campbell graduated L.D.S. Yet the number of medical graduates remained small. Only nine passed in the summer of 1928, and it is of interest that the age-old propensity of the St Andrews M.D. to attract aspirants carried on: seven passed the clinical part of the M.D. and one the clinical part of the Ch.M.

In October, 1928, Professor John McGibbon was appointed to the Chair of Midwifery and Gynaecology. He was a further Edinburgh graduate—his father a prominent general practitioner in that city. Born in 1876, he graduated in 1898 and joined his father's practice, but after working as a houseman at the Royal Maternity Hospital in Edinburgh he became so interested in obstetrics that he decided to make this his career. He had returned to St Andrews from the University of Witwatersrand, Johannesburg, where he had gone to be Professor in 1922. So he was not already on the staff of Dundee Royal Infirmary when appointed to his Chair; like Professor Patrick he was an incomer who had to be appointed directly to the charge of beds by the Governors. Dr. Alfred Pitkeathly, who was his house-surgeon, found him a short, rather pompous man with a recurrent laryngeal nerve palsy—this nerve to the muscles of his voice-box had been cut, he used to say, by his best friend. As a result, he had a hoarse croaking voice.[3]

The shortage of medical students was disappointing to both sides of the University. Only eight graduated in the summer of 1929; they included W.G. Campbell, and Andrew Logan, who became thoracic surgeon in Edinburgh and after the Second World War performed the first lung transplant on a boy who had swallowed paraquat weed-killer. But in the previous October, at the beginning of the new session, the University had set in motion a scheme—which would be the first of several continuing to the end of the century—by which United States students came to St Andrews for study. These young men were all Jewish, and many came from the Eastern Seaboard of the United States—from the State of New York—others from Michigan and Alabama. The first mention of these was in October 1928, and it was Sir James who had offered places in a medical faculty to these Jewish men who were refused entry to a medical school

in their own country—seventeen of them came into the second year of the course in November, including Abraham Heller, who with his compatriots never forgot the kindness of St Andrews to them.[4]

At the start of the Martinmas Term of 1928-29, there were the following numbers of students matriculating:

	Male	Female	Total
Medical School	63	9	72
First Year United College		10	
First Year University College		6	+ 17 U.S. students for 2nd Year

The totals for the United College had now increased very much over University College—435 compared with 256; St Mary's had 18 and the Dental School 1 only. The preponderance was entirely due to Arts students at the United College *and* to the failure of the Science and Engineering Faculties in Dundee to increase their numbers; from now on, the numbers at St Andrews would consistently predominate. But while criticism would in later years be made of this predominance of the Arts side, no criticism could be made of policy in the Medical Faculty, where the numbers seeking entrance to the United College and 'The Bute' would now consistently be greater than those seeking to begin their careers in University College. Ample resources continued to be put into the part of the Medical School in Dundee—ample for the numbers involved—and as most degrees (including M.A.) were taken by local schoolgirls and schoolboys, there was no question of the United College side being filled by Southern English applicants. The Conjoint Medical School was well supported by the Court in these years, and this support was if anything relatively better for the Dundee than the St Andrews side. Nor was there any favouritism over the United States entrants. In May of 1929, it was agreed to admit twenty-three more U.S. students into the second year of the medical course—eleven to St Andrews, and twelve to Dundee. Finally, thirty-one arrived; fourteen locals began at St Andrews and five in Dundee at the start of the session.

Because of the presence of these overseas students, its was decided by Senate to appoint 'Regents' to look after their education and welfare. But these were appointed only in St Andrews and not in Dundee and this was a bad decision. The Harkness Scholars had Regents, but no others. Their status was maintained at as high a level as possible, the aim being to equate them with the Rhodes Scholars of another University.

Sir James Irvine had as one of his aims the maintenance of the picturesque attributes of the Old University. He drew into practical service the pageantry and colour of 'the College of the Scarlet Gown' which *alumni* from Napier of Merchiston and the Admirable Crichton, through Montrose and down to Andrew Lang and R.F. Murray, had loved and revered. He encouraged the revival of the Kate Kennedy Pageant, and this attracted students from University College and from the Medical School who did not otherwise make the journey to St Andrews from Dundee. By an express provision of the Harkness benefaction he had St Salvator's Chapel restored and enriched in 1929-31, and in 1940 would have the ancient Katharine and Elizabeth bells recast. His term of office was marked in these early years by a wonderful series of Rectors—Barrie,

Kipling, Nansen, Grenfell and Smuts, all of the greatest distinction. A particularly important personal achievement was the system of student residences which he developed at St Andrews and which had been adopted by the new foundations of the nineteen sixties, and by most of the older foundations which never previously possessed them. As he would write twenty years later 'Beyond question the Collegiate system has been of great advantage to St Andrews, giving the university a characteristic quality denied to her younger sisters and binding her sons, now her daughters also, into a corporate life which strengthens their allegiance to the University of which Colleges are part'.[5] The whole series of Halls—St Salvator's, Chattan, St Regulus, Dean's Court—and those of newer date—began to be instituted in the next decade. But in Dundee, because of the considerably reduced numbers of women medical students, the Airlie Place residence to show a financial loss. Indeed, Mr Bonar at a College Council meeting suggested it be closed. Principal Mackay explained that a number of the women students living in bunks might be encouraged to use the hostel, and it was agreed that a survey of their places of residence be made.

As part of this heightening of ceremonial, the Senate decided upon special robes for the Deans of the various Faculties in 1929. That for the Dean of Medicine was crimson silk with white facings, and the coat of arms of St Leonard's College on the left lapel. No hood was to be worn, but the round cap or birettum of black velvet of the University of Paris—'as anciently and long worn in this University'.

The most important even in the University in 1930 was the death on March 30th of Principal John Yule Mackay. University posts being held *ad vitam aut culpam*, he had died in office. He had held the Principalship of University College for thirty-five years—as well, of course, as his Chair of Anatomy. Undoubtedly a man of high character, and always anxious to do the best, he had also had the ability to see the enlarged University in a way many in both Council and Senate did not. The Dundee Council recalled him as a man 'always anxious to do the best for the *College* he loved so dearly', and remembered how his task was not easy. 'It says much for the conciliatory spirit of Dr. Mackay that the difficulties, arising chiefly in the early years of his office, were surmounted so successfully'. The Senatus' minute took a much broader and more university view, and was more explicit. 'While, on the one hand the Senatus cannot forget the peaceful influence which, after the re-union of 1897, he exerted during the anxious stages thro' which the University passed just 30 years ago, or the quiet but valuable work he then did; on the other hand, they will always remember the kindly feeling that he showed towards his colleagues, his undepressing confidence in our country during the Great War, and his generosity towards soldiers and others who had toiled and suffered in our defence. Nor do they fail to appreciate that cheerful and fearless spirit with which he met, if he could not arrest, the gradual advance of that feeblement in health that marked his later years. Till within a recent date he attended with his usual care and grasp of detail to the administrative duties of his position, until finally without repining or complaint he passed quietly away, exhibiting to the last that consideration and courtesy to his colleagues which had always marked his life'. Both Council and Senate were

right in their assessment that a greater debt was owed to him than might appear, as his work had always been done quietly and without ostentation. Principal Mackay had much of the vision and sense of Sir Thomas Thornton about him, and can be given no higher praise. Sir William McCormick, who had been Professor of English for a short time in 1890 in Dundee, and had recently been the Chairman of the University Grants Committee, died the same week.

The committee to appoint the new Dundee Principal was formed in April. It consisted of the Chairman Mr J. Ernest Cox, Principal Irvine, Dr. J.C. Buist, William C. Lang, Dr. William Low of Blebo, Sheriff McDonald, and Mr James Prain. They reported in June that they had held three meetings, had considered all aspects of the question carefully, but were not prepared to make a recommendation. Instead, they decided to ask Sir James to undertake the duties on a temporary basis. In reply and acceptance, he said he regarded the invitation as a signal mark of confidence and as an expression of the mutual good-will which bound the constituent parts of the University together.

As 1930 was the start of a quinquennium, the Carnegie Trust gave the University £43,000. Of this £10,500 was given to University College—and from it money was to be made available to endow a Chair of Geology at Dundee. Only twelve graduated M.B. Ch.B. in June, but J. Douglas Robertson was awarded a Rutherford Gold Medal for his M.D. thesis on 'An historical and experimental study of gastric acidity'. In October there were one hundred and five students in the Medical and Dental School—the highest so far, with fifteen entrants in the United and University Colleges, and a further seventeen Americans expected. Once again the number of students on the St Andrews side had increased—this time to 540 compared with 274 in Dundee. Those in Engineering remained disappointingly few—one in St Andrews and 6 in Dundee, but there were now 30 students doing Scots law in Dundee.

In the pre-clinical years, in the 1930s, R.A. Robertson, now Professor of Botany, was a good teacher, and Professor Herring—when his health permitted—even better. Professor Waymouth Reid had become what could only be called an eccentric—his lectures dramatic and often coarse. He had done no research for many years. His brown bowler hat was known to all the students. He had a cat, and hung a flag outside his room when the animal was on heat. His caricatures of colleagues irritated them. Professor Waterston was considered a good formal lecturer, and was liked and respected. Dow, on the other hand, was a good tutor in the dissecting room where he could be much more incisive and interesting than in the lecture room. Professor Patrick was regarded as the best of physicians, who included Dr. Frankie Milne, Dr. Charlie Kerr, Mackie Whyte the neurologist, and Dr. Foggie the dermatologist. Professor Kynoch had had two assistants—Dr. Margaret Fairlie and Dr. Chisholm—the former more decisive and a very clear teacher; the arrival of Professor McGibbon had produced some rivalry between him and these two. On the surgical side, William (Pinkie) Robertson was deservedly popular (his nephew, Mr Lewis Robertson, became Chairman of the Eastern Regional Hospital Board in the 1960s) but died of septicaemia after pricking his finger. Jock Anderson was highly regarded as a teacher, good technical operator, and clinician with an eye to research.[6]

But the dominant figure in the nineteen twenties and early thirties in the Medical Faculty was Professor Price. His brother was the Price of *Price's Medicine*. He was to some extent an aloof man, but 'so good', said Peter Robertson. Technically he was a very good surgeon, but his young private assistant, Mr F.R. Brown, looked set to be even better. Dr. Robertson recalls how the junior staff would give Price and Brown a patient a-piece requiring the same operation, and would later argue about which of them had done the operation better. But unlike his younger colleague John Anderson, Professor Price was apparently somewhat unwilling to try new techniques, and by the nineteen thirties he was beginning to appear fixed in his procedure by Alfred Pitkeathly, who came up in 1930 and knew him until his death. Dr. Pitkeathly remembers his dislike of the American students, who suffered verbal abuse from him but kept coming back for more, and his arrival by taxi at the College precisely at nine a.m. His car was washed for him each day between nine and ten; he began lecturing at five minutes past nine, precisely from where he had left off the previous day, and, with a cigarette in his mouth, continued until five minutes to ten. On his way to his wards—6 and 7 in the old part of the Infirmary, he called at Weir's the tobacconist for a box of one hundred Balkan Sobranie. He bought antiques in various parts of Angus, Perthshire, and Fife, and these made up a good deal of his estate after his death. He was breeder of setters and spaniels, and shot with the aristocracy. He not infrequently chartered the Tay Ferryboat—the 'Fifie'—to take him over to see a patient or to operate, and the ferry would wait for him to come back. Dr. Margaret Fairlie and he were friendly and she used to go to the main theatre to watch him operate; this was in later years said to be one of the reasons why Professor Fairlie was such a fine surgeon, who 'operated like a man'.[7]

His untimely death followed a surgical operation. Concerned about abdominal symptoms, he persuaded Sir John Fraser, the Professor of Surgery in Edinburgh, to operate on him. Post-operative coughing after a duodenal ulcer was found burst his wound; he later developed pneumonia and died on 26th February 1933, at the age of fifty-eight. He was a figure larger than life, and was a representative Professor of Surgery for St Andrews—one respected by all students, liked by many, less well liked by others. Perhaps the sarcasm—described in detail by Dr. Menzies Campbell in some of her lectures—was the most unlikeable feature about him. From the academic point of view, moreover, he did not develop post-graduate research, and in spite of travelling on the Continent, he did not bring back new advances nor develop any original operations. His greatest gifts were his fine operative technique, his sympathy to patients and especially to children, and his courtesy and charm of manner. When he died tributes were sincere, from Senate, the Dundee Council, and colleagues.

Two years later, a new Professor arrived in Dundee who was to become one of the greatest pathologists in the United Kingdom. This was Daniel Fowler Cappell, successor to the quiet Professor Sutherland. He was born in Glasgow, the son of a pharmacist, on 28th February, 1900. Educated at Hillhead High School and at Glasgow Academy, where he was Dux, he showed such promise

as a teacher of Anatomy while a student in Glasgow that he was reserved from call-up in the last year of the War. He was awarded the Struthers Gold Medal at the age of nineteen, graduated M.B. with Honours in 1921, M.D. with a Gold Medal in 1930, and now moved from Professor Robert Muir's department, at the time probably the best in the country, to become Professor at St Andrews.

The important event of 1931 which had its effect on the Medical Faculty and upon the whole University was the beginning of the world recession. This at once reduced the money available for salaries of staff and for development of buildings and equipment. Professor Cappell was one who was particularly affected by this. He had plans to increase the facilities at the Royal Infirmary—then very small and restricted—for both teaching and research—but there was just not the money available to do so. The whole city of Dundee would continue to suffer, and suffer severely, for much of this decade of depression, and this, too, made for a background of poverty and restriction. The Dundee Council—aware more certainly of the implications of what was happening than the academics on the Senatus Academicus, proposed on October 7th that salaries for Professors and lecturers be cut by 2½%, subject to the University Court agreeing to reduce the salaries of the staff under its jurisdiction by a similar amount. The previous year, in 1930, the Carnegie Trust had released £43,000 for the University, of which a quarter was for University College, but as ever revenue costs had to be kept viable, and Dundee was just not able to attract enough students to its technical departments to make up for the large and increasing preponderance of Arts students electing to study at United College.

One event which raised morale in Dundee but which also emphasised the divergence now developing between the two sides of the University was the Senate meeting in the Caird Hall on the occasion of the Jubilee of the Dundee College. It took place in 1932, the year Professor Stalker died. This was the first time the maces had been carried and the Senatus walked in procession in Dundee since Principal Tulloch had suggested St Andrews and Dundee share graduations and ceremonies so many years before. The L.L.Ds. were the Earl of Strathmore, James Brebner the former Rector of the Harris Academy, and W.C. Leng, Esq. of the Dundee newspaper firm. Doctors of Divinity were Rev. Charles Cooper of Paisley Abbey, and the Rev. Allan Campbell Don, former Rector and Provost of St Paul's Cathedral in Dundee, now private secretary and chaplain to the Archbishop of Canterbury, and later to become a Scottish Dean of St Paul's. This ceremony apart, there was no visible sign of the University of St Andrews in the City of Dundee—University College and its students were much as they had always been, and the medicals—who were not members of the College—were seen all together perhaps only at Charities Days. The red gown was not worn, but this was only because students did not seem to want to wear it. The College authorities and Council could certainly have made an effort to have the wearing of this badge as necessary in Dundee as it was in the United College. The annual College photographs of these years had a St Andrews Cross in the middle and in front, and students, especially women, wore the undergraduate tie of the University, but gowns were not worn by men

or women. Had more University ceremonies taken place, the gown might have appeared. But sadly these were all in St Andrews.

The man who would succeed Professor Price was perhaps the Professor of Surgery in St Andrews more uniformly respected and well thought of by the students—and by others within and without the University—than any other. Perhaps he would not have fulfilled the promise expected of him, but there was no means of knowing, as he died tragically of tuberculosis only two years after his appointment. John Anderson was born in 1886 in Macduff, in Banffshire, and was the first senior member of clinical staff to come to St Andrews from Aberdeen University, where he had graduated in 1908. He had been in Dundee Royal Infirmary as a house surgeon, but had then trained in England and Germany. He was appointed a surgeon to D.R.I. in 1911 at the early age of twenty-five, and was also surgeon to the Perth Hospital, King's Cross Fever Hospital, Ashludie and Glenlomond Sanatoria, and Arbroath Infirmary. He had gained very real success and prestige as an army surgeon, beginning as a surgeon at No. 20 Casualty Clearing Station, and later, in spite of not yet being a Fellow of a Royal College of Surgeons, was made consulting surgeon to the 3rd Army. He was awarded the D.S.O. in 1918—an unusual and high award for a surgeon, and was mentioned twice in despatches. He wrote the chapter on cranial wounds and penetrating wounds of the chest in the official book of War Surgery. In 1919 he became a Fellow of the Edinburgh College, and his ability was recognised quickly when he was elected a member of the Moynihan Surgical Club.

This was the new Professor. He was forward-looking in the clinical and administrative fields—he used the new electrical diathermy machine in Dundee, began to look for research projects, and, it was said, thought towards a system of State Medicine in a manner which put him well ahead of his times. In the major Medical School of Edinburgh he was highly regarded by senior surgeons there who recall his great potential and regret his early death on 17th August 1935. In the opinion of his students 'Jock Anderson would have been a star turn if he had not died'.

His successor, Richard Charles Alexander, was another Edinburgh graduate. Born in Edinburgh on 18th September 1884, he was educated at George Watson's College and Edinburgh and Paris Universities. Like Professor Patrick, he took an M.A. first in 1904, before his M.B. in 1908 with honours. After further study in Paris, house posts in the Royal Infirmary and Royal Maternity Hospital, he became a Fellow of the Royal College of Surgeons of Edinburgh in 1911. Until called up for war service, he was assistant to Professor H. Alexis Thomson, and Resident Surgical Officer at the Chalmers Hospital. He served for three years with a Casualty Clearing Station and was mentioned twice in despatches. It was during this period that he carried out an immense amount of surgery, and acquired the speed as an operator which was to be so characteristic of him. He was also, in 1913, Crichton Research Scholar in Edinburgh, and studied problems of gall-bladder disease. When additional beds became available in Dundee he obtained charge of them as a visiting surgeon in 1921, and now, in the year of the King's Silver Jubilee, he was appointed Professor of Surgery in

the University of St Andrews.

These were the days when staff at the Infirmary were small in numbers, and when those in post held a relatively much higher position in society than do their opposite numbers of today. The senior staff were large figures, held in awe by patients, nursing staff and students. They could indulge in personal idiosyncrasies, too, to a degree not seen—and perhaps not acceptable—today. Dr. Alfred Pitkeathly and Professor Sir Donald Douglas both recall how Mr Saunders Melville, who was assistant surgeon to Mr Jock Anderson, used to kick the door of the anaesthetic room while they—the unfortunate residents— were trying to anaesthetise an emergency case for theatre and he thought they were taking too long. Both of these men were strong minded enough to refuse to be intimidated by this behaviour, and Mr Melville respected them for it. But those who were intimidated were treated harshly. In the same way, students in the wards and 'big clinics' were subjected to fierce and stinging interrogation. This was the way teaching was done, and some staff members were less kind than others. Senior staff members were also openly critical of their colleagues to a degree not seen so regularly in later years, and this sometimes led to antagonisms being all too obvious to the students. Professor McGibbon and Dr. Fairlie had a certain rivalry, perhaps because the younger person was so good at her work. Dr. Frank Milne was unfairly critical of Professor Patrick. A little later, Professor Alexander, Mr Brown, Mr Robb and Mr Melville all showed rivalry for one another.

The wards were full of the same sort of diseases as had been seen for all the century—tuberculosis, lobar pneumonia, strokes, severe valvular disease of the heart with heart failure. The myocardial infarction had not yet arrived on the medical scene. Carcinoma of the lung was a rare disease, and Peter Robertson was shown a patient with one when he took his M.D. In surgery and obstetrics, sepsis could still run out of control. Members of staff aged and failed in their capacity. Professor Kynoch had two strokes and in his last years was a shadow of his previous self as an operator. He also lost his fluidity and wit as a lecturer. Clinical diagnosis rested largely upon the elucidation of physical signs, and the schools of heavy percussion—as practised by Drs. Milne and Charlie Kerr— and light percussion—as taught by Adam Patrick—had their respective adherents. Laboratory tests were primitive; Dr. Frank Milne carried out blood sugar estimations in the side-room, and Professor Patrick, who had a considerable laboratory experience, would take his houseman and students in procession to his small ward laboratory to check what results the laboratory staff had reported. Professor Charteris fitted a polygraph for diagnosis of cardiac irregularities, but attended the wards rarely to use it. There was an electrocardiograph available from the 1920s, in charge of a technician called Malcolm. Professor Patrick had his own, complete with heavy wet batteries to produce the electricity. The heavy machine was taken round with him to all his consultations.

Then as now the laboratory technicians were invaluable members of the preclinical departments. Professor Waterson had a laboratory attendant Mr Cross, who was a white-bearded old fisherman. He was very proud of an antomical

specimen which he described to the students as the LAIRNYNX and the FAYRNYNX with the NASAL FUSSIL. Student prosectors were used; Peter Robertson dissected a lower limb with Duke Elder dissecting the other side— 'his speed of hand reflected his speed of mind'. As in later years, the technicians would inform these student dissectors, in the quiet of the summer vacation, of just how important they were to the running of the department, and how entirely dependent the Professor was upon them. Mr James Brown took Mr Cross' place and his cheerful chaff and stories of the famous whom he knew 'very well' kept Bute students amused till his retiral to Shetland a quarter of a century later. Tom Izzard, the opposite number in Professor Mackay's and later Professor Dow's Department, went to the Royal College of Surgeons of Edinburgh to a senior technician post. Mr Cameron, with his spectacles, was well known for working the lantern for Professor Charteris, and Mr Hogg, with his thin light hair, coughed and spluttered almost as much as his boss Willie John Tulloch. But the greatest characters of all these, and the most respected and loved, were James Corkhill on the Dundee side in Pathology and Frank Weston on the St Andrews in Physiology. They had the happiest and kindest personalities, and were both rewarded by Honorary Science Degrees at the end of their University careers.

The last major staff change in the years before the Second World War was that of the Professor of Physiology in University College. This, with Anatomy, was a *true* U.C.D. Chair. Although all the other Professors of the Medical Faculty are described in University of Dundee Archives as 'Professor of —— University College Dundee' this is incorrect; they were all Professors of the University of St Andrews. In March 1935 Professor Waymouth Reid announced that he would resign at the end of the current academical year. He had been 47 years in his Chair, and was the last of the initial University College appointments—Professor Steggall having had his jubilee in 1932 and retired in 1933. His early work on osmosis and intestinal obstruction produced classic papers, and he was elected a Fellow of the Royal Society at an early age, but for many years now he had produced no original work in his department. He had not pressed for funds or developed his equipment except in a somewhat off-hand manner, and as always, university departments which stand still quickly regress. The somewhat limited academic standing of these two pre-clinical departments, Anatomy and Physiology, had not helped the status of University College as far as the outside world was concerned. Nor had his eccentricities and his quarrels with colleagues helped; the effigies of other staff members he hung on miniature gibbets did not endear him to them. And further, the Principal of the University, Sir James Irvine, had learned to be unimpressed. This rather sad failure on Professor Reid's part had perhaps more repercussions than might be immediately obvious.

His successor was a complete contrast, and one who, though remaining only a limited time in Dundee, would make a considerable mark while in post and continue his interest in a way which will be recorded later. Robert Campbell Garry was born in 1900 in Glasgow, his father being a B.Sc. of the University. After his own graduation there in 1925 he became lecturer in Physiology, took a

D.Sc. rather than the usual M.D., and in 1933 went to Aberdeen as head of the Rowett Research Institute there. He was an excellent scientist and one very concerned with the education in School as well as in University. He quickly set about modernising the Physiology Department and its library, and became a friend of Professor Peacock, with whom he would later collaborate in lectures and books of science for children. From soon after his arrival he became dedicated to improving the status of University College, and this led him later into conflict with Sir James Irvine. For he felt that students on the Dundee side of the University deserved better facilities, and was quite prepared to say so. He tried to introduce lines of research which would complement what was done in Professor Herring's department, and tried to encourage science students doing Physiology to study in one or other department if it suited their interests or special needs. This was indeed a novel approach, but it did not commend itself to some of the staff working in the United College—Professor Herring, sadly, would not co-operate—or indeed to the Principal.

All the Professors had their foibles which students remembered. 'My Good Woman', Professor McGibbon would say to a woman patient in the maternity 'only God and I can save you'. Professor Patrick's quietness and paucity of words went with his gentlemanly academic personality. 'You'll get this job on one condition', he told Alfred Pitkeathly, 'that you don't smoke before noon'. His slowness while driving was a source of great entertainment, for he must have been one of the slowest drivers in Dundee or anywhere else. Taken out to a visit by a surgical colleague who owned one of the faster cars of the time he confided to his houseman next day 'I don't think I'm getting the best out of my car'. Professor Alexander's contempt for 'the surgeons in the South' (by which he appeared to mean all surgeons working south of Edinburgh) continued over the years, as did his wagging finger to emphasise a point. In other departments, too, there were characters. Dr. R.P. (Bobby) Mathers' Ear Nose and Throat Clinic was dramatic in setting and action—the various chairs had to be correctly placed to the nearest millimetre, and the shifting of the light was a pantomime in itself. Professor Cappell's precise West of Scotland accent remained with a generation of students, and Professor Tulloch's habit of almost swallowing cigarettes as he smoked them remained with two generations. A lecturer much criticised was Dr. Lennox, in Forensic Medicine, and Dr. Tuach McKenzie, the medical superintendent of Westgreen Asylum, had the worst teaching reputation of all. Professor Dow was remembered for his reply, when an Anatomy inspector asked why plastic dissection tables were not available in his rooms 'Ah, but there's something *warm* about wood'. Professor Herring's stated intention, at his first lecture 'to get as many of you through the Second Professional Examination as possible' earned him annual applause. Dr. W. Fyffe Dorward, who succeeded Dr. Lennox, was remembered for his admonition for students to 'take the bull by the horns' and to 'wear a dark suit' when in the witness box. 'Batty' Bell—who succeeded Dr. Tuach McKenzie, used to shut the lecture room door with a dramatic gesture—one year a rubber stop was nailed against the wall and the door kept coming back at him instead of closing. Students had to sign an attendance roll for his class—which was unusual—and

many celebrated names were included. Dr. Burgess' sartorial elegance was remembered, along with his very clear lecturing style. Professor Waymouth Reid's Rabelaisian remarks are remembered but not recorded.

A feature of the 1930s was the appearance of South African students, following Jan Smut's Rectorship in 1931 and his subsequent encouragement of young men to come to St Andrews. Those who were medicals included the brothers Dick and Tom Venning, both Presidents of Bute, and their contribution to St Andrews rugby was considerable. 1935 was the year when Mussolini invaded Abyssinia, and the re-arming of Germany under Adolf Hitler was commencing. In the next three years, the European tensions would worsen into a second major war: Hitler would re-occupy the Rhineland in 1936, and the Spanish Civil War would begin. In March 1938 Hitler would annex Austria, and in September Mr Neville Chamberlain would fly to Munich to sign a treaty with him. Against these the small progress of St Andrews—some increase in medical graduates in 1935—twenty four with only seven United States students— and the University total reaching over a thousand for the first time—might be of no importance. But a state of affairs was coming about in the University which, like that in the outside world, would lead in coming years to an unhappy war also. And the Medical School would be closely involved.

13

Pre-War Developments. The 1939-1945 War

Major-General Wimberley, Principal of University College, Dundee

During the 1930s there began to be established an imbalance between the St Andrews and Dundee Colleges which had not existed in the previous decade. Some of this was due to the technical departments in Dundee failing to develop, and this was to a certain extent associated with the slump of the 1930s which affected Dundee so badly. But it was also due to the considerable and progressive increase in the Arts Faculty in United College. Those students in the Conjoint (now called Senior) Medical School were increasing in numbers also and they were students of St Andrews University and not of University College Dundee. They tipped the imbalance farther. And because of the Constitution of University College, *all* new Chairs or lecturer's posts were of necessity University ones. Even had a whole series of Arts Chairs been created by the Court with the full authority of the University Grants Committee, these would all have been St Andrews University posts, just as all the Medical Chairs were Chairs of the University of St Andrews. They could have no more 'belonged' to University College and its Council that these Medical ones did. They would have been a part of the University but with no constitutional relationship to University College or to United College or St Mary's College. These constitutional difficulties were the result of the terms of the original foundation, which Principal Tulloch and after him Principal Donaldson had sought unsuccessfully to modify. So much of the imbalance which was developing was not the 'fault' of the University of St Andrews; it was inherent in the limitations of the original Dundee foundation.

In the post-war 1918 decade, all the running was made by Court and Senate—Council records relate to quite local Dundee events or administrative needs, and the Council reacted periodically to proposals sent it from what was in law and in fact the principal part of the University. Yet most of these were positive proposals and aimed at progress—following the initiative of Principal Herkless. They covered a wide range, from the physical welfare fund for students, and library grants of 1930, to the provisions of what was a health service for *all* undergraduates in 1933.[1] Later they included suggestions that a Commerce Degree be offered, and Law classes begun. Improvements in the bacteriology department, both for teaching and for service provision, were suggested in 1933, and were to be a charge on the Court. The electrocardiograph for the Infirmary was bought with Court money. In 1934, following the retiral

of R.A. Robertson, Robert James Douglas Graham from Edinburgh was appointed to a new Joint Chair in Botany for both sides, and later that year a Joint Chair of Geology was proposed. Later again, as will be seen, another residence for medical students was opened in Dudhope Terrace near the Infirmary. This was a logical provision for senior students who had formerly been in the United College, and did not affect adversely University College students, as the large majority of these had lived at home since their first year. In 1937 came a proposal from the Principal to equalise laboratory fees and increase a number of Dundee ones to St Andrews levels. In 1937, too, the Court arranged that the Medical School be completely rewired, at a cost of £1600. And in 1939, a new joint handbook with details of all subjects offered, in all three Colleges, was prepared by Professor Garry and Professor Copson (the new Mathematics Professor at University College) and accepted by the Principal. Against this the Court had held up Dundee developments in Arts, and refused to follow the lead of Mr George Bonar over the School of Economics he wished to associate with the University. There was a genuine difficulty here over Bonar's wish to include non-graduating students—though, with good will on both sides, this could probably have been overcome.

The Faculty of Medicine, perhaps because of its increasing confidence despite small student numbers, produced positive suggestions for academic development within the University. Its confidence contrasted with that of the other faculties physically located in Dundee. A very long memorandum was prepared in the summer of 1936 stressing the need to increase teaching space at the Royal Infirmary and accommodate more medical students. The Faculty described two types of teachers in what it itself described as 'the Advanced Medical School': professors and lecturers appointed by the Court, and other staff members with no university appointment who nevertheless were potential teachers of merit. While there were at this time no full-time university teachers in clinical subjects at St Andrews, the memorandum advised that those hospital specialists with no university connection be given honorary teaching status with the designation of clinical tutor, clinical instructor, and so on. This method of increasing the teaching potential without involving the University in significant financial outlays continues to be present, and is of course employed in all Medical Schools in the National Health Service era. While noting that medical student numbers (Professor Charteris used the Materia Medica class numbers as the example) had reached a peak of eighty four in 1921 but had fallen to forty eight in 1922 and to twenty eight in 1923, and remained in the twenties until the influx of United States students increased them again, the Faculty warned that the clinical faculties in Dundee were inadequate both for teaching and examining any higher number than sixty. They suggested the numbers be reduced to not more than forty in a year. After long discussion the University agreed with many of the points made, but did not wish the admission of medicals to fall below fifty.

From about 1935, however, the Dundee Council began to show interest in developing policies of its own. It had always maintained a tight discipline on its own appointed staff. For example, on 17th March 1933 Dr. Kenneth Hayens,

the German lecturer, had asked permission to live in St Andrews, but had been refused and told he must reside in Dundee. Post-graduate Fellowships appeared in late 1935, and certain students who applied for these when intending to study in St Andrews had their requests refused or restricted; one medical because Council would not allow a Dundee Scholarship to go to research in a department over which it had NO control! The same applied to students asking to take certain Arts subjects at St Andrews while holding a 'Dundee' bursary, and on one occasion (1937) to an engineering student who made a similar request about science subjects. It had also, because of its independent status, maintained a different method of meeting class grants (expenses requested by heads of departments to run their class in the coming year) than the other Colleges or the Medical School. In November of 1935 Mr J. Ernest Cox reported that a General Meeting of the Governors (as distinct from the College Council) had proposed both to have the Principal of the University an *ex officio* member of Council, and to increase to three the number of academic representatives on Council elected by the Principal. This would strengthen the academic content of Council and give its deliberations wider scope.

In January of 1935, the old question of duplication of Medical Chairs reappeared. But on this occasion it was on very different lines from those of a quarter of a century before. The University Grants Committee expressed itself more than happy with the University at this visitation:

> It was evident, both from the proceedings at meetings and from informal conversations, that the Committee was favourably impressed with the progress recently made by the University. Approval was given to the policy of the Court under which any increased financial resources are applied in the first instance to strengthen existing departments of study; and the principle was approved that new ventures should be undertaken only when the necessary financial provision is forthcoming from internal sources without being dependent upon increased Government Grants.

Because of a suggestion from the General Medical Council that additional Anatomy and Physiology should be given to students in their years of clinical study, i.e. after they had passed their Second Professional Examination, the University Grants Committee studied very particularly the situation in St Andrews, where there was a duplication of Anatomy and Physiology departments. They came to the conclusion that, with the number of students at present passing through, the existing arrangement could be justified on both financial and educational grounds, but recommended that 'in both subjects the teaching for the Second M.B. Ch.B. Examination should be given in St Andrews alone'. According to the report, this was a calculated decision urged upon the UGC by Sir Humphrey Rolleston, and was given added weight on account of the impending resignation of Professor Waymouth Reid. The Court, however, did not by any means rush to agree that all pre-clinical Anatomy and Physiology teaching be given in the United College alone, but saw the advantages of having Chairs in Dundee which could be adapted to providing instruction in clinical Anatomy and Physiology. In this they looked to the good of the enlarged Uni-

A. M. Paterson

A. Waymouth Reid FRS

C. R. Marshall

Lewis R. Sutherland

D. McEwan

A. M. Stalker

J. A. C. Kynoch

John McGibbon

Principal J. Yule Mackay

James Musgrove

versity in a way which would have pleased Sir Thomas Thornton, and they argued in precisely the opposite manner to Principal Peterson when the same question was being argued by him.

It is suggested that the proposals should be discussed at the earliest possible date by the Joint Committee of Court and Council, in consultation with the Faculty of Medicine. To carry on as at present is much simpler than any modification on the lines suggested by the Grants Committee, but there can be little doubt that if worked with harmony and with good-will a more modern and more effective medical course would result. On the other hand, to ignore the suggestion of the Grants Committee without a thorough exploration of its workability would be hazardous. The Committee has had this scheme in mind for some time and its views are shared by the General Medical Council; these bodies are aware of the impending vacancy in the Chair of Physiology in Dundee and recognise that this is a timely opportunity to give effect to a teaching policy to which general approval has been given throughout the country. The fact, almost accidental, that we have two Chairs of Anatomy and two of Physiology makes it possible to develop the new policy in this University and places the Grants Committee in a powerful position to enforce a change in the allocation of the duties attached to the Chairs.

Sensible discussions between Council and Court came to the conclusion that the proposal to concentrate Anatomy and Physiology in St Andrews alone be not proceeded with, and Professor Garry was, as has been seen, appointed in Professor Reid's place. And so the University College Medical Chairs were *not* removed, and the pre-clinical part of Medicine continued there unharassed. To alter the arrangements would have had no merit, would have caused justified alarm in the City of Dundee, and would have made implementation of the G.M.C.'s suggestion about clinical teaching of the two subjects of Anatomy and Physiology very difficult.

On 7th October 1937, at a Special Meeting of Council, Dr. W.C. Leng proposed 'that the Council take measures for the appointment of a Principal resident in Dundee (a) because there was an increased administrative amount of work requiring to be done in Dundee (b) because of the desirability of keeping the College before the public and (c) because of the importance of fostering the corporate life of the College which, while being a member of the University of St Andrews, has its own individuality'. In proposing this, he acknowledged gratefully the work done by Sir James Irvine towards the provision of equipment, in stimulating the collective social life of the students, and in enlarging and refurbishing the women's hostel. Mr J. Ernest Cox moved a direct negative, which was passed by eleven votes to five. But Dr. Leng's proposal was an important and significant one, especially its clause (c).

There was other evidence at this time of the beginning of the movement to ask for expansion and development in Dundee University College. A committee of the College Council was set up 'charged with investigating the lines along which University College Dundee could most usefully expand and develop'

though its existence was only revealed publicly when one of its members, Mr George Bonar, died very suddenly in 1938. On the purely academic side, the main issue was the provision of more departments in the Faculty of Arts in Dundee. History had been asked for since the 1920s, and requests came later for Greek. Although lecturers travelled from St Andrews to lecture in philosophy, the provisions were felt to be insufficient. These requests, especially that for history, which applied particularly to students intending to go to the Teachers' Training College and teach the subjects in school later, were entirely reasonable. The Council saw no point in their students travelling to St Andrews for classes, pointing out that they lived at home and could not afford the expense. There were also feelings that more residences be provided in Dundee, especially since the St Andrews Colleges now had St Salvator's, Dean's Court, Swallowgate and Edgecliff West, with a £46,000 extension to St Salvator's Hall to be begun in 1937. It was the reverse of the 1890s—now it was St Andrews' turn to enjoy the help of rich benefactors—exactly as Dundee had done in the past.

All this was one side of the question of increased teaching and opportunity in University College—the attitude and policy of the business men of the Governors and Council. The other side was the attitude and policy of the Principal of the University. It seems likely that events in the two years before the outbreak of the Second World War finally decided him upon a policy of disinterest in University College, though *not in the Medical School.* He had done an enormous amount of work in the St Andrews side of the University, to such an extent that the Colleges there had almost avoided the reductions of the economic depression which had halted developments in most other British Universities. The St Andrews Colleges had enjoyed expansion or at the least, had suffered no really disastrous cut-backs. But now, by Martinmas of 1938, there were 194 medical and dental students in the Senior Medical School, and the total of 274 under-graduates in University College included some sixty pre-clinical medicals who would join the Medical School as soon as they reached their third year. University College did not seem worth great investment—certain of the staff the Principal looked down upon, and the lack of involvement by so many of the citizens in the University College their city possessed did nothing to increase his respect. In 1937 he had to inform the Council that since University College had been invited to send representatives to the Coronation Service in Dundee Parish Church, and the notices sent out to all Council members had resulted in only two saying they could attend, the Joint Education Board had decided that University College should not be represented at the Service. To use an illustration anticipating 1946, he felt the Dundee Council were prepared to wear the uniform, but had not joined the Regiment.

And so, on June 5th, 1939, Sir James Irvine wrote to resign as interim Principal of University College with effect from July 31st. This action of his was clearly unexpected, and the minutes of the Council Meeting a fortnight later reflect this. In their discussion, it was revealed that nine years previously they had felt they could not afford the salary of a full-time Principal (although they had at once paid Sir James an Honorarium of five hundred pounds *per annum*—the same amount as they would pay his successor). The Council noted

that Sir James was the nominee of the Privy Council for the post of interim Principal. He had had, it was said, two ideals—the first, to improve the relationship between the College and the University, the second, to make University College a more efficient unit within the University. The first had been done. The second was progressing, and the care for Dundee students, the institution of the Chair in Dental Surgery, the first in Scotland, Mr Henry Gordon Campbell having been appointed Professor the previous year after prolonged negotiations and the provision of an endowment, and the beginning of a Law (B.L.) Degree, were instanced as evidence of this. 'That he had visions of a greater and worthier College reveals itself in the way in which he advocates the building up of an Extension Fund, used eventually to purchase ground for future developments, and the memorandum on a building programme which he presented to the Council not many weeks ago'.

'His many friends on the Council recognised him as a man of wide vision, with a quick perception of the kernel of the immediate problem, and above all, a grit and determination to strain every nerve to put into effect what he believed to be the correct solution'. At this June meeting, Mr J. Ernest Cox submitted his resignation as Chairman as from the end of July. At the meeting on the 17th of July, the Report of a Special Committee to consider future policy of University College Dundee was not proceeded with, and it seemed as if the Council had not yet got over the shock of Sir James' resignation. Had they engineered his resignation, they would surely have proceeded smartly in the Peterson tradition. The Special Committee members were Mr W.H. Valentine, Dr. James Lawson, Professors Dow, Peacock and Copson. Instead, with Mr Cox in the Chair for the last time—he refused to alter his decision to resign though pressed to do so— the Council asked Professor Fulton, of the Department of Engineering, to fill the vacancy. He was to be a full-time Principal, but otherwise conditions were not specified. His appointment was confirmed on August 21st, when he was to be paid five hundred pounds *per annum* and was 'to observe and conform to all competent requests and instructions which may from time to time be given by Council'. It was also stated, somewhat inconsistently, that 'his Professorship was to be in no way affected by his Principalship'. Lastly, it was noted that he was due to retire, on age, in 1941.

This then was the general background in the University at the outbreak of the Second World War, but there was one appointment in the Medical Faculty important enough to deserve special analysis and comment before the war years are described: namely the appointment of Professor McGibbon's successor to the Chair of Midwifery and Gynaecology.

This story had in fact begun as long ago as May 1936. Because Professor McGibbon's health had become so bad, the question of a successor was discussed, or at least of someone to undertake the running of his department. The possibility of a woman candidate for the post was raised, in general terms, and the University saw no reason why a woman should not be appointed, if her other qualifications were suitable. On July 7th applications had been lodged for the Chair of Midwifery in the University, and a short list of four—Mr Chisholm, Miss Fairlie, Dr. Seager and Dr. Taylor was drawn up. The minute stated that

they were to be interviewed in the Senate room at St Andrews on July 20th. And then, on July 10th, a letter was received from the Dundee Infirmary members of the Joint Appointing Committee—the University being required, by an agreement made after the end of the War, to include three representatives of the Infirmary Directors. It was certainly not the sort of letter University Senates are used to receive in connection with the appointment of one of their own members.

> The Infirmary members of the Joint Committee are unanimously of the opinion that on the merits and experience of the applicants they are not prepared to recommend to the Directors the appointment to the Infirmary post of any but Dr. Margaret Fairlie. They feel that in Dr. Fairlie they have a candidate of proved ability and of long experience in the work of the Infirmary ... Dr. Fairlie is held in high esteem by the community.
>
> Also, taking into consideration what was said at our meeting on 7th instant, it does not seem that any purpose would be served by my representatives taking part in any interviews.
>
> Further, my representatives consider it unfortunate that it was thought necessary to re-advertise the joint appointment and extend the date for applications.
>
> William F. Ferguson, Secretary to Directors

In reply, the Court did no more than point out that the Directors were in fact wrong in refusing to attend the interviews under the terms of an agreement they had signed with the University in 1922. The University had their way and on October 10th, Mr William Air, Mr James Prain, Mr Henderson and Mr Athole Stewart, representing the Directors, attended a special meeting to interview the four candidates. The Joint Committee recommended Dr. Fairlie first and Dr. Taylor second. The D.R.I. members again stated strongly that Dr. Fairlie was the candidate 'who would fill the post in the interests of the community of Dundee'. Lord Provost Phin supported them. Mr Air then moved that Dr. Fairlie be appointed. The Lord Rector, Lord Macgregor Mitchell, seconded by Professor Herring, moved that the Court proceed. The Principal, seconded by Dr. Angus MacGillivray (one of the Dundee ophthalmologists) then moved that the University Court delay the appointment. This was then passed by five votes to four. Dr. Taylor later asked to withdraw his name. Next month, on November 16th, Mr William Ferguson wrote on behalf of the Directors to say they now felt that, since there had been no agreement on an appointment, each party should make its own appointment. Further, the directors must have their appointment made by the 17th December. At the same time, Dr. Taylor wrote to the University stating that he was still willing to be considered for the Chair. The next letter from the Directors arrived in December, confirming that they were appointing Dr. Fairlie to be Medical Officer in charge of the Department of Obstetrics and Gynaecology in the Infirmary. Their letter contained an important sentence, in view of the true background to the situation: 'This failure has arisen from a difference of opinion which cannot be resolved by the submission of names of candidates who did not present themselves in response to the

advertisement, the terms and conditions of which, and the date for application, were jointly agreed upon'. They saw no reason to depart from their position.

The rest of the story can be told shortly. The Directors refused to make clinical cases available for the Final Examinations of 1937. They would not allocate them to anyone other than the Medical Officer in charge, and therefore the examination could only be conducted by Dr. Fairlie. Because of this, the Faculty had to make arrangements for the examination to be held elsewhere, and Maryfield Hospital (the city or poor-law hospital) was used. In the summer of 1937, the Dundee Town Council approached the University, possible following promptings by the Principal, about the use of Maryfield Hospital as a Teaching Institution. It was interesting that they did so readily. In November the Court stated its case clearly: a successor was needed to Dr. R.C. Buist, and as there was a vacancy in the Chair of Midwifery and Gynaecology, the prospect was opened of filling these two positions with one and the same person. 'From the point of view of the City, the combined stipend and professional status would attract an obstetrician of high merit and greater experience. A week after this, Dr. Fairlie approached the University to say she was anxious to co-operate with teaching and examining, and the Court agreed to give her a post as lecturer with the status of an internal examiner—without prejudice to the Chair or to possible Maryfield Hospital development. Miss Jean Herring, a daughter of Professor Herring, was appointed a clinical tutor in Gynaecology.

Meetings of the University and Town Council took place the next February, on the 21st, but nothing came of them. Professor McGibbon continued to teach and examine, and meetings took place between the University and the Directors of the Infirmary. It was not however until June of 1940 that the Chairman Mr Henderson and Sir James Irvine finally agreed on a draft—that a Joint Committee of equal numbers nominated by Court and Directors should be appointed, with equal voting power, and that this Committee should act in the event of a vacancy occurring in the Professorships of Medicine, Surgery, Midwifery, or Pathology within three months of the vacancy occurring so that the appointment should be made within four months at the latest. The details of how the Committee would make its recommendations were also laid down. This was sealed and signed[2] and on June 20th, 1940, Principal Irvine proposed that Miss Margaret Fairlie, M.B. Ch.B. F.R.C.O.G. be Professor of Midwifery and Gynaecology in the University of St Andrews. Mr Henderson seconded, and the motion was passed unanimously. She was however to retire at the age of sixty or if she should cease to hold the post of a Medical Officer to Dundee Royal Infirmary.

This meeting was also told that Professor Garry was appointed to become a visiting Medical Officer to the Infirmary 'for special duties of a physiological nature'. The coincidence was of interest, as Professor Garry has provided the background to this very unfortunate affair. While the very long account in Dr. Southgate's book[3] leaves the impression that Principal Irvine was the main source of trouble, and was customarily acting in a manner as detrimental to

Dundee as possible, Professor Garry gives an entirely different account. Because he was so closely involved, he remembers the situation very clearly.

The University staff had to go cap in hand to the Board of Governors of Dundee Royal Infirmary every five years to have their professional staff's appointments continued. Principal Irvine was bitterly opposed to this, and I worked with him to try to stop it. The threat to go to Maryfield was an attempt to overcome this. The candidate whom Irvine had in mind for St Andrews was Dugald Baird—I pushed Baird as I knew how outstanding he was. But beds were given by the Board and any new Professor would have no beds if they did not wish. They gave the beds to Dr. Fairlie, who had looked after many families of Dundee people. They could not see outside Dundee—or did not care. Principal Irvine had academic standards which were very sound and very high—he saw the chance of having someone with a first-class record at Dundee.[4]

This then was the background to the appointment and all the argument which surrounded it. Professor Fairlie would make an excellent Professor—the first woman to hold a Clinical Chair in Scotland. But it was not chauvinism or antagonism which caused the Principal to query the appointee forced upon him by the letter from the Infirmary Directors telling the University whom they were to appoint—it was simply that he had a candidate in mind who had greater potential. That Sir James was correct in his judgement, and that Professor Garry was correct also, was shown in the subsequent career of Sir Dugald Baird at Aberdeen. Professor Garry, a stern critic of Sir James, was entirely behind him on this occasion. The protracted arguments, and the suspicion they created on both sides—especially when reported by the *Courier*—sadly hardened the attitude of Court and Council further against each other. In this instance the faults were by no means all on the side of the Principal.

In 1940, the first year of the war, the fall of France and the evacuation of Dunkirk were followed by the long hot summer of the Battle of Britain, as long and hot as that of 1984. The war was very real that summer. Squads of schoolboys, and some students, toiled day and night erecting concrete anti-tank barriers against the expected invasion around the coast of Fife; open areas such as golf courses had high wooden tree trunks set up as a defence against gliders—and the Rules of Golf were hurriedly altered to take account of a ball striking one of them, and the action to be followed by the player. Earlier, in March, Professor George Duncan became Principal of St Mary's College— Principal Irvine tried to delay his appointment but was outvoted. Principal Duncan's proposer on Court was a new member, Dr. James Lawson, B.Sc., M.D., M.R.C.P.Ed., who had been a physician at Tor-na-dee Sanatorium but had given up medicine to return to Dundee and share in the running of a family drapers, Lawsons Limited. He had been a member of the Council of University College since May of 1939, where his professional background and business skills had been seen as a valuable source of added strength.

The Second World War produced the same sort of staff difficulties as those of the first. By 1940, a whole range of staff had left for service—in Anatomy

Lieutenant-Colonel Thomas John Mitchell, DSO, M.D. Ch.M., the University's first Master of Surgery, and Drs. John Henry Mulligan and Bruce Robertson; in Ophthalmology, Drs. A.R. Moodie and A.A.B. Scott; in Medicine Dr. Macklin; in Dermatology Dr. John Kinnear; and in Surgery Mr W.G. Campbell. Dr. George Smith was RMO to a unit which held the perimeter at Dunkirk; William Walker, later Professor Walker, was evacuated semi-conscious from France with a head injury. And also as in 1914, their work was carried out by deputies; Dr. William Smyly for Dr. Bruce Robertson, Dr. Alastair MacGillivray for Dr. Moodie,[5] Dr. David Hay for Dr. Macklin, Mr Stanley F. Souter for Mr Campbell. Dr. J. Gordon Clark became a temporary lecturer in medicine, and Mr A.E. Chisholm was made a clinical lecturer in obstetrics for twelve months. He had been appointed to the vacant post at Maryfield Hospital. Not all eligible Dundee Staff members left to go to war service; Mr R. Saunders Melville resigned from his post as visiting surgeon in June after complaints had been made by the nursing staff about his excessive rudeness. He was succeeded as a Chief by Mr John Robb. A retired RAMC officer, Colonel Hugh Richardson, came to the Anatomy Department in the Bute to help out. Dr. Peter Robertson, M.D. returned to service for the second time. He was selected by a Lieutenant-Colonel Ian Hill, an Edinburgh assistant physician, as suitable for training as a medical specialist. While in France in No. 5 General Hospital, beside the Somme, he was visited by Professor Edgar Dickie, M.C. of St Mary's College when he went to France to visit Church of Scotland huts and canteens.

The Emergency Medical Service for the Eastern Region of Scotland was set up in 1940. It comprised two large hutted hospitals, one at Bridge of Earn, outside Perth, and another at Stracathro, near Brechin in Angus, for the expected casualties. Professor Alexander was largely responsible for this Service, which he did with his great personal energy and selfless dedication. His tremendous capacity for work and man management made him an ideal choice for this highly important task. One of the University physicians, Dr. James Stalker, was so busy at Bridge of Earn that he had to leave his lecturer's work. Later in the war, an orthopaedic unit was established in Gleneagles Hotel, and a Mr Ian Smillie was one of the surgeons who worked in it, carrying out definitive orthopaedic operations and supervising rehabilitation for wounded service-men.

In 1939-40 there were the following numbers of students in the University:

	Men	Women	Total
United College	256	242	498
St Mary's College	25	1	26
Medical and Dental School	133	53	186
University College	190	94	284

If pre-clinical students were included, however, by now more than half those studying in Dundee were medicals. The First Year medicals were 44 in the United College and 30 in University College.

In February of 1940, Dr. Edward Harkness of New York died. His bene-factions had totalled £160,000, and of this, £100,000 had gone towards the

provision of residences in St Andrews town, to restoring and improving St Salvator's Chapel, and part of the remainder had gone to endow a Chair of History. By the standards of the Baxter benefactions to Dundee, and those of Mr Cox, Mr Whyte and others, Dr. Harkness' bequests were not outstanding. But just as the bequest in Dundee had created envy in St Andrews in the 1880s, so the bequest in St Andrews in the 1930s had created envy in Dundee. So often in the history of these two sides of the University what had happened in or to one was repeated at another date to the other, and this similarity was not confined to favours: faults were as often as not shared equally by both.

Some progress was made in improving residences for medical students in Dundee. The William Low Residence for medical students was originally bought in October 1937 from a bequest by Dr. Low. The cost then of the house and all necessary alterations and arrangements was a little under £4,600. The warden, Dr. Hutchison, was in Professor Cappell's department. Now in 1940, the next door house, No. 11 was acquired. The Committee responsible for supervising further alterations was Principal Irvine, Mr J.B. Salmond, Professor Cappell, Dr. Hutchison, and Dr. James Lawson. It was hoped to extend the building to take about thirty residents, but the steel necessary was refused by the Government—being required for war purposes. However, this pair of residences was established before and during the War and not, as was sometimes believed, bought by Dr. James Lawson later as part of his policy of isolating medical students. Those few obliged to live in residence—Harkness Scholars—used the 'Willie Low' and one or two students who were employed on medical work of national importance in the summer vacation lived there. One of these was Kenneth G. Lowe, a Harkness Scholar of 1936. Professor Cappell used him in connection with his department's setting up the war-time Blood Transfusion Service, and because he was helping in this way he was granted a rebate of twelve shillings a week from his residence fees.

On October 25th 1940, four high explosive bombs were dropped on the town of St Andrews and two of these fell on the University. One landed in the quadrangle of St Mary's, damaging the Library, the other in West Burn Lane, close to the Natural Science extension of the Bute complex. Their combined effect was to wreck the departments of Botany and Geology, while many windows in the remainder of the group were blown out. Arrangements had to be made for movements of classes. The O.T.C. under Lieutenant J.W. Nisbet mounted guard over the damaged buildings. Urgent thought was given to protection of the books in the Library. The Royal and Ancient Golf Club had taken the earlier precaution of asking the University to safeguard their important paintings, and these were already in the basement of St Salvator's Hall. All this brought the reality of the war close to St Andrews, and from now onwards, constant attention was paid to Air Raid Precautions.[6]

Once Professor Fairlie was appointed, she received every support from the University Court in the replenishment of her Department in the Medical School. She was voted £100 at once, and a further £300 was sought from the Carnegie Trust. Coinciding with this, changes were made in the inside of the Medical School—Physiology remained on the ground floor and Anatomy at the top,

but Materia Medica went to the first floor and Pathology to the second. On the second floor the room formerly occupied by the Department of Midwifery was furnished as a room for the Dean of the Faculty, and the Midwifery Department was given the north-east laboratory with the animal room in the Materia Medica Department as a demonstration room and a private room for the Professor. The Ophthalmology lecturer's room was given to the Otolaryngology lecturer for his use in the Martinmas Term, for the Anaesthetic lecturer in the Candlemas, and for the lecturer in Mental Disease, Dr. Bell, in the Whitsunday Term. In the Old Technical Institute, used by Surgery, the O.T.C., and Professor Tulloch's Department, the O.T.C. premises were given to Professor Tulloch and on the Surgery floor, a small room was given to Dr. Kinnear for his Dermatology Department. The Officers Training Corps, or Senior Training Corps as it was called at this time, went into larger premises in Park Place—from 1941 onwards male students were all enlisted into this unit, and its training commitment became progressively more demanding. In 1941 also the University Air Squadron was formed, and this expanded slowly during the rest of the War.

All the individual personal items continued. Professor Alexander was authorised to spend six guineas for a cadaver for his department—this was the cost in 1941. The Air Ministry Training Scheme began, and the 'Air Bejants' arrived. Dr. R.P. Cook was appointed as lecturer in Biochemistry in Professor Garry's Department—Dr. A. Hynd was already lecturing on this subject in Professor Herring's Department in a joint appointment shared with the Mackenzie Institute. In the Bute also, Frank Weston and James Brown were employed as temporary lecturers. Mr Husband, the janitor, was called up. The William Low Residence was used for summer courses, but participants had to bring their own food coupons. Rationing of food and clothing went on through the War; indeed until 1954 students brought their ration books with them to their residence or bunk. Coupons were needed for gowns, and each scarlet gown required sixteen. In 1942 the University ordered thirty-eight from R.W. Forsyth of Edinburgh in a bulk buy, in order that the gown would still be seen.

Professor Waterston died in Edinburgh on September 4th 1942. At the memorial service in St Salvator's Chapel Professor Cappell, now Dean of the Faculty of Medicine, led the representatives of the Medical Faculty. Professor Dow was asked to take over charge of the Department in the Bute, where he had worked before moving to UCD, and he continued in this joint charge until the end of the War. It was interesting that he appeared to have no difficulty in carrying out this role—he was always very fond of St Andrews and especially of the Bute—so it was certainly possible for a shared department to succeed, if the person involved wanted it to do so.

As the War continued, the depths of early 1942, with the Fall of Singapore, the greatest disaster to British Arms in the country's history, and the German advance into Russia, were succeeded by the increasing co-operation by the United States in Europe and the gradual turn of the tide. The defeat and resignation of Mussolini in July 1943, following the North African victories of October 1942 and the Allied invasion of Italy, marked the first unmistakable sign of the breakdown of the Axis powers. Decisive victories in January 1943 by

the Russians at Stalingrad marked the turn of the War in Russia also. Casualties to British troops were never on anything resembling the scale of those of 1916-18, and the policy of the Government towards medical students was much more uniform than the stops and starts of twenty-five years earlier. More new names appeared in the Medical Faculty. Dr. D.H. Smith became a clinical tutor in Tuberculosis in July 1944, Dr. Susan Wilson an assistant in Anatomy at University College, and Mrs Agnes Dow a temporary assistant at the Bute. Dr. George Grant was appointed lecturer in Radiology, Dr. James Brodie in Bacteriology; Drs. Henry Goodall and James G. Lawson became temporary lecturers in Bacteriology and Pathology. In Anaesthetics, Dr. John McDonald Clark, Dr. John Duke Stewart, and Dr. James Ferguson were clinical lecturers throughout the War. In Ear, Nose and Throat Mr M.J. Gibson was second in charge to Dr. Mathers, and Dr. George Henderson of the Department left for War Service. Of significance was the decision of the Infirmary Directors, who were now considerably more co-operative to the University since their Midwifery appointment days, to agree to extend the appointments of Professors Patrick and Alexander for a further year from October 1944, although they were over age to continue to be visiting Medical Officers.

Remarkably, the Charities Campaign, which belonged especially to the Dundee side of the enlarged University, was carried on during the war with even more fervour than previously. Drs. J.D.M. Ross and G.R. Tudhope had acted as permanent secretaries to the Campaign throughout the 1930s, and the University must be forever grateful to them for all the work they did. Their reward was not only the respect, but also the love of two generations of students. The St Andrews side had the Kate Kennedy procession, but nothing to compare with the excitement and enthusiasm of 'Charities'. It was the one occasion when Dundee people became really aware that they had a great University in their midst. In 1944, when money was short, war-weariness evident, and young school-leavers thin with five years of food rationing, £4261 were raised in Dundee and the surrounding burghs. The total credit for this went to Dundee's student body.

As the end of the war came into sight, the same features appeared as in 1918—proposals for teaching doctors returning from H.M. Forces, for example, and a certain lessening of the rigours of S.T.C. training. But the most important series of proposals by far were those of the Goodenough Report of April, 1943. This report was from the Inter-Departmental Committee on Medical Schools, and looked towards the post-war period with the inception of a Health Service and changes in medical training. The conception of a new University Teaching Hospital was formally stated as the next stage in the development of medical teaching for the University, and the memorandum issued by the University through its Court envisaged development of the Medical School on a very considerable scale indeed. This memorandum is of such historic importance that it deserves quotation *in extenso*:

1. The (Goodenough) proposals are therefore directed to the attainment of two related objectives (a) the improvement of medical training, both undergraduate and postgraduate, in the

University, and (b) an extension of the Health Services provided in this area. It may be stated, however, that the policy now outlined has been for long regarded by us as the natural development of the Medical School and has not been framed merely to meet the circumstance that the whole problem of Medical Service is now being examined by Government. No essential change in our policy has been found necessary in envisaging the creation of a Consolidated Medical Service, and even in the absence of such a movement our plans for the future would be little different although their prospect of realisation would be remote. We are therefore glad to take advantage of the suggestion made by the Committee that we should outline what is in our opinion the ideal scheme applicable to our academic conditions and our public environment, without consideration as to whether or not the proposals are financially possible. Of necessity we have included certain projects which concern the Teaching Hospital rather than the University, but there is no clean-cut line of demarcation and without reference to these projects the picture would be incomplete. The corresponding financial estimates, so far as they affect University expenditure, are given in the appendix.

2. In making the recommendations which follow we have kept before us the idea that in the interests of teaching efficiency the present dimensions of the Medical School ought not to be increased to any great extent. Under existing arrangements, pre-clinical studies are concluded both in St Andrews and in Dundee, and, in terms of a domestic concordat, students are now divided in approximately equal numbers between the two centres. Entrant medical students are restricted to about 30 in each centre and at the beginning of the 3rd year these groups are combined so that the number proceeding to clinical studies may be taken as 60 annually. The arrangements work satisfactorily and any suggestion that the subjects of Anatomy and Physiology should be concentrated in one centre can be ruled out. Experience has convinced us of the educational efficiency which is secured when classes are of relatively small dimensions and by the instruction of medical students in the fundamental sciences along with students of pure science. These advantages would be lost by concentrating pre-clinical medical students in one college. Further, any trivial economy in annual expenditure which might follow from the amalgamation of the duplicate departments of Anatomy and Physiology would be extinguished by the loss of endowment revenues and by the heavy capital cost incurred in doubling the capacity of the laboratories and other buildings.

3. When the new medical curriculum is introduced after the War, and the course is extended to 5½ or 6 years, there is likely to be

considerable modification of the time-table but there will be little
reason to alter in any profound sense the teaching work of the
pre-clinical years, especially as we hold the opinion that the
fundamental sciences introductory to Medicine should be taught
in a University and not studied at School. Attention is therefore
directed to the arrangements for the three clinical years.

4.   Before discussing the details of individual departments, some
primary aspects of our general problem require consideration.

(a) *Locus of the Medical School:*

The Medical School building, erected nearly fifty years ago, is
situated in the grounds of University College, Dundee, and is
nearly a mile distant from the main teaching hospital. The
building was designed on unambitious lines and the growth of the
School, both in numbers and in the scope of the curriculum, has
rendered the accommodation entirely inadequate. The site does
not readily permit of building expansion and, in any event, it
would be undesirable to rectify the present situation merely by
structural enlargement. By so doing, an arrangement which we
regard as fundamentally unsatisfactory would be perpetuated and
there can be no doubt that the whole of the teaching in the three
final years of the medical course should be conducted in the
immediate vicinity of the main teaching hospital. Our plans for
the future therefore depend largely for their realisation on the
erection of a new Medical Institute or Institutes in the
neighbourhood of the Dundee Royal Infirmary. The building
should house all the subjects of the Third Year and upwards; it
should contain the Medical Library together with the
Administrative Offices relating to the School, and the fabric
should be readily capable of expansion or modification to suit
changing conditions. Although the activities of this projected
Medical Institute would be closely associated with those of the
hospital it would continue to be administered solely by the
University Court.

(b) *Staffing:*

From the third year of study and upwards the staffing of each
teaching department in the Medical School is designed mainly to
meet the academic requirements. This system is capable of
improvement by the division of staff into definite Units which
would co-ordinate more effectively the activities of both
University and Hospital. In Medicine and in Surgery the adoption
of a Unit system would demand both an increase and a complete
re-organisation of staff. The department of Midwifery is in
progress of being organised on this model, but recent legislation
has tended more and more to increase institutional midwifery and
the staff of the department, although recently enlarged and
adequate for teaching purposes, falls short of what is required.

The ideal major Clinical Unit would consist of:

    The Chief (who might be a Regional Consultant)
    Senior Assistant (who might be a Regional Consultant)
    One full-time Assistant
    One Registrar (with experience as House Officer)
    Two Resident House Officers (recent Graduates)

The framework of a major Unit should be flexible to an extent which would allow members of the staff in any department to be seconded to other departments or to other associated hospitals. For example, a Senior Assistant in a medical Unit might be attached to a hospital for chronic diseases or for infectious diseases, or to a department engaged with scientific studies, e.g. Pharmacology. Two other points should be mentioned in this connection. Each Unit should undertake Out-Patient work so as to preserve continuity in the diagnosis, treatment and after-care of each case. The expansion of the teaching staff on the lines indicated above and the enlargement of the radius of their duties would involve, of necessity, the provision of an increased number of trained technicians. To this requirement should be added secretarial assistance on a scale substantially larger than at present. These suggestions are not trivial; they follow naturally as part of the policy to conserve in every possible way the time of experts so that they may devote their full energy to the teaching of students and to the care of patients.

It is also our opinion that an Almoner's department should be instituted both in the public interest and in the interest of the Medical School, but as this is a project which concerns the teaching hospital rather than the University the item is not included in the financial estimates.

(c) *Whole-Time Appointments to Chairs:*

We are of the opinion that the three major subjects (Medicine, Surgery and Midwifery) should be held by full-time Professors. The arguments in favour of this are well-known and do not require repetition but we recognise that much would be lost if a professor in these subjects were restricted by the terms of his appointment to the practice of his specialty in any one hospital. The description "full-time Professor" ought in consequence to be elastic in its interpretation and capable of modification in terms of local conditions. An opportunity for preserving the merit of the existing part-time system while relieving the Professor of the necessity to earn professional fees may well be opened out by the new organisation of Consultants which is envisaged as part of the national scheme. In the event, which we consider desirable, of University professors participating as consultants in any Regional Scheme we would regard such dual service as discharging the functions of a full-time professorship.

(d) *Method of Making Appointments*

Office holders in the Medical School will normally have Hospital duties and this raises the problem of how such appointments should be made. Our position is that by far the greatest proportion of the clinical teaching is carried out in the Dundee Royal Infirmary and through a harmonious arrangement with the Directors all appointments (major and minor) to positions involving both hospitals and teaching duties are made by the parent bodies on the recommendation of a Joint Committee composed of equal numbers from the University Court and the Dundee Royal Infirmary. The scheme works smoothly, and it is our hope that such modification in medical training as may emerge from a comprehensive State Medical Service will not interfere with the continuance of the arrangement. Dependent as we are primarily on co-operation with a single general hospital, we consider that the existing method of filling appointments is preferable to a centralised scheme in which a Regional Appointments Board would make the recommendation leading to these appointments. It is recognised that, in future, local authority hospitals of varying type will probably become more closely associated with the University training of medical students and that it will be necessary to devise similar machinery for filling the corresponding teaching positions. This ought not to present any serious difficulty.

5.   *Rearrangements of Existing Departments:*

Applying the above principles to the existing departments of study we make the following recommendations:

Materia Medica: The professor should be "full-time" as defined in para. 4 (c) but need not of necessity be a Chief Officer in a hospital with all the duties and responsibilities of the Chief of a Unit. Considering the research possibilities of modern therapeutics it is our opinion that the professor of Materia Medica should have a special interest and competency in experimental science and that his function as a physician should be complementary to his scientific work. We are not satisfied that "Materia Medica" is now a sufficiently accurate description of this professorship and we prefer Pharmacology, it being understood that the activities of the department will also include Therapeutics. Until such time as a new medical institute is provided, the adoption of this policy will involve the re-equipment of the existing department for experimental research, including the provision of adequate animal-house accommodation.

Pathology and Bacteriology:

As close co-operation and integration of their work is desirable, these departments are considered together.

    In both subjects progressive fundamental research is curtailed

through the claims of other duties. Much of the routine testing for the hospitals of the region and in connection with Public Health examinations is conducted in these departments, and, as the work has grown in recent years, the burden thrown on the professors has become excessive. It would be short-sighted, however, to rectify this situation by removing from the University departments the responsibility for carrying out examinations for the Public Health authorities of Dundee and adjacent regions. Not only would this tend (to take the case of Bacteriology as an example) to restrict the scope of the work of purely academic scientific study but, by removing the contact with epidemic and infective disease in the community, would deprive the department of access to material which is utilised in a steady succession of valuable researches. Further, it is the considered opinion of the professors of Pathology and Bacteriology in Scotland that the development of Regional Medical organisation requires the active participation of the University departments if the highest standards of work are to be maintained. We consider therefore that the position can be best met by separating the teaching and research duties from those of Public Health Services; this will entail an increase of staff in both departments, with circulation of the various members between different types of duty so as to ensure a thorough all-round experience in teaching, routine work and reasearch. Co-ordination of academic and Public Health duties is essential in view of the need for laboratory control of epidemiology investigations and it may reasonably be expected that the increased costs of these developments will be fully met from the Regional Scheme by payment for services rendered. The proposals of the professors of Pathology and Bacteriology also provide for the seconding of men to posts of varying degrees of responsibility within the Region. One such post would be that of Resident Clinical Assistant in Pathology and Bacteriology in the main Teaching Hospital. It may be recalled that among the requirements proposed for the future training of medical and surgical specialities is a year spent in the study of one of the basic sciences and we consider that a post of the type envisaged above would be one valuable means of providing this part of the training.

Within the department of Pathology, Clinical Pathology should be sub-divided into Clinical Haematology and Clinical Biochemistry. There would thus be four main divisions, viz., Morbid Anatomy, Pathological Histology, Haematology and Biochemistry, and, as far as possible, the staff would undertake duty in each section in rotation, and would take part in developing Experimental Pathology. The importance of modern Haematology as an aid to the physician need not be stressed and

we have drawn up a detailed scheme which would ensure that the teaching of the subjects and the conduct of clinical examinations would be undertaken with the thoroughness they deserve. With regard to Clinical Chemistry it is our belief that if the subject is to progress as a science it is essential that it should be pursued by one who has a trained outlook on and experience in chemical research. He should not be burdened with routine biochemical analyses required for clinical diagnosis but should have access to hospital material to enable him to carry out fundamental research on selected subjects. The operation of such a department, particularly if it collaborated with the Pharmacologist and Therapeutist in the study of modern chemotherapeutic problems, would go far to provide continuous instruction in Chemistry during the clinical years of the medical students' course.

It will be generally agreed that the Regional Blood Transfusion Service has become a permanent requirement and recent developments have indicated the desirability of applying blood grouping tests as a routine in connection with maternity services. This work might well continue to be undertaken by the enlarged Pathology Department now envisaged.

It is impossible at this stage to give an exact estimate of the staff required for the associated departments of Pathology and Bacteriology as much will depend on how the Regional Scheme develops, and whether any subsidiary laboratory centres are established in the Region. There is, however, one condition which should be attached to any arrangement under which the departments of Pathology and Bacteriology conduct work on behalf of Hospitals, Public Health Authorities and Practitioners. In each case the Professor must remain Head of the Department as a whole, responsible for all teaching and research, and directing the conduct of the routine investigations; there should be no bifurcation of administrative authority. Only in this way can the fullest use be made of the resources of the Department and can researches be initiated which arise directly out of the routine study of disease.

Surgery, Midwifery and Medicine:

All three departments should be reconstituted on the Unit principle as defined in para. 4 (b); the detailed duties attached to each member of these units need not be elaborated here as they are already sufficiently standardised.

6. *Developments:*

At present all the subjects mentioned below are included in the curriculum but we believe that their importance warrants a much more comprehensive and intensive effort on the lines indicated. Staffing details are omitted from the synopsis as the relation of the teaching and adminsitration to existing departments must be left for future consideration.

(a) *Human Nutrition and Dietetics:*
Conditions in Dundee render the area peculiarly suitable for
investigation of the problems of human nutrition and a good
opportunity presents itself to establish a University department in
the above subjects. The adoption of this project would require
trained dieticians in the Dundee Royal Infirmary where, in all
probability, new equipment would be necessary. The suggested
University department would work in collaboration with the
Hospital Almoner system and would have intimate connection
with the Infant and Child Health departments and with the Ante-
Natal and Maternity departments both of the Royal Infirmary
and of the Public Health Authorities Hospitals.

(b) *Child Health and Welfare:*
The above subject requires the whole-time services of a Senior
Physician with an adequate staff and its importance justifies the
establishment of a professorship to co-ordinate the studies of all
aspects of Child Care throughout the region. The Professor
should be a Regional Consultant and the Department should
work in conjunction with all the activities in the area which are
concerned with the health and welfare of children. A Paediatrician
of skill and experience is required and as, under existing
conditions, there is no prospect that the occupant of the Chair
could build up an adequate consulting practice it is evident that
the establishment of a professorship will involve a close liaison
between University, Voluntary Hospital and Public Authorities.
As a matter of public policy the creation of a department on the
lines now indicated is justified.

(c) *Orthopaedic and Traumatic Surgery:*
This development is one which primarily concerns the Teaching
Hospital but it has an important bearing on the training of
medical students. A new Unit in the Dundee Royal Infirmary
should be established to deal with accident cases; it should
comprise a Ward Unit with O.P. department and Casualty Room
and should work in conjunction with long-term Orthopaedic
Hospitals and with Rehabilitation Centres. The department would
take all the accident and fracture cases and in order to provide a
24-hour service a duplicate staff would be necessary. The Chief
and Sub-Chiefs would be Consultants for the Regional Scheme
and the junior members would take duty in rotation at the
Receiving section for acute cases and at the Orthopaedic and
Rehabilitation hospitals for recovery cases. Facilities for
instruction of students in all branches of this work are of obvious
importance and to meet the requirements of teaching it would be
necessary for the University to institute a Lectureship in
Orthopaedic Surgery and also certain junior appointments.

(d) *Industrial Health Services:*

Although the present section of our Report is concerned primarily with the improvement of certain aspects of medical training already undertaken and is not devoted to the suggestion of new developments, we think it only right to state here that the study of Occupational Disease and the problems of Industrial Health generally are worthy of immediate inclusion in the teaching programme. Details have not yet been fully adjusted but a minimum start with the project would involve the creation of at least one additional lectureship.

(e) *Radiology:*

Regional Medical Schemes will involve additional provision for Radiology, both diagnostic and therapeutic. The staff of such a service should be associated with University teaching and close collaboration should be established with the departments of Natural Philosophy in the University. The Chief of the Unit should have the status of University Lecturer and his stipend should be sufficient to make the teaching of students an important duty. The Senior Radio-therapist should also be a paid teacher and the arrangements must be such as will be readily adaptable to the requirements of the Cancer Act when it comes into operation.

(f) *Mental Health Services:*

There is an urgent need for two Outpatient Clinics, one at Dundee Royal Infirmary and one at the Public Authority Hospital; these would co-operate with the Child Guidance Clinics and with the department of Child Health. Teaching of students should include instruction of psychiatric outpatients work of all types.

(g) *Experimental Psychology:*

Instruction in psychology will be provided for more effectively in the new curriculum to be introduced after the war. As the department of Experimental Psychology in St Andrews is among the best equipped in the country it is proposed to arrange that the instruction should be given in the United College and that students from Dundee should travel to take the course.

7. *University Residence:*

So far there has been in use only one small official residence attached to the Medical School. The scheme has been successful to an extent which justifies the University Court taking steps to incorporate the neighbouring house but this expansion is meanwhile in abeyance owing to the war. Everything points to the advisability of extending the Residence System for the benefit of students in their clinical years and, for obvious reasons, the locus of such a residence should be in the vicinity of the main Teaching Hospital. It is a general experience that the best results follow when a residence is built to a plan designed for the special purpose in view and that the adaptation of existing houses is

rarely satisfactory. There is no reason why men and women should not be accommodated in separate residential wings of one building equipped with common kitchen, dining-room and library, an arrangement which is economical both in capital cost and in recurring expenditure. In the case of the Medical School of this University it is estimated that each residential wing should be capable of accommodating about 50 students. This represents a residential unit of suitable size and the design can be readily adjusted to meet the condition that the ratio of men to women students may fluctuate. The existing residence could than have as its first purpose the housing of students during their period of compulsory residence in their final year.

Residence in the Infirmary:

In discussion with the Committee reference was made to the desirability of all medical graduates holding House appointments for at least six months after graduation and it is possible that such a period of post-graduate training may become compulsory before the granting of a licence to practice independently. The provision of necessary facilities, including residential accommodation, is outwith the province of the University and in consequence the item is not included in the financial estimates which follow.

APPENDIX

Financial Estimates

Of necessity, the estimates are approximate but they are not entirely conjectural. Capital costs of buildings are based on actual expenditure on similar projects from 1928 to 1938 and the amount of stipend is assessed on figures quoted by the Committee on Post-War Organisation of Hospitals in Scotland.

PART I—CAPITAL EXPENDITURE

Medical Institute: Although reference is made in the text to a Medical Institute which would accommodate all the subjects of the third year and upwards we recognise that certain advantages follow from the division of a Medical School into separate Institutes each designed to meet the special requirements of a single subject or a group of associated subjects. The latter method is, however, expensive both in initial capital cost and in recurring expenditure. For this reason, the estimates now submitted are restricted to the cost of a single building to house the subjects of the three (or four) final years of study.

To provide such a building, with lecture-rooms and laboratories appropriate to the various departments together with accommodation for administration, the offices of the Dean and the Medical Library would cost approximately £105,000. The estimate is exclusive of the cost of the site or of equipment other than permanent fittings which would form part of the structure.

The above figure is based on the working space necessary for the

instruction of 300 students. This total, while allowing for some expansion, assumes that students are recruited to the Medical School at the rate of 60 annually and that the course which now lasts for three years may in future be extended to four years.

Residence for Medical Students: The proposed residence for medical students embodies a somewhat unusual design but this need not add unduly to the standard rate being applied of an initial capital cost of £500 to £600 per student. Allowing £12,000 for the centre block of the building, this brings out a total of £72,000 exclusive of site and furnishings beyond those which form part of the structure.

The cost of the Residences for Students conducting cases of labour has already been met by the University.

PART II—RECURRING EXPENDITURE

The expenditure on salaries necessary to give effect to the various schemes is detailed below. Superannuation charges have been added but additional overhead and maintenance charges are not included. In each case the expenditure at present incurred by the University is deducted from the total cost of each department so as to bring out the new financial liabilities which would be incurred to operate the proposals.

Anatomy and Physiology have not been included in the estimates as the provision already made in these subjects is adequate for teaching up to the standard of Honours B.Sc. and the retention of this standard is a natural charge on University funds.

Materia Medica (Pharmacology) and Therapeutics: To restore the Chair of Materia Medica to a full-time Professorship, to institute a Readership in Therapeutics and to provide adequate laboratory staff would involve increased annual expenditure of £1,595.

Pathology: The additional stipends for enlargement of the staff on the lines laid down in the memorandum are estimated at £2,230 p.a.

Resident Clinical Assistant in Pathology and Bacteriology: This post may possibly be regarded as a charge on Infirmary funds but meantime it is included in the University returns. The estimated cost is £440 p.a. (with residence).

Bacteriology: Exclusive of a separate staff to carry out examinations on behalf of Public Health Authorities, it is estimated that the re-organisation of the Department as indicated in the memorandum would cost £1,570 p.a.

Surgery and Medicine: To introduce the Unit system in its simplest form would raise the existing salary payments by £2,815 p.a. in each department, i.e. at total of £5,630 p.a.

Midwifery: As the Unit system is already partly in operation the additional annual charge to complete the scheme would be £2,080 p.a.

Child Health and Welfare: The creation of a full-time Professorship in this subject, together with adequate assistance would cost £1,870 p.a.

Orthopaedic Surgery: Cost of Lectureship and two Resident

Assistants may be taken at £650 p.a. As this staff has to be
duplicated to provide continuous service, the total becomes
£1,300 p.a.
Dietetics £550 p.a.
Radiology £1,100 p.a.
*Ophthalmology, Public Health, Forensic Medicine and Medical
Psychology:* Of the above subjects, only the first mentioned need at
present be administered on the Unit system but extra staff will be
necessary in all the departments of study. Estimated increase in
salaries *£2,750* p.a.

The total charges enumerated above amount to £21,115 per
annum and this may be regarded as £22,000 *per annum* when
account is taken of extra minor charges as, for example, secretarial
assistance. It must be pointed out, however, that in arriving at the
above figures we have adhered to the salary scales now operative in
this University for Professors, Readers, and Lecturers. If the scale of
salaries recommended by the Hetherington Committee is adopted the
total is substantially larger (£31,930) and may be taken as at least
£32,000 *per annum.*

All subsequent post-war developments which actually took place are
foreshadowed in this memorandum, which was issued with the agreement of the
Faculty. It produced a sense of expectation; the Medical School of the enlarged
University of St Andrews, now moving towards its Jubilee, had every prospect
of 'taking off'. The University's own graduates were becoming mature enough
to be eligible for senior academic posts, and reliance on others from the longer-
established major schools for St Andrews Chairs would be reduced. The small
numbers so far in the Faculty—and they *were* small, it must be remembered,
against the hundreds of medicals graduating yearly from Glasgow and Edinburgh—were showing no evidence of lack of ability; perhaps the family
tradition of the small university, so long the feature of St Andrews, was working
for her medical graduates also. Principal Fulton asked that his dissent be
recorded from the Court's decision about the site of the Advanced Medical
School—he and the Council wished no change from the present location. In this
instance at least, the Court were far-seeing and adventurous, the Council
inward-looking and negative. Far from St Andrews denying progress to
Dundee, the Dundee party were denying progress to their own side of Sir
Thomas Thornton's enlarged University.

The University Grants Committee was due to visit St Andrews again in
1944. This meeting led to a complaint from the Council of University College
that it was not to be able to give its views on post-war developments, and a letter
was written in March to Mr D.J.B. Ritchie, the Secretary to the University
Court:

27th March, 1944.

Principal Fulton had told the Council that the University Court had
been asked to give its views on post-war and future developments. He
further intimated that the Council should not be invited as a body to

make any formal statement regarding the needs of University College.

Council profoundly regrets this departure from the procedure followed on similar occasions in the past and begs to state that it cannot be held to agree that this arrangement be considered a precedent for the future.

They forwarded a report on Post-War Policy prepared by Principal Fulton and by the Professors teaching in the College, which they had unanimously adopted as an interim statement...

Patrick Cumming

Professor Fulton complained that the Court had accepted a Chair in Scots Law and one in Electrical Engineering, but that the additional matters he had asked for had been rejected. These again concerned provisions for more Arts subjects at University College, especially in History. The Dundee Council agreed that after consultation with its own Law Agents, it send a letter direct to the University Grants Commission 'with the recommendations from University College Dundee, so that the Council's voice might be heard'. Later, on 24th May, the Chairman of Council, Mr W.H. Valentine, wrote to Sir Walter Moberley, the Chairman of the UGC, saying that his Council now understood that 'the St Andrews University Memorandum would not be considered until some time after the return of Principal Irvine to enable the matter to be discussed here, and I hope, agreement to be reached. I was also able to inform the Council that this enquiry was different from the usual quinquennial survey, and subsequent grants would not be reserved exclusively for objects dealt with in the present memorandum'. The Council, he continued, had therefore agreed that his letter to the UGC of 29th March be withdrawn meantime. In late November, however, the Council decided, at a meeting at which Sir James was present, to send a letter from University College directly to the Conference of Scottish Universities from its College Education Board about a common syllabus for Mathematics, Physics and Chemistry, and pressing once more for a lectureship in History. The Council was by this tactic distancing itself from the University, and was acting as an independent body. And although the University Court agreed in February of the next year to appoint a lecturer in History at £600 salary *per annum* at University College, a further break in relations had occurred.

One further event occurring while the war was still in progress was an inspection by the General Medical Council Examiners. This was the first inspection of its kind since 1930, when the three inspectors had pronounced themselves 'satisfied', and took place in 1944. For the Medical Finals, Professor A.W. Harrington of Glasgow was the External Examiner. The method of choosing written questions was now for the local and external examiners to submit four questions from which his colleague selected three. All six questions had to be answered, and the answers were marked by the Examiners who had not set them. Any great discrepancy in the marking, or in the marks obtained in the clinical and oral parts of the examination, led to a joint discussion and further scrutiny. (See note 7 for details of papers). The clinical examinations were shared between 'the Municipal Hospital, Maryfield,' and the Royal. 'This in-

novation increased the number of patients available in an admirable way, and reduced the intrusion into the wards of the Royal Infirmary'. The orals were held in the Pathology Department at the Infirmary.

The Examiner from the G.M.C. was obviously impressed with the arrangements for the examination, and with the high standard of the candidates in all three parts. At the clinical, each student was given a 'long' case and allowed at least one and a half hours for its investigation. At the end of the first hour, the candidate was called away for a side-room examination conducted by the two Examiners. At this part of the examination, six slides were shown, as well as charts, X-rays, and instruments.

> I was interested to observe that in the investigation of the "long" cases also candidates carried out excellent side-room examinations, including full urine analysis (qualitative), microscopic reports on deposits, stained blood films, and sputum films. In one instance a candidate put up a beautifully stained Ziehl-Neelsen film showing tubercle bacilli in the sputum of a patient in whom repeated examinations had failed to discover Koch's bacillus previously. I mention this incident not as the performance of an exceptional candidate, but as an illustration of the high standard of clinical work attained by many of the candidates.

The short cases were then examined in front of each Examiner separately, but discussion of the final marking was done jointly. The G.M.C. Inspector was highly impressed by the informal notes students made, when writing up their long cases. 'The standards were high and I fully agreed with the marks awarded'. 'None the less', he went on, after praising the actual running of the medical final, 'I consider that the examination of 63 candidates by the Examiners, lasting from 9.00 a.m. till 7.00 p.m. or later on four consecutive days, with the morning of a fifth in addition (seven clinical and two oral sessions) taken in conjunction with the marking of 63 scripts, is too heavy a task'. How different this examination sounds, and how somehow more searching, than the production line of forty years later where one hundred are put through in one day! The emphasis on side-room work was very much a feature of Professor Patrick's era—Dr. Alfred Pitkeathly's recollections of his time as a houseman come to mind—and credit for skill in performing laboratory stains must also go to the intensive training which Professor Tulloch gave his bacteriology class. In this year, 36 of the total 63 passed, and 18 obtained 'Conditional Passes' in Medicine. Of this last group, 9 passed in the other two subjects and so passed in all three. Of the remaining 9, 3 finally failed in all subjects, one failed surgery and 5 midwifery.

The Inspector in Medicine was Professor J.A. Nixon, C.M.G., M.D., F.R.C.P.(London). The Surgery Inspector was Mr Harold Collinson, C.B., C.M.G., D.S.O., F.R.C.S. Eng. The Surgery written paper was prepared similarly to the Medicine one, but there were four compulsory questions. The maximum was 100 marks. Mr Paterson Brown was the External, with Professor Alexander. In the clinical, one 'long' and several 'short' cases were examined, together with X-rays of fractures and dislocations, alimentary and renal

conditions, and various instruments and surgical applicances. The short cases and X-rays were taken alternatively by each Examiner, but both were present and the mark was decided between them. The long case questions were asked by one Examiner acting alone, but the examination was arranged so that this part of the clinical was taken by the examiner who had not read the candidate's paper. 'The cases utilised were varied and very suitable, the questioning detailed and searching, and in almost every case the candidate was asked to demonstrate his method of physical examination'. This brought out Professor Alexander's immense skill as a teacher of clinical examination—he would show his students precisely how to place their fingers and hands on the area they were examining. His *forte* was clinical examination and diagnosis. The 'orals' included surgical pathology, and Mr George Sturrock assisted the senior members by testing candidates in surface markings on a living model. 'The examination impressed me as a carefully conducted and thorough test of the candidates' knowledge, and the standard demanded was adequate'.

Sir William Fletcher Shaw, M.D., F.R.C.P., F.R.C.O.G. was the Midwifery Inspector. His report included the fact that of the 65 who began the medical course each year at St Andrews, only 55 might still be involved by the final year. He also noted that the clinical three years had been reduced by three months as a war-time measure, with the finals being taken that March instead of in June, but that this was to revert to the full time in 1945. The necessary certificates of residence for a month in a Maternity Hospital, and of taking twenty deliveries, were detailed, as was the part of the course about care of the new-born. With Professor Fairlie as External was Professor Cameron of Glasgow, and the examination covered the same parts as medicine and surgery—written, clinical and oral. A difference between this Final and the others was that it took place in September 1944 and not March, and was therefore a re-sit. The Examiners corrected his or her own written questions—five in all—but both read a doubtul answer. A gynaecological case was seen, followed by one in the maternity, in the clinical part. The orals were held by both Examiners together in the Department in the Medical School.

Some criticisms were made of this Final Examination by Sir William. The Examiners did not work to a time-table, and so did not see an equal number of candidates—some students had the same Examiner for both cases. In the oral, too, although each candidate was given about ten minutes, there was no bell and the time varied. The possible disadvantages of this were noted. However, 'the examination is thorough and has a sound clinical test, and I was satisfied with all the marks given'.

It fell to the new Dean, Professor Tulloch, to sign the formal comments 'on behalf of the licensing body' in February 1945. He defended certain of the written questions—'on the infant and on Endocrines' which had been commented upon by the Inspector. But apart from these replies to some criticism, very little had had to be said by the Senate, and Professor Cappell's earlier letters to the General Medical Council needed no comments at all. The Medical School was now mature. Its new Dean was a graduate of its own, and would become an excellent holder of the post in the next years. The student numbers

were still small, but the standard of examinations high. Questions mirrored the practice and problems of the day. The records of 1944 reflect confidence, looking forward to a yet higher level of graduate coming through the Faculty.

In February of 1946, Principal Fulton resigned. He had been in Dundee all his life—first as a student, then as a lecturer. His only departure was as a Royal Flying Corps adviser in the 1914-18 War. He would continue as a member of Court, however, and would become an active agent in post-war University politics.[8] The Council decided at once that a full-time Principal should be appointed, at a salary of £1,500 *per annum*, with a free residence, and a further £250 towards his special expenses. Professor Garry was to be a member of the Principalship Sub-Committee, as was Mr Robin Thomson, B.A., C.A., the new Council Chairman. On March 19th, 1946, the advertisement was drawn up and approved. And on 15th July, a Special Council Meeting reported that Mr W.L. Ferrar, M.A. Bursar of Hertford College Oxford, and Major-General D.N. Wimberley, C.B., D.S.O., M.C., Director of Infantry, the War Office, had been interviewed for the post. Major-General Wimberley was unanimously elected.

14

The post-war period in the University

The Third Party
The Cooper Report and the Royal Commission

The difficulties which arose in the post-1945 period had their origins in long-standing internal conditions and in recent external factors. In the 'Deed of Endowment and Trust of University College Dundee' the Governors of the College were to be the Supreme Governing Body[1] and every governor was to be a member of the College. Governors could elect themselves for life simply by donating £50 or more to University College. The Managing Body of the College were the Council, 'responsible to the Governors for the proper discharge of their functions'[2]. The Education Board were to organise and direct the education of the College and in this were responsible to the Council alone. Appointment of the Principal—'who need not be or have been a Professor of the College'[3]—and the Professors of the College, was in the power of the Council, at such salaries and upon such terms as they though fit, as indeed was removal or termination of contract of such employees. It was the Council who were given power, subject to the sanction of the Governors in General Meeting, 'to affiliate or unite the College with the University, College, Society or Institute having objects similar to any of the subjects of the College hereby instituted, and upon any terms that may be desirable'. And although University College was finally affiliated to the University of St Andrews in 1897, no mention of that University appeared in the Deed until the Special Resolution of 27th November 1935, when a sub-section was added to Section XVII to provide for the Principal of the University of St Andrews to be an *ex officio* Member of the Council[4].

Following the affiliation, University College Dundee retained its autonomy under the terms of its Deed. Although called a 'College' in this Deed of Endowment, it never received a Charter nor was it ever incorporated—even though it was set up on lines similar to comparable institutions in English cities; it *continued* as a Trust under the administration of its Trustees, Governors and Council. Furthermore, it was not an independent College such as Southampton or Exeter, but a constituent part of a University rather like University College London. While it enjoyed the advantages of being a part of the University of St Andrews, it also claimed the privileges of independence. While 2 of its members could serve on the Senate and Court of the University, no reciprocal privilege was allowed to members of the United and St Mary's Colleges. There were real difficulties inherent in the unsatisfactory compromise arrangement of the late

250

1890s which Principal Donaldson and Sir Thomas Thornton had both recognised and which could not be resolved without fundamental constitutional change. Although successive Principals of the University of St Andrews had been present at Council meetings, they had no *direct* power to order the College in any way; the Court, however, on the advice of the Senate, was in charge of general university policy, and the development of the Medical and later the Dental School was in its direct power, since these Schools were not parts of University College. Thus as well as being in a difficult constitutional position as far as expansion of University College was concerned, the University was in a difficult position on financial grounds, since the College guarded its own endowments and paid its own staff. Further, the economic depression between the Wars meant that the pre-1914 financial support was lost over the 1920s and 1930s, and there was a corresponding loss in local interest also. The wealthy supporters of university development in Dundee who had done so much at the end of the 19th century and whose active advice and interest continued into the earlier years of the 20th century, were no longer there. St Andrews University, apart from the Berry Bequest, had had no corresponding wealthy benefactors until Sir James Irvine induced Dr Harkness to give the University the very considerable sums he did from 1927 onwards.

Criticism of the Court, and therefore of 'St Andrews' began in Council when in the pre-1945 years the teaching of various Arts subjects, and developments in the teaching of Economics, were denied to University College. Some criticism of Dundee Arts restrictions also came from the Quaestor and Factor in the United College between the wars.[5] Initially, there was no criticism of the fact that the Medical School was developing faster than University College; medical student numbers, though small, were a vital element in university life in Dundee. The pre-clinical students were an essential element in boosting University College and the combined senior years were an essential element too, even though they were technically no longer College members.

These were the internal long-standing factors. An external factor which became evident after 1945 was the feeling among prominent Dundee citizens that the town merited a larger University presence; rivalry with Aberdeen about which city was to be third in Scotland made Lord Provosts, Town Councillors, and business men all too aware that while Aberdeen boasted a flourishing University, Dundee had only a College. Even the Advanced Medical School—which though a part of St Andrews University in a way that University College was not—could be esteemed one of Dundee's academic institutions—did not compare with the antiquity of the Aberdeen Medico-Chirurgical Society and its fine headquarters in King Street, nor indeed with the splendid new Medical School built not long before the Second War. But the major external factor was the campaign by the local Dundee Press.

Medical students of the 1920s and early 1930s recalled that Mr D.C. Thomson's *Dundee Courier and Advertiser* from time to time ran series of articles on various local issues for short periods, and then dropped the subject. But from 1938 the state of the College Council became an object of the newspaper's interest, and this coincided with the delay in the appointment to the

Chair of Midwifery and Gynaecology. On 11th January 1938, about the same time as golf plans for a 'Super New Course' were proposed 'to consolidate St Andrews as the world's finest golfing centre', a headline 'What's wrong with the University College Council—Too many "Yes" men' became the first shot in what was to become a prolonged campaign of great bitterness. 'At one time', the article began, 'University College Dundee had "live wires" at the head of affairs. They made sure that the citizens knew all about their College with remarkable results'. The newspaper reminded its readers that local support 36 years previously had paid the debt of £12,500 the College was then owing. It mentioned also the payment of £6,000 towards the new Medical School building, and the liberality of Sir George Baxter and Mr J. Martin Whyte. It contrasted the 102 governors of 1903 with the 22 of the day, and complained of the lack of a resident Principal. The article continued:

> Today the interest of the citizens is frozen, and frozen by the inaction of the Council. The interest was alive in 1901. It has to be restored now. It is not the blame of the citizens. One business man was heard to say that "Yes" men predominated ... the governors meet annually ... and nod approval to the Council. Everyone is agreed on the need for reawakening public interest today. The Council has the remedy in its own hands—appoint a resident Principal.

At this stage the Council was the object of criticism in the series of articles following—a cartoon on the 14th, a headline 'U.C.D. at the crossroads' on the 7th, 'Hush-hush and Rip Van Winkleism' on the 25th. In the last of these unnamed business men were again quoted and the abolition of two Professorships[6] at U.C.D. and their replacement by lectureships brought to the public's attention. The question of the Midwifery Chair was taken up the same month, when the appointment of the Dundee gynaecologist was described as 'the obvious and proper course', Maryfield Hospital attacked as entirely unsuitable for teaching and Dr. J.D Saggar, a local doctor who was a Town Councillor, applauded for stating that 'the Court's purpose was to attract somebody from outside'. But after Professor Fairlie's appointment was confirmed as gynaecologist to Dundee Royal Infirmary, the *Courier* turned its attention to the neglect of U.C.D.:

> No use blinking it. University College is one of Dundee's neglected opportunities ... St Andrews is a great source of strength to University College Dundee and University College Dundee should equally be a great source of strength to St Andrews. The two are partners. Together they should provide the finest University in the Kingdom. Each is dependent on the other. Each has its own particular problems. Above all, there must be frankness between the partners. And there must be fairness to U.C.D. ... What is wanted is real leadership. He who leads will do a big service for Dundee and for St Andrews University.

This was one side of the new campaign. The other and less fair side was the policy of denigrating those who spoke against it. In November 1938 Professor McKenzie, the recently retired and distinguished Professor of Chemistry at University College, stoutly defended progress made there. In 50 years, he said,

University College had grown to 245 students—as many as had been at St Andrews in his bejant year. He denied any lack of enthusiasm amongst the College staff, and made the point that the strained state of *University College* finances—which remained independent of those of the rest of the University—made expansion difficult. These last remarks were characteristically ignored by the *Courier* in its subsequent attack on him on 9 December.

Thus, even before the 1939-45 War, the Third Party was entering upon a campaign similar to that which had been so unhelpful in the 1880s. Over one year, criticism of the Council was replaced by criticism of the University, and the hint of a demand for a change in the relationship of University College to the rest of the University appeared in November with the remark that 'critics should enquire as to the actual responsibilities of the College in its relationship to the University of St Andrews'. In this year too, criticism of Sir James Irvine began.

All this is entirely pertinent to post-war troubles. By the end of the War, it was becoming clear that the *Courier's* aim was to bring about the formation of a separate University in the City of Dundee. The Third Party was able to point, with justification, to the denial of development in Arts in University College. But it must not be forgotten that much of the reason for this poor development lay in the unsatisfactory relationship of the College and its Council to the Court of the enlarged University. Even had the Court wished to develop University College on a massive scale it was prevented by the terms of the Deed of Endowment from founding Chairs without financial backing being available from Council sources, and by the provisions of the pre-war University Grants Committee, whose own lack of financial resources undoubtedly refused duplication of departments. The only part of the enlarged University physically in Dundee over which it had complete control was the Medical School, and this element could not be said to have been unfairly held back. Had the Third Party adopted a more constructive press campaign, the other two parties could well have worked out a useful compromise. But this was not to be:

> A fire is kept hot by stoking
> and a quarrel by persistence
> Blow on a spark to make it glow,
> or spit on it to put it out
> both results come from one mouth
> The talk of a third party has brought divorce on
> staunch wives and deprived them of all they have laboured for[7]

With the arrival of Principal Wimberley at the beginning of the Michaelmas term 1946, the scene was set for eight of the saddest years in the history of the University of St Andrews. The Medical Faculty was to be a real though not a declared issue in the struggle now to begin. Principal Wimberley's account of these years 'from my own point of view' is a full and very frank one, and was to be made public in 1985. He had commanded the 51st (Highland) Division with the greatest distinction in 1943 in North Africa from the Battle of Alamein onwards, and in Sicily. He had become a living legend in that year, and 'Tartan

Tam' would retain his place in military history for ever afterwards. He was however not promoted higher in the field, but returned to become Commandant of the Staff College and later in 1944, Director of Infantry.

Principal Wimberley came to Dundee in 1946 with the firm belief that University College should not be split off from St Andrews as Dundee elements were demanding. He had reassured the Principal that this was his view when the two men met while Wimberley was still working at the War Office. He was greatly attracted to Sir James when he arrived, but had no such feelings for Mr D.C. Thomson . . .

> I outlined the plans I had begun to formulate for the expansion of the College, asking for his newspaper's support to help achieve these. I continued, however, by saying that I was against a separate University for Dundee, as both impractical and unwise, and further that I could not be a party to a plan which, in my opinion, would do grave harm to Scotland's oldest University. I ended by saying that I had already told Irvine, at the time of my appointment, that I was strongly against a split. I was at once left in no doubt whatever that such a policy was anathema to D.C. Thomson, and it became clear that there was no love lost between him and Sir James. If the latter had considerable outward charm of manner, the former certainly had none. He was downright and blunt to a degree. When I had finished speaking, he turned to his henchman beside him, and said to him firmly that he was to continue to press at every opportunity in the newspaper's columns for a separate university, and a complete break away from St Andrews; but he added that, in doing this, he was nevertheless not to attack Principal Wimberley personally or by name.
>
> As our interview went on the atmosphere perceptibly cooled, and I realised the curious little man was totally inflexible in his purpose, and he and his newspaper were now likely to be a considerable thorn in the flesh. He did, however, have the grace to say that he was glad that I had come to see him and tell him of my views, face to face, however much he disagreed with me over the question of separation. His last words to me were somewhat at follows . . ."Well, Principal Wimberley, I would have you know that I am for Dundee, only Dundee, and nothing but Dundee". To this outburst I remember replying . . . "Well, Mr Thomson, if you are for Dundee, I am first and foremost for the good of Scotland". In all the eight years I was to be resident in Dundee, we never had another interview, and indeed hardly exchanged a word.[8]

The importance of the *Courier* campaign over the next years cannot be over-emphasised. The Third Party became the most important Party in this period. Everyone was afraid of the Thomson press—Principal Wimberley certainly was, as were probably more Dundee men than would admit[9]—and Sir James Irvine's attitude to Dundee was one of exasperated fury, in addition to fear. 'No-one could make any arrangements or plans so long as D.C. Thomson was alive'[10]. The medicals, as the longest-serving undergraduates on the Dundee

side of the University, were more often than not Presidents of the Students' Representative Council and a succession of them were deeply concerned at the way things were going. Dr. David Green recalls how his committee protested in vain against the almost daily unfair and partisan articles appearing in the *Courier* attacking the University of St Andrews. In 1945 they wrote to all the other major Scottish papers complaining about the refusal of the *Courier* to print their side of the arguments, but these papers would not support them and took no action. His successor J.J.A. Reid (later Chief Medical Officer at the Scottish Home and Health Department) wrote to Mr Strachey, M.P. for Dundee West, and also to Mr Walter Elliot, one of the Scottish University M.P.s likewise protesting at the *Courier's* campaign. Mr Strachey replied in rather vague terms on 13th December 1946, and Mr Elliot much more helpfully the next day. He suggested writing to *The Scotsman* and asking Mr Murray Watson, its editor, to write a leader on the matter, and then having a motion in specific terms passed by the Dundee Committee of the S.R.C. and sent to the Secretary of State, the three University Members, and to the Chancellor and Vice-Chancellor. He also advised the seeking of an interview with the Secretary of State for Scotland, when the S.R.C. could put its case. Sir John Anderson likewise wrote sympathetically. There was also correspondence between the students 'on the Dundee side' and Sir James Irvine, and Dundee representatives went over to St Andrews to discuss their fears directly with him. As a result of their discussion, Sir James wrote personally to Mr Reid about the inaccuracy of the *Courier* article which appeared on Saturday 14th December 1946 and stated that of the 15 members of the University Court, only 2 directly represented Dundee. This article was certainly untrue[11]. There is no doubt that over the war and post-war years until the Royal Commission, and indeed after, the overwhelming majority of the students were strongly opposed to the separation of the two parts of the University. In the 1946 Rectorial campaign, an effigy of Mr D.C. Thomson was burned in Dundee[12] and in 1948 a large banner was placed by students on the Albert Institute, opposite the *Courier* office—'United we stand. D.C. Thomson take note'. It was removed very quickly by *Courier* staff.

Nevertheless, hostility was not on one side alone. The personality of Sir James Irvine was a strange one in several respects, but none perhaps more than in his different attitude to students and staff on the Dundee side of the University. Students were fascinated by his charms. 'The buzz would go up' recalls Dr David Green 'Jimmy the Princ's in Dines'. And the U.C.D. Union would fill with students, who would hang on his words as long as he sat there. This fascination was equally felt by students on the St Andrews side. Although he was regarded to some degree as one who saw to it that he got his own way, his students always felt a strange confidence when he appeared, and sensed that he had a real interest in them.

But with staff it was different. University College staff sensed his hostility, even when he greeted them with apparent friendliness. They knew that he regarded them as inferior, and that he would reduce their departments if the opportunity arose. They sensed that while he was quite prepared to accept the

real contributions they were making to teaching in the University, he would give them no credit and certainly no honour: if there was a conflict between the United College and University College, he would always favour the former. And they knew he would talk down their requests, sometimes with anger. If an item unfavourable to Dundee could be discussed in Court or Senate after the Dundee representatives had left for their train, he would do so[13]. He was increasingly antagonistic to Dundee developments[14]. The failure to see the potential for development of the enlarged University was Irvine's greatest failing. In this failure he was a lesser man than Tulloch, Donaldson or Sir Thomas Thornton. Had he not lost his only son Nigel in the war he might have overcome his increasing bitterness; his house became a mausoleum to his dead son and he was never the same man again. His policy of reducing departments in University College was not based on U.G.C. directives alone. 'Undoubtedly' recalls Dr. Eric Mackay, whose father, Major W.M. Mackay, was head of the Electrical Engineering Department under the Professor of Physics,

> this provided ammunition for the Thomson press based in Dundee, and for local City Councillors for whom it provided a platform to boost civic aggrandisement by having a university. In retrospect, I feel that if Sir James had shown a little bit more restraint, the construction, or even the promise of construction of the Tay Road Bridge would have killed the idea of a separate Dundee University, and we would have had a perfect balance...

Eric Mackay was a successor to David Green and John Reid as S.R.C. President in the Dundee Committee, and held the same views as they did. In this capacity he led the student witnesses in 1951.

The next individual to become involved in this struggle was Principal Douglas Wimberley. He was soon the figurehead of the Second Party—and unlike the Third and First, a newcomer to the local scene. He began by losing his trust in Principal Irvine; this occurred at an early stage in his own Principalship. Quickly taking up the cause of his College, he set in train a series of measures for its improvement, some of these logistic—such as provision of residences for College lecturers, some public relations, such as institution of formal public events, and social occasions of which all grades of college staff mingled together. But of his academic subordinates (as he saw them) he had little understanding and his involvement in their problems irritated some and led him into conflict with the University Court. From an early stage he saw the Medical School as something which did not fit into his concept of what the Dundee side of the university should be. He saw the medicals as not belonging to his College, and sought to have them included.

In this he encountered particular opposition from Dr. James Lawson who was the Chairman of a new body called the Medical Planning Committee. This had been set up on 17th January 1946, the reasoning behind its establishment being that the Court could not delegate the solution of administrative problems solely to the Faculty of Medicine—the Faculty was seen as dealing primarily with teaching matters and reporting to the Senate; the Court believed a smaller committee would give advice directly to it, and so be more useful. The members

L. Turton Price

A. M. Patrick

F. J. Charteris

W. J. Tulloch

Bute Class picture 1920 showing P. C. Robertson, H. Graham, W. F. Dorward, B. Rycroft, W. Cunningham, P. T. Herring, D. Waterston, D. R. Dow

Bute Class picture 1952-53 showing J. Taylor, S. Bayne, A. E. Ritchie, J. H. Mulligan, R. Walmsley

included the Dean of the Faculty, most of the Professors, and one or two senior non-professorial staff. The majority of the members were Dundee-based, as was its Chairman at this time. An equivalent, smaller Dental Planning Committee was set up for the same reasons. While Principal Wimberley felt very deeply the slights he undoubtedly received from Sir James once the two men had distanced themselves from each other, he was quite prepared to speak disparagingly of Dr. Lawson, whom he disliked and looked down upon; he described him as being engaged in a 'never-never business'—alluding to the family drapery firm. He regarded Dr. Lawson as an unsavoury assertive individual who had somehow ingratiated himself with Sir James Irvine and was now his ally in doing everything possible to undermine University College. The fact that Dr. James Lawson had first been a member of the College Council— from 1939—and was now a member of Court made him seem even more untrustworthy. Principal Wimberley saw him as one who was out to wreck University College's chance of expansion by setting up a 'Medical College' (called by Wimberley 'St Luke's', though the name does not appear elsewhere)[14], for the medical students domiciled in Dundee[15]. He was suspicious of all Dr. Lawson's proposals—his move to establish additional medical student residential accommodation especially angered him, as did his refusal to co-opt him on to his Medical Planning Committee[16]. Principal Wimberley saw too the appointment of a Medical Administrative Officer for Dundee, who was to work under the Secretary of the University and not under him, as 'driving a wedge between University College and the Medical School', and 'prejudicing the talks between the University Court and the Council which were to take place on the basis of my memorandum.'[17]

The person appointed to this new post was Mr R.N.M. Robertson, who had returned from war service to be Assistant Quaestor and Factor at St Andrews. He was a Law graduate of Glasgow who had represented his University at rugby and had been an outstanding athlete, holding for several years the Scottish long-jump record. He had never taken to the town and had applied for the new post, as he told Sir James Irvine when he asked him why on earth he wished to leave St Andrews for Dundee, 'only to broaden my experience and increase my salary'. He recalls arriving in Dundee in March 1948, being met by Dr. Lawson on his first morning, introduced to one or two people, and then left in the hall of the Senior Medical School building with no idea of his duties and no office or clerical help. He later learned that his duties included administration of Medical (and Dental) Planning Committees, the William Low Residence Committee, and Joint Secretaryship, with the Secretary of the Eastern Regional Hospital Board, of the Medical Education Committee of that Board. The Hospital Board was the new Statutory Body appointed to run the hospital part of the new National Health Service; Dr. James Lawson, inevitably, was the University representative on the Regional Board[18].

Mr Robertson was ignored by Professor Tulloch who had succeeded Professor Cappell as Dean in 1945 on the latter's return to Glasgow to take the Chair held previously by his very own teacher and chief, Sir Robert Muir. He got an office only after Principal Wimberley had found him a 'cubby hole in the

attic of the Old Technical Institute above Surgery'. He was ignored by Professor Tulloch because his post was, yet again, the creation of Dr. James Lawson, and Tulloch hated Lawson[19].

Professor Cappell, however brilliant, was not popular with students, and because of his unblinking eyes, was known as 'The snake'. His successor as Dean, since he smoked constantly, inhaling deeply, blowing out through his nostrils, and often shouting loudly to his staff, was nick-named 'The dragon'. William John Tulloch was born in Dundee on 12th November 1887, the son of Henry Tulloch, a local business man, and Coralie van Wassenhove of Waerschoot, a Belgian lady. It may well have been his mother who gave him his strong personality, his dramatic sense, and his fierce wit, as well as his Roman Catholicism. Educated at Dundee High School and St Andrews University, he graduated M.B. Ch.B. in 1909, worked initially as an assistant to Professor Sutherland and then left in 1911 to be assistant to the Professor of Comparative Pathology in Durham. He returned to Dundee, married in 1915, but spent the war years at the Royal Army Medical College, Millbank, where he did outstanding work on meningococcal meningitis, anaerobic infection of wounds, and tetanus prophylaxis, and was awarded the O.B.E. (Military Division). He had been promoted Professor of Bacteriology in 1921, and his laboratory had had a huge work load, serving the public health laboratories of Angus, Fife and Perth as well as of Dundee. Always the dramatic teacher, and remembered by students with fear at his often barbed wit as well as with affection, he now became Dean of the Faculty at this critical period when the old University was to try to hold its course against continuing attack. 'Willie John' had shown his teaching and research ability, but now had to show his capacity as Dean. Forthcoming in debate, and loyal to Principal Wimberley, he would speak disdainfully of those he disliked: St Andrews was 'The Holy City' (or 'The Hub of the Universe') and Braeknowe, Headquarters of the Regional Board, 'The Kremlin'. But he was not as strong a man as Professor Garry; Professor Garry had a firmness and consistency in action Tulloch never had. Unfortunately Tulloch, too, had learned to distrust Sir James Irvine.

The next years of unhappiness can be briefly summarised. Within six months of his arrival Principal Wimberley wrote and made public his memorandum criticising the division in Dundee between the Medical School and the College, attacking the move as he saw it to form a new Medical College, and putting forward his own ideas for reform. He went so far in this paper as to say that there were only two courses open to the College Council—the first to proclaim a desire and an intention to have a separate University by means of a Royal Commission, the second, while stating openly to the University what the Council thought required to be put right, to give an assurance, and loyally work to it, that we 'would have no truck with any movement aiming or hinting or threatening that way'; he went on to state that he looked to a broad federal system as the solution. His paper included his significant paragraph about 'the junior partner whose ideas put forward time and again . . . are never accepted . . . he must in the end apply to break the contract and set up afresh'[20]

His narrative sets out the progress of events; the talks between Court and

Council of 1947-48, his preparation of arguments for one unified College in Dundee, his constant fear at the skill and resolution of the Third Party, the breakdown of talks, Lord Cooper's enquiry of 1949, and the emergence of Professor T.M. Knox as a leader for the University's case. In their proposals to Lord Cooper, Principal Wimberley and the Council had urged the 'federal solution'. They had also urged that the Council have an increased number of representatives on Court, and that the unified College in Dundee include the Medical School. They claimed that St Andrews had starved Dundee financially. It is of interest that when the two sides were preparing their cases Sir James called Mr Robertson aside after a meeting, and asked him to modify the Dundee case to suit his point of view[21].

The Cooper Report's general theme, that the College system be abandoned in favour of a completely unified university, albeit in two places, was not accepted. Continuing demands from Principal Wimberley and the Council and Governors led to the Royal Commission of 1950 and to the subsequent Tedder Report. In both of these the Medical School was of paramount importance. In evidence to Lord Cooper, the University referred to 'the *Courier's* undisguised intention of depriving the Court of St Andrews of its endowments and properties in the Medical and Dental Schools'. It mentioned the hypothetical possibilities of using Perth Royal Infirmary and the large hospital at Bridge of Earn as St Andrews hospitals, but dismissed this idea as 'too speculative to be realistic'. It mentioned, too, the fact that Oxford and Cambridge students were able to go elsewhere to hospitals or medical colleges for clinical teaching and then return for graduation, relating this to the need to retain Anatomy and Physiology at St Andrews. The University submission went so far as to continue:

> Apart from this difficulty about the Medical and Dental Schools, however, the University Court would not object, *from the point of view of St Andrews alone*, to a dissolution of the connection with University College and the creation of a University of Dundee. If faced with a choice, it would greatly prefer this solution to Principal Wimberley's because, while the latter only perpetuates and indeed strengthens the *imperium in imperio*, the former does at least remove it.

> However, the Court has no doubt that the creation of such a University is not in the public interest[22].

Behind all the argument and wrangling over these years was the fact that the campaign by the *Dundee Courier and Advertiser* continued without ceasing. It was ruthless and uncompromising—in fact, a verbal terrorist campaign.

Principal Wimberley's account includes his frequent criticisms of it[23]. As far as the University was concerned, the prospect was an unhappy one. It was clearly realised, as it was realised later at the time of the Royal Commission, just how much the University stood to lose. This perhaps accounts for the absence of counter-attack. Whatever the Old University did could be called wrong. If, for example, large sums *had* been put into the Dundee side before the war, this could easily have been used by the *Courier* as an excellent reason for separation;

the facilities were already there in Dundee, so why not acknowledge its independence? On the other hand, failure to put large sums into Dundee for development could equally be used to instance the injustice of St Andrews' attitude, and so demonstrate the absolute necessity for separation so that justice be achieved. The constant propaganda could not fail to influence local feeling and opinion, and produced exasperation in the University parties who wished for peace and progress.

It therefore says a great deal for the University of St Andrews that the loyalty of both staff and students remained as high as it did. Perhaps the very fact that no adequate contrary view was permitted expression in the columns of the *Courier* angered the students and offended their sense of fairness, as did response to some criticism they did make[24]. While the distrust of Sir James was so great that what amounted to a mythology grew up about him—it was even believed that he had deliberately arranged General Wimberley's appointment, considering him as an easy option to be manipulated—and then found him too difficult to handle[25], the personality and behaviour of Principal Wimberley was also not without fault. He was, and is, so respected by the public at large that any hint of criticism seems almost an irreverence. But he was wrong, and seen to be wrong, in so many ways by the students and academic staff, that their criticism has to be recorded. He probably never 'got into' the academic world. He was impetuous—as his memorandum of 1947 showed—and made plans without first obtaining the facts by reconnaissance—as in his proposal to introduce the teaching of Russian in University College[26]. His practice of seeking information about candidates for posts produced a great deal of irritation—not the fact that he sought information, but the way he went about it. Many students were annoyed at his military style of managing the College. Some regarded his request for students to donate a piece of silver to the College on leaving as ridiculous, and some medicals due to leave for National Service were turned off by his exhortation to be sure to get attached to a *good* regiment. Whatever view of him was held initially—and the view of Senior members of Medical Faculty staff was ambivalent[27]—and whatever view was held of his sincere efforts to better his College, the fact remains that he became more and more partisan against the Enlarged University. This is evident in his journal. It was also evident from the fact that advantages obtained for College staff in the provision of houses for new University College staff were denied to Medical School staff[28]. Even Lord Cooper advised him: 'The problem is essentially an academic one, and best left in the hands of academic people ... Sir James Irvine is entitled to much sympathy' ...[29]. As so often in relations between the First and Second Parties, there were faults on both sides. And at this date in the history of St Andrews University, the contestants were few in number but high in authority. Prisoners of their own personalities and prejudices, they were in a situation where their differences and inability to concede could do immense harm. The Third Party compounded the difficulties.

But perhaps Principal Wimberley's greatest failing—apart from falling into the trap of becoming too partisan—was his inability to realise that the students on the Dundee side of the University did *not* regard themselves as 'Wimberley's

men'. Though he referred to them as 'his chaps', they did not regard themselves as such. The witness of Dr. John Reid is repeated time after time; the students all regarded themselves as one, but the 'one' implied that they were *cives* of the University of St Andrews. This even applied to those who did not visit St Andrews town, for academic purposes, until they went to the Younger Hall to graduate.

For the Royal Commission, the same ground was gone over. The many witnesses produced predictable opinions. Irvine's memorandum was autocratic, short, clear, pointed; his contempt for the limitations of the business men of the Council and for the Third Party, evident. Principal Wimberley's very long submissions, set out in military paragraphs, acknowledged the importance of the Medical School. He claimed it had suffered in the 1930's, because, he thought, it had no direct representation either on the University Court or the Council. This he thought was the reason for its failure to develop. He felt that the Court was prepared to abandon the institution of a separate Medical College provided it maintained control of administration. He clearly felt that a Medical College would attract 'better' students fed to it from the United College, that it would attract better teachers because of its higher salaries, and so would overshadow University College in the future. 'As Medicine' he said, 'while possible the most important, is by no means the only subject taught in Dundee, the Dean (of Medicine) cannot also undertake the duties of a Vice-Principal'— he was strongly antagonistic to the concept of a university Vice-Principal in Dundee (as proposed by Lord Cooper) who was a figurehead only.

The Court's submission demanded full incorporation of University College within the University by the abolition of its Trust Deed, and the closure of Arts Departments in that College. It attacked the Council's desire to absorb the Medical and Dental Schools, as this would, in its view, produce dual control of them as well as U.C.D. The Court submitted its view:

> That the Medical School and the Dental School should be incorporated as a second College in Dundee, on the basis, for example, of the Medical College of St Bartholomew's Hospital. The students would continue to enjoy Students' Union and athletic facilities in common with those of University College just as those of both Colleges in St Andrews enjoy such facilities in common there. There is thus no more segregation of medical students than exists at present, and in any case the proposal only affects medical students after they have spent three years alongside students of the other Faculties during their pre-clinical studies in one of the other Colleges.

Such a College would let the Medical School 'belong'. A minority report was signed by Principal Wimberley, Dr. A.R. Moodie and Professor Dow.

The Governors naturally saw things the other way round and were political, not academic, in their views. To them, the present administrative arrangements for the Medical School were designed to keep that school in the hands of St Andrews and to avoid its falling into the hands of Dundee. In support, they quoted paragraph 37 of the Cooper Report, which said this very thing. They criticised the smaller number of medical students starting at Dundee, attacked

the St Andrews staff as having no interest in Dundee, and laid great stress on the recent cash benefits to St Andrews. They pointed out that 'it was Dundee that enabled St Andrews to give a Medical Degree on the same footing as other Scottish Universities'. They attacked the suggestion of a separate Medical College. In essence, they—but only *half of them*—wanted separation. The Council, in a separate report, again asked for federation—those in favour included Professor G.H. Bell, and a minority were against and asked for separation: Messrs R. Fenton, T. Cook (the Member of Parliament), William Hughes, John Gray and Sheriff H.F. Ford. U.C.D. Professors asked for federation and a distinctive name for the whole Dundee side of the University.

Of the large number of smaller submissions, three only are of interest in a history of medical teaching. Sir Garnet Wilson, the former Lord Provost and a supporter of Principal Wimberley's, described how the Court 'today administers the Medical School from St Andrews with great pride of possessiveness'. He wrote largely of the need to introduce help from business men and busines interests, and ended: 'It is doubtful if the Medical School, if designed to become part of the University of Dundee, would altogether welcome dissociation from the University of St Andrews'. Although Principal Wimberley believed Sir Garnet to be a federalist like himself, Sir Garnet's later comments in his autobiography showed that in his heart he was in fact a separatist[30]. Professor Garry wrote from Glasgow and listed a number of instances of Irvine's antagonism. He also made the assertions that it was Irvine who had, without previous notice, altered the balance of bejants entering Medicine in the United and University Colleges after the war in favour of the former. He was against separation, but thought there should be two equal halves to the University. Professor Cappell wrote a disappointingly peevish letter which in effect was a series of complaints against poor funding in Dundee between the wars compared with St Andrews. It included a number of inaccurate criticisms such as those of the Berry Fund and of the Professors of Anatomy and Physiology—Dow and Garry—who had served on the Court.

The view of the Faculty of Medicine was clear and unequivocal.

1.   The Faculty expresses emphatically the opinion that it would be disastrous to divide the University into St Andrews and Dundee, i.e. to have a separate University in each centre.

2.   In the event of it being decided to establish a purely technological section of the University of St Andrews in Dundee, then the Faculty of Medicine would prefer to be incorporated as a separate entity from such a (technological) institution. (This referred to the suggestion that Arts be withdrawn in Dundee and Applied Sciences developed alone there).

3.   Assuming that the Departments of the University situated in Dundee were not purely technological, the Faculty favours the establishment in Dundee of a unit to which specific administrative duties could be delegated.

4.   The Dean of the Faculty of Medicine should be on the Court; a Deputy Dean would then be required.

The Faculty also expressed the belief that the Medical Planning Committee should *continue*, and 'should cover the whole Medical Faculty'; it should be under the Chairmanship of the Dean.

This was signed by Professors Dow, Alexander, Walmsley, Bell, Lendrum, Hunter, Ritchie, Hill, and Drs. Dorward, Tudhope and Kinnear (Dermatology). It was further agreed that Professors Bell, Burgess (Public Health), Walmsley, and Tulloch the Dean, would give oral evidence in support. (Professor Tulloch submitted a paper as Dean which however said relatively little beyond stating that he was against a separate Medical College but was decidedly against a separation of the University).

This Faculty view was reinforced by an even stronger one from other teachers in the Faculty. These were:

> Unanimously of the opinion that the establishment of a University of Dundee entailing the separation of the Medical School from the University of St Andrews would be a disaster.
>
> The University of St Andrews would, by separation, lose a Faculty which contributes both a significant part of the biological studies carried on in that University, and a fair measure of wisdom of its councils. Similarly the Medical School could ill afford to lose its association with the most venerable of the Scottish Universities and those tradiitons which are so beneficial to students and which attract applicants to the staff.

This was signed by Mr F.R. Brown, Mr John Grieve, Dr. I.D. Easton, Dr. W.M. Jamieson, Mr G.M. Sturrock, and Professors Hill and Lendrum.[31]

The solidarity of the student body came out in their evidence to the Tedder Committee. On 3rd October, 1951, at 10.15 a.m. the Students Representative Council met the Committee:

'Since we do come from both Dundee and St Andrews', said Mr D.D. Ruddy, the vice-president,

> may I say that from the St Andrews' point of view I think the whole dispute is most unfortunate indeed. We realise the reasons that have brought this thing to a focus at this time, and we only wish that the authorities in the University could see eye to eye as the students, we feel, do. There are differences of opinion as Mr Mackay has said: they can be forgotten and they are submerged in a common unity of the students. There is very little feeling amongst the students that the University is divided into two halves. The distinction between the two sections of the University is considered an obstacle, but not one that cannot be got over ...

The 'Mr Mackay' referred to was a recent medical graduate, and was the S.R.C. president. He had been born and brought up in Dundee, begun his studies at University College, yet regarded himself as a St Andrews student. The certainty of this feeling comes out clearly in the record of the discussion, as does the certainty the four students had that they were truly representing the views of their fellows. Thus, they dismissed as irrelevant the political strivings of Dundee for position. They insisted that the primary purpose of the University was

education, that a change of name was not required, saw the Colleges as adminstrative organisations, which if so regarded would not interfere with student unity, reported no demand for a Dundee graduation ceremonial, and considered the geographical difficulties had been overstated. They did not favour a separate Medical College. They looked forward much more realistically than their elders to the day when it would take only half an hour to reach one place from the other. They agreed that the ancient building and institution of St Andrews town was a bait to attract medicals and they also felt that if all pre-medical work was done in Dundee, there would not be so many seeking entry. They did not think fusion of the Medical School into a Dundee College would affect students. Questioned about the numbers of students from England coming to St Andrews or Dundee, they realistically admitted that some of these had come only because they had failed to get a place in the south. In summary, they emphasised the complementary nature of St Andrews and Dundee.[32]

After everyone had said his piece, the Commission deliberated and then reported (in 1952). The Report noted that present difficulties were only the most recent form of the old dispute of the late 19th century, and that no solution was possible until the constitutional structure was changed. It noted that University College had no access to grants except through the University Court—there having been no benefactions from Dundee since the foundation of the College Chairs 60 years previously—and that it had followed an acadmic policy which the Court had not been prepared to endorse. It noted, too, that there was in Dundee 'little reason to be dissatisfied with the physical expansion of University College in the last quinquennium—an expansion which had been in part foreseen before the present Principal of the College took office in 1946, but which has owed much of its scope and rapidity to him'. So Principal Wimberley's claims of an unfair restriction of resources were dismissed. And it noted that the 'habit of mind which goes with (Dundee's sense of being second best) is in some ways the most important element in the situation'.

As far as the Advanced Medical School was concerned, Lord Tedder's Report agreed with that of Lord Cooper that 'the Advanced Medical School was the prize for which St Andrews and Dundee were competing, each being determined that it should not fall into the hands of the other, and academic considerations and the welfare of the teaching of medicine being subordinate'. It thus saw the formation and method of working of the Medical—and to a lesser extent the Dental-Planning Committee, as being 'a manifestation of the malady from which the University is suffering'. And since it rejected devolution of power to Colleges constructed on an Oxford or Cambridge model, it rejected a separate Medical College in Dundee. As far as the University as a whole was concerned, it proposed a remodelled collegiate system in which there would be two, and only two, subordinate administrative bodies, one in Dundee and one in St Andrews. The Advanced Medical School, and the Dental School, would become part of the Dundee sub-division; the Committee did not accept the University Court's argument that compelling reasons existed for placing all the medicals in their own Medical College, because these arguments were based on the false premise that the Medical School would be placed under the Governors

and Council. The Governors and Council were to disappear. The Dundee sub-division would then be a 'new' College, whose name would later be Queen's College.

As far as pre-clinical teaching was concerned, the duplication of Departments of Physiology and Anatomy was criticised.

> No immediate change is possible because both departments are fully occupied by the present intake of students and no new building can be erected in the near future, but if a clear policy is not worked out now disagreement will certainly arise when the plans are drawn up for the new Medical School which the University proposes to build when the main teaching hospital in Dundee is moved to a new site on the outskirts of the City. We recommend that all teaching of medical and dental students in Anatomy and Physiology up to the standard of the Second Professional Examination should be concentrated in the new College in Dundee when it becomes practicable to do so. This recommendation is independent of any decision that may be taken whether the future developments of Anatomy and Physiology should be housed with the clinical departments in this new Medical School, or remain beside the Pure Science Departments; this is a separate issue on which we express no opinion'.

On the other hand, complementary departments of Physics, Chemistry, Botany and Zoology for both sides of the University would allow first-year medicals to start at St Andrews . . .

> There is no reason why entrants should not be encouraged to study the pre-medical sciences in the United College before migrating to the new College in Dundee for Anatomy and Physiology. An arrangement like this would be in line with our suggestions for other classes of students, and would give the University an advantage unique in Scotland.

The other great feature of this Report concerned the governance and administration of the University, the place of the Rector, and academic development. The Dundee Trust, with Governors and Council, would go. The Dundee side would be equated in numbers and influence with the St Andrews—this was important, having regard to the specially vulnerable position St Andrews had always had over student numbers. Most striking of all, however, was the total rejection of the movement for an independent University in Dundee. Although Mr D.C. Thomson naturally refused to acknowledge this rejection[33] all other parties who mattered were pleased that the separatist campaign by the Third Party was defeated. The other major Scottish newspapers, and *The Times* of London, applauded the good sense of the Tedder Report[34].

The University Court unanimously resolved, at its meeting on 13th May 1952 to accept the conclusions and recommendations of the Report in its entirety. After this meeting, Sir James Irvine suffered a heart attack and was at once placed under the care of Professor Hill. He died a month later.

At the meeting of the Dundee Governors on 16th June Sir Garnet Wilson, seconded by Mr Robin Thomson, moved that the Governors approve in

principle the findings and recommendations of the Tedder Commission. This was countered by the Lord Provost, William Black, seconded by ex-Lord Provost Fenton, and asking the Secretary of State for Scotland to give more consideration to their request for a separate University. Education and the good of the University were not pre-eminent in their horizon. They were defeated by 41 votes to 17, thanks, as Principal Wimberley recorded, 'to the system of plural voting based on money paid over by certain Governors'[36]

In due course the necessary bill passed through the Houses of Parliament and received the Royal Assent on 31st July, 1953. Principal Wimberley was not re-employed by the University, and this rejection produced a considerable local outcry. It is difficult to say what would have happened had he remained; Mr R.N.M. Robertson considered his rejection an enormous mistake by the University, holding the view that he would have been totally loyal to Principal Knox, Sir James' successor. Professor Garry, too, considered that he would have been 'a breath of fresh air'. On the other hand, Miss Janet Allan considered his actions noted over the years made the new Principal unwilling to take the risk of retaining him[37]. In 1954 Mr D.C. Thomson died; the harassment by his newspaper against the University carried on for some months further, but then it too died away.

The Old University had suffered a severe shock, but the future now seemed brighter than it had done for fifty years. The new Principal, Sir Malcolm Knox, would work as hard as he could to right previous wrongs, both imagined and real, and to make it clear to the citizens of St Andrews and the citizens of Dundee that both must make concessions and acknowledge the contribution of the other. Morale improved remarkably, on the St Andrews side, because the University was saved, and the more percipient members of staff began to be aware of the potential excellence in Queen's College; on the Dundee side, because they had sought recognition and had deservedly won their case.

15

Immediate post-war developments in the Medical School

The Third Missed Chance—the National Health Service

Professor Cappell had been made Dean of the Faculty of Medicine in the first year of the war, in succession to Professor Charteris. 'Piggy' Charteris was so called because when he laughed his blue eyes tended to disappear into his fresh cheeks and face like those of a pig. He had always been extremely inactive as Head of an Academic Department. This may have been partly because his request for a whole-time clinical post had been refused; there is no doubt that residents who worked on the wards he had nominal charge of respected his ability as a physician. His wards were in Maryfield Hospital but he seldom went there. He also had a consultant physician's appointment at St Andrews Cottage Hospital, but he rarely visited there either. He lived in St Andrews—the only clinical professor to do so,[1] travelled to Dundee for lectures and committee work, but returning at the earliest opportunity. Students, however, found his lectures stimulating for like Sir James MacKenzie, he taught them to be critical of the drugs and remedies as habitually prescribed, and to think for themselves. His students recall that his lectures were more stimulating than those of his successor as Dean. Professor Cappell had however an energy and vision which was exactly what was required in this post. Although he was very restricted in pre-war days at the Infirmary by the Directors there, of whom he had had a poor opinion,[2] his University department enjoyed, as has been seen, a good share of University financial support. This continued during the war years. The Blood Transfusion Service he developed in the eastern region of Scotland was a model for the whole country and anticipated both war and post-war transfusion needs.

This was the man of ability and enterprise who went to Sir James Irvine in 1944, when the progress of the war held the certainty of military victory, to discuss future developments in the Medical School. A number of versions of the discussion are given, from the blunt reply of the Principal 'I am not interested in Dundee'; in Professor K.G. Lowe's account,[3] through Professor A.C. Lendrum's 'but the Principal replied that he was not particularly interested',[4] to Mr R.N.M. Robertson's recollection. These replies were to Professor Cappell's statement that the Medical Faculty was now ready to take off—an opportunity to make it, for its size, one of the best in Britain was there to be seized if finance were available to establish full-time Clinical Chairs. Mr Robertson's account of the

267

Principal's reply, when in later years as Secretary of Dundee University he talked with Professor Cappell at his retiral home in Edzell and heard the tale told again, was that 'this did not fit in with the priorities he had in mind for post-war developments of the University'. The Dean of Medicine had retorted that he would resign his St Andrews Chair and return to Glasgow to take Sir Robert Muir's Chair, which had been offered to him.[5] In Professor Lowe's version, Professor Garry had accompanied the Dean, but this is denied by Professor Garry[6].

The story is of interest for two reasons. The first is that it does not accord in the slightest with the policy of development which actually took place in the post-war years, and this discrepancy was noted particularly by Mr Robertson from his personal experience as administrator of the post-war Medical Planning Committee. Nor does it accord in any way with the University Court's previous comments on the Goodenough Report. The second is that it is clear evidence of the dislike which Sir James Irvine engendered in so many of the staff, and of the deep distrust, already described, which more and more individuals at all levels felt in their dealings with him. In addition, it seems unlikely that Professor Cappell would have turned down the offer to succeed the Chief he revered so much, even if he had been told by Sir James that the small St Andrews School's future was assured.

For there is no doubt that development began as soon as the war with Japan ended. In September 1945 a meeting was called by the University to inform the Infirmary Directors of the U.G.C. recommendations for additional medical education expenditure. Of the £1M available for medical education in the United Kingdom for 1945-46, £10,000 were to go to St Andrews. But the U.G.C., while agreeing in principal with full-time Clinical Chairs, considered that there should be no undue haste in establishing these and so were making no immediate grant for them. Much the same view was expressed about salaries for part-time clinical teachers and indeed for posts for demobilised doctors. So the delay at this time was due to the U.G.C. and not to the University. On the other hand, the U.G.C. had made money immediately available to improve teaching hospitals—£225,000 country wide. This was to be given in proportion to the number of students in the particular school, and so St Andrews was allocated £7,871, which was raised to £8,027 in January 1946. It was recorded at their January meeting that 'Sir James Irvine assured Mr Lewis F. Robertson (the Chairman of the Directors) that the University would favourably consider claims of Dundee Royal Infirmary.' This was perhaps only said to impress, as the money had been allocated to the Infirmary whatever the Principal's views had been. At the September meeting in 1946 the Directors agreed that fees for students' hospital tickets should be discontinued—a long overdue reform— and both sides agreed that the advertisement for a specialist orthopaedic surgeon should be delayed to give time for ex-service candidates to apply.

For this was the start of the return from war service of many staff. Dr. Macklin was to come back but soon to leave when he found his path blocked by those who had not been away. Dr. J. Gordon Clark was appointed a visiting physician, and Dr. J.B. Gyle, a First War soldier, succeeded to Dr. Clark's

clinical assistant's post. Dr. Janet B. Conn, also returned from RAMC service, was appointed a Grade I lecturer in Midwifery and Gynaecology. Dr. George H. Smith (who had been invalided out of the Forces earlier) continued as a lecturer in Pathology, supporting Dr. G.R. Tudhope. Dr. Tudhope was once again carrying the work of the Department, since Professor Cappell's successor, Professor Stuart McDonald, was ill. The only son of Professor Stuart McDonald, Professor of Pathology at Durham College of Medicine, he was born in Edinburgh in 1905, took a BA at Cambridge in 1926 and MA, MB BChir in 1930. He had next worked in Durham University, at the Royal Victoria Infirmary in Newcastle, and later in Birmingham. In 1938 he took his MD and later PhD of Birmingham. A pre-war Territorial Army Officer, his career had flourished during the war. He went with the 14th British General Hospital (TA) to France in 1939, later went to India, and there did a great deal of research into sulphonamide and antibiotic therapy, and tropical diseases, finishing the war as a Lieutenant-Colonel Assistant Director of Pathology. Dr. McDonald had been interviewed by a Committee of the Court in 1944 while still serving and on a liaison visit to the India and War Offices and the Medical Research Council, and though appointed Professor in March 1945, had not taken up duty until September, after demobilisation from the RAMC.

In 1945 Mr W.G. Campbell was released from Royal Naval Medical Service on November 15, following Dr. B.S. Robertson in Anatomy on October 18. Two staff surgeons had their posts confirmed: Mr George Sturrock as a tutor, and Mr S.F. Soutar as an interim tutor, in Clinical Surgery. Some new posts apart from Dr. Janet Conn's were authorised—a Grade 1 lecturer in Materia Medica, and a registrar, resident, and technician for the new Orthopaedic Department. Even when these were costed, there was still £5000 left from University sources, and so laboratory assistance in bacteriology, and secretaries for the Pathology and Orthopaedic Department, were all approved. In University College 25 men and 10 women students went into first year medicine, and 27 and 13 in the Bute.

At the end of 1945, Professor McDonald's salary was £1,250, maintaining the differential the Pathology Chair enjoyed. This compared with £1,200 for Sir D'Arcy Thompson, Professor Herring, and Professor Tulloch who was now Dean. The Bute Professor of Anatomy received £1,050, and Professor Dow's Cox Chair had £100 *per annum* more. The salary of Professor Garry's Physiology Chair was £1,100 and Professor Peacock had £1,150; there was thus very little difference in the salaries of the pre-clinical chairs on the two sides of the Faculty of Medicine. A year later, in October 1946, the salaries of the Professors of Medicine and Surgery were raised to £600 *per annum*. This was without prejudice to further payment as a lecturer in the clinical subject, and the increase was in anticipation of the likelihood of a change in the status of these Chairs. Other clinical scales were:[7]

		£	
Readers		230-260	
Lecturers	Grade I	200-230	for a 5 year appointment
	II	110-140	
	III	80-100	

Assistants   Grade   I   50-70
                         II   25-40   for a 3 year appointment.

In this year, Dr. James S. Lawson's name appears on more and more influential committees of the University and Medical Faculty. His unhappy relationship with Principal Wimberley and Professor Tulloch has already been described, but the account of the efforts he undoubtedly made from now on to develop and strengthen the Medical School shows the other side of him, as one of the most important figures in the history of the Faculty of Medicine. That he was so distrusted and disliked by the two main personalities on the Dundee side constitutes the third missed chance and equates with the failure of Simson and the accident to Day. Had someone else been available to chair committees than Dr. Lawson, or had he established a secure friendship and trust with Principal Wimberley and the Dean of the Faculty, a very different history might have been told.

He was on the Joint Committee of the Court and Dundee Royal Infirmary. In February 1946 this committee agreed that there might be more teaching hospitals required than the Dundee Infirmary, and if so then the UGC Grant would have to be split. The question of teaching hospitals was now a high priority in the development of Medical Schools, and would remain so for very much longer than any member of Dr. Lawson's Medical Planning Committee realised. The national Goodenough Report had been followed by the local Aitken Report, and in the light of these, it was agreed in October 1946 to approach Mr Lionel Pearson of Messrs Adams, Holden and Pearson, a London firm of Architects, and seek his help as an expert to advise on short and long term policy. He accepted in November. Although he was to advise on a new Teaching Hospital for Medicine, plans continued for a teaching hospital for Dentistry, where Mr A.D. Hitchin succeeded Professor Gordon Campbell from 31st December, 1946. Mr Ramsay, the janitor of U.C.D. and the Senior Medical School, also retired at this time. On 23rd October, Professor Stuart McDonald died, in sad circumstances.

Professor McDonald's death meant that a new Professor would be needed in Pathology. Earlier in the year, yet another new Professor had appeared who would become an important figure in the Faculty's history and who would share the anxieties of twenty years in the future with his opposite number in Physiology in the Bute. This was Professor Robert Walmsley. He was born in 1906, the son of Thomas Walmsley, a marine engineer. Educated at Greenock Academy, he was an Edinburgh graduate of 1931, and took his M.D. with gold medal in 1937. In the Anatomy Department of Edinburgh he had been successively demonstrator, lecturer, and senior lecturer. He was a Goodsir Fellow in 1933, and held a Rockefeller Fellowship from 1935 to 1936, during which time he studied embryology at the Carnegie Institute in Baltimore. Professor Walmsley had joined the Edinburgh General Hospital (Territorial Army) before the outbreak of war, and had served in it as pathologist in the Middle East. His older brother, Thomas, had been a lecturer in Anatomy in Glasgow and later moved as Professor to Queen's University, Belfast. The third Bute Professor was thus very much an Edinburgh man, and carried with him to

St Andrews the proud tradition of the Medical School of Edinburgh and its Anatomy Department in particular. Professor Dow, also a candidate for this Chair, resumed his post in University College. Professor Dow—with Professor Tulloch the first St Andrews medical graduate of modern times to hold a Chair in the enlarged University—remained at his best in the dissecting room. He had never been an inspiring lecturer. O.B.D. would place his dissector in a structure and ask 'Come, come, student', when the reply was not forthcoming quickly. Once it is recorded that a student accidently cut his forearm in the rooms, when Professor Dow called out, 'Gather round, students, gather round. Now, Mr Fyfe, what structures are likely to be pierced here?' David Rutherford Dow was born in 1887 in Crail, the only son of the local doctor there. He was educated at Waid Academy in Anstruther. To the end of his life he would retain a great affection and regard for St Andrews, while in the near future becoming a principal figure in the Dundee side of the University.

Professor Walmsley, like Professor Dow, was less happy in the formal lecture than in the dissecting rooms where he could get nearer the students. They quickly sensed the very real sincerity and interest which his shy rather austere presence overlaid. He was supported by another shy man, John Henry Mulligan M.B. Ch.B., who had arrived at the Bute just before the war and had been a prisoner of war throughout, taken with others of the First Highland Division at St Valery. He was a keen scholar of German, and a brilliant neuro-anatomist, believed by Professor Jim Smith, a later Professor in the Department, to be as brilliant as any Anatomist in either side of the University in the twentieth century. His shyness was almost embarassing, yet covered a cheerful artistic personality. It was he who developed the technique of blackboard chalk drawing to become such a feature of the Department's teaching for forty years; students remembered how he would put a little arrow at the side of his drawings, to show where the light was coming from, before throwing chalk on the board with all the intensity of a Renaissance artist. Professor Dow was likewise supported by Dr. John Henry McDougall, a kind and extremely able man whose career was dogged by ill health, and who was remembered with the very highest affection by students he taught 'on the Dundee side'. Dr. Stephen Bayne, a former Harkness Scholar, was appointed a lecturer in Physiology in 1946, in Professor Herring's Department.

The provision of new Teaching Hospital facilities exercised the minds of the Medical Planning Committee not only because of changes required by the academic world but also because of changes about to take place in the provision of medical services for the entire nation. One of the main aims in the minds of the deeply caring ministers of the Labour Government of the day concerned the provision of medical help—this was to be provided free to every child and adult in the country and remove forever the obstacle of payment for service given; a National Health Service. The concept of 'A General Medical Service for the Nation' was not the politicians' alone; in 1938 the British Medical Association published a report[8] which was incorporated in many of its aspects into the Beveridge Report later.

And so as well as a division of finance being agreed in 1947 between the

Royal Infirmary and Maryfield Hospital—still the Poor Law Hospital—the medical planners looked for the first time outside the city boundary, thinking ahead towards the larger Eastern Hospital Region which was envisaged:

> The necessity will arise under the new curriculum regulations and the proposed Medical Act of allowing students closer association with a general hospital both in pre-graduation and pre-registration periods. The Committee feel that every effort must be made, now, to secure for this University the hospital facilities of this Region. The main general hospital outside Dundee is Perth Infirmary. It has been suggested that other Universities might wish to place students in this Hospital and as half the students (medical) coming from Perthshire matriculate in Edinburgh a case might be made for such students attending Perth Royal Infirmary while living at home. The Committee strongly recommends an approach to the Directors of Perth Infirmary with a view to a limited number of students being attached during one term of the final year.

The recommendation then gave details of all that Perth Royal Infirmary offered, and went on:

> No other hospital in the Region, outside Dundee, offers the same advantages. It would be necessary to invite the medical staff to become Grade 3 lecturers and to make every effort to have the Infirmary classified as a Teaching Hospital when opportunity offers. There would be no difficulty with teaching, as Heads of Divisions (Professors Alexander and Patrick) are consultants there. 10-15 students could, each term, use Perth Royal Infirmary—the cost would not be greater than £700 per annum or less than the salary of one full-time Grade 3 lecturer.
>
> If the University Court agrees, it should pursue the matter before Perth Royal Infirmary passes to the proposed new Regional Hospital Board.

This move of Dr. James Lawson was approved, and a 'P.R.I. Committee' of Professor Tulloch as Dean, Professors Patrick and Alexander, Sir George Cunningham the Rector, and Dr. Lawson as Chairman met representatives of the Perth Directors, Mr S. Norrie-Miller, Mr R. Martin Bates, Mr J. Little; and Mr Conal Charleson and Dr. Ian Easton, surgeon and physician. A draft agreement for admission of students to Perth, and for appointments of medical staff, soon followed.

Nor was there a shortage of available money. Of the U.G.C. grant to St Andrews, £25,000 was allocated by the Court to the Advanced Medical School, and equal amounts of £30,000 each to St Andrews Colleges and University College Dundee. In 1947, too, provision of whole-time medical officers to serve the students were agreed, at an initial cost of £1,000, and an expected annual expenditure of £2,600. One was to work in Dundee and one in St Andrews. Comments upon the new Medical Act were sent to the Department of Health for Scotland. Apart from the above grants, further money was recieved in 1947 as interim non-recurrent grants towards capital expenditure.

These were allocated by the Court following Dr. Lawson's prompting, for St Andrews projects—£45,000, and for Dundee projects—£57,000. Even in appointments to the Faculty, Dr. Lawson's power was evident. When Dr. W.M. Jamieson, recently returned from post-war service, was appointed assistant in Fevers and Public Health, the 'Court was invited to approve, provided Dr. Lawson is satisfied'.

The rest of 1947 was taken up with further planning of the new Teaching Hospital, extensions to the Dental School, early negotiation with the proposed Eastern Regional Hospital Board, and the re-institution of the Diploma in Public Health, which had been discontinued at the start of the war.

On March 31st 1947, the Medical Planning Committee met at D.R.I. The University representatives were Dr. Lawson, Professors Tulloch, Garry, Patrick, and Margaret Fairlie, and the Department of Health for Scotland representatives were Dr. Peters, Mr Norman Graham, and Miss L.C. Watson. Mr Athole Stewart, the Chairman of the Infirmary Directors, Mr Lewis Robertson, and Dr. Henry J.C. Gibson the Medical Superintendent, attended by invitation. This was an important meeting. The Aitken Report on Hospitals in the Eastern Region of the proposed National Health Service had been published without reference to the University. Its recommendation was that it would not be possible to bring Dundee Royal Infirmary or Maryfield Hospital to modern standards on their present sites, and therefore that only minor alterations be undertaken until a long-term policy of removal of the Medical School and Infirmary to the outskirts of the city could be brought about.[9] Mr Pearson, the architect already engaged by the University, said in his interim report that 'the balance of advantage' was heavily on the side of developing these two existing hospitals and grouping the other medical buildings with them. The University—in this instance Dr. James Lawson—believed that the 500 beds available in Maryfield made this the correct view. The representatives of the Department replied that while they had no commitment to the recommendations of the Aitken Report, and while teaching requirements would have to be met by any area hospital scheme, the provision of a new hospital to meet the needs of the region would be the first consideration of the Regional Hospital Board, and the Board's decision could well be to build some distance from the city centre. Arguments went back and forward, and the progress of the debate foreshadowed the state of things to come—the civil service representatives stating options which clearly would have ministerial backing and which they would put into effect in spite of the University view. The disadvantages of a country hospital for medical students—of their having to travel 'to and fro for say five miles'—were raised by Dr. Lawson. He also instanced the need for quick action if the Goodenough proposals and those of the G.M.C. for curriculum changes were to be effective. He pressed for agreement with Mr Pearson's proposals, for the provision of the new Medical School adjacent to the Infirmary, and for enlargement of the William Low Residence just above Dudhope Park—also close to the Infirmary. Perhaps if Dr. Lawson had been intent on a completely separate 'St. Luke's College' he might have taken the chance of an entirely new and more distant site, but he did not. But all the Department of Health officers

would concede was that they saw no objection to extending the William Low Residence on the lines suggested. For the rest, 'they promised to consider carefully the proposals of the University and to communicate their opinion to the University'.

There were also extensions to the Dental School at this time. At the end of the bitterly cold and long 1946-47 winter, when St Andrews was actually cut off by snow from both rail and road for a short time, a meeting in April, 1947, between representatives of Court and Dundee Council agreed that the premises of the Seaforth Club should be sold by the Council to the Court for £5,000 to extend the Dental School. The present 'Dental Hospital and School' was to be used and described as the Dundee Dental Hospital, and the new premises developed after their sale was complete.

Through the summer of 1947, considerable activity and progress continued. Dr. Tudhope asked for alterations to the Pathology Department which were originally estimated at £410; £697 were finally approved in May. Messrs Adams, Holden and Pearson produced their report at the same time, including block plans for the Dundee Hospitals, a Nurses' Hostel at Dudhope House, and a new Medical School on a site adjoining Dudhope Castle. Their fee was £840. The Perth Royal Infirmary Directors and the University completed their agreement on the establishment of that Infirmary as a Teaching Hospital; Dr. Ian D. Easton OBE, Messrs Conal Charleston and E.R.G. Kirkpatrick, surgeons, all became Grade 3 lecturers. Ten students were to go to Perth per term, and a list of suitable lodgings was to be obtained from the Town Clerk of the City of Perth. Students were to be selected by Professors Patrick and Alexander. Long term policy was also agreed. P.R.I. as a Teaching Hospital now received a grant for £400. The University proposed the Principal, Dr. James Lawson, Professors Tulloch and Walmsley, Principal Wimberley, Mr Athole Stewart and Mr Lewis F. Robertson as possible nominees for the new Regional Hospital Board.

As has been noted, the Diploma in Public Health, suspended during the war, was now to re-open. As ever, the G.M.C. had produced its inevitable new regulations. Two sorts of staff, equally inevitably, had to be found and paid for—university, and extra-mural teachers. Each group would need £1,000, and Sir James, with the constantly present Dr. Lawson, proposed £2,100.

Apart from the death of Earl Baldwin, the Chancellor of the University, there were two more events of importance for the Faculty in 1947. These were the appointment of two Professors. On May 15, four of the eight candidates for the Chair in Pathology were short-listed for interview; Dr. A.C. Lendrum, Dr. G.L. Montgomery, Dr. J.G. Thompson and Dr. G.R. Tudhope who was running the Department at the time. Dr. James Lawson was the Chairman of the interviewing committee. In July, Dr. Alan Chalmers Lendrum, MA MD BSc ARPS was appointed, at a salary of £1,450, to the Chair of Pathology in the University of St Andrews. He was allowed to receive professional fees of £100 for work done on behalf of other hospitals than those of the Medical School, had to reside in Dundee, to retire at 65 years of age and 'was not to lecture or teach Pathology elsewhere than in the University of St Andrews'. His contract

was not so very different from that of the Chandos Professors of the 18th century, as far as this last restriction went. Born in 1906, his father was the Rev. Dr. Robert Alexander Lendrum, and his mother Anna was the eldest daughter of James Guthrie of Pitforthie, Angus. After schooling at Glasgow High School, he went to the University of Glasgow, and on graduation in 1933 had become an assistant in Sir Robert Muir's Department. Just as Professor Walmsley had come from a proud Department, so had Professor Lendrum come from what was probably the greatest School of Pathology in Great Britain at the time. He remained proud, too, of his ecclesiastical connections, was widely read and a witty lecturer, and was a talented photographer.

Also in July, a successor to Professor Garry was appointed. He had announced his intention to resign as from the end of September, and he also, like Professor Cappell, would return to Glasgow, his *alma mater*. Although Professor Herring, now aged seventy-five, had announced his retiral as from the end of the summer vacation, Professor Garry, though considering a possible transfer to the Bute, decided against. He would, he felt, have been a traitor to Dundee had he moved, so strongly antagonistic had he become to Sir James Irvine. His antagonism was especially marked because of his status as a 'University College' Professor, for he had been made aware of this distinction too often. Professor Garry had also become personally involved with Principal Wimberley's efforts on behalf of his College, and supported these efforts loyally. Unlike Professor Dow, he had had no association with the Bute, and so had no division of loyalty from that side of the Medical School. Of all Sir James' critics, he remains probably the most fair and objective, and he retained a corresponding sympathy for the Principal, especially with regard to the campaign of the Dundee Press.[10]

Professor Garry's successor was invited to meet the Court and the Dundee members of its Joint Committee with the College Council on July 22nd. Professor George Howard Bell was also from Glasgow. Born in 1905 in Ayr, he was educated at the Academy there. He had taken his B.Sc. in Glasgow University in 1929, and M.B. with Honours in 1930 and M.D. also with Honours in 1943. After a house physician's post in the Royal Sick Children's Hospital in Glasgow he had gone straight into the Department of Physiology, had left for a year in 1934 to be a lecturer in Bristol, and then returned as senior lecturer in Glasgow in 1935. Not being absent on military service he had spent therefore virtually the whole of his life in the Glasgow School; he was now invited to take the Chair in University College. Two facts about Professor Bell had commended him to the Principal—he had recently become a Fellow of the Royal Society of Edinburgh, and he was a member of the Senatus Academicus of the University of Glasgow, although not a Professor. Whereas Sir James had had no place for non-professorial staff on the Senatus in St Andrews as a regular feature this was by no means so in Glasgow, where Sir Hector Hetherington had encouraged their appointment. Sir James was apparentrly unaware of this. Professor Bell was another new appointee destined to play a significant part in events to come. For the present, he moved quietly into the ground floor of the Medical School, and Professor Garry returned to Glasgow.

Professor Bell's opposite number in the Bute, though not to be appointed till March 1948, can be introduced now. The sub-committee to consider the vacancy was Professor Graham, the Botany Professor as Chairman, with Sir James, Dr. Lawson, and Professors Read (Chemistry), Walmsley, and Bell. Anthony Elliot Ritchie, an Edinburgh man, was appointed to succeed the much loved Professor Herring. He was ten years younger than Professor Bell—born on 30th March 1915, the son of Professor James Ritchie, Professor of Zoology in Aberdeen and later Edinburgh. Though educated in Edinburgh at the Academy, he took the M.A. of Aberdeen in 1933 and B.Sc. in 1936. He then graduated in Medicine at Edinburgh in 1940. His brilliance ensured quick progress—he was a Carnegie Research Scholar in 1940-41, assistant lecturer in 1941, lecturer in 1942, and senior lecturer in 1946. In 1945 he took the M.D. with the customary gold medal. During the war he had been concerned with nerve injuries as part of a specially picked team, and this gave him a clinical interest recognised both in Edinburgh, where he was a lecturer in electrotherapy, and subsequently in Dundee as an Honorary Consultant to the Eastern Regional Hospital Board. He would stand in antithesis to Professor Bell in years to come, and became an important figure in the continuance of medical teaching in St Andrews University.

Sir James Irvine sailed to the West Indies in December of 1947, to found the new University College there. It is further evidence of Dr. James Lawson's position and power that he was designated, with Principal Duncan of St Mary's and Principal Wimberley of University College, as one of the three-man committee to act during Principal Irvine's absence. His medical planning committee had met regularly to the end of the year—Professor Lendrum's request for an increase in his class grant from £300-£350 was agreed, as was his request for £80 for an animal house. Professor Patrick was to continue in post until September 1950, and Professor Alexander until 30th September, 1951. The Student Health Scheme for Dundee and St Andrews was begun, and Dr. Henry Q.C. Wheeler was appointed as an anaesthetic assistant at Perth Royal Infirmary on Professor Alexander's recommendation. Medical numbers entering increased a little—44 in the Bute and 30 in University College. And gowns cost under £6 each. 1948 was an even busier year. U.G.C. Grants totalled £99,000 to Dundee and £37,500 to St Andrews. Grants for teaching hospitals were £2,500 to Dundee Royal, £300 to Perth Royal, and £900 to Maryfield. The first ever research report from a clinical department came from the Department of Surgery to Faculty and Senate, and included research instituted by Mr John Grieve, the lecturer. The Medicine and Midwifery Departments gave no reports, as no research whatever was done by them. Apart from the appointment of the full-time Administrative Officer of the Advanced Medical School, the main happening was the inception of the National Health Service. In March the Duke of Hamilton became the new Chancellor, and on June 21 D'Arcy Thompson died in his home at 44 South Street.

Many personalities appeared in the Faculty in 1948. Just as in the 1880s, it was as if there were two worlds in the University—the public world of antagonism and hatred and the world of quiet progress. Dr. John O. Forfar,

who had been awarded the M.C. as a member of 47 Royal Marine Commando in 1944, was a St Andrews graduate of 1941. He had come back as a registrar in 1946, then senior registrar, and was now appointed senior lecturer in Child Health. Dr. W. Cameron Swanson, who would develop a first-class radiotherapy service in D.R.I. in later years, also became a lecturer. Professor Lendrum asked to increase his establishment because of his rapidly increasing work load, and was allowed to promote Drs. Prain and Inglis to Scale 2 lecturers, and Drs. W. Walker and Leslie to Scale 3. The Dental Planning Committee discussed the establishment of a new Department of Operative Dental Surgery. Mr Walter Campbell, the son of Professor Campbell, was appointed Honorary Visiting Surgeon at D.R.I. and his assistant was Mr James S. Kinnear. Mr Kinnear's temporary post terminated on January 3rd and he was now appointed permanently in succession to Mr J.J. Robb, who died suddenly on January 2. Dr. Douglas Adamson was promoted Associate Assistant Visiting Physician. In Bacteriology, Drs. David Stiven and James Brodie were to become assistants. Professors Dow and Bell were granted a lecturer of higher status—Dr. J.D.B. McDougall, and a new lecturer, respectively. Dr. Steve Bayne transferred his Physiology lectureship to Biochemistry. Grants for teaching hospitals for 1948 were fixed at £2,500 for Dundee Royal, £300 for Perth Royal, and £900 for Maryfield, identical to the amounts for 1947. Later in the year, a lectureship in the History of Medicine was suggested by Dr. James Lawson, as part of his continuing hard work to improve every feature of the Faculty. Dr. James Thomson was encouraged to convert a room in the Infirmary in Dundee as a laboratory for his Child Health Department. Drs. W.F. Mair and H.J. Gibson were appointed medical officers for the student health service in the two halves of the University. While the three upstairs parties were arguing, those on the ground—to use another military term—were already treating the enlarged University as having two equivalent parts to it. And all the time, too, the students continued to regard themsevles as *cives* of the University of St Andrews.

The inception of the National Health Service altered profoundly the delivery of medical care to the public. As far as the Faculty of Medicine was concerned, however, it was the Hospital part of the service which was important—the General Practitioner Service was not yet included in formal undergraduate or post-graduate teaching. The State took over all hospitals, and these were henceforth to be managed by Boards of Management. In overall control was the Eastern Regional Hospital Board, with its headquarters in Dundee but its area extending to Montrose in the North East, Stracathro Hospital in North Angus., Perth Royal Infirmary in the West, and St Andrews in the South. The Boards of Directors of the Royal Infirmaries of Dundee and Perth would disappear; the control of Maryfield Hospital and the several clinics—chest, venereal disease, childrens'—would pass from the Corporation of Dundee to the State. The Hospital Board was supported by public funds in financial terms and by the Scottish Home and Health Department in administrative terms. But the composition of Regional Boards and Boards of Management was to some degree dependent upon politics, both local and national, since various bodies

had to be represented by Statute, and key appointments were made by the Secretary of State. Since one of the basic aims of the National Health Service was to *develop* medical care in the community, with a view to both treatment and prevention of disease, new projects, specialities, and service were encouraged. Since the aim was to bring medical care to more patients and especially to previously less privileged members of society, this increase in service had a high priority. These would be provided out of National Health Contributions but only to a limited extent, it was thought, out of general taxation. At this early stage of the Health Service, it was still believed that the Service would so decrease the incidence of disease that in a few short years its costs would diminish.

The first priority for the new organisation was to provide a service, and thus teaching was a secondary consideration. If there was a conflict between the needs of teaching and the needs of the *Service*, the Service would have to be put first. A new hierarchy of posts was established. There would no longer be 'Honoraries', who were paid a nominal sum for their service to the hospital patients. Now there were to be full-time consultants, for the various specialties, all paid on the same scale. Such staff would be employed *wholly* by the National Health Service; if a consultant wished to undertake private practice, he could choose to be paid on a part-time basis. But the bulk of a part-timer's income, too, would be paid by his employer, the State. Further, such staff could earn 'distinction awards' which would increase their income considerably. Training grades were junior registrar, registrar, and senior registrar. All these National Health Service employees could be given a teaching appointment by the University, and paid a nominal rate of remuneration. University staff, by contrast, would be paid an amount equivalent to a full-time National Health Service opposite number, (usually rather less), and would be given an Honorary National Health Service appointment, providing a clinical status equivalent in N.H.S. terms to their University appointment. In Scotland, where unlike England the teaching hospitals had always been service hospitals, there was no great difficulty in the new organisation. The big difference was that non-University staff could, and did, achieve the same or higher seniority in the Service by virtue of their N.H.S. rank as did University Staff. It was all part of the levelling out process which was being applied in all walks of life by Government policy. Requests for new equipment, and new *service* developments, now had to be made to the Boards and not to Directors, and this necessity to bid for a share of public funds affected University Departments also.

With the setting up of these new Administrative Boards of Management for individual hospitals and Regional Boards for the whole Eastern Region of Scotland, there inevitably emerged a new type of individual, the administrative medical officer. These were not the same as the traditional medical superinten-dents, who had served their small or large hospitals with distinction and who were, on account of their often considerable clinical experience and distinction, respected by senior consultant staff and respected and feared by juniors. These new individuals were appointed by Regional or other Boards and so had no loyalty to a local hospital or institution; their loyalty was to the Board and to the

Board's superiors in Central Government. The first of these Senior Administrative Medical Officers for the Eastern Region was Dr. F.F. Main. By the application of Parkinson's first law[11] these administrators very soon had appointed numbers of assistants. The same process applied to lay administrators of all kinds, and in ten years, jobs presently done by one or two staff would find an establishment of many more essential to carry out much the same work load.

A result of this very large change was therefore to increase staff levels considerably. There were still returned ex-service doctors looking for training posts, and additional short-term registrar posts were created for them. Many of these made the life of the unfortunate houseman a misery, by ordering numerous laboratory tests which he had to perform. So this period, too, saw the application of Parkinson's first law to laboratory and other investigative services. But there were to be created many more senior posts as 'consultants'—all with very worth-while salaries—and this necessitated a large number of junior posts being created also, both to train the potential consultant and also to do much of his routine work for him once he was appointed. All these new posts required additional money to pay for them, but this presented no problems for the Government in the need to develop this entirely new system of State provision which was basic to the Socialist system.

But there was not yet equality for University staff salaries. These had to be applied for locally, and St Andrews could not offer as high a salary for a Professor as the more famous schools of Glasgow or Edinburgh, for example. But the Scottish Universities had to protect their own staff's interests, and had to agree a reasonable scale which would compete with the new N.H.S. scale and continue to encourage those of high calibre to seek University as distinct from State posts. On November 27th 1948, a Conference of the Courts of all the Scottish Universities was held, when the rates proposed by the Spens Report[12] were referred to, and the following observations made:

1) £3000 *per annum* was 'a not unreasonable salary' for a full-time Professor (This gave a differential of ten times over the salary of a newly-qualified assistant. Over the next thirty years, this differential would steadily diminish.)

2) When compared with the salaries of young specialists (in 'training' grades) as set out in the Spens Report, existing scales for full-time non-professional clinical staff was inadequate. Such should be £1500 to £2500 *per annum*.

3) All full-time University teachers should be eligible for distinction awards (This had, in fact, already been agreed by the Ministry of Health.)

4) Full-time non-clinical teachers must be paid more—Professors should receive £2000 to £2500 *per annum* and the non-professional staffs £1200 to £1800 *per annum*.

All these proposals were to safeguard the salaries of University staffs, and it is of interest that the same problems were a source of difficulty for the next fifty years—most of all, perhaps, the need to pay pre-clinical teachers an adequate

salary and so retain the medically qualified personnel so essential in a good Medical Faculty.

The Medical Planning Committee also involved itself in discussions with the new Senior Adminsitrative Medical Officer at the Regional Board, Dr. Main. The grading of hospital appointments between N.H.S. and University appointees was argued for, as was the relationship of the grades of specialist and potential specialist as set out in the Spens Report. The University also insisted that it should have maximum representation on any Advisory Appointments Committee if a post with a University component or honorary teaching appointment was advertised. In all these, Dr. James Lawson continued to be the moving force, and succeeding generations must not forget just how much he did for the Faculty of Medicine in these years.

Dr. Lawson was also responsible for arranging for the provision of a Mace for the School of Medicine of the University. Its final design was submitted to the Court, and accepted by it, on December 14th, 1948. In 1947 'an anonymous benefactor' had approached one of the Assessors of the General Council with the offer of a Mace for the School of Medicine. This was to be the fifth Mace of the University, the first being the ancient Mace of the Faculty of Arts, regarded as the Mace of the University, and dating from 1418. The second is the Mace of the Faculty of Canon Law, and is the Mace of St Mary's College, and the third is the Mace of St Salvator's College—the most magnificent of all. The fourth Mace was presented in 1912 to University College by Dr. Randolph Polack, a German who also bequeathed prizes for the High School of Dundee and elsewhere. The knop of this mace is octagonal in section and displays the patron saints of the University and of the three older Colleges, alternating with figures symbolic of the four main branches of study in the College. The knop is surmounted by a figure of the Virgin as patron saint of the City of Dundee. The new Medical Mace was designed by Mr Pilkington Jackson and created by Messrs Hamilton and Inches of Edinburgh. The figure of St Andrew forms the pinnacle above a shrine containing the Fountain of Healing, with a symbol of the Earth repeated six times. On the upper stage of the knop is an extract from the Hippocratic Oath: In purity and holiness will I guard my life and my art, and below this, are six beautiful Coats of Arms—The University, The Chancellor, Pope Benedict XIII, The Rector, The Founder of the first Chair of Medicine, and the Principal and Vice-Chancellor. On the lower stage beneath the Arms of the University is the rod and serpent, and on the other faces are symbols of medical subjects taught. Spiralling down the shaft are nine panels of ornament based on vegetable sources of the principal medical herbs, and on the collar of the fleuron are thistles, and the fleuron itself is composed of the Winged Ox of St Luke repeated three times. Work was begun in January 1949, and the Medical Mace formally accepted by the University at the Graduation Ceremony on 14th October, 1949.

1949, the year of the Cooper Report, was a less busy one for the Faculty of Medicine. The sought-after salaries for staff were confirmed from 1st April and were in fact better than those requested the previous year except for Professors', whose upper limit was fixed at £2750. In March, the James Mackenzie Institute

for Clinical Research was finally wound up in St Andrews—it had failed for want of support by the local practitioners. The Directors transferred to the University the securities of the Institute, totalling £15,353—and with this money, two new Medical Chairs were to be endowed—the James Mackenzie Chair of Child Health and the James Mackenzie Chair of Public Health and Social Medicine. The money was split equally and invested by the Court, in whose patronage the Chairs were.

One more Professor who would become a great servant of St Andrews was appointed in this post-war period. He was the successor to Professor Adam Patrick, who had had his tour of duty quite considerably extended, and was now 66 years old. He had worked very hard as a clinician, in ways unbelieveable to future generations. He wrote his peripheral clinic letters by hand, and left them for the local practitioners to collect as soon as he had left. He was always the quiet scholar, decisive in clinical teaching but perhaps, because of his delivery, less effective in formal lectures. He retained his keen interest in laboratory investigation and in Pathology, and would take his quite considerable retinue to the post-mortem room, where he would record the shape of the mitral valve in a case of rheumatic carditis, and would give the members of the Pathology Department present the benefit of his great experience if it was asked for. Because of his quiet manner, the bulk of students were unaware of the flashes of humour his residents and registrars came to know well. After his retiral from the Chair of Medicine, he continued to lecture in Medical History for several years, and to be the honoured guest at the Maryfield Christmas parties.

His successor was a complete contrast. Professor Ian G.W. Hill was an Edinburgh man, small in stature but a dynamic personality and a dynamic teacher. Ian George Wilson Hill was born on 7th September 1904, in Edinburgh, where he was at George Watson's College and the University. He took his M.B. with Honours in 1928 and was elected F.R.C.P. Ed. in 1933. He left Edinburgh for Aberdeen in 1933, returned in 1937, and was appointed lecturer in the Department of Therapeutics. From 1938, he was an assistant physician in Edinburgh Royal and from 1946 a physician at the Deaconess Hospital. A pre-war Territorial like Professor Walmsley, he had had a particularly distinguished career in the War, first as Officer in Charge of medical divisions in the U.K., Middle East, and India, and he had ended the War as consulting physician to the 14th Army in Burma. In 1945 he was awarded the C.B.E. (Military Division) for his RAMC service. Dr. Peter Robertson met him during the early part of the War when he was sent to his unit as a potential medical specialist, and recalls what a stimulating and yet rather alarming person he was. Professor Hill's special interest was cardiology, and he would create a Department of Medicine where for the first time clinical research would be developed in St Andrews, and whose fame would become widely known. His very first 'big clinic' was inevitably on a case of cardiac failure, and his sharp, clear, and vivid description of types of patient, causes of failure, prognosis, and treatment would be recalled by those who attended for the rest of their professional lives. He pushed knowledge into his students with as much ferocity as 'Sonny' Alexander or Willie John Tulloch.

The first five years after the Second World War ended with the Faculty undoubtedly 'taking off'. A series of new, able, and active staff at all levels were now in post, and the National Health Service, far from being the disaster some had predicted, had by making considerably increased funds and staff available, by itself created new activity and energy in Medicine. It had now its own share of N.H.S. senior staff, and these were men of ability and activity also. There still however loomed the threat of further major trouble for the University after the non-acceptance of the Cooper Report, and the obvious determination of members of the Second and Third parties to take their campaign further.

But this threat seemed to have disappeared with the recommendations of the Tedder Report, and it looked as if an age of fulfilment for medical teaching, and for the whole University, was at hand.

16

The post-1945 students and their teachers

More developments

The first post-war academic session began in October 1945. This first year contained students who had secured entry while the war was still in progress, and was mainly composed of school leavers. But as in 1919 there was about to be a large increase in those seeking entry, made up almost entirely of those who had begun their course earlier in the war, left for service with the Armed Forces and were now returning, or of those ex-service men and women coming up to University for the first time. A memorandum from Professor Tulloch, the Dean, typed on the large-letter print typewriter which everyone of these years grew to know so well—and by a young typist called Miss Judy Grieg—was discussed at Faculty on October 22nd, 1945.[1] It was concerned with the need for fairly balancing places between returning and new ex-service students, the effect of National Service, and the admission of women. In effect, it made the conditions of entry very tight, and the need to pass examinations on time very strict also. (It was in fact modelled on the system used in Aberdeen's Medical Faculty). As a result, the only chance a schoolboy or schoolgirl had of gaining entry in October 1946, was to win a Scholarship or Bursary. Prospective students, especially those from schools in Dundee, Fife, or Perthshire, sat both Dundee and St Andrews Entrance competitions, and where they started—in University or the United College—depended upon where they won their scholarship. All other young men were called up for the new compulsory requirement of National Service: this great leveller would continue until 1959. Because school-girls were not involved in National Service, there were extra places available for them.

All bejants and bejantines of 1946 were therefore aware of just how privileged they were. The ex-service remembered friends or relatives lost during the war years, and their thankfulness at being alive, and sound in mind and body, and their awareness of having to make up time for the years slipped away, made them the most determined undergradutates to appear for a quarter of a century. The returned doctors—appearing as post-graduate students—were equally determined. The entry was, in fact, a specially selected group. Their standard of examination performance was high, and made higher by their relentlessly hard work. Against this a few, especially those who were some years older, found the sudden discipline of academic work, different from their recent

external service discipline, too hard for them to accept, and fell by the wayside.

For new first-year students, things were the same as had always been. The arrival, settling into accommodation, buying of books—the excitement and anxieties of all this were as they had been for Duncan Dewar. They queued to matriculate, and had their class cards duly completed. Most had their fees paid, as they were supported financially by 'ex-service grants'. Although many had held positions of authority in the recent past, they happily found the red gown now their common badge, as it had been for Elizabeth MacDonald. It effaced all other inequalities. They fitted in without complaint to the indignities of the first year at St Andrews—the hecklings, the Kate Kennedy interviews, the require-ment to be in Hall by 10 p.m. They remained polite to the impositions of senior men and senior women even though some of these were callow youths by the standards and experience of their own past four years. Their deep sense of privilege at being where they were did not reduce in any way their capacity for fun and pleasure. Sir D'Arcy Thompson wrote to *The Times* to say that in his sixty years as a Professor he could not remember a medical class with a greater thirst for knowledge and determination to learn. In University College, the first year of ex-service did not take part in the heckling and shoe removing function for bejants, with the result that the engineering semis who had hoped for their support to defeat the seniors, were themselves sadly defeated. There, too, was the coming-up ball, the early elections for Students' Representative Council, and the activists prepared to enlist whoever they could get for their own student society or organisation. The St Andrews University Medical Society was largely a society for third-year and more senior students of the Conjoint Medical School, and so the bejants took little part in its activities. In sport, the rugby teams were largely of schoolboys, but the association football team was soon led by Jimmy Walker D.F.C., a former RAF navigator, now medical student, who was one of its greatest-ever captains. St Andrews as the world capital of golf, a position it had earned through the years, had hosted the 1939 Open Championship and Walker Cup match. In the summer of 1946, it had hosted the first post-war Open, won by Sam Snead with 290 strokes. And in the Whitsun term of 1946-47, students would leave their classes to see the first of many United States victories in the post-war Walker Cup, when the red gowns coloured the fairways of the links of St Andrews for perhaps the last time before spectators were roped off from the play.

The first or Martinmas term at United College began with the 9 o'clock Botany lecture taken usually by Professor Graham. Astonishment was expressed by students when he told them they could take the class notebooks into the Degree Examination in December. Some failed in spite of this! At ten, the class of forty went through the corridor to sit at the feet of Sir D'Arcy. His first lecture, on 'the little amoeba', held them spell-bound. At the start of his second, he began 'Today I am going to tell you about the Amphioxus. How easy that would be if you knew Greek. But you don't know Greek'. Then, turning from the blackboard, he asked 'Does anyone here know Greek?' John Leckie put up his hand. 'You see', said D'Arcy blandly, 'No-one here knows Greek!' He came

in the next week to talk about the structure of bones and birds' wings, and with two pieces of paper, folded like a child's paper aeroplane or rolled into a cylinder, reduced his great learning to terms the simplest could understand. (Unlike Professor Walmsley who related 'form is the expression of function' to John Hunter, D'Arcy related it to Plato.) Another day he was late. When he arrived, he said he had to hurry to London. 'But I will leave you with a thought', he said. He then pulled something out of his pocket. 'Here out of my right-hand pocket is my live frog', he said, 'and a very jolly little fellow he is too.' 'And here out of my left-hand pocket is my dead frog', he went on, putting one in the bench. 'And there is a vast difference between 'em'. In the practical class, various zoological objects were laid out for description. 'Try again, my dear' said D'Arcy to a girl who had written 'horse spermatozoon' as an answer. When he came back later to find she had written 'elephant spermatozoon', he said to her, with his eyes twinkling, 'It's a tadpole, silly'. On the other hand, he had the occasional outburst of temper, and two former aircrew recalled asking him innocently about homing pigeons, when, because he did not know the answer, he stamped angrily out of the laboratory. He remained a rather awesome figure, even to the shy and trembling young scholars allocated him as regent, to whom he was so kind. And it was during the winter of this session, when he journeyed to India by plane, that a succession of illnesses began which would later lead to his death.

Professor Graham's Botany Department was shared between the two Colleges, and so he was responsible for the UCD medicals also. The small, bright-eyed person of Professor Peacock (Zoology) was a teacher who also had the gift of making things simple. His north-country speech came through as he spoke and he was a friend and compatriot of Professor Garry—a total contrast in size. Of the University College pre-clinical Professors, it was Professor Garry who was favourite. Clear, didactic, he taught physiology which was up-to-date and apposite to clinical medicine. 'Everyone went to his lectures.' He was respected as a man both strong and fair, who would have made an excellent Dean had he not left for Glasgow. Professor Bell was a less commanding figure; 'he read his lectures'. He was the senior author of a standard text-book 'Bell Davidson and Scarborough' which continued in use for many years.

The 1946-7 winter was one of the coldest of the twentieth century. When the Chemistry degree examinations were held before Easter, there was still deep snow on the ground. Anatomy began in the Candlemas term and a whole term was used to dissect upper limb. Lower limb was dissected in the Whitsun term. For Professor Walmsley's lectures all wore gowns—they were worn in the Bute for all classes except practicals. Everyone bought and wore the Bute tie. The dissecting rooms had their own atmosphere of mystery: 'No admittance except to members of the Anatomy Class.' Unlike the Medical Society at Dundee, the Bute Medical Society was a pre-clinical students' scientific society, and a social one too. In October 1947, Miss Mary Whitfield was elected its first woman president. Professor J.C. Brash of Edinburgh lectured on 'The Ruxton Case', Professor Alexander on 'Opening the Abdomen' and Professor Fairlie ('who sat where you are sitting' as Professor Walmsley reminded the audience) on 'The Pelvis'.

But of all these pre-clinical lecturers in United College, Professor Herring was perhaps the best loved. Now an old man, his obvious delight in histology, his happy and always kindly humour in the practical class, and his ability to teach a list of essentials which students would remember for a life-time, made him one of those very few Professors whom generations of students genuinely loved. He had no detractors. As the little bent old lady who was the cleaner in the Department described Professor Herring: 'He was a gentleman to his back bone'. He took all lectures himself—except those in Biochemistry given by Dr. Hynd. Dr. Hynd lacked the agreeable personality and pawky humour of Dr. R.F. Cook, his University College opposite number. 'Cookie' worked in what could only be called a broken down building in Small's Lane, known to all as 'Dirty Dicks'. He collaborated with Professor Tulloch on studies relating to the still new antibiotic, penicillin, and produced marvellous work in such a limited laboratory.

Students continued to do other things besides attend classes. The Bute Ball was the main social event of the Martinmas term in United College. Medicals took a full part in the affrays which preceded each Rectorial election. Society meetings of every sort had their devotees, as had the Mermaid Dramatic Society, the Chapel Choir or the pipe band. For a whole session's golf over any of the courses of the links of St Andrews, an undergraduate in the post-1945 years had only to pay 30 shillings (£1.50p). St Salvator's Hall fees were £60 a year—£20 a term, and for £100 a student could pay all his accommodation, all fees and books, the cost of clothes and still have some spending money left. University College had the most famous pub in the entire University—Ma Strachan's in Small's Wynd. This hostelry was used by all students, not only medical ones, and remained the meeting place of meeting places until the street was finally taken over in the Queen's College Development. Though the UCD students had no equivalent to University Chapel and the pier walk, a graduation service was held before Principal Wimberley's time, organised by a medical student, K.P. Duncan, the son of Dr. J.H. Duncan of St Mary's. Afterwards the Principal organised these formally.

Airlie Hall Residence gradually increased in size as successive houses in the street were taken over. It started as a women medical students' residence, but after 1945 was for men. To it came young men from many overseas countries—especially from Nigeria, the Sudan and Ethiopia. Senior male medical students lived in No 10 Dudhope Terrace—the 'Willie Low'—and the girls lived in the house next door at No 11—the 'Willie High'. These were small residences by St Andrews standards, holding about a dozen students each, and so places in them were hard to get. They had the great advantage of being beside the Infirmary, and so ideal for the final year. In their third year, students from the two sides merged. In these merged years, there was no conflict, no them-and-us. Friendships and romances were made between the now allied University and United College students. The medical world they were now in was a clinical one. Third year was Pathology, Bacteriology and Pharmacology and Therapeutics—the Third M.B. Degree subjects. But there was also a class in systematic and clinical surgery, and in clinical diagnosis. At 9.05 every morning, Professor Alexander

lectured in the old Institute theatre above the bacteriology department. He had a list of subjects written in chalk on the blackboard and went through them lecture by lecture, beginning each day when he had left off the day before, and wagging his forefinger to emphasise a point. Mr John (Jack) Grieve lectured also, and Mr Ian Smillie gave the course in fractures—general orthopaedics being still covered by the Professor.

The class then left, and walked the same route St Andrews students had covered since the First War. Now there was the thrill of the Infirmary, and real patients at last! In the Caird block, Professor Alexander had wards 15 and 16, Mr Walter Campbell 13 and 14, and each had half 17, the children's surgical ward. Mr Sturrock, as short of words as the Professor was talkative, was the sub-chief on 15 and 16, and Mr James Kinnear, who had succeeded the late John Robb, Mr Campbell's assistant. In the main part of the Infirmary, Mr F.R. Brown had charge of 6 and 7, with Mr Soutar, returned from National Service, his assistant. Ward teaching was held each morning, when the personalities of the various staff members became evident, and students were questioned with varying degrees of charity. Once a week was the 'double' or 'big' clinic, shared with the final year surgical intensives. These were taken in turn by the Chiefs, then by the sub-Chiefs, and Mr Smillie was included. The Professor showed at the first clinic of all a patient with a tumour of the kidney, and then took his class of 70 to the West Theatre where he proceeded to remove it. At the end, his black shoes stained with blood, he said, noting that three students had fainted; 'there were five last year'. Mr Brown showed a patient with both femoral shafts fractured, at his first double clinic. After discussing treatment and prognosis, he said in his quiet way, looking down at his fingers, 'I've a particular interest in this man. You see, I ran him over last night'.

Pathology and Bacteriology were regarded by most as more important subjects than Materia Medica, but this belief was soon changed when the new Professor of Pharmacology and Therapeutics, Robert Brockie Hunter, failed one-third of his first 1948 year. The rather reduced circumstances of the Materia Medica Department under Professor Charteris were rapidly altered by the activity and drive of his successor. Professor Hunter was born on 4th July, 1915, the son of Robert Marshall Hunter and Margaret Brockie. Educated at George Watson's College in Edinburgh, he graduated M.B. Ch.B. in 1938. During the war, he had for a time acted as personal physician to General Montgomery in North Africa, and, in 1945, he was awarded the M.B.E. (Military Division). Returning to Edinburgh, he took the membership there and became a lecturer in the Department of Therapeutics under Sir Derrick Dunlop. His interest in post-graduate training led him to become assistant-director of the Edinburgh Post-Graduate Board in Medicine. And now, at the early age of 33, he was appointed to the Chair in St Andrews.

Dr. George Ranken Tudhope was the most universally admired and indeed loved figure amongst the Third Professional subject teachers. While Professor Lendrum's lectures were witty and entertaining, students preferred Dr. Tudhope's solid instruction, with his cells acting like policemen, firemen, or milkmen, with minds of their own—however much his similes might offend the purist academic,

they made his students remember the disease *processes*, as he used to repeat in his well-recalled voice. There was nothing superficial about him, in formal or informal teaching, and the transparent honesty of his character was the same as that of Professor Herring. How frequently in the often heartless world of university ambition a man or woman like this is loved when much more worldly-successful colleagues achieve only a degree of respect at best, and universal dislike at worst.

Professor Hunter was very quick to obtain an increase in his own departmental staff, and he was also quick to designate an entirely new medical firm—the Therapeutics Unit. He established this in Wards 1 and 2 at Maryfield Hospital. There was no room for an additional medical unit in the Royal Infirmary, but any disappointment he may have had at not obtaining beds there was soon overcome by the challenge of developing Maryfield. When he arrived, patients were carried to his teaching clinics on litters, covered by faded Dundee Corporation blankets; he made it plain to his students that he intended this to change. But apart altogether from Professor Hunter's aim to build his Therapeutics unit, there was a progressive development at Maryfield as University policy, and many other Departments with first-class staff moved in: Mr Walter Campbell's Surgical Service in Wards 3 and 5, Miss Herring's Department of Obstetrics and Gynaecology in 7, 10 and 14, Ward 9, the acute mental ward, the only one in Dundee, under the charge of Dr. G.D. Fraser Steele, the other Medical Unit under the charge of Professor Hill in 6 and 8, and the Department of Pathology under Dr. George Smith. Dr. James Frew came from a brilliant undergraduate career in Glasgow as senior lecturer in the Therapeutics Unit, but later 'moved to the NHS'. Such movement, in effect a promotion, became common. He had five beds only; 'Frew's few' as they were called; in 1961, he joined Dr. Robert Semple in the Wards 6 and 8 unit. Maryfield became the location of a new speciality, Geriatric Medicine; former Poor House blocks were taken over by Dr. Oswald Taylor Brown in 1950 and that especially able physician built a major service from this unlikely beginning.

In the fourth year, Systematic Medicine and Medical Clinics took the place of Surgery and Surgical. As well as Professor Patrick and Dr. Douglas Adamson in Wards 8 and 9 at the Infirmary, there was Dr. John Morgan, whose clinics were a succession of jokes but would end on a serious note. With him in Wards 2 and 5 was Dr. Gordon Clark, quieter, but firm and practical. In later years, both Professor Hunter and Professor Patrick's successor were at fault in undervaluing his clinical acumen and teaching ability. The teaching in Professor Fairlie's Department of Obstetrics and Gynaecology continued to be one of the best in the Faculty. 'The Madam' continued to wear the neat suits and silk tie-neck blouses of pre-war years, but she could carry off this fashion as very few women could. Her black Bentley car appeared at this time. Her grin, with a tongue pushed against a tooth, students remembered, as they also remembered the occasions when she could be very angry indeed. Sandy Buchan, her lecturer, was an Aberdeen graduate and a favourite for many years; he had a knack of putting words together in unlikely combinations rather as Professor Kynoch had done. The midwifery students—in groups of three—

D. F. Cappell

John Anderson

M. Fairlie

R. C. Alexander

R. C. Garry

G. H. Bell

G. R. Tudhope A. J. Pitkeathly Margaret Dickie J. D. M. Ross D. R. Dow

Major-General D. Wimberley,
Principal, U.C.D.

Old Medical School

spent two weeks in residence at the Willie Low in No 11 when doing their deliveries at D.R.I. under the fearful figure of Sister McKiddie. Whereas during the war they had had to cycle at top speed to Maryfield from the Low Residence for cases 'coming off' during the second fortnight of their month's practical, there was now accommodation in 'The Cottage' at Maryfield Hospital itself. Here they met the inimitable Jenny, the senior maid. 'They students', she used to say, 'is a' the same. There's aye a saft yin, aye a hard yin, and aye an in-between yin'.

The fourth year also included Ophthalmology, taught by Dr. A.A.B. Scott, Dr. Robin Mathers, son of 'Bobby' Mathers of ENT, and Mental Diseases, taught by 'Batty' Bell. Saturday mornings took the class by bus to Westgreen where clinical cases were shown. The lecture course was one of the very few where a roll was taken. The course remained rather restricted in the 1940s and '50s as treatment was limited to electro-convulsive therapy and most drugs were sedative ones.

Degree subjects of the fourth year were Forensic Medicine and Public Health. Forensic was still taught by 'Daddy' Dorward, commonly believed to be the 'Doc' in the *Sunday Post*, though there was no real evidence that this was so. He was an extremely diligent teacher, concerned about student welfare, and as well as being Police Surgeon in Dundee, was a busy general practitioner. When he died, crowds lined the streets along his funeral route in a way they never did for any Professor, so greatly was he loved by the Dundee public. Public Health was beautifully and explicitly taught by Dr. W.L. Burgess, who deserves special mention. He was born in Aberdeen in 1886 and graduated M.B. with First Class Honours in Edinburgh in 1909. In 1911, he took both the Diploma in Tropical Medicine and Hygiene and the Diploma in Public Health, and his M.D. with commendation the next year. He became Chief Tuberculosis Officer for Dundee in 1913 and Medical Officer of Health in 1918. He was appointed lecturer in Public Health in St Andrews University in 1913, and promoted reader in 1930. During the 1939-45 war, he served on Government Committees at a high level, and was awarded the C.B.E. in 1944. For many years he was in medical charge at King's Cross Hospital. Dr. Burgess was as distinguished in his field as Professors Patrick, Hill, Alexander and Douglas— in some ways more so—and with Professor Alexander was the first St Andrews medical Professor to achieve an award in the Civil Honours List. Being a Corpora-tion employee—as M.O.H.—he found two of his junior trainees Dr. W.M. Jamieson and Dr. David Smith, created consultants in Infectious Diseases and Tuber-culosis at the beginning of the National Health Service, and so it was very fair and fitting that he was appointed as the first holder of the James Mackenzie Chair in his subject in 1950.

In the final year, the class was divided into three groups, and did an 'intensive' term in each of the major subjects. There was also Ear, Nose and Throat, taught by Mr M.J. Gibson, Bobby Mather's successor, with George Henderson; and Dermatology, taught by Dr. John Kinnear and Dr. John Rogers. Dermatology was the only subject which had no class examination. After the appointment of the Professor of Child Health, Paediatrics was an extra

examination subject in the final year; before this it was a fourth year subject, taught by Dr. James ('Jas') Thomson. He ran the Department well, and began clinical research at an early date. Anaesthetics was taught in a course of lectures by Dr. Willie Shearer, and all students had to give at least twelve anaesthetics before graduation. Also in the final year, infectious fevers were taught at King's Cross Hospital by Dr. W.M. Jamieson and his staff, and Tuberculosis at Ashludie by Dr. D.H. Smith. From 1949, Mr Martin Fallon, O.B.E. M.A. Ch.M. FRCSI, the first Regional Board appointed Thoracic Surgeon, also taught there in his engaging personal way. In one or other of their intensive terms groups of students went to Perth Royal Infirmary for a three week period. This was possible because all major subjects began to be taught there from the late 1940s when Mr Ian T. Fraser was appointed assistant lecturer in Obstetrics and Gynaecology. The large amount of clinical material available surprised everyone; it was commonly believed amongst the students that Perth was being developed as an alternative sourse of patients by the University should the *Courier's* campaign succeed.

Professor Alexander did not retire until October 1951—a year later than Professor Patrick. While not a good technical operator, Sonny Alexander cared deeply for his patients and had an amazing clinical sense. His social foibles and class-consciousness amused some students and staff, but the majority were aware that he was the only Professor who actually *taught* them how to behave as doctors—how to conduct themselves towards patients, how to listen to them, and how to look for clues. His loyalty to his own staff was absolute even in their absence. Woe betide the stranger who criticised his house-surgeon. If angry he was very angry, but once his anger had cooled he bore no malice— this, too, his students and staff sensed. Of all the clinical Professors in the Faculty of Medicine he was the one who had the deepest and most sincere interest in his students—he had an encyclopaedic knowledge of them for years into the past. Because of this, he shares with Professor Price the highest place of all St Andrews surgical Professors; though lacking Price's pre-eminence in the Faculty, he excelled him in his concern for his students. Many years after he retired he rebuked his last house-surgeon, while they were playing golf at St Andrews. 'Stop calling me "Sir" ', he said. 'You are a consultant now'.

All the final years had their 'Year Clubs'. Before and during the 1939-45 war, these were as small as their graduating year. A composite photograph showed the members, with the Professors and the Principal in the front row. Informal graduation dinners were held until 1946—from that summer onwards formal dinners were held in Dines—the Professors attending as guests. From then on came the Year Books, with photographs, plus a suitable quotation or comment for each member.

Once graduated, a minority of the year held local house officer posts. There were very few in the early post-war years—2 medical, 2 surgical, one gynae-cological/maternity, one paediatric, and 3 casualty officers in D.R.I. Of the casualty officers, one was the principal, and the other 2 did the ENT and Opthalmology houseman's work in addition. Maryfield had 6 residents on the same basis, one surgical, 2 medical, 2 maternity and one paediatric. Perth had 3

or 4. Work was extremely hard. The medical house officer had 60 beds—2 adult wards—to look after, and had to do all the routine side-room testing of bloods and urines himself. The surgical in D.R.I. had 70 beds—60 adult plus 10 or even 15 surgical childrens', and on arrival the new incumbent was presented with a cut-throat razor by the hospital barber with which to shave the operation site of all male patients. An afternoon off per week was allowed. Nevertheless the Gilroy and Maryfield Residences were happy places. Although the salaries had gone up from £60 per annum pre-war to £1 per day, there was no charge for accommodation or food, and a meal would be cooked at any hour of the day or night by the House Sister or her staff for the residents. On Sundays, the mess president for the week carved the roast, but these and other favours gradually disappeared as the numbers of residents rose and commercial requirements for cost-effectiveness in the Health Service loomed larger. At Perth Royal Infirmary, the two house-surgeons were on emergency call every day—the two units alternating, and the shift ending or beginning every midnight. The accommodation in Perth—an especially well-endowed hospital in pre-N.H.S. years by the wealthy and supportive shire community—was grander than the tiny rooms in the Gilroy at Maryfield. At Perth, too, there was a fine medical library, established many years before Maryfield's (1963) and Dundee Royal's (1964).

In October, 1951, Professor Alexander was succeeded by Professor Donald Macleod Douglas. He was the fifth St Andrews graduate to hold a Chair in the Medical Faculty.[1] Born on June 28th, 1911, in St Andrews, Fife, he was educated at Madras College in St Andrews and so was a local boy. His father, William Douglas, was Rector of Bell-Baxter School in Cupar. Like Alfred Pitkeathly, he graduated in 1935. His contemporaries remembered him as very genial, a good organiser, and ambitious, and unlike Sonny, that he became more distant as he rose in the academic world. He was a rugby blue. He left Dundee soon after graduation and went first to London and then to the Mayo Clinic as a Commonwealth Fellow in 1937, returning as a first assistant in Surgery at the British Post-graduate Medical School in 1939. While in the RAMC, he was seconded as a Professor of Surgery in Baghdad, and was awarded the M.B.E. (Military Division) in 1945. He then went to Edinburgh as Reader in Experimental Surgery, and was Professor James Learmonth's assistant in 1951 on his appointment to St Andrews. Now at the age of forty he was back in his own Medical School, as the first whole-time Surgical Professor.

Admitted by the Senatus Academicus on the same day was the first James Mackenzie Professor of Child Health, John Louis Henderson. He was four years older than Professor Douglas, being born on 25th March, 1907, educated at Reading and Edinburgh University, graduating in 1933, and taking his M.D. with commendation in 1938. During the 1939-45 war, he was a lecturer in the Department of Child Health in Edinburgh, and in 1946 went to the United States as a Rockefeller Travelling Fellow. Since 1947, he had been a senior lecturer in Child Health at Edinburgh. St Andrews thus was supplied with five clinical Professors from Edinburgh, in these immediate post-war years, and this was university policy.[2]

A little earlier that summer, on June 16th, Professor Hill wrote a memorandum

for the Faculty of Medicine about the teaching of Psychiatry. Dr. G.D. Fraser Steele was a Regional Board Consultant, appointed without reference to the University, who had charge of the acute psychiatric ward at Maryfield Hospital and of Gowrie House, the former private mental hospital. Dr. Bell, the lecturer, was still physician superintendent at Westgreen. Dr. J.D. Uytman was also a University lecturer, unassociated with either of them. Professor Hill's memorandum looked towards the appointment of a Professor of Psychiatry with a proper department such as had not so far existed. He suggested that psychiatry become a final M.B. subject, and that training in Mental Deficiency be included. In these views, he said, he was supported by Sir David Henderson, Professor of Psychiatry in Edinburgh. It would not, however, be until 1955 that a Chair of Psychiatry was formally proposed in Senate.

In 1950, the invitation of visiting lecturers from abroad was discussed. It is noteworthy that the first formal proposal for this came from Dr. James Lawson's Medical Planning Committee. Professor Hunter was by now interesting himself in external lecturers, and the concept of inviting distinguished men to visit; following the Medical Committee's initiative and the Faculty's agreement, he asked R.N.M. Robertson to arrange that money be set aside for a visit; £300 was suggested to cover an air fare, and £150 to pay for the visitor's 6 weeks' stay. Later, at Professor Douglas' suggestion, the surgeon Sir Heneage Ogilvie was appointed Visiting Lecturer in the Faculty of Medicine for 1952-53.

Teaching of Diagnostic Radiology was next on the list of new requirements. In 1951, Dr. Cecil Pickard, a Leeds graduate of 1939, was appointed by the Regional Board as the first full-time consultant radiologist. Before his appointment, this service had been given by two part-time specialists, Dr. Grant and Dr. Sprunt. Dr. Grant's retiral and Dr. Sprunt's appointment as consultant to Maryfield and Arbroath had left the way open for yet another soon-to-develop service to be put on a secure basis. It was agreed that Dr. Pickard should co-ordinate Diagnostic Radiology teaching, and Dr. W. Camerson Swanson co-ordinate Radiotherapy, both as full-time consultants.

Professor Henderson raised the question, in November of 1952, of Child Health becoming a Fourth M.B. subject. The Faculty decided against doing this, but agreed that each group of final year doing intensive medicine could sit a special Child Health examination at the end of their medicine term. These marks would then be carried forward to the Final examination.

In June, 1953, when the University of St Andrews Act became law, the last major innovation in teaching was brought before the Faculty. This was the teaching of General Practice. As so often, the senior Medical Schools of Edinburgh and Glasgow already had this, and Edinburgh had a General Practice Teaching Unit. In discussion on June 12th, Professor Burgess doubted whether the Faculty should approve the immediate setting up of such a unit in St Andrews, but suggested that the building of a Health Centre should be considered. What could be done, he suggested, was that medical students should be sent out to the practices of suitably chosen general practitioners. This could begin at once. Pressure was coming from the College of General Practitioners also for such new teaching. In 1953, the usual sub-committee agreed

that students from St Andrews could be seconded to selected general practitioners for instruction and familiarisation, and by February of the next year the Eastern Regional Faculty of the College of General Practitioners wrote formally to welcome the start of this important new departure in teaching.

With this huge increase in teaching, with so many newly-appointed Professors and Heads of Departments eager to insist on time being made available for their subjects, it is not surprising that these years saw an increase in the length of the curriculum. The Medical Act of 1950 laid down new regulations for admittance to the Medical Register, with 'provisional registration' and time spent in approved hospitals after graduation, before 'Certified Experience' was confirmed and 'full registration' allowed. This meant that medical graduates could no longer practice as legally registered practitioners as soon as they graduated, but now had to spend a year in approved posts. The setting up of this, the approval of 'pre-registration house jobs' as they came to be called, took a great deal of time and hard work. Not only had hospital posts to be approved by the GMC, but various *definitions* (e.g. of what was exactly meant by 'house officer') had to be discussed by the Faculty; this latter was done on June 16th, 1951. The new six year course required a whole new time-table. There were now three pre-clinical and three clinical years. In the new fourth year, Medicine replaced Surgery as the first course of lectures and the subsequent years were re-arranged[4].

All the final year subjects except paediatrics were tested together at the time of the Fourth Professional Examination. The written papers immediately preceded the clinicals and orals. The form of these did not change in the 1950s and '60s, but the examination remained a hard and searching one. It was not uncommon for students who had had a smooth passage in earlier years to fail the Finals. The newly graduated pre-registration house officer was given recognition by a salute from the famous head porters—Mr Yule of D.R.I., Mr Hosie of Maryfield—both former Black Watch men, and the stately Mr Geddes of P.R.I., ex-Scots Guards as befitted the social standing of that hospital! With the need to provide graduates with pre-registration posts obligatory for the University, numbers of residents increased, and so the excessive hours of work of earlier decades were reduced. The new residents also discovered the worth of famous ward sisters of these decades—at D.R.I., Sister Wallace in Ward 2 and 5, Sister Farquhar in 8 and 9, Sister Elder in 6 and Sister Pearson in 7, Sister Brummidge in 13 and 14, Sister Buist in 15 and 16, Sister Jean Sturrock in 17, and Sister Crichton in 18. Sister McKiddie in maternity, Sister Lowe, later Sister Kiddie, and Sister Hardie in 3, Sister Rose Gardiner in 10, and Sister Young in casualty, all had an experience and an authority unmatched by successors. In Maryfield, there were Sister Thompson in 1 and 2, Sister Welsh in 3, Sister Stobie in 5, Sister Russell in 7, Sister Wood in 8, Sister Potter in 10, Sister Dolly Wilson in 11, and Sister Mair in 14, as their equivalents.

Professor Burgess died on April 27th, 1954. His successor, appointed on July 27th, was Dr. Alex. Mair, M.D. D.P.H. He was an Aberdeen graduate of 1942 who was currently the Senior Lecturer in the Department. In the war, he had served in the RAMC, and returned to the Public Health Department in

Aberdeen after graduating M.D. with Honours as he moved to St Andrews on promotion in 1952. He continued the good work of his predecessor and also developed many aspects in Social Medicine of growing importance now that the serious problems of infectious diseases were overcome—Medical School Work, The Industrial Health Unit, and Rehabilitation Services. He was never at ease or successful in Faculty discussion and debate in putting his views over to colleagues, and it was for this reason that his ability and his very real and important contributions were not recognized as they deserved to be.

The medical curriculum was now firmly established as a six-year one. Medical Student numbers remained the same, though other Faculties, especially in Queen's College, expanded. In 1955-56, 34 men and 12 women entered the Faculty at the United College and 28 and 8 at Queen's. The Queen's numbers were balanced by the 28 dentals who also needed teaching there in the pre-clinical departments. This was the simple logistic reason for the discrepancy in medical intakes since 1946. In 1956-57, the numbers were 30 and 12, 20 and 10, respectively; one dental student began at the United College and 28 at Queen's. In 1959-60, there were 28 and 11, and 26 and 8 respectively; 2 dentals began in St Andrews and 27 in Dundee. Students themselves remained the same as ever. One Anatomy student at the Bute was a little behind with his dissection of the upper limb, so took the part, wrapped in its oilcloth, home with him to his bunk in Crail. Unfortunately, a dog in the seat behind began to chew the cloth. Human fingers were revealed, a woman screamed, and the bus driver drove the bus to the police station on arrival at Crail. Professor Walmsley did not find the incident amusing! A staff member on the Dundee side, due to be married the next day, found the drawn blinds of his lecture room covered with various observations. When he released them, he found further remarks pasted on the glass behind; he left the lecture.

As senior staff members retired or left, other took their places. Dr. A.A. Douglas, Professor Douglas' elder brother, who graduated at St Andrews in 1925, was appointed to the ophthalmologist's post in Perth in 1951 and moved to Dundee Royal in 1953 on the retiral of Dr. A.A.B. Scott. Mr George Sturrock succeeded Mr F.R. Brown as Chief in Wards 6 and 7 and Mr S.F. Soutar moved from 15 and 16 to join him. Dr. A.A. Kirkland ('papa K') retired from the Professional Medical Unit but continued as Visiting Physician to the terminal care and young chronic sick Royal Victoria Hospital; he in turn was succeeded there by John Morgan in the early 1960s when Dr. Morgan left D.R.I. In Perth Royal Infirmary, surgical teaching continued under Mr Conal Charleson and Mr Roger Kirkpatrick. These two surgeons were technically as good and in their range of skills better than any in Dundee Royal; both were offered posts elsewhere—Mr Kirkpatrick a Chair in Australia where he was born—but refused these as they found their country practice so rewarding. In 1954, Dr. W.M. Wilson was appointed lecturer in Medicine, on Professor Hill's recommendation. With Dr. Ian Easton, these two also made a team as good as any in Dundee Royal or Maryfield. Students were sent from the Bute to their wards for clinical instruction. In the 1950s, staff of the Emergency Medical Service Hospital at Bridge of Earn were given University posts; Dr. Gordon Malcolm the physician,

Dr. Harry Graham of the large and extremely busy rehabilitation unit, and Mr Ian Sutherland in Mr Smillie's Orthopaedic Unit.

This last unit was the biggest single charge in the Eastern Region; Mr Smillie's beds numbered 250 at the height of his career. Since his facilities remained so limited in Dundee Royal, he developed this first-class unit for elective surgery, to which he sent patients from North Angus as well as Dundee and Perth. This development, far from the noise and dirt of the town, was encouraged by the Regional Hospital Board, and represented a significant shift of medical political power away from Dundee. His other staff, Mr Saville, Mr Colin Campbell and Mr Logan Clark, were joined by Dundee Orthopaedic Surgeons who went to Bridge of Earn to operate on their Dundee patients; Messrs. Dick Muckart, George Murdoch, James Hutchison. Bridge of Earn was further strengthened by Mr Ian Maitland; in 1 958, he came from Glasgow to Tayside as the first fully trained urological surgeon in the region, ten years before any specialist equivalent service began to appear in Dundee. But being far in the periphery, his talents went un-noticed. Later again, in the summer of 1960, Mr John Kirk became the first locally appointed plastic surgeon; he had come earlier as Senior Registrar to Mr Batchelor from Bangour on a visiting basis. Mr Kirk's hard work and firmness of decision resulted in the continuing acquisition of a whole range of equipment for this altogether new service. He attended the Dundee Hospitals as a visiting surgeon, but kept his base in Perthshire: Bridge of Earn was the centre of the plastic surgery service.

Maryfield Hospital continued its expansion of staff and facilities. Dr. George Smith had gone there in 1952, and from nothing developed a unit which grew steadily to include, at the time of its closure twenty years later, a second consultant, as well as supporting staff; the unit became the specialist centre for cytology in Tayside. Professor Henderson appointed Drs. Ross Mitchell and Constance Forsyth as Senior Lecturers in Child Health and, in 1961, Dr. Kenneth Rhaney as a specialist pathologist for his Department. In 1952, Professor Fairlie appointed Dr. S. Reid, from Middlesborough, to a consultant and Honorary Lecturer's post, and later Sandy Buchan was promoted from Senior Lecturer to N.H.S. Consultant.

Professor Margaret Fairlie was approaching her retirement. She was born in the farm of Stotfaulds in Monikie on March 13th, 1891. Her undergraduate career is already recorded. All her clinical career had been spent in Angus apart from a spell as Resident Surgical Officer at St Mary's in Manchester, where her Chief was W.E. Fothergill, and in 1926 when she went to Paris to the Marie Curie Institute to learn the use of Radium in gynaecological malignant disease. After the rather unsatisfactory events which preceded her eventual appointment as the first woman to hold a medical professorial Chair in any Scottish University, she had built a good teaching department. For a short spell in 1955 she served as Warden of the Women's Residence at Westpark Hall, but after a serious illness moved her home to St Andrews. Professor Adam Patrick, and her successor Professor James Walker said of her: 'She served her city and her hospital well. To her speciality she brought distinction, to her Chair dignity, and to her University a record of work well done'.

He successor was to be one of the relatively few professors of whom students were genuinely fond. James Walker was born on March 8th, 1916, in Stirling, and was educated at Falkirk and Stirling High Schools and Glasgow University. Here he had a more than usually brilliant career—B.Sc. 1935, M.B. with Honours and the Brunton Memorial Prize in 1938, and M.D. with Honours in 1954. He served in the RAF during the war in the United Kingdom and in India, and took his M.R.C.O.G. in 1947, the year after his return. He was appointed senior lecturer in Professor Dugald Baird's great Department in Aberdeen in 1948, and Reader at the Hammersmith Hospital the next year. He brought with him to St Andrews a reputation as a first-class research worker, already known nationally for his work on foetal haemoglobin, but also a reputation amongst Aberdeen students for kindness, friendliness, genuine interest, and lectures packed with useful information. Physically, he was a big cheerful man. His students quickly came to like their new Midwifery Professor and continued to do so throughout his years in his Chair.

Other Professors continued in their careers. Professor George Bell played his record of oesophageal speech to successive years. Professor Walmsley and his staff worked to develop one of the best Anatomical museums in the country. Modelled to some degree on that of Professor Thomas Walmsley, in Belfast, it anticipated the C.A.T. scan by twenty-five years. He also shared work with Dr. Hamish Watson, Professor Hill's senior registrar and later junior colleague in Cardiology, on the heart; the specimens of congenital cardiac defects in the Bute were beautifully presented. Professor Anthony Ritchie's Physiology Department became a more purely scientific one, but its primary function was to teach the physiology medical students required. Dr. John Taylor was his senior lecturer in Physiology, and Dr. George Roland Tristram his senior lecturer in Biochemistry—he became the first Professor of Biochemistry in 1965. He took up his post as Professor on 1st January, 1966, and, in Queen's College, Dr. R.P. Cook was appointed Head of a separate Department of Biochemistry exactly one month later. In 1965-66, Dr. D.R. Burt of the Zoology Department carried out the very large task or reorganising the Bell-Pettigrew Museum.

Two Professors retired; first, Professor Dow in October, 1958. Although first Master of Queen's College, he had continued to teach. He was succeeded on October 1st by Professor Rex Ernest Coupland. A Leeds graduate of 1947 with Honours, and a distinction for his M.D. in 1952, he was a demonstrator in Leeds till 1948, spent the next two years' National Service in the RAF, and then returned to Leeds as a lecturer. There was some thought in the Faculty of not filling the Cox Chair, in view of the Tedder recommendation that Anatomy transfer to Dundee, by moving Professor Walmsley's department from the Bute. Providentially for St Andrews, the Faculty felt a move at that time was premature.

The other retiral was Professor Tulloch in 1962. Since leaving office as Dean, he had become the elder statesman of the Faculty. He later left Dundee to live with his daughter in Southampton, where Mr R.N.M. Robertson, who had moved there as secretary of the new university when his Medical Administrative post disappeared in 1954, recalled meeting him and giving him snippets of news

from home. The Honorary D.Sc. conferred on him was the first in the long history of the Medical Faculty. Certainly 'never entirely happy in the office chair' (as Dean), as was said on his obituary in 1966, he remained the outstanding research brain of the Faculty of Medicine in the thirty years and more he held his Chair. His department produced more Gold Medal M.D.s than all the others put together. His successor, James Paris Duguid was an Edinburgh graduate of 1942, and gained his Gold Medal M.D. in 1949. He had been a Crichton Research Scholar and was Reader in Bacteriology at Edinburgh University. In later years, he would be appointed C.B.E. for his important contributions to the Scottish Home and Health Department as an adviser in microbiology problems. As different as chalk from cheese from 'W.J. Tulloch' he was liked by students and staff, served in the Dundee University period, and was then succeeded by a 1957 St Andrews graduate, Mrs Heather Dick.

One death merits special mention. Dr. George Ranken Tudhope died suddenly on December 12th, 1955. He had married Miss Christian Bisset, his first wife having died previously after being an invalid for many years, and the marriage was a happy one. Perhaps helped by the influence of this charming and talented lady, his authority had increased and his confidence blossomed, and he was repeatedly reappointed to more and more prestigious committees of the University. 'Of all my colleagues', said Professor Tulloch to his staff at the time, 'Dr. Tudhope was the most honest and best'. Professor Lendrum, in a kind obituary in the 'British Medical Journal' mentioned his real goodness, and his dedication to the Church of Scotland 'which he served so unswervingly'. His son, George Ranken Tudhope, was awarded a Rutherford Gold Medal for his M.D. Thesis in 1958, when he returned from Sheffield to the Therapeutics Unit, and his grandson Douglas took a brilliant First Class Honours, in his turn, in Computer Studies at the University of Edinburgh.

The traditional major clinical departments blossomed in the good and trouble-free years after the Tedder Report. The large majority of the staff in the Medical Faculty were delighted with the recommendations which, while guaranteeing the future of St Andrews Medical School, gave Dundee a real say in University government. They were confirmed in this view by the success of Professor Dow as the first Master of Queen's College and by their realisation that the new Principal, unlike his predecessor, was entirely fair. But it has to be emphasised that the very different circumstances of the '50s and '60s allowed academic departments scope which was just not possible to the earlier generation. In pre-war days, Professors were part-time and lectured every day of every week. They had no supporting staff apart from their housemen and the assistant visiting staff member. In pre-war or war-time days, there was little or no guidance to graduates; in this respect Professor Cappell was one who promoted the interests of students whom he thought merited support; three such were Douglas Black, Sheila Callendar and Kenneth Lowe. But after the war, the new generation of whole-time Professors had considerably bigger staffs. They were expected to raise academic standards, and promote research in their departments. They now had registrars, employees of the NHS, as well as lecturers to do their routine work. But they were no better or bigger men than their pre-war

counterparts, Patrick and Alexander, Macklin and Brown and before them, Anderson, Saunders Melville and Price.[5]

In the whole range of departments the *Senior Lecturers* did the research— Wallace Park came to Professor Bell's department and then went to Professor Lendrum's as a pathologist. In the middle 1960s, he was awarded a Scottish Hospitals Endowment Research Trust grant of £1,100 for research into Human Cytogenetics; in due course, he gained a Personal Chair. Dr. Basil Andrew followed him in Physiology research in Queen's and John McDougall continued in Anatomy. In the Bute, Dr. Jim Smith did outstanding work on posture and later on collagen with Dr. Serafini-Fracassini of Biochemistry. Dr. Alex McQueen carried the lecturing load in Physiology for Professor Bell. Dr. Gemmel Morgan, Dr. John Morgan's son, did a great deal to improve Clinical Chemistry as a specialist subject; unappreciated by his seniors he went to Glasgow as Professor. A.P.M. Forrest's standard of work as a lecturer gained him Professor Douglas' support first to train in United States, and in due course, to flourish in Glasgow and Cardiff. He broke into Edinburgh Surgery as the first non-Edinburgh Regius Professor of surgery; later another distinguished and younger St Andrews graduate, G.D. Chisholm, was appointed to the Chair of Surgical Science in Edinburgh—a unique honour for the St Andrews Medical School.

The whole-time Professors, perhaps because they had no private practice rivalries, co-operated better with clinical colleagues than their predecessors. Yet some tension remained. Professor Douglas respected Mr F.R. Brown, Mr S.F. Soutar at DRI and his own Senior, Mr W.G. Campbell at Maryfield. Professor Hill respected Dr. John Morgan though Dr. Gordon Clark somewhat less. He learned to respect Drs. R. Semple and J.S. Frew at Maryfield. Professor Hill's interest in heart disease was supported by Professor Douglas' aim, as soon as he arrived in 1952, to start a cardiac surgery service in Dundee. But these two professors adopted a somewhat different policy in their staff selection for new enterprises; Professor Douglas sent his own protegees for training, Professor Hill imported already trained doctors from outside with the skill and experience he required. Thus he brought Dr. K.G. Lowe from the Hammersmith Hospital to develop the cardiac catheterisation he had been taught there; Dr. Cecil Pickard, the radiologist from Leeds, he brought to Dundee to carry out the radiological procedures. He later brought Dr. Oswald Taylor Brown to develop the new specialty of Geriatric Medicine. Next, he brought Dr. John Stowers from University College Hospital to Maryfield as a trained expert in Endocrine Diseases and Diabetes, and may have had a hand in encouraging Dr. Bill Wilson of Perth in the same special interest; later again, Dr. Andrew Lenman, previously assistant to Professor Ritchie, was brought in to start the neurology service. He therefore converted the entire medical scene from the older arrangement of general physicians covering all aspects to the modern approach of high quality specialist clinical care. He also saw to it that he appointed staff with research interests.

By contrast, Professor Douglas had himself to learn the rudiments of cardiac surgery after his appointment. He learned first from Mr F.R. Brown.

Later, he went to the London Hospitals, and in 1952, from March to May, was given leave to go to the United States for further training. He then put his newly appointed Senior Lecturer, W.F. Walker, through the same process. But while this short training period was suitable for closed cardiac surgery, it was not adequate for the next step of open heart procedures. Mr Walker was in fact appointed as a consultant cardiac surgeon with the Professor's support when he had not gone through a normal length of special training.[6] And so, although Professor Hill and Dr. Lowe supported the cardiac unit loyally by referring them cases, two younger staff members with cardiological interests in the medical unit, Drs. Hamish Watson and D. Emslie-Smith, sent their cases elsewhere. The unit ultimately failed for lack of support; although a National Report on Cardiac Surgery in Scotland by Professor Sir Andrew Watt Kay, Sir Charles Illingworth's successor in Glasgow, advised cardiac surgery centres in Glasgow and Edinburgh only, local insufficiency was the significant reason for failure in Dundee. Aberdeen, by contrast, maintained its cardio-thoracic unit. The Regional Board accepted the situation and, instead of providing further support for cardiac surgery, instituted a neurosurgery service; the first appointee was Mr Joe Block in 1962.[7] Professor Douglas also saw Mr John Grieve develop an interest in urological surgery—he too was a local surgeon who developed his own field first by abstracting from foreign literature for the Britsh Journal of Urology, later by training in London, and, in 1960, by three months' study in Sweden. So his course of training followed the same lines as those of Mr Walker in cardiac surgery. In 1969, he was appointed specialist urological surgeon and went to Maryfield.

There seems no doubt that Professor Hill's policy was more far-seeing and more effective than Professor Douglas'. It is of interest that Mr Grieve's successor in post-St Andrews years, J.P.A. Weaver, was appointed urological surgeon when he too had done a bare minimum of specialist training. But it was Professor Hill who provided the clinical and political initiative—he was appointed Queen's Physician for Scotland in 1963; Professor Douglas was later taken on as Surgeon to Her Majesty the Queen, and, on Professor Sir Ian Hill's retirement, Professor Sir Donald Douglas in turn was glad to sponsor Dr. K.G. Lowe, Professor Hill's first assistant, as Queen's Physician, in his turn. Professor Douglas, too, had the signal honour to become President of the Royal College of Surgeons in 1971—in this, he broke the centuries-old monopoly of Edinburgh men holding the top positions in their Corporations, and did so as a St Andrews graduate. He was later knighted for his services to surgery.

These were the years when the Medical Faculty of the University of St Andrews was flourishing indeed, when the efforts of the previous hundred years seemed to be coming to fruition. Though the numbers of graduates remained small, their quality was high, and they carried with them the authority of the enlarged University now greatly strengthened. A succession of problems have been described—that of the M.D. of the nineteenth century, that of the birth of the Conjoint Medical School against the practice and policy of Principal Peterson, that of the shortage of medical undergraduates between the two World Wars—when Sir James Irvine's contribution, by arranging the matricula-

tion of United States students, kept the Faculty viable—a fact conveniently forgotten; that of the 1946-52 crisis, following Sir James' ill-considered policies— and all had been overcome by the Old University in its own time. The next crisis was about to erupt, not the last in our long history. But first a large development in another major specialty, and another in a smaller, require to be recorded.

Mental Diseases had been a poor relation in St Andrews University medical teaching. As ever, Edinburgh and Glasgow had already had men of the highest distinction in their Departments. Of those teaching in St Andrews, the first, Dr. Rorie, had been the best. Gowrie House still has the arms of his family carved on its tower. Dr. Tuach McKenzie was an alcoholic. Dr. Bell, although a very learned man, widely read, and a hard worker—with his assistant Dr. Boyd, he ran Westgreen single-handed during the 1939-45 war—was not effective as a teacher; after the war, he had more than one serious and damaging disagreement with the Board and with the University. Gowrie House was looked after largely by General Practitioners until the start of the National Health Service. It was then incorporated with Maryfield on Dr. G.D. Fraser Steele's appointment. He wished to do research but leave all the routine patient care to Dr. Bell; this was obviously totally unsatisfactory and, as a result, there was no cooperation beteen the two mental hospital groups of Westgreen and Gowrie House with Maryfield. In 1954, Dr. Alastair Rae was appointed Dr. Bell's deputy, but did no teaching; Dr. Murray Lyon, later superintendent at Sunnyside in Montrose, worked for a short time with Dr. Steele. After various disagreements, Dr. Steele left for England, and, in 1956, Dr. Ivor Ralph Campbell Batchelor F.R.C.P. Ed. D.P.M. was appointed Physician Superintendent in clinical charge of Gowrie House. Born in Edinburgh in 29th November, 1916, he was a son of the large family of Dr. R.C.L. Batchelor, F.R.C.S. Ed., F.R.C.P. Ed., head of the Venereal Diseases Department in Edinburgh. He graduated at Edinburgh University in 1940, and served from 1941-46 as a squadron leader in the Royal Air Force. In 1945, he publsihed a text-book of Aviation Neuropsychiatry. He returned to Edinburgh to the Royal Mental Hospital in 1947, and remained there as assistant physician and deputy physician superintendent until his appointment as a National Health Consultant in Dundee. He was a protegee of Sir David Henderson—who, like Sir Robert Muir, placed his juniors widely in senior posts. Dr. Harry Stalker, his deputy before Dr. Batchelor, went to Perth as superintendent of Murray Royal. Dr. Murray Lyon was another, who went to Sunnyside after Dundee. Then Dr. Bell retired in 1961, and, after a year's delay, Dr. Batchelor was appointed Professor as from October 1st, 1962, with joint charge over Westgreen—now named Royal Dundee Mental Hospital— and Gowrie House.

His appointment was marked by division in the appointing committee, with disagreement between Regional Board and University members. The Board representatives had their way and their choice was proved a good one. Under his powerful and in some respects relentless leadership the Department of Psychiatry increased to a full establishment. All new N.H.S. consultants were given honorary teaching appointments to swell the total of clinical teachers. Dr. Peter Aungle became Physician Superintendent; the only staff member to

elect not to teach, Dr. Rae, remained as deputy. Dr. J.D. Uytman, who was until then for practical purposes a member of the Department of Medicine, became a Senior Lecturer and continued to teach medical psychology and lecture especially on neuroses. By 1968, there was a second senior lecturer, Dr. Hugh McNamee, three lecturers—Dr. James Stuart Lawson, a non-medical, Dr. Graham Naylor who subsequently became a reader and an expert in the biochemistry of mental disorders, and Dr. David le Poidevin. Clinical lecturers, as well as Dr. Aungle, were Dr. J.F. McHarg, Drs. J.P. Mellon and H.G. Smyth in Mental Deficiency, Dr. Helen Matthewson in Child Psychiatry, Dr. P.D. Whatmore in Forensic Psychiatry, and Dr. S. Catterall in Psychotherapy. Later Dr. McGhie from Glasgow brought with him a succession of clinical psychologists; this became a semi-autonomous department. So, in six years, Professor Batchelor had twelve on his staff—excepting assistants and tutors—which compared with the eighteen Professor Lendrum's Pathology Department had reached in twice as long. For a short time, indeed, in the middle sixties. Psychiatric teaching made its way, as it were, into all syllabuses of the curriculum. These were the years when the psychiatrists 'believed their specialty was the all-embracing gospel'[8] and were prepared to advise even politicians. Professor Batchelor became the reviser of Henderson and Gillespie's *Text-Book of Psychiatry* from its 8th edition in 1956 on its 10th edition in 1969; his clinical views were very much those of the Edinburgh school. With a particularly clear and persuasive spoken and especially written style, and with a particular ability in committee, Professor Batchelor was soon chosen to serve on a succession of these of increasing status; he was on the Royal Commission on the National Health Service, 1976-79, and on the Medical Research Council Health Services Panel, 1981-82. In 1977, he was awarded the C.B.E., and, in 1981, was knighted. His students remembered him as a didactic teacher with somewhat fixed views on certain aspects of mental disease. Like Professor Fairlie, he moved to St Andrews on his retiral.

While Psychiatry was a large subject, there remains one smaller subject for mention to complete the picture. This was Forensic Medicine. Dr. W. Fyfe Dorward died in office in November of 1964. He had worked almost unbelievably hard both as police surgeon and as senior partner in one of the best general practices in Dundee. Two of his assistants, Dr. Priscilla E. Turnbull, and his eldest son, Dr. W. Morrison Dorward, had given him their support. They took over both his police surgeon's post and the University Department and ran them through to the 1965 Degree Examinations in June and October. The Department was then taken over by Dr. Donald Gregory Rushton, a King's College London graduate of 1948, who had been a research fellow at Guy's Hospital and a lecturer in Morbid Anatomy and Senior Lecturer in Forensic Medicine at King's College Medical School. Dr. Rushton became the Senior Lecturer of the St Andrews Department, but remained primarily a Forensic Pathologist; while he gave the systematic lecture course, he had the assistance of Dr. Turnbull for a year to do the practical police surgeon's work, and thereafter had two general practitioner assistants, Dr. D.C. Marshall and Dr. H. Leadbitter.

Here then was the Faculty complete. All Departments, in the 1960's, were in the charge of men of distinction, who, like their opposite numbers elsewhere, saw the need to exalt their calling and to exalt their University. In undergraduate and post-graduate teaching, there was healthy activity. In the early sixties, a post-graduate society flourished, with meetings in D.R.I. and Maryfield in the Martinmas and Candlemas terms, and, significantly, in the Bute in the Whitsun term—so that all members of the Faculty had the means of getting to know one another. At these meetings, registrars, lecturers, and their seniors presented papers on subjects of their theses, or as a trial run for a paper for an external society or external body. They were useful and popular. In the 50s and 60s, there was an upsurge in the numbers of those seeking higher degrees—M.D.s mostly, with one or two Ch.M.s and Ph.D.s. The St Andrews M.D. was coming into its own, it seemed, at long last. In 1960, the regulations for the M.D. and Ch.M. were made even more stringent. There were to be four grades of each: (a) an ordinary thesis (b) a commendation (c) a high commendation (d) an Honours which would automatically be awarded a Gold Medal. The older Silver Medals thus disappeared, and their status was replaced by High Commendation. If a thesis was thought worthy of grades (a) and (b), one external would examine it, but if it were thought worthy of grades (c) or (d), it had to be sent to a second additional external examiner.

The Faculty though complete and busy with activity must not, however, be described as if it was the only Faculty of Medicine in Scotland, let alone Great Britain, where first-class work and staff of high distinction existed. To do otherwise would be local and limited in outlook.[9] But with the range of ability and activity higher than St Andrews Medicine had ever known before there was bounding confidence. When as Professors Hill and Hunter would 'fly the flag' with enthusiasm to visitors at all levels of importance and from all countries, they could point with truth to the contribution the academic departments and the N.H.S. consultant staff were making to the whole Faculty. As at the turn of the twentieth century, the events of fifteen years earlier had somehow lost their previous importance, and were apparently soon to be forgotten now the Faculty of Medicine, and the whole University under Sir Malcolm Knox's fair leadership, seemed set to become a force to be reckoned with[10].

17

Queen's College

Sir Malcolm Knox, Principal

Ninewells Teaching Hospital and Medical School; The Medical Sciences Building

Thomas Malcolm Knox, Professor of Moral Philosophy in the United College, was appointed Principal of the University from 1 October, 1953, and began at once to fulfil the requirements of the Tedder Report and the St Andrews University Act which followed it. There were many immediate advantages. The now three-College University—Queen's College being the name for the new Arts, Science, Engineering, Law and Medicine College located in Dundee, and ranking of equal status with the United College and St Mary's in St Andrews—contained elements formerly separated by the old division of University College and the Conjoint Medical School. More important, the anomaly of the position of UCD's Council, and especially its Governors, was resolved. The two administrative Heads of Queen's and the United Colleges were called 'Masters', and Professors Dow and Copson, (Copson had moved from the Mathematics Chair in UCD to that in United College) were appointed to hold these offices. Time showed that these were satisfactory choices. The title 'Queen's College' related to the new Queen—Queen Elizabeth II had ascended to the throne on 6th February, 1952, and this choice of title, too, was a happy one.

As well as administrative advantages, there were financial advantages also. Endowments from University College were taken over by the University and the difficulty of its individual funding disappeared. But when Principal Knox gained access to the University's investments, he found much to cause concern. Money had been invested in very limited ways, and Sir James had not pursued any policy of re-investment for growth. As a result, much investment had actually lost in value. The new Principal, who had worked in the business world for Lord Leverhulme in his early years, realised that there would have to be a sensible policy of investment in the Stock Exchange, and that there would have to be a pause in spending until profits started to show.[1]

Nevertheless, Queen's College developed quickly. On February 12th, 1954, the Graduation was held in the Caird Hall when 2600 persons were present. The Principal made an optimistic and forward-looking speech. The SRC had earlier suggested that a garden party should accompany graduations, but nothing came of this at the time. Over the next years, Queen's College Tower would be built as visible evidence of the new status of this part of St Andrews University.

Behind the tower, new building was begun and further land acquired. But it was the Tower which became the symbol of Queen's College. It was a showplace such as had not existed before. Functions held there were popular, and visitors to the Staff Club on the top floor appreciated, some for the first time, just what a magnificent situation on a hillside the City of Dundee had. Everyone was conscious of a new optimism and the fact that the recent years of antagonism were past. On the telephone exchange, the telephonists answered 'Queen's College' with confidence in their voices. The Principal was in Queen's College every week, and when No. 1 Airlie Place became his official residence, he began to hold social functions for his staff, which he financed out of his own pocket, once a month. Unlike his predecessor, however, he had no charisma; he was aware of his inability to meet and talk to people easily and the knowledge saddened him. Most people failed to understand what a desperately shy person he was. Some Dundee staff thought he was the subject of antagonism in St Andrews on account of his active policy towards Queen's College, but this was not so at this time.[2]

In the Faculty of Medicine, the main excitement was the prospect of a new Teaching Hospital and Medical School. New staff were also very concerned with clinical and research developments which they were determined would increase the status of their departments and of themselves in consequence. In May 1954, Professor Bell was appointed Dean in place of 'Willie John', and his principal responsibility was to be in connection with the plans for the new hospital. His sudden rise in status in the project was the result of the disappearance of Dr. James Lawson's Medical Planning Committee following the passing of the St Andrews University Act.

The first notification of a new teaching hospital had appeared as long ago as the University Court's comments on the war-time Goodenough Report.[3] Following the creation of the Eastern Regional Hospital Board in November 1947 to run the hospital side of the National Health Service, hospital development had had a high priority. The first Board Chairman was Councillor William Hughes, with Dr. Frank Main as Senior Administrative Officer, Robert Moore as Secretary, and W.E. McCracken as treasurer. They had discussed future development of D.R.I. in particular on November 3rd, 1948, and December 18th, and in that year the ever-present Dr. Lawson was the chairman of their planning committee as well as of the university one. The view which he had initially held, that new building take place on and adjacent to the present site of D.R.I. has already been described; this was the university committee's view also. But the Scottish Home and Health Department had not agreed with this decision, and at once came back to the Board and the University with an alternative view, that the new Teaching Hospital was to be built on the periphery of the town. On September 28th, 1949, the Regional Board, and Dr. Lawson, agreed that 'the proposed new hospital centre at Dundee should take place ... on a new site in preference to restructuring D.R.I. on its present site ... to provide adequate residential accommodation for staff and the erection by the University of a new medical school'.[4] 'As the approval of the Secretary of State may be confidently expected', the decision went on, 'it is obviously desirable

that some consideration should be given immediately to the next steps so that the amount of time which must inevitably be involved in the planning stage may be kept to the minimum really necessary'. The policy of building major hospitals at the periphery of large cities was supported by central government thinking, including possible requirements in the event of nuclear attack.[5]

Mr R.N.M. Robertson, in his then capacity as medical planning committee administrator, recalls 'looking over a stone wall at the green fields of a farm', together with the Dean and others, 'on a cold day in 1950'. Many other members of staff would also recall looking at this site, in its transition from green fields to the largest teaching hospital complex in Scotland, over many more years. In 1950 the land in question was part of the Invergowrie estate, a farm owned by Mr Jack, father of Dr. Henry Jack, a lecturer in Mathematics at Queen's College. 'Ninewells' was better known to locals as the site of the tram terminus on the Perth road near its junction with Riverside Drive. Over the whole of 1950 negotiations continued over its acquisition for a new role. The Agricultural Executive Committee objected at the end of 1949 to the site selected, and their suggestion of an alternative necessitated several meetings and inspections by their own representatives and those of the Board—Dr. Lawson, Professors Adam Patrick and Tulloch, Mr Hughes, Baillie Ross, and Dr. Burgess. No progress had been made by September, and on 22nd the Board pressed the Department at St Andrew's House for a decision. They also asked that an investigation into the National Health Service requirements of the whole region be set up. In November, the Department informed the Board that 'for the purposes of planning it would not be unreasonable to assume that building work on the new hospital would begin in the year 1956-57'. It was not until 10th April, 1951, that the procedure for acquisition of the site was approved—far less the actual acquisition, and the Secretary of State introduced the prospect of still more delay by suggesting that a Public Inquiry be held.

During the summer of 1951, Regional Board members and others visited hospitals in Sweden. At the Board meeting on 13th of November, Mr Hughes gave his views on the type of hospital he considered desirable. Two types were possible, in his opinion; one of two or three storeys over a large acreage, the other of nine storeys occupying less space. In discussion, a hospital of 700-800 beds was envisaged, of four to six storeys in height, incorporating features of both horizontal and vertical types of design and with residential accommodation for only a proportion of the staff. The original 240 acres presented to the Secretary of State as the site had by now been reduced in the interests of agriculture. Also, the Town Council were now proposing that a new road be built, which would pass over the site! It was in fact only at this stage that the Board agreed formally to communicate with the University to find out what amount of ground work would be needed for the Medical School; they also asked their own Regional architect to prepare a plan showing the area necessary for hospital and medical school purposes. Through 1951, more visits took place to Swedish hospitals, help was sought from the Nuffield foundation, and plans of recently built hospitals elsewhere in the United Kingdom were obtained. But movement was extremely slow. More talks were held with the Agricultural

Committee. Additional members were co-opted to the Board Planning Committee, and Professors Hill and Dow and Dr. Lawson were appointed members of a Technical Committee. Professor Patrick reported by 30th September, 1952, that although 'the site for the new hospital had now been approved by the Secretary of State, he had done so with some reluctance, and the amount of agricultural land used was to be kept to a minimum'. Nothing happened in 1953, and on 24th of May, 1954, it was announced that there was 'delay in the acquisition pending a decision of the Secretary of State on a proposal by the Corporation of Dundee for the acquisition of other land forming part of the same estate'. The Secretary of State had approved this land for housing development. Planning permission for private developers to take over a section at the south-east corner of the site had also been given by the Secretary of State; this meant that further ground was now lost. By the end of October, 1954, it was stated that work was unlikely to begin on the actual building until 1960 or later, and that a short list of possible architects was to be drawn up. In early January of 1955, the Secretary of State postponed a meeting in Dundee on the grounds that he 'expected to be in a position very soon to make a definite statement about the date for commencement of the work'. However, 1955 did see some progress. A new Senior Administrative Medical Officer (SAMO), Dr. Cyril Bainbridge, appeared in January. By the end of September the missives of sale and purchase of the site were completed. The area was reduced to 201 acres. And, on 23rd November, Robert H. Matthew, C.B.E. M.A., F.R.I.B.A. of Edinburgh was 'invited to accept the commission as architect, subject to the agreement of the University Court'. Of importance for later years was the fact that the Regional Board concluded the architect's contract, for both the new hospital and the medical school, and were to 'act as agents for the University in respect of their interests'. The fees were to be in proportion to the share of combined capital costs between the University and the Regional Hospital Board.

Nevertheless, active planning by university staff was beginning to take place in anticipation of building starting at some date in the near future. The rather sorry tale just described of the initial delays might perhaps have reduced optimism, but there is no evidence that it did so. From the middle '50s, no effort or expense was to be spared in making Ninewells in every respect the finest hospital in Great Britain if not in Europe. This intention was very much that of the Regional Board, Dundee and Angus-based as it was, and was shared by the local business interests and the local press. The 1950s were years of Conservative rule in Central Government—Sir Winston Churchill retired in 1955 and was succeeded by Sir Anthony Eden; after the Suez crisis of July to November, 1956, he in turn was succeeded, in January of 1957, by Mr Harold Macmillan. Though the post-war years of enormous spending were over, there still seemed ample money and political will available for academic and many other sorts of expansion.

Although Dr. James Lawson's University Planning Committee disappeared after the University of St Andrews Act became law, he himself remained on the University Court and the Regional Hospital Board. From these he continued to

give support and favour to the Medical Faculty and its Deans; of the contestants of the 1946-52 period, he was the only one to survive in post until illness overtook him in the early 1960s. This remarkable man saw not only General Wimberley, but also Professor Tulloch and even Mr D.C. Thomson, come and go. He deserves a fairer memorial than those individuals were prepared to give him.

But now that the Queen's College era had arrived, it was the Dean of the day whose committees would act. On 23rd April, 1956, the U.G.C. Medical Sub-Committee visited St Andrews University. Professor G.H. Bell led the local representatives—Professor Dow, Master of Queen's, Professor A.D. Hitchin of the Dental Faculty, Professors Hill, Hunter, Lendrum and Walmsley, and Messrs. I.S. Smillie and J. Grieve. Student representatives from both St Salvator's and Queen's were also present. As well as visiting the Bute, the Medical Departments in Queen's College, the Dental School, Maryfield and D.R.I., they went to visit the site still only proposed for the 'New Hospital and Medical School'.

The significance of Professor Bell being Dean at this time was that he was strongly anti-St Andrews, and was looking to the elimination of medical teaching there as soon as this could be achieved. Professor Walmsley, conscious of the implications in the memorandum the Dean had prepared for submission to the U.G.C., wrote personally to him on April 19th 'be wise at a time when the reputation of the Medical School is being established, because the majority of applicants for admission to the Faculty of Medicine opt to take the preclinical course in St Salvator's College' and asked for the memorandum to be altered. Professor Walmsley was on sure ground in making this statement, since he and Professor Coupland went through all the applications together and allocated first year students to the two colleges personally. There were two other points of discord; one concerned increase of staff. Professor Lendrum pressed very hard—as he had consistently done over the years—for a continuing increase in staff for his Department. He quoted the levels obtaining in Glasgow, asked that his technicians be paid National Health Service rates, and complained about the amount of hospital duties his staff had to do—these, he said, encroached on their time required for teaching and research. Letters passed around over the summer months, and Professor Lendrum received no support from colleagues— Professor Tulloch said that although routine work put a strain on his staff, it did not interfere with teaching, Professor Hill said frankly that the NHS staff did the bulk of the routine work, and Professor Walker agreed that, as he put it, 'active clinical duty is part of the job'.

The other discord was also expressed by Professor Lendrum, who did not agree with the siting of the new hospital. He wrote to the Dean in February:

> Explain to them that a man at a desk in Edinburgh in 1938 (by which time the fashion for peri-urban general hospitals had died . . .) decided to have a District Hospital outside Dundee. The local Lord Provost had pledged himself to this prior to being made Chairman of the Regional Hospital Board—he was then an active socialist candidate for political office—he knew nothing of hospitals and less of the

character of a Teaching Hospital.

The new peri-urban hospital is not wanted by the medicals—it is not wanted by those who wish to see the Medical School become a living part of the University. It will certainly be cursed by the public when they realise what it means in general inconvenience and inefficiency. Can the U.G.C. not say to the Department of Health (and here he quoted Oliver Cromwell) . . . 'Think it possible you may be mistaken'.[6]

The U.G.C., however, made its position plain in its report after its April visit: 'Confronting the Medical School would be the construction of an entirely new Teaching Hospital in the Ninewells area'. This should be a complete and self-contained unit (here the report detailed the clinical departments concerned) . . . including *student residences*. What disadvantages there would be in the segregation of the clinical teaching from the rest of the College and especially the pre-clinical departments would be outweighed by the immense advantage of having all the facilities for clinical teaching and research on the one site.

'The U.G.C. could not hold out hope of a start being made to the medical school part of the Teaching Hospital in the next few years if it was the responsibility of the U.G.C. to finance the project.

Because of heavy commitments for building elsewhere, the Committee could not at present accord a high priority to the new Medical School in Dundee'. The Principal, writing to the Dean on May 2, reiterated these points: 'close contact at Ninewells Hospital will be an asset of the greatest importance to our University', he said. And he went on to introduce a concept which would have considerable significance on all subsequent building and political plans: 'It is essential in the views of the U.G.C. that the Medical School should be "embedded" in the hospital, so that the wards, laboratories, lecture rooms, retiring rooms and students' amenities will all be in the same building'. Finally, confirming that no specific date for funding was yet available, Principal Knox ended:

It is clear that the U.G.C. is hoping to induce the Department of Health to meet the cost of a Medical School, embedded within the hospital. Since it is important that the U.G.C. negotiations with the Department of Health should not be prejudiced by any action on the part of the University, I have been instructed by the U.G.C. in writing that we are not at present to pay out any sums in connection with the new Medical School, even Architect's fees.

At the same time, Principal Knox wrote to Professor Bell, on May 2, telling him that 'the U.G.C. considered the Medical School outstanding'.

Lack of immediate funding was nothing new to St Andrews—the Old University had known this problem for centuries. But it was a source of concern to the Medical Faculty Professors, and of course to the local Dundee councillors and others. For this new Medical School and Teaching Hospital at Ninewells was already hailed as a major status symbol for Dundee, and in this decade of prosperity in the city, with a range of new industries started after the war now established, confidence was high. While Ninewells was the major development, others in the Faculty planned for the 1957-62 quinquennium were a new

Department of Midwifery at Dudhope Terrace, at a cost of fifteen thousand pounds, with seven to ten thousand pounds *per annum* to meet salaries, three thousand pounds for a Department of Orthopaedics, including a room for Mr Smillie, a museum and laboratory, and smaller sums for the Departments of Anaesthetics and Dermatology. Profesor A.C. Lendrum became Dean from January, 1957, and that June a record number of M.D.s for recent years graduated—ten, including two medallists.[7]

In the autumn came the news from the University Court that financial restrictions would require a cut in the proposed number of beds at Ninewells from eight hundred to five hundred and fifty, and that urgent plans would have to be made for accommodating teaching to this new figure. At its meeting on October 2nd, the Faculty 'received with dismay (the news) and regretted the consequent postponement of the long hoped for integration of the Medical School'. One interim site for research was made available in this year, however. This was the 'Clinical Investigation Unit' (C.I.U.) at Maryfield Hospital, and its funding and running costs were borne by the Board. In the next ten years, it made available good if small facilities for not only staff of the powerful Medical and Therapeutics Department, but also for one or two members of other clinical units, to carry out research. Dr. W.K. Stewart's Renal Dialysis Unit began its life here, Dr. R.S. McNeill carried out his pulmonary function studies, Miss Margaret Browning, and Alexander Brownie, their endocrine studies in what came to be called 'the isotopes lab', and in later years Dr. G.R. Tudhope and Dr. Charles Rizza their haematological work. It was a great change, Dr. Tudhope recalled, from the shed which had existed before he left in 1954 for Sheffield.[8] Two members of Mr Walter Campbell's N.H.S. surgical unit worked there; J.S.G. Blair, who studied the slipperiness of human fat, and J.S. Kinnear, who set up the Yttrium implant service, for advanced breast cancer patients, for the Eastern Region.

Although the Teaching Hospital's site, if not its date of building, was now agreed, there still remained the question of provision of a Medical Sciences Centre for pre-clinical subjects. The location of pre-clinical Departments was dependent on the honouring of one of the provisions of the Tedder Report, that, when possible, Anatomy and Physiology would be transferred to Queen's from the United College. Principal Knox was proving strictly fair in his policy of carrying out the Tedder recommendations; even Dr. D.G. Southgate himself could not fault him in this respect.[9] The United College's professors had agreed to the move. Professor Anthony Ritchie sent a long memorandum on the subject to Faculty on December 9th, 1955, and Professor Callan, Sir D'Arcy's successor, and Burnett (Botany) sent individual memoranda at the same time. A little earlier, at the end of July, 1955, Principal Knox had written to Sir Keith Murray, the Chairman of the U.G.C., to ask whether the new Ninewells Medical School should include pre-clinical as well as clinical departments, and in reply Sir Keith had quoted their letter to St Andrews of the earlier date of October 23rd, 1953, to the effect that while they agreed to support the scheme for a new Teaching Hospital, the site of the future locality of pre-clinical departments would be considered later. Sir Edward Hale, the U.G.C. Secretary,

then wrote that the Committee had given full and careful consideration to the siting of a pre-clinical centre; their main objection was the isolation of medical students at their pre-clinical stage if they were placed in the new Medical School Complex. It was also important to keep the pre-clinical departments near those of basic sciences. Any new Medical Sciences Building to replace the old Medical School building in Dundee would therefore have to be within the Queen's College complex and not at Ninewells.

The other factor, the number of students to be catered for, was dependent on Central Government policy. On February 28th, 1958, the U.G.C. reported to the Principal the advice of the Willink Committee. This was first, that there be a reduction by about a tenth in medical student intake from as early a date as practicable after 1961, and second, that the intake would have to be raised again from about the year 1970. (The McNair Report, on the other hand, had advised a large increase in the number of dental students). Following this, the Faculty had concluded that, at present, the maximum number of medical students in a year, at the University of St Andrews, should be seventy-five.

On December 15th, 1959, there was a full discussion in the Faculty on the future development of Anatomy, Physiology and Biochemistry, and the location of their Departments. It was recommended that when practicable to do so, not only should pre-clinical subjects be taught at Queen's College, but pre-medical ones also. This, therefore, went farther than the Tedder proposals. The thinking behind the recommendation was expressed as follows:

> Ten years ago it was fair to state that recruitment to the Faculty of Medicine was influenced enormously by the fact that students might spend the first three years in St Andrews. In June, 1957, when the Cox Chair became vacant, it was agreed that the recommendations of the Royal Commission could not be implemented then ... by a majority ...[10] Now it is agreed that duplication is wasteful, that the move of the Department of Anatomy in the Bute to Dundee will help the Dentals[11] ... Recruitment to a Medical School depends to a large degree on the eminence of its Clinical School ... at present this is high ... this with the provision of the best facilities in the new Medical School and Hospital in the whole of Great Britain plus the increased residential accommodation for medical students, will influence recruitment.

> Anatomy to move to Queen's College, plus the major Physiology Department. But some Physiology be retained at St Salvator's College for Science students.

> The opinion was expressed that if the 2nd M.B. subjects were to be taught entirely at Queen's College, it would be advisable for all the 1st M.B. subjects to be taught there also. There will be space available.

These recommendations were signed by Professor R.B. Hunter, who had become Dean in 1958. Later, Principal T.M. Knox agreed with 'the confident expectation the medical students will be transferred from St Salvator's'. It is important to emphasise this agreement; it was part of the honest endeavours being made by those 'on the St Andrews side' to make the Tedder Report work.

In spite of the volume of earlier misrepresentation that St Andrews has been the evil-doer in refusing to accept agreements and make them work, the next few years would show clearly that it was those on the Dundee side—especially those in the Arts Departments who were determined to split the University—who broke them if it did not suit their intentions.

It is also important to notice, yet again, the expectations continuing to build up emotionally about Ninewells, even though actual building had not even a date for contract, let alone for starting work on the site. It was already being hailed not only as has been said by Dundee Councillors and citizens, but by the Faculty of Medicine, and indeed by Queen's College staff generally, as the showplace school and hospital which would establish Dundee as the greatest attraction to intending medical students in the whole land.

Yet two years later there was little movement. Through 1960, the Principal and the Chairman of the Eastern Regional Hospital Board continued to discuss matters of policy. The start of actual building seemed as far off as ever. Four major problems were discussed over the summer and finally agreed. Organisation and administration had to be integrated between the two main partners 'to avoid the risk of duplication with friction resulting in factions', as the Prinicipal realistically put it. While the University was to have freedom in academic matters and responsibility for student fees and discipline, the Board was to have responsibility for the logistic necessities of weekly payments of staff, issues of stores and re-supply, lighting, heating, kitchens and laundry. Ninewells was to have a Board of Management just like other N.H.S. hospitals; the idea of a special Joint University and E.R.H.B. Board of Governors was floated in July, but was dropped. Appointments of senior staff, anticipating the opening in 1968, were discussed, and the University confirmed the fifty per cent representation on appointment committees for posts with an honorary teaching appointment which it has continued to enjoy.

During this period of planning the idea of 'NWH' as the all-sufficient hospital for Eastern Scotland grew more and more evident. There was anxiety even then that enough patients would be available for teaching, and the Regional Board, thinking in Dundee terms as its members habitually did, expressed by way of their Senior Administrative medically-qualified Officer of the day, Dr. R. Glyn Thomas: 'It is important to us that the Regional Board introduce a satisfactory system whereby patients from the Perth and Angus hospitals are sent to Dundee for diagnosis and treatment. We want to avoid the possibility of competition for teaching material between Dundee and the Perth and Angus hospitals'. So long as things were to be done to suit Dundee, they saw no problem. It was however decided later, and agreed by the Principal, that consultants with clinical charge at Perth and the nearer Blairgowrie and Meigle Cottage Hospitals, or at 'the new Angus hospital' (sic), should come to NWH to do their clinical teaching. This, it was believed, would encourage such staff to transfer their interesting cases. In September of 1960 the expansion of the Dental Hospital and School planning was taken further, as were plans for the expansion of Maryfield Hospital. The possibility of a new hospital for North East Fife was considered. In the near future, there was the prospect of the next

quinquennial visit to the University on May 29th, 1961.

1961 however saw a very large step forward. In July of that year an International Symposium on Hospital and Medical School Design was held at Queen's College, under the Chairmanship of Sir Malcolm Knox. The Nuffield Hospital Research Foundation's work in processing new ideas was made use of by the University, but an International Symposium held locally seemed a useful way of collecting and then assessing the latest experience. Those with experience of recent Teaching Hospital Design from England, Wales and the United States were to speak. Professor Robert Matthew, John Musgrove, and Dr. Tom Sommerville were to open on the architect's brief, design of research laboratories, and student teaching facilities respectively. Professor Douglas spoke on operating theatre design, and Mr Alan Wightman on ward unit design. Dr. R. Glyn Thomas, the SAMO, spoke on outpatient department design; the ideas for this, later used in the actual building, came however from Dr. James Hunter, his deputy.

This conference was extremely valuable, both as a public relations exercise for St Andrews and Dundee and also because final planning decisions came from it. Once planning was done, the work in fact proceeded very smoothly and well[12]. Robert Matthew's paper covered the points which were the basis of this planning. As well as the principle of 'embedding' there was that of the 'open door' of Scottish Teaching Hospitals which unlike their English counterparts were service hospitals taking in all who came to them for medical care; Professor Douglas was especially concerned that this principle apply to Nine-wells. From this concept, patient care provision was a primary aim; in design a clear distinction was to be made between patient care and supporting servicing and supply organisation. As far as embedding was concerned, architectural problems would arise primarily in the relationship of the clinical academic departments to the wards. Because there were to be some eighteen ward units with complicated relationships within the hospital—paediatric and maternity wards relating to premature baby units, for example, and ENT and Eye wards relating to the polyclinic, in turn associated with six clinical departments, it was considered that a group of low buildings would be needed to allow for future expansion. Because of the high cost of mechanical services to laboratories, the clinical departments would have to be grouped together. For ease of movement each clinical department should be on the same level as its ward unit.

Professor Matthew's plan depended upon four objectives:

1.   A predominantly horizontal lay-out to be used to ease traffic movement, ensure ease of expansion, to group linked departments on the same level, and relate the wards to the hillside landscape.

2.   The achievement of compactness by providing many rooms and spaces with artificial lighting and ventilation, so that they could be fitted into the hillside below ground level.

3.   Vertical segregation of various types of traffic to be achieved by three main 'levels'—top, the 'Contact' or 'Main Deck' level, for outpatients, visitors and staff; 'Mid level' for treatment—in-

patient and casualty traffic; 'low level' for supply and
distribution traffic.

4.   The obtaining of the closest possible integration of the whole by
planning for functional needs and close sharing of common
facilities and services.[13]

From this again came the concept of the five-storey Concourse
Block—the centre of this, the Main Concourse, was a grouping
of entrances for all users of the Hospital, and containing all the
facilities (reception, cloakrooms, waiting areas, buffet and shops)
serving everyone arriving or departing from Hospital or Medical
School. Below this was to be the casualty and administration
department served by the ambulance bay. The remainder of the
Concourse Block would consist of the central kitchen at the
supply level, and the restaurants, administration and records
department on the top two floors. The middle tier would, as the
treatment level, be used mostly by in-patients and the lower tier
become the 'supply street'.

From this concept Ninewells Hospital and Medical School would be built
for the University of St Andrews and for the citizens of Eastern Scotland. And
from this plan, it was so built.

During this period of planning and progress, the Faculty had the immense
advantage of having as Dean Professor R.B. Hunter. As a clinician he was
limited in experience by comparison with those holding the other clinical
chairs. He was in some ways an antithesis to Sir James Irvine—generally
unpopular with students and junior staff—unpopularity did not however seem
to bother him—but acknowledged and favoured by the senior staff who realised
what a superb organiser he was. Thus, while his juniors remembered his great
ability to select staff who would be of maximum use to his unit, and then use
them to produce a succession of papers and publications, and his student class
remembered his announcements that certain subjects would not form part of
the Degree Examination—and then found a few days later these very subjects
appeared in the paper they had to answer—he was deservedly the friend and
confidant of the Principal, was supported by Dr. James Lawson, and was
recognised by those in authority outside the University for the strong, shrewd,
and far-seeing person he undoubtedly was. Because Sir Ian Hill was also a
strong personality, there was an inevitable polarisation within the medical side
of the Faculty—which did not help intra-hospital cooperation and was often
awkward for staff obliged to transfer from one of the blocs to the other. But
while Professor Hill's contribution was to exalt the prestige of the Medical
School in clinical terms, Professor Hunter's was to plan in logistic and medical
political terms; his reputation in this field was complementary and no less
significant. His further contribution was, as has been seen, in the development
of post-graduate teaching, but this, too, was in public relations and wider-world
terms; the first post-graduate teaching done in St Andrews Medical School on a
regular basis was in fact carried out in Maryfield Hospital by Dr. Lowe, one of
Professor Hill's staff.

Throughout 1961, regular planning continued both in foreground and in background. By April, the staffing structures for the Dundee General Hospitals, and development of clinical research, Psychiatry, and Paediatrics were all agreed. Following the visit of the U.G.C., and the July Symposium, the equipping of Ninewells, the distribution of maternity beds there, and the professorial charge in Psychiatry were taken a little further. It was now agreed that there were three units requiring staffing for teaching purposes; Ninewells, Maryfield Hospital, and Perth Royal Infirmary. A major 'Eastern Regional Hospital Board Paper on Medical Staffing in the Region' appeared on January 4th, 1962. As well as the teaching needs of the three main units, the provision of the increasing numbers of specialist units required new staff provision. While some of these had appeared following University initiative, many were the result of policy decisions by the Board over the years following 1948—Neurosurgery, Thoracic surgery, Geriatric medicine, Orthopaedic surgery, and neo-natal Paediatrics. By now it seemed that twelve hundred beds were going to become available in Dundee itself—just over seven hundred in the new hospital, and just under five hundred in Maryfield. At this stage in the story, it was proposed to develop Maryfield, on its present site, to provide a comprehensive Accident Centre, and house the specialties of Cardiology, Neurology, Cardio-vascular Surgery, Neurosurgery, Thoracic Surgery, Oral and Plastic Surgery, some Gynaecology, one hundred and twenty Orthopaedic beds, Geriatric Medicine, and all Radio-Therapy. Outpatient clinics would also be held at Maryfield to save the citizens the necessity of a bus journey out of town. While twelve neurosurgery beds were to remain at Dundee Royal, there were to be thirty at Maryfield. The present Orthopaedic beds at the Infirmary would close. The concept was for Ninewells to be the the general unit hospital, Maryfield the special unit hospital.

The most important consideration of all—finance—was now to make itself felt. Professor Hunter's hand-written marginal notes, when as Dean he conferred with Principal Knox and Mr Lewis Robertson, noted in January 1962 that the £9m limit agreed by the Department of Health for Scotland six months previously was now exceeded by £162,000. Another new District Hospital, in Kirkcaldy, was having its cost quoted as between six and thirteen million pounds. 'NW much more complex' the Dean wrote, 'DHS saying 9M *the limit*'. By now detailed cost plans, with their steady increases as time went by, were becoming a cause for concern. It was starting to become evident that delay, probably serious delay, was inevitable. 'It has generally been accepted so far', wrote Mr Robertson to the Principal on June 14th 1962, 'that the buildings at Ninewells Hospital will not be occupied until the whole scheme has been completed. It might be useful to get confirmation that the University will accept this principle in relation to the Medical School Accommodation'.[14] On August 12th, a list of thirteen firms was submitted, one of which would be offered the main contract. The final sketch plans were expected that month. The Dean noted in the margin, 'Main contractor appointed April '63; Start work August '63'.

On August 28th 1962, Mr J.K. Johnston, now the Secretary of the Board

since Mr Moore had retired, wrote to Professor Hunter confidentially, enclosing a copy of the contractual procedure recommended by the Board to the Scottish Home and Health Department, a preliminary list of firms recommended by the Consulting Architect for the Main Contract, and 'the questionnaire suggested by Robert Matthew, Johnson, Marshall and Partners, Architects for issue to these firms'. The contractual procedure had still to be approved by the Department, and Mr Andrew Hughes, from St Andrews House, who was one of the civil servants responsible for planning from the civil service side, was expected to give its view at the next Regional Board meeting. 'Without prejudice to the generality of the procedure', said Mr Johnston, 'it is open to us to add firms to Matthew's preliminary list, or, alternatively, to consider whether the preliminary enquiry stage might not be omitted altogether. This would mean inviting the Architect to agree with the Board and the University a shorter list of firms who would be invited to tender without prior formal enquiry from them'. Mr Johnston was well aware of the need to save as much time as possible.

The recommended list of thirteen firms to be considered for the Main Contract included some of the largest in the land. The contract would be of such importance that this was felt to be essential, and the firm would have to be chosen with the greatest care.

While these negotiations were being carried on and decisions made at this higher level, work was proceeding at a lower level by those whom General Wimberley would have described as 'staff officers'. These had been working since the later 1950s, but began to be coordinated more formally by the appointment of a planning team which began to function in 1959. This consisted of a representative from the Regional Board 'officers', as they were designated—Mr J.K. Johnston (initially assistant secretary, later secretary to the Board), Mr Alan Wightman the Architect, and Dr. James Hunter, the Deputy SAMO. Dr. Sommerville, now a Senior Lecturer in the Bacteriology Department, but formerly a Major in the Indian Medical Service and so especially well qualified in planning and staff duties, was the University representative. He was seconded from his Department as a full-time member of the planning team, and was brought in 'when things were rolling slowly'. These four developed a loyalty amongst themselves and to their own team which became extremely valuable—not only did they respect one another, but their team spirit enabled them to 'resist attempts at division'.[15] Professor Douglas had already been authorised to prepare departmental briefs from the various medical departments for the architects, which briefs the various departments had decided covered their future requirements. The planning team thus began with the 'raw material'; this varied from detailed careful bids at one end of the spectrum to that of a professor who said to Dr. Sommerville: 'I don't know exactly what I require. But see that I get as good as anyone else'.

The team had then to prepare documents and memoranda for the next higher staff level, the Joint Planning Committee. This consisted of about seven Board members, including the Chairman, Mr Lewis Robertson, and medically qualified members—initially Dr. Gordon Clark, later Dr. Ian Easton—and Professors Hunter, Douglas, and the Dean of the day. Various of the Board

officers—Architect, Regional Engineer, Treasurer, Senior Administrative
Medical Officer, as well as Mr J.K. Johnston also attended, as did other lay
representatives from the University including Mr Alan J.G. Brown, the Medical
Faculty Secretary. Not only were there these various experts and representatives,
but there were also representatives from the Scottish Home and Health Department. The reason for the presence of senior civil servants, plus, of course, their
own architect, engineer, and so on, was because of the public accountability of
the whole project. The share of costs between U.G.C. and Government has
already been referred to and will be referred to again. Not only was public
accountability in general a large consideration but also the detail of who was to
pay for what. However, as far as the lower planning team was concerned, they
were assured by the Pater Formula[16] that there was no need to worry about
relative distribution of cost between the University and the Scottish Home and
Health Department.

From the University's point of view, it was the teaching and research
accommodation which was important. But Dr. Sommerville was aware that the
first priority was to build a *hospital*, where patients came to be treated. The
student had to arrive and find he was studying *within a hospital*—this was the
embedding concept—and had to realise that patient care came first. Dr.
Sommerville believed that the peripheral site of the hospital was chosen partly
because the patients from Perth and Angus who were to boost the teaching
supply could reach it by the peripheral road system. The notion that all teaching
would be embedded within the hospital was in the minds of his fellow team
members at this stage also. They had, from the Faculty point of view, to plan
five elements, central teaching accommodation, a library and museum, laboratories, the clinical departments adjacent to their own wards, and the paraclinical
departments; these last were grouped with what were thought to be their related
clinical departments—bacteriology with surgery, pathology with medicine.
The Ninewells Hospital library was to be a branch of the Queen's College one—
this initially raised no difficulties, but difficulties arose in the later 1960s. The
museum was to be so built that specimens corresponding to teaching of the
hour could be laid out for the several student years.

At this early stage, too, provision for future expansion was felt to be highly
important. The belief in ever-increasing funding of universities was just beginning
to appear with the decade of the 60s. The team's belief was that if bed expansion
became necessary, clinical departments could spill over into paraclinical, and
new paraclinical departments could then be built elsewhere. In general, it was
found as planning time went by that each clinical department had to be more or
less the same size—thus, they enlarged rather than reduced. 'We erred on the
big side'.[17] This principle presented some anomalies—the Paediatrics Department, for example, was finally made three times its original size. The final brief
would then be passed to St Andrews University, for transmission to the U.G.C.,
and to the Eastern Regional Hospital Board, for passage upwards to the
Department in Edinburgh.

By March 1962, a great deal of initial planning for Ninewells had been done.
As well as university departments and lecture theatres, there was the planning

of ward units, maternity department, operating theatres, diagnostic radiology department, the Concourse block with treatment and admissions, physiotherapy, canteens, kitchen, cloakrooms, stores, almoner's department, mortuary, and later a chapel, not forgetting the services of engineering, heat, light, and laundry. And all this was for the first major hospital to be built since the start of the National Health Service.

By the summer of 1962, what could be described as the 'preliminaries to the contract' were completed. A meeting was held that September at Queen's College to review progress to date. Principal Knox had by then been in contact with the U.G.C. over the latest report from the architects. This report (in fact the fourth given) was acceptable to the University, but because the cost of the scheme was now so clearly above the stipulated cost limit, the whole of the university accommodation was being re-examined to see if any economies could be made. The Scottish Home and Health Department had also given their views on this latest architects' report. They too had stressed that they wished the scheme to be modified, as it was to cost so much more than their own cost limit. They raised many questions of detail in the final designs submitted, and stated plainly which parts of the scheme they considered too costly. Mr Lewis Robertson considered that the whole scheme should be agreed and approved by both the Regional Board and the University even if the cost could not be reduced to the £9 million limit. Dr. R. Glyn Thomas said that the architects' report covered only part of the scheme; final designs still to come for many departments could require even higher costs. Mr Johnston added another source of extra cost; he expected the Department to give approval soon to the appointment of a Teaching Hospital Planning Officer at a salary of £1901 rising to £2244—more than that of a newly appointed hospital consultant. There were also discussions proceeding with the National Federation of Building Trade Employees, who had their own views on the contractual procedure being proposed.[18] The contract with the Architect was finally signed in October 1962.

The second Teaching Hospital in Dundee had also to be kept in mind, and in late 1962, this was still Maryfield Hospital. Sir Malcolm was anxious to have a lecture theatre built there. The Regional Board however were less anxious to proceed with Maryfield's development. They wanted the Maryfield scheme, instead of being undertaken progressively over the next ten years, to be delayed till after the completion of Ninewells. Departments at Maryfield could be transferred to D.R.I., argued Dr. Glyn Thomas, the Maryfield buildings demolished, and a new hospital then built on the site. This was an important new idea which would have important consequences.

By June 1963 the main sub-contractors had been appointed. Professor Mair had pointed out the previous year that the sketch plans showed the main Lochee sewer to be running within fifteen feet of the location of main ward blocks, and by the next summer an arrangement had been made with the Corporation of Dundee over the provision of a private water main for Ninewells, and over how the special supply would be paid for. In June also it was agreed that a mock-up should be built, to give the users an idea of what certain chosen features of the

hospital would look like, and give them the chance of making their comments before the yet more final design was confirmed. The mock-up contained a 6-bed ward bay, a single-bed bay, the central core of a standard ward unit, a treatment area, nurses' station, nurse's bedsitting room, and a nurse's study bedroom. A standard maternity delivery room was also to be built in mock-up. The cost of all these was to be fifty thousand pounds. Staff at every level were in turn detailed to go onto the site, look over the mock-up, and write down their impressions and suggestions on paper pads using pencils specially provided. Nothing was to be left to chance, the captions declared.[19]

On June 30th Messrs. Crudens Ltd., of Musselburgh were declared 'acceptable to the design team as main contractors'. The final selection process—apart altogether from the long-continued earlier process—had gone on for four months. Sir Malcolm, plus the University Architect, had been present at every stage. In early March 1962 the Consulting Architects had actually advised that Messrs. Holland, Hannen and Cubitts (Scotland) should be invited to tender for the main contract. A local Dundee builder, Charles Gray Ltd., had been supported by local interest. So the 'final' final list had included:

Gilbert Ash (Scotland) Ltd.
Crudens Ltd.
Charles Gray (Builders) Ltd., Dundee.
Holland, Hannen and Cubitts (Scotland) Ltd.
Sir Robert MacAlpine and Sons Ltd.

Crudens offer was to carry out the work for £10,595,000; although economies of £60-70,000 were already planned, the cost of the Radiotherapy Centre was now £200,000 extra.[20] The first sod was cut on 10th August 1964 (it was minuted on November 27th, 1963 at the Board that this ceremony was to take place in early 1964).[21] Sir Malcolm Knox and Mr Lewis Robertson were present to represent the University of St Andrews and the Eastern Regional Hospital Board. A photopraph taken at the ceremony showed the Principal on a digger machine, looking extremely uneasy.

From now on building continued; the important planning was over. On 9th June 1965 Lord Hughes of Hawkhill, as Mr Hughes now was, came from London to lay the foundation stone in the base of the Concourse Tower:

This foundation stone was laid on behalf of the Eastern Regional Hospital Board and the University of St Andrews by Lord Hughes of Hawkhill, C.B.E., D.L., J.P., LL.D. (St. And.) on 9/6/65.

By spring of 1966, however, building was proceeding more slowly. The report of that spring (NW 2/66 dated 3/2/66) suggested that the engineering and laundry departments were sufficiently well completed that they would shortly be brought into use. The new governing body—in fact an enlarged Dundee General Hospital Board of Management—was detailed. It would be concerned with final equipment schedules, estimates of future running costs, advanced recruitment, redeployment of present staff. Thus, the Scottish system of hospital government was to be imposed on this new Teaching Hospital. The Home and Health Department laid down the responsibilities of the clients clearly: 'All the buildings on the Ninewells site will belong to the Secretary of

State, and the parts of the complex paid for and occupied by the University will be leased to them at a nominal rent. Despite this, the University cannot be regarded as an ordinary tenant; for future management purposes they must be regarded in some measure as part owners'.[22] While it had been agreed initially that two-thirds of the building costs were to be borne by the Scottish Home and Health Department and one-third by the University, the steady increase in costs had made both the Department and the U.G.C. ask, in early 1966, for the apportionment to be reviewed, since neither wished to have to make a substantial adjustment. On 10th May 1966, it was agreed that 70% was to be paid by the Department and 30% by the University, but Sir Malcolm said the U.G.C. considered the University share too high, when compared with other projects elsewhere. (The University Hospital of Wales was building in Cardiff at this same period. It had been started later, was progressing faster, and costing less). The U.G.C. had instanced the cost of the laboratory block as being charged wholly to the University, when it obviously had a large service component for patient care and investigation. By October the Regional Board agreed to accept responsibility for 30% of the laboratory block, and the Board and University shares were adjusted to 74% and 26% respectively; by 30th September, £1,597,830 of the work was completed.

The full break-down, with costs in pounds sterling at 1966 values, are interesting to compare with costs of seventy years earlier:

Hospital £				School £
1,143,910		Main Ward Block		—
495,720		Minor Specialty Block		—
430,000		Radiotherapy Department		—
418.650		Maternity Block		—
1.277.450		Polyclinic		—
994,194	85%	Concourse Block	15%	175,446
531,140		Main Theatre Block		—
—		Lecture Theatre		325,750
35,800	10%	Library and Museum	90%	322,200
—		Laboratory Block		1,829,070
280,410		Medical Physics		—
141,290		Nurse Training and Recreation Block		—
325,134	90%	Residences	10%	36,126
35,230		Staff Houses		—
39,230		Mortuary Chapel		—
264,570	90%	Laundry	10%	29,400
6,412,728	70%		30% (29.7%)	2,717,992
267,520	70%	Engineering Group	30%	115,080
178,625	70%	Main Distribution	30%	77,025
58,616	70%	Main Plant	30%	25,164
388,738	70%	External Works and Landscaping	30%	166,602
168,847	70%	Corridors for connecting Blocks and Services Supplies	30%	72,363
7,475,074		Total £10,649,300		3,174,226
70%				30%

The rest of the Ninewells story is a less happy one. Even by November 1965 there were serious doubts about the rate at which construction was taking place. 'By the end of 1965', said the Joint Planning Committee minute, 'it had become evident that the rate of construction was *not* increasing, and that the priced information being passed to the contractor had reduced to a mere trickle'. From then on there continued a decade of argument, later recrimination, and finally legal actions between the Board as client, main and other contractors—especially Ove Arup and Partners, as well as Crudens—and the Consultant Architect. The progress note of September 1966 showed that delays were increasing in all sections—the Concourse Tower was 43 weeks late, the main wards 4-12 weeks late, the operating theatres 19 weeks late. But not all work was behind—laboratories and lecture theatres were being completed on time. There are 'difficulties in resolving user requirements' problems within the unit costs' the Design Team complained. The Design Team were called to the Board offices to 'discuss the rate of progress on which the Regional Hospital Board had expressed profound dissatisfaction'. The Design Team was asked 'to verify whether there were solid grounds for expecting completion on time, or whether there was to be a revised Contract Span'. At the Joint Planning Committee meeting of 13th October 1966, both Board and University agreed that the conclusion of the contractors, that the work would be completed within the time limit allowed, was 'unlikely'.

And so it proved. The Comptroller and Auditor General were called in, in August 1967. By now, there was 24 weeks of delay on the wards, 22 on the operating threatres, 14 on lecture theatres, and 13 weeks on laboratories. Mr P.J. Westmore was appointed Project Administrator, with a full time watching brief. A re-constituted Joint Planning Committee in October 1967 met frequently; letters came from the architects, contractors, and back again from the Board. In 1968, under new university management, Mr Alan Brown and his Faculty administration were questioned about failure to produce adequate information from the medical side, and were able to prove positively that there had been no fault on the part of this capable and experienced man or his colleagues. The criticism came from Mr P.J. Westmore, a Regional Board appointee as Joint Planning Officer of 1963. Mr Westmore was however obliged by the nature of his contract to refer any query in the first place to the Faculty Secretary, and this particular query concerned fears by the Board that the University were causing delay by continually altering plans and upsetting the contractors. This sort of incident was a symptom of the unease felt about the continuing delays, and existed at all levels. It was not to be until 24th October, 1974, that Ninewells Teaching Hospital and Medical School was formally opened, and by now the client group was a new and young one, in whom St Andrews University had no share.

The story of the building of Ninewells could very easily be made use of by a third party, if such party so wished, to demonstrate the inefficiency and stupidity of the Regional Board, the University, the town, and the contractors involved. But the difficulties were considerable, and though mistakes were made, they were largely due to inexperience and not to misdemeanour. Mr Lewis

Sir James Irvine FRS

W. L. Burgess

A. C. Lendrum

Sir Ian Hill

R. B. Hunter (Lord Hunter)

Sir Donald Douglas

Alex. Mair

Robertson and Sir Malcolm Knox, whose extremely close and happy friendship continued and in fact strengthened further in subsequent years until the Principal's death, were capable men, whose judgements about division of responsibility were admirable. Mr Robertson was aware that the National Health Service was still 'new' while this pioneering project was being undertaken. Ninewells was in his view a proving ground in cooperation between a University Faculty of Medicine and a Public Controlled Health Service as had not previously occurred on such a scale. 'The whole machinery of design had to be invented'. Sir Malcolm Knox took a very responsible part in focussing the St Andrews University side of the matter. He was acknowledged by all the Board members and employees as a conscientious contributor, very keen to see Ninewells succeed, and excellent at resolving the potentially tricky interface between old University and new Hospital Board. As far as the Board itself was concerned, members over the 1950-67 period were generally good natured and harmonious, and were surprisingly little affected by background feeling in Dundee. On the other hand,

> premature announcements of one kind or another, very often inspired by the public expectation in Dundee that the thing should get on and happen, were made before adequate thought had been given ... the press took a great interest as the project was *locally* important as a big thing Dundee needed to help its image—as it always needs this sort of help ... The means of making estimates (of cost) were pretty limited—so at each stage the price appeared to shoot up ... [23]

But, just as the senior staff officer often fails to be aware of just what is happening in the field, Mr Lewis Robertson was unaware of the difficulties the four-man design team had to face. They were more conscious than he was of background discontent. One result of the delays in Ninewells building was to convince the Board that the Maryfield site could not be developed as had been earlier envisaged. When this fact became apparent in the early 60s, the Radio-therapy Department had to be transferred to the Ninewells site as a huge new planning requirement. This compounded the planning team's difficulties. The Government decision to double the medical student intake about the same time required further hurried revisions. The team were all too aware of inadequacies in the drafting of the contract, which allowed the contractor to influence design and made no requirement as to the sequences of completion. And since Crudens' bid was too low, arguments with that firm began at once; Crudens recognised they had under-priced the job and would have great difficulty avoiding financial loss—and tried to reduce accordingly. The Civil Service element in planning made for delays also; twenty years later, the development of Perth Royal Infirmary as the Second Teaching Hospital was similarly delayed by the unbelievable slowness of the Home and Health Department to agree its various cost limits, with the result that once a decision had been taken, the cost had inevitably increased to such an extent that the design had to be modified; the reductions in *their* turn took so long to be agreed that in the end they cost more than the original. [24]

Ninewells Hospital was in spite of all difficulties a great project, well built,

strikingly individual in concept and design. For this the credit goes to the four man planning team, the clerks of works, those working on the site, and to the collaboration between successive lay officers of the Regional Board, Board members and Sir Malcolm Knox. It was also one of the most daring and adventurous enterprises ever undertaken by the University of St Andrews in her long history. It was all the sadder, then, when the wall plaque in the entrance hall of the Concourse was made to read:

> The crests of the Eastern Regional Hospital Board and the University
> of Dundee who were responsible for the planning of Ninewells
> Hospital and Medical School.

The Medical Sciences Building, though not a responsibility of Regional Board or Central Government but rather a University one as far as planning and payment were concerned, will be mentioned later in this history of St Andrews Medicine. But while its concept, planning, size and cost were tiny in comparison to those of Ninewells, its political importance was not very far short and in some respects was even greater. The Court's development plans of war-time years for the Medical School had included not only a new Teaching Hospital but a new building in the College to replace the old 1902 Medical School and Institute Building next door, so the idea was nothing new. The location was also fixed; both U.G.C. and University agreed it must be within the main college area. It was only the number of departments it was to contain which was uncertain; uncertain too was the number of students to be catered for, dentals as well as medicals. It was therefore not until the decision was taken to transfer all pre-clinical medicine to Queen's College and until the likely increase in dentals was agreed, that the final size could be decided. Planning thus did not begin in earnest until 1966, and the Institute was to be completed in two phases, according to the concept of that date.

While the politics and costings of the building will be described later, the details of its planning and construction can be conveniently included now. The original aim was to house Physiology, Anatomy and Biochemistry, together with Pharmacology and Microbiology, and Medical Biophysics, in the Medical Sciences Block. An Aberdeen firm of architects, Mackie, Robertson and Taylor, prepared drawings in 1967 and 1968, and an annual intake of 70-80 students, the total St Andrews intake, would be catered for. Construction began early in 1968. The main contractor was C. Gray, of Francis Street Dundee, and the Project and Management Sub-Committee was under the convenership of Professor J.P. Duguid. The Institute was completed by 1970, and on completion, now for the University of Dundee, it housed only Anatomy and Biochemistry, the others having had space made for them in Ninewells. It was therefore a very much smaller and more restricted building than originally planned.

Perhaps the most important thing about Ninewells, as far as the whole University and the Faculty was concerned, was the fact that it was 'there'. It was as it were the backcloth against which the whole of the rest of Faculty policy was set. Once the College became Dundee University, Ninewells would remain for some years its greatest wonder. Principal Drever recalled later how he 'always took visitors to admire Ninewells'.[25] In the early 1970s, students

would also be taken there, especially by members of Professor Mair's staff, and shown around, also to wonder and admire. Not all the senior staff were totally mesmerised by it; Mr Walter Campbell, the surgeon at Maryfield, pointed out to his staff in the early 1960s the large and basic planning error in making the ward units for the major surgical and medical firms too small. 'They are mad', he used to say, from his Maryfield experience. 'We cannot cope with our emergency load with the bed numbers *we* have—they will not cope in Ninewells. The units should have 30 beds to each adult ward.' Time proved him correct. Dr. (later Professor) K.G. Lowe saw the enterprise equally critically as far as time was concerned; he compared the building of Ninewells with the building of the Road Bridge: 'History ran past them', he said, 'while Ninewells was being built. They did not see what was happening—the changes in the world oil economy. The fact that the optimistic forecast on how Dundee would prosper which Professor Archie Campbell wrote was being proved wrong'.[26] Years later Dr. Tom Sommerville was also critical of the size of the ward unit, and of the huge size of the hospital: 'A hospital this size is no longer necessary', he said. The Staff Common Room was a great disappointment, and a Senior Staff Common Room and Dining Room were refused for political reasons by the Labour Administration. (In fact, the three large dining rooms, on different levels, became divided by natural selection into those for different grades of staff). 'No-one knows anybody' was his view. 'Gaps remain between the departments—no different from those in the old Medical School, in Maryfield or D.R.I.'[27]

For in the last analysis, there was a certain disappointment that Ninewells Teaching Hospital and Medical School was as Dr. Sommerville has just described. As bus fares increased and waiting times for outpatients lengthened, the local citizens lost some of their early enthusiasm. Beds blocked by elderly patients frustrated nurses and doctors to an increasing degree through the 80s. Wound sepsis rates were sadly high for a building whose design had been claimed as the last word in ventilation systems and whose operating theatres were said to be the most modern available. The huge early hopes have been alluded to repeatedly. Students and newly-qualified doctors, unaware of how great these had been, felt no disappointment but only the soul-lessness, the absence of atmosphere of Ninewells when they compared it to D.R.I. or King's Cross, in the 1970s and 1980s. They were prudent enough not to be critical about the hospital to Ninewells staff who *did* believe in it, but spoke more honestly when they were out of Dundee in other parts of the country or even in what certain of the Ninewells staff described as 'the provinces'—Angus or Perth. For many Ninewells staff, on the other hand, the hospital was a great one; over a period of ten years from the middle 70s to the middle 80s such would repeatedly tell visitors how undergraduates and graduates 'were becoming increasingly aware of just how fine Ninewells is'. Such held a genuine belief that to be on the consultant staff, or even registrar staff there meant to be very much above the average in status and importance. This superior attitude of some Dundee medical minds equated, as far as hospital doctors working in other parts of the region were concerned, to the very same attitude of St Andrews staff so bitterly resented by those in University College in earlier times. The Dundee

staff involved, like their St Andrews predecessors, just could not understand such feelings and dismissed them as small-minded envy. It was an interesting change of attitude with change of status; and it followed the change from Queen's College into the University of Dundee.

18

The Disruption

Its immediate consequences for Medicine

The 1972 Graduation

'One day TMK came into the office and said "Take down this memorandum". He then dictated to me his view that Queen's College should split off from St Andrews as a separate University of Dundee. It was all carefully and logically worked out as all his memoranda were, and needed hardly any changes after it was typed. It was a bombshell'. So recalled Miss Janet Allan, the Principal's secretary, of a day in October, 1963. She just could not understand his change of mind, for although there had been for at least a year past a movement, educational but also very much political, that university curricula be revised and made less academic, and in parallel that a very large number of additional universities places be created, Sir Malcolm had expressed the strongest antagonism to it. Such a view was anathema to him, an open proponent of élitism in academic matters as he was.[1] He had rounded on the 'enemies', as he called the pressure group for a huge increase in university places, the previous January, and his speech was recorded and praised by the *Courier* on January 26th. At this early period in the year, the University of St Andrews appeal was starting to gather momentum, and the *Courier* reported on February 2nd that over seven hundred pounds per day were now coming into it from the surrounding parts of Scotland and from much farther afield. Sir Malcolm had continued to encourage this at all opportunities. In the summer, at the Graduation, he spoke out as strongly as could be imagined:

> It had been suggested that the universities of Scotland could be increased by one if this University were divided into two. If this happened, the number of Scottish Universities would be diminished by one, because this University is like an organism, its parts on either side of the Tay being complementary and supplementary to one another.
>
> To sunder them would be like taking an axe and cleaving a human being in two from head to toe. This would leave you with two pieces in your hands, both dead, and not with two human beings.
>
> Those who talk of building up Queen's College into an independent University must be told that, in that event, St Salvator's and St Mary's would have to be built up too.

He went on to criticise the groups of persons who were urging that *all* school leavers in Britain go to a university.

What the Principal was saying was entirely true. It must have been bitter for him to find that in spite of all his meticulous fairness in fulfilling the provisions of the Tedder Report, there was a continued undercurrent in the Arts Faculty, and in the developing Social Sciences Faculty in Queen's. In spite of all the visible evidence of recent years, there was still the myth being fostered, and still believed, that 'The University Court' was starving Queen's College of funds. Dr. John Mills, a graduate of 1966, recalled his own father, then a member of the Department of Mathematics, holding this view; for himself, then and always afterwards, he was against the split.[2] Perhaps the only thing which Professors have in common is a blind, sometimes entirely inward-looking attitude to their own Departments, which makes them unable to see that other slices must of necessity be cut from the cake. Even as excellent a Professor as Professor Walker spoke in later years of the feeling that 'we were competing against St Andrews for funds'. It was inevitable therefore that professors and particularly lecturers, lulled as they were by the political background which was currently promising apparently endless expansion in staff, resources, salaries—and so in prestige—would feel that independence would unlock treasures presently denied them.

With these were those biassed against St Andrews, which included not only some university staff but also the local municipal and business element, some of whom had never accepted the Tedder Report,[3] and who, while attacking St Andrews for allegedly failing to honour aspects of that Report, were entirely prepared to refuse to honour aspects which they themselves did not like. The number of departmental alterations which U.G.C. instructions had brought about, and which were imposed upon the University and in no way 'its fault', could be used and were used as a stick to beat the unfortunate University Court of St Andrews. Indeed, it is probable that some of the municipal elements did not understand the function of the U.G.C. nor appreciate its power. Thus, the maximum use was made of the moves to develop Arts subjects in St Andrews as the Tedder Report had advised, in provoking 'deep concern' in Queen's College; even the large developing Social Science Faculty in Queen's could be used in evidence against St Andrews by those anxious enough to cause trouble. On the other hand, there was no concern felt over the move of Medicine into Queen's College, even beyond the terms of the Tedder Report's recommendation. No blame can be fairly attached to the St Andrews side of the enlarged University over this period. The faults of envy and suspicion, and failure to see beyond very local interest, belonged to these three elements on the Dundee side.[4]

It is of interest that the *Courier and Advertiser* took a restrained and reasonable line in its comments at this time. It quoted Sir Malcolm's Graduation speech with approval, especially his argument against expansion at too fast a pace:

'That is why it is reckless to dangle a plan for twenty new universities as political bait. Where are the staff, the libraries, equipment and buildings to come from? . . . Standards would be lowered', said its leader prophetically. Nevertheless the newspaper saw that a split of the University was not necessarily ruled out for all time, but might later be achieved with advantages to both:

'St Andrews might out-Oxbridge Oxbridge ... and Dundee might develop applied subjects'. In this the *Courier* showed a better grasp of division of function than those college and town council individuals who saw diminution in 'pure' subject availability as a calculated insult to Dundee. Such individuals, like others concerned with plans for Ninewells Hospital, did not see 'history run past them as the road bridge was going up'. Some did not know enough, or perhaps did not want to know.[5] The *Courier* leader went on 'But both would be whole universities covering a full range of subjects ... but this is in the long term. Expansion should proceed slowly'.

Both at the time and in retrospect, it seemed inconceivable that Sir Malcolm Knox was urging the disruption of what he had worked hard to build. The view that he had had prior knowledge from government sources that a split was to come, and that his Graduation speech of June 1963 was a last attempt to avert it,[6] does not seem to be the correct one. Nor does there seem to be any foundation for the view that he was tired after the events of 1948-52, fearful of a renewal of them, and 'lost his nerve'. It seems likely that he made up his mind on a course of action which he saw no reason to change, and which he believed was the correct one from then onwards—much as it saddened him to do so.[7] After he had dictated his memorandum to Miss Allan in his office at College Gate (the Nerve Centre as it was called at the time) events moved swiftly. A verbal statement was made to the Senate Meeting in Queen's College on 8th November 1963, and his printed memorandum was considered at the January Senate in St Salvator's College. The new factor was the Robbins Report on University expansion, which looked to a huge increase in universities and student numbers— the latter to rise to half a million by 1970. This report published in October 1963, but whose contents were known many months earlier, led to the U.G.C. requiring St Andrews to expand student numbers to at least 2,300 in St Andrews and at least 3,000 in Dundee in 4 years. The Principal's memorandum— objective in its content and form—argued:

A college of 3000 students would exceed in size some existing universities and therefore there would be a legitimate criticism, at that stage, of a policy aimed at keeping together, and developing complementarily, two centres of activity of that order of magnitude. But if, once they have grown, independent development in both centres seems reasonable, why should they not become altogether independent? To try to maintain a tie between two independently developing centres must give rise to strains and tensions that might be better avoided.

An academic institution ought to have vision and to plan ahead. If it seems that growth in two centres will lead to the independence of both in a few years, the right academic view may be to recognise this now, to endeavour to convince the U.G.C. and the Scottish Office accordingly, and then, if this endeavour succeeds, to allow both centres, as soon as independent development becomes possible, to develop in whatever way each thinks necessary to enable it in due course to stand on its own feet and become an independent university ...

3rd January 1964

T.M.KNOX

The minute continued:

> Motion made and question proposed that the separation of the two sides of the University of St Andrews and the foundation of a University of Dundee are desirable; (moved by Professor Hitchin, seconded by Professor Preston); and agreed to unanimously.

Those present remember a seemingly long silence. Ian Adamson remembers Professor James Walker raising his hand 'as if to try to vote against'; others remember the sadness of the occasion.

The reactions were predictable. Of those most biassed against St Andrews, Dr. Southgate and Professor Bell remain strong spokesmen: 'It seemed almost an insult to insist (should anybody do so) that Dundee's university institution remain harnessed to St Andrews and, as it were, concealed under the name of St Andrews'.[8] 'Never again' said Professor Bell, 'would they be able to lord it over us'.[9]

At the other end of the spectrum, Mr John Grieve, the Senior Lecturer in Surgery, wrote twenty years later: 'I was on the Senate for four years prior to the bisection. In the period of 15+ years before the schism a vast amount had been done to make the two parts complementary. It has always been my considered opinion that the breaking up of the original St Andrews University was the biggest mistake in Scottish University History'.[10]

The claims of student feeling against movements of departments to St Salvator's (or the United College) are not borne out by the students of the day's accounts, nor by the recall of student wardens and subwardens.[11] This applied to all students—the few attending meetings were a tiny minority. 'There do not seem to be any stronger arguments for a split than in 1952' said the official student publication 'Aien'; 'although there is the prospect of Dundee taking more students, the other arguments (for union) still stand'. The position in London University was quoted, where a large increase in students did not result in any separatist demand, and the prospect of the Tay Road Bridge being completed at the very time the disruption was expected to be completed 'made the whole thing seem daft'. And whatever views may have been held by younger staff and some older staff in the Arts and Science, there is no doubt of the feeling of almost incredulity in very many of the Medical Faculty, both students and staff. The Secretary of the Faculty, Mr Alan Brown, summed up the feelings of the medicals when he said 'No-one who mattered was for the split. There may have been some in the Arts Departments, Social Science or Maths. It was said "There was a large body of opinion for a University of Dundee whose views had to be met" but where *was* this large body? Who were they all?'[12] On the other hand, there was the wonder by some members of the Arts Faculty, which still continues, why medicals whose entire field of academic activity was centred in Dundee remained 'St Andrews Professors (or staff) first, second and last'. 'It was a sad day when without any consultation or warning (other than rumours) the split was announced. There were no sensible arguments which could justify the establishment of two universities twelve miles apart (with a road bridge connecting them) on a sparsely populated East coast of Scotland. Indeed it ensured that neither of the Universities would be really viable' said Professor

Sir Donald Douglas.[13] Sir Ian Hill was especially saddened by the disruption, and perhaps expressed his feelings more strongly and more openly than any of his colleagues.[14] Professor Lendrum, strong critic of St Andrews as he was, called the split 'silly'.[15] Professor Walker, though feeling at the time that his Department and others in the Faculty would gain access to funds for equipment and staff as the result of separation, stated 'We did not realise how much we lost when we lost St Andrews'.[16]

Through 1964, the Senate became divided into Dundee and St Andrews sub-committees, each tasked with planning towards the implementation of the disruption. And very soon it was the position of the medical students, yet again, which produced problems. St Andrews would have let University College go its way years before but for their presence; St Andrews however retained 'the wish for Medicine' which had been a recurring theme in its history for five and a half centuries.

There were three possibilities open to the University. First, St Andrews would abandon medical teaching altogether. Second, a small Faculty could be formed, but with its own clinical school elsewhere. Third, there could be a pre-clinical school, based upon the medical building Lord Bute had bequeathed 60 years before, with students going on for clinical training in another university. Because it was at once clear that 'there would no longer be a complete Medical Faculty in this University' the medicals would have to be incorporated into the Faculty of Science. It could therefore be a decision of the Faculty of Science whether Medicine would continue. There would however in the meantime be a period during which students matriculated at St Andrews University would continue to have their clinical training in Dundee. The Universities (Scotland) Act, 10th March 1966, would make the disruption statutory, but would not take effect until 1st August 1967. There would therefore be St Andrews medical graduations—if any students so wished—continuing to take place until 1972.

In the short phase between the decision to disrupt and the inauguration of the independent University of Dundee, the Faculty of Medicine remained that of the University of St Andrews. In January 1964, Professor J.L. Henderson, Professor of Paediatrics, became Dean. A less able administrator than several of his colleagues, he was helped in the Ninewells Joint Planning Committee by the powerful personality of Professor Hunter, who was given a special continuing appointment of coordinator on that committee by the Court.

In 1964 the University of Colorado Medical Centre gave £8,000 towards the cost of equipment for a neonatal nursery and unit for research into problems of prematurity and the newborn, and Dr. Colin Walker took over its clinical charge. In 1964 the Association of Surgeons of Great Britain and Ireland had its meeting in the University of St Andrews, when Professor Douglas welcomed them to 'this far-off place', and the Association of Physicians and the British Cardiac Society also visited the University and its Medical School, at Professor Hill's invitations, in 1962 and 1963 respectively. 1965 saw progress made in the creation of Departments of Biochemistry independent of those of Physiology. Approaches were made for the appointment of Heads of these independent Departments in June.

At the Graduation Ceremony in July 1965 the Arts/Science/Divinity took place in the Younger Hall on July 1 and the Medicals joined the other Faculties in the Caird Hall on July 2. The Dundee limb-fitting centre in Broughty Ferry was opened on September 29th by Group Captain Douglas Bader, and work was continuing on the enlarged Dental School to increase its student intake from 25 to 50 *per annum* as the 1962-67 Quinquennial proposals had decided.

At the Court Meeting on October 19th, George Roland Tristram, BSc PhD FRSE was appointed Professor of Biochemistry in St Salvator's. He was to be appointed from 1st January 1966: he will be heard about later for his great contribution to St Andrews Medicine. At this meeting also a good deal of difficulty was reported over the means of appointing the first Principal of Dundee University. The Queen's College Council had not agreed with Sir John Wolfenden's suggestion, as Chairman of the U.G.C., that the Academic Advisory Committee put up a name. After various letters had crossed back and forwards, Professor James Drever, Professor of Psychology in the University of Edinburgh, and a member of the Robbins Committee whose decisions had provoked the Disruption, was later nominated, and formally appointed by the Secretary of State for Scotland.

The question of another part of the Medical Faculty building programme was also discussed. Sir Malcolm had written to Sir John Wolfenden on June 24th in connection with moves being made about possible retention of preclinical medical departments in St Andrews. The U.G.C. Chairman had now replied that this would have to await his Committee's considered response. He also raised the question of the building of a Medical Sciences Block, in Queen's College and complementary to the clinical Medical School of Ninewells, as a high priority. The Government of the day was very determined that more doctors were required urgently, and this explained the urgency of building. The complete scheme was to cost £1,500,000, and was to be phased in two initial stages of £300,000 each. His letter asked if St Andrews could start in 1967-68 or 1968-69. He also asked if, should money be made available by the U.G.C., they could take a revised student entry of 100-110 as soon as the two stages were completed.

The building of a Medical Sciences—as well as a Biological Sciences—block in Queen's College had already been gone into, as soon in fact as the decision to concentrate both pre-clinical and pre-medical students had been taken. The Principal was thus able to reply that 'Schedule I was in active preparation'. But, as ever, tender prices had gone up and the cost of the first two stages was now £650,000 instead of £600,000. Further, the intake of 100-110 students could not be assured unless further alterations were made in other existing buildings, the cost of which was £50,000. St Andrews would therefore need £700,000 and not £600,000. The Medical Sciences Institute was approved with the important proviso that the medical students from the Bute would be taught in it, as had been agreed. Building did not begin till 1967 at the western end of Dundee University and back towards the Hawkhill; it provided for Anatomy and for the Biochemistry Department which became one of the centres of excellence of the new University; Physiology however remained in the Old

Medical School. From the point of view of St Andrews University, the size of this Institute was a factor against the transfer of St Andrews medical students to Dundee for clinical teaching, although it was not the only one. 'There was a desire to expand the preclinical school in Dundee to provide the maximum back up for the clinical school and the clinical school places were limited by the hospital bed numbers. Dundee had plans, as soon as independent and even before, to use all its clinical places'.[17]

On 4 April 1966 Professor John Steven Watson MA FRHistS was appointed Principal of the University of St Andrews. He was educated at Merchant Taylor's School and St John's College, Oxford. Unfit for military service as a result of his leg amputation following a road accident, he had served as Private Secretary to Ministers of Fuel and Power in 1942-45 and had lately been an historian of the highest distinction at Christ Church, Oxford, before coming to St Andrews. Sir Malcolm Knox had also been born in the northern half of England, though on the opposite side of the country in Birkenhead in 1900, and he too, had been an Oxford scholar before coming to St Andrews in 1936 as Professor of Moral Philosophy. He was now retiring prematurely. The new Principal, J. Steven Watson, would therefore be Head of the existing enlarged University for a year, and would become a friend and colleague of James Drever, the first Principal of Dundee. In that transition year Professor Tulloch died, in August 1966, and Professor Hill was knighted. In October 1966 the entry to Medicine was:

| St Salvator's College | Men | 27 | Women | 11 |
| Queen's College | Men | 30 | Women | 10 |

3 men entered St Salvator's as Dental students, and 30 men and 12 women entered Queen's.

As 1967, the year when the Disruption would take place continued, the first doubts about the creation of new universities appeared. Dundee was of course only one of a large number, up and down the country, of new foundations or technical colleges now given university status. This latter sometimes meant that an old technical college of distinction became a new university with considerable lack of seniority. The U.G.C. stated the St Andrews-Dundee position plainly:

> The circumstances in which the decision to create two universities was made have changed. The policy pursued actively after 1957 of avoiding duplication in St Salvator's and Queen's was very successful; but its very success has made each of these Colleges less fit to stand as a university without an extensive reconstruction of academic activity which, in 1964, was thought to be easily accomplished but which now, in conditions of financial stringency and decellaration of expansion, is seen to be difficult. The Programme for 1962-67 has been steadily followed. Of 18 Chairs asked for, 14 have been filled, and 2 more will be soon. Of 270 Readers and Lecturers asked for, all but 36 have been added.

The U.G.C. noted the spread of Faculties Dundee would have, and that it would have no Humanities. It advised Dundee to build up its biological departments. As far as St Andrews was concerned, the U.G.C. noted how 'even more lop-sided' it would be, losing Law, Education, Social Sciences, Medicine

and Dentistry, and losing six of the degrees it had hitherto awarded. 'The University will be in danger of losing the contacts with the world around it which are essential to it and to Scotland'.

Of the Chairs to be filled, one was the last Chair in the Faculty of Medicine to which an appointment was made before the Disruption was completed. This was the Chair of Orthopaedic and Traumatic Surgery, into which Ian Scott Smillie, OBE, ChM, FRCS Glasgow and Edinburgh was inducted at the Caird Hall in Dundee on 4th July 1967. He was born in Dublin of Scottish parents on 5th April 1907, and educated at Merchiston Castle School and Edinburgh University, where he graduated in 1931. He did not win the usual undergraduate honours, and his house appointments were at Chester and Grimsby, as well as Edinburgh. In 1935 he took his Fellowship and in 1936 was clinical assistant to Sir Walter Mercer when the Orthopaedic Department in Edinburgh was inaugurated. During the 1939-45 war he was in charge of the Orthopaedic E.M.S. Hospital at Larbert, and was awarded the OBE for his services there. In 1948 he took the ChM with a Gold Medal and Chiene Medal; in this year he became the surgeon in charge of the Eastern Region Orthopaedic Service. Because of his limited beds in D.R.I. he had made his main headquarters at Bridge of Earn, and he had never entered university planning as Professor Douglas did. Nor had he made any attempt to scale the political heights of the College of Surgeons. But he was undoubtedly the only surgeon in Dundee and in the University with a world-wide reputation, and this was on account of his fame as a knee surgeon. His textbooks on Injuries of the Knee Joint and Diseases of the Knee Joint were translated into four European languages, and he would in 1981 be elected President of the International Society of the Knee. One of the clearest lecturers any student ever heard, he was didactic in teaching and an Emperor among surgical chiefs. His reputation as a world authority increased the status of the Medical School in these early 1960s very considerably.

Earlier in 1967 there was agreement that a Standing Committee of the Faculty of Medicine be set up 'to coordinate pre-medical and pre-clinical courses at Dundee and St Andrews, so long as the division of responsibility continues. It should include dentals, for a few start at St Andrews'. On May 12th, the Senatus met in Belmont Hall, Dundee, 'for the last meeting of the Senatus in Queen's College before the elevation of the College to the status of an independent University'. The formal foundation took place on a wet day in October. The new University had secured the enormous privilege of having H.M. Queen Elizabeth the Queen Mother as its first Chancellor, and this Royal Superstar graced the proceedings as she always did on such occasions. The University Officers' Training Corps—still as it has remained a joint enterprise— provided a Guard of Honour for her in the City Square. As far as these members of the student body were concerned, the events of the day did not signal any change; they were part of one university organisation which had been more solidly united over the whole century than any single other. But for the staff of Dundee University it was a happy day, full of high expectation for great and continuing expansion into the future. Principal Drever followed the Mace, from which he had had removed all emblems pertaining to St Andrews,

and the Dundee University Flag flew from the flagpole at Belmont Hall. All Dundee interests were united in their warm approval; Cairds in Reform Street had available a stock of new undergraduate gowns—modelled on the St Andrews pattern but with a darker insert at the back, and it seemed that the prophecy of the *Advertiser* of the 1890s, that the student gown would now be seen in the streets of a university city, was to be fulfilled.

Although the G.M.C. had approved 'the abolition of qualifying degrees in Medicine etc. in the University of St Andrews' as long before as May 23rd, 1966, there was the proviso

a)   that a students who has matriculated in the Faculty of Medicine in the University of St Andrews before the appointed day shall for a period of five years from the start of the academic session next following that day be entitled, subject to his compliance with the rules and regulations of the University of Dundee from time to time in force, to take any qualifying examinations in those subjects in the University of Dundee.

b)   The University of St Andrews shall on the appointed day cease to grant degrees in Medicine, Surgery or Midwifery and degrees and licences in Dentistry other than to students who have matriculated in the Faculty of Medicine in the University of St Andrews or the University of Dundee or partly in the one and partly in the other.[18]

There would therefore in this new University be a remnant of St Andrews students—the medicals, who would graduate along with their class-mates on the Dundee side each year from now until 1972—or 1973 if a re-sit was necessary. They would do this as they had done since the previous century—the only students in the enlarged University of Sir Thomas Thornton who *inevitably* moved from one side to the other. Previously, all had perforce to take a St Andrews medical degree; now all could if they wished graduate M.B. Ch.B. (Dundee). There was every incentive for them to do so. All their examination papers would from now be titled 'University of Dundee'. The new Ninewells Hospital was being built for their clinical training. All clinical teaching staff were staff of the University of Dundee. It seemed very likely indeed that the bulk of these medicals, especially first year students starting at Queen's—now Dundee— would choose the exciting new University in preference to the old one.

But the notion that 'the "unity" of the University meant little in practice for students' and that 'students had no interest in a matter which, after all, would concern future, not existing students' applied as little to the medicals of these few short years as did the notion that Dundee students had only participated vigorously in three recent Rectorial elections.[19] Even before the Disruption took place, the students were aware of its coming and of its implications. From 1964 student sports teams from the two main colleges began to play each other as if they were members of different universities. The medical teaching staff did not talk to students of the split, and for the three or four years from then till 1968 there was no strong feeling amongst the students that anything had changed at all. Principal Drever recalled in later years being aware of this, as well as of the

feeling which so many students had that the Disruption was unnecessary. But the views of the students were not taken into account at any stage.[20]

From 1968 it was possible for a medical student, from whichever side she or he had started, to elect to graduate M.B. Ch.B. (Dundee) or M.B. Ch.B. (St Andrews). The last bejants or bejantines who retained the option were those who matriculated first in October 1966, and they would thus in due course graduate at St Andrews in 1972—if they had any wish to. But 'direct entry' students who joined the same year course in October 1967 (those who entered the 2nd M.B. course directly without taking 1st M.B. subjects at university) were forbidden the choice—they *had* to take a Dundee Medical M.B. And this applied to those who began their course at St Andrews as well as to those who began at Dundee.

In 1968, two medicals elected to graduate from Dundee—James Douglas Stewart, of Deanston near Stirling, and Robert J. Kent, B.A. Robert Kent was from New York. His father, Edward Katz, was one of the Jewish students from New York who had come to St Andrews to study medicine. He graduated in 1936, changed his name to Kent, and had always an ambition that his son, too, would go to St Andrews University and graduate in medicine there as he had. His son's decision was a great sorrow to him.[21] No graduate in July 1969 elected to take the Dundee degree—the whole year chose St Andrews. In December 1969, however, James D.K. Morton decided to graduate M.B. from Dundee. He was already a B.D.S. of St Andrews, and then and in later years gave as his reason the feeling that he was acting fairly towards the place where his entire Dental and Medical training had been carried out. 'But if I had not had a St Andrews degree already', James Morton recalled, 'I would certainly not have taken my medical one at Dundee'. In 1970, however, eleven students decided to graduate as from the New University; they included Thomas Walmsley, the younger son of Professor Walmsley, and in 1971, eleven chose to do so, nine in the summer and two at the December-January re-sits.

During these years the Faculty of Medicine began to change. In 1968, Professor Hunter left, having secured the Vice-Chancellorship of the University of Birmingham. He would in due course be knighted and later still be created a life peer. He seems to have quickly forgotten the Dundee scene—Mr R.N.M. Robertson, who had worked very closely with him as administrator of the post-war Medical Planning Committee, met him as Secretary of Dundee University at a conference in Birmingham and found Principal Hunter had forgotten who he was. Professor Hill was approaching his retirement the next year—his Edinburgh commitments as President of the College of Physicians there were now over, so he had no requirements out of Dundee to enforce his absence. But he began to reduce the commitment to teaching he had previously held to be his prime function. His contributions to the Ninewells planning were over. The cardiac electrophysiology he had pioneered was now carried out by his assistants. He gave only one lecture—on malaria—to the 1970 graduating class—and students felt that he had lost interest in them. Part of this reduced activity was due to his sense that the new University and its Faculty was not as it had been in earlier years. That he was by no means failing in mental or physical

powers was shown by his active work after retirement, in Iran and later in Ethiopia as Faculty Dean. But though his contributions to St Andrews were great and his personality formidable, he is not the greatest Professor of Medicine to serve St Andrews so far—that accolade must go to George Day.

1968 and 1969 also saw changes of organisation and technology which would start a new attitude to administration and diagnosis in medicine. The Salmon Scheme for Nursing organisation and the Divisional system for Doctors appeared at this time, and imposed the administrative nurse or doctor on the profession in a manner not wholly beneficial. The first automatic blood counting and sampling equipment appeared—the earliest stage in what would lead to progressive automation of laboratory work and increasing belief in laboratory tests as the *sine qua non* of clinical diagnosis. On October 17th, 1968, H.M. The Queen Mother, as Chancellor of the University of Dundee, opened the completed Dundee Dental Hospital building.

Professor Hunter was succeeded by Professor James Crooks. He had served as a soldier during the 1939-45 war, and had been a survivor of the Siam railway of death. But he never spoke of this period as a prisoner-of-war to fellow prisoners after the war, and the significance of this was not lost upon them. He graduated M.B. at Glasgow in 1951, and took his M.D. with Honours and the Bellahouston Gold Medal in 1959. Students quickly developed the same feelings about him as they had towards Professor Hunter, and this opinion of him was remarkably uniform. Dr. Tudhope and especially Dr. Gordon Sprunt were greatly preferred as Therapeutics lecturers, both in style and content.

Sir Ian Hill was succeeded by Oliver Murray Wrong, a B.M. of Oxford of 1947 and D.M. of 1964. His interest was in renal disease, and his appointment an unhappy one. As soon as he arrived he was openly critical of Dundee University and the City of Dundee, and his teaching course was as openly criticised by his students and by colleagues. He ran no proper lecture course, and instituted a multiple choice paper to his class without any prior warning. Members of the 1970 and 1971 years were especially angry. 'Fortunately he came to Dundee towards the end of our training, so was unable to wreck our careers by the abandonment of systematic lectures' was a consensus student opinion. Clinical teaching in Medicine was happily saved by the bedside teaching of Professor Kenneth Lowe, who was given a Personal Chair after Professor Wrong appeared; he was regarded however as less effective in formal lecturing. Students also felt they were preserved by the teaching of the non-professorial medical units of Dr. J. Gordon Clark and Douglas Adamson at D.R.I. and of Drs. Semple and Frew at Maryfield. Drs. Jamieson and Mary Kerr at King's Cross earned increasing respect and praise.

Professor Douglas was also felt by his students of these years to be progressively less committed to them, though he remained popular and respected. His lecturing became reduced to his own vascular interests. He, like Professor Hill, was saddened by the Disruption, and his interests in the later 1960s and early 1970s seemed to his students to be more taken up with his career outwith Dundee. He was knighted in 1972. Professor Batchelor's course remained an

excellent one, and was warmly praised, as were those of Obstetrics, Social Medicine, and Pathology. Professor Duguid's Bacteriology course was well planned and well appreciated. Professor Smillie's lectures, though progressively limited to his knee-joint interests, were recalled as clear and memorable. Professor Lendrum, too, in those years continued to give his lectures with a philosophic content which were appreciated both then and in subsequent recollection. His 'Occam's razor' was remembered by many students who could remember little or nothing of his Pathology matter.[22] Drs. Park, Guthrie and Goodall continued to teach the factual Patholgy.

At the pre-clinical stage of the course, both Anatomy and Physiology remained much as before, although students regretted the leaving of Professor Coupland in Queen's College and Dundee University very much. Biochemistry on both sides was regarded as non-memorable; this feeling applied to Dundee students in particular, and to Clinical Chemistry even more so.

Perhaps the lecturer of these years who gained the most uniform applause was Dr. Rushton. His Forensic Medicine lectures were described as 'wonderful'. In the fifth year Social Science and Forensic Medicine lectures were double—2 hours with an interval half-way through, and this arrangement, which could so easily have become boring, never became so because of the interest and vitality of the lectures.

But overall was a certain lessening of the confidence and authority which had so enlivened the Faculty in the first half of the 1960s. Appointments which were less than satisfactory were as always sensed immediately by the student body. This may have been due to the lessening of interest by the principal professors after the first burst of enthusiasm which characterised the new University, perhaps to the frustrating delays over the building of Ninewells, and perhaps to the realisation by the staff that independence from St Andrews had not unlocked the key to treasures they had expected. There was certainly indignation when the Principal decided to allocate funds elsewhere, which some medical departments had believed would come their way.[23] This frustration on the part of some of the staff began to rub off on the students, and some Dundee Medical Faculty staff began, in the 1970s, to express their concern about St Andrews to their students as had not occurred in the 1967-69 period.[24]

In spite of the formal Disruption, a most surprising degree of what can only be called fellowship continued to exist amongst the medicals, both within their own year and extending to the year below. The slight initial rivalry when the St Andrews students appeared quickly vanished, as it had always done. After the 2nd Professional subjects were passed there was what was described as 'a poor third term' of Economics, Statistics, and Sociology. These were thinly attended subjects. There were also introductory lectures in Bacteriology and Pathology— the former more popular, plus some introductory time on the wards. As well as the registrars on Dr. Semple's unit at Maryfield, the general practitioners Dr. J.A.R. Lawson and Dr. W. Morrison Dorward were especially good clinical instructors on Dr. J.G. Clark's unit at D.R.I. In this term, Dundee students travelled to St Andrews for social functions arranged by the St Andrews side; this happened in several years. Student views gave no comfort to the ardent

separatist: 'We all realised St Andrews was St Andrews—a tremendous name abroad more than it ever had at home—no-one knew where Dundee was'; 'Oxford and Cambridge sort of thing—you were talking about the same as them when you spoke of St Andrews'; 'I considered myself a Queen's College graduate of the University of St Andrews'; 'We made a deliberate attempt to integrate our year'; 'we had mixed flats of Dundee and St Andrews'; 'Can't remember *anyone* anti-St Andrews—if this had been so, they would not have mixed'; 'The St Andrews lot thought they were mildly superior—but we were very keen to have a St Andrews degree'; 'many Dundee students went to St Andrews'—and so on. This list of views is not carefully selected; it was very hard to find students who did not express them. The consensus can be summed up quite simply: 'I disapproved of the split, especially with the Road Bridge'. Of those who elected to graduate at Dundee, there were no recriminations against St Andrews either; they felt simply that fairness required they graduate in the location where they had been trained. 'But we were booed by our class-mates' recalled Karalyn Stewart (Mrs McNeill).

1972 was to be an especial graduation: the last Medical Graduation in the University of St Andrews. Invitations were sent out to alumni and accommodation was booked in the main halls of residence. A special Graduation Dinner was to be held. This function was arranged by the Principal's staff and by the university chaplain of the day; there was a degree of resentment in the Bute that their staff were not given a larger share in making the arrangements. Honorary Doctor of Science Degrees were to be conferred upon Professor Douglas Black of the University of Manchester, Sir Donald Douglas, Professor (now Doctor) Anthony Ritchie, who had left the Bute to become Secretary of the Carnegie Trust for Scotland, and Professor Robert Walmsley. The higher degree of Doctor of Medicine was to be conferred on William Kinnear Stewart, M.B. (St Andrews) with Honours, for his Thesis 'The Role of Magnesium in Biological Fluids'. Ch.M.s were to be given to John Maxwell Anderson, M.B. (St Andrews) with Commendation for his Thesis 'The Transplantation Immunology of Certain Mammalian Mothers and Progeny' and on Benson Okeke Igwebe, M.D. (St Andrews) for his on 'An Account of Tropical Ulceration'. The final Examinations were labelled 'University of Dundee'.[24] Of the 82 candidates for these M.B. degrees, 22 were direct entry into second year and so could not take a St Andrews Degree. 56 graduated in the Younger Hall on June 30. It was a bright day, and the audience well behaved as befitted the fact that they were all relatives of the graduands or alumni. For some, their own graduation was almost forgotten; was it really so long?[25] The congregation stood, the Academic Staff entered, the Deputy Secretary, Dundee, Members of the St Andrews and Dundee Senates, and Members of the St Andrews Court followed. Then came the maces, including the Medical Mace which St Andrews had retained on the instruction of its benefactor. Last came the Chancellor, Lord Ballantrae, or as he was better known to many, Brigadier Bernard Fergusson. Of the three who chose to graduate at the Caird Hall in Dundee, two had begun their under-graduate career in the Bute and one in Queen's College. Andrew H. Reid, a graduate of 1965 and later a psychiatrist at Royal Liff Hospital, chose to

graduate M.D. at Dundee. He felt that, although he already had a St Andrews degree, he should now give his allegiance to the new University. As so often, all made up their own minds about things, and the large majority of this graduation year elected, in spite of pressure from students in other Dundee Faculties, to take the Old University degree.

19

Survival

The Manchester Agreement

The Dundee connection had been a short one in the long history of St Andrews University. As far as Medicine was concerned, it spanned about the same period of time as the professorships of Simson *primus* and *secundus*. But in this shortest of periods of time the complete Medical School within Sir Thomas Thornton's enlarged University had increased in status out of all proportion to its student numbers. These began very small, increased after the Great War, and then fell once again until increased by the intake of young Jewish students from the Eastern United States in the 1930s. After the Second World War the increase was maintained, and the numbers applying for the seventy-five places increased steadily in the 1960s.

1945	346	1954	361
1946	618	1959	362
1947	521	1962	859
1948	572	1963	1,016
1950	495	1964	1,056

Of these a significant number were from England or farther afield: 'The large English entry', said Sir John McNee in his report as G.M.C. visitor in 1954, 'is no doubt accounted for by the attractions of St Andrews for pre-clinical studies'. Sir John was from Glasgow, whose student population was more entirely local than that of any other Scottish University. This fact was of course not new. Thirty years before, in the 1924 intake, forty-five students came from Dundee, Angus and Fife, twenty-three from elsewhere in Scotland and from England, and four from the then Indian sub-continent. But while St Andrews was in some odd way considered blameworthy because it attracted a high English intake, Edinburgh, which took fifty per cent of its medical intake in some years from England, was somehow not.[1]

While the total number of St Andrews medical graduates had remained small, their achievements had been a source of pride to the University and to their fellows. This became yet another reason for sadness amongst St Andrews graduates after the Disruption. It became another reason for sadness within the Medical Faculty in Dundee; 'we realised later just how much we lost when we lost St Andrews'. Medicals from Edinburgh especially had the same feeling of loss and indignation that it had happened.

Not only were there some major figures—Sir Stewart Duke-Elder (1919), the ophthalmologist; Sir James Webster (1919), Spilsbury's successor as Home Office Pathologist; Sir Douglas Black (1933), President of the Royal College of

Physicians of London and Chief Scientist as the Department of Health; Sir James Cameron (1929), the B.M.A. statesman; Sir Francis Ibian (1934) of Nigeria; Sir John Reid (1944), Chairman of the Executive Board of the World Health Organisation and Scottish Chief Medical Officer; Sir James Black (1946), the Pharmacologist; Walter L. Perry (1943), who as Lord Perry of Walton became Vice-Chancellor of the Open University, but in the academic world there was a wide range of professors, including, in Anatomy D.R. Dow (1911) and J.W. Smith (1942); Community Health G.O. Sofoluwe (1957) and S. Morrison (1951); Pathology J.R. Anderson (1937) and G.L. Montgomery (1936), professors at Glasgow and Edinburgh respectively; J.B.W. Halley (1949) in New South Wales, H.D. Attwood (1951) in Melbourne and J.S. Henderson (1951) in Winnipeg; Clinical Pharmacology A.M. Breckenridge (1961); Pathological Biochemsitry H.G. Morgan (1946); Paediatrics J.O. Forfar (1938); Forensic Psychiatry R.S. Bluglass (1957); Dean of the London School of Hygiene and Tropical Medicine G.S. Nelson (1938) and C.E. Gordon Smith (1947); Medicine K.G. Lowe (1938), W. Walker (1942) holder of the Regius Chair in Aberdeen, and Sir Christopher Booth (1951) of the Royal Postgraduate Medical School in London; Ophthalmology Alexander G. Watson (1944) Ottowa; Surgery G. Smith (1942) in Aberdeen, and Sir Donald Douglas (1934); A.P.M. Forrest later Sir Patrick Forrest (1942) and G.D. Chisholm (1955) who currently held the Chairs in Edinburgh; T. Solanke (1956) in Ibadan, D.C. Carter (1964) in Glasgow Royal Infirmary; Obstetrics D.C. Fairweather (1949) and Margaret Fairlie (1915).

In the wider and as many would argue more challenging world outside the universities, St Andrews medical graduates spanned as wide a field of endeavour as could be imagined—W.A. Young (1911) the tropical diseases pioneer, Margaret Shirlaw (Mrs Menzies Campbell) (1918) the historian; Mildred Clark (1918) the diarist and co-founder of the Bute Medical Society; Peter Robertson (1923) and Alfred Pitkeathly (1934)—as clever as many Professors of Medicine and with a wonderful sense of humour into the bargain; Noel Nelson (1923), Christopher Grant (1949), Alexander Maclean (1941) of South Uist and Wilfred Dally (1952) of Edzell, Keith Thompson (1952) and Jeremy Gillingham (1972)— all general practitioners of distinction in various ways; John Lawson (1943) President of the Royal College of General Practitioners; Air Marshall Sir Ernest Sidey (1935) and Lieutenant-General Sir Alexander Drummond (1924), respective heads of the R.A.F. and Army Medical Services of their day; Sir Daniel Thompson (1934) Chief Medical Officer to the Treasury; the Dickson brothers (D.C. and J.W.L. 1926 and 1928)—hockey internationalists; Alan Lindsay (1949)—who hopped, stepped and jumped for Great Britain in the 1948 Olympic Games; Duncan Macrae (1939)—the extra great rugby three-quarter whose career was cut short by the war and captivity with the rest of the Highland Division after St Valery; George Blair (1940)—decorated for gallantry while a Japanese Prisoner-of-War; Albert Davies (1951)—mission hospital doctor in the Transvaal; Abe Heller (1934)—the New York doctor; Jane Anwan (Mrs Odia) (1959)—the Nigerian anaesthetist; George Cowan (1963)—the Army physician, Alistair Law (1947)—Chairman of the Scottish Council of the B.M.A., and

Derek Buchanan (1946) its Scottish Secretary; James C. Anderson (1922)—the urologist (Anderson: Hines operation); Andrew Logan (1926)—who performed the first lung transplant in Britain; Elizabeth MacDonald (Bryson) (1905)—the first M.D. of the twentieth century and pioneer of Social Medicine in New Zealand, were some of these.

St Andrews medical graduates' pride was especially a pride in the University and its long seniority as a place of learning. The period when the pride in the Medical School itself, so actively promoted by Professors Hill and Hunter in the 1960s, was evident, lasted only a very short time and disappeared with the Disruption and with the retiral or movement elsewhere of these vigorous promoters of its excellence. St Andrews graduates had never been told how prestigious their degree was, as Edinburgh students always were, nor had they the contrastingly more cheerful and less superior confidence in their school which Glasgow students enjoyed. Their degree was not so prestigious, though it was catching up when the split came. They had not the strong local confidence of Aberdeen graduates, since the City of Dundee was never identified with the University in the manner which is one of Aberdeen's great advantages over Dundee. Perhaps where they scored most of all was over the graduates of the English and especially the proud London Medical Schools, if one of such decided that social or university status was a subject for comparison. Here it was the name of St Andrews University which gave them the certainty of quiet superiority, as well as letting them share the immediate loyalty to the other Scottish schools which Scottish graduates display in these situations as they close ranks in face of the Southron.

Yet it has to be said that not everyone had this feeling for St Andrews as 'the beloved University'. Mr R.N.M. Robertson, though living in the town for a short spell when assistant questor, felt no affection for it. Professor C.C. Booth, later Sir Christopher Booth, Director of the Clinical Research Centre at Northwick Park, said of St Andrews at a reunion in 1983 'it is just a repository for children of the bourgeois who fail to get into Oxford or Cambridge', and of Dundee, 'when I came here I was surprised to find so many men of ability in a place so far off'. Professor Lendrum spoke of 'these St Andreans (referring to students) who came over to us for their clinical training' and considered that 'St Andrews got its Medical faculty but did not really care afterwards'. Mr Gordon Wilson, the Scottish National Party President and M.P. for Dundee East, said in a speech as Dundee Rector in November 1984: 'There is no point in thinking of St Andrews as a truly Scottish University, as it is full of students from south of the Border'. (In the 1984-85 final year, fifty per cent of the students were English, in the Dundee Medical Faculty).

But all this was past history. As soon as the Senatus and Court had confirmed the Disruption, one immediate question was whether Medicine would continue at St Andrews or whether it would at long last disappear. Professor Anthony Ritchie, Chandos Professor of Physiology and then Dean of the Faculty of Science, wrote a personal note by hand to Dr. Stephen Bayne, the Senior Lecturer in Biochemistry in his own Physiology Department, on January 14th 1964—within a week of the Senate Meeting at which the Disruption

had been agreed. He was very aware, as were all the staff of the old University, that things were going to be very much more difficult for St Andrews than for Dundee in the near future. 'It is likely' he wrote

—though not certain—that in the course of the next few years the St Andrews and Dundee Colleges will separate into two distinct and autonomous Universities. We will not *know* whether this is definite for something like a year. Nevertheless, the implications are so vast in scope and complexity that it seems necessary to establish, quite soon, enquiries into what a University in St Andrews could usefully teach and investigate when on its own. One important and fairly urgent facet of this is an advance determination of whether to operate a pre-clinical school or not—à la Cambridge—i.e. feeding other clinical hospital schools anywhere, not in any way linked with Dundee. It may be necessary to devise a new Medical Sciences B.Sc. (and an appropriate standard of entry) in order to ensure that our medicals are acceptable anywhere else on account of their better or fuller pre-clinical training. This would probably mean a drop in numbers from our present 50 to something like 25 *pro tem*, but if a good job was made of the Medical B.Sc. concept, numbers might build up again later . . . This "retention of pre-clinical Medicine" report will need to have representation from Anatomy, Biochemistry and Physiology in the first instance—though of course complications like Pharmacology arise, in that some English Universities do it, or start it, before commencing clinical work . . . Please let me know if you would be willing to serve as representative of Biochemistry in such as enquiry . . .

Dr. Bayne wrote back in biro three days later thanking Professor Ritchie: 'The idea of a Medical Sciences B.Sc. is a very attractive one. We discussed it first in relation to your concept of a pre-clinical institute about ten years ago and again at the time when the decision to transfer pre-clinical teaching to Dundee was made.' He said, realistically, that such a project would require a much happier degree of inter-departmental and even intra-departmental cooperation than existed at present—'Desirable though such a course would be, and much as I would like to see it introduced', he wrote, 'I have grave doubts about the necessary agreement being reached, and enthusiasm aroused'. Professor Ritchie returned at once:

the prospective situation differs in one signal respect from all other previous ones, as it is . . . a case of "a good B.Sc. Med. or Die!" It is not, in my view, a matter of inventing a cheap B.Sc. terminology for 2nd M.B. Professor Walmsley has publicly stated that Biochemistry is the important future facet of high-grade pre-clinical education, and it may be that the pressures involved will assist fusion to some degree . . . it is a matter of survival!

This then was the first decision within the Bute—that a new type of degree be devised. In a more formal document of January 20th, Professor Ritchie enlarged on his ideas of the last week. Any new sort of pre-clinical training would have to secure entry to clinical schools 'by reason of the candidates being

that small amount better than the standard pre-clinical students elsewhere'. Current medical students did not specially care for pre-medical science—they wanted to get into clinical work as soon as they could. Special conditions of entry would therefore have to be devised for the new science degree. A possibility was for entry to the course to be entirely by pre-medical exemption. An élite pre-clinical degree might boost the reputation of the pre-clinical school and so raise the numbers from the inevitably small level they would be initially. A critical element in this new degree would be Biochemistry, and a Chair for St Salvator's College had been requested for 1966.

In 1964, thought and action went on. Professor Ritchie and Dr. Bayne were not the only individuals concerned about the retention of Medicine in St Andrews. Professor Walmsley was also thinking hard. The Principal's support had been forthcoming from the start; Miss Janet Allan remembered clearly herself and Sir Malcolm, in the 'Nerve Centre' at College Gate, drawing concentric circles on a map of Fife in an attempt to see whether a reasonable radius would encompass a population large enough to support the clinical component of a complete Medical School. Although Kirkcaldy hospital was building, and would contain an almost complete range of specialities, it was felt that it would be too much within the orbit of Edinburgh to be a serious source of clinical material. Perth, too, it was believed would remain within the orbit of Dundee. Over the weeks of the earlier part of this year, members of the Science Faculty had informal discussions about whether they would in fact agree to support the continuation of Medical Teaching. There was real doubt for a while that they might return to their early eighteenth or late nineteenth century attitudes—that there were more important scientific subjects to be taught than medical ones. Professor Allen (Physics) and Professor Callan (Zoology) supported by Dr. Colin Muir, were three who voiced antagonism publicly. Professor Callan in particular had looked on the Anatomy Department accommodation, which would become available when that subject was moved to Queen's College, as suitable for expansion from his own Department. These staff members, plus some chemists, had felt for a number of years that the pre-medical courses taken by medical students were something of a nuisance as far as their Departments were concerned—the courses were short, light in content when compared to those of the pure Science course, and the students, they thought, less intelligent and less able. This was the difference between the era of Sir D'Arcy, Professors Robertson, Graham, and Irvine, when the Professor took the medical class himself. Now a junior lecturer tended to be delegated. There was also a difference in the pre-clinical subjects between the time of Professor Herring, who gave all the Medical Physiology lectures week by week and Professor Ritchie, who lectured seldom by contrast. In Biochemistry too, Dr. G.R. Tristram believed in 'getting rid of the medicals as soon as possible'.

While there was feeling against Medicine on the part of the pure Science Departments, there was decided support from not only the Arts Faculty in St Salvator's but also from St Mary's College. The Professors and staff here had always preserved a liberal attitude towards the twentieth century discords much in the Tulloch tradition—Principal Duncan, with especially Professors Dickie

and Forrester, were sympathetic towards many of Principal Wimberley's anxieties. Now St Mary's support for Medicine helped in tipping the balance towards its retention for St Andrews.

But while the other major problem was what would continue being taught at the pre-clinical level, and how it would be put together for presentation to the U.G.C., the other was where the hypothetical Medical Science graduates were to go to follow their clinical studies. Professor Bell—Dean by chance again in this 1963-64 period—was well known for his attitude. Professor Lendrum too was unsympathetic. These two would in later years refer to 'those Edinburgh Professors'—meaning Walmsley, Hunter, Hill, Douglas and Ritchie, who were 'pro-St Andrews and who were always going over to St Andrews[2] and were friendly with Knox'. Professor Dow's attitude at this special time was also felt to be equivocal—his views perhaps differing somewhat if in St Andrews or if in Dundee. Professor Walmsley's feelings were clear; he would never approach Professor Bell—or indeed any of the Queen's College Professors—to ask if medical students from St Andrews could continue to go to the new Dundee University, because he did not wish to be humiliated by them. He felt he had as a strong card the knowledge that so many students wished to go to St Salvator's for their pre-clinical studies. This knowledge had been reinforced by his recent experience of jointly allocating entrants with Professor Rex Coupland. So he never feared that students would all of a sudden cease to want to begin their medical careers at St Andrews. His immediate action was therefore to approach informally, by letter or personal visit, Medical Schools where he had personal friends—especially graduates of his own University of Edinburgh, and ask if they were prepared to take the proposed Medical Sciences graduates for clinical training.

Professor Ritchie, in his current post as Dean of the Faculty of Science, pursued his aim on a more formal basis. He prepared a written case for the retention of pre-clinical teaching in St Andrews and sent it to Sir Melville Arnot, Professor of Medicine at Birmingham, and presently Chairman of the Medicial Sub-Committee of the U.G.C. He wrote formally to Professor Bell, Dean of the Medical Faculty, and received 'a gratuitously offensive letter saying they (Dundee) would take one or two'.[3] This finally confirmed the view of the two Medical Professors that they must make other arrangements. With the knowledge and agreement of the Principal, they discussed the Oxbridge idea of students going elsewhere for hospital training but returning to St Andrews to graduate—but rejected it. They did consider whether the M.D. and Ch.M. be retained, but decided against. Perhaps they could have been a little more enterprising and determined, and explored the clinical potential of Kirkcaldy and Dunfermline plus Perth—but they did not even try this possibility. This was an instance of the background importance of the Ninewells project—in 1964 it was still unsullied by the delays and recriminations of the post-Disruption years, and it overwhelmed the thinking in the Bute as well as in the Queen's Medical School—Ninewells was not only out of reach of St Andrews itself but made the smaller, other, possible clinical locations for St Andrews seems ridiculously inappropriate when set beside its coming magnificence.

The paper recommended:

(1) that a School of Medical Sciences be established within the framework of developments in the Biological Sciences in St Andrews.

(2) that a three year course leading to a B.Sc.(Med.Sci.) should be offered.

Provision should also be made for an Honours year of study in any one, or in a combination of two, of the main degree course subjects. Implicit in the recommendation was the necessity for these pre-clinical medical studies to be within the course structure and regulations of the Faculty of Science.

In justification for these recommendations it was argued that the need for more medical graduates was recognized; the block was at pre-clinical level and therefore it was irrational to discontinue the established pre-clinical school in St Andrews. It was also argued that such a degree would meet the increasing demand from hospital laboratories, medical research institutes, and from industry, for scientists professionally orientated towards human biology. Sixty students was suggested as the starting number. Details of admission requirements, subjects of study, exemptions, honours courses and postgraduate studies were also included. It was stressed that this degree was not to be regarded as simply a continuation of the present M.B. Ch.B. 2nd Professional Examination, but now was a new project with new implications. The need to incorporate Microbiology, Pharmacology, and Pathology so as to satisfy the entry requirements to most clinical schools was also indicated, and recommendations for the institution of these were included. While the proposals in this paper were welcomed by the Medical Sub-Committee of the U.G.C. in December 1965 and by a large number of universities, they were not by the Academic Advisory Committee, which was concerned with the apportioning of subjects and teaching between the shortly-to-be split St Andrews and Dundee. The Academic Advisory Committee seemed to take the view that its primary obligation was to the new University of Dundee. The old University, however, firmly disagreed with this advice, and in its proposals for the 1967-72 Quinquennium, gave 'high priority to the establishment of a B.Sc. Degree in Medical Sciences . . . The Degree, which should be in the Faculty of Science but under its own Ordinance, should provide for Ordinary and Honours graduates, and should be so designed that its holder is qualified to apply for entry to the majority of British Teaching Hospitals' . . . The Bute staff won this argument against considerable opposition from Professor Callan in Faculty, and the establishment of the new degree was finally agreed in principle.

But this was only one half of the quest. The other was the outlet. The immediate response to the Disruption, the proposal for and acceptance locally for a Medical Sciences Degree, had come and gone. Details of the course would be worked out later. But as far as the outlet for St Andrews graduates was concerned, it was Professor Walmsley who had made all the investigations and who was thought to have made good progress. Professor Ritchie had also written, more formally, during his period as Science Dean. Walmsley assured

colleagues there would be no problems. He went around his many friends and came back with what appeared to be their agreement to absorb the St Andrews output—London schools, in particular, were to be a safe clinical placing. But as 1965 passed and 1966 began, the non-professorial staff in the Bute began to wonder if they had not been lulled into a false sense of security. As 1966 progressed, informal soundings showed that, for example, Oxford and Cambridge Universities were only prepared to accept Honours graduates from St Andrews, and there was increasing doubt as to how secure the other outlets really would be. Professor Walmsley was unwell over this year, and his illness raised doubts further.

Dr. Tristram had been appointed Professor of Biochemistry in St Salvator's College from the beginning of January 1966. He is such an important figure in the continuation of medical teaching in the University of St Andrews that he requires as full an introduction as any of his predecessors. Born in 1912, in Whitwell in Derbyshire, he was educated first at a Church of England School in Derbyshire and later won a scholarship to Brunts School in Mansfield. He was a student at Liverpool, taking his B.Sc. and later Ph.D. In 1936 he made the discovery that squalene was a precursor of cholesterol. In 1937 he went to Imperial College, to Cambridge in 1943, and thence to St Andrews in 1950 as a lecturer in Physiology. In 1962, he was elected F.R.S.E.—a rare honour for a non-professor. His brothers, father, grandfather and great-grandfather had all been Derbyshire miners, and so his was a very different background from that of the average Scottish member of academic staff in St Andrews.

It was Professor Tristram who, with Dr. Bayne, Dr. John Taylor the Senior Lecturer in Physiology and Dr. Jim Smith the Senior Lecturer in Regional Anatomy, became increasingly concerned. One day Sheena Douglas, Professor Douglas' daughter, asked him before he began his lecture if he could tell the class anything about the future prospects for Medicine in St Andrews. She was shortly to attend a British Medical Students' Association Meeting and wanted any information she could get. He put away his lecture notes, and spoke for most of the time which should have been given to Biochemistry of his views— his thoughts on the content of the B.Sc. Medical Science Degree, his ideas on the range of new subjects which would have to be introduced if the degree was to become truly acceptable, and most of all his fears that no effective means had been worked out of ensuring that St Andrews graduates with this degree would actually get into a Medical School for clinical study.

What he said reached the ears of Professor Walmsley, who left a message for him that he would be in his room at 3 o'clock that afternoon. One of the weaknesses of the old University was, and to a large degree still is, the rather quaint notion that its Professors are on a higher level than any other members of staff. In the small medical world of the Bute the Professors were, and to a degree still are, unable to accept the ability and good sense of non-professorial—or as in this instance, of *junior* professorial staff. In the larger world of the clinical Medical School the presence of other staff kept this balloon firmly deflated— Professor Alexander had the knowledge that Mr F.R. Brown was technically a much better surgeon; Professor Douglas was aware that the same applied to

Mr Walter Campbell, whose beautiful neatness was a joy to behold; Professor Hill was aware of Dr. John Morgan's shrewdness and experience, and was big enough to call him in consultation soon after he arrived; Professor Lendrum was sensible enough to accept Dr. George Smith's opinion, and later those of Dr. Guthrie and Professor Wallace Park, on a histological section, and so on.

Professor Walmsley was very displeased with Professor Tristram, and told him so; as a result of this meeting, they exchanged no words for a further six months. And as a result of this, in turn, the anger Professor Tristram felt at his exchanges with Professor Walmsley led him, with Drs. Bayne and Taylor, to approach Mr George Clark the secretary to the Middlesex Hospital in London who was attached to the Secretariat of the Royal (Todd) Commission on Medical Education of the day, and ask for information on entry requirements to the London Schools. When Mr Clark told these three that it was not in fact the case that St Andrews graduates would be easily accepted in London, and that they would all have to re-sit the 2nd M.B. Professional examination first, Tristram went straight to Dr. Steven Watson and persuaded him to arrange a meeting. This was done; Mr Clark came to St Andrews, and one of the most critical meetings in the history of Medicine in the University of St Andrews took place in the Department of Physiology, on Thursday, 23rd February 1967.[4] Neither senior Professor was present, though aware of the meeting. It was therefore Drs. Bayne, Taylor, Smith and Tristram who heard from their London visitor that there was no certainty that any St Andrews B.Sc. Med.Sci. graduate had an assured outlet to a Medical School in Britain. The reason was simple and had been overlooked by Professor Walmsley and also by Professor Ritchie in his earlier thoughts on the Degree; the curriculum at St Andrews did not marry with the various curricula of the possible recipient Medical Schools. They could thus give no guarantee of acceptance.

Great credit attaches to these members of the Physiology and Biochemistry Departments—and to Dr. Smith of Anatomy who was also one of their number but had a certain conflict of loyalty. In the subsequent days, the hero of the hour must be Professor Tristram. He went straight back to the Principal and put the problem to him. There was clearly no easy answer and the range of possibilities was again pondered. Nothing was immediately done, as the B.Sc. in Medicine had not been finally approved, and its firm approval was the pre-requisite for the attempt to establish the clinical connection. When the Quinquennial memorandum was prepared at the end of 1966, the arguments for the degree were summarised as just described, and all that was said about clinical medical training was 'We hope to turn the general assurances which we have received, all the way from Aberdeen to London, into three or four definite agreements from clinical departments to take those trained at St Andrews'.[5] This 'hope' was a calculated risk. The assurances given to Professor Walmsley—and some informal ones to Professor Ritchie—were now known to be unrealistic. But St Andrews University had to give an indication of clinical outlets becoming available to support their bid for their proposed degree; if they had not, it would have lessened the degree's chances of acceptance by the U.G.C.

However, all was well. Faculty and Senate supported the new degree. Informal communications suggested the degree would be accepted outside the University. But by now it was the spring of 1967, and on April 5th the Principal, after consultation with Professor Tristram and Dr. Bayne, wrote to the Vice-Chancellors of Birmingham, Bristol, Cambridge, Leeds, Liverpool, London, Manchester, Newcastle-upon-Tyne, Nottingham, Sheffield, to the Master of Queen's College Dundee, and to Glasgow, Aberdeen and Edinburgh:

> I venture to ask your help in the problem about the pre-clinical
> school at St Andrews arising from the division from Dundee next
> August ... We will have in St Andrews the established Departments
> of Anatomy, Biochemistry, Physiology (plus strong pre-medical
> Departments of Chemistry and Physics) ... Our long-term plan is to
> set up a B.Sc. in Medical Sciences which would serve a dual purpose
> [here he listed the arguments already described] ... if we do not I fear
> that existing strength may wither away ... Thus the particular
> benefits which St Andrews can offer would be lost to Medicine ...
> The question is: which Universities feel themselves able to accept
> qualified pre-clinicals from St Andrews, how many students, and on
> what terms? Would your University be willing to cooperate with us?

The Principal then explained the position of the loss of places in Dundee, and repeated the arguments for retaining 'the long-established pre-clinical School in St Andrews'. He said nothing about the saturation of pre-clinical places in Dundee which a number of lecturers in the Bute felt were being protested for just a little too much by certain members of the Faculty of Medicine and by certain members of Dundee staff in other Faculties. There was a distinct feeling that one or two Dundee Professors would be only too happy to see the attempt by St Andrews to retain Medicine fail. This feeling was probably unfair to most of their Dundee medical colleagues, certainly to those who were still shocked at the approaching Disruption.

Principal Watson went on to detail four possibilities. The first was the Oxbridge arrangement where the University with the Medical School recognised the St Andrews training as qualifying for entrance to it, but the Medical Degree would remain that of St Andrews. The second involved acceptance of the Medical Science Degree but required the graduate to take the other University's 2nd M.B. Professional Examination. The third was similar to the first—transfer to a Clinical School—but completion of all Professional Examinations at the University of St Andrews. This was precluded by the recent Universities (Scotland) Act, but the sentence following did not exclude for all time (as the Courier might have put it) the possibility: 'Any idea of the establishment by the University of St Andrews of a Faculty of Medicine with an Examining Board in clinical subjects carrying out examinations for its own degrees in Medicine must therefore be dismissed to the long term future. Even more distant is a Clinical School in Fife, though facilities in Fife are increasing'. The fourth was a firm agreement between the University of St Andrews and an existing Medical School in which an increase in clinical places was planned, or one of the several new Medical Schools, by which St Andrews would contribute part or all of the

intake into that Clinical School. St Andrews was having to offer its students to whoever was prepared to take them. It had no other choice.

By June 8th, the Principal reported that replies had been received by all the Universities approached; Bristol, Oxford, and Sheffield were sympathetic, as was Glasgow—which gave 'a probable promise to take a share'. Aberdeen could take 8 or 10 but not more, Edinburgh 15, Newcastle 20, and Dundee 5-10 but no more. Manchester University had written to say they wished to enter discussions for a joint school, and to investigate the fourth option further. June was going to be a busy month, for the Royal Commission on Medical Education were due to visit St Andrews in July. On June 16th and July 4th a 'pre-clinical curriculum Committee' of the Faculty of Science met to agree details of the new degree. The Dean, Professor J.A. MacDonald (Botany) was in the Chair. Professors Ritchie and Tristram, and Drs. J.W. Smith and J. Frame representing Professor Walmsley, were joined at the first meeting by Drs. S. Bayne and J. Taylor. The curriculum, terms, and arrangements for enrolment were agreed— the last were to be the same as those for students in the Faculty of Science. Students enrolling for medical studies starting in October 1968 were to be eligible for the Degree. The students of the previous year—October 1967— would take their 2nd M.B. in March of 1970 and the 'Ninth Term' (the one so many students disliked, the 'transition term') would be in the new University of Dundee. They would then graduate from Dundee.

In the meantime, the visit of the Royal Commission members was arranged for July 10th at St Andrews. There is good evidence from the letters exchanged of their sympathy for St Andrews, and their sincere desire to help. Sir Edward Collingwood, and Professors Fleming and Carstairs, were received by the Principal and by Professor Tristram and Professor Ritchie, who was also making a good deal of the running at this time, in their efforts to retain Medicine.

The very next day, with the blessing of the Commissioners, a deputation of Professors Ritchie and Tristram, and Dr. J.W. Smith (Professor Walmsley was abroad) met the Dean of the Manchester Faculty of Medicine, Professor A.C.P. Campbell, a friend and former fellow-lecturer of Professor Walmsley at Edinburgh, Dr. F.B. Beswick, the Deputy Dean, and Mr A.R. Anscombe, Dean of Clinical Studies and Lecturer, in the Dean's room of the Medical School at Manchester. Tuesday, 11th July 1967 became one of the most important days in St Andrews' long history of Medicine. Both sides were filled with pleasure at the smooth and almost unbelievably quick progress in agreeing option four of Principal Watson's letter:

> We are convinced that such a union is desirable, eminently
> practicable, and in the interests of both Universities. It is
> recommended that an agreement whereby all suitable St Andrews
> graduates be admitted to courses leading to the degrees of M.B. Ch.B.
> of the University of Manchester should be considered as soon as
> possible ... a small informal liason committee will be set up ... we
> believe that the combination of a degree in basic medical sciences
> from a residential Scottish University with the clinical training in a

large provincial university has much to offer to the applicants,
students, and staff of both universities.

There could be no greater contrast with the Peterson meeting of 9th December,
1886, than this. Here was cooperation with no hint of dishonesty or self-seeking.
Manchester saw what St Andrews had to offer, and was sympathetic to the
difficulties of the older University. St Andrews, given cooperation, would
respond at once. It would be easy to sneer that St Andrews had no other option,
but Manchester, too, was in real difficulty. It had more than ample *clinical*
material but lacked pre-clinical facilities sufficient to increase the number of
medical students to the level it desperately wanted. The parallel between 1967
and 1886 should not be missed, nor the contrast ignored.

The first output of St Andrews graduates to come to Manchester would
arrive in June of 1971 or earlier, and forty-five or fifty would be the total. The
meeting planned to increase this number to a maximum of one hundred by 1973
at the earliest. Professor Tristram, in his hand-written notes of this meeting,
said:

'Great cordiality. Various suggestions re cooperation. Required to develop
behavioural sciences in St Andrews—should be stimulus to development of
Psychology.' (The Department of Psychology, apart from a tiny remnant, had
been closed in St Andrews as part of the fulfilment of the Tedder Commission's
requirements. The Department of Education had also been closed and transferred
to Dundee). 'All senior medical teachers in M. v. enthusiastic (have been
consulted by Dean). Contents of pre-clinical courses need not be *completely*
similar. U.G.C. to be approached at any time by both U's acting in concert.'

He also noted the longer term possibilities when he got back:

The 1975 total of 110 is 10% of the stated national requirement and
could be achieved if further additional facilities were provided in
Manchester by the conversion of further hospitals to "teaching"
status. This possibility is an attractive feature of the proposed
union—attainable at relatively small cost. £90,000-£120,000 required
to modify the Bute and Chemistry. There would not be more than two
extra lecturers needed for each department. £90,000 has already been
allocated by the U.G.C. Microbiology, Pharmacology, will stimulate
development of more extensive course for pure science students.
Should attract good staff

his hand written notes of July 13th recorded.

The Principal wrote at once to Sir Edward Collingwood, on July 14th:

'We now have a draft union . . . better than I dared hope . . . I will see the Vice
Chancellor of Manchester (Professor Sir William Mansfield Cooper) on Monday
and then we will write together to the Royal Commission and the University
Grants Committee'. Sir Edwards replied by return with an enthusiastic
letter.

But the cheerfulness of the Principal was as nothing compared to that of the
emissaries and their Manchester colleagues. 'We got on so well that we were
finished by lunch-time', recalled Professor Tristram. 'So we spent the afternoon
celebrating with several drinks and cheerful chatting'.

On July 26th, the Principal wrote a confidential letter to Professor Walmsley, who was still out of the country, informing him of the treaty, as Professor Walmsley had made his contribution by earlier personal contacts with Professor Campbell. Principal Watson told Professor Walmsley that he was about to inform the U.G.C. formally, but that he thought it was unecessary and in fact undesirable to say anything to the Dundee side. He had had a number of complaints from individuals there, saying that St Andrews should not feel hurt at their attitude, and had replied 'that they (Dundee) had done the legal minimum but had been rather less cooperative than other universities'. He had also had a request from a member of Dundee staff who wished to write an article for the *Courier* about the future of Medicine in St Andrews which he had turned down. Sir William Mansfield Cooper wrote on his own behalf to Sir John Wolfenden about the treaty, and he certainly showed sympathy with St Andrews over its medical students' 'future difficulty in completing medical qualifications' as he put it. Various letters passed over the summer. Sir Edward Collingwood wrote formally at the end of July to say that the Royal Commission had received the St Andrews news 'with enthusiasm'. 'There will be no hitches from our side', he wrote. On August 24th Dr. Beswick wrote to Professor Tristram to say that Mr Symons, the Chairman of the University Council of Manchester, wanted his daughter to begin Medicine at St Andrews. On September 29th Principal Steven Watson with Professors MacDonald, Ritchie and Tristram met Professor Campbell, Dr. Beswick and Mr Anscombe at the Cumberland Hotel in London. Professor Hunter was also present, heading the U.G.C. Medical Sub-Committee. The St Andrews Senate approved the confidential news enthusiastically on October 2nd. Although there had been no press leak, Principal Watson wrote humorously to Professor Campbell later that month to say that at the Dundee inaugural celebrations, several Medical Faculty members knew all about it! Manchester's Faculty Board agreed on October 18th and its University Council on November 15th; St Andrews' Court agreed in turn on December 13th.

The University now prepared to give its success maximum publicity. Professor Ritchie wrote an amusing letter to the Principal at the end of October, with suggestions about how the press releases should be handled. He wrote very fairly about the separation imposed by Dundee, advising it be mentioned in the least controversial terms if at all, and indeed against saying anything which could be a source of resentment. He believed the comparison with Oxford and Cambridge should be stressed, as the three oldest universities having this Medical Science degree—and showed unashamed élitism in his advice on stressing the fact that applicants for it must be of sufficient merit if they were to be accepted. In December, articles from Manchester and St Andrews were published. Dr. Beswick wrote for *The Lancet*, 'playing down', as he put it 'Dundee's saturation of pre-clinical places'. Steven Watson's article was an excellent one:

'St Andrews is perhaps the last University, in the full mediaeval sense, in these islands. It absorbs its young people from Scotland, from England, or from any part of the world, into an intense and distinctive community; it has a very

high proportion of students living in residences and its remaining colleges can rival Oxbridge in length of pedigree'. But he was realistic enough to note its danger of proud parochialism. Of the actual agreement, he spoke of the two styles of life:

> Most (medical students) will go to Manchester, that is, those who first enter St Andrews in 1970. Until then, in the interim, they will go to several clinical schools; a few, the outriders, will go to Manchester and a sizeable party, the rearguard of a grand army, will go to Dundee.
>
> I will not dilate upon the distinction and advantages of St Andrews—or at least, on second thoughts, I will only note that it provides contacts between students of different disciplines in a way which Oxford might, if it lifted its eyes so far, envy.
>
> Manchester has a world wide reputation for clinical teaching which the human resources of the district are ample to maintain. It aims to provide hospital residence for students in a way which London may think necessary perhaps the day after tomorrow

... and he ended by referring to 'the four hundred year tradition of Medicine in St Andrews'. In this he was right. St Andrews had 'had the wish for Medicine' and Medicine in St Andrews would yet again not die.

Now that it was public knowledge that medical teaching was to continue, the next step was to work out the details of the curriculum. There was no longer any feeling of anxiety as there had been, and this made for easier and confident planning. A permanent pre-clinical committee was formed of the three professors. In May, 1968, an *ad hoc* committee was appointed by the Dean, Professor MacDonald, consisting of Dr. J. Smith (convener), Dr. Bayne, Dr. Taylor, Dr. Frame of Anatomy, Dr. Goodlad and Dr. Ingram of Biochemistry and Physiology. This latter committee suggested in late November that candidates for the ordinary degree of B.Sc. in Medical Science should attend three courses qualifying for 1st Science Examinations, four courses qualifying for 2nd Science Examinations, and short courses in three additional subjects. These last were to fit the medicals for their entry into the Manchester or other medical schools. Statistics and Sociology were suggested—these were taught to Manchester University pre-clinicals. The first year of study would therefore comprise 1st Science courses in Chemistry, Physics, and Biology. The second would consist of a 2nd Science course in Anatomy—systematic histology, basic embryology, and of a 2nd Science course in Physiology. Each would be about 240 hours of study and be open to both Science and Medical streams. In the third year would be a 2nd Science course in Biochemistry (including Microbiology) and of at least 280 hours. There would also be, for B.Sc. Medical Science students only, a course in 'Medical Science'. This would consist of Physiology and Pharmacology, of about 120 hours, and Regional Anatomy, Embryology, with Basic Pathology and Medical Genetics, of about 300 hours. Of all these, only Basic Pathology was wholly new. It was obvious that a professional pathologist, as would be found in a hospital of any size, would not be available in St Andrews, so it seemed best that this course should be taught as an

extension of Histology. For Medical examination purposes, the Physiology and Pharmacology could be examined by the Physiology Department, and Anatomy and Pathology by the Anatomy Department. Microbiology and Human Genetics would be examined along with Biochemistry. The ordinary Degree would then qualify for entry to clinical study.

As far as Honours Degrees were concerned, various possibilities were considered and some were rejected as too long for anyone going on to an M.B. Ch.B. course later. The best acceptable was thought to be a four years course with an Honours year in one subject of the Biochemistry, Physiology or Anatomy group. While this would imply less depth of knowledge in a single subject than the usual B.Sc., it would imply considerable knowledge of a number of subjects. Thought was also given to providing what came to be called 'exposure to clinical material' for these new medical students. The only element which had caused a slight difficulty during the Manchester—St Andrews meeting of July 1967 was the Psychology staff at Manchester. They had raised queries about just how much of their subject was going to be taught at St Andrews. To overcome their queries, staff of the psychiatric hospital at Stratheden near Cupar readily agreed to undertake Psychology teaching until Professor Jeeves, later an outstanding member of staff, could re-build the University Department recently transferred to Dundee. Dr. Dugald McColl Macgregor, consultant psychiatrist at Stratheden, undertook to give these lectures from 1971, by which time the first Medical Science group of students would be ready for them. Medical Sociology lectures were also required by Manchester, and as early as 1969 Dr. George Steedman Riddell, M.D. Aberdeen, of the Community Health and Epidemiology Unit of the Fife Health Board, was appointed an Honorary Senior Lecturer for that course. Help with Bacteriology was given by Proffessor T. Beswick (Virology) and Professor P. Collard (Microbiology) of Manchester, and Dr. Harris of the Medical Genetics Department there also undertook to travel to St Andrews to lecture; Dr. Moore of the St Andrews Botany Department was another who taught Genetics in the earliest years of the new course.

In these interim years, when the St Andrews pre-clinical students were still being accepted by Dundee University to complete their Medicine there, the University had also to cure its 'lop-sidedness' by extensions in some Departments and the opening of some new. In essence it meant that the number of Science students would increase in number until they equalled those in the Arts Faculty and in St Mary's. These were the years of sadness for Sir Malcolm Knox—he was regarded with disfavour as the architect of the Disruption by many in St Andrews—citizens as well as university staff. His early retiral was held against him by these critics also, certain of whom recalled what they believed were the great days of Sir james Irvine. It was not the difficulties of the West Burn Lane scheme of the 1950s—abandoned after public feeling had sought and obtained a Commission of Enquiry—which produced feeling against him, but the events of 1964 and 1965. Nor were his relations with his successor happy. But just as time would remove diehards from the Dundee scene in the subsequent years, so it would remove diehards from the St Andrews scene. These sad years made

Sir Malcolm feel happier in Dundee than in St Andrews, and his final retiral was to Crieff in Perthshire.

1969 would be the last year of entry for medicals whose course would end in Dundee. In this year, when the new Degree was being consolidated in preparation for the entrants of October 1970, Professor Ritchie resigned to become Secretary of the Carnegie Trust for Scotland. He had been an important figure in these recent years, quick to see the difficulties for Medicine and quick to realise the way through them. His was the sharp mind which grasped the essential need of a new type of degree, and he was the man who wrote the very first plea for retention of Medical training and sent it to the U.G.C. From his new post he continued to maintain an interest in St Andrews, an interest which was warm, sincere, and which he never lost.

His successor was also an Edinburgh graduate. Joseph Fairweather Lamb was however from North Angus. He was born on 18th July, 1928 at Balnacake, near Brechin, educated first at Aldbar Public School and from 1941-47 at Brechin High School, where he was Dux. He went straight from school into National Service in the R.A.F., and did his medical degree at Edinburgh, graduating in 1955. His house posts were in Dumfries and the Eastern General Hospital Edinburgh. In 1957 he graduated with Honours in Physiology at Edinburgh, became a junior research fellow in the Department there, and after a spell as lecturer in Physiology at the Royal (Dick) School of Veterinary Studies, he took a Ph.D. in 1960, went to Glasgow and was there as lecturer and senior lecturer before being appointed to the Chandos Chair. In 1969, too, Dr. James William Smith was appointed to a Personal Chair in Regional Anatomy. St Andrews had been slow to make such appointments compared to other universities, and this appointment was overdue. He was born in Shrewsbury in 1919, and matriculated first at St Andrews in 1937. As a student he had had an excellent academic record, and played rugby for the University. After graduation in 1942 he served in the R.A.M.C. in India. Returning after the war he had had thoughts of a career in surgery, but did not proceed with it. He had been at the Bute since 1946, and had established an international reputation for his work on the joints of the foot, for which his M.D. thesis was awarded a Gold Medal, and more recently for his work on collagen, including electron microscope and biochemical studies, with Dr. Serafini-Fracassini. In 1968 he had been made a Reader. He was an outstanding lecturer, following in the wake of Dr. John Mulligan as an illustrator in chalk in addition. No lecturer in Anatomy, perhaps before and certainly not since, has drawn the crowds as he did.

The fact of the new Degree was now widely known, and before its first students destined for Manchester had even appeared, a request was made from another university for inclusion too. In the summer of 1969, because of continuing Central Government demands that more places be created for medical students, the U.G.C. raised the possibility of additional B.Sc. Med.Sci. undergraduates being matriculated at St Andrews, to proceed after graduation there to Sheffield University. It was in fact a proposal to extend the new Pre-Clinical School before it had even begun. Flattering as this may have been to St Andrews, it was not a helpful proposal and created some alarm in Manchester.

For the arrangement was a firm one; St Andrews would supply the whole of its Pre-Clinical School to the University of Manchester Medical School from 1973 onwards. Manchester was to take no more than 50 students in 1973, no more than 60 in 1974, and in 1975 and subsequent years, no more than 75. The arrangement with Manchester was entered into on the basis that it was an exclusive arrangement, and both sides, especially, it must be noted, Manchester, were insistent it remain so. While it was feasible to produce a pre-clinical course at St Andrews to integrate with one other University's clinical one, it was not, certainly not at this time, possible to integrate with the pre-clinical course of a second, different university. While Principal Watson did consider the possibility of increasing the St Andrews intake to feed into other Medical Schools, further consideration, plus correspondence with Manchester, showed him that it was not possible. He informed the U.G.C. accordingly.[6] He did indicate to them, however, that St Andrews wished to increase its intake in later years to 90 students annually, when it could build the necessary accommodation and be given the necessary money for revenue expenditure. What the various negotiations did do was to cause Manchester to agree to increase the number of students from St Andrews from 50 to 75, to take over the 25 originally sought by the U.G.C. for Sheffield. This overcame the U.G.C.s problem of how to achieve the target of 3700 pre-clinical places by 1975, which the Government had demanded.[7]

Not only did Sheffield ask St Andrews to provide extra places. On March 17th, 1970 Principal James Drever of the new University of Dundee wrote to the Principal:

Dear Steven,   17/3/70

We have been taking our forward look towards 1980 and trying to establish some pattern of student intake for which provision must be made, suggested by Todd report that medical intake go up from 110-150. In this connection it was thought that I might approach you informally to see whether you thought it a good idea to allow any pre-clinical expansion that might be needed for this to take place in the University of St Andrews rather than here. I know that you have no difficulty in finding clinical places for your medical science graduates at present, but the old arrangement was a good one in many ways and you might like to consider returning to it in some measure.

It would mean in effect that we might earmark some 45 places for St Andrews graduates sometime after the middle 70s.

Yours,
James.

Principal Drever on his arrival had puzzled over why the St Andrews side medical students were not to continue crossing to the Dundee side; he said many years later that he had been able to see no good cause why they should not, but had been assured by Professor Hunter that the Medical Sciences Building arrangement could not be altered.[8] He and Principal Watson were good colleagues, and wrote to each other in terms which were friendly, in

contrast to the usual rather formal communications between academic staff.

Principal Watson, who on his arrival had found it hard to see the need for the Disruption, recalled, also many years later, his genuine sorrow at being unable to repair a medical bridge with Dundee. He had conversations with the Bute staff—especially with Professor Tristram. The opinion was that nothing could be done because the Treaty with Manchester could not be altered. The staff expressed their feelings sharply; they still felt they could have had just a little more cooperation in their anxious months of 1964 and 65.[9] So on April 28th he replied:

Dear Jim,   28/4/70
    This is all very awkward. You will remember that my original wish was to continue pre-clinical students going from here to clinical work in Dundee on the good old plan. At that time, however, it seemed that Dundee would not have any room for them. I had to cast round urgently to preserve our Clinical School. As you will know, we signed a Treaty with Manchester which will have the effect of sending our people from St Andrews after their B.Sc. Medical Sciences to their clinical work in Manchester. When it seemed that our expansion of Pre-Clinical Med. would go further than the outlets could be widened, we did have some discussion of a second Treaty. Manchester were alarmed at this and we have revised our arrangements with them to accommodate all our planned Pre-Clinical development for the next few years. Everyone recognized that there may be some students who do not want to go to Manchester who may make arrangements for themselves for their clinical training. But I think I am honour bound not to make any regular arrangement so long as our Manchester Treaty exists. If our figures should go up more rapidly than we detailed to Manchester, then we would have some surplus which we would be only too happy to see crossing the Tay Bridge. This would not certainly amount to anything of the order of 45 in the middle 70s. I am afraid this letter sounds a rather disappointing answer, but in the circumstances it cannot be anything else.

Best wishes,
Yours ever,
Steven.

Dear Steven,   30/4/70
    Thank you for your letter.
    I quite understand your problem, and if we are asked to increase our medical intake we shall take account of the full medical course and not merely its clinical stages . . . I shall try to leave some flexibility in the arrangements which may allow individual students to come here from St Andrews if they wish. The position in St Andrews will not slow down our growth in any way. It was simply that some of the Medical Faculty, themselves St Andrews graduates, felt that this

might be an opportunity to restore some elements of the old arrangement.

Best wishes,

James Drever.

On 21st April, 1970, the Medical Sub-Committee of the U.G.C. of the day visited St Andrews. Their members included Sir Robert Aitken the Chairman, Professor A.P.M. Forrest, Professor R.J. Scothorne of Glasgow, a friend of Professor Smith, and Sir Charles Stuart-Harris, Professor of Medicine in Sheffield. Stuart-Harris addressed the pre-clinical staff in the Bute and praised the experiment which the U.G.C. had in some quarters doubted would succeed. A small number—about ten—St Andrews graduates had arrived in Manchester, and had created an extremely favourable impression—these were those who became the first post-St Andrews Manchester graduates of 1974.

This visit set the seal of approval on the arrangement. From now the Pre-Clinical School would take off—Anatomy would include Pathology, Physiology, Pharmacology to an increasing degree, and Biochemistry with Microbiology. In this 1969-70 session clinical consultant advisers and helpers appeared on the scene, their skills covering a wide range. The 'home-based' staff included in Biochemistry, Professor Tristram; Drs. Steve Bayne, M.B., F.R.S.E. and George Goodlad as Senior Lecturers; David Thirkell, Ph.D., St Andrews, Augusto Serafini-Fracassini M.D. Padua, Ph.D. St Andrews, John Gilbert (St Andrews, later Professor at Heriot-Watt University), William Hornby (London), David Worsnip, and William Ledingham (St Andrews) as lecturers. In Physiology, there was Professor Lamb; Dr. John Taylor, M.R.C.P. Ed. and Dr. Charles Ingram, M.B. Aberdeen as Senior Lecturers, and Dr. W.G.S. Stephens, Ph.D. St Andrews, Mrs Cynthia Reid, M.B. St Andrews, John J. Ferguson, B.Sc. St Andrews, M.B. Edinburgh, and Martin Stanton, M.B. Cantab. as Lecturers. Dr. Glen Cottrell, B.Sc. Ph.D. (Southampton) was lecturer in Pharmacology. The Anatomy Department was smaller; Professor Walmsley and Professor Smith, Dr. John Frame, M.B. Glasgow, and Dr. Tom Murphy, M.D.S. Edinburgh, as Senior Lecturers, and Edward W.T. Morris, F.R.C.S. M.R.C.S. London, as Maitland Ramsay Scholar.[10] The Demonstrators were Allan Lloyd (Bristol) William Mair and Stephen John Tristram (St Andrews). In 1971 Dr. James Begg, M.R.C.Path., the Consultant Pathologist at Kirkcaldy became an Honorary Anatomy Lecturer, and Drs. John W. Buchanan, M.D. Edinburgh, F.R.C.P. Edinburgh, Alan W.M. Smith, M.B. Edinburgh, F.R.C.P. Edinburgh, and Gordon Mackenzie, M.D. Edinburgh, M.R.C.P. Edinburgh, M.R.C.P. London—Consultant Physicians—joined the Physiology Staff, in addition to Dr. Riddell. In 1973 Dr. A. Marr, a Radiologist, joined the Anatomy Department; Drs. Mark Fraser, F.R.C.P. Ed. and A.W. Blair, M.R.C.P. Ed. Paediatricians, Dr. P.N. Edmunds, another Consultant Bacteriologist, and Dr. J.C.G. Mercer, the Medical Administrator (SAMO for Fife) joined the Biochemistry Department. In 1974 a further Bacteriologist, Dr. John D. Barrie, joined the Honorary Lecturer staff.

A disappointment at this time was the loss of a place on the Scottish Council of Post-Graduate Education. Professor E.C. Meikle, once a candidate for a post

in Dundee before the War and through it a Japanese Prisoner-of-War in Singapore where he went to become Professor of Surgery, was now setting this new Council up. He sent the proposed establishment from Edinburgh in February; Professor Tristram wrote back to ask if St Andrews could be included. He pointed out that St Andrews was trying to establish Senior and Junior Fellowships to attract graduates at Senior Registrar and Senior House Officer levels. 'It is our hope', he wrote, 'that staff and students can be kept aware of clinical problems and that the incumbent physicians can be brought into contact with basic research of direct clinical importance. It would ease our task and provide encouragement if St Andrews University had a place on the proposed Council'. There was no reply from Professor Meikle.

The first B.Sc. Medical Science Graduates completed their Manchester Degrees in 1974. The 'lost legion' as they were called at first, integrated well enough but perhaps never to the extent that students from St Andrews and Dundee had done. Their high excellence impressed on all sides; Manchester staff agreed that their most striking attribute was their knowledge of Anatomy. For this they had Professor Smith to continue to thank as long as he was in the Department; Dr. Cynthia Reid, too, who moved to Anatomy from Physiology very soon after Professor Lamb's arrival, was also a first-class tutor and lecturer.

In 1973, Professor Tristram, now Vice-Principal of the University, realised that the Manchester agreement, which had been for three years in the first instance, was set to run out unless it was extended and put on a truly permanent basis. As things stood in 1973, students who had just matriculated for the first time in St Andrews that year might find themselves with no outlet if this was not done. Once again credit has to go to Professor Tristram for his prompt assessment and his prompt action. The story can be shortly told: he negotiated a permanent Treaty, requiring five years' notice by either side for revocation. Because of its importance, it merits recording in full detail.[11, 12]

As can be imagined, its preparation went through several drafts. The University and its medicals were grateful for the help given them by Walter Borthwick, the University Solicitor. It was he who was the legal adviser, and who made the document what it finally was. In May of 1973, Professor Lionel Butler as Vice-Principal wrote to Sir Robert Aitken of the U.G.C. with the news that this definitive agreement was in prospect between St Andrews and Manchester. The slightly difficult question of numbers was included—the previous month Sir Robert had written mentioning the possibility that 'extra' St Andrews students might be diverted to the Welsh National School of Medicine—but as with Dundee, the possibility had to be excluded. Nevertheless, a number of St Andrews graduates did go to on to the National University of Wales, establishing a short-lived Welsh connection. But the Manchester connection was the important one, and Professor Tristram went there on May 16th to ensure that the agreement would be reviewed for 1975 and onwards from that date. St Andrews will for all time be in his debt for his contribution to the continuance of Medical Teaching; this continuation in itself was of real and lasting significance to the Old University, as future years might very well show. With his name must

go those of Dr. Steve Bayne, Dr. John Taylor, and, especially for his help in constructing the new curriculum and in the next years for giving St Andrews Medical Science graduates their outstanding reputation as anatomists, Professor Jim Smith.

20

Consolidation and Expansion after the first chance taken: 1974-85

In the twenty years from the end of the Second World War until the Disruption, the substance of the Medical Curriculum in the clinical years changed enormously. At the end of 'Sonny' Alexander's time as Professor of Surgery, his operation list still included weekly dissections of tuberculous neck glands in children; the antibiotic treatment of tuberculosis and the era of safe milk were just arriving. After operations, patients received fluid replacement by rectal infusions; intravenous infusions were reserved for those most seriously ill. In Medicine, the ravages of rheumatic valvular disease of the heart still led to congestive cardiac failure, and oedema was treated by Southey's tubes inserted beneath the skin of the legs. In Obstetrics, patients with the fits of eclampsia were treated by rectal infusions of the drug Avertin. The Resident Medical Officers' duties were laid down in strict detail which had not changed for the previous twenty years; 'every Visiting Medical Officer' had it 'in his power summarily to suspend the Resident Medical Officer who has been assigned to him, for any insubordination or dereliction of professional duty'; Professor Fairlie dismissed on the spot a girl resident who asked leave to get married.[1] By 1965 so much had changed; some diseases had all but gone, and other new ones had appeared. Therapy and diagnosis were revolutionised.

But in the 1964-65 Academic Year, the syllabus for Anatomy, and the syllabus for Physiology, and those for Pathology and Bacteriology, were as they had been for fifty years:

> Every course (in Anatomy) includes lecture demonstrations, dissections, radiographic demonstrations, and tutorials ... The Principles of Anatomy, tissue and systems of the body, early stages of development ... lectures are correlated with the part of the body being dissected and the functional, developmental, and microscopic anatomy of the various regions are considered in conjunction with their topographical Anatomy ... In the senior course special consideration is given to the Anatomy of the central and peripheral nervous systems ...

> The Course of Physiology and Biochemistry for medical students extends over 5 terms ... Junior Daily Lectures throughout the first 3 terms cover the function and regulation of the organs and systems of

the living body, supplemented by tutorial classes and appropriate demonstrations ... in the Senior Class, courses in applied Physiology and Biochemistry emphasise the application of certain aspects of the subjects and introduce the medical student to physiological methods used in clinical practice ...

In Pathology, fundamental facts and principles of Pathology are first taught, followed by Pathology of Special Systems ...

In Bacteriology, fundamental and biological aspects of bacteriology, general principles of infection, immunity and allergy are taught ... Later, the systematic study of the principal disease-producing bacteria, viruses, protozoa, and fungi is carried on ...

St Andrews would now have to include all three subjects in its B.Sc. Med. Sci. Degree, and would have to move forward very fast to keep pace with rapid developments in these same pre-clinical and early clinical subjects. The course would not only have to teach the traditional Anatomy and Physiology, but Biology, Genetics, and not only the new Physiology and Biochemistry, but the new Micro-biology, as Bacteriology was beginning to be called, with Pathology and Pharmacology in addition. While the Physiology Department had already incorporated all the new Biochemistry and Pharmacology into it, the Anatomy Department had now to begin its conversion, with Pathology as its other major arm.

Pathology began to be incorporated with help from Professor Colin Campbell of Manchester, the Dean at the time of the original treaty. Specimens from Manchester were supplemented with a number from Kirkcaldy and a few from Perth. Dr. John Frame, the lecturer in Histology, began to teach basic Pathology both naked-eye and microscopic. Professor Walmsley's war-time experience as a histopathologist proved valuable at this time, but the brunt of the teaching was borne by Dr. Frame. His Pathology 'department' in the 'cabin' on the right of the front door of the Bute was regarded with horror by graduates of previous years or by members of reunion clubs, who remembered the pleasant botanical gardens Professor Geddes had envied so many years before. But there was nowhere else for it to go. It housed the electron microscope, where Professor Smith and Dr. Serafini-Fracassini carried out much of their research work on the structure of collagen.

In 1972 Professor Walmsley retired. His health had not been good in the recent past, but improved considerably then and indeed in later years. Totally honourable, punctilious in manners and in his dealings with others, and showing a generous loyalty to his students and especially to his staff—who trusted him in turn—he was the embodiment of the best type of Edinburgh medical man, and though never losing his first love for his own University, he embodied, too, Professor Hill's dictum of loyalty and love to St Andrews. He recalled his thrill when, in the post-war years, he went with Professor J.H. Baxter of St Mary's to inspect some bones unearthed between South Street and Market Street. They discovered a skull, and other bones, which had been wired for anatomical display. The material was thought to be about a century old, and this proof of Anatomical teaching at that time in St Andrews brought very near to him one of

his special heroes, his predecessor Dr. Reid. He looked forward too: 'My proudest service to St Andrews', he said twelve years after his retiral, 'was to have helped to preserve Medicine for her. I know I only helped a little'.[2]

But a new sort of professor was going to be required. It was a little like the time of Dr. Briggs, a century and a half before. The new appointee would require to develop not only Anatomy but another subject—this time Pathology, as well. And so Professor Walmsley's successor would have to be very different from him; Professor David Brynmor Thomas came to this role and did prove himself very different, both in character and in his management of the department. He was born on 11th October 1930, at Cefn-Coed-y-Cymmer in Brecon-shire. After schooling in Wales, he went to University College in the University of London in 1949, when he was awarded a Bucknill Scholarship, and in 1955 he won the Suckling Prize in Obstetrics and Gynaecology and was editor of the students' magazine. After graduating B.Sc. with Anatomy as a special Honours subject, and M.B., B.S., in 1956, he held pre-registration house posts in U.C.H. including one with Professor W.C.W. Nixon, Professor of Obstetrics and Gynaecology and a famous teacher. He did no National Service. After a further house surgeon's post in the Royal Northern Hospital in 1957, he went to Neath as a surgical registrar, but then turned to Anatomy. He was a demonstrator in Bristol University in 1959-61, and then again altered direction, becoming an assistant in Pathology in Oxford in 1963-65, and finally lecturer and senior lecturer in Anatomy once again in Birmingham till 1967, when he was appointed senior lecturer in charge of the Sub-Department of Histology and Cellular Biology. Before his appointment to St Andrews, he took the M.R.C. Path. As much of his experience had been in Pathology as in Anatomy, he regarded himself as a Pathologist—he did not even take orals in the Anatomy Degree Examination after his arrival at the Bute—a Pathologist tasked with developing the other arm of the Bute Chair. The Pathology he introduced was, as the new title of the Department indicated, 'Experimental'—it included basic research in Cell Biology, Immunology, but not the traditional organ Pathology or micro-scopic Pathology of the hospital routine reporting bench. There was a degree of division, inevitably, between this new element in the Department and the traditional anatomists, and each of these pursued their own lines of research. The new element was however just what was required for the B.Sc. Med. Sci. with its emphasis on a high grade of knowledge in Cell Biology; the introduction, and development of it was Professor Thomas' considerable and welcome contribution. Since Manchester University did not want specialised organ Pathology taught to the St Andrews students, there was no need to extend the teaching side beyond Dr. Frame's course; in fact, after Professor Thomas' arrival, many of the large specimens used in Professor Walmsley's time were no longer required.

Now that Anatomy had its other arm developed, the years could come and go as they had done before 1967, except that the main clinical school was not twenty-five minutes away, but six or seven hours. The aim of the curriculum, to match the Manchester one but in greater depth, was achieved. The Department of Bacteriology and Virology in Manchester, in fact, requested that St Andrews

teach a little less—the knowledge St Andrews students were bringing with them was sufficiently greater than that of their pre-clinical opposite numbers that difficulties arose when the groups merged. The clinical back-up from Kirkcaldy was very good; Dr. Serafini-Fracassini on his arrival was particularly impressed how high the standard was. This was not surprising since the Kirkcaldy senior staff were largely Edinburgh trained, and several had teaching connections with the Medical Faculty in Edinburgh or clinical sessions in Edinburgh hospitals. Physiology, Biochemistry and Microbiology, and Anatomy and Pathology all maintained their Honorary Lecturers in subjects usefully associated with their own curricula. These lecturers brought patients to the Bute for clinical demonstrations of appropriate conditions; inborn errors of metabolism, endocrine disease, special eye and ear conditions, radiological studies including the new invasive techniques as they came along, and so on. Dr. J.D. Barrie played a great part in the development of Medical Microbiology and deserves special mention. St Andrews pre-clinical medicals enjoyed a good deal more clinical input than they had ever done in the days before 1967. The extent of this input was largely unknown, and merits recognition and record.

Not all communications with Dundee were lost, however. St Andrews staff attended the funeral of Professor Alexander in 1968—Professor Lowe remembered with respect his dignified, gentlemanly manners when he attended him during his last illness, and St Andrews staff mourned the death of Professor Patrick the next year. Mr F.R. Brown died at this time also. Over the 1970s enough graduates in the Dundee Medical Faculty to matter continued to regret the futility of the Disruption. This decade saw the decline in financial support and political enthusiasm for the Robbins expansion of the previous one, and towards its end, the recognition that a University degree was in certain respects almost a disadvantage in obtaining one's first employment began to dawn on the current generation of graduates, especially those from the new universities. Reductions in Dundee could no longer be blamed on the policy of the University Court of St Andrews—this reality also dawned on Dundee staff—and the lopsidedness of St Andrews remained a nagging fear to her staff also.

In 1973, a revision of the Medical Science curriculum was undertaken by a sub-committee of the Faculty of Science under the convenership of Professor F.D. Gunstone, a member of staff more aware than many of the necessity of high standards if St Andrews was to survive. The principle already laid down, that medical students must take the full *Science Faculty* courses in their pre-medical subjects and not, as before 1967, modified 'medical' ones, was confirmed; the Faculty of Science continued to insist on this. Thus all medical students were to take the First Science Course in Chemistry and also the First Science Courses in Physics and in Biology (Zoology) unless exempted from either of these on the basis of high level G.C.E. or S.C.E. passes. The course in Biology was not now to include that part of the course previously taught in the Department of Botany. In practice medical students attended the same First Science Zoology Course as science students. Genetics was to continue being taught—finally in the Department of Biochemistry—Professor Harris of the Department of Medical Genetics in Manchester, and a noted expert in the field, not only helped

to organise this course, but continued to come to St Andrews to teach. The Curriculum was now as follows:

Year I	First Science Chemistry
	First Science Physics
	First Science Zoology
	Medical Science Psychology/Statistics
	Medical Science Introduction to Anatomy and Physiology
Year II	Medical Science Anatomy
	Medical Science Histology
	Second Science Physiology
Year III	Medical Science Anatomy/Pathology
	Second Science Biochemistry Microbiology
	Medical Science Physiology/Pharmacology
Year IV	Medical Science Honours Anatomy
	Medical Science Honours Biochemistry
	Medical Science Honours Physiology

Those students who were exempted from a pre-medical subject took an Arts or even occasionally a Divinity Faculty subject in lieu. This impressed visiting older members of the U.G.C., who recalled past times when a broad education was necessary before a student could be accepted for the study of Medicine. But over the next years the subject chosen tended to become an easy option—such as physical education—or the subject from which they had been offered exemption.

Within a few years there were further changes. The Chemistry Course for first year medical students was separated from the First Science Course. The Medical Science Introductory Course in the first year included Anatomy, Biochemistry and Social Medicine (the last taught by visiting clinical staff). Biochemistry was transferred to the second year and a new Half-Course in Medical Microbiology was introduced in the third year. Human Genetics was (for timetable reasons) a somewhat unlikely component of their Medical Microbiology course—it was later transferred to form part of the Second Medical Science Biochemistry Course. In the later 1970s the subject matter of the courses was kept rigorously up-to-date. Professor Lamb, Tristram and Thomas were alert to maintain the impetus. Regular contributions from Fife medical staff continued. From 1978 medical students attended a Biochemistry course completely separated from the Second Science Biochemistry course. Practical Biochemistry followed traditional lines involving the acquisition of laboratory skills—this was seen as an essential difference between a basic qualification in medical science and a purely vocational course. This was very different from the system developed by the Department of Biochemistry in the new University of Dundee. This Department, one of the two there to achieve high academic distinction, introduced tape slide sequences, practical experiments, and assessment exercises providing structured units which students could move through at their individual pace of learning. In St Andrews, the Dundee system was

adopted by the Department of Physiology and Pharmacology in which audio-tutorial units were developed and a suite of computer simulations based upon that developed in St Bartholomew's Hospital in London was adapted to run on the Bute microcomputers.

1977 saw two events of interest for Medicine; the beginning, or perhaps more accurately the reawakening of an argument between other Science Faculty Departments and those of the Medicals over resources, and the first offer of re-amalgamation with the separated University of Dundee.

The resources argument continued into the next decade and its interest lay in the fact that it mirrored very greatly the arguments and counter-arguments of a century earlier. Then, Professors Bell-Pettigrew and McIntosh had waged a running battle in Senate over the allocation of resources, a battle only won for them by the far-seeing provisions of the Marquess of Bute and by the development of the Conjoint Medical School in Dundee. Now it was the turn of Professors Lamb and Tristram, with support from Professor Thomas, to fight against Professor Callan of Zoology, Lord Tedder of Chemistry, and other members of the Faculty of Science.

The overt argument was over Full-Time Equivalents. Each student for whose instruction a department is fully concerned is termed a 'Full-Time Equivalent' for resource allocation. Thus, the more Full-Time Equivalents (FTEs) a department has, the greater its resources in staff and money have to be, if it is to fulfil its teaching obligations to those students. The medical argument was simply stated: pre-clinical medical students do three full courses in their second year of curriculum while pure science students do two full courses in their second year. Therefore the Medical Sciences Departments should get corresponding amounts of financial support and staff. The Science Faculty in reply argued that the second year Science student does two second year courses and therefore spends half his time in one Department and half in another. Therefore each Department gets only one-half of a Full-Time Equivalent, as the student spends one-half of his total time at university in each. They then applied the same logic to the Medical Departments and said that because the student spends one-third of his time in each (Medical) Department, those Departments should get only one-third of a Full-Time Equivalent. Therefore, their arguments continued, the funding of these Medical Departments should be less. Since the U.G.C. did not give the University the extra money which would be needed, and if the Medical Science Departments chose to teach three courses instead of two, then it was for them to make the necessary economies. In reply, the medicals argued that the courses taught by them for Pure Science and Medical Science were the same in quantity and quality and therefore that Medical Science should be given the same funding as Pure Science.

Professor Callan, opposed to the continuation of Medicine in St Andrews after the Disruption, remained antagonistic ten years later. On 2nd November 1977 he wrote to the Dean of the Science Faculty:

Dear Dean,

Now that a new season of student/staff ratio calculations is about to begin, I would like to propose that Faculty debate the vexed

question of the weighting to be given to Med. Sci. students. When I first came to hear a few years ago that 2nd year Med. Sci. students each counted ½ despite the fact they were studying 3 subjects, this struck me as anomalous, and I have not changed my opinion. I see no good reason why undergraduate weightings should not be in strict accord with the number of subjects studied instead of as now, being dependent on the year of study. If there is justification for present practice, then I would like to hear that justification clearly spelled out, and its proponents available for questioning and debate at the Faculty.

Yours sincerely,
H.G. Callan

When the Science Faculty Establishments Committee met on the 21st November, they noted the current weighting for second and third year medical students as one and a half equivalents for each student in those years. While accepting that the higher loading of what they described as 'professional courses such as medicine and engineering is a general feature of such courses' (and this was a give-away remark; had *any* medical student who had been through UCD or the Bute in the days of the enlarged University walked into the meeting, he or she could have quickly told them how much more intensely medicals were obliged to work in their pre-clinical years compared to their opposite numbers in Pure Science) the Committee decided that 'the arguments for and against higher weighting for medicals was finely balanced', and that they would send a list of discussion points to the Faculty Council 'with no recommendation either way'.

Professor Tristram, who had not been present at the Committee meeting, was quick to reply. He criticised the implications in several of the points being sent to Faculty Council that the Medical Departments gave lesser 'medical' than 'science' student courses—the number of hours of lectures and practicals were the same for medicals as for second Science, not 'about the same'; they gave *full* courses, not 'almost full' and so on. 'Whoever stated that course preparation applies to lectures and not to practical work cannot have seen this department. Each year each experiment must be checked and in the Microbiology courses the academic staff work long hours'. The opposition clearly did not or would not understand the fact that the 'Medical' Departments taught Science and Medical Sciences at the same level and had identical laboratory costs for each group.

Professor Lamb, too, replied quickly. On 25th November he circulated a paper for a Joint Meeting of Pre-Clinical Departments to take place in the Bute on the 30th. He noted Professor Callan's bid to reduce the medical students' FTEs. As a counter, he suggested that Medical Science teaching be converted to a 'unit structure'. Medical students could then take all units spread over three years, whereas Pure Science students in each department would take some of the units in the appropriate year and Medical Biologists would take more units. More significantly, he wrote: 'It seems inappropriate that a grouping such as Social Sciences are represented on all University bodies, whereas Medical Sciences are not represented'.

While these arguments and counter-arguments were symptomatic of the realisation that money shortage would become worse not better, they also brought out yet again the unhelpful, rather jealous attitude which many academic staff had towards Medicine. For while the Medical Departments recognized the discrepancy between the calculated FTEs and actual student numbers created by the weighting of their students, the facts of the matter were that these medical students were attending courses and half courses which were fully equivalent to 2nd B.Sc. courses. The medical courses involved the same amount of informal teaching and tutorial work as the pure science courses in the same departments. Every second or third year medical student required exactly the same amount of staff time, and cost the departments in laboratory expenses and overheads exactly the same as a 2nd B.Sc. student. Professors Lamb, Thomas, Smith, Tristram and their staffs feared most of all that a devaluation of the FTE of medical students would make it impossible for them to continue to honour the Manchester Agreement.

The medically qualified staff in the Bute undoubtedly had a feeling of isolation. Although they got on so well with their Manchester colleagues, they had no academic clinicians nearby to give them support. The Kirkcaldy staff were no help—their appointments were entirely 'Honorary'. Had they received payment from the University even to a limited degree, it might have been possible for them to find a place on Faculty as occurred in Dundee. The Bute and Biochemistry doctors voiced their fears in their submission to the U.G.C. Medical Sub-Committee when it visited St Andrews on 6th June 1978. Their submission paper, under the signatures of Professor J.M. Howie, the Science Dean, and Dr. C.G. Ingram, the Pro-Dean for Medical Science, detailed the curriculum. This had been modified since 1973, as has been seen, but modification had been imposed from without; the fact that 'medical' subjects were now in the first year was a requirement of a statutory body—the G.M.C.—and not a personal wish of St Andrews medical staff. The figure of 80 students starting each year allowed for wastage and for the fact that a number elected to do their clinical training at Schools other than Manchester. The *minimum* intake to Manchester had to remain guaranteed so some extra students were essential to allow for wastage. Over a thousand applicants sought entry to this course at St Andrews each year; the entrance requirements were higher than for Pure Science students.[3] A new development since 1973 was the Honours course in Medical Biology—not a Pre-Clinical Course but nevertheless one taught in the Pre-Clinical Departments. Concern was expressed that a further increase in clinical teaching would be required by the G.M.C. in the early years of Medical courses, for this would strain local resources. On the other hand, the 1974 reorganisation of the National Health Service had given Fife the chance to develop its medical services and this chance was being happily taken; Fife was, like the Central Region of Scotland, making up ground considerably on more favoured regions of the country. But most concern of all was expressed at the poor resources being offered to the Pre-Clinical Departments both in financial provision and in staff provision—and student/staff ratios were quoted to support this claim.[4] Professor Lamb went further in his views; he asked for a

separate Faculty or Sub-Faculty of Medicine with an appropriate U.G.C. rating for its students. He and his colleagues also asked for improved travel allowances and facilities (noting as ever that allowances to NHS staff were much higher), increased provision of medical journals, and of audiovisual aids.

The Medical Sub-Committee of the U.G.C., under the Chairmanship of Professor A.D.N. Greenfield from Nottingham, included Professor G.J. Romanes from Edinburgh and Professor A.C. Turnbull, once a colleague of Professor James Walker, from the Maternity Department in Oxford. While they were not prepared as yet to agree to the institution of a Medical Faculty with its own Ordinances, they deplored the inadequate resources provided to the St Andrews Pre-Clinical Department. They described as 'appalling' the student/staff ratios, for of course the U.G.C., in recognition of the fact that medical students cover more work than science students, weighted them higher at 8/1 instead of the 10/1 for Pure Science. (This fact was ignored by the anti-medical voices in the Science Faculty). The U.G.C. Sub-Committee agreed also with the medically-qualified staff that the teaching of two subjects within one Department was unsatisfactory, and they made it clear that, for proper teaching coverage of each of these subjects, a minimum number of staff was essential and that St Andrews was operating below that minimum.

The other event of 1977 was the 'open letter' sent by Professor Lord Tedder to the University Court of Dundee University. Lord Tedder, son of Marshal of the Royal Air Force Viscount Tedder whose report resulted in the setting up of Queen's College and the dissolution of the U.C.D. Council and Governors, and who had moved from the Chair of Chemistry in Dundee to the Purdie Chair in St Andrews, wrote to Dundee proposing that re-amalgamation of the Universities be considered. As well as writing to the Court, he wrote publicly to the Association of University Teachers in the two Universities, 'just in case the Dundee Court suppressed my letter'.[5] When news of the letter became known in Dundee, Mr Alan Brown, Secretary to the Faculty of Medicine from 1962 to May 1982, wrote to Lord Tedder pledging his support: 'more power to your elbow', he said. He was well aware of where the feelings of the medicals still lay.[6] As Professor Sir Donald Douglas put it: 'We missed the interesting students we used to get from the Bute'. The St Andrews input to the Faculty of Medicine was something perhaps no-one had really appreciated until it disappeared. Mr Lewis Robertson, a member of the original Court of the New University, held the same view in retrospect: 'I could never understand what Dundee gained on being separated from St Andrews'.[7]

At the Dundee Court Meeting on 21st February Lord Tedder's open letter appeared on the agenda. It was clear from the outset that Principal Drever did not wish it to be discussed and he suggested that the Court should move on to the next item of business. At the request of members of the Court the document was in fact discussed briefly and received with interest. It was agreed that a Joint Committee should be set up and in due course this was done. In addition two developments resulted from the letter; the first was the provision of a bus to facilitate the regular transport of staff and students of all Faculties between

the two Universities and this is still in operation; the second was a much closer relationship and co-operation between the two Libraries covering not only books but journals and publications and this has proved invaluable and a great success. The Tedder letter was also discussed at length by the Senate.[8] In the next decade disagreement on student 'equivalents' and resource allocations within the Faculty of Science continued. The points made by the Medical Sub-Committee of the U.G.C. in 1978 were never taken up. On January 21st, 1980, Professor Tedder wrote from his large new Department on the North Haugh to the Dean:

'After years of expansion we live in a world in which the resources available to the University will, at best, remain static and at worst decline rapidly . . . one department can only gain staff, space or finance as the result of a corresponding loss by another department . . . The current demands for more staff, more space, and more money come from the pre-clinical departments . . .' He then went on to attack the Medical Sciences Degree. The main stream in Manchester did two years before starting clinical work, the St Andrews element did three. He attacked the 'norms' for medical students compared to science in their second and third years. He deplored the fact that while, when the B.Sc. Med. Sci. course first started, its students did exactly the same as other first year science students and were 45 in number, the numbers had increased to 75 and one third of the first year course was now 'given over to medical subjects'. The psychology and statistics courses should have been kept in the second and third years, he said. He further attacked the increase of new intake to 80, saying that if the medical departments had difficulty handling this number they should reduce it to 60. And as far as the Manchester agreement was concerned, he criticised the fact that forty per cent of the first year medicals came from the Manchester area and would return there. 'With the pressure for cuts the three year clinical course appears to be in real jeopardy unless we can establish that our course really is a medical *science* course and not just an elongated pre-clinical course'. He noted next that the British Medical Association had suggested there was an over-production of doctors, but that the current Secretary of State for Education, Mr Mark Carlisle, was worried 'about the serious shortages of teachers of mathematics, physical science and modern languages'. This was not a time, therefore, wrote Professor Tedder, to divert resources 'away from mathematics and the physical sciences'. In conclusion, he said that 'the pre-clinical departments are continually demanding more staff, more space, and more money, principally for students who are using St Andrews as a Junior College of the University of Manchester'. He asked that the numbers of medicals be assessed with a view to their reduction. The medical staff were quick to point out that the 'norms' were laid down by the U.G.C., as was the presence of medical subjects in the first year by the G.M.C. The points about student numbers, too they claimed were incorrect and misleading.

Professor Tedder's letter is of interest as evidence of the normal efforts which professorial members of universities make to obtain resources for their own departments—Professor Tedder was in effect demanding support for his own and related departments by attacking Medicine. But it is also of interest

as evidence of antipathy to Medicine and perhaps especially to medically qualified staff. Professor Tedder himself believed that most of the opposition to his 1977 suggestion of re-amalgamation from within St Andrews came 'from the medicals';[9] it is possible this belief affected his attitude to some degree in 1980. The picture remained that of the 1880s, with Professor Heddle being replaced in 1980 by Professor Tedder. The 1980 incumbent of the Chandos Chair, Professor Lamb, in the tradition of his predecessor Professor Pettigrew, replied at once in a paper to his colleagues but designed for a wider circulation, on January 31st 1980:

Medical Science in St Andrews

In my view there is a continuing problem about the distribution of resources within the Faculty of Science. On most issues we are simply outvoted. I think our situation will worsen with time, as medical students are set to increase to the mid-1980s, whereas the general student numbers are set to decline.

One possible solution is to form a Faculty of Medical Science containing our 6 subject groups. This is the pattern in all other U.K. medical schools . . .

Medical students are unique in the University in being dedicated to one course, with none changing to other subjects. The students attracted to St Andrews to do Medicine are, therefore, attracted by us, who then teach them. (Medical Biology students are probably similar in this respect). The presence of these students has not, in the past, kept out pure science students, as we have never met our target. The current income from Medical Science and Medical Biology is about £1,000,000 per annum (10% of total income). Of this, about half is spent on our departments (salaries of staff, secretaries, and technicians); the rest, and all our Pure Science money, goes elsewhere. This clear picture of underfunding has been pointed out by both the U.G.C., the Quaestor, myself, Professor Tristram and Professor Thomas, with remarkably little result. In a separate Faculty I think we would stand a better chance of getting it, as it is then a 1 to 1 situation . . .

The style and word usage in this paper dates it clearly in the 1975-85 decade. Like Professor Tedder, Professor Lamb made contentions which were not strictly true—the uniqueness of the medical student, for example, in the part of the paper quoted being hardly accurate. He too used special pleading. But on the question of the amount of income the medicals brought into the Faculty and so into the University he was, as will be seen, on surer ground.

It is however necessary to see this conflict against a much wider background. If this is not done, the opinion of Professor Lendrum, that 'St Andrews always said it wanted a Faculty of Medicine but when it got one gave it no help whatever'[10] might well be correct, and very just. But the antagonism against Medicine in St Andrews was not an isolated phenomenon. Jealousy is not unknown amongst academics, and the medically-qualified members of university staffs had incurred jealousy because of their higher rates of pay and in more

recent years the growing power and skill of the British Medical Association as their Trade Union. The Association of University Teachers had refused and would continue to refuse to allow the pre-clinical medical teachers to be represented by the B.M.A. in negotiations over pay and conditions of service, and in the next years would refuse to allow pay increases to clinical teachers granted by the Doctors' and Dentists' Pay Review Body. This conflict remains a source of considerable trouble in British Universities. One result has been an inevitable diminution in numbers of the best medical graduates entering Pre-Clinical Medicine. The problem was certainly not confined to St Andrews alone. The particular difficulty in St Andrews was that there was no *clinical* staff component in support.[11]

Although many in St Andrews were unaware of the fact, the Pre-Clinical School was beginning to attract an interest out of all proportion to its size and precarious constitution. In Manchester, one of the most solidly based universities in the kingdom, St Andrews was by no means a 'Junior College' as far as its Medical Science students were concerned. While many Manchester staff and students were bred in a very large city, relations between them and the University of St Andrews remained cordial and cooperative. Manchester as a great industrial city and cultural centre had no sense of inferiority towards St Andrews, and so looked for no insults. 'We were always on the same wavelength with Manchester' said Professor Serafini-Fracassini. This friendship gave the lie to the assertion that St Andrews, because of its isolation and sense of snobbish superiority, would always be unable to achieve happy relations with an industrial city and the attitudes found in such a city. Certain individuals in Dundee, as the years passed and fewer and fewer medical staff were left who remembered the enlarged University of Sir Thomas Thornton, undoubtedly retained a suspicious attitude of this sort. Professor R.G. Mitchell, the second James Mackenzie Professor of Child Health and arguably the best Dundee Medical Faculty Dean since the Disruption, felt uneasy that certain totally new members of Dundee medical staff were going to live in St Andrews, and that some had declared warmth for the University there. He argued that it was wrong for staff to live so far from their work[12]—while it was apparently quite satisfactory for a person to live fifteen or twenty miles distant from Ninewells in Carnoustie or Perth, it was somehow wrong for them to live fourteen miles distant in St Andrews.

St Andrews Medical Science graduates certainly travelled more than fourteen miles when they moved to Manchester. For those born and schooled there or in surrounding areas, they were returning home. But the substantial number who were from elsewhere found a great difference. The first contrast was size. 'From small classes in which everyone knows everyone, and their teachers, suddenly everything is much more formalised—an inevitable consequence of such a large institution', was the first impression. It was also an interesting one; St Andrews is regarded by many cities as a place full of formality. The change in standards of accommodation—'Victorian terraces where students had their digs'—was the second impression, and not a favourable one, when students remembered the residence life, and the mixing with others from other faculties, which they had formerly enjoyed. The first clinical year's mornings were taken up with

teaching sessions where groups of a dozen or so students were allocated to hospitals throughout the city; teaching was found to be 'a little haphazard', with teachers who had heavy clinical responsibilities tending to be less patient than they might have been. The considerable distances between hospitals meant hurried, even daunting, journeys on local buses to reach lectures. These too were very different in Manchester: 'the afternoon in a lecture theatre—enormous, crowded, 300 anonymous students and a very overcrowded coffee bar—none of this is guaranteed to create much of a comradely atmosphere ...' was the common feeling of this first clinical year. There was not the bonding there had once been with fellows on the Dundee side. But by now, size of Clinical School was all-important, and the bigger the School, the surer its future.

By their second clinical year, however, the St Andrews students were beginning to feel they belonged to their Medical School. Manchester's unique and excellent system of clinical attachments of two or three students in hospitals over a wide area—involving distances much much longer than fourteen miles—was described by several as being 'the high spot of my student career'. Students were welcomed to a degree unknown in the central hospitals, and St Andrews graduates were quick to appreciate this welcome. The best resident 'slots', as they were called, were in Medicine and Surgery; Psychiatry and Paediatrics were less enjoyable. The final year of revision reverted to nine o'clock lectures—attended with varying degrees of interest from those giving useful instruction to the occasional surgeon's unit which was simply not attended. In the afternoons they were on the 'snake'—the complicated rotation system which again involved travelling around the city. Internal assessments, because of the very large student numbers, allowed those who obtained a good report and passed the Spring month-long written and clinical examination in addition, to be exempted from the finals proper. About forty-five percent of the final year were so exempted 'giving us' as one put it, 'our last long summer holiday'. Their lasting happy impression was of the huge size and scope of clinical material in the North-West Region of England; this complemented their Pre-Clinical years in St Andrews admirably.

It was remarkable in these years of the 1980s that the name of the School stood so high. In a series of articles in the *British Medical Journal* in early 1984 giving advice to prospective entrants to Medicine, St Andrews attracted considerable space and favourable comment—bracketed with Oxford and Cambridge—and the agreement with Manchester was praised. Most other schools including Dundee were listed but not mentioned otherwise.[13] Young doctors began to appear once again in Scotland and England flying the flag of the graduates' tie after a gap of several years. Hospital doctors in various parts of the United Kingdom announced their Pre-Clinical School with pride. Older graduates in Dundee and district continued to deplore the Disruption, and were virtually unanimous in looking forward to the day when it might be healed. The policy of Professor Thomas in encouraging high-quality research staff in Pathology enhanced this arm of the Bute teaching; Dr. E.G. Wright's work, with Dr. A.C. Riches, on the regulation of growth in blood cells earned their team a place in a small select group in Britain and the U.S.A. collaborating in

that field. Dr. Clive Evans was another member of staff whose project on the adhesiveness of malignant cells carried great potential. Dr. J.R. Kinghorn of the Biochemistry and Microbiology Department carried out pioneer work in Genetic Engineering. In Anatomy, Dr. James R. Rintoul returned in the winter of 1979 from being Head of the Anatomy Department in Adelaide. His return strengthened both the anatomical and the medically qualified staff in the Bute; shortage of medically trained teachers became critical in the 1980's. But the main figure in Anatomy was undoubtedly Professor Jim Smith, whose research work had earned him an international reputation. His lectures became legendary—students from other Faculties came to hear him—and a generation of medicals testified to his memory as one of the best lecturers, in any Faculty, they had heard. Of interest too was the fact that his commissioned textbook 'Regional Anatomy Illustrated' was the largest, indeed the only major textbook to have come from the Faculty in the twentieth century. It was ironic that this book was not written and completed until after the Medical Faculty had disappeared. It was written with the help of two other St Andrews graduates, J.S.G. Blair, a surgeon, and Professor K.G. Lowe, the retired physician from Dundee. The drawings were the work of Dr. Tom Murphy, whose illustrations had completed smaller dissection manuals shared with Professor Walmsley. Sadly, Professor Smith, who had suffered progressive ill-health from respiratory disease while the book was being written, died before its publication in 1983.

Three other Professors appeared on the scene in the 1980s. The first was Professor Augusto Serafini-Fracassini, 'Gus' to his many friends. Born in Turin on February 26th 1934, he graduated M.D. at the University of Padua in 1959 and so could pull university rank on any British graduate. He lectured in Padua in Histology for the next six years, and in 1965 was appointed lecturer in Biochemistry at St Andrews. With Dr. Bayne, he was the only medical doctor in that Department. His work with Professor Smith on collagen has already been mentioned; his research interests in proteoglycans from normal and osteoarthritic cartilege, and in analysis of the enzymatic properties of connective tissue microfibrillin, continued. In August 1985 he was appointed Dean of the Faculty of Science. The second was Professor William Russell, who succeeded Professor Tristram in the Chair of Biochemistry in October of 1984. Professor Tristram's administrative activities had meant that he had given a rather disappointing amount of time to his Department in the years before his retiral in 1982. St Andrews was fortunate to capture as successor one of the greatest virologists in the country. Born on 9th August 1930, he took first class honours in Glasgow in Pure Science in 1952, quickly followed by his Ph.D. in 1956. He was a pupil of Alan Glen's School as Sir James Irvine had been. After a short spell in industry he became a research fellow in the Glasgow College of Physicians and Surgeons, next an international cancer fellow in Toronto, and next a member of research staff at Mill Hill in London, in 1963. By 1973, he had become head of the Division of Virology at the National Institute of Medical Reseach, a post he left to take the St Andrews Chair. He was a member of the Grants Committee of the Medical Research Council. Professor Russell was thus an established figure in the world of major virus research, and on coming to St Andrews he quickly

established research contacts with Ninewells and Kirkcaldy, as well as his already established collaboration with the Central Middlesex Hospital in London. A factor which had attracted him to St Andrews was the unusual strength of the Department in both Biochemistry and Microbiology.

Professor Glen Cottrell was promoted to a Personal Chair in Neuro-Pharmacology in 1985. Born in London in 1938, he took successively a B.Sc., Ph.D., and D.Sc. at Southampton in 1960, 1963, and 1981, had worked at Harvard University before coming to St Andrews in 1965, and had been promoted to Senior Lecturer and finally Reader in 1972 for his successive contributions to research and teaching. His Chair raised the level of Pharmacology towards the independent Department which the U.G.C. had looked for in 1978, as a consolidation of Medical Science teaching.

The contribution of another person to the maintenance and expansion of Medicine in the University of St Andrews during these years cannot be forgotten. This person was Principal Steven Watson. It was he who had written the early vital requests for help. It was he who had put the case for Medicine so excellently in formal and informal negotiations. Unlike the scientists who argued against Medicine, he saw the University over its five hundred and seventy years as a continuing *studium generale.* And as well as all this, it was the Principal who by his overseas contacts opened another door for reinforcement of Medicine.

The University of Glasgow Medical Faculty had like others the problem of a shortfall in clinical year entrants because of failures by students in their pre-clinical examinations. In late 1981, Professor Jennet of Glasgow approached Professor Lamb about the possibility of St Andrews Pre-Clinical School taking about 10 students each year who could make this shortfall up. The students were to be from overseas. And so in 1982, three United States, one Canadian, and one New Zealander came into the second year of the Medical Science course, to go on to Glasgow in due time. Nine came in 1983—again all from overseas. In 1984, the University of St Andrews was asked to take no more. But following the interest in St Andrews the Principal had created during his public relations visits to North America, Stanford University in California and the University if Virginia began negotiations to send about ten or twelve of their good students to take the St Andrews B.Sc. Medical Science and then return home for the clinical years. In 1984 the Public Service Department of Malaysia asked St Andrews to take twelve Malaysians into the first year of the Medical Sciences course—these were to return also in due time, and would in subsequent years form the nucleus of a University of Malaysia Medical Faculty. A small intake of Omani students, sent from their country with the same long-term aim, arrived that year also. A similar project was mooted for students from Malawi. This new source of students increased the numbers at a time when U.K. medical student numbers were set to fall—any such fall in home-born students on a national scale affected St Andrews, vulnerable as ever in respect of her Medicine. St Andrews was also under obligation not to take more than 20% of her total intake from these categories of overseas students.

As in the earlier centuries, the Old University was able to alter her ground

as the situation changed, but now had an established and well-respected Pre-Clinical School—which was not so a hundred years earlier. And so the period after the Disruption had seen not the missed chances in Medicine of previous centuries, but instead a succession of chances taken—the resolve not to lose medical teaching, the victory over the scientists who were eager to see Medicine in St Andrews die, the Manchester Agreement, and the transition to the modern Pre-Clinical Departments of Microbiology, Pharmacology, and Experimental Pathology, all of whose staff overcame their isolation from clinical academic Departments by their own initiative and excellence—all these retrieved for the University that element in her teaching which Bishop Wardlaw had instituted so long ago.

Of all these, it was the Manchester Agreement which had enabled Medicine to survive, and the Pre-Clinical School to begin to make its name. It was the subject of scorn by some, not surprisingly. Dr. Hamish Watson, the able and confident Post-Graduate Dean in the Faculty of Medicine in Dundee and a strong critic in 1967 of the Disruption, ridiculed it and dismissed the Fife clinicians who supported it as 'mice'; the St Andrews graduates who went on to Manchester 'were of course all sent to the lesser Manchester hospitals—to the equivalent of Maryfield'.[14] Totally untrue statements of this type were unkind and unhelpful. Certain Glasgow clinicians, in the tradition of some of their predecessors who had been glad to accept Chairs in the enlarged University but who were cruelly antagonistic towards her, had no doubt that St Andrews Medicine should be closed forthwith. (It has to be recorded that an equal number of Glasgow staff held the same opinion about Medicine in Dundee.)[15] On the other hand, General Medical Council opinion was strongly in favour of the continuation of Medicine in St Andrews, both because they considered its standards high and also because they saw it as a link to restore that broken at the Disruption.[16] In 1985, a further series of negotiations between St Andrews and Dundee could well have led to a restoration. Opinion of former medical graduates of St Andrews in Dundee was that while there was rank-and-file support for re-amalgamation there was not at Professorial and Deputy Principal level. It must be recorded that Dr. Adam Neville, the outstanding Principal of the University of Dundee, who had worked hard to bring Dundee University staff and Dundee citizens together without a great deal of success, did everything he could to make re-amalgamation possible if the negotiators desired it. The conclusion was, however, that 'the time was not yet ripe'.

Pre-Clinical Medicine was not only a good student element in the University of St Andrews; by 1985 it had become the source of a significantly large income for the University—another parallel with the nineteenth century—and of the three hundred or so students now entering the Faculty of Science each year, the eighty-six medicals were a significant proportion in numbers also. Research income from major Grant-providing Bodies for 1985, for the Faculty of Science, was weighted very markedly indeed towards the research in the Pre-Clinical Medical Departments. They overshadowed the others in this year. The Medicals were worth their inclusion; of that there was no doubt. But Medicine in St Andrews remained in these years as precarious as it had ever been.

Reductions in medical school intake, demanded yearly by the B.M.A. and the policy of the Government of the day to enforce cost-effectiveness in all things,[17] put not only Medicine but much of what St Andrews had taught so well over the centuries at risk of extinction. The shopkeeper attitude to work without the need for holidays or the frivolities of non-measurable activities then prevalent at high level in Government insisted that subjects taught at universities be 'useful' with an end-product in practical terms.

In May of 1985, a London *Times* leader threatened closure of St Andrews Medicine; this was nothing new. St Andrews could survive. Similar leaders and London-led demands had appeared regularly for two hundred years. But the Dundee Medical Faculty was also reported as being under threat of closure; this was something new for *them*. It was a serious threat; the Medical Faculty was the pre-eminent one in Dundee, Arts never having taken off there and much applied science never having challenged the more favoured Glasgow and Edinburgh centres of applied science or engineering excellence. Perhaps continuing threats would bring change and sharing from Dundee. Time would tell. During 1985, indeed, some Dundee medical students began to voice the opinion that 'two universities were a nonsense and should amalgamate' What is certain is that the old Medicals, who were the only students in the enlarged University of Sir Thomas Thornton who *necessarily* shared their undergraduate years between the then two sides, were with few exceptions proud to be St Andrews graduates, who looked forward and would continue to look forward to the sensible solution of Dr. Eric Mackay and his fellows coming to pass. If they die out with the passage of the years, this book is their record for posterity. But St Andrews Medicine has shown its ability to survive since Bishop Wardlaw's time, and if that ability continues, this record is its hope for the future.

References

CHAPTER 1

1 Dr. R.G. Cant—personal communication
2 *University of St Andrews—A Short History* (R.G. Cant) Part 1 p 5
3 *The Discarded Image* (C.S. Lewis) Chapter VII
4 Cant, *op cit,* Part II
5 *Votiva Tabella* p 130
6 *The Origins of Modern Science* (Herbert Butterfield) p 34
7 *William Shevez, Physician Archbishop* (G.O. Cowan) Practitioner *220* 816, May 1978
8 *Acta Facultatis Artium U. St. A 1413-1588* (A.I. Dunlop) Oliver and Boyd 1964 pp 157-159
9 For details of the hospitals existing in and beside St Andrews in Mediaeval times see History of Fife and Kinross (Sibbald) London 1803 pp 179, 270, 282 and Proceedings of the Society of Antiquaries of Scotland *X*, s 294
10 *The First Book of Discipline* (James K. Cameron) 1972 p 137 ff
11 At the time of the Reformation John Douglas, Provost of New (St Mary's) College, was a Bachelor of Medicine. *Acta Facultatis Artium,* above.
12 ibid, as above; Dr. R.G. Cant—personal communication
13 'Dr. John Makluire and the 1630 Attempt to Establish the College' (J.F. McHarg) *Proceedings of the Royal College of Physicians of Edinburgh Tercentenary Congress 1981,* ed. R. Passmore, Royal College of Physicians Publication No. 6, 1982, 44-58
14 *Votiva Tabella* p 199
15 ibid p 129 ff

CHAPTER 2

1 *On Scotland and the Scotch Intellect* (H.J. Buckle) p 42
2 See R.G. Cant in *The Origins and Nature of the Scottish Enlightenment* (ed. R.H. Campbell and A.S. Skinner) John Donald, Edinburgh, 1982 esp pp 51-55
3 *Memories of the Old College of Glasgow* (David Murray) p 170
4 *Royal College of Physicians of Edinburgh Historical Sketch 1925* p 41
5 *History of the Royal College of Physicians of Edinburgh* (W.S. Craig) p 359
6 *Votiva Tabella* Part II p 117
7 Craig, *op cit,* p 424.
8 'That in case the University will admit none graduates of medicine at any of their Universities untill they have a Professor of Medicine of their own but such as comes from the College of Physicians with a recommendation and a declaration of their being tryd by the said college and found qualified and that the College of Physicians will oblige themselves to admit none other

licentiate or fellow of the said College, but those that have taken their degrees at one of the Universities at home, and will join their interest with the Universities to obtain one Act of Parliament that none shall be capable to practice medicine within this Kingdome but such as have taken their degrees at one of the four Universities'.

'And when the foresaid universities or any one of them have gott a professor of medicine then the said College of Physicians shall be upon the same termes with which the Universities as though the College of Physicians of London and with the Universities of Oxford and Cambridge viz., they examine all their graduates that come to reside within the said Colleges' Librarys before they are allowed to practise physicion'.

'And last the College of Edinburgh as being the nearest to the College of Physicians should have most of the advantage of this proposal and therefore it is proposed to the Universities that they agree among themselves that the whole emoluments be divided equally among them'.

9   *The Social Life of Scotland in the Eighteenth Century* (Henry Gray Graham) p 457. At St Andrews, masters and seconders ate wheatbread, and terners ate oat bread

10   Perhaps the most outstanding Dundee Surgeon of the century, Patrick Blair wrote the first scientific account of congenital pyloric stenosis. This is a condition occurring in infants in their first months of life and now treated by operation.

11   Craig, *op cit,* p. 424.

CHAPTER 3

1   Craig, *op cit,* p. 242.
2   *Johnson's Journal of a Tour to the Hebrides* (Oxford) p 200
3   Craig, *op cit,* p. 242.
4   *Votiva Tabella* p 197 ff
5   Letter from Edward Harrison M.D. F.R.C.S. Ed, Meeting of Medical Graduates of the Scotch Universities held in London 5/4/1827.
6   Letter from Council of the Royal College of Surgeons of England, Council of Apothecaries, General Practitioners and Accoucheurs 14/4/1827.

CHAPTER 4

1   Craig, *op city,* p. 573.
2   *The Early Days of the Royal College of Physicians of Edinburgh* (R. Peel 1899, Pitcher) p 93-95
3   *Life of Sir Robert Christison, Bart. Vol. 1 p 159* (Blackwood 1885)

CHAPTER 5

1   The applications, with references, for Drs. Day, Paterson and Redfern are in the library of the Royal Faculty (College) of Physicians and Surgeons of Glasgow: Royal F.P.S.G. *Testimonials,* Volume 4. Two points of great interest arise from a study of these testimonials. The first is the large, extensive, and enthusiastic support for Dr. Day from sixty-four supporters,

ranging from Thomas Addison the Senior Physician at Guy's Hospital, through William Bowman, F.R.C.S., F.R.S. (of Bowman's capsule in the kidney), F. le Gros Clark, Surgeon to St Thomas' Hospital, William Sharpey, Professor of Anatomy and Physiology in University College London, William Fergusson F.R.S., Surgeon to King's College Hospital, James Paget, Professor of Surgery at the Royal College of Surgeons of England, to Robert Gordon Latham, M.D. Cantab., F.R.C.P., F.R.S., later Professor of English Literature at University College and late Fellow of King's—Physician to the Middlesex Hospital. Professor Day was also strongly supported from the continent. By contrast, the support for Dr. Paterson and Dr. Redfern is very restricted—from Edinburgh and Glasgow and a few English provincial specialists.

The second, perhaps more significantly because it is unexpected, is the clear evidence of the considerable status of the Chandos Chair and of its recent holder, Professor Reid. By the distinguished London medical men especially, Professor Reid's work and character were known and respected to a degree which can only be described as extraordinary. St Andrews and its medical teaching was seen in a very different light from its traditionally believed position of inferiority, although its limitations were also clearly spelled out. Sir James Clark, Physician to H.M. Queen Victoria and Prince Albert, wrote as significantly as any when he said: ... 'There should be a Chair at every University for the general student on a course of Anatomy and Physiological Hygiene: St Andrews can never be a Medical School and I shall be very glad to hear that she sets an example to other non-medical Universities by making available this teaching ...'

2 *The Healers* (David Hamilton) p 162 ff
3 ibid. p 166
4 University Library 13th June 1857
Sederunt Rev. Dr. Brown, Rector, Very Rev. Principal Tulloch, Mr Mitchell, Dr. Day. The Minutes of the 9th, 11th, 16th of May and 4th and 5th June were read and confirmed. Dr. Day read the Medical Circular as amended—which was approved of.

University of St Andrews

Regulations of the Senatus Academicus respecting the Education of Candidates for the Degree of Doctor of Medicine

I   Every Candidate for a Diploma in Medicine, upon presenting himself for examination, shall produce satisfactory evidence—
  1) Of unexceptional moral character
  2) Of having had a liberal and classical education
  3) Of having completed the twenty-second year of his age

II   Fellows, Members, and Licentiates of the Royal College of Surgeons of England, Edinburgh, and Dublin—of the Royal College of Physicians of London—of the Faculty of Physicians and Surgeons of Glasgow—and of the London Apothecaries' Company—are eligible as Candidates for the Degree of Doctor of Medicine, on producing their Diploma or Licence.

N.B.—Notice to Students. In 1860, the following regulation will come into force: Every Candidate whose Diploma or Licence bears a date later than 1859 will also be requested to produce satisfactory evidence from the Physicians in attendance, that he has regularly attended the Medical Practice of a recognised Hospital for at least eighteen months.

III   Candidates not holding any of the qualifications enumerated in the above Clause, must produce satisfactory proof that they have regularly attended lectures delivered by Professors in some University, or by Fellows of the Royal College of Physicians or Surgeons of London, Edinburgh, or Dublin, for four complete Winter Sessions, or for three Winter and three Summer Sessions, on the following branches:

1)	Anatomy	2 courses of six months each
2)	Practical Anatomy or Dissections	12 months
3)	Physiology	1 course of 6 months
4)	Chemistry	1 course of 6 months
5)	Practical Chemistry	1 course of 3 months
6)	Botany	1 course of 3 months
7)	Natural History or Comparative Anatomy	1 course of 3 months
8)	Materia Medica and Pharmacy	1 course of 3 months
9)	Midwifery and Diseases of Women and Children	1 course of 3 months
10)	Medical Jurisprudence	1 course of 3 months
11)	Surgery	1 course of 6 months
12)	Clinical Surgery	1 course of 6 months
13)	Practice of Medicine	1 course of 6 months
14)	Clinical Medicine	1 course of 6 months

and that they have diligently attended for at least two entire years the Medical Practice in some Public Hospital in Great Britain or Ireland, containing not less than one hundred beds, and having a regular Establishment of Physicians, as well as Surgeons.

Regulations respecting the Examinations

Examiners for Degrees in Medicine:	George E. Day, M.D. F.R.S. Professor of Anatomy and Medicine. Arthur Connell, F.R.S.S. L.V.E., Professor of Chemistry. William Pyper, L.L.D., Professor of Latin.
Assistant Examiners:	Andrew Anderson, M.D., Professor of Medicine in the Andersonian University, Glasgow.

William T. Gairdner, M.D.,
Lecturer on the Practice of
Medicine, and on Clinical
Medicine, Ed.

The examinations take place twice in the year,
commencing on the first Monday in May, and the third
Monday in October. The graduation fee is Twenty five
Guineas. In the event of a Candidate being found unqualified,
he shall forfeit one-third of the graduation fee, which,
however, will be accounted for to him when he passes his
examination at a subsequent trial.

Candidates can only be admitted to examination at other
periods by a special grace of the Senatus Academicus. The
graduation fee in this case in Fifty Guineas.

The examination by printed paper extends over three days,
after which each Candidate is submitted to an oral
examination.

All Candidates are required to give a written translation of
a passage from Celsus, to write Prescriptions in Latin with
accuracy, and to be so far acquainted with Greek as to be
able to give the meanings of Scientific and Medical Terms
derived from that language.

During the first two days of the examination, the
Candidates answer printed questions on (1) Chemistry and
Materia Medica, (2) Anatomy and Physiology, (3) The
Practice of Medicine, (4) The Principles of Surgery and
Midwifery. On the third day, they are required to write a
short commentary on a Medical and on a Surgical or
Midwifery case.

The Degree is conferred at the conclusion of the oral
examination by the Rector, in the Hall of the Public Library
of the University, and the Diplomas are signed by the
Professors of the University.

Every Candidate is required to present himself for
registration to the Secretary, on or before the Saturday
preceding the examination, and to communicate by Letter
with the Professor of Medicine, at least a fortnight previously,
stating what Diploma or Certificates he intends to produce.

JAMES McBEAN, A.M., Sec.

As the examiners receive very frequent applications
respecting the course of reading to be perused, they beg to
recommend the following works as especially deserving of
perusal:

Fowne's Manual of Chemistry (Candidates who have been
long engaged in practice are expected to possess, at least, a

knowledge of the general principles of the Science, and an
acquaintance with the ordinary Chemical Compounds used in
Medicine).
Christison's Dispensatory, or Pereira's Materia Medica
(especially the sections treating of the mode of action, uses,
and administration of Medicines) and the London, Edinburgh,
or Dublin Pharmacopoeia.

5　*Veterum Laudes* (ed. J.B. Salmond) Oliver & Boyd, 1950
6　St. A.U.L.Ms 37106/3
7　*Dundee Royal Infirmary 1798-1948* (Dr. H.J.C. Gibson) Wm. Kidd & Sons,
　1948, p 41
8　*University Education in Dundee—a Centenary History* (D.G. Southgate)
　Edinburgh University Press, p 119
9　*Twenty-five Years of St Andrews* (Dr. A.H.K. Boyd) Longman 1893
10　*Veterum Laudes*
11　Of interest is the series of illustrated guide books of Scotland, written by
　English visitors, at this time in the nineteenth century, which extolled 'the
　Links of St Andrews'. Dr. Samuel G. Green, in his guide book published in
　1886, wrote: 'But we shall be accused of giving way to the tendency of the
　times by thus presenting St Andrews as famous for its golfing ground rather
　than its University'. (Reprint 1985, p 161).

CHAPTER 6
1　*The Scottish Reformation* (Gordon Donaldson) 1960 p 49
2　*The Worship of the Scottish Reformed Church 1550-1638* (William McMillan)
　1931 Chapter I
3　Southgate, *op cit* pp 14-15
4　*ibid,* p 15
5　*ibid,* p 119
6　Jan. 8th 1876. Upon the table the following statement from the non-
　professorial Medical examiners:

　　　　　　　　Edinburgh, December 21st 1875.
　　　The extra-professorial Medical Examiners of the University of
　St Andrews have had under their consideration the report of the
　Visitors appointed by the General Medical Council in regard to the
　examination for the degree of M.D. held at St Andrews in April
　1875.
　　　In the report both the nature and the quality of this
　examination has been called in question and the extra-professorial
　Examiners therefore feel it to be their duty to submit to the Senatus
　a few observations in reply to the strictures of the Visitors.
　　　The Degree of Doctor of Medicine being attainable from the
　University of St Andrews under the two following different and
　very distinct conditions, namely:
　　I)　According to Section 18, page 45 of the Calendar for 1875-
　　　　76, the Degree of M.D. may be conferred under conditions

very similar to those existing in other Universities and upon any candidate who has previously obtained the Degree of M.B., the Degree of M.B. being itself obtainable under conditions and regulations very similar to those under which the like Degree is conferred in the University of Edinburgh.

II) The Degree of Doctor of Medicine according to Section 1, Degree of M.D., page 45 of the Calendar for 1875-76 may be conferred by the University of St Andrews on any registered Medical practitioner above the age of forty years whose professional position and experience are such as in the estimation of the University to entitle him to that Degree and who shall on examination satisfy the Medical Examiners of the sufficiency of his professional knowledge, provided always that Degrees shall not be conferred under this section on a greater number than ten in any one year; it is obviously enough, under the statute, that the University of St Andrews is satisfied with the status of its graduates as persons who have satisfied the requirements of the Medical Examiners—men whose position in the Medical profession, and whose mature experience as Examinees at various other Licensing Boards have secured the confidence of the University. Accordingly acting on the opinion and guided by the advice of its Examiners in medicine, the University has on several occasions, restricted the number of its graduates, notwithstanding the excellent testimonials by which the claims of these candidates were supported.

The Examiners submit that while a quite satisfactory amount of theoretical knowledge was required from the candidates, the positive assertion of the visitors that only 'a moderate amount of *practical* knowledge of their profession was required' is inaccurate and unjustifiable. The Examiners also emphatically repel the insinuation that the 'Answers given were of no high order, especially in Surgery and Anatomy' as one wholly at variance with the facts. They would simply refer to the printed questions which will bear comparison with any questions that proceed from any other board in the United Kingdom, while the written answers and the thoroughly testing oral examinations were sufficient in the opinion of the Examiners to justify the University of St Andrews in conferring the Degree of Doctor of Medicine upon its successful recipients.

As to the suggestion of the Visitors that preparations of morbid anatomy, microscopic or otherwise, should be employed in the course of examination, the Examiners see no objection to the adoption of the suggestion.

This reply was signed by Dr. Keiller, the senior external examiner.

[7] Southgate, *op cit,* Chapter 4

[8] *ibid,* pp 25, 26

[9] *ibid,* p 26

[10] *Dundee Advertiser* January-February 1881

[11] Southgate, *op cit* p 57

[12] *William Carmichael McIntosh M.D. F.R.S.* (A.E. Gunther) p 9

[13] *D'Arcy Wentworth Thompson, The Scholar–Naturalist 1860—1948* (Ruth D'Arcy Thompson) p 63

CHAPTER 7

[1] *Dundee Advertiser* 16th December 1874

[2] Dundee Royal Infirmary Minute Books—Regulations for Medical Students and Dressers, 1867.

[3] *University Education in Dundee,* D.G. Southgate p 65

[4]

M.D. DEGREE AT THE UNIVERSITY OF ST ANDREWS,
APRIL 23 & 24, 1885

Paper No. 1

MATERIA MEDICA

1.	EMMENAGOGUES	(a) Meaning of the term; (b) name specimens of the class; (c) the doses; and (d) indications for their administration
2.	HYDROCYANIC ACID	Give (a) its composition; (b) its usual strength; (c) doses; and (d) its incompatibles.
3.	DIURETICS	Specify (a) those which are applied externally; (b) those which are given internally; (c) their doses and modes of administration.
	WRITE IN FULL AND IN LATIN	Two Prescriptions (a) for an Emmenagogue mixture (b) for a diuretic in Cardiac dropsy

---

MEDICAL JURISPRUDENCE

1. A person is found dead in a ditch at the roadside with his mouth just covered with water. What appearances would justify you in certifying that the case was one of Accidental Suffocation during intoxication?

2. What are the chief points to be attended to in the examination of an infant at full time found dead under suspicious circumstances?

3. Severe pain and vomiting are complained of by a young woman after a meal, and death occurs in thirty hours. What is the probable cause of death? What poisons might have occasioned the symptoms? How is your diagnosis made?

Paper No. 2
SURGERY

1. In what thoracic conditions may Paracentesis Thoracis be required? Indicate the situation most appropriate for puncture in each, and describe the operation.
2. What are the symptoms of Potts' Disease of the Vertebrae (Kyphosis)? Describe its causes, progress, and treatment.
3. Describe any one of the partial Amputations of the Foot; give its ordinary distinctive name; indicate its anatomical relations. State the circumstances in which it may be required and the objections taken to its results.
4. Give the symptoms, diagnosis, and treatment of Calculus in the Kidney. Describe the operations of Nephrectomy and Nephrotomy.

CASES
   1. A patient with several 'stumps' in the upper jaw is affected with swelling over the antrum, on the same side, and inability to open the mouth. The stumps are extracted, but the disability in the movements of the lower jaw continues, and further swelling develops itself in the parotid region. The introduction of the finger through a gap in the line of teeth posteriorly admits of the recognition of a painful resistant massive swelling behind the hard palate, and on the inner side of the hamular process of the sphenoid bone there is an elastic point in this swelling. When this part of the swelling is incised a very copious discharge of foetid pus takes place. Some days afterwards smart and repeated haemorrhage comes from the opening in the palate. This is permanently arrested by local treatment. The introduction of the finger into the cavity recognises the articular process of the lower jaw as the external boundary of the suppurating area, and the bare pterygoid plate prominent in its anterior wall, while the internal maxillary and the carotid vessels can be recognised pulsating and effectively covered with soft parts. The patient dies three weeks after this bleeding, of a diffuse capillary broncho-pneumonia affecting chiefly the pulmonary bases. Explain the nature of the case, and correlate the phenomena to each other and the fatal result. Give your opinion as to the details of treatment which should be adopted.
   2. A patient, upwards of sixty years of age, subject to a supposed Diarrhoea, after exposure, experiences a chill, followed by vomiting and constipation. This continues in spite of opiates and laxatives. A distending enema, which does not exceed a pint in amount, brings away nothing from the lower bowel. No flatus passes downwards. There

is slight tympanitis over the area of the small intestines. As the case goes on the temperature is normal or subnormal. The pulse tends to rise in number; there is developed a little uneasiness, hardly amounting to pain, on pressure at one point over the junction of the right hypogastric with the middle hypogastric region. At various intervals the contents of the stomach are emptied. The amount of urine excreted is diminished, but about twenty ounces are passed in twenty-four hours. What is the nature of this case? What its most probable cause? Where would you expect to find that cause? What plan of treatment should be adopted? Discuss the facts stated as bearing on the prognosis.

Paper No. 3
MEDICINE

1. Describe the physical signs distinctive of dilatation of the right ventricle of the heart, the causes which give rise to it, the results which depend upon it, and its treatment generally.
2. Describe the appearances distinctive of Herpes, giving the pathology and treatment of Herpes Zoster.
3. What is the signification of the term Hyperpyrexia? State the disease in the course of which it is most liable to occur, and its treatment.

CASES

1. A young lady, aged twenty, complains of an uneasy pulsation in the abdomen; on palpation the girl is found to be somewhat thin, the aorta easily felt and pulsating forcibly, there is no bruit audible except on compression with the stethoscope, there is no pain anywhere, there is slight leucorrhoea. What is her complaint, and how would you treat it?
2. A boy, aged eleven, has had a hard, barking, and spasmodic cough which recurs in fits. His larynx, trachea, and lungs are perfectly healthy. He has a venous hum in his neck, a systolic basic murmur in his heart, and his external muscles are somewhat flabby. The disease has lasted a fortnight. What name would you give it, and how would you treat it?

Paper No. 4
MIDWIFERY

1. What are the difficulties usually encountered in determining the existence of Pregnancy, and give its undoubted evidence about the sixth month.
2. What different kinds of Haemorrhage may occur during

Gestation and Parturition, and how are they to be diagnosed and treated?
3.   In what case and when would you induce Premature Labour, and what are the ordinary methods of induction?
4.   Describe a case of Phegmasia Dolens, the usual time of its occurence, and treatment.
[5] University Education in Dundee D.G. Southgate p 121
[6] This device, of sending a memorandum to *all* members of a Committee, is used—and still is used—when there is suspicion on the part of the memorandum's sponsors that its contents will not be made available to all members of the Committee they wish informed of their views. It is also used if there is fear that only a selected part of their views may be passed on.
[7] See p 257
[8] University Education in Dundee, D.G. Southgate p 121
[9] Mrs C.J. Tudhope, O.B.E., M.A., LL.B. Personal Communication
[10] *A Memorial of Sir Thomas Thornton,* Prof Knight (Wm. Kidd) 1905
[11] *St Andrews University OTC—A History by J.S.G. Blair* (Scottish Academic Press) 1981

CHAPTER 8

[1] *A Memorial of Sir Thomas Thornton* Wm. Knight (William Kidd, Dundee) 1905
[2] Minutes of Glasgow University Medico-Chirurgical Society of 26th November, 1875. (Supplied by Dr. Derek A. Dow, Archivist, Greater Glasgow Health Board)
[3] The letter added that this might need an Act of Parliament for its achievement
[4] U.C.D. Council Minutes—July-Sept. 1891
[5] University Education in Dundee. D.G. Southgate. Plate 3.

CHAPTER 9

[1] St Andrews University Court Minutes 19/10/98
[2] Mr R.N. Smart, Personal Communication. Mr Smart has made a particular study of the life of de Wytt
[3] Southgate, *op cit* p 93
[4] U.C.D. Council Minutes 8th January 1902
[5] *ibid;* Dundee U Rec A/336/1
[6] The examination in Clinical Medicine for the Degree of Doctor of Medicine consists, for each candidate, of a written report and commentary upon at least three cases. In the reports the candidate is expected to show an intimate acquaintance with the advanced and recent methods of diagnosis, including the chemical, microscopical, and bacteriological examination of the excreta, the blood and other fluids of the body; the use of the opthalmoscope, laryngoscope and other special instruments; the applications of electricity etc. Candidates may be examined orally on the cases given them for report, or upon any other cases selected for the purpose.
At the time of entering for the examination a candidate may request that one

of the cases be selected from the following Departments viz. Diseases of Women, Diseases of Children, Mental Diseases, Zymotic Disease, Diseases of Eye, of Throat, of Ear, of Skin. Should the candidates specialise in one of these Departments he will be expected to show high proficiency in it.

The examination in Clinical Medicine will be held at the end of the Summer Session in each year.

For the Ch.M. or Master of Surgery, the student could elect surgical diseases of Women, of Children, Eye, Throat and Ear diseases, and similarly would be expected to show special skill in a chosen specialty. Otherwise the regulations were equivalent

[7] *Votiva Tabella* p 335—The romance of St Andrews

CHAPTER 10

[1] Duncan Dewar's Accounts 1819-27 (Lang) Jackson Wylie 1926

[2] Grierson's *Delineations of St Andrews*, 1838 ed. Gillespie et al

[3] For details of University Finances and student numbers, see 'Supplement to the University of St Andrews—a Historical Sketch' by J. Maitland Anderson (Citizen, 1883)

[4] Southgate, *op cit* p 17

[5] *University Life in St Andrews 1880-1890.* Rev. J.R. Strachan (Blairgowrie Advertiser) August 1924.

[6] *Look Back in Wonder* Elizabeth Bryson (David Winter) Part III

[7] This Poet Laureate was Austin Dobson. One of these daughters became warden of University Hall

[8] *Look Back in Wonder*, Part IV; Medical Women—essays by Sophia Jex-Blake

[9]

EXAMINATION PAPERS
UNIVERSITY OF ST ANDREWS

FOURTH PROFESSIONAL EXAMINATION FOR THE
DEGREE OF M.B., Ch.B.

SYSTEMATIC MEDICINE
Friday, June 24, 1904—9 a.m. to 12 noon
(Only FIVE questions to be attempted)

1. In what diseases is Haematemesis an important symptom? Describe the morbid anatomy, clinical history, and treatment of any *one* of these diseases.

2. Measles—
   (a) Describe the clinical history of an attack, mentioning the duration of the various stages from the time of infection onwards.
   (b) What are the chief complications that may accompany or follow the attack?
   (c) How long should the patient be kept away from school to prevent risk to the other scholars?

3. Describe the chief symptoms of Exophthalmic Goitre. Indicate the appropriate treatment of the disease, and write one prescription for it as it should be sent to the druggist
4. Describe the morbid anatomy, clinical history, and treatment of Infantile Paralysis.
5. Give the grounds for a differential diagnosis between Acute Bronchitis, Croupous Pneumonia, and Pleurisy with effusion. Describe fully the treatment of the last disease.
6. Describe the clinical history and treatment of an attack of Acute Nephritis, and write two appropriate prescriptions as they should be sent to the druggist.

SURGERY
SATURDAY, JUNE 25th, 1904—9 a.m. to 12 noon
(FIVE questions are to be answered, of which No. 6 must be one.)
1. Give the clinical and pathological features of a case of Enlarged Prostate, and describe the treatment.
2. Describe the symptoms and signs of a case of Chronic Tubercular Arthritis of the Hip Joint.
3. Enumerate the more common deformities of the bones resulting from Rickets, and describe the operation of Osteotomy for Genu Valgum.
4. Give the symptoms, and signs, and treatment of Acute Appendicitis.
5. How would you distinguish Simple, Tubercular, Syphilitic, and Malignant Ulcer of the Tongue?
6. Give the symptoms and treatment of a case of Acute Plastic Iritis of syphilitic origin, and state how you would distinguish it from a case of Acute Primary Glaucoma.

MIDWIFERY AND DISEASES OF WOMEN
MONDAY, JUNE 27th, 1904—9 a.m. to 12 noon
(FIVE questions only to be answered, one of which must be No. 6)
1. Describe the structure, position, and relations of the healthy Ovary.
2. Describe the Mechanism, and give the diagnosis and treatment in right-occipito-posterior position, of the Vertex.
3. Give the causes, diagnosis, dangers, and treatment in a Labour complicated with Prolapse of the Cord.
4. Give the indications for the Induction of Premature Labour; describe the best methods of carrying out the operation, and mention any precautions to be observed.
5. Describe fully the management of a case of Labour complicated with Mitral Stenosis.
6. What are the symptoms and physical signs of Cancer of the Cervix Uteri?

ST ANDREWS UNIVERSITY

SCHEME FOR MARKING FOR THE FOURTH PROFESSIONAL EXAMINATION FOR THE DEGREE OF M.B., Ch.B.

MEDICINE		SURGERY		MIDWIFERY AND GYNAECOLOGY	
Paper	100	Paper	100	Paper	100
CLINICAL (Case 1 . . . 50)		CLINICAL (Case 1 . . . 40)		Oral	100
(Case 2 . . . 30)		(Cases 2 and 3 . 50)	100		
(Urines . . 10)	100	(Instruments . 10)			
(Microscopes . 10)		Oral	70		
Oral	60	Clinical Ophthalmology .	30		
Mental Diseases .	20	Laryngology, Otology, Rhinology . .	20		
Skins	20	Operative Surgery .	40		
		Surface Anatomy and Marking . .	20		
		Bandaging, Fractures, and Dislocations .	20		
	300		400		200

No candidate to be passed in the subjects of Medicine or Surgery unless he obtains at least 50% of the marks in the Clinical portion of the Examination in these subjects.

10 At St Andrews a first year student is a bejant (ine), a second year a semi, a third year a tertian (senior woman or senior man; more recently, an academic mother or academic father), and a fourth year a magistrand

11 Dr. Margaret W. Menzies Campbell M.B. Hon. F.D.S.R.C.S. Ed.—Personal Communication

12 Dr. P.C. Robertson—Personal Communication

CHAPTER 11
1 British Association—Dundee Meeting 1912 (D. Winter & Son)
2 *St Andrews University Officers Training Corps—a History* by J.S.G. Blair (Scottish Academic Press)
3 Mrs C.J. Tudhope, O.B.E., M.A., LL.B.—Personal communication
4 Rabbits were also used for mustard gas research. The work was carried out on the grass north of Lower College Hall, then a tennis court, and known to students of the later twentieth century as the lawn where graduation teas were held. Dr. S. Bayne recalled Sir James Irvine explaining dramatically how he was asked to be prepared to open the first unexploded mustard gas shell received from France, and collect its contents. He set up his equipment in the expectation that mustard gas was a gas, and was horrified to discover

that it was a liquid. The shell case can still be seen in the Department of Biochemistry and Microbiology in the Irvine Building

5   Sec. Proc. Roy. Soc. B, 1917-1919: J. Roy. Army Med. Corps. 1916-17-18. 'Tulloch types' are still the recognized classification of Cl. Tetani, the causative organism of Tetanus

6   *D'Arcy Wentworth Thompson—The Scholar-Naturalist* (Ruth D'Arcy Thompson) (Oxford 1958) p 163

7   ibid. p 165

8   Dr. W.B. Cunningham, M.D.—Personal Communication

9   Dr. John Pryde later became Professor of Biochemistry at Cardiff

10 Peterson letters made available by David Hunt, Archivist's Department, University of Dundee

CHAPTER 12

1   Southgate, *op cit*

2   ibid. p 124, 133-4, 161

3   Dr. A.J. Pitkeathly, O.B.E., Personal Communication

4   In the late 1960s, the St Andrews American Medical Graduates' Association endowed money to found a prestigious North American Travelling Fellowship. This was open to St Andrews and later Dundee medical graduates. Dr. A.B. Heller, by then an eminent New York General Practitioner, was a leader in the venture. The first Travelling Fellowship was awarded in 1971 to J.S.G. Blair. American medical graduates of these years continued to attend reunions of the After Many Days Club, and all maintained their deep affection for their *alma mater*

5   Obituary notices of Fellows of the Royal Society, 8 November 1953

6   Professor E.C. Meikie, Dr. A.S. Davie, Dr. A.J. Pitkeathly, Dr. P.C. Robertson, Personal Communications

7   In his will, written on February 21st during his last illness, he appointed 'Margaret Fairlie, who has promised to become my wife' and Dr. Sam Cameron, the Glasgow Gynaecologist, as his executors. The settlement continues sadly . . . 'I leave and bequeath the whole of my means and estate heritable and movable real and personal to the said Margaret Fairlie, whom I had hoped to marry shortly . . .'

CHAPTER 13

1   U.C.D. Council 20/2/33—report by Professor Waterson's Committee, including provision of a nurse in University Hall, a physician attached to the mens' residences, and the suggestion that a lay member of the Council assist in negotiations with the Governors of D.R.I. over health provision in Dundee

2   University Court Minutes 1939-40, p 106

3   Southgate, *op cit* pp 189-195

4   Professor R.C. Garry—personal communication

5   Referred to as 'The Macgillivray' by Dr. Southgate

6   Dr. S. Bayne, then a student, recalls: 'I was in St Salvator's Hall when the

bombs fell. The one which demolished the corner of the library removed a very fine tree. The one which fell in West Burn Lane caused a lot of damage in the Biochemistry Laboratory on the east side of the building. With others I helped Hynd to clear up the broken glass'.

7

UNIVERSITY OF ST ANDREWS
Fourth Professional Examination for the Degree of M.B., Ch.B.

MEDICINE
Thursday, 9th March, 1944—10 a.m. to 1 p.m.

1. Describe the signs, symptoms, and treatment of laryngeal diptheria.
2. A patient, aged fifty, complains of dyspepsia of recent origin, and has become rather pale and thinner. Describe how you would investigate the case, and discuss the differential diagnosis.
3. Describe the signs and symptoms found in a case of pleurisy with effusion occurring in a young adult. Discuss the aetiology and the treatment.
4. Discuss the aetiology, and describe the symptoms and treatment of angina pectoris.
5. Classify the leukaemias, and state shortly how you would distinguish between them.
6. How would you recognise and treat coma occurring in untreated diabetes mellitus?

SURGERY
Wednesday, 8th March, 1944—10 a.m. to 1 p.m.

1. Discuss the aetiology, clinical features, and treatment of an early case of acute pyogenic osteomyelitis affecting the tibia.
2. Discuss the mode of production, clinical features, and treatment of compression fracture of the vertebral column.
3. A patient receives a blow on the left loin; describe the clinical features which would indicate that the kidney had been injured, and discuss the treatment.
4. Give brief descriptions of the following terms:
   (a) Cholecystography.
   (b) Ganglion.
   (c) Dupuytren's contracture.
   (d) Ranula.
   (e) March foot.

MIDWIFERY AND GYNAECOLOGY
Tuesday, 12th September, 1944—10 a.m. 1 p.m.

1. Give the aetiology, diagnosis, and treatment of pyelitis during pregnancy.
2. Describe the physiological action and therapeutic uses of progesterone.

3. Give the diagnosis of a right occipito-posterior position during the later weeks of pregnancy. Discuss the management of such a case during labour, when the occiput has failed to rotate to the front.
4. Describe the appearance of a baby born in a severe state of asphyxia. What treatment would you adopt in such a case?
5. How would you differentiate chronic inversion of the uterus from a fibromyomatous polyp? Give the treatment of inversion of the uterus as met with in obstetrical and gynaecological practice.

[8] Professor R.C. Garry—personal communication. He described Professor Fulton, with Professor Wynne-Jones, Professor of Chemistry at UCD, as moles who regularly leaked confidential university information to the *Dundee Courier* and *Advertiser*.

CHAPTER 14

[1] Deed of Endowment and Trust of University College Dundee 1881 (printed by John Leng & Co. Bank Street Dundee 1882: reprinted 1949) p 10 Sec. IV ff
[2] *ibid* p 14 Sec XVI, XVII
[3] *ibid* p 20 Sec XLIII
[4] *ibid* p 44
[5] John Grieve—the Quaestor's son. Personal Communication
[6] Botany and English. There was in fact a third—Peterson's Chair of Classics
[7] Ecclesiasticus 28; 10, 12, 14 (New English Bible Translation)
[8] Memoirs of Major-General Douglas Wimberley Vol III p 2
[9] ibid p 96
[10] Miss Janet Allan, Secretary to Principal Sir Malcolm Knox—Personal Communication
[11] Dr. J.J.A. Reid, Chief Medical Officer, St Andrew's House. Personal Communication
[12] Dr. J.J.A. Reid, Dr. B.K. Dean, Dr. W.E.A. Buchanan, Professor H.D. Attwood—Personal Communications
[13] Professor R.C. Garry—Personal Communication; Memoirs of Major-General Douglas Wimberley Vol III p 19
[14] Royal Commission on University Education in Dundee 1952—Written Evidence Paper No 23. Professor Garry recorded that when members of the Faculty of Science from both sides of the University pressed that their Faculty Meetings be held in Dundee, the Principal threatened legal action against them if they persisted with their bid
[15] ibid Papers 1, 2, 14, 15
[16] Wimberley Memoirs Vol III p 24
[17] *ibid* pp 41, 42
[18] *ibid* p 42
[19] Mr R.N.M. Robertson, Medical Administrative Officer; later Secretary, University of Dundee—Personal Communication

20 *ibid*
21 Wimberley Memoirs Vol III p 25
22 Mr R.N.M. Robertson—Personal Communication
23 Evidence of University Court to Lord Cooper's Enquiry 1949
24 Wimberley Memoirs Vol III pp 48, 63, 65, 84, 87, 95, 96, 98, 104, 116, 117, 119, 135, 186, 187, 188, 226, 228, 263
25 ibid p 95; Drs. D.M. Green, J.J.A. Reid, E.J. Mackay—Personal Communications
26 Dr. E.J. Mackay—Personal Communication
27 Wimberley Memoirs Vol III p 38
28 Dr. D.M. Alexander, Dr. J.S. Henderson—Personal Communications
29 Dr. D.M. Green—Personal Communication
30 Wimberley Memoirs Vol III p 103 Lord Cooper wrote 'It will be a pity if the prospects of an early rapprochement are adversely affected by local politics in Dundee. The problem is essentially an academic one and best left in the hands of academic people. I would venture one last word. Sir James Irvine is entitled to much sympathy. He has lived for United College and achieved wonders there. He cannot be there much longer and it will not be easy for him in his closing days to adopt a new policy. Do your best to make it easy for him'. It is of interest that Wimberley never once alluded to the effect the loss of his son had had on Sir James, especially as he must have seen University House, with its memorials
31 *The Making of a Lord Provost* Garnet Wilson (David Winter, Dundee 1966). 'Time brought revenge to those who, in 1952 and before then had called for a University of Dundee, for their hopes are at last being realised' (p 58)
32 Royal Commission on University Education in Dundee 1952—Written Evidence Papers Nos 18, 19/20, 1, 5/6, 8, 21, 14, 46, 15, 4
33 ibid Paper 14; SRC Transcript of Oral Evidence (No 46) kindly lent by Dr. E.J. Mackay
34 Wimberly Memoirs Vol III p 118
35 Principal Wimberley was concerned that the *Times* leader seemed to favour St Andrews, and that it had suggested that not all the recommendations need necessarily be followed by the University. He suspected the *Times* 'must keep a University correspondent or adviser of their own; resident in St Andrews' (p 187)
36 ibid p 205
37 Miss Janet Allan—Personal Communication

CHAPTER 15

1 Principal Wimberley believed that a large number of professors lived in St Andrews but this belief was erroneous. A number of staff were members of the Golf Club, but resided in Dundee
2 Professor A.C. Lendrum, Personal Communication
3 Professor K.G. Lowe, Personal Communication (as recounted to him by Professor Cappell)

[4] Professor A.C. Lendrum, Personal Communication

[5] Mr R.N.M. Robertson, Personal Communication

[6] Professor R.C. Garry, O.B.E., Personal Communication

[7] Pre-Clinical salaries were:

Grade I	£700	4 of £25 to £800
Grade II	£500	4 of £25 to £600
Grade III	£450—	no increments
Assistants	£350—	no increments

[8] A General Medical Service for the Nation, November 1938 (British Medical Association, London)

[9] A hospital survey was carried out in 1945 in preparation for the establishment of the National Health Service. A group of eminent doctors were involved and their terms of reference were 'to review the hospitals (other than mental hospitals and mental deficiency institutions) and, within a policy aimed at post-war development of a comprehensive and co-ordinated hospital service, to advise the Secretary of State what modifications or extensions of the existing hospital facilities are necessary or desirable'. The work of the group was divided by geographical regions, and Professor R.S. Aitken and Dr. H. Hislop Thomson produced the report on the Eastern Region (Dr. J.J.A. Reid, Chief Medical Officer, Scottish Home and Health Department, Personal Communication)

[10] Which he described as 'malignant'. (Professor R.C. Garry, Personal Communication)

[11] 'Work expands to fill the time available for its completion', (C. Northcote Parkinson, 1958, John Murray, London)

[12] Remuneration of Consultants and Specialists, Inter-Departmental Committee (Chairman: Sir Will Spens, C.B.E.) Report May 19, 1948. Session 1947-48: Cmd. 7420

CHAPTER 16

[1] Miss Judy Greig became in due course the secretary to the Dean. Her main responsibility was to the students. As such she became one of the best-known members of the Faculty and one of the best-loved helpers and advisers of two generations of St Andrews medical students

[2] The others were W.C. McIntosh, W.J. Tulloch, D.R. Dow and M. Fairlie.

[3] Professor Anthony Ritchie 1984. Personal Communication

[4]

10th Term (Martinmas)

9.00-10 a.m.	Medicine Lecture—Monday-Friday
10.00-11 a.m.	Pathology Lecture—Monday-Friday
11.15- 1 p.m.	Clinical instruction in Medicine
2.00- 3 p.m.	Materia Medica (Pharmacology and Therapeutics) 4 days per week
3.00- 4 p.m.	Materia Medica, Pathology, Bacteriology-Group
4.00- 5 p.m.	Practicals

11th Term (Candlemas)

9.00-10 a.m.	Surgery Lecture—Monday-Friday

10.00-11 a.m.	Pathology Lecture—Monday-Friday
11.15- 1 p.m.	Clinical Surgery
Afternoons	As Martinmas Term

12th Term   (Whitsun)

9-10-11 a.m.	Tutorials in Pharmacology, Pathology, Bacteriology
11.15- 1 p.m.	Clinical Medicine
Afternoons	As above

Fifth Year   (Martinmas)

9.00-10 a.m.	Surgery Lecture—Monday-Friday
10.00-11 a.m.	Various
11.15- 1 p.m.	Clinical Surgery
2.00- 3 p.m.	Obstetrics and Gynaecology Lecture 4 days per week
3.00- 4 p.m.	Monday, Tuesday: Fevers. Thursday: ENT. Friday: Fevers
4.00- 5 p.m.	Fevers 3 days per week + Vaccinations

(Candlemas)

9.00-10 a.m.	Medicine Lecture—Monday-Friday
10.00-11 a.m.	Clinical Ophthalmology—2 days per week
11.15- 1 p.m.	Clinical Medicine
Afternoons	As above: Dermatology added
Saturdays	
10.00-12 p.m.	Tuberculosis

(Whitsun)

9.00-10 a.m.	Surgery Lecture 3 days per week. Therapeutics 2 days
10.00-11 a.m.	Clinical Ophthalmology
11.15- 1 p.m.	Clinical Surgery
2.00- 3 p.m.	Public Health—Monday-Friday
3.00- 4 p.m.	Forensic Medicine—Monday-Friday
4.00- 5 p.m.	Mental Diseases: 2 days per week. Vaccinations. Venereal Diseases. Tuberculosis

Saturdays

| 10.00-12 p.m. | Mental Diseases |

The sixth year was divided into intensive terms as before, with Clinical Pathology each term and Paediatrics in the Medicine term.

[5] Professor K.G. Lowe 1984. Personal Communication

[6] Professor Hunter's pencil notes in Faculty Minutes express concern felt by the medical side over the cardiac surgery appointment; see also E.R.H.B. Minutes Vol 18, 1965-66, for Professor Hill's misgivings about the cardiac surgery service's administration later

[7] Mr Block had one of the most frustrating introductions a new specialist could ever experience. For many months he had no beds—only being allowed one or two in the Professorial wards at D.R.I.—and had to operate when and

where he could find free space and time. Later he developed an excellent service, for which the region should be always grateful

[8] Dr. A.S.L. Rae. Personal Communication

[9] At Aberdeen, in addition to Sir David Campbell in Therapeutics and Sir Dugald Baird in Obstetrics and Gynaecology, there were Professor J.Z. Young in Pathology and Professor Craig in Paediatrics. In Edinburgh there were Sir Stanley Davidson in Medicine, Sir James Learmonth followed by Sir John Bruce and Sir Michael Woodruffe in Surgery, Sir Derrick Dunlop in Therapeutics and later Professor Ronald Girdwood; Sir Walter Mercer in Orthopaedics, followed by Professor J.I.P. James; Professor Norman Dott in Surgical Neurology, Professor McWhirter in Radiotherapy, Professor Carstairs in Psychiatry; all large names and many of them world figures. Glasgow had the largest number of all, as befitted its size and importance; Sir Charles Illingworth in Surgery, followed by Sir Drew Kay; Professor Arthur Mackie; Sir John McNee followed by Sir Edward Wayne and Professor Eddie McGirr in Medicine; Dr. Joe Wright of the Scottish Consultant Staffing Report, Professor James Hutchinson in Paediatrics, Professor J. Norman Davidson, F.R.S. in Biochemistry, Alex. Forrester in Anaesthetics, Professor Ian Donald and Sir Hector McLennan in Obstetrics, plus a range of non-professorial clinicians of great distinction—Dr. Paddy Macluskey, the doctors' physician, Wallace Dennison, the Paediatric surgeon, Andrew Tindal, the Anaesthetist. All of these and others were better and better-known than their St Andrews opposite numbers

[10] 'For a short period in the middle 1960s St Andrews was probably the best Medical School in Scotland' was the opinion of Mr Lewis Robertson, as he viewed it from his position of Chairman of the Regional Board. In later years, he saw no need to alter that view. (Personal Communication 1984)

CHAPTER 17

[1] Miss Peggy Sturrock, Finance Department, University of St Andrews, 1941-65—Personal Communication

[2] Miss Janet Allan, Personal Secretary to Principal Sir Malcolm Knox—Personal Communication

[3] Goodenough Report p 234

[4] Eastern Regional Hospital Board Minutes, Vol 2, 1949-50, pp 202-204

[5] Dr. JJ.A Reid, Chief Medical Officer,. Scottish Home and Health Department—Personal Communication

[6] Recs. A/318/4. File ERB/CHA U of D

[7] One reason for the considerable increase in the number of higher degrees from this time onwards had nothing to do with the University. From the middle 1950s, for thirty years and longer, promotion to consultant status in the Health Service became very slow, with more trained and competent individuals in the senior registrar grade than there were consultant posts. Extra qualifications such as multiple Memberships or Fellowships, and especially a higher degree, carried extra weight at interview

[8] Dr. G.R. Tudhope, 1984—Personal Communication

[9] Southgate, *op cit* p 325

[10] Professors Bell, Hitchin and Lendrum wished the move to take place earlier. Dr. Southgate's assertion about the reason for the appointment of Professor Coupland is the opposite of the facts. It was the *Faculty* which recommended that the Cox Chair be filled, ibid p 361

[11] It was for this reason, as well as on account of the increasing preference for the Bute by intending medical students, that had led to the imbalance after 1946; the reduction on the Dundee side was balanced by the dental students who required teaching space and time in University and later Queen's College in their increasing post-war numbers

[12] Mr Alan Wightman, Architect of Ninewells Hospital—Personal Communication

[13] Hospital and Medical School Design—International Symposium, Dundee, 1961. Vol I, 40-43

[14] Recs A/318/2/5 University of Dundee. Meetings between the Principal and the Chairman of the Eastern Regional Hospital Board; from 1960, Mr Lewis Robertson became Board Chairman in succession to Lord Provost William Hughes

[15] Dr. T. Sommerville, Mr Alan Wightman—Personal Communications

[16] The 'Pater Formula' is named after Mr John E. Pater, C.B., who was later an Under Secretary, after working successively in the Ministry of Health and DHSS from 1947-73. His formula is concerned with the apportionment of costs between the health authority and the universities, taking into account their respective responsibilities. Dr. J.J.A. Reid, SHHD—Personal Communication

[17] Dr. T. Sommerville: Personal Communication

[18] Domestic Minutes of Faculty Board of Medicine, 2nd October 1962. 'On the question of contracts procedure the (University Grants) Committee confirmed that this was a matter primarily for the Department of Home and Health and that they had no comments on the procedure at present proposed'

[19] The mock-ups were in fact continued into 1964. The first group began to be erected on the site in August, 1963. Another set—of laboratories—was due to be ready by March 1964. These were late: their order of building was changed more than once. 'The mock-ups, after a series of stops and starts, are now said to be re-opening on 4th May. The first will be the Operating Theatres Suite. The sequence for subsequent mock-ups is Joint Clinical Investigation Unit, Out-Patient Consultation Suite and standard laboratories. The date for these will be announced in due course'.
ibid 29th April, 1964

[20] The principal contractors were:

Structural Engineers:	Ove Arup & Partners
Services Engineers:	Steensen Varming Mulcahy & Partners
Quantity Surveyors:	W.J.R. Christie & Partners
Main Contractor:	Crudens Ltd of Musselburgh

[21] Domestic Minutes of Faculty of Medicine, 27/11/63

[22] Joint Planning Committee Minutes, NW 2/66 dated 3/2/66

[23] Mr Lewis Robertson—Personal Communication
[24] Perth Royal Infirmary Development, 1981-84
[25] Principal James Drever—Personal Communication
[26] Professor K.G. Lowe—Personal Communication
[27] Dr. T. Sommerville—Personal Communication

CHAPTER 18

[1] Miss Janet Allan, Personal Communication
[2] Dr. John Mills (1966) Personal Communication
[3] Mrs C.J. Tudhope, Personal Communication
Articles by Lord Provost McManus (Courier, 14th November, 1963) including his address to students in the Queen's College Union:
'Dundee was a progressive city and in several aspects was emerging as one of the most important in the country. There could be no question but that university status would play its part in this ... could provide 5000 places ... The policy of the St Andrews University Court had been to allow only one part of the university to develop in Dundee ... the removal of the Arts Faculty from Queen's last year caused bitter resentment, particularly in the Corporation'.
Courier, 6th December 1963:
'Oxford and Cambridge had a lower incidence of first year failures than any other because they were complete communities in themselves and there was free intermingling of ideas from different faculties—This did not and could not exist in Queen's College because of the separation of certain faculties between Queen's and St Andrews University (sic). Being the Second Industrial City in Scotland and the fourth largest, and the three larger towns already having separate universities, Dundee had a first-class claim for Queen's College being upgraded'.
[4] Southgate, *op cit* p 348 ff
[5] Dr. Ian Adamson (1949), Senior Lecturer in Mathematical Sciences who approved of the disruption at the time, expressed the positive side of the wish for a separate University in Dundee. He and others felt that Queen's College had enough size and merit to require independent status; the growing size of the Social Science Faculty, under the governance of Professor Archie Campbell, the outstanding Professor bar none on the early Dundee Senatus whose early sudden death robbed him of a career almost certain to lead to the top of the academic world, was producing an 'Arts element' large enough to stand on its feet. Dr. Adamson saw the sense of transferring the small Arts language departments to St Salvator's College so criticised by Dr. Southgate and the Dundee Corporation, and actually was about to put a motion to the General Council Meeting approving the transfer until pressure from colleagues in Queen's College caused him to withdraw it
[6] Professor A. Ritchie, Personal Communication
[7] Miss Janet Allan, Mr Lewis Robertson, Major-General Douglas Wimberley, Professor A.M. Moodie, Dr. Ian T. Adamson, Professor Erskine Wright, Dr. R.G. Cant, Professor Norman Gash—personal communications.

Miss Allan's recollection of the time deserves a particular record. 'The Principal thought things were at last going well, in the 1960s, with Queen's College getting their deserved share. "I don't travel to Dundee. I live in Dundee", he used to say. There was no background antagonism to Dundee in the 1960s—TMK had it running as well as it could. Although it was shortly after he got his knighthood that he turned his attention to the division of the University, this had nothing to do with it. But he was thought by some people in St Andrews to have stopped working for the whole University because he had got his knighthood and was looking to his retirement. In fact it was TMK who thought out very well the entire picture of development for both universities. He never quoted anyone in government having had anything to do with the split'.

Mr Lewis Robertson and Professor Moodie (Professor of Politics at the University of York, a St Andrews graduate of 1946 who was at one time in Professor Knox' Department and kept in close touch with him over the years) both witness to the Principal's continuing clarity and force of view over the split; Dr. Ian Adamson has the same recollection as did General Wimberley during personal discussions in 1983.

In Dr. Cant's view the Principal quite probably had some forewarning: but his apparent *volte face* derived from his Hegelian philosophy in accordance with which anyone in his position had an obligation to assist 'state policy' to prevail over his own personal views. Professor Gash, 'always one of those who deplored the parting of the ways', said: 'I never quite knew what induced T.M. Knox to make his sudden *volte face* and decide that the joint university was inoperable. The Senate meeting at which he announced this is still vivid in my memory. It took us all by surprise and we never had the chance to discuss it calmly'. Professor Gash, in contrast to Dr. Cant, believed that Sir Malcolm's action may have been a very emotional decision, perhaps related to personal disappointments

[8] Southgate, *op cit* p 356

[9] Professor G.H. Bell, 1984—Personal Communication

[10] Mr J. Grieve, 1984—Personal Communication

[11] Mrs C.J. Tudhope, Dr. A. Simmons—Personal Communications

[12] Mr A.J.G. Brown—Personal Communication

[13] Sir Donald Douglas—Personal Communication

[14] See obituary by Professor K.G. Lowe in the Alumnus Chronicle of 1983. 'Like the majority of his clinical colleagues in the Medical School he had greatly regretted the split in the University and was heard to remark that he would prefer to be remembered as the last Professor of Medicine in St Andrews than the first in Dundee'. 'There was no comparison between a place where students had been taught for five hundred years and any new set-up institution, however well endowed'. (said to Dr. P.C. Robertson)

[15] Professor A.C. Lendrum—Personal Communication

[16] Professor James Walker, C.B.E.—Personal Communication

[17] Lord Hunter, Miss Janet Allan, Mr Alan Brown—Personal Communications

[18] Universities (Scotland) Act 1966, para 17 of Schedule 6

[19] Southgate, *op cit* p 357

[20] Principal James Drever (1984)—Personal Communication

[21] Dr. T. Sommerville (1984, 85)—Personal Communication

[22] William Occam or Ockham (died ? 1349): a Franciscan and philosopher; condemned the doctrine of Realism without accepting the extravagances of Nominalism. The real is always individual, not universal. The universal is *quoddam fictum*, a 'term' or 'sign', not a 'thing', and 'entities must not be unnecessarily multiplied'—the principle of *Occam's razor*. Professor Lendrum's view that individuals do not suffer from multiple disease processes has been overtaken by the more recent findings of geriatric physicians.

[23] For the graduates whose written and spoken recollections form the substance of these paragraphs, see Acknowledgements.

[24]   *University of Dundee Medicine 9-12 noon, 9 June 1972*
          (All questions to be answered)
          1.   Discuss the aetiology of hepatitis.
          2.   A man of 40 complains of headaches and dizziness and is found on examination to have bilateral papilloedema and a blood pressure of 260/155 mm.Hg. Discuss how this patient should be investigated and the treatment which you would adopt.
          3.   Give a brief account of the causes of pleural effusion. State how you would investigate a man of 45 years who complains of dyspnoea for four weeks and who is found to have a right-sided pleural effusion.
          4.   Write short notes on the following:
               a) lassitude; b) syncope; c) haematuria; d) ketosis;
               e) exophthalmos

          University of Dundee Surgery 9-12 noon, 12 June 1972
          (All questions to be answered)
          1.   Discuss the aetiology, pathology, clinical features, diagnosis and treatment of carcinoma of the bronchus.
          2.   Describe the management of a compound (open) fracture of the femoral shaft due to a road traffic accident. What are the possible complications?
          3.   Discuss the recognition and treatment for acute perforated appendicitis.
          4.   A patient develops anuria after a major operation. What are the possible causes of this? Indicate how the diagnosis may be reached in each case and the treatment required.

          University of Dundee Obstetrics and Gynaecology 9-12 noon,
          13 June 1972
          Answer BOTH questions in Part A in one book and select ONE question from Part B and ONE question from Part C and answer in a second book.

Part A—Both Questions 1 and 2 must be answered
1. Discuss the clinical features, haematology, complications and management of a patient with abruptio placentae.
2. Describe the clinical features of a malignant ovarian tumour. What methods of treatment are currently available?

Part B—Please answer Question 3 OR 4
3. Discuss the management of a Rhesus negative pregnant woman who has had a previous baby seriously affected with haemolytic disease.
4. Describe the normal human placenta and give a brief account of its functions.

Part C—Please answer Questions 5 OR 6
5. Discuss the factors predisposing to ileo-femoral thrombosis in obstetrics and gynaecology and the techniques of diagnosis and treatment.
6. What are the legal 'permissions' for termination of pregnancy in the United Kingdom? Discuss the methods employed to terminate a pregnancy of more than 14 weeks' gestation.

The Final Examination also included a paper in Child Health. There were in fact three of these each year, since one third of the year sat the Child Health paper during their intensive term in Medicine. The June paper was:

University of Dundee Child Health 9-11 a.m., 5 June 1972
1. Describe the clinical features and possible complications of congenital hypertrophic pyloric stenosis.
2. Discuss the differential diagnosis of jaundice occurring in the neonatal period.
3. How would you investigate a persistent cough in a 6-year-old child?
4. Discuss the emotional implications in childhood of going to school.

[25] *Isti quinam sunt* heads the annual summer newsletter of the After Many Days Club, the oldest University Alumnus Society. Eligibility for membership is reached twenty-five years after the person's first matriculation date.

CHAPTER 19

[1] The Conference of representatives of Senates of the Scottish Universities met on February 14th 1959 to discuss exemptions from courses of study and from certain examinations. This related especially to English students whose school standard of work gave them direct entry into second year. Professor John Brotherston of Edinburgh said that 'In Edinburgh they always drew a considerable proportion of their medical students from England—now about 50%; they wished a competitive choice, so that Edinburgh could compete with English Universities for the best students'. Many Edinburgh medical graduate witnesses confirm their very high proportion of English students.

[2] Professors A.C. Lendrum and G.R. Bell, Personal Communications

[3] Professor A.E. Ritchie, Dr. R.G. Cant, Personal Communications

[4] See Mr A.J.B. Brown's letter of 3rd February 1967 from the Faculty of Medicine's Office in Queen's College to Professor Walmsley:
'This is to confirm the arrangements made yesterday that Mr George Clark, acting on a remit from the Royal Commission will visit you and some of your preclinical colleagues on Thursday 23rd February . . .
I am not sure about what precisely Mr Clark will want to talk. His remit from the Royal Commission is to make "an intensive study of the organisation and administration of medical schools" . . . I am writing to Mr Clark telling him of what I have arranged about his visit to St Andrews and will ask him . . . to raise any points concerning the future of the preclinical department in St Andrews direct with you'

[5] Quinquennial Memorandum: See Miss Allan's covering note on the Principal's behalf to Professor Tristram on 17th November, 1966

[6] See Principal Watson's letter of 4th November 1969 to Sir Robert Aitken, Deputy Chairman of the U.G.C.

[7] See Sir Kenneth Berrill's letter to the Principal, from U.G.C. (1095/10/01 of 25th November, 1969)

[8] Lord Hunter, Principal Drever—Personal Communications

[9] Professors Ritchie, Tristram; Dr. Bayne, Personal Communications

[10] A Post-Graduate Scholarship in B.Sc. Med. Sci. subjects or in Gynaecology or Ophthalmology

[11] Additional details of this period are found in UY WATSON 875 U of St A.

[12]   MEMORANDUM OF AGREEMENT
                                       between
              THE COUNCIL OF THE UNIVERSITY OF MANCHESTER
                 (hereinafter referred to as 'the University of Manchester')
                                         and
              THE UNIVERSITY COURT OF THE UNIVERSITY OF
                                   ST ANDREWS
                 (hereinafter referred to as 'the University of St Andrews')
                        WHEREAS the classes provided by the University of St
                        Andrews leading to an Ordinary or Honours Degree of
                        Bachelor of Science in Medical Science of that University
                        form a pre-clinical course qualifying students to proceed
                        to clinical studies and the degree of Bachelor of
                        Medicine, and of Surgery (M.B., Ch.B.) in the University
                        of Manchester AND WHEREAS under an informal
                        arrangement made between the parties hereto and
                        approved by the Royal Commission on Medical
                        Education and by the University Grants Committee the
                        University of Manchester agreed inter alia to admit each
                        year to clinical studies all those students of the
                        University of St Andrews who in that year had
                        completed the said pre-clinical course in the University

for the purpose of enabling them to proceed to clinical studies and the degrees of Bachelor of Medicine, and of Surgery in the University of Manchester AND WHEREAS the parties hereto now wish to make proper and formal provision for the foregoing arrangement THEREFORE the parties hereto are agreed as follows videlicet:—

FIRST   The University of Manchester hereby undertakes at the date of the commencement of each session, beginning from the commencement of Session Nineteen hundred and seventy-four/seventy-five, to admit to its clinical courses all those students of the University of St Andrews who have applied to be so admitted and who by the date of the commencement of each Session have successfully completed either an ordinary or an Honours Degree of Bachelor of Science in Medical Science of the University of St Andrews for the purpose of enabling them to proceed to clinical studies and the degrees of Batchelor of Medicine, and of Surgery of the University of Manchester: provided always that

(1) the number of such students to be so admitted at the date of the commencement Session Nineteen hundred and seventy-four/seventy-five shall not exceed Sixty-five;

(2) the number of such students to be so admitted at the date of the commencement of Session Nineteen hundred and seventy-five/seventy-six shall not exceed Seventy-five;

(3) the number of such students to be so admitted at the commencement of each Session thereafter shall not exceed Seventy-five, unless the parties hereto by mutual consent agree to increase such number.

SECOND In order to provide for the high degree of integration necessary in the teaching programmes and curricula of the pre-clinical departments in the Universities of Manchester and St Andrews respectively, and for satisfactory collaboration and liaison generally between the said Universities, the parties hereto agree as follows:—

(1) that the Dean of the Faculty of Medicine in the University of Manchester or his representative and the Dean of the Faculty of Science in the University of St Andrews or his representative shall meet regularly and at least once each academic year.

(2) that, similarly, representatives of each of the pre-clinical teaching departments in each University shall

meet at least once each academic year at the request
of either University.

(3) that each year such pre-clinical department shall
appoint its representative for the succeeding year
and the representative so appointed will be the
person who should, in the first instance, be
approached on any matter or problem arising from
the course provided by his department.

(4) that copies of the reports of the meeting prescribed
in sub-paragraphs (1) and (2) above shall be lodged
for reference purposes in the offices of the Dean of
the Faculty of Medicine of the University of
Manchester and the Dean of the Faculty of Science
of the University of St Andrews respectively.

(5) that the Dean of the Faculty of Science of the
University of St Andrews or his representative shall
have the right to attend meetings and shall be
provided with copies of the relative agendas and
supporting papers of the Curriculum Committee of
the Faculty of Medicine of the University of
Manchester. Similarly, the Dean of the Faculty of
Medicine of the University of Manchester or his
representative shall have the right to attend meetings
of the Pre-Clinical Committee of the Council of the
Faculty of Science of the University of St Andrews
and shall be provided with copies of the relative
agendas and supporting papers.

(6) that the Dean of the Faculty of Medicine of the
University of Manchester shall be invited to those
graduation ceremonies in the University of St
Andrews at which degrees are to be conferred on
medical science students; and the Dean of the
Faculty of Science of the University of St Andrews
shall be invited to graduation ceremonies in the
University of Manchester at which medical degrees
are to be conferred on former graduates of the
University of St Andrews.

(7) that each University will encourage collaboration
between their respective medical student societies,
namely, the Medical Students Representative
Council in Manchester and the Bute Medical Society
in St Andrews.

THIRD   During the subsistence of this Agreement, the University
of St Andrews undertakes not to enter into any similar
agreement or arrangement, whether formal or informal,
with any University or Medical School other than the

University of Manchester without first obtaining the consent in writing of the University of Manchester.

FOURTH It shall be open to the parties hereto to modify, revise or alter any of the terms of this Agreement by mutual consent, but any modification to, revision of or alteration so agreed shall not take effect until a period of five years has elapsed from and after the date upon which such modification, revision or alteration has received the final approval of both parties: provided always that in particular cases, the parties may by mutual agreement reduce the said period of five years which must elapse before a modification, revision or alteration takes effect so long as the interests of any student or students are not thereby detrimentally affected.

FIFTH This Agreement shall continue in force unless and until terminated by either side giving to the other written notice of not less than five years. Such written notice must be given on or before the First day of October in any year, in which event this Agreement shall terminate on the Thirtieth day of September in the fifth year following such First day of October. IN WITNESS WHEREOF these presents typewritten upon this and the two preceding pages are executed as follows:—They are sealed with the common seal of the said University Court of the University of St Andrews and subsribed for it and on its behalf by Principal John Steven Watson and Professor George Roland Tristram, two of its members, and by David McDonald Devine, its Secretary, all at St Andrews on the Thirteenth June Nineteen hundred and seventy-four before these witnesses Miss Margaret Mackenzie Forrester and Miss Helen Elizabeth Margaret Lynch, both secretaries of College Gate, St Andrews; and they are sealed with the common seal of the said Council of the University of Manchester and subscribed for it and on its behalf by Arthur Llewellyn Armitage, Vice-Chancellor of the said University of Manchester and by Vincent Knowles, its Registrar, all at Manchester on the Twenty-fifth day of the month and year last mentioned before these witnesses Frederick Bakewell Beswick, Associate Dean of Medicine, Medical School, Manchester and David A. Richardson, University Administrator, The University, Manchester.

CHAPTER 20

[1] This occurred in the summer of 1951. The resident had in fact spent two years in the Services before coming to study Medicine

[2] Professor R. Walmsley—Personal Communication, 1985

[3] In 1978, 1,025 applied for entry into Medical Science. Of these, 26.8% gave St Andrews as a first choice, and 30% were Scots

[4] See Appendix III of the submission to the U.G.C. dated 12th May, 1978. Students/Staff Ratios were

Anatomy	16.9
Biochemistry	13.9
Physiology	13.1

The Faculty of Science student/staff ratio was 10.1

[5] Professor Lord Tedder—Personal Communication

[6] Mr A.J.G. Brown, T.D.—Personal Communication

[7] Mr Lewis Robertson, C.B.E.—Personal Communication, 1985

[8] Dr. H. Wilson—Personal Communication

[9] Comparisons made at this time between the two years at Manchester and the three years at St Andrews overlooked the fact that the actual number of teaching weeks in Manchester's two years was only 20-25% less than St Andrews' three years. So there was relatively little difference in study time between the Manchester and St Andrews pre-clinical courses.

[10] Professor A.C. Lendrum—Personal Communication

[11] See Proceedings of Annual Representative Meetings of the British Medical Association, especially Reports of its Academic Sub-Committee, 1983-4-5

[12] Professor R.G. Mitchell—Personal Communication

[13] *Learning Medicine* (B.M.A. Publications) p 21 ff

[14] Dr. H. Watson—Personal Communication

[15] Mr J. Macarthur, Dr. A. Simmons—Personal Communications

[16] Mr J. Cook, F.R.C.S.—Personal Communication

[17] In the mid-1980s, 'League Tables' of Universities, showing their ratings for cost, courses, graduate unemployment, etc., were actually drawn up—see for example *The Sunday Times' Good University Guide*, September-October, 1983

Acknowledgements

I wish to thank first Professor Norman Gash, Professor of Modern History at St Andrews, for asking me to begin this work in 1979. Next I wish to thank the Senates of the Universities of St Andrews and Dundee for allowing me access to their original documents, minutes, and correspondence, which provided the greatest part of my source material; especially valuable in this context was the opportunity to study, side by side, St Andrews Senate and Dundee College Council records of the late nineteenth and middle twentieth centuries. My especial thanks go to Mr Robert Smart and Miss Joan Auld, the keepers of muniments of St Andrews/Dundee Universities for their patience and help; to Mr Smart particularly for reading and correcting the earlier chapters.

May I next thank particularly Major-General Douglas Wimberley for the several long conversations and recollections he kindly shared with me, at his house at Coupar Angus, and for allowing me access to his personal papers, and Miss Janet Allan, former private secretary to Sir Malcolm Knox and Principal J. Steven Watson, for invaluable help, advice and support.

Among the very many others to whom I am indebted are: Principals and Professors: Principal James Drever, first Principal of the University of Dundee, and Principal J. Steven Watson, Principal of the University of St Andrews; Professors A. Ritchie, R. Walmsley, G.R. Tristram, K.G. Lowe, R.G. Mitchell, Sir Donald Douglas, A.C. Lendrum, G.H. Bell, J.W. Smith, I.G. Kidd, and A. Serafini-Fracassini.

Dr. J.J.A. Reid 1944, Dr. D.M. Green 1947, and Dr. E.J. MacKay 1951, successive medical presidents of the S.R.C. in University College, gave me a very considerable amount of help, both by the provision of personal documents of the highest importance, and by their comments and written recollections. Dr. Reid (Sir John Reid) has also provided information from the Scottish Home and Health Department of high value.

Dr. S. Bayne 1941 also provided me with unique personal papers relating to the Distruption of 1964, and subsequent happenings in University medical teaching. I am very grateful to these four.

Other graduates and staff: M. Menzies-Campbell 1918, P.C. Robertson 1923, H.A. Graham 1923, W. Cunningham 1924, J.W.L. Dickson 1928, W.G. Campbell 1929, M. Dickie 1934, A.J. Pitkeathly 1934, J.S. Kinnear 1935, Colonel Mary Munro 1935, A.S. Davie 1936, D.G. Adamson 1938, Alan Douglas 1938, G.H. Smith 1938, J.M. McInroy 1940, W.C. Smith 1940, J.E. Taylor 1940, W.E.A. Buchanan 1943, R. Summers 1943, L. Troup 1943, R.M. Milne 1944, A.M. Stalker 1944, G.R. Tudhope 1944 (Dundee), J. Scott Innes 1945, D.W.K. Buchanan 1946, A.C. Millar 1946, G.S. Caithness 1947, A.G.R. Law 1947, E. Mathieson 1947, W.F. Walker 1948, C.W. Grant 1949, W.M. Anderson 1950, J.D. Macgregor 1950, J.S. Henderson 1951, D.M. Murray 1951, J. Robertson Rintoul 1944, 51, D.A.R. Simmons 1951, D.M. Alexander

1952, B. Ashworth 1952, B.K. Dean 1952, J. Langlands 1952, I.R. McLellan 1952, N. Macleod 1952, H.M. Sprunt 1956, A.J. Chalmers 1957, J. Curt 1957, I. Harper 1957, I. Huddleston 1957, R.R. Sturrock 1957 (Dundee), D.W. Nisbet 1958, E.J.H. Moore 1961, J.D.K. Morton 1961 (Dundee), D.R.P. Bushby 1962, C. Doig 1962, G.O. Cowan 1963, M. Lyle 1965, C. Macfarlane 1965, J.A. Mills 1966, A.L. Goostrey 1968, D. Whalley 1968, D.A. Ingram 1970, D. Irvine 1970, K. MacNeill 1970 (Dundee), J.D. Cannon 1972, J. Gillingham 1972, J. Griffith 1972 (Dundee), S. Hewit 1972, N. Jack 1972, R.H. MacDougall 1972, A. McKerrigan 1972, P.J. Latham 1972 (Dundee), I. Lightbody 1972, T. Naidoo 1972 (Dundee), P. Riley 1972 (Dundee) all provided comments and information either in past years or following recent written requests. I thank them all.

In a special group I would like to thank the North American Medical Alumni, whose loyalty to the University remains absolute and whose sadness at the Disruption is unanimous; Dr. Sydney Bassin (1933) has been their recent spokesman.

The St Andrews medical science graduates who gave information about their Manchester training have asked to remain anonymous; their contribution was very valuable.

One person who must have a special and personal acknowledgement is Mrs Christian Tudhope. Not only did she provide a great deal of unique information which no-one else could have given, but she read the whole account, gave invaluable advice on the 1897-1952 period, and supported and encouraged me throughout.

I am also indebted to recollections and comments from several non-St Andrews graduates, and these are Dr. John Taylor (Edinburgh) of the Department of Physiology in St Salvator's College, Dr. Tom Sommerville (Edinburgh) of the planning team for Ninewells, Dr. H.L.D. Duguid (Aberdeen), Dr. H.P. Tait (Edinburgh) Honorary President of the Scottish Society of the History of Medicine, Dr. Hamish Watson, Professor Hunter's successor as Post-Graduate Dean in Dundee, and Dr. G. Forwell (Glasgow), Senior Administrative Medical Officer 1961-66.

Mr Alan Brown deserves special thanks. He was Secretary to the Faculty from 1962 to 1982 and provided a large amount of objective and fair recollection and comment. Mr R.N.M. Robertson, administrator of the post-1945 Medical Planning Committee of the University, and later Secretary of Dundee University, gave me considerable help most willingly. Dr. J.F. McHarg provided evidence of medical teaching in the earlier centuries at the University.

Dr. Derek Dow, Archivist, Glasgow Health Board, kindly sent me papers and information relating to the University of Glasgow. Dr. J.L. Potter, the Executive Dean of the Faculty of Medicine in Edinburgh gave similar help. Mrs V. James, of the General Medical Council, obtained reports of the G.M.C. from 1875 onwards relating to St Andrews, and other papers.

The Keeper of the Records of Scotland, at H.M. General Register House in Edinburgh, and H.M. Stationery Office in Scotland, sought and obtained a number of important documents and references.

J.W. Jolliffe, Librarian of the Bodleian Library, Oxford, gave help in obtaining information about the diaries of Rev. Andrew Clark concerning his daughter Mildred's years at St Andrews in the 1914-18 War.

Mr Edward Flint, of Edinburgh, gave family information relating to Professor James Flint, Chandos Professor of Medicine in St Andrews. Mr Lewis Robertson was particularly helpful with information about the building of Ninewells Hospital; I also received help from Mr J.K. Johnson and Mr A. Wightman, Regional Board Secretary and Ninewells architect respectively. Mr Wightman gave me a good deal of his time most willingly, as well as providing additional papers not otherwise available.

Mrs Marjorie Anderson kindly made a contribution from Mr Fred Cunningham's trust towards the cost of publication and the Scottish Society of the History of Medicine and the Carnegie Trust also gave me grants. These helped me to fund the work and I am very indebted to them.

Next may I thank those who typed the script; the late Miss Jean Palmer, who did so much so willingly, and Mrs M. Tallach who completed the later chapters.

Lastly, I have to thank very sincerely Dr. R.G. Cant, St Andrews University's historian, for the immense care he took in reading my text, correcting my errors, supporting my conclusions, and approving the work on behalf of the University.

Index

411